Conflict of Nor
How WTO Law I

One of the most prominent and urgent problems in international governance is how the different branches and norms of international law interact, and what to do in the event of conflict. With no single 'international legislator' and a multitude of states, international organisations and tribunals making and enforcing the law, the international legal system is decentralised. This leads to a wide variety of international norms, ranging from customary international law and general principles of law, to multilateral and bilateral treaties on trade, the environment, human rights, the law of the sea, etc. Pauwelyn provides a framework on how these different norms interact, focusing on the relationship between the law of the World Trade Organization (WTO) and other rules of international law. He also examines the hierarchy of norms within the WTO treaty. His recurring theme is how to marry trade and non-trade rules, or economic and non-economic objectives, at the international level.

JOOST PAUWELYN is Associate Professor of Law at Duke University School of Law. His areas of interest are public international law and the law of the WTO. He was previously Legal Affairs Officer for the WTO in Geneva (1996–2002).

CAMBRIDGE STUDIES IN INTERNATIONAL AND COMPARATIVE LAW

Established in 1946, this series produces high quality scholarship in the fields of public and private international law and comparative law. Although these are distinct legal sub-disciplines, developments since 1946 confirm their interrelation.

Comparative law is increasingly used as a tool in the making of law at national, regional and international levels. Private international law is now often affected by international conventions, and the issues faced by classical conflicts rules are frequently dealt with by substantive harmonisation of law under international auspices. Mixed international arbitrations, especially those involving state economic activity, raise mixed questions of public and private international law, while in many fields (such as the protection of human rights and democratic standards, investment guarantees and international criminal law) international and national systems interact. National constitutional arrangements relating to 'foreign affairs', and to the implementation of international norms, are a focus of attention.

Professor Sir Robert Jennings edited the series from 1981. Following his retirement as General Editor, an editorial board has been created and Cambridge University Press has recommitted itself to the series, affirming its broad scope.

The Board welcomes works of a theoretical or interdisciplinary character, and those focusing on new approaches to international or comparative law or conflicts of law. Studies of particular institutions or problems are equally welcome, as are translations of the best work published in other languages.

General Editors	James Crawford SC FBA
	Whewell Professor of International Law,
	Faculty of Law and Director, Lauterpacht Research Centre for
	International Law, University of Cambridge
	John S. Bell FBA
	Professor of Law, Faculty of Law, University of Cambridge
Editorial Board	Professor Hilary Charlesworth *University of Adelaide*
	Professor Lori Damrosch *Columbia University Law School*
	Professor John Dugard *Universiteit Leiden*
	Professor Mary-Ann Glendon *Harvard Law School*
	Professor Christopher Greenwood *London School of Economics*
	Professor David Johnston *University of Edinburgh*
	Professor Hein Kötz *Max-Planck-Institut, Hamburg*
	Professor Donald McRae *University of Ottawa*
	Professor Onuma Yasuaki *University of Tokyo*
	Professor Reinhard Zimmermann *Universität Regensburg*
Advisory Committee	Professor D. W. Bowett QC
	Judge Rosalyn Higgins QC
	Professor Sir Robert Jennings QC
	Professor J. A. Jolowicz QC
	Professor Sir Elihu Lauterpacht CBE QC
	Professor Kurt Lipstein
	Judge Stephen Schwebel

A list of books in the series can be found at the end of this volume

Conflict of Norms in Public International Law
How WTO Law Relates to other Rules of International Law

Joost Pauwelyn

CAMBRIDGE UNIVERSITY PRESS
Cambridge, New York, Melbourne, Madrid, Cape Town, Singapore, São Paulo, Delhi

Cambridge University Press
The Edinburgh Building, Cambridge CB2 8RU, UK

Published in the United States of America by Cambridge University Press, New York

www.cambridge.org
Information on this title: www.cambridge.org/9780521824880

© Joost Pauwelyn 2003

This publication is in copyright. Subject to statutory exception
and to the provisions of relevant collective licensing agreements,
no reproduction of any part may take place without the written
permission of Cambridge University Press.

First published 2003
Fifth printing 2006
This digitally printed version 2008

A catalogue record for this publication is available from the British Library

ISBN 978-0-521-82488-0 hardback
ISBN 978-0-521-10047-2 paperback

Cambridge University Press has no responsibility for the persistence or
accuracy of URLs for external or third-party Internet websites referred to in
this publication, and does not guarantee that any content on such websites is,
or will remain, accurate or appropriate.

Contents

	Preface	*page* xi
	Table of cases	xiii
	List of abbreviations	xxvi
	Introduction	**1**
1	**The topic and its importance: conflict of norms in public international law**	**5**
	Conflict	5
	Conflict of norms	6
	Conflict of norms in public international law	10
	The importance of the topic	12
2	**The case study: the law of the World Trade Organization**	**25**
	WTO law as 'just' another branch of public international law	25
	The WTO legal system is not a 'closed legal circuit'	35
	The sources of WTO law	40
	The nature of WTO obligations: reciprocal or integral?	52
3	**Hierarchy of sources**	**89**
	The continuing uncertainty as to the sources of international law	89
	Are there any *a priori* hierarchies in international law?	94
	Judicial decisions and doctrine	109
	General principles of law	124
	Custom and treaties	131

	Unilateral acts of states and acts of international organisations	143
	From 'sources' of international law to 'general' versus 'particular' international law	147
4	**Accumulation and conflict of norms**	158
	The function of norms	158
	How norms interact	161
	Accumulation	161
	Conflict	164
	Accumulation and conflict with general international law	200
	Accumulation: 'fall-back' on other norms of international law	201
	Conflict: 'contracting out' of general international law	212
5	**Conflict-avoidance techniques**	237
	Co-ordination *ex ante* (conflict prevention)	237
	The presumption against conflict	240
	Treaty interpretation as a conflict-avoidance tool	244
6	**Resolving 'inherent normative conflict'**	275
	Preliminary classifications for conflict resolution	275
	One of the two norms ceases to exist	278
	One of the two norms is 'illegal'	298
7	**Resolving 'conflict in the applicable law'**	327
	One of the two norms 'prevails'	327
	Explicit conflict clauses	328
	Lex posterior	361
	Lex specialis	385
	Both norms are 'equal'	418
	Conclusion on conflict resolution	436
8	**Conflict of norms in WTO dispute settlement**	440
	The judicial settlement of disputes	441
	The jurisdiction of WTO panels	443
	The applicable law before a GATT/WTO panel	456
	Practical consequences of the approach suggested	472

A closer look at certain past disputes in the light of the
    theory presented here   478

Conclusions   487

Bibliography   493
Index   506

Preface

At heart, this book is inspired by a willingness to see more to life than money. Trade is a money-making exercise. The statistics show that trade liberalisation, the WTO's leitmotif, does increase welfare. The WTO is 'good for you'. This cannot be, and has not been, stressed enough. Even if the WTO undoubtedly needs improvement, it would be disastrous to turn back the clock and revert to escalating protectionism. Trade between nations makes the world a better place. It also makes it a safer place. But at the same time, trade is but an instrument to achieve nobler goals: the prevention of war; raising standards of living and the creation of jobs, not just in the rich countries but also in the developing world; political freedom and respect for human rights; social protection and an equitable distribution of wealth; the fight against environmental degradation and the protection of public health; etc. Given the diversity of WTO members, these goals must, in the first place, be set by each member individually, preferably, of course, in co-operation with other members. When genuinely pursued, that is, when not abused as a disguised restriction on trade, such goals must trump the instrument of trade, even if they are not set out in the WTO treaty itself. This should be particularly so in case these goals have been defined in other, non-WTO rules of international law as between WTO members that have agreed to those rules. WTO law is not a secluded island but part of the territorial domain of international law. The WTO, important as it may be, must thus be put in perspective. For public international law at large, this approach pleads for the unity of international law, not its fragmentation. However, to achieve this unitary view, rules must be developed on how norms of international law interact. This is what this study attempts to do.

I am much indebted to the supervisors of the thesis which is at the origin of this book: Joseph H. H. Weiler, Jan Wouters and, particularly, Petros C. Mavroidis, who has supported me enormously throughout the production of this work. This is an opportunity also to thank those who nurtured my fascination for the law: Alan E. Boyle, Ian Brownlie, William J. Davey and Cornelius Van der Merwe. Thanks also to my former colleagues at the WTO Legal Affairs and Appellate Body divisions. Without the support and motivation offered by Fanny, Luka and Marit, my wife and two daughters, as well as my parents, this book would not have seen the light of day.

Table of cases

PCIJ cases

Chorzów Factory (Merits), PCIJ, Ser. A, No. 17 (1928)	page 205, 448
Customs Regime between Germany and Austria, PCIJ, Ser. A/B, No. 41 (1931)	57, 300–1, 423
Delimitation of the Polish–Czechoslovakian Frontier (Question of Jaworzina), PCIJ, Advisory Opinion, Ser. B, No. 8 (1923)	257
Eastern Greenland, PCIJ, Ser. A/B, No. 53 (1933)	144
Electricity Company of Sofia and Bulgaria, PCIJ, Ser. A/B, No. 77 (1939)	283
Employment of Women during the Night, PCIJ, Ser. A/B, No. 50 (1932)	151
Free Zones of Upper Savoy and the District of Gex, PCIJ, Ser. A/B, No. 46 (1932)	151
German Interests in Polish Upper Silesia (Merits), PCIJ, Ser. A, No. 7 (1926)	205
Jurisdiction of the European Commission of the Danube, PCIJ, Ser. B, No. 14 (1927)	288, 396
Lighthouses between France and Greece, PCIJ, Ser. A/B, No. 62 (1934)	151
Lotus, PCIJ, Ser. A, No. 10 (1927)	150
Mavrommatis Palestine Concessions (Jurisdiction), PCIJ, Ser. A, No. 2 (1924)	395
Oscar Chinn, PCIJ, Ser. A/B, No. 63 (1934)	57, 277, 308–9
Polish Postal Service in Danzig, PCIJ, Ser. B, No. 11 (1925)	395–6
Polish Upper Silesia case, PCIJ, Ser. A, No. 6 (1925)	116
Serbian Loans Issued in France, PCIJ, Ser. A, Nos. 20/21 (1929)	414

xiv TABLE OF CASES

Upper Silesia Minorities, PCIJ, Ser. A, No. 15 (1928) 415
Wimbledon, PCIJ, Ser. A, No. 1 (1923) 57, 103

ICJ cases

Admissions case (Conditions for Admission of a State to
 Membership in the United Nations), Advisory Opinion,
 ICJ Reports 1948, 57 206
Aegean Sea Continental Shelf (Greece v. Turkey), ICJ Reports
 1978, 1 143, 266
Ambatielos case (Preliminary Objection), ICJ Reports 1952, 28 397
Arbitral Award of 31 July 1989 (Guinea-Bissau v. Senegal), ICJ Reports
 1991, 53 245
Barcelona Traction, ICJ Reports 1970, 3 61, 62
Border and Transborder Armed Actions (Nicaragua v. Honduras), ICJ
 Reports 1988, 76 450
Certain Expenses of the United Nations, Advisory Opinion, ICJ
 Reports 1962, 151 50, 241, 288, 290–1, 292
Continental Shelf (Tunisia v. Libya), ICJ Reports 1982, 18 126, 262, 468
Corfu Channel (Merits), ICJ Reports 1949, 4 248
East Timor case (Portugal v. Australia), ICJ Reports 1995, 90 61, 62,
 425–6, 454
Effect of Awards of Compensation Made by the UN Administrative
 Tribunal, Advisory Opinion, ICJ Reports 1954, 47 110, 112
Elettronica Sicula SpA (ELSI), ICJ Reports 1989, 42 206
Fisheries Jurisdiction (Spain v. Canada), ICJ Reports 1998, 432 245, 453
Fisheries Jurisdiction (United Kingdom v. Iceland) (Jurisdiction of the
 Court), ICJ Reports 1973, 3; (Merits), ICJ Reports 1974, 3 139
Gabcíkovo–Nagymaros Project (Hungary v. Slovakia), ICJ
 Reports 1997, 7 203, 206, 217, 265, 266, 385, 462–3
Genocide Convention case (Application of the Convention on the
 Prevention and Punishment of the Crime of Genocide (Bosnia and
 Herzegovina v. Yugoslovia)) (Preliminary Objections), ICJ
 Reports 1996, 625 61, 74, 101, 308
Interpretation of Peace Treaties, Advisory Opinion, ICJ Reports 1950,
 221 206, 248, 353
LaGrand case (Germany v. United States of America) (Jurisdiction and
 Admissibility), Judgment of 27 June 2001, posted on the
 internet at http://www.icj-cij.org/icjwww/idocket 59, 224, 226,
 245, 253, 448

Legality of the Threat or Use of Nuclear Weapons, ICJ Reports 1996, 66
    (request by the WHO), 226 (request by the UN General
    Assembly)   150–1, 286–7, 288, 292, 408–9, 415–6, 417–8
Lockerbie cases *(Questions of Interpretation and Application of the 1971*
    Montreal Convention Arising from the Aerial Incident at Lockerbie,
    Libyan Arab Jamahiriya v. US and UK) (Provisional Measures),
    ICJ Reports 1992, 3 (UK), 114 (US); (Preliminary Objections),
    ICJ Reports 1998, 9 (UK), 115 (US)   121, 171, 186–7, 203–4, 241,
                                              286, 291–3, 339–42, 386–7, 461
Maritime Delimitation between Nicaragua and Honduras in the
    Caribbean Sea (Nicaragua v. Honduras), pending before the ICJ,
    http://www.icj-cij.org/icjwww/idocket   20, 450
Maritime Delimitation in the Area between Greenland and Jan Mayen,
    ICJ Reports 1993, 38   138
Maritime Delimitation and Territorial Questions between Qatar and
    Bahrain, ICJ Reports 1995, 6   257
Monetary Gold, ICJ Reports 1954, 19   454
Namibia case *(Legal Consequences for States of the Continued Presence*
    of South Africa in Namibia (South West Africa)), Advisory
    Opinion, ICJ Reports 1971, 16   50, 61, 143, 206, 266, 292
Nicaragua case *(Case concerning Military and Paramilitary Activities in*
    and against Nicaragua) (Jurisdiction and Admissibility), ICJ
    Reports 1984, 392; (Merits), ICJ Reports 1986, 14   36–7, 124,
                                                              155, 449, 452, 458, 467
Northern Cameroons (Judgment), ICJ Reports 1963, 27   448
Nuclear Tests case, ICJ Reports 1973, 99   143
Nuclear Tests cases, ICJ Reports 1974, 253 *(Australia v. France)*,
    457 *(New Zealand v. France)*   144, 448, 453, 483
Reparations for Injuries, Advisory Opinion, ICJ Reports 1949, 179   287–8
Request for Revision of Judgement No. 273 of the UN Administrative
    Tribunal (Mortished), ICJ Reports 1982, 321   112
Reservations to the Genocide Convention, Advisory Opinion, ICJ
    Reports 1951, 23   56
Right of Passage (Portugal v. India), ICJ Reports 1960, 6   127–8,
                                                                    241, 391, 394
South West Africa (Second Phase), ICJ Reports 1966, 6   127, 130, 354
South West Africa (Voting Procedure), ICJ Reports 1955, 67   268
Teheran Hostages (US Diplomatic and Consular Staff in Teheran), ICJ
    Reports 1980, 3   36, 79, 84, 107, 452, 458
United States Nationals in Morocco, ICJ Reports 1952, 189   264–5

xvi TABLE OF CASES

GATT 1947 panel reports

Canada – Administration of the Foreign Investment Review Act,
adopted on 7 February 1984, L/5504, BISD 30S/140   457
Canada – Import Restrictions on Ice Cream and Yoghurt, adopted on 4
December 1989, BISD 36S/68   250
*Canada – Measures Affecting Exports of Unprocessed Herring
and Salmon*, adopted on 22 March 1988, L/6268,
BISD 35S/98   458
Canada – Measures Affecting the Sale of Gold Coins, not adopted,
report circulated on 17 September 1985, L/5863   207
Canada/European Communities Article XXVIII Rights (DS12/R), BISD
37S/80   444, 457
Grey Portland Cement, GATT doc. ADP/82   207
*United States – Countervailing Duties on Fresh, Chilled and
Frozen Pork from Canada*, adopted on 11 July 1991,
BISD 38S/30   250
*United States – Countervailing Duties on Non-Rubber Footwear from
Brazil*, adopted on 13 June 1995, BISD 42S/208   207
United States – Imports of Sugar from Nicaragua, adopted on 13
March 1984, L/5607, BISD 31S/67   457–8
*United States – Restrictions on Importation of Sugar (US–Sugar
Headnote)*, adopted on 22 June 1989, BISD 36S/331   357–8
United States – Restrictions on Imports of Tuna, DS 29/R, not adopted,
report circulated on 16 June 1994   35, 258–9, 268, 456–7
United States – Taxes on Petroleum and Certain Imported Substances,
adopted on 17 June 1987, BISD 34S/136   86, 458

WTO cases

The italicised case name is the short name referred to in the text. Each WTO dispute has a DS number (set out in the list below). The document reference for panel reports is "WT/DS_/R"; for Appellate Body reports it is "WT/DS_/AB/R". All WTO dispute settlement reports can be found on the WTO webpage at www.wto.org.

Argentina – Footwear: Argentina – Certain Measures Affecting
Imports of Footwear, Textiles, Apparel and Other Items,
complaint by the United States (WT/DS56), panel and
Appellate Body reports adopted on 22 April 1998   2, 51,
347–8, 376, 411, 471, 479–81

Argentina – Safeguards: Argentina – Safeguard Measures on
   Imports of Footwear, complaint by the European
   Communities (WT/DS121), Panel and Appellate Body reports
   adopted on 12 January 2000   164, 412–3
Australia – Leather: Australia – Subsidies Provided to Producers
   and Exporters of Automotive Leather, complaint by the
   United States (WT/DS126), panel and Appellate Body reports
   adopted on 16 June 1999. Panel report on implementation
   (DSU Art. 21.5) requested by the United States, adopted on
   11 February 2000 (WT/DS126/RW) (no appeal)   221, 223,
                                                                   225, 226, 317
Australia – Salmon: Australia – Measures Affecting the
   Importation of Salmon, complaint by Canada (WT/DS18),
   panel and Appellate Body reports adopted on 6 November
   1998   33, 109, 208, 403, 446
Brazil – Aircraft: Brazil – Export Financing Programme for
   Aircraft, complaint by Canada (WT/DS46), panel and
   Appellate Body reports adopted on 20 August 1999   795–6, 200
Brazil – Aircraft (Article 21.5 – Canada): Brazil – Export Financing
   Programme for Aircraft – Recourse by Canada to Article 21.5
   of the DSU, WT/DS46/RW and AB/RW, panel and Appellate
   Body reports adopted on 4 August 2000   348–9
Brazil – Aircraft (Article 21.5 – Canada II): Brazil – Export
   Financing Programme for Aircraft – Second Recourse by
   Canada to Article 21.5 of the DSU (WT/DS46/RW/2), panel
   report adopted on 23 August 2001   265–6, 348
Brazil – Aircraft (Article 22.6): Arbitrators report on suspension of
   concessions (DSU Art. 22.6), proposal by Canada
   (WT/DS46/ARB), circulated on 28 August 2000   210, 220,
                                                                  233, 270, 271, 470
Brazil – Desiccated Coconut: Brazil – Measures Affecting
   Desiccated Coconut, complaint by the Philippines
   (WT/DS22), panel and Appellate Body reports adopted
   on 20 March 1997   210, 470
Canada – Aircraft: Canada – Measures Affecting the Export of
   Civilian Aircraft, complaint by Brazil (WT/DS70), panel and
   Appellate Body reports adopted on 20 August 1999. Panel
   and Appellate Body reports on implementation (DSU Art.
   21.5) requested by Brazil (WT/DS70/RW), adopted on 4
   August 2000   111, 209, 446, 470

Canada – Autos: Canada – Certain Measures Affecting the
Automotive Industry, complaints by the European
Communities (WT/DS142) and Japan (WT/DS139), panel and
Appellate Body reports adopted on 19 June 2000   403–4

Canada – Dairy Products: Canada – Measures Affecting the
Importation of Milk and the Exportation of Dairy Products
(WT/DS103), complaints by the United States and New
Zealand (WT/DS113), panel and Appellate Body reports
adopted on 27 October 1999   253, 470

Canada – Patent: Canada – Term of Patent Protection, complaint
by the United States (WT/DS170), panel and Appellate Body
reports adopted on 12 October 2000   210, 470

Canada – Periodicals: Canada – Certain Measures Concerning
Periodicals, complaint by the United States (WT/DS31), panel
and Appellate Body reports adopted on 30 July 1997   401, 404–5

Chile – Price Band System: Chile – Price Band System and
Safeguard Measures Relating to Certain Agricultural
Products (WT/DS 207), panel and Appellate Body reports
adopted on 23 October 2002   260–2, 264

Chile – Swordfish: Chile – Measures Affecting the Transit and
Importation of Swordfish, complaint by the European
Communities (WT/DS193), panel established at the DSB
meeting of 12 December 2000, proceedings suspended on 23
March 2001   3, 20, 116, 450, 452

Chile – Taxes: Chile – Taxes on Alcoholic Beverages, Appellate
Body report, WT/DS87/AB/R, WT/DS110/AB/R, adopted
12 January 2000   32

EC – Asbestos: European Communities – Measures Affecting the
Prohibition of Asbestos and Asbestos Products, complaint by
Canada (WT/DS135), panel and Appellate Body reports
adopted on 5 April 2001   108, 119, 198, 398,
411, 445, 453, 456

EC – Bananas: European Communities – Regime for the
Importation, Sale and Distribution of Bananas, complaints
by Ecuador, Guatemala, Honduras, Mexico and the United
States (WT/DS27), panel and Appellate Body reports adopted
on 25 September 1997. Panel report on implementation
(DSU Art. 21.5) requested by Ecuador (WT/DS27/RW/ECU),
adopted on 6 May 1999 (no appeal). Arbitrators report on
suspension of concessions (DSU Art. 22.6), proposal by the

United States (WT/DS27/ARB/US), circulated on 9 April 1999, and proposal by Ecuador (WT/DS27/ARB/ECU), circulated on 24 March 2000   77, 80–3, 190–3, 200, 208, 210, 220, 223, 233, 271, 346–7, 357, 358, 401–3, 404, 411, 421, 446, 447, 470, 471

EC – *Computer Equipment*: European Communities – Customs Classification of Certain Computer Equipment, complaint by the United States (WT/DS62, 67, 68), panel and Appellate Body reports adopted on 22 June 1998   42, 76, 253, 257, 269, 270–1, 357

EC – *Hormones*: European Communities – Measures Affecting Livestock and Meat (Hormones), complaints by Canada (WT/DS48) and the United States (WT/DS26), panel and Appellate Body reports adopted on 13 February 1998. Arbitrators report on suspension of concessions (DSU Art. 22.6), proposals by the United States (WT/DS26/ARB) and Canada (WT/DS48/ARB), circulated on 12 July 1999   1–2, 32, 86, 109, 132, 163, 186, 220, 233, 241, 242, 249–50, 270, 317, 349, 411, 412, 479, 481–2

EC – *Poultry*: European Communities – Measures Affecting Importation of Certain Poultry Products, complaint by Brazil (WT/DS69), panel and Appellate Body reports adopted on 23 July 1998   252, 260, 268, 272, 345, 358, 478–9

EC – *Sardines*: European Communities – Trade Description of Sardines, complaint by Peru (WT/DS231), panel report circulated on 29 May 2002 (under appeal)   349

Guatemala – Cement I: Guatemala – Anti-Dumping Investigation Regarding Imports of Portland Cement from Mexico, complaint by Mexico (WT/DS60), panel and Appellate Body reports adopted on 25 November 1998   194–7, 200, 224

Guatemala – Cement II: Guatemala – Definitive Anti-dumping Measure regarding Grey Portland Cement from Mexico, complaint by Mexico (WT/DS156), panel report adopted on 17 November 2000   225

India – Autos: India – Measures Affecting the Automotive Sector, complaint by the United States and the EC (WT/DS146/R and Corr.1, WT/DS175/R and Corr.1), panel report adopted on 5 April 2002   51, 111

India – Patent (EC complaint): India – Patent Protection for Pharmaceutical and Agricultural Chemical Products,

complaint by the European Communities (WT/DS79), panel
report adopted on 2 September 1998 (no appeal) 121–2
India – Patent (US complaint): India – Patent Protection for
Pharmaceutical and Agricultural Chemical Products,
complaint by the United States (WT/DS50), panel and
Appellate Body reports adopted on 16 January 1998 208, 249, 470
India – Quantitative Restrictions: India – Quantitative
Restrictions on Imports of Agricultural, Textile and
Industrial Products, complaint by the United States
(WT/DS90), panel and Appellate Body reports adopted
on 22 September 1999 119, 294–5
Indonesia – Autos: Indonesia – Certain Measures Affecting the
Automobile Industry, complaints by the European
Communities (WT/DS54), the United States (WT/DS59) and
Japan (WT/DS64), panel report adopted on 23 July 1998 189–90,
193–4, 240, 366–7, 412
Japan – Alcoholic Beverages: Japan – Taxes on Alcoholic Beverages,
complaints by the European Communities (WT/DS8), Canada
(WT/DS10) and the United States (WT/DS11), panel and
Appellate Body reports adopted on 1 November 1996 28, 46,
49, 51, 52, 110, 223, 245, 249
Japan – Varietals: Japan – Measures Affecting Agricultural
Products (WT/DS76/AB/R), Appellate Body report adopted
19 March 1999, DSR 1999: I, 277 109
Korea – Beef: Korea – Measures Affecting Imports of Fresh,
Chilled and Frozen Beef, complaints by the United States
(WT/DS161) and Australia (WT/DS169), panel and Appellate
Body reports adopted on 10 January 2001 108
Korea – Government Procurement: Korea – Measures Affecting
Government Procurement, complaint by the United States
(WT/DS163), panel report adopted on 19 June 2000
(no appeal) 210–1, 467, 470, 482–4
Korea – Safeguards: Korea – Definitive Safeguard Measure on
Imports of Certain Dairy Products, complaint by the
European Communities (WT/DS98), panel and Appellate
Body reports adopted on 12 January 2000 164
Mexico – Corn Syrup (Article 21.5 – US): Mexico – Anti-Dumping
Investigation of High Fructose Corn Syrup (HFCS) from the
United States – Recourse to Article 21.5 of the DSU by the

United States (WT/DS132/RW and AB/RW), panel and
Appellate Body reports adopted on 21 November 2001   209, 294,
297–8, 442, 448–9

Nicaragua – Measures Affecting Imports from Honduras and Colombia:
complaint by Colombia (WT/DS188), panel established at the
DSB meeting of 18 May 2000, complaint by Honduras
(WT/DS201), consultations formally still pending   20, 450

Philippines – Autos: Philippines – Measures Affecting Trade and
Investment in the Motor Vehicle Sector, complaint by the
United States (WT/DS195), panel established at the DSB
meeting of 17 November 2000   296

Turkey – Textile: Turkey – Restrictions on Imports of Textile and
Clothing Products, complaint by India (WT/DS34), panel and
Appellate Body reports adopted on 19 November 1999   198,
295–6, 303, 454, 470

United States – The Cuban Liberty and Democratic Solidarity Act:
complaint by the European Communities (WT/DS38), the
panel's authority lapsed on 22 April 1998 (no panel findings
issued)   20

United States – Measures Affecting Government Procurement:
(WT/DS88 and 95)   20

US – Anti-Dumping Act of 1916: United States – Anti-Dumping Act
of 1916, complaints by the European Communities
(WT/DS136) and Japan (WT/DS162), panel and Appellate Body
reports adopted on 26 September 2000   209, 294, 448–9, 470

US – Certain Products: United States – Import Measures on
Certain Products from the European Communities,
complaint by the European Communities (WT/DS165), panel
and Appellate Body reports adopted on 10 January 2001   224,
225, 226, 235, 236, 420–1, 446

US – Copyright: United States – Section 110(5) of the US
Copyright Act, complaint by the European Communities
(WT/DS160), panel report adopted on 27 July 2000   118, 445

US – Cotton Yarn: United States – Transitional Safeguard
Measure on Combed Cotton Yarn from Pakistan, complaint
by Pakistan (WT/DS192), panel and Appellate Body reports
adopted on 5 November 2001   270, 271

US – FSC: United States – Tax Treatment for 'Foreign Sales
Corporations' complaint by the European Communities

(WT/DS108), panel and Appellate Body reports adopted on
20 March 2000   51, 110, 112, 196–7, 200, 269–70, 297, 317
US – FSC (Article 21.5 – EC):   United States – Tax Treatment for
'Foreign Sales Corporations' – Recourse to Article 21.5 of the
DSU by the European Communities (WT/DS108/RW and
AB/RW), panel and Appellate Body reports adopted on
29 January 2002   260
US – Gasoline: United States – Standards for Reformulated and
Conventional Gasoline, complaints by Venezuela (WT/DS2)
and Brazil (WT/DS4), panel and Appellate Body reports
adopted on 20 May 1996   29, 245, 249
US – Hot-Rolled Steel: United States – Anti-Dumping Measures on
Certain Hot-Rolled Steel Products from Japan, complaint by
Japan (DS184), panel and Appellate Body reports adopted on
23 August 2001   153, 211–2, 215, 224, 225, 270, 469
US – Line Pipe: United States – Definitive Safeguard Measures on
Imports of Circular Welded Carbon Quality Line Pipe from
Korea, complaint by Korea (WT/DS202), panel and Appellate
Body reports adopted on 8 March 2002   84, 271–2
US – Section 211 Appropriations Act: United States – Section 211
Omnibus Appropriations Act of 1998, complaint by the
European Communities (WT/DS176), panel and Appellate
Body reports adopted on 1 February 2002   84, 118–9, 208
US – Section 301:   United States – Sections 301–10 of the Trade
Act of 1974, complaint by the European Communities
(WT/DS152), panel report adopted on 27 January 2000
(no appeal)   52, 68, 74, 235, 421, 451, 471
US – Shirts and Blouses: United States – Measure Affecting
Imports of Woven Wool Shirts and Blouses, complaint by
India (WT/DS33), panel and Appellate Body reports adopted
on 23 May 1997   51, 86, 197, 207–8, 449, 470
US – Shrimp: United States – Import Prohibition of Certain
Shrimp and Shrimp Products, complaints by India, Malaysia,
Pakistan and Thailand (WT/DS58), panel and Appellate Body
reports adopted on 6 November 1998   1, 20, 32–3, 209, 245,
                         255, 256, 260, 266–7, 269, 411–2, 470, 484–6
US – Shrimp (Article 21.5):   United States – Import Prohibition of
Certain Shrimp and Shrimp Products – Recourse to Article
21.5 of the DSU by Malaysia, panel and Appellate Body

reports (WT/DS58/RW and WT/DS58/AB/RW) adopted on
21 November 2001   50, 51, 111, 259–60, 268, 269, 464–5, 485

US – Underwear: United States – Restrictions on Imports of
Cotton and Man-made Fibre Underwear, complaint by Costa
Rica (WT/DS24), panel and Appellate Body reports adopted
on 25 February 1997   197, 270

Other cases

Aaland Islands (Dispute on the Regime of Demilitarization for the),
report of the International Committee of Jurists entrusted
by the Council of the League of Nations with the task of
giving an advisory opinion upon the legal aspects of the
Aaland Islands Question, *League of Nations Official Journal*,
Special Supplement No. 3, October 1920   57, 103

Air Transport Services Agreement arbitration (*United States v. France*)
(1969) 38 ILR 182   143

Al-Adsani v. The United Kingdom, judgment by the ECtHR of 21
November 2001, http://www.echr.coe.int/Eng/Judgments.htm   3, 255–6

Amoco Int. Finance Corp. v. Iran (1987) 15 IRAN–US CTR 189   206, 392

Chemin de Fer Zeltweg (Austria v. Yugoslavia) (1934) 3 RIAA 1795   396

Costa v. ENEL, Case 6/64 [1964] ECR 585   75, 246

Costa Rica v. Nicaragua case, Central American Court of Justice,
reprinted in (1917) 11 AJIL 181   301, 423, 425–6, 433

DeBartolo Corp. v. Florida Gulf Coast Building and Trades Council,
(1988) 485 US 568   246

*Decision of the Commission as to the Admissibility of Application
No. 788/60 lodged by the Government of the Republic of Italy* (1961)
4 Yearbook of the ECHR 116   74

Defrenne v. SABENA, Case 43/75 [1976] ECR 455   127, 227

El Salvador v. Nicaragua case, Central American Court of Justice,
reprinted in (1917) 11 AJIL 674   301

Espahanian v. Bank Tejarat (1983–I) 2 IRAN–US CTR 157   255

Footwear Distributors and Retailers of America v. United States, 852
F. Supp. 1078 (CIT), appeal dismissed, 43 F.3d 1486 (Table)
(Fed. Cir. 1994)   246

Georges Pinson case, Franco-Mexican Commission, AD 1927–8,
No. 292   205

Golder case, European Court of Human Rights (1975),
   57 ILR 201   255
Guinea-Bissau/Senegal Maritime Boundary arbitration (Award of
   31 July 1989) (1990) 83 ILR 1   246, 265, 266
Hermès International v. FHT Marketing Choice BV, Case C-53/96 [1998]
   ECR I-3603   246
INA Corp. v. Iran, (1985) 8 IRAN–US CTR 373   392–3
*Iran–United States (Case A/2), Jurisdiction over Claims filed by Iran
   against US Nationals* (1981) 1 IRAN–US CTR 101   396
Iran v. United States (Case A18), (1984–I) 5 IRAN–US CTR 251   255
Island of Palmas arbitration (*Netherlands v. United States*), (1928)
   2 RIAA 831   264
Johnston and Others v. Ireland, European Court of Human Rights,
   Series A no. 112   255
*Kronprins Gustaf Adolf and Pacific (Arbitration of a Difference
   Concerning Swedish Motor Ships)*, 18 July 1932 (1935)
   29 AJIL 835   462
La Bretagne arbitration decision (1986) 90 RGDIP 716   139, 204
Loizidou v. Turkey, European Court of Human Rights, judgment of
   18 December 1996, Reports 1996-VI, para. 44   255, 256
Mox Plant case (*Ireland v. United Kingdom*), Order on Provisional
   Measures by ITLOS, 13 November 2001, posted on the
   internet at www.itlos.org   3
Murray v. Schooner Charming Betsy, 6 US (2 Branch) 64 (1804)   246
Opel Austria v. Council, CT–115/94, REC. 1997, 11–39   40
Opinion on the Draft Agreement on a European Economic Area,
   Opinion 1/91, [1991] ECR I-6079, [1992] 1 CMLR 245   75
Parliament v. Council, Case C-70/88, [1990] ECR 2073   285
Phillips v. NIOC and Iran, Case No. 39, Chamber Two, Award no.
   425–39–2, 29 June 1989 (1989–I) 21 IRAN–US CTR 79   393
Racke (A.) GmbH v. Hauptzollamt Mainz, Case C-162/96 [1998] ECR
   I-3655   40, 246
Rainbow Warrior arbitration award (30 April 1990), 20 UNRIAA 217   448
*Regina v. Bow Street Metropolitan Stipendiary Magistrate and Others,
   ex parte Pinochet Ugarte (No. 3)*, judgment by the House of
   Lords of 24 March 1999 [2000] AC 147   3
Southern Bluefin Tuna case (*Australia and New Zealand v. Japan*)
   (Jurisdiction and Admissibility), Arbitral Tribunal
   constituted under Annex VIII of the UN Convention on the

Law of the Sea, posted on the internet at
www.worldbank.org/icsid/bluefintuna/main.htm   22, 118, 132,
214, 413, 450, 453–4
Spanish Fishermen's cases, including Case 812/79, *Attorney-General
v. Burgoa*, [1980] ECR   139
Tadić case, *Prosecutor v. Duško Tadić*, International Criminal
Tribunal for the Former Yugoslavia, Trial Chamber, Decision
of 10 August 1995, IT-94-I-T; Appeals Chamber, Decision of
2 October 1995, IT-94-1-AR72 (1997) 105 ILR 419   124, 294, 448–9
Tariffs Applied by Canada to Certain US-Origin Agricultural Products,
final report of the Arbitration Panel Established Pursuant to
Article 2008 of NAFTA, 2 December 1996   265
UK–France Continental Shelf Arbitration (1979) 18 ILM 397   139
Van Gend en Loos, Case 26/62 [1963] ECR 1   75
Von Colson and Kamann v. Land Nordrhein-Westfalen, Case 14/83
[1984] ECR 1891   247

Abbreviations

AD	Annual Digest of Public International Law Cases (now ILR)
AJIL	American Journal of International Law
ASDI	Annuaire Suisse de Droit International
ASIL	American Society of International Law
BISD	Basic Instruments and Selected Documents
BOP	balance of payments
BYIL	British Yearbook of International Law
CITES	Convention on International Trade in Endangered Species of Wild Fauna and Flora
CMLR	Common Market Law Review
CTE	Committee on Trade and Environment
DSB	Dispute Settlement Body
DSU	Understanding on Rules and Procedures Governing the Settlement of Disputes
EC	European Communities
ECHR	European Convention on Human Rights
ECtHR	European Court of Human Rights
ECJ	European Court of Justice
ECR	European Court Reports
EJIL	European Journal of International Law
FAO	Food and Agriculture Organization
GATS	General Agreement on Trade in Services
GATT	General Agreement on Tariffs and Trade
GYIL	German Yearbook of International Law
ICJ	International Court of Justice
ICLQ	International and Comparative Law Quarterly

ICTY	International Criminal Tribunal for the Former Yugoslavia
IIL	Institute of International Law
ILC	International Law Commission
ILC Draft 1996	Draft Articles on State Responsibility adopted on first reading, ILC 48th session, 1996
ILC Draft 2000	Draft Articles on State Responsibility provisionally adopted by the Drafting Committee on second reading, ILC 52nd session, 2000
ILM	International Legal Materials
ILO	International Labour Office
ILR	International Law Reports
IMF	International Monetary Fund
IRAN–US CTR	Iran–United States Claims Tribunal Reports
ITLOS	International Tribunal on the Law of the Sea
JIEL	Journal of International Economic Law
JWT	Journal of World Trade
MEA	multilateral environmental agreement
MFN	most favoured nation
NAFTA	North American Free Trade Agreement
NBER	National Bureau for Economic Research
NGO	non-governmental organisation
NILR	Netherlands International Law Review
NYIL	Netherlands Yearbook of International Law
OECD	Organization for Economic Cooperation and Development
PCIJ	Permanent Court of International Justice
REC	Recueil of the Judgments of the ECJ
Recueil des Cours	Recueil des Cours de l'Académie de Droit International (The Hague)
RGDIP	Revue Général de Droit International Public
RIAA	Reports of International Arbitral Awards
SCM agreement	Agreement on Subsidies and Countervailing Measures
SPS agreement	Agreement on the Application of Sanitary and Phytosanitary Measures
TBT agreement	Agreement on Technical Barriers to Trade
TRIMS	Trade-Related Investment Measures
TRIPS	Trade-Related Intellectual Property Rights
UN	United Nations

UNCIO	United Nations Conference on International Organization
UNCLOS	United Nations Convention on the Law of the Sea, 1982
UNCTAD	United Nations Cooperation on Trade and Development
UNEP	United Nations Environment Programme
UNRIAA	United Nations Reports of International Arbitral Awards
UNTS	United Nations Treaty Series
WHO	World Health Organization
WIPO	World Intellectual Property Organization
WTO	World Trade Organization
YBILC	Yearbook of the International Law Commission
YIEL	Yearbook of International Environmental Law

Introduction

> Certainly, international law must adapt itself to the variety of fields with which it has to deal, as national law has done. It must also adapt itself to local and regional requirements. Nonetheless, it must preserve its unity and provide the players on the international stage with a secure framework.[1]

How should a WTO panel react when faced with the argument that an allegedly WTO inconsistent trade restriction is justified under an environmental treaty, IMF rules or customary international law? How should they react when parties make objections, claims or defences based on rules of general international law, not explicitly covered in the WTO treaty itself, such as rules on burden of proof, standing, good faith, due process, error in treaty formation or the binding nature of unilateral declarations? Those are the type of questions that gave rise to this book. They are very real and practical questions and as a legal adviser to WTO panels, I was often asked to answer them. In the *US – Shrimp* dispute, for example, the United States invoked a number of multilateral environmental treaties in defence of its import ban on shrimp coming from countries which, in the US view, did not sufficiently protect endangered turtles. In *EC – Hormones*, the European Communities claimed that their ban on hormone-treated beef, allegedly inconsistent with WTO rules for not being based on sound science, was justified with reference to the 'precautionary principle', a principle which, in the EC's view, was

---

[1] 'The Proliferation of International Judicial Bodies: The Outlook for the International Legal Order', Speech by His Excellency Judge Gilbert Guillaume, President of the ICJ, to the Sixth Committee of the UN General Assembly, 27 October 2000, p. 4, posted on the internet at http://www.icj-cij.org/icjwww/ipresscom/SPEECHES/iSpeechPresident_Guillaume_SixthCommittee_20001027.htm.

part of customary international law. In *Argentina – Footwear*, the statistical tax imposed on imports was, according to Argentina, nothing more than an implementation of an agreement it had reached with the IMF. The relationship between WTO rules and other rules of international law is at the forefront also of the ongoing Doha Development Round. The Doha Declaration explicitly listed 'the relationship between existing WTO rules and specific trade obligations set out in multilateral agreements (MEAs)' as one of the topics on the negotiating agenda.[2] The relationship between the three pillars of trade, environment and development, and the norms that each of these pillars may produce, is at the heart also of the 2002 Johannesburg Summit on Sustainable Development.

An answer to those questions of relationship between WTO rules and other rules of international law goes beyond the specifics of a trade dispute, even beyond the peculiarities of the WTO legal system. Answering those questions necessarily implies an expression of one's view of international law as a whole. Should a trade dispute before the WTO be examined only in the light of WTO rules? Is there such a thing as general international law that binds all states and could it be a uniting factor as between the different branches of international law so that it should apply also to the WTO treaty? Or should the WTO rather be left untouched and operate only within its limited sphere of trade rules? These are considerations of extreme systemic importance for the system of international law. In addition, they are heavily value-laden and go to the heart of much of the critique against globalisation: is globalisation only about the economy and making profits or is it counterbalanced also by other factors such as environmental protection, development of weaker regions, social protection and safety nets?

The above-mentioned problems related to the interplay between different treaty regimes and between treaties and custom or general principles of law, not only surface in the WTO. Given the increased overlap as between different regimes of international law – be it the UN Security Council dealing with human rights and war crimes; the World Bank addressing environmental sustainability; or the WHO negotiating a treaty to regulate the sale of tobacco products – the question of how different norms of international law interact is omnipresent. On 8 May 2002, the International Law Commission even set up a Study Group

---

[2] Doha Ministerial Declaration, paragraph 31(i), adopted on 14 November 2001, WT/MIN(01)/DEC/1 dated 20 November 2001.

on the topic of the 'Fragmentation of international law', to be chaired by Professor Bruno Simma.[3] In terms of specific disputes the question was raised prominently also before, for example, the European Court of Human Rights (in the *Al-Adsani* case where the prohibition on torture set out in the Convention played out against customary international law rules on state immunity) and the House of Lords in the *Pinochet* case (where the relationship between the Torture Convention and customary rules on immunity for heads of state were at stake). ITLOS, as well, has been asked to deal with disputes that raise questions under treaty regimes other than UNCLOS (see, for example, the *Swordfish* dispute, a dispute that was brought also before the WTO; and the more recent *MOX Plant* case, raising questions not only under UNCLOS but also under the Convention for the Protection of the Marine Environment of the North-East Atlantic (OSPAR Convention), the EC treaty and the Euratom treaty).

This book does not go into specific cases of interplay or conflict between WTO rules and other rules of international law. Rather, it attempts to provide a conceptual framework within which the interplay between norms can be examined. It is hoped that this framework will be useful also for the resolution of conflicts not involving WTO norms.

Chapter 1 sets out the parameters of this book, limiting its scope, in particular, to situations of 'conflict' as between two established 'norms' or 'rules' of international law. This first chapter also elaborates on a number of reasons why conflict of norms is a field of study of both systemic and practical importance in modern international law and, more particularly so, in WTO law.

Chapter 2 introduces the specific case study that will be used throughout this book, namely the law of the World Trade Organization. It assesses the place of WTO law in the wider spectrum of public international law, sums up the different sources of what will be referred to as 'WTO law' and, of crucial importance, introduces the distinction between 'reciprocal' and 'integral' obligations and the legal consequences attached to it.

In chapter 3, we examine whether there is, as in most domestic legal systems, a hierarchy of 'sources' of international law, that is, formal hierarchies depending on the source of the norm in question. We examine the relative importance of judicial decisions and doctrine as a

---

[3] Daily Bulletin, Fifty-fourth session of the ILC, posted on the internet at http://www.un.org/law/ilc/sessions/54/jourchr.htm.

'source of law', including the question of 'conflicting judicial decisions'; the status of 'general principles of law'; and the intricate relationship between custom and treaties.

In chapter 4, the focus is shifted away from 'sources' of law, to specific 'norms' of law. We examine the process and definition of 'accumulation' and 'conflict' of norms and highlight the importance of 'fall-back' and 'contracting out' of general international law for a theory on conflict of norms.

Moving then to the specific problem of 'conflict' of norms, chapter 5 stresses the exceptional nature of 'conflict', given the presumption against conflict and the process of treaty interpretation to be resorted to in order to avoid a conflict between two norms. For those cases where genuine conflict nonetheless arises, chapters 6 and 7 attempt to set out solutions. Chapter 6 deals with what we will call 'inherent normative conflicts'; chapter 7 with 'conflict in the applicable law'.

We conclude this book with one of its most important chapters, namely that on how the general theories developed earlier apply in the concrete circumstances of WTO dispute settlement. In this final chapter we will come back to some of the specific WTO disputes referred to earlier in this introduction and explain them in the light of the theory defended in this book.

1 The topic and its importance: conflict of norms in public international law

> The measure of success which is achieved in eliminating and resolving conflicts between law-making treaties will have a major bearing on the prospect of developing, despite the imperfections of the international legislative process, a coherent law of nations adequate to modern needs.[1]

What follows is about 'conflict', more particularly conflict between 'norms' of 'public international law'. The prime example referred to will be the law of the World Trade Organization. The crucial question in this case study is: how does WTO law relate to other rules of public international law? The internal hierarchy between norms which are part of the WTO treaty[2] is also addressed. We not only examine these questions *in abstracto*. We also assess them in the more concrete context of WTO dispute settlement.

Conflict

The scope of this work is limited to situations of 'conflict' between legal norms. The main question is, therefore: when there is a conflict between two norms, which of the two norms should be applied? This question relates to the hierarchy of norms in international law.

Before suggesting ways to resolve conflict of norms, we shall have to define first what is meant by 'conflict'. In many instances, what may

---

[1] Wilfred Jenks, 'Conflict of Law-Making Treaties' (1953) 30 BYIL 401 at 453.
[2] When referring to the 'WTO treaty' we mean the Final Act Embodying the Results of the Uruguay Round of Multilateral Trade Negotiations, concluded in Marrakesh, Morocco, on 15 April 1994, published in WTO Secretariat, *The Results of the Uruguay Round of Multilateral Trade Negotiations, The Legal Texts* (Geneva, 1995). The sources of the wider notion of 'WTO law' are discussed in chapter 2 below, pp. 40–52.

seem like a conflict will not *be* a conflict but only a divergence which can be streamlined by means of, for example, treaty interpretation. This necessary exercise of identifying when exactly two norms are 'in conflict' means that we cannot limit this study to setting out a number of rules of priority in international law. In addition, we shall need to address the definition of conflict and the different avenues that may lead to convergence of norms in a conflict that is apparent only, not real.

Conflict of norms

Norms versus the pre-normative and norms versus process

Crucially, only conflict between *legally binding norms* is dealt with. We use the notion of 'norms' and that of 'rules' interchangeably. We shall not address the interplay between norms and elements of a pre-normative character. As a result, this work does not generally address, for example, the influence of pre-normative elements (such as the *travaux préparatoires* of a treaty or state practice) on the interpretation, modification or termination of norms.[3] Nor shall we address the impact of what is referred to as 'soft law' even though an increasing number of authors consider this soft law to be of a normative value, albeit not legally binding in and of itself.[4] Others, in contrast, are of the opinion that soft law is of a pre-normative value only and is, in fact, not law at all.[5] Pre-normative elements, as well as norms that are not legally binding, may well be crucial in treaty interpretation so as to resolve apparent (but not genuine) conflicts. Yet, our focus here will be on what to do in case such harmonious interpretation is *not* possible, that is, on what to do in case an international adjudicator is faced with a genuine conflict between two legally binding norms.

---

[3] For an overview of the impact of subsequent practice on treaties, see Wolfram Karl, *Vertrag und Spätere Praxis im Völkerrecht* (Berlin: Springer, 1983).

[4] See, for example, Alain Pellet, 'The Normative Dilemma: Will and Consent in International Law-Making' (1991) 12 *Australian Yearbook of International Law* 22. Elsewhere, Pellet makes a distinction between 'le juridique' and 'l'obligatoire', soft law being part of the former, not the latter (Nguyen Quoc Dinh, P. Daillier and A. Pellet, *Droit International Public* (Montreal: Wilson & Lafleur, 1999), para. 254).

[5] In this sense, see, particularly, Prosper Weil, 'Towards Relative Normativity in International Law?' (1983) 77 AJIL 413, who is of the view that acts that 'do not create rights or obligations on which reliance may be placed before an international court of justice or of arbitration' and acts '[the] failure to live up to [which] does not give rise to international responsibility' are of a pre-normative character only (*ibid.*, at 415).

Our focus on legally binding norms, and the conflicts that may arise between them, results from the need to delimit the scope of this study. It does not in any way imply that international law is, or should be, limited to a number of positive rules. As Rosalyn Higgins expressed in the first two sentences of her general course at The Hague: 'International law is not rules. It is a normative system...harnessed to the achievement of common values.'[6] That international law is not just 'rules' – or what Higgins refers to as 'accumulated past decisions' – but rather a continuous 'process' – from the formation of rules to their refinement by means of application in specific cases, with multiple actors, institutions and legally relevant instruments and conduct at play – will become apparent across this work.[7] Still, the topic of this book is conflict and hierarchy between legally binding norms, in particular, *as they may be invoked before an international court or tribunal*. The hierarchy of actors, institutions and values will shed valuable light on this examination, but is not our main concern here.[8]

In the words of Bos, the standpoint taken in this study is that of the 'consumer' of international law, not that of the 'producer' of international law.[9] States before an international court or tribunal, where conflicting norms may be invoked, are, indeed, 'consumers' of international law or 'law-takers'. From that perspective, it is crucial to know what the law is, where it can be found and how the judge will apply it

---

[6] Rosalyn Higgins, 'General Course on Public International Law' (1991-V) 230 *Recueil des Cours* 23.

[7] Criticising the traditional theory on the sources of international law, Abi-Saab phrased it thus: 'Elle [the traditional theory] représente le développement du droit en termes d'explosions et de ruptures, plutôt que de transitions et de transformations, ou comme un processus continu et en constante évolution...Nous aboutissons ainsi à une théorie de création juridique par "big bang"...En réalité cependant, le droit international, comme tout droit, ne provient pas d'un "néant" ou d'un vide social' (Georges Abi-Saab, 'Les Sources du Droit International: Essai de Déconstruction', in *Le Droit International dans un Monde en Mutation, Mélanges E. J. De Arechaga* (Montevideo: Fundación de Cultura Universitaria, 1994), 29 at 47).

[8] As Weiler and Paulus remarked on the question put to them, 'Is there a hierarchy of norms in international law?': 'Should we not also be thinking of international law as process rather than, or as well as, norms? Operationally, does the image of the lawyer determining the content of norms and actors behaving or misbehaving accordingly really capture international legal process? Normatively, is the hierarchy of norms going to tell the true story of what is important and what is unimportant in international law rather than, say, the hierarchy of actors or of institutions?' (Joseph Weiler and A. L. Paulus, 'The Structure of Change in International Law or Is There a Hierarchy of Norms in International Law?' (1997) 8 EJIL 545 at 554).

[9] Maarten Bos, 'The Recognized Manifestations of International Law' (1977) 20 GYIL 9 at 11–13.

in case there is, for example, a conflict of norms. However, given the lack of a centralised 'legislator' in international law, as well as the optional nature of international adjudication, states are also, even mostly, 'producers' of international law or 'law-givers'. From that perspective, clearly circumscribing what international law is and is not, is of less importance. The 'law-giver' can give her own interpretation to existing norms and always produce new norms to her liking. International law from this abstract 'producer's' viewpoint – the one we will *not* adopt here – is more open to extra-legal considerations and corresponds perhaps better with everyday reality in international relations. Nevertheless, the narrower 'consumer's' approach, increasingly important in fields, such as the WTO, with compulsory dispute settlement procedures, is what will preoccupy us in this study. As Peter Hulsroj warned:

> Clearly a question on how a state can be expected to react in a given situation cannot be answered by purely analysing the norms that would follow from Art. 38 of the Statute of the ICJ, but must embrace norms dictated by history, self-interest, potential political fall-out, etc. Only, I believe that law pragmatically must be understood to be the norms that an ultimate arbiter, the courts, will find to apply to a given legal conflict – and this again means that legal norms are the ones that in some form or another can be derived from the source definition in Art. 38 of the Statute of the ICJ. All other norms are then extra-legal norms and it would be dangerous to ask an ultimate arbiter to disregard this distinction... since predictability will be lost and the ultimate arbiter will be put on an almost impossible task, namely to define norms based on all-encompassing empiricalism.[10]

Norms versus laws and norms versus obligations

As far as the title of this study is concerned, it was tempting to use the term 'conflict of international *laws*', as opposed to 'conflict of *norms* in public international law'. The temptation is there, for the term 'conflict of international *laws*' would echo the more familiar field of study known as 'conflict of laws' or 'private international law': that is, the discipline dealing with conflict between different *domestic* laws in disputes having links with two or more *domestic* legal systems. Wilfred Jenks seems to have succumbed to this temptation when entitling his seminal piece 'Conflict of Law-Making Treaties'. He noted, for example, that 'some of the problems which [law-making treaties] involve may present a closer

---

[10] Peter Hulsroj, 'Three Sources – No River, A Hard Look at the Sources of Public International Law with Particular Emphasis on Custom and "General Principles of Law"', (1999) 54 *Zeitschrift für öffentliches Recht* 219 at 236.

analogy with the problem of the conflict of laws than with the problem of conflicting obligations within the same legal system'.[11]

Modern international law is, indeed, composed increasingly of treaty-based *sub-systems* (such as that of the WTO, the Framework Convention on Climate Change or the World Intellectual Property Organization). These sub-systems could be said to have their own sector-specific 'international law', law-maker and law-enforcement mechanism. Like national laws within the discipline of 'conflict of laws', these sub-systems of public international law interact and may give rise to conflict. It is, indeed, this type of conflict (say, between WTO law and the law developed under the Framework Convention on Climate Change) that inspired this work and will attract most of our attention. Nevertheless, to talk of these sub-regimes as being separate 'international laws' which may 'conflict' would give the wrong signal. First, it would lose sight of *general* international law in creating the impression that these sub-regimes are 'self-contained regimes' to be evaluated exclusively with reference to norms created *within* the particular sub-regime. Second, it could be understood by some as elevating what are basically treaty norms (say, WTO provisions) of a *contractual* nature to the status of 'law' in the strict domestic law sense of norms imposed by an independent 'legislator' on all subjects (i.e. states) of the sub-regime independently of their will.[12]

Another alternative to 'conflict of norms' (besides 'conflict of international laws') could have been 'conflict of obligations'. However, to talk of conflict of *obligations* would obscure the fact that international law is composed of obligations *and* rights. As we shall see below, a conflict may consequently arise not only as between two contradictory obligations, but also as between an obligation and an explicit right.[13] At the same time, it is worth noting that in practice a conflict of norms will always boil down to, and need examination in terms of, a conflict between *rights* and/or *obligations* resting on one or several states. There is no such thing as norms 'in the air'. Norms, at least those we shall further examine (that is, those that are legally binding), are imposing obligations on, or

---

[11] Jenks, 'Conflict', 403.
[12] Sir Gerald Fitzmaurice has argued, for example, that treaties, including so-called 'law-making treaties', are not, in the proper sense of the word, formal sources of *law*: 'They may, according to circumstances, afford evidence of what the law is, or they may lead to the formation of law and thus be material sources. But they are in themselves sources of obligation rather than sources of law' (Gerald Fitzmaurice, 'Some Problems Regarding the Formal Sources of International Law', in *Symbolae Verzijl* (The Hague: Nijhoff, 1958) 153 at 154).
[13] See chapter 4 below, pp. 184–8.

granting rights to, particular states. They are in that sense 'subjective'. But this does not mean that norms can always be reduced to the form of bilateral right–duty relations between two states, of a contract-type nature. Increasingly, the rights and obligations set out in norms of international law are of a collective or communitarian character. As a result, their breach can then, for example, be invoked by all (participating) states.[14]

The fact that a conflict of norms can hence be reduced to conflict of rights and/or obligations resting on one or several states – albeit not always of a *contract*-type nature – is another reason *not* to talk of 'conflict of international *laws*', or 'conflict of *treaties*'. Although the general nature of the treaties in question may well determine whether or not a given norm in one treaty should prevail over that in another treaty, in the end, conflict must be narrowed down to a conflict between two given norms: more particularly, the rights and/or obligations set out by these norms as they apply between particular states. A conflict is rarely one between treaties or sub-systems of international law *in their entirety*, where one treaty or sub-system *in its entirety* needs to give way to another treaty or sub-system, that is, the way one domestic law may need to give way to another domestic law in the field of conflict of laws.[15] Although some conflicts may lead to the invalidity, termination or non-application of an entire treaty,[16] all conflicts require at least some examination of the specific rights and obligations set out in the relevant treaties.

Conflict of norms in public international law

Importantly, this study is *not* about the vertical conflict between *national law* and *international law*, such as the question of whether a *national* regulation enacted to protect the environment is in conflict with WTO rules.

---

[14] See, for example, Article 42 (defining the notion of 'injured state') and Article 48 (on invocation of responsibility by a state other than an injured state) of the ILC's Draft Articles on Responsibility of States for Internationally Wrongful Acts, adopted by the ILC at its 53rd session, 2001 (Report of the ILC on the work of its 53rd session, General Assembly Official Records, 56th session, Supplement No. 10 (A/56/10), chapter IV.E.1, hereafter '2001 Draft Articles on State Responsibility').

[15] For an exception, see Article 59(1) of the Vienna Convention on the Law of Treaties dealing with the termination of a treaty implied by the conclusion of a later treaty (for example, in case 'the provisions of the later treaty are so far incompatible with those of the earlier treaty that the two treaties are not capable of being applied at the same time').

[16] See, for example, Arts. 53, 59 and 63 of the Vienna Convention on the Law of Treaties.

We deal only with the horizontal conflict between two norms of international law (for example, a provision in an environmental convention which contradicts a WTO rule). We shall, in addition, focus on specific subjects of international law, namely states and separate customs territories (such as Hong Kong, China or the European Communities), the latter also being able to join the WTO.[17] The rights and obligations incumbent on other subjects of international law (such as international organisations or, in some instances, individuals), and their potential for conflict, will not be addressed.

The norms of international law subject to examination will not, however, be limited to those derived from treaties.[18] We shall address also norms produced by other sources of international law.[19] What these sources are, and how they may influence the outcome of conflict of norms, is examined in chapter 3.

---

[17] The *Explanatory Notes* to the Marrakesh Agreement Establishing the WTO (hereafter 'Marrakesh Agreement') define the term 'country', as it is used in WTO agreements, 'to be understood to include any separate customs territory Member of the WTO'. Article XII of the Marrakesh Agreement allows any state or 'separate customs territory possessing full autonomy in the conduct of its external commercial relations and of the other matters provided for in this Agreement and the Multilateral Trade Agreements' to accede to the WTO. Hereinafter when the word 'state' or 'country' is used in the context of the WTO treaty, it should be read as including separate customs territories.

[18] Some of the major contributions in the field of conflict of norms in international law were, however, limited to conflict of treaty norms. See, in chronological order: Charles Rousseau, 'De la Compatibilité des Normes Juridiques Contradictoires dans l'Ordre International' (1932) 39 RGDIP 133; Hans Aufricht, 'Supersession of Treaties in International Law' (1952) 37 *Cornell Law Quarterly* 655; Jenks, 'Conflict'; Nguyen Quoc Dinh, 'Evolution de la Jurisprudence de la Cour Internationale de La Haye Relative au Problème de la Hiérarchie des Normes Conventionnelles', in *Mélanges Offerts à Marcel Waline, Le Juge et Le Droit Public* (Paris, Librairie générale de droit et de jurisprudence, 1974, 2 vols.), I, 215; M. Zuleeg, 'Vertragskonkurrenz im Völkerrecht, Teil I: Verträge zwischen souveränen Staaten' (1977) 20 GYIL 246; Dirk Falke, 'Vertragskonkurrenz und Vertragskonflikt im Recht der WTO' (2000) 3 *Zeitschrift für Europarechtliche Studien* 307; and Jan Neumann, 'Die Koordination des WTO-Rechts mit anderen völkerrechtlichen Ordnungen – Konflikte des materiellen Rechts und Konkurrenzen der Streitbeilegung', unpublished doctoral thesis (Münster, 2001).

[19] This wider approach to conflict in international law so as to include other sources of international law was adopted also by: Michael Akehurst, 'The Hierarchy of the Sources of International Law' (1974–5) 47 BYIL 273; Maarten Bos, 'The Hierarchy among the Recognized Manifestations ("Sources") of International Law' (1978) 25 NILR 334; Emmanuel Roucounas, 'Engagements Parallèles et Contradictoires' (1987-VI) 206 *Recueil des Cours* 9; and W. Czaplinski and G. Danilenko, 'Conflict of Norms in International Law' (1990) 21 NYIL 3.

The importance of the topic

The potential for conflict between norms seems inherent in *any* legal system. In domestic law, many conflicts are avoided since the law-maker will, in many cases, abrogate conflicting norms or explicitly regulate the hierarchy as between different norms. Still, even in domestic law, it is impossible to foresee how a newly created norm will interact with each and every other norm, not just because of the sheer number of norms, but also because of the general and vague nature of many legal norms, whose scope of application and effect may change with society. Conflict is, therefore, not an *anomaly* in the law, nor always an intended contradiction as between two expressions of legislative will. It is, rather, *inherent* in a system of law, that is, a system intended to cover all constellations of fact with a limited number of generally phrased rules. To give one example, often legislators are keen to include as many transactions as possible under one law, creating the risk of 'over-inclusion' of the law. At the same time, given the inherent weakness of the human mind, when enacting a new law, the legislator cannot always foresee all future transactions that are to fall under the new law, creating the risk of 'under-inclusion'.[20] This over-inclusion of some norms, and under-inclusion of others, makes conflict between norms unavoidable, even in the most developed of legal systems.

As far as norms of *international law* are concerned, there are a number of variables that make conflict an even more inevitable occurrence. Most of the reasons why conflict arises in international law are inherent in the nature of international law. The first three described below relate to the law-*making* process of international norms. A fourth reason that comes to mind relates to their *enforcement*. In addition to those inherent reasons, four additional reasons can be pointed to which have emerged more recently with the development of modern international law. They are particularly relevant to conflict involving WTO rules.

That conflict of norms in international law is a topic deserving attention at the highest levels was recently confirmed by the ILC. On 8 May 2002 it set up a Study Group on the topic of the 'Fragmentation of international law', chaired by Professor Bruno Simma.[21]

---

[20] Richard Posner, *Overcoming Law* (Cambridge, Mass.: Harvard University Press, 1995).
[21] Daily Bulletin, 54th session of the ILC, posted on the internet at http://www.un.org/law/ilc/sessions/54/jourchr.htm. See also Gerhard Hafner, 'Risk Ensuing from Fragmentation of International Law', ILC, Report on the Work of its 52nd session, General Assembly Official Records, 56th session, Supplement No. 10 (A/55/10), 321–39.

Four reasons inherent in the nature of international law

Multitude of law-makers at the international level

First, international law does not have one central legislator, nor one central executive. It has essentially as many law-makers as there are states. As a result, since each state is largely its own law-maker, the legal relationship between states varies enormously depending on the states involved; much more, for example, than the relationship between individuals under domestic law where legislation and other generally applicable law largely outweighs private contracts. This multitude of law-makers and legal relationships, in particular in the current context of proliferation of international organisations, obviously increases the risk of conflict between norms. But this is not necessarily a bad thing. Given the diverse interests and characteristics of the almost 190 states that exist today, it is to be expected that as many legal relationships exist. Because of that diversity, the time is not ripe for international law to become a monolithic bloc of rules created by some world legislator or government, equally applying to all states the way, for example, Belgian law applies to all Belgians. The *equality* between states and the resulting equality between the law they create, as well as the *neutrality* of international law (other than *jus cogens*) resulting in all norms being of the same legal value, are, indeed, essential elements for international law to fulfil its dual function. This dual function is (i) ensuring the peaceful co-existence between states and (ii) enhancing the co-operation between states in pursuit of goals they consider as common between them. However, the price to be paid for this diversity in international law is the increased risk of conflict between norms.

A more practical consequence of international law essentially being created only by state consent is that many international norms are left unclear and in potential conflict with other norms. The need for consensus among a wide variety of states for norms to be enacted, combined with an often heavy time pressure for conclusion of a treaty, may, indeed, explain a great number of the inconsistencies in international law. Interestingly, the more states join a particular treaty regime (as is the case, for example, with the WTO), the more difficult it becomes to arrive at a consensus within that regime and the higher the risk for vague and open-ended rules that are potentially in conflict with other rules, either within or outside that treaty regime. In addition, the more states join a regime, the more difficult it becomes to agree on explicit conflict clauses dealing with the question of how the regime relates to other rules of international law and, hence, the more conflicts that remain potentially unresolved.

The time factor

Second, international law is not only made by a multitude of states, resulting in a multitude of legal relationships. As with any law, *it may change over time*. The fact that all international norms have essentially the same binding value makes time an even more important variable in international law than it is in domestic law. As a result, any later norm can, in principle, overrule an earlier one (*lex posterior derogat legi priori*). To put it differently, international law is not only dependent, in one way or the other, on the consent of (some or all 190) states. These states can, in addition, change their mind *at any point in time* (subject to *jus cogens* and the principle *pacta tertiis nec nocent nec prosunt*). Hence, the potential for conflict to arise must be multiplied by a time factor: an earlier norm may conflict with a later one (even if created by the same states), the same way an older norm may need to be interpreted and applied in the background of a newer norm.

There are, of course, a multitude of reasons why states may change their minds over time. Realist theories would posit that states will change their positions depending on how they perceive their own national interests at any given point in time. Since realists believe that states constantly struggle to achieve and maintain power, they would submit that the international legal system and the norms it produces over time arise from balancing state interests, preservation and mutual quests for power.[22] Liberal theories, in contrast, do not so much focus on a constantly changing power struggle *as between states*, but envision rather that states act as agents for the benefit of their domestic constituencies and are therefore subject to change through the liberal functioning of the *domestic* system.[23] As a result, in their view, international norms will change over time mainly as a consequence of domestic evolution. Finally, constructivism would add that states may change their mind also as a result of their experiences in the international arena, their national interest being influenced over time either by the

---

[22] See, for example, Anne-Marie Slaughter, 'International Law in a World of Liberal States' (1995) 6 EJIL 503 at 507 (discussing realism).

[23] See, for example, Andrew Moravcsik, 'Taking Preferences Seriously: A Liberal Theory of International Politics' (1997) 51 *International Organization* 513 at 516.

expectations and understandings of *other states* or by the international *institutions* that they have joined.²⁴

Multitude of law-makers at the domestic level

Third, and still within the process of law-*making*, not only elements at the *international* level enhance the potential for conflict, but also *domestic* factors must be considered. Most prominently, there is the fact that states, although considered under international law to constitute one single entity, are, in practice, represented by a multitude of domestic actors in the international law-making process. Even if for most treaties parliament's approval may be required, the fact remains that treaties are not normally negotiated by members of parliament but by diplomats or civil servants. And the delegates representing a state in the WTO context are mostly not the same as those representing the same state in UNEP, the WHO or WIPO. These different negotiators operating in different law-making contexts are often tempted, as Jenks put it, 'to secure fuller satisfaction for their own views on debatable questions of detail at the price of conflict between different instruments and incoherence in the body of related instruments'.²⁵ Especially in highly technical fields such as GATT/WTO law, negotiators have, indeed, felt the urge to portray 'their' treaty as something that is delinked from the wider corpus of international law, be it out of professional jealousy or ignorance. In this respect, Jenks' call for negotiators to 'form the habit of regarding proposed new instruments from the standpoint of their effect on the international statute book as a whole'²⁶ has not always been heard. It must be repeated here.

In addition, looking beyond the veil of different *government* officials negotiating different treaties, it is often the case also that different *private* interest groups are at play in different treaty settings. In the WTO, it may be predominantly industry; in UNEP, predominantly environmental interest groups. As Benvenisti has observed, 'states are not monolithic entities;...many of the pervasive conflicts of interest are in fact more internal than external, stemming from the heterogeneity within,

---

[24] See, for example, Jutta Brunnée and Stephen Toope, 'International Law and Constructivism: Elements of an Interactional Theory of International Law' (2000) 39 *Columbia Journal of Transnational Law* 19. On so-called 'modified constructivism', see Claire Kelly, 'The Value Vacuum: Self-enforcing Regimes and the Dilution of the Normative Feedback Loop' (2001) 23 *Michigan Journal of International Law* 673.
[25] Jenks, 'Conflict', 452. [26] *Ibid*.

rather than among, states... The transnational conflict paradigm shows how domestic interest groups often cooperate with similarly situated *foreign* interest groups in order to impose externalities on rival *domestic* groups.'[27] The fact that different types of domestic pressure groups may be at work in the creation of different international law rules, once again, enhances the risk of conflict between these rules: each of these groups tends to focus on their own interests, without necessarily taking into account the interests of other domestic groups and the rules they give rise to.

When it comes to the creation of customary international law, the variety of actors is arguably even wider. Customary international law does not require approval by parliaments. It simply emerges as a result of state practice, recognised as binding. All actors on the international scene may play a role in this custom-creating process, including lower state officials, international organisations and civil servants, as well as international adjudicators, NGOs and academics.

In sum, the multitude of actors at play in the construction of one and the same state's 'consent' is, therefore, another factor that increases the risk of inconsistencies arising as between *different* norms or expressions of the same state's consent. This consent may, indeed, find its source either in a different coalition of domestic interest groups, in a different institutional setting (parliament, the ministry of foreign affairs or that of trade), at a different point in time (parliaments as well as civil servants change over time) or at a different level (higher versus lower state officials).

No centralised adjudicator

Fourth, and focusing now on law *enforcement*, international law does not only lack a centralised legislator and executive. In addition, it does not have a centralised court system with general and compulsory jurisdiction. Such a court system, especially if combined with a centrally organised sanctions regime, could have created some order in the multifaceted international law-making process. There is, of course, the ICJ, the 'principal judicial organ of the United Nations'.[28] But this court only has compulsory jurisdiction as between some states and in respect of certain subject matters (as, for example, defined under the optional clause

---

[27] Eyal Benvenisti, 'Exit and Voice in the Age of Globalization' (1999) 98 *Michigan Law Review* 167 at 169.
[28] UN Charter, Art. 92.

system of Art. 36(2) of the ICJ Statute). In addition, international law knows of a multitude of international enforcement mechanisms, most of them treaty-based (such as the WTO dispute settlement system under the WTO treaty), others being set up on an *ad hoc* basis.

This lack of a centralised international adjudicator means, firstly, that there is, in most cases, no judge to bring order in the multiple legal relationships present in international law. Secondly, the existence of different international tribunals creates the risk that conflict arises also in the way international law is construed or enforced.[29] At worst, it may lead even to conflict of norms being resolved in favour of one norm by one adjudicator and in favour of the other norm by another tribunal.

Four additional reasons in the context of modern international law

The above four variables at the origin of conflict between international norms are inherent in the system of international law. They have been present ever since international law emerged as a system of law. Four additional elements can be pointed to which show that, in modern times, the potential for conflict is even more significant. It is under these elements that the particular importance of conflict in the WTO context becomes apparent. In 1976 Akehurst wrote that 'the problem of hierarchy of the sources of international law has seldom given rise to difficulties in practice'. Akehurst was careful and right, however, to add that 'there is no guarantee that that state of affairs will continue'.[30]

The move from a law on 'co-existence' to a law on 'co-operation'

First, international law has witnessed a shift from being a law on 'co-existence' between sovereign states – dealing with issues such as territorial sovereignty, diplomatic relations, the law on war and peace treaties – to a law regulating also the 'co-operation' between states in pursuit of common goals, such as the law created under the auspices of international trade, environmental and human rights organisations. This evolution, allowing for deeper co-operation as between states, was spearheaded in particular by the end of the cold war.[31] It led, first of all, to an exponential increase in the number of international law norms created; hence, an increase in the potential for conflict between these

---

[29] For examples, see Shane Spelliscy, 'The Proliferation of International Tribunals: A Chink in the Armor' (2001) 40 *Columbia Journal of Transnational Law* 143.
[30] Akehurst, 'Hierarchy', 274.
[31] See Hafner, 'Risk', 321 and Michael Reisman, 'International Law after the Cold War' (1990) 84 AJIL 859.

norms. From 1970 to 1997, the number of international treaties more than tripled, with some 1,500 *multilateral* treaties being in existence as of 1995.[32] The rising number of specific treaty norms also highlighted the problem of potential conflict between international custom and supervening treaty norms. Witness, for example, the *Pinochet* case before the House of Lords[33] and the *Al-Adsani* case before the ECtHR,[34] where the relationship between specific treaties banning torture and customary rules on state immunity was at play.

Moreover, under the traditional law on co-existence between states, composed mainly of a myriad of bilateral agreements, the typical case of conflict arose in the form of conflicting obligations held *by one state towards two or more different states*, for example, under different peace, neutrality or mutual assistance agreements. This type of conflict – referred to below as an 'AB/AC conflict', A being a state with conflicting obligations vis-à-vis B and C[35] – can be compared to a conflict between two contracts concluded by one and the same person A with two different persons B and C under domestic law. The two contracts are only common to person A and conflict arises because A promised something to B that is not consistent with what he promised to C: for example, the cession by A of sovereignty over the same piece of land to both B and C or a promise made by A to assist B in case he is at war with C when the same promise is made towards C in the event that he is at war with B.

Under more recent international law on co-operation, constituted increasingly of *multilateral* treaties dealing with different *common* goals, additional types of conflict arose. Today the typical conflict between norms is, indeed, that between norms deriving from different treaty-based sub-systems (say, a conflict between a WTO rule and a rule of an environmental convention). Here, both conflicting norms are binding on states A and B but state A invokes one norm in its favour, whereas state B relies on the other, contradictory norm. Hence, we are no longer faced with a conflict between two contracts concluded by one state vis-à-vis two different states, but two sub-systems, binding on all states involved, under which contradictory law was made. The best domestic law analogy may be that of two legislators, each creating contradictory laws.

---

[32] José Alvarez, 'The New Treaty Makers' (2002) 25 *Boston College International and Comparative Law Journal* 213 at 216.
[33] *Regina v. Bow Street Metropolitan Stipendiary Magistrate and Others, ex parte Pinochet Ugarte (No. 3)*, judgment by the House of Lords of 24 March 1999 [2000] AC 147.
[34] *Al-Adsani v. The United Kingdom*, judgment by the ECtHR of 21 November 2001.
[35] See, in particular, chapter 7, below, pp. 422–36.

Besides such conflict of norms part of *different* sub-systems, conflict increasingly arises also as between norms within the *same* sub-system (say, between two norms of WTO law) or between a norm of general international law (say, customary law on the law of treaties) and a norm of a given sub-system (say, a WTO rule on how to amend the WTO treaty). Of course, the old type of conflict (state A making one promise to state B but another, contradictory promise to state C) continues to exist. It is of importance, for example, when state A concludes an environmental agreement with state B in which A promises B to restrict certain trade flows also with third parties (including state C), whereas state A has, in another context (say, the WTO), made a contradictory promise towards state C not to restrict those same trade flows.

In sum, with the transformation of international law into a law on both co-existence and co-operation, the potential as well as types of conflict between norms has increased significantly. As Jenks put it:

the conflict of law-making treaties, while obviously an anomaly which every possible precaution should be taken to avoid, must be accepted as being in certain circumstances an inevitable incident of growth, and it becomes an essential part of the duty of international lawyers, while encouraging the adoption of procedures which will minimize the occurrence of such conflict, also to formulate principles for resolving such conflict when it arises.[36]

Finally, although we witness an unmistakable increase in the number of norms created, it remains the case that international law has a 'lacunary character', as Hafner explained, 'due to the fact that rules of international law or standards are produced only if States feel the urge to create new rules, with the result that the international legal order hardly qualifies as a system inspired by rational and logical choices'.[37] This chaotic feature of international law contributes to the potential for conflict of norms.

Globalisation

Second, and related to the need for co-operation between states so as to tackle today's global problems – of protecting the environment, human rights or stimulating economic development – the ever-increasing interdependence between states, *as well as between regulatory areas*, has resulted

---

[36] Jenks, 'Conflict', 405.
[37] Gerhard Hafner, 'Should One Fear the Proliferation of Mechanisms for the Peaceful Settlement of Disputes?', in L. Caflisch (ed.), *The Settlement of Disputes between States: Universal and European Perspectives* (The Hague: Kluwer, 1998), 25 at 33.

in a proportional boost to the potential for conflict between norms of international law in different sectors. As Alvarez noted, 'states are driven to regulate at the international level by ever-rising movements of people, goods, and capital across borders, along with the positive and negative externalities emerging from such flows – from the rise in a common human rights ideal to emerging threats to the global commons'.[38] As a result, '[i]n light of the growing factual integration of world community on the one hand, and the proliferation of subsystems on the other, it is to be expected that the need to take measures to ensure the unity of the international legal order will increase'.[39]

The potential for conflict is particularly acute for WTO rules. WTO rules regulate the *trade* relations between states. In today's highly interdependent world, a great number, if not most, state regulations in one way or another affect trade flows between states. Hence, WTO rules, essentially aimed at liberalising trade, have a potential impact on almost all other segments of society and law. For example, liberalising trade may sometimes jeopardise respect for the environment or human rights. Equally, enforcing respect for human rights or environmental standards may sometimes require the imposition of trade barriers. Moreover, trade restrictions are resorted to increasingly in pursuit of all kinds of non-trade objectives, ranging from respect for human rights[40] and the environment[41] to confirmation of territorial borders.[42] As a result, the potential for interplay and conflict between WTO rules and other rules of international law is huge: WTO rules are rules that cut across almost all other rules of international law.

---

[38] Alvarez, 'New', 217.   [39] Hafner, 'Risk', 335.
[40] See, for example, the disputes on *United States – Measures Affecting Government Procurement*, WT/DS88 and 95 (involving US trade sanctions against Myanmar); and *United States – The Cuban Liberty and Democratic Solidarity Act*, WT/DS38 (involving US trade sanctions against Cuba).
[41] See the panel and Appellate Body reports on *US – Shrimp* and the dispute on *Chile – Measures Affecting the Transit and Importation of Swordfish*, WT/DS193 (panel suspended on 23 March 2001) (hereafter *Chile – Swordfish*), brought also before the International Tribunal for the Law of the Sea (now suspended, on the basis of a provisional arrangement, by Order of 15 March 2001, http://www.un.org/Depts/los/ITLOS/Order1-2001).
[42] See the dispute on *Nicaragua – Measures Affecting Imports from Honduras and Colombia*, WT/DS188 and 201 (this panel was never activated), involving trade sanctions as a result of a maritime delimitation dispute, pending also before the ICJ (*Maritime Delimitation between Nicaragua and Honduras in the Caribbean Sea (Nicaragua v. Honduras)*), http://www.icj-cij.org.

These first two factors as they apply to WTO rules – first, the move from a law on 'co-existence' to a law on 'co-operation' and, second, globalisation – were aptly summarised by Leebron as follows:

> The growth of the 'trade and...' business derives from two converging forces. First, more issues are now regarded as trade related in the narrow sense that the norms governing those issues affect trade, or conversely, that changes in trade flows affect the realisation of those norms. Second, an increasing number of substantive areas are the subject of international coordinated action or multilateral agreements. Even if conduct in such areas does not directly affect trade flows, the creation of formalized regimes governing them raises the question of how such regimes should be related to the trade regime and whether, for example, trade sanctions should be employed to enforce nontrade policies and agreements.[43]

An emerging hierarchy of values

Third, the emergence of the concept of *jus cogens*, essentially in the second half of the twentieth century, corresponds to an awareness that not all norms of international law should have the same status. Some of them protect so important and universal a value, such as the prohibition on genocide, that they have a hierarchical standing that is higher than other norms.

Also *within* the sphere of human rights, an increasing hierarchy of norms takes shape, some being 'normal' human rights, others being 'non-derogable' human rights or human rights from which state parties to the convention in question cannot deviate even in time of public emergency.[44] Article 4(1) of the International Covenant on Civil and Political Rights, for example, allows for derogations in emergency situations. However, a select group of enumerated rights, such as the right to life or freedom from torture or slavery, may never be suspended or limited, even during times of national emergency. Obviously, this hierarchy among human rights is explicitly provided for in certain treaties. Nonetheless, it does express a tendency towards what Weil coined 'relative normativity'.[45]

Finally, also in the recently adopted Draft Articles on Responsibility of States for Internationally Wrongful Acts, a scale as between different

---

[43] David Leebron, 'Linkages' (part of the Symposium: The Boundaries of the WTO) (2002) 96 AJIL 5.
[44] See Ian Siederman, *Hierarchy in International Law – The Human Rights Dimension* (Antwerp: Intersentia, 2001), 66–84.
[45] Weil, 'Normativity'.

international law obligations emerges. Although the Articles no longer include the notion of 'crimes', particular importance is attached to obligations 'established for the protection of a collective interest' or obligations 'owed to the international community as a whole'.[46] The distinction thus made between bilateral or reciprocal obligations, on the one hand, and multilateral or integral obligations, on the other, is one of the focal points of this study. It is further discussed in chapter 2 below, pp. 52–88.

The shift from all norms of international law being equal towards the recognition that some norms, based on their substantive content, are more important than others, has further contributed to the potential for conflict between norms. Since, for example, *jus cogens* cannot be deviated from, one norm can no longer replace any other norm, even with the mutual consent of the states involved. On the one hand, this development has increased the potential for conflict (even if the practical application of the supremacy of *jus cogens* remains to be put to the test). On the other hand, it has offered new solutions to contradictory evolutions in the law and brought about a certain normative order in the often chaotic world resulting from the contractual freedom of states.

An increase in the judicial settlement of disputes

Fourth, modern times have seen an increase in compulsory dispute settlement systems as well as a renewed eagerness to resort to international courts or tribunals for the *ad hoc* resolution of disputes. The fact that international adjudicators are hence more frequently asked to resolve matters of international law means also that issues of conflict between norms are more likely to arise *in concreto*, before these adjudicators. In a first instance, this will accentuate the problem of conflict and make the establishment of coherent rules on conflict an urgency. At the same time, decisions by international adjudicators on how to resolve particular conflicts will contribute to the establishment of such conflict rules.

In this respect, the importance of the WTO judiciary holding compulsory jurisdiction for all claims under WTO covered agreements cannot be overestimated.[47] As noted earlier, WTO rules have an 'all affecting'

---

[46] See Article 48 of the 2001 Draft Articles on State Responsibility.
[47] Also, for example, as compared to Part XV of UNCLOS. See, in particular, the recent Arbitration Award in the *Southern Bluefin Tuna* case (*Australia and New Zealand v. Japan*), 4 August 2000 (www.worldbank.org/icsid) where the arbitrators held *not* to have jurisdiction.

character.⁴⁸ Because of this, even disputes with only a relatively limited trade aspect can be brought to the WTO, such as the trade aspects of human rights disputes or disputes over high seas fishing or territorial borders.⁴⁹ In addition, compulsory jurisdiction is available to a state *against which* trade restrictions are imposed. But a state wanting to enforce compliance, for example, with most environmental rules, often has no recourse to international adjudication.⁵⁰ In the alternative, trade sanctions could be imposed, but there again the *victim* of the sanction (i.e., the alleged violator of the environmental rule) may complain at the WTO. The state imposing the sanction cannot, in most instances, resort to, say, UNEP for judicial settlement.

Why is conflict between WTO norms a problem?

When assessing the potential for intra-WTO conflicts, or problems of internal hierarchy between WTO norms, two additional factors that have given rise to such conflicts must be pointed to.⁵¹

First, the WTO treaty, although it constitutes a 'single package' binding on all WTO members, is composed of some sixty different legal instruments. These instruments range from the Marrakesh Agreement itself, to agreements on goods, services and intellectual property rights and understandings or decisions on dispute settlement, financial services or the interpretation of specific GATT provisions. In addition, there are the country-specific schedules of commitments which also form an integral part of the WTO treaty. Many of these instruments were negotiated during the Uruguay Round. Others, such as GATT 1947, were simply incorporated without change. Obviously, the more legal instruments one is faced with, especially when these instruments were negotiated at different points in time, the greater the risk of conflict.

Secondly, during the Uruguay Round negotiations many of the legal instruments were negotiated side by side with the original intention that they would operate as autonomous agreements, much the same way as the previous Tokyo Round Codes. These Codes were binding only on a number of like-minded states, not even necessarily GATT Contracting

---

⁴⁸ See above, p. 20.   ⁴⁹ See above, notes 40–2.
⁵⁰ In this respect, see Joost Pauwelyn, 'A World Environment Court?', Working Paper for the United Nations University, in *International Environmental Governance – Gaps and Weaknessses, Proposals for Reform* (Tokyo, 2002).
⁵¹ On the causes of intra-WTO conflicts, see Elisabetta Montaguti and Maurits Lugard, 'The GATT 1994 and Other Annex 1A Agreements: Four Different Relationships?' (2000) 3 JIEL 473, in particular at 474–5.

Parties, who wanted to liberalise further in a certain area. As autonomous legal instruments, created subsequently to the original GATT 1947, these Uruguay Round agreements sometimes derogated from, and often repeated, partly or fully, their parent GATT provisions. Only at a very late stage of the negotiations was it decided to bring all the results of the Uruguay Round together under one umbrella agreement, to be binding equally on all WTO members. This had the unintended result of creating repetitions, omissions and possible conflicts. No time was left to work out the complex interrelationship between the different legal texts. To reopen the negotiations for that purpose would have jeopardised the delicate consensus reached under each of these legal instruments. This separate consensus was, moreover, not always reached by the same negotiators. GATT, GATS and TRIPS negotiators are, in most WTO members, different people. This may explain also why, in particular, the relationship between the three WTO pillars – GATT–GATS–TRIPS – is not explicitly addressed in the WTO treaty.

In sum, the potential for intra-WTO conflict is a textbook example of a variety of law-makers at work, both internationally (146 states with widely diverging interests) and internally (representatives coming from diverse domestic backgrounds), at different points in time (GATT 1947 and a succession of trade negotiation rounds culminating in the 1994 WTO treaty), in different substantive contexts (goods, services and intellectual property rights, as well as different sub-sectors in each of those fields) and operating under serious time pressure in order to come to a consensus on a wide variety of issues. It provides an ideal case study for the topic of conflict of norms.

2 The case study: the law of the World Trade Organization

> We can sit down and look at the realistic possibility of making the WTO work for the whole world. We should be realistic. We shouldn't be kidding ourselves that the WTO is all right at the moment. It's not all right.[1]

In this chapter, we make a first attempt to posit WTO law in the wider context of public international law. The sources of WTO law are summed up and some of the special features of WTO law, of particular importance to conflict of norms, are examined.

WTO law as 'just' another branch of public international law

For WTO law to be a relevant example in this study on conflict of norms in public international law, it should be established first that WTO law is, indeed, part of public international law.

With one possible exception, no academic author, WTO decision or document disputes that WTO rules are part of the wider corpus of public international law.[2] Like international environmental law and human

---

[1] Supacha Panitchpakdi (WTO Director-General as of September 2002), 'Keynote Address: The Evolving Multilateral Trade System in the New Millennium' (2001) 33 *George Washington International Law Review* 419 at 432.
[2] See John Jackson, *The World Trading System* (Cambridge, Mass.: MIT Press, 1997), p. 25; Ernst-Ulrich Petersmann, 'Dispute Settlement in International Economic Law – Lessons for Strengthening International Dispute Settlement in Non-Economic Areas' (1999) 2 JIEL 189; Donald McRae, 'The WTO in International Law: Tradition Continued or New Frontier?' (2000) 3 JIEL 27 and 'The Contribution of International Trade Law to the Development of International Law' (1996) 260 *Recueil des Cours* 111. For earlier sources confirming that GATT was no more than a specialised branch of public international law, see: Georg Schwarzenberger, 'The Principles and Standards of International

rights law, WTO law is 'just' a branch of public international law. To public international lawyers, my call in the April 2000 issue of the *American Journal of International Law* for WTO rules to 'be considered as creating international legal obligations that are part of public international law'[3] is a truism. As one author noted in response: 'It is difficult... to envisage any other possible status for rules emanating from a treaty concluded among States under international law, as the WTO Agreement.'[4] To many negotiators and other WTO experts in Geneva, however, the fact that WTO law is 'just' a branch of the wider corpus of international law comes as a surprise. Not a single legal argument has been (or, in my view, can be) put forward in their support. The fact that many negotiators of the WTO treaty – in numerous countries, representatives from a trade ministry delinked from that of foreign affairs – did not *think* of public international law when drafting the WTO treaty is not a valid legal argument. At most, it amounts to an excuse for the WTO treaty not to have dealt more explicitly with the relationship between WTO rules and other rules of international law.[5]

The Bello–Jackson debate: are WTO rules 'binding'?

The possible exception referred to in the previous paragraph is Judith Bello. She expressed the view that 'WTO rules are simply not "binding" in the traditional sense. When a panel established under the WTO Dispute Settlement Understanding issues a ruling adverse to a member, there is no prospect of incarceration, injunctive relief, damages for harm inflicted or police enforcement.'[6] In her opinion, '[t]he only truly binding WTO obligation is to maintain the balance of concessions negotiated

---

Economic Law' (1966-I) 87 *Recueil des Cours* 1; Société Française pour le Droit International, Colloque d'Orléans, *Aspects du droit international économique* (1972) (the Rapporteur, Prosper Weil, concluded that '[s]ur le plan scientifique, le droit international économique ne constitue qu'un chapitre parmi d'autres du droit international général'); and Ignaz Seidl-Hohenveldern, *International Economic Law* (Dordrecht: Nijhoff, 1989).

[3] Joost Pauwelyn, 'Enforcement and Countermeasures in the WTO: Rules are Rules – Toward a More Collective Approach' (2000) 94 AJIL 335 at 336.

[4] Mariano Garcia Rubio, *Unilateral Measures as a Means of Enforcement of WTO Recommendations and Decisions* (The Hague: Academy of International Law, 2001), footnote 22.

[5] Compare, for example, the WTO treaty to UNCLOS, an equally broad and universal regulatory treaty that carefully regulates its relationship with other rules of international law in Art. 311 (containing no less than six paragraphs).

[6] Judith Bello, 'The WTO Dispute Settlement Understanding: Less is More' (1996) 90 AJIL 416.

among members'.⁷ As a result, when a law or measure of a WTO member is successfully challenged in WTO dispute settlement, the member concerned has, in Bello's view, three choices: to withdraw the law or measure, to provide compensatory benefits or to suffer retaliation against its exports.

First, it is unclear whether Bello thereby wanted to classify the WTO treaty as one that is *not* part of public international law, the only issue of interest for present purposes. It seems, rather, that her point was directed more specifically at the question of whether WTO dispute settlement decisions are legally binding in the sense that they oblige a losing member to cease WTO inconsistent conduct. Second, as pointed out by John Jackson in a direct response to Bello, the enforcement of rules in international law is inherently different from that in domestic law and may, indeed, not always be as effective.⁸ However, 'that is a different issue from the question of whether the "WTO rules are... 'binding' in the traditional sense". Certainly they are binding in the traditional *international law* sense.'⁹

That WTO rules are legally binding rules part of international law must, indeed, stand beyond doubt. They derive from a treaty and, pursuant to Article 26 of the Vienna Convention on the Law of Treaties, '[e]very treaty in force is binding upon the parties to it and must be performed by them in good faith' (that is, the *pacta sunt servanda* principle). Whether WTO rules are as effectively enforced and complied with as domestic law or other rules of international law is another issue.

It is important, in this respect, to distinguish the question of whether the *WTO treaty* is a legally binding instrument part of international law, from two other issues. First, the nature of the WTO treaty must be distinguished from the secondary obligation of cessation which, in my view, necessarily follows breach of a WTO obligation. The fact that if cessation does not immediately occur the opposing party may retaliate, does not mean that somehow the rule breached is not legally binding, let alone not a rule of international law.¹⁰ Secondly, the legally binding nature of the WTO treaty is different from the question of whether a WTO

---

⁷ *Ibid.*, 418.
⁸ Bello is, of course, correct when pointing out that '[t]he WTO has no jailhouse, no bail bondsmen, no blue helmets, no truncheons or tear gas' (*ibid.*, 417).
⁹ John Jackson, 'The WTO Dispute Settlement Understanding – Misunderstandings on the Nature of Legal Obligation' (1997) 91 AJIL 60 at 63.
¹⁰ Pauwelyn, 'Enforcement', 342 ('Can there be no decision that a *binding* international treaty has been breached, just because the injured party can, in response to such breach, suspend the treaty (equalize the balance), in whole or in part? Obviously not').

dispute settlement decision conclusively establishes breach, i.e., whether such decision is a judicial one, binding on the parties, having the character of *res judicata*. In my view it is, and not only the WTO treaty is legally binding, but also WTO dispute settlement decisions are binding, at least as between the disputing parties. As the Appellate Body noted in *Japan – Alcoholic Beverages*, adopted panel reports 'are not binding, *except with respect to resolving the particular dispute between the parties to that dispute*'.[11]

Confirmation in the definition of international law, the law of treaties and the WTO treaty itself

To be entirely sure that WTO law is public international law, let us consider briefly the abstract definition of public international law. Take Guggenheim's uncontroversial definition: 'public international law is the aggregate of the legal norms governing international relations';[12] or that of Quoc Dinh, Daillier and Pellet: 'le droit international se définit comme le droit applicable à la société internationale'.[13] No one can deny that WTO agreements govern a particular aspect of 'international relations' and, in that sense, are relevant for, and apply to, the 'société internationale'. They regulate and govern the *trade* relations of states and independent customs territories. No one can deny either that WTO agreements set out 'legal norms' or 'droit', not merely a collection of gentlemen's agreements, usages or rules of etiquette.

---

[11] Appellate Body report, *Japan – Alcoholic Beverages*, at 14, emphasis added, confirmed in the Appellate Body report on *US – FSC*, para. 108. See further in this chapter, pp. 40–52. Moreover, on what seems to be the real debate between Bello and Jackson – do WTO dispute settlement decisions create a legally binding obligation *to cease WTO inconsistent conduct?* – the answer must also be yes, as Jackson pointed out (with reference to DSU Arts. 3.7, 19.1, 21.1, 22.1, 22.8 and 26.1(b)). As I stated elsewhere: 'WTO rules, as well as DSB recommendations, should be considered binding legal obligations. That is, if the DSB finds a breach of WTO rules, the member concerned should be considered to be violating its obligations under international law, as a consequence of which the member would be obligated, in turn, to stop the violation by bringing the inconsistent measure into conformity with WTO rules. This approach accords with the DSU's unambiguously providing that compensation and retaliation are only "temporary measures" that are not to be preferred to full compliance [DSU Arts. 22.1 and 3.7]... residual international law rules... make clear beyond doubt that in case wrongful conduct is found, the state concerned has to stop that conduct. The DSU determines, in turn, the means by which the prevailing WTO member is authorized to obtain fulfilment of that secondary legal obligation of cessation' (Pauwelyn, 'Enforcement', 341).

[12] Paul Guggenheim, *Traite de Droit International Public* (Geneva: Georg, 1967), 1.

[13] Nguyen Quoc Dinh, P. Daillier and A. Pellet, *Droit International Public* (Montreal: Wilson & Lafleur, 1999), 35.

That WTO agreements are, indeed, international 'legal norms' or 'droit' is confirmed in the Vienna Convention on the Law of Treaties. The concept of 'treaty' – a recognised source of public international law – is defined there as: 'an international agreement concluded between states in written form and governed by international law, whether embodied in a single instrument or in two or more related instruments and whatever its particular designation'.[14]

Turning next to the concrete text of the WTO treaty itself, all doubts as to whether WTO law is part of public international law are cleared. Article 3.2 of the WTO's Understanding on Rules and Procedures Governing the Settlement of Disputes (DSU) explicitly directs panels and the Appellate Body to 'clarify the existing provisions of [the covered WTO] agreements in accordance with customary rules of interpretation of public international law'. For those maintaining that WTO rules are *not* rules of international law this is, indeed, a death-blow. For if WTO rules must be *interpreted* in accordance with rules of public international law, surely, they must *be* rules of public international law. What is more, Art. 3.2 of the DSU not only proves that WTO law is a part of public international law, it also indicates that WTO law is to be considered, not in isolation, but with reference to other, non-WTO rules part of public international law. As the Appellate Body acknowledged in its very first report, '[t]hat direction [in Art. 3.2 of the DSU] reflects a measure of recognition that the *General Agreement* [GATT] is not to be read in clinical isolation from public international law'.[15]

Why has GATT/WTO law often been seen as distinct from public international law?

A critique of Donald McRae

Donald McRae in his 1996 Hague lecture examined why 'the field of international trade law [has nonetheless] traditionally been regarded as outside the mainstream of international law'.[16] He provides three reasons.

---

[14] Article 2.1(a). The criterion 'governed by international law' in this definition of a 'treaty' arguably begs the question we try to answer here, namely is WTO law part of public international law? Any doubt in this respect is taken away though by the other considerations set out in this section which establish that this question is to be answered in the affirmative.

[15] Appellate Body report on *US – Gasoline*, at 17. John Jackson refers to this report as one where 'the Appellate Body stated flatly that WTO/GATT law is part of international law generally' (John Jackson, 'Comments on Shrimp/Turtle and the Product/Process Distinction' (2000) 11 EJIL 303 at 305).

[16] McRae, 'Contribution'.

First, McRae points to social traditions – 'In some countries the idea of commerce, of buying and selling, or of economic matters generally, was not viewed with favour' – combined with the view often held by traditional international lawyers that trade law is too 'technical' and that held by trade lawyers that their field is 'special'.[17] One could add to this set of reasons that trade relations are in many countries overseen by the economic, trade or commerce ministry which is detached from that of foreign affairs, the former being staffed largely with economists, the latter being the traditional feeding ground of public international lawyers.

Second, McRae refers to the 'insidious distinction between the public and the private' pursuant to which 'trade was a matter for the private sphere, not a matter for Governments'. McRae himself refers to the 'emergence of the economic state' based on socialist theories to show that governments also engage in commerce. However, one need not go that far. Governments not only trade themselves (albeit decreasingly so), more importantly, it is governments that *regulate* by their laws and regulations the conduct of private commercial transactions, including transactions across borders. State regulations imposed in respect of imports and exports and other commercial transactions that may affect foreigners or foreign products represent a major part of domestic law. Commerce is, hence, a matter also for governments and *public* international law. The rules concluded in the WTO are not contractual rules applying as between two private traders in respect of a certain transaction. WTO rules discipline *government* regulations affecting trade, not private commercial contracts. Surely, the fact that a rule regulates the conduct of individuals or private economic operators does not necessarily make that rule a rule of private law, let alone a purely contractual rule as between private parties.

Nonetheless, it remains true that often GATT/WTO law has been seen as 'private' in nature in that it affects mainly private economic operators subject to the government regulations involved, more so than it affects government-to-government relationships such as, for example, diplomatic law does. In addition, GATT/WTO rules are often negotiated, and enforced, as a direct result of lobbying by private operators (sometimes one company or one sector), that is, actors who are not always well

---

[17] This mutual distrust is aptly illustrated by Antonio Cassese, *International Law in a Divided World* (Oxford: Clarendon, 1986), at 317: 'international economic relations are usually the hunting ground of a few specialists, who often jealously hold for themselves the key to this abstruse admixture of law and economics'.

versed in public international law. Hence, the private aspect of WTO law is easily overrated and the wider context to which it belongs – *public international law* – often overseen.

Third, and in McRae's view most important, there is

the problem of fitting international trade and economic law into a discipline that defined itself in terms of peace and security, in terms of the territorial integrity and political independence of States, in terms of sovereignty. The rationale of international trade law has nothing to do with sovereignty. International trade law does not rest on that primary assumption of international law, that the world is composed of sovereign nation States, each surrounded by territorial borders within which it exercises plenary authority. International trade law is founded on the primary value of promoting individual economic exchanges, about the value of specialization and the economic welfare that results from specialization and exchange. Rather than focusing on the independence of States, international trade law highlights the concept of interdependence. In fact, when we talk of international trade law and of international law we are dealing with two régimes, with two systems that in quite a fundamental way are talking about different things.[18]

Whereas McRae's first and second reasons – explaining why GATT/WTO law has been kept on the sidelines of public international law – are convincing, this third reason is both misleading and erroneous. It falls into the very trap McRae himself has warned about, namely the trap for trade lawyers to portray 'their' discipline as something 'special'. He thereby risks perpetuating the erroneous viewpoint that GATT/WTO law is really a different 'regime' and not international law at all.

First, McRae uses the wrong benchmark to compare trade law to international law. The international law he refers to is the international law of 'co-existence' prevalent up to the end of the First World War ('a discipline that defined itself in terms of peace and security...territorial integrity and political independence'[19]). Since then international law has expanded its scope so as to include also law on 'co-operation'.[20] Together with disciplines such as international human rights law and environmental law, international trade law is testimony to this expansion into new fields where states realised the need to 'co-operate' in order to tackle common problems, that is, fields which 'highlight the concept of interdependence'.[21] Hence, the 'different assumptions' McRae is referring to are those underlying, on the one hand, the traditional

---

[18] McRae, 'Contribution', 116–17.   [19] *Ibid.*, 117.
[20] See chapter 1, above pp. 17–19.   [21] McRae, 'Contribution', 117.

international law of 'co-existence' and, on the other hand, the modern international law of 'co-operation' *including GATT/WTO law*. In other words, McRae is not comparing international law to trade law, but old international law to new international law. It is not because GATT/WTO law does not fit well in the nineteenth-century mould of international law – a time at which GATT/WTO law did not even exist – that it is not part of today's international law where, indeed, many of its branches highlight not so much independence and sovereignty, but interdependence and co-operation across borders that may well limit sovereignty. If international trade law were, on these grounds, not international law, then also talking about international law, on the one hand, and international human rights and environmental law, on the other, would be 'dealing with two régimes, with two systems that in quite a fundamental way are talking about different things'.[22]

Second, notwithstanding the evolution of international law from a law on 'co-existence' to one on 'co-operation', the basic principles of this international law, including those underlying GATT/WTO law, have remained the same, in particular the presumption of sovereignty of a state over its own territory until proof to the contrary is provided. Two random examples in WTO jurisprudence prove this point. In *Chile – Taxes*, the Appellate Body stated: 'Members of the WTO have the sovereign authority to determine the basis or bases on which they will tax goods, such as, for example, distilled alcoholic beverages, and to classify such goods accordingly, provided of course that the Members respect their WTO commitments.'[23] In *US – Shrimp*, as well, the Appellate Body noted that '[i]t appears to us...that conditioning access to a Member's domestic market on whether exporting Members comply with, or adopt, a policy or policies unilaterally prescribed by the importing Member may, to some degree, be a common aspect of measures falling within the scope

---

[22] The same is true when McRae refers to the fact that 'trade is not, or at least primarily not, an inter-State activity', but 'about voluntary exchanges between individuals that take place across borders' (*ibid.*, 123). To derive from this that trade law is not public international law would necessitate the same conclusion for international human rights and environmental law where private individuals are the subjects of protection and, in terms of environmental degradation, most often also the perpetrators.

[23] Appellate Body report on *Chile – Taxes*, para. 60. See also Appellate Body report on *US – FSC*, para. 90. In *EC – Hormones*, the arbitrators examining a US proposal to retaliate against the EC remarked: 'WTO Members, as sovereign entities, can be presumed to act in conformity with their WTO obligations. A party claiming that a Member had acted *inconsistently* with WTO rules bears the burden of proving that inconsistency' (WT/DS26/ARB, 12 July 1999, para. 9).

of one or another of the exceptions (a) to (j) of Article XX'.²⁴ Accordingly, McRae's statement that 'international trade law...is a discipline whose rationale is inconsistent with or even fundamentally opposed to the idea of sovereignty'²⁵ is wrong. As Bello noted, the WTO is there for a reason: 'sovereign nations choose to cooperate across borders because, without such cooperation, in the interdependent global economy they are helpless to promote economic growth and prosperity most effectively'.²⁶ In other words, the WTO is driven by sovereign states who, in the exercise of self-interest, realised that co-operation with a view to mutual trade liberalisation is beneficial for all of them, even if it implies curtailing their rights to impose certain trade barriers. The WTO is not a construct detached from the sovereignty or self-interest of its members. It is not something states have agreed to against their national interests, but rather a trade-off between limiting their sovereign rights to regulate activity on their territory (including products entering their territory) and increasing their economic well-being.²⁷

McRae confuses the *assumption* underlying international trade law with the *consequence* of international trade law. The underlying *assumption* is *not*, as McRae puts it, 'the *irrelevance* of the sovereignty of States'.²⁸ As is the case for *all* international law, the assumption underlying trade law is the sovereignty and self-interest of states. The limitation on state sovereignty is only the *consequence* of certain international trade law. The *consequence* of *traditional* international law (such as the law on the use of force) may safeguard and increase this sovereignty. However, the consequence of most *modern* international law, including WTO law, is to limit sovereignty so as to tackle cross-border problems internationally in the interest of all states involved. This limitation on sovereignty is a consequence of the exercise of sovereignty, *not* the underlying assumption of international trade law.²⁹

---

²⁴ Appellate Body report on *US – Shrimp*, at para. 121. In the same vein, see the Appellate Body report on *Australia – Salmon*, at para. 199 ('The determination of the appropriate level of protection...is a *prerogative* of the member concerned and not of a panel or the Appellate Body').
²⁵ McRae, 'Contribution', 118.   ²⁶ Bello, 'WTO Dispute', 417.
²⁷ For an economic account of why states co-operate in the WTO (i.e., why it is in their economic interest to do so) and why they would not otherwise (i.e. unilaterally) achieve the same economic benefits, see Kyle Bagwell and Robert Staiger, *GATT-Think*, NBER Discussion Paper No. 8005 (November 2000) and Kyle Bagwell, Petros Mavroidis and Robert Staiger, 'It's a Question of Market Access' (2002) 96 AJIL 56.
²⁸ McRae, 'Contribution', 123.
²⁹ If trade law is not international law because it limits state sovereignty to regulate trade with other countries, what then about human rights law? There, states go much

'Embedded liberalism'

As noted, some of the reasons put forward by McRae do offer an explanation of why the GATT/WTO remained for so long on the sidelines of public international law. Perhaps the most important reason, however, is, in my view, historical, linked both to the ideology that inspired the founding fathers of the GATT 1947 and the institutional outlook held until recently by GATT/WTO 'insiders'.

The ideology behind the original GATT 1947 is closely related to what John Ruggie calls the 'embedded liberalism' bargain.[30] As Howse pointed out, 'trade liberalization was embedded within a *political* commitment, broadly shared among the major players in the trading system of that era, to the progressive, interventionist welfare state'.[31] In particular the government and trade policy 'elite' shared this ideology and further developed it, gradually losing sight of the part of the bargain which linked freer trade to the welfare state and interventionism based on non-trade concerns. To return to Howse,

> [a]s persons with the bent of managers and technical specialists, they ['this new trade policy elite'] tended to understand the trade system in terms of the policy science of economics, not a grand normative political vision. A sense of pride developed that an international regime was being evolved that stood above the 'madhouse' of politics...a regime grounded in the insights of economic 'science', and not vulnerable to the open-ended normative controversies and conflicts that plagued most international institutions and regimes, most notably, for instance, the United Nations.[32]

This ideology of 'embedded liberalism', fuelled by an inward-looking institutional elite, may well be the main reason for the GATT's seclusion from other areas of public international law. In this setting, the 'trade and...' challenge somehow disappeared from view and was managed, mainly by technocrats and experts, *within* the system. As Joseph Weiler put it:

> further: they not only limit their powers to regulate foreigners, but also restrict themselves in what they can do vis-à-vis *their own nationals* (without any foreign element involved).

[30] John Ruggie, 'Embedded Liberalism and the Postwar Economic Regimes', in *Constructing the World Polity: Essays on International Institutionalization* (London: Routledge, 1998), 62.
[31] Robert Howse, 'From Politics to Technocracy – and Back Again: The Fate of the Multilateral Trading Regime' (part of the Symposium: The Boundaries of the WTO) (2002) 96 AJIL 94 at 97.
[32] *Ibid.*, 98.

The GATT successfully managed a relative insulation from the 'outside' world of international relations and established among its practitioners a closely knit environment revolving round a certain set of shared normative values (of free trade) and shared institutional (and personal) ambitions...Within this ethos there was an institutional goal to prevent trade disputes from spilling over or, indeed, spilling out into the wider circles of international relations.[33]

Over time, and especially since the 1990s and the controversial GATT panel report on *United States – Restrictions on Imports of Tuna*,[34] the 'trade and...' challenge and the way it had been dealt with so far became known to the wider public, culminating in the Seattle and Genoa protests. This evolution of traditional 'outsiders' becoming involved in WTO affairs, combined with WTO insiders opening doors to non-trade concerns, manoeuvred the WTO from the fringes of international law to the very forefront of it.

The WTO legal system is not a 'closed legal circuit'

Although nowadays few people would disagree that WTO law is part of public international law, a lot of confusion remains as to whether the WTO legal system is a 'closed' or 'self-contained' regime.[35] It is one thing to say that WTO law is international law, quite another to determine whether international law other than WTO law has a role to play in the WTO.

The concept of being 'self-contained' was first referred to by the PCIJ in the *Wimbledon* case, where the provisions relating to the Kiel Canal in the Treaty of Versailles were labelled as 'self-contained' in the sense that they could not be supplemented or interpreted by the aid of other provisions referring to the inland navigable waterways of Germany.[36] The

---

[33] Joseph Weiler, 'The Rule of Lawyers and the Ethos of Diplomats: Reflections on the Internal and External Legitimacy of Dispute Settlement', in Roger Porter, Pierre Sauvé, Arvind Subramanian and Americo Zampetti (eds.), *Efficiency, Equity, and Legitimacy: The Multilateral Trading System at the Millennium* (Washington: Brookings Institution Press, 2001), 334 at 337.

[34] *United States – Restrictions on Imports of Tuna*, DS 29/R, circulated on 10 June 1994, not adopted (condemning US trade restrictions on imports of tuna for purposes of protecting dolphins).

[35] On the notion of 'self-contained' regimes, see Max Srenson, 'Autonomous Legal Orders: Some Considerations Relating to a Systems Analysis of International Organisations in the World Legal Order' (1983) 32 ICLQ 559–76 and Bruno Simma, 'Self-Contained Regimes' (1985) 16 NYIL 115.

[36] PCIJ, Series A, No. 1, at 24 (1923).

ICJ endorsed the notion of 'self-contained regime' in the *Teheran Hostages* case. However, it did so exclusively in terms of state responsibility:

> diplomatic law itself provides the necessary means of defence against, and sanction for, illicit activities by members of diplomatic or consular missions [in particular, measures of declaration of *persona non grata* and the breaking-off of diplomatic relations]...The rules of diplomatic law, in short, constitute a self-contained régime which, on the one hand, lays down the receiving State's obligations regarding the facilities, privileges and immunities to be accorded to diplomatic missions and, on the other, foresees their possible abuse by members of the mission and specifies the means at the disposal of the receiving State to counter any such abuse. These means are, by their nature, entirely efficacious.[37]

In other words, the Court found that diplomatic law constitutes a 'self-contained regime', but only in the sense that 'diplomatic law itself provides the necessary means of defence against, and sanction for, illicit activities by members of diplomatic or consular missions',[38] including declaring such persons *persona non grata*, but *excluding* the occupation of the embassy or the detention of its staff. Respect for diplomatic law, notwithstanding other breaches, is, indeed, of crucial importance to maintain the possibility of a peaceful settlement. If all diplomatic channels were interrupted, communication so as to achieve a settlement would become difficult, if not impossible.[39] Hence, the Court did not find that diplomatic law was a self-contained regime in the sense of a regime that is completely detached from other rules of international law. It only concluded that in the particular circumstances of the *Teheran Hostages* case the remedies to be resorted to for breach of diplomatic law had to be limited to those available under diplomatic law, not any other remedies such as occupation of the embassy.

In the *Nicaragua* case, the ICJ made another reference to certain regimes of international law that provide for their own enforcement mechanism. There, the ICJ noted that

---

[37] ICJ Reports 1980, 3, at para. 86. But see Simma, 'Self-Contained', 120–3, for arguments that even diplomatic law is not a 'self-contained regime', not even in the limited sphere of state responsibility. In the same sense, see also L. A. N. M. Barnhoorn, 'Diplomatic Law and Unilateral Remedies' (1994) 25 NYIL 39.

[38] ICJ Reports 1980, 3, para. 83.

[39] But this does not mean that in instances where, for example, a diplomatic agent is caught in the act of committing an assault, his or her immunity must be sacredly respected. The Court recognised that in this event the agent can be briefly arrested so as to prevent commission of the crime. ICJ Reports 1980, 41, para. 86. See also Barnhoorn, 'Diplomatic Law'.

where human rights are protected by international conventions, that protection takes the form of such arrangements for monitoring or ensuring respect for human rights as are provided for in the conventions themselves...The mechanisms provided for therein have functioned...In any event, while the United States might form its own appraisal of the situation as to respect for human rights in Nicaragua, the use of force could not be the appropriate method to monitor or ensure such respect.[40]

In that case, the ICJ did not, however, use the words 'self-contained regime', nor did it make a general statement to the effect that no remedy other than those provided for in human rights conventions could be resorted to. It only found that the use of force was not an 'appropriate method'.

As soon as states contract with one another, they do so automatically and necessarily *within* the system of international law. This is why WTO law is international law. It is not a 'self-contained regime' in the sense of a regime *existing outside of international law*. As Pieter Jan Kuijper noted:

The GATT, as is the case with all those international organizations which have their own substantive law and are not merely vehicles for international negotiation and co-ordination, inevitably is a special branch of international law. As with all such branches it develops rules which deviate from general international law and which further refine and adapt the rules and principles of international law.[41]

As further explained below,[42] in their treaty relations states can 'contract out' of one, more or, in theory, all *rules* of international law (other than those of *jus cogens*), but they cannot contract out of the *system* of international law. This limitation, directly linked to the *pacta sunt servanda* principle, could be construed as one of *jus cogens*. Indeed, at a 2002 conference, a former WTO Appellate Body member and expert in public international law expressed the view that the *pacta sunt servanda* principle has the standing of *jus cogens*.[43] The prohibition on setting up a treaty regime *outside* international law can, to some extent, be compared to the prohibition on a limited number of individuals under domestic law setting up their own 'state-within-the state'.

---

[40] ICJ Reports 1986, 14, paras. 267–8.
[41] Pieter Jan Kuijper, 'The Law of GATT as a Special Field of International Law, Ignorance, Further Refinement or Self-Contained System of International Law?' (1994) 25 NYIL 227 at 228.
[42] See chapter 4 below, pp. 212–18.
[43] Statement by Florentino Feliciano at the Second Annual WTO Conference of the British Institute of International and Comparative Law, London, 15 May 2002.

This 'unitary' view of international law – prohibiting the creation of sub-systems completely delinked from international law rules agreed upon elsewhere – is crucial to avoiding the situation where a particular regime of international law, say, the WTO, becomes a safe haven, either for states to escape obligations entered into elsewhere or for domestic pressure groups to circumvent domestic legal constraints by insulating their particular interests in a trade-only WTO cocoon, impermeable to limitations or restrictions that they may face even under domestic law. Such a view of international law is, therefore, not only crucial to upholding the *pacta sunt servanda* principle as between states, but also to avoiding international law becoming what Benvenisti calls 'a convenient exit option for those finding domestic controls too stringent'.[44] In other words, it goes to the heart of the legitimacy and democratic content of international law. Crucially, however, the fact that all treaties are necessarily a part of the corpus of international law does not prevent states, in the exercise of their contractual freedom, from agreeing that one particular regime, treaty or provision prevails over another.[45]

Since the WTO treaty is by definition part of the corpus of international law, and the relationship depends essentially on the contractual freedom of WTO members which is to be exercised within the bounds of the *pacta sunt servanda* principle, the question of 'self-contained regimes' becomes one of degrees, namely: to what extent has WTO law *not* contracted out of international law? In other words, to what extent is international law still relevant to WTO law? Following Riphagen's distinction between a 'system' and a 'sub-system',[46] WTO law is, therefore, not a 'system' in and of itself but a 'sub-system' of international law. The remaining problem is, more particularly: to what extent is this 'sub-system' influenced by (i) the general features of the 'system' to which it belongs (i.e., 'general international law') and (ii) the *other* 'sub-systems' of international law (say, international environmental law or the law of the sea)?

---

[44] Eyal Benvenisti, 'Exit and Voice in the Age of Globalization' (1999) 98 *Michigan Law Review* 167 at 169.
[45] See chapter 7 below, pp. 328–43.
[46] Riphagen provides the following definitions: 'a system was an ordered set of conduct rules, procedural rules and status provisions, which formed a closed legal circuit for a particular field of factual relationships. A subsystem, then, was the same as a system, but not closed in as much as it had an interrelationship with other subsystems' (W. Riphagen, Special Rapporteur to the ILC on State Responsibility, Fourth Report, YBILC 1982, vol. 2, p. 202, para. 16).

This problem is, both in the literature and international case law, mostly addressed from the angle of state responsibility, that is, to what extent are general international law rules on state responsibility (in particular, countermeasures) still relevant for the enforcement of WTO rules? Some authors have argued in this respect that WTO law is a 'self-contained regime' in the sense of 'a certain category of subsystems, namely those embracing, in principle, a full (exhaustive and definite) set of secondary rules...which is intended to exclude more or less totally the application of the general legal consequences of wrongful acts'.[47] James Crawford, for example, submits that the DSU is, in terms of state responsibility, an example where it is 'clear from the language of a treaty or other text that only the consequences specified flow'.[48] Kuijper also expressed the view that '[t]he intention to move further towards a self-contained system certainly underlies the WTO Agreement and its Dispute Settlement Understanding, but it remains to be seen how the WTO Members will make it function'.[49] Other authors, in contrast, argue that general international law remedies are still relevant also in WTO dispute settlement.[50]

Crucially, however, the fact that WTO law may exclude general international law rules on state responsibility (something we examine further below)[51] and may, in that specific sense, be a 'self-contained regime', does not mean that the *entire field* of general international law no longer applies to the WTO treaty, nor that other 'sub-systems' of international law, such as international environmental law or human rights law, cannot influence the WTO treaty. It is one thing to be self-contained in terms of the law on state responsibility, quite another to be self-contained in terms of, for example, the law on treaties or the judicial settlement of disputes, two other branches of 'general international law'.[52] As much

---

[47] This is the definition of 'self-contained regime' introduced by Bruno Simma (Simma, 'Self-Contained', 117).
[48] Third Report on State Responsibility, ILC, A/CN.4/507/Add.4, para. 420.
[49] Kuijper, 'Law of GATT', 257.
[50] Petros Mavroidis, 'Remedies in the WTO Legal System: Between a Rock and a Hard Place' (2000) 11 EJIL 763 and Garcia Rubio, *Unilateral Measures*.
[51] See chapter 4 below, pp. 218–36.
[52] As Dominique Carreau pointed out at the 1971 Colloque d'Orléans: 'M. Weil s'est battu conte une conception qui voudrait faire du droit international économique une discipline tout à fait autonome, qui emprunterait peut-être au droit international classique, mais qui devrait être autonome, avec des modes de création autonomes, des règles propres, des techniques propres. C'est là être très exigeant, et effectivement si on prend de tels critères la réponse ne peut être négative: le droit international économique est un mythe.' (Société Française pour le Droit International, *Aspects*, 124).

as no one nowadays can maintain that WTO law is not international law, no one has submitted so far that the WTO legal system is self-contained in terms of international law other than state responsibility. Kuijper, for example, although expressing the view that the WTO was intended to be self-contained *in terms of state responsibility*, is a strong proponent of examining 'sub-systems' of international law (including WTO and, even, EC law) in the wider context of general international law, in particular the law of treaties.[53] In addition, one must consider these different 'sub-systems' not only in the light of the overall 'system' of international law, but also as they play out against each other, one sub-system being capable of influencing and changing another.

The WTO treaty has contracted out of parts of international law and this contracting out is an important instance of 'conflict' which we will examine below. But contracting out of *some rules* of international law does not mean contracting out of *all* of them, let alone contracting out of the *system* of international law.

The sources of WTO law

We know now that WTO law is but a special branch of public international law. The problem examined in this work is how this WTO law relates to other international law. In order to conduct this exercise we must define up front what we understand by WTO law. Below, it will be explained that all international law can be relevant as applicable law before a WTO panel.[54] However, when referring to WTO law we do not mean all law that may be relevant before a WTO panel. Rather, we limit the concept of WTO law to the law created within, and special to, the WTO context. This law consists mainly of the WTO treaty. But it is also composed of other elements, in particular acts of the WTO as an international organisation.

The single most important dividing line between elements of WTO law is that between WTO law which is part of WTO 'covered agreements' and WTO law which does not belong to these 'covered agreements'.[55] This dividing line is crucial since only claims under WTO 'covered agreements'

---

[53] See Kuijper, 'Law of GATT' and also Pieter Jan Kuijper, 'The Court and the Tribunal of the EC and the Vienna Convention on the Law of Treaties 1969' (1998) 25 *Legal Issues of European Integration* 1. In support of examining also EC law in the wider context of public international law, see: Judgments in *Racke v. Hauptzollamt Mainz* (C-162/96, [1998] ECR I-3655) and *Opel Austria v. Council* (CT-115/94, REC. 1997, 11-39).

[54] See chapter 8 below, pp. 456-72.   [55] See Annex 1 to the DSU.

fall within the substantive jurisdiction of WTO panels and the Appellate Body. WTO 'covered agreements' include only a number of *WTO agreements*. *Non*-WTO rules are excluded and so are WTO rules that *do not* derive from the WTO treaty itself.

WTO agreements

WTO treaty provisions are by far the main source of WTO law. The results of the Uruguay Round negotiations constitute around 30,000 pages of text. One must distinguish, first, the Final Act[56] which includes all of the results of the Uruguay Round as concluded on 15 April 1994, and, second, any post-1994 agreements that may emerge in the WTO context.

The Final Act, the Marrakesh Agreement, WTO 'covered agreements' and WTO 'schedules'

The Final Act Embodying the Results of the Uruguay Round of Multilateral Trade Negotiations includes some sixty 'treaties', two of which have now been terminated.[57] The drafters used varying terms to designate the more or less sixty legal instruments, such as agreement, understanding, protocol, decision, declaration or even mechanism. However, according to the Vienna Convention,[58] whatever the denomination given, they can all be considered as 'treaties'.

Even if some sixty different instruments or 'treaties' were negotiated, the combined result of the Uruguay Round negotiations is set out as part of one single framework agreement, namely the 'Final Act'. This Final Act incorporates all WTO agreements. All WTO members have adopted and are bound by this 'single package' with the exception of the two so-called plurilateral agreements to which less than half of the WTO membership is signatory.

Some thirty of the sixty 'treaties' part of the Final Act constitute what is called the Marrakesh Agreement Establishing the WTO, referred to here as the 'Marrakesh Agreement'. Those thirty 'treaties' are by far the most important ones. They range from the Marrakesh Agreement itself, to GATT 1994 with its specific Understandings, the specific agreements on trade in goods, the General Agreement on Trade in Services (GATS),

---

[56] Final Act Embodying the Results of the Uruguay Round of Multilateral Trade Negotiations, concluded in Marrakesh, Morocco, on 15 April 1994.
[57] The International Dairy Agreement and the International Bovine Meat Agreement.
[58] The Vienna Convention defines the term 'treaty' without reference to its particular designation, that is, 'whatever its particular designation' (Art. 2.1(a)).

the Agreement on Trade-Related Intellectual Property Rights (TRIPS), the DSU, the Trade Policy Review Mechanism and the two remaining plurilateral agreements. The remaining thirty legal instruments, not part of the Marrakesh Agreement, are mainly ministerial decisions and declarations.

The single most important distinguishing feature among WTO treaties is whether or not they are listed in Appendix 1 to the DSU as 'covered agreements', that is, agreements that are subject to, and can be invoked before, the WTO dispute settlement mechanism.[59] Of the sixty or so WTO treaties, only the treaties incorporated in the Marrakesh Agreement (with the exception of the Trade Policy Review Mechanism) are 'covered agreements'. The other thirty or so treaties part of the Final Act, but not part of the Marrakesh Agreement, are not 'covered agreements' and cannot, therefore, be enforced under the DSU.

Besides the treaty provisions themselves, some WTO agreements part of the Final Act – more specifically those incorporated in the Marrakesh Agreement (such as GATT 1994, GATS and the agreement on agriculture) – include annexes setting out, not multilateral treaty text applying to all WTO members, but member-specific schedules specifying so-called trade concessions or specific commitments. These concessions take the form, for example, of tariff or export subsidy reduction commitments or national treatment commitments in specific service sectors. They are the result of mainly bilaterally negotiated trade deals which under the MFN clause are then 'multilateralised'. They are drafted by the WTO members negotiating the concessions, but thereafter verified and accepted by the entire WTO membership as a full part of the Marrakesh Agreement.

In 1998 the Appellate Body made an important statement when it declared that these country-specific schedules of concessions set out *treaty text* to be interpreted like any other norm of the WTO treaty, that is, in line with the Vienna Convention rules on treaty interpretation and notwithstanding the special features of these member-specific schedules.[60]

---

[59] Article 1.1 of the DSU provides: 'The rules and procedures of this Understanding shall apply to disputes brought pursuant to the consultation and dispute settlement provisions of the agreements listed in Appendix 1 to this Understanding (referred to in this Understanding as the "covered agreements").'

[60] Appellate Body report on *EC – Computer Equipment*, para. 84 ('the only rules which may be applied in interpreting the meaning of a concession [being part of WTO covered agreements] are the general rules of treaty interpretation set out in the *Vienna Convention*').

Agreements concluded in the WTO context subsequent to 15 April 1994

WTO agreements are not static. First, pursuant to the Marrakesh Agreement, the WTO treaty concluded in 1994 can be amended[61] and new members can accede to it.[62] Amendments, in so far as they relate to 'covered agreements', would then become themselves, per definition, an integral part of the 'covered agreement' in question and fall thereby under the DSU's coverage.[63] Accessions result, in turn, in the annexing of a Protocol of Accession and new country-specific schedules of concessions to the Marrakesh Agreement, making the Protocol and schedules an integral part of WTO 'covered agreements'.[64] Both these post-1994 amendments and accessions are thus enforceable as 'covered agreements' under the DSU.

Secondly, separate protocols or entirely new WTO agreements may be concluded post-1994. Under GATS, for example, new protocols on financial services and telecommunications have been added. The actual substantive obligations under these protocols are reflected, though, in the country-specific schedules of commitments where new commitments have been made in the areas of financial services and telecommunications. In addition, entirely new WTO agreements, say, a treaty on trade and competition, could be added to, for example, the Annex 1A list of Multilateral Agreements on Trade in Goods. To do so, the amendment procedures in Art. X of the Marrakesh Agreement must be followed, in particular those relating to amending the Marrakesh Agreement itself, since adding a new multilateral trade agreement is not explicitly regulated in Art. X.[65] In case the new agreement is to be binding only on a limited number of WTO members, Art. X:9 explicitly regulates the adding of so-called plurilateral agreements. This can occur only where there is a consensus among all WTO members. The agreement

---

[61] Article X of the Marrakesh Agreement.   [62] Article XII of the Marrakesh Agreement.
[63] At the time of writing, not a single amendment had been made to the 1994 WTO treaty.
[64] In principle, the report of the Working Party that negotiated the accession does not become a 'covered agreement'. But in practice the important paragraphs of that report are explicitly referred to and incorporated in the Protocol of Accession so that indirectly those paragraphs of the Working Party report can also be enforced through the DSU.
[65] In the absence of such explicit rules, adding a new agreement (assuming that this new agreement is to be an integral part of the Marrakesh Agreement binding on all WTO members) then involves, indeed, amending the Marrakesh Agreement itself, not any of the other more specific multilateral trade agreements.

as between the parties to a plurilateral agreement suffices to *delete* such agreement from Annex 4 to the Marrakesh Agreement. It does not suffice to *add* such new agreement to Annex 4. The latter can be done 'exclusively by consensus'.

There may also be post-1994 treaties concluded in the WTO context that do not become part of the Marrakesh Agreement nor, *a fortiori*, of WTO covered agreements enforceable under the DSU. One may think here especially of bilateral agreements between disputing members, such as a mutually agreed solution, an agreement in respect of the reasonable period of time for implementation of reports or an agreement on the procedures to be followed in case of an implementation dispute. Such agreements cannot be the subject of *claims* before a WTO panel, but, as explained below,[66] they may play a role as part of the *applicable law* before a WTO panel when examining claims that do fall under the 'covered agreements'. The fact that bilateral settlements cannot be enforced under the DSU represents a serious flaw. It would, indeed, be very beneficial for the implementation of WTO rules if a WTO member who, for example, obtained concessions in a mutually agreed solution and, as a result, withdrew its request for a panel, could enforce that solution through the DSU mechanism in case of non-respect by the other member. When agreeing on such solution (a solution that may, of course, not affect the rights of other WTO members: see Art. 3.5 DSU), parties could, however, include an arbitration clause to this effect, say, an agreement to arbitrate any disputes under the mutually agreed solution pursuant to DSU Art. 25.

Acts of WTO organs

As opposed to GATT 1947, the WTO is an international organisation with legal personality, specific functions and an organic structure. Its organs are law-creating bodies. The law they create must be clearly distinguished from that created by the WTO treaty itself.[67] A treaty concluded as between WTO members does not have the same legal standing as an act by a WTO organ, even if this organ is constituted by delegates

---

[66] See chapter 8 below, pp. 456–72.
[67] For an interesting approach to the sources of *GATT law*, see Wolfgang Benedek, *Die Rechtsordnung des GATT aus Völkerrechtlicher Sicht* (Berlin: Springer, 1990). Based on the law of international organisations – and, it would seem, in particular the law of the EC – Benedek divided the sources of GATT law into primary sources (essentially GATT itself and other agreements) and secondary sources (mainly decisions of the GATT Contracting Parties acting as *de facto* organs of an international organisation) (*ibid.*, 94–125).

of all WTO members. In practice, this distinction and the importance of the WTO as a now fully fledged international organisation is often overlooked. Too often, it is considered that a consensus of WTO members acting, for example, in the form of the Council for Trade in Services, can simply overrule or amend a WTO treaty provision, without respecting the amendment provisions in the Marrakesh Agreement. The agreement of WTO members *as states*, required, for example, to amend the WTO treaty, cannot be equated to an agreement among WTO members *acting as a WTO organ*. As explained below, acts of a WTO organ must respect and are subject to their constituent WTO treaty instruments. They cannot change them. On the contrary, acts of WTO organs taken in disrespect of the relevant WTO treaty provisions could be said to be invalid or to be taken *ultra vires*, even if to date no procedure exists to challenge the validity of WTO acts. In that sense, the WTO is not a 'member-driven' organisation where the will of members, whatever form it takes, can overrule previous state consent.

The distinction between actual WTO treaty norms and acts of WTO organs is crucial in terms of the substantive jurisdiction of WTO panels. Only claims under WTO covered agreements, not claims under acts of WTO organs, fall within this jurisdiction. As noted below, however, the fact that claims under such acts of WTO organs do not fall within a panel's jurisdiction does not mean that these acts cannot be part of the applicable law before a panel, to be resorted to when deciding on the validity of claims that do fall under WTO covered agreements.[68] For example, a WTO waiver cannot itself be the subject of a WTO claim before a panel, but it may be invoked in defence against another claim of, say, violation of GATT Art. I, as was done by the EC in *EC – Bananas* in respect of the Lomé waiver.

Examples of norms enacted by WTO organs are: waivers granted by the WTO Ministerial Conference to a specific WTO member (pursuant to the three-quarters majority rule in Art. IX:3 of the Marrakesh Agreement), decisions adopted by specialised WTO committees (such as the adoption by the SPS committee of Guidelines under Article 5.5 of the SPS agreement), interpretations of WTO agreements adopted by the Ministerial Conference or General Council (pursuant to the three-quarters majority rule in Art. IX:2 of the Marrakesh Agreement) or decisions taken by the DSB in respect of dispute settlement. In addition, reference could be made to the increasing number of international agreements the WTO

[68] See chapter 8 below, pp. 456–72.

as an institution concludes with other international institutions, such as the World Bank, the IMF, the International Office for Epizootics, etc.

DSB decisions may be of a general nature, such as the adoption of rules on how to count DSU deadlines or the imposition of a ten-day deadline for requests to be a third party in panel proceedings. They may also relate to particular disputes, such as the decision to refer a matter to a panel or arbitrator. DSB decisions that actually adopt panel or Appellate Body rulings and recommendations, on the other hand, ought to be classified rather as decisions of the WTO judiciary, not decisions of WTO political organs. This was confirmed by the Appellate Body in respect of decisions by GATT Contracting Parties in which GATT panel reports were adopted. The panel on *Japan – Alcoholic Beverages* found that such decisions are an integral part of GATT 1994 since they are 'other decisions of the CONTRACTING PARTIES to GATT 1947' which, pursuant to Article 1(b)(iv) of GATT 1994, have been incorporated in GATT 1994.[69] In other words, the panel considered such decisions and, hence, indirectly, GATT panel reports, to be fully fledged WTO treaty norms, applicable and binding as to a particular set of circumstances.[70] The Appellate Body reversed this panel finding, concluding instead that adopted reports are 'an important part of the GATT *acquis*' but that 'they are not binding, except with respect to resolving the particular dispute between the parties to that dispute'.[71] The same reasoning must, *a fortiori*, apply to DSB decisions in which WTO panel and Appellate Body reports are adopted. Such decisions, taken virtually automatically pursuant to the negative consensus rule, are not decisions of the DSB as a political WTO organ binding on all WTO members. They are a mere rubber-stamping or confirmation of the work conducted by the judicial branch of the WTO. To that extent, the DSB can, indeed, be said to be part of the WTO judiciary. The fact that the Appellate Body confirmed that panel reports and the decisions adopting them are binding only on the parties to the dispute does not only mean that such decisions cannot be seen as acts of WTO political organs. It also confirms that such decisions, and hence panels and the Appellate Body, are judicial in nature since bestowed with the power to make legally binding rulings as between the disputing parties.

[69] Panel report on *Japan – Alcoholic Beverages*, para. 6.10.
[70] Benedek, *Rechtsordnung*, 94–125, seems to have made the same mistake, classifying decisions by GATT Contracting Parties in the field of dispute settlement as 'secondary law', instead of judicial decisions binding only on the parties to the dispute.
[71] Appellate Body report on *Japan – Alcoholic Beverages*, p. 14.

That it is not always an easy task to distinguish between an agreement as between WTO members and an act of a WTO organ, witness the Declaration on the TRIPS Agreement and Public Health, adopted by the Ministerial Conference at Doha on 14 November 2002.[72] This 'declaration' does not specify the legal basis pursuant to which it was adopted, nor does it specify whether it is an amendment or an interpretation of the TRIPS agreement. The language of the Declaration seems to imply that it simply interprets the TRIPS agreement. However, if this is what the Declaration does, Art. IX:2 of the Marrakesh Agreement stipulates that any interpretation of the TRIPS agreement must be made 'on the basis of a recommendation by the Council overseeing the functioning of that Agreement', that is, the TRIPS Council. This formality does not seem to be complied with. The example shows also that in the WTO the prevailing view remains that, with the consensus of WTO members, everything can be done, an attitude that must be changed if the WTO is to distinguish itself as an international organisation whose organs have law-making capacities.

GATT/WTO 'custom' and 'subsequent practice'

It is questionable whether there exists any GATT/WTO-particular customary international law, as referred to, for example, by Benedek[73] and Palmeter and Mavroidis.[74] In terms of 'GATT custom', Benedek makes reference to the practice of consensus decisions instead of majority voting or the practice on dispute settlement under GATT Arts. XXII–III later codified in 1979. Palmeter and Mavroidis make reference to the 'customary practices' cited in Article XVI:1 of the Marrakesh Agreement, which provides: 'Except as otherwise provided under this Agreement or the Multilateral Trade Agreements, the WTO shall be guided by the decisions, procedures and *customary practices* followed by the CONTRACTING PARTIES to the GATT 1947 and the bodies established in the framework of GATT 1947' (emphasis added).[75]

In the view of Palmeter and Mavroidis, '[i]t is doubtful that the "customary practices" referred to would be recognised as customary

---

[72] WTO document WT/MIN(01)/DEC/2, dated 20 November 2001.
[73] Benedek, *Rechtsordnung*, 123–31.
[74] David Palmeter and Petros Mavroidis, 'The WTO Legal System: Sources of Law' (1998) 92 AJIL 398 at 407.
[75] Note that DSU Art. 3.1 also incorporates certain GATT 'principles': 'Members affirm their adherence to the principles for the management of disputes heretofore applied under Articles XXII and XXIII of GATT 1947...'

international law. Although the customary practices of GATT might meet some of the requirements of custom, it is doubtful that they were accepted by the parties to GATT or are viewed by the members of the WTO "as law".'

However, that it is quite difficult for there to be GATT/WTO custom is not so much linked to the absence of the psychological or subjective element for custom to exist, namely *opinio juris* or the existence of a general practice 'accepted [by GATT Contracting Parties/WTO members] as law' (Art. 38(1)(b) of the ICJ Statute). It is related rather to the fact that custom is a source of law *independent of treaty norms*. The ICJ in the *Nicaragua* case made it clear that custom and treaty are two sources of law that exist independently of each other.[76] The fact that a norm of customary international law (in that case, the principle of non-use of force) was codified in a treaty does not thereby extinguish the customary norm. Both norms continue to exist side by side. Equally, in case subsequently the treaty were to be terminated, this does not mean that also the custom automatically ceases to exist. Custom cannot be completely dependent on the existence and operation of a particular treaty (*in casu*, the WTO treaty). If WTO custom were, indeed, to exist as a source of law independent of GATT/WTO treaties, it would mean, for example, that in case a WTO member were to leave the WTO, it would no longer be bound by WTO treaties, but still be bound by GATT/WTO custom. It is difficult to imagine that such GATT/WTO custom exists today, custom that would then arguably also be binding as between WTO members and states, such as Russia or Saudi Arabia, that are not yet WTO members.

The fact that it is, on these grounds, difficult to see any WTO-specific custom emerge, leading a life independent of the WTO treaty, is not to say though that there can be no custom in the area of trade altogether. Such custom could emerge *with reference to GATT/WTO law*, such as, arguably, basic principles of non-discrimination, or be constituted by parts of the so-called *lex mercatoria*.[77] Such custom would then be binding on all states, irrespective of whether they were WTO members. This is a question not further examined in this work. What could be added, though, is that given the reciprocal nature of most WTO obligations, a feature discussed below, it is less likely that WTO rules become an engine of growth for customary international law. As Schachter pointed out,

---

[76] ICJ Reports 1986, 95.
[77] See S. Zamora, 'Is there Customary International Economic Law?' (1989) 22 GYIL 9.

[a] persuasive common sense argument can be made that such treaties [which are essentially reciprocal in character] should not be construed as including rules that are declaratory or constitutive of customary law binding on non-parties. The reason is that the rules in those treaties are meant to be intra-dependent and therefore should not be abstracted from the treaty as independent rules.[78]

The normative elements that may have developed under the operation of GATT, or now the WTO, are better described as 'subsequent practice' to be taken into account in the interpretation of GATT/WTO treaty rules, in the sense referred to by Art. 31(3)(b) of the Vienna Convention, namely 'subsequent practice in the application of the treaty which establishes the agreement of the parties regarding its interpretation'. Article XVI:1 of the Marrakesh Agreement itself uses the words 'shall be *guided by*... customary practice'; not, for example, 'shall abide by'. If these practices were to constitute custom they would not only 'guide' the WTO, but 'bind' WTO members. Some of the other normative elements often alleged to be WTO custom, such as the ten-day deadline for requests to join panel proceedings as a third party, are a mix of 'subsequent practice' under the DSU and normative value to be attributed to General Council and DSB decisions as acts of WTO organs.[79]

In *Japan – Alcoholic Beverages*, the Appellate Body explained what it understood by 'subsequent practice' as referred to in Art. 31(3)(b) of the Vienna Convention:

the essence of subsequent practice in interpreting a treaty has been recognized as a 'concordant, common and consistent' sequence of acts or pronouncements which is sufficient to establish a discernible pattern implying the agreement of the parties regarding its interpretation. An isolated act is generally not sufficient to establish subsequent practice; it is a sequence of acts establishing the agreement of the parties that is relevant.[80]

It is important to recall that, in the context of international organisations, evidence of 'subsequent practice' may be found either in *state* practice or in the practice of the international organisation itself, *in casu*, WTO organs. It is generally accepted today – and confirmed by the

---

[78] Oscar Schachter, 'Entangled Treaty and Custom', in Yoram Dinstein and Mala Tabory (eds.), *International Law at a Time of Perplexity – Essays in Honour of Shabtai Rosenne* (Dordrecht: Nijhoff, 1998), 717 at 735.

[79] A 1994 decision of the GATT General Council makes reference to this rule as a practice. Moreover, each time the DSB establishes a panel, the DSB chairperson reminds WTO members that they have ten days to exercise their third-party rights under DSU Art. 10.

[80] Appellate Body report on *Japan – Alcoholic Beverages*, p. 13, footnotes omitted.

ICJ in, for example, the *Certain Expenses* and *Namibia* cases[81] – that the constituent instruments of international organisations must be interpreted not only with reference to subsequent practice of the *individual states* that are members of the organisation, but also the subsequent practice of the international organisation itself or its organs. The latter is understood to occur pursuant to customary international law, not as part of the law of treaties but as part of international institutional law.[82] As a result, the discussion often heard in WTO circles as to whether a decision or practice is one of WTO members or one of the WTO as an institution (for example, the General Council or the DSB) is not relevant for purposes of determining the normative value of 'subsequent practice'. Both practice of WTO members and practice of the WTO as an institution can be referred to in the interpretation of WTO law.[83]

Subsequent practice can lead to further clarification of treaty rules, certain treaty gaps being filled or even the desuetude of WTO obligations.[84] Following international case law, such 'subsequent practice' is capable also of actually changing treaty norms.[85] In that instance, subsequent practice can be equated with an implicit agreement to change the law and operates, not pursuant to Art. 31 of the Vienna Convention on treaty *interpretation*, but pursuant to the rule of customary international law allowing for the *modification* of treaties by means of subsequent practice.

WTO judicial decisions and doctrine

Academic writings are increasingly referred to in panel and Appellate Body decisions. Such decisions refer even more frequently to previous panel and, in particular, Appellate Body reports. Reference has also been

---

[81] Respectively, ICJ Reports 1962, 168 and 1971, 22.
[82] See Elihu Lauterpacht, 'The Development of the Law of International Organization by the Decisions of International Tribunals' (1976) 152 *Recueil des Cours* 379 and Tetsuo Sato, *Evolving Constitutions of International Organizations* (Dordrecht: Kluwer, 1996), 232–43.
[83] For an example, see the panel report on *US – Shrimp (Article 21.5)*, at para. 5.56, which referred to the 1996 Report of the CTE in its interpretation of GATT Art. XX, either as 'subsequent practice' or as 'the expression of a common opinion' of WTO members.
[84] Kuijper has questioned, for example, whether, as between European states, the freedom of road transit as prescribed in GATT Art. V cannot be said to have fallen into desuetude (Kuijper, 'Law of GATT', 231).
[85] See the ICJ *Namibia* case, ICJ Reports 1971, 22 (in respect of voting practices of the UN Security Council which were effectively found to have changed the UN Charter provisions).

made to judicial decisions of other courts or tribunals, such as the ICJ and the ECJ.

As far as judicial decisions are concerned, we noted earlier that GATT and WTO panel and Appellate Body reports, as well as the DSB decisions adopting these reports, are not acts of WTO political organs or 'subsequent practice' legally binding on all WTO members, but rather judicial decisions binding only on the parties to a particular dispute. The Appellate Body, in its report on *US – Shrimp (Article 21.5)*, confirmed that 'Appellate Body Reports that are adopted by the DSB are, as Article 17.14 provides, "...unconditionally accepted by the parties to the dispute", and, therefore, must be treated by the parties to a particular dispute as a final resolution to that dispute.'[86]

Judicial decisions and teachings of publicists do *not* in and of themselves constitute legal norms. Nonetheless, they are influential in the process of determining what the law is. The same applies in the context of WTO law. As the Appellate Body stated in *US – Shirts and Blouses*: 'Given the explicit aim of dispute settlement that permeates the *DSU*, we do not consider that...the *DSU* is meant to encourage either panels or the Appellate Body to "make law" by clarifying existing provisions of the *WTO Agreement* outside the context of resolving a particular dispute.'[87]

Be this as it may, the Appellate Body made it equally clear that '[a]dopted panel reports are an important part of the GATT *acquis*. They are often considered by subsequent panels. They create legitimate expectations among WTO Members, and, therefore, should be taken into account where they are relevant to any dispute.'[88] The Appellate Body, in a footnote, referred explicitly to Art. 59 of the ICJ Statute (pursuant

---

[86] Appellate Body report on *US – Shrimp (Article 21.5)*, para. 97. For a more detailed, but inconclusive, discussion of the principle of *res judicata* as it operates in the WTO, see panel report on *India – Autos*, paras. 7.42 ff.

[87] Appellate Body report, p. 19. In *US – FSC* (footnote 127), the Appellate Body stressed the importance of distinguishing between authoritative interpretations under Art. IX of the Marrakesh Agreement and interpretations by the WTO judiciary in a particular case.

[88] Appellate Body report on *Japan – Alcoholic Beverages*, p. 14. As far as *unadopted* GATT panel reports are concerned (non-adoption being virtually excluded under the WTO's DSU), the Appellate Body stated that these 'have no legal status in the GATT or WTO system' but that 'a panel could nevertheless find useful guidance in the reasoning of an unadopted panel report that it considered to be relevant' (*ibid.*, 14–15). In *Argentina – Footwear* (at para. 43), it specified that panels may not go beyond deriving 'useful guidance' from the reasoning employed in *unadopted* panel reports, criticising the panel in that case on the ground that it 'in fact, *relies* upon the [unadopted] *Bananas II* panel report'.

to which ICJ decisions are binding only as between the parties to the particular dispute), adding that this provision 'has not inhibited the development by that Court (and its predecessor) of a body of case law in which considerable reliance on the value of previous decisions is readily discernible'.[89] In the WTO, no equivalent to Art. 59 can be found, nor is there an equivalent to Art. 38(1)(d), explicitly stating that judicial decisions are 'subsidiary means for the determination of rules of law'. Nonetheless, through its case law the Appellate Body has clearly incorporated this 'subsidiary means' into WTO law.

Unilateral acts of WTO members

Unilateral acts of WTO members have occasionally played a role in WTO dispute settlement. In the panel report on *US – Section 301*, for example, a US declaration solemnly made and repeated several times during the panel's proceedings – to the effect that the US administration would not use its discretion under section 301 to act contrary to the DSU – was accepted as a US undertaking that confirmed the panel's interpretation of section 301 in a way that was consistent with DSU provisions. As a result, the EC's challenge failed, but the panel added that this result was only warranted in so far as the US undertakings were maintained.[90]

The nature of WTO obligations: reciprocal or integral?[91]

Introduction: consequences and relevance for the topic of conflict of norms

WTO law is international law. The WTO legal system is not a closed legal circuit. But, of course, WTO law does have special features, both in terms of the rights and obligations it imposes on WTO members and in its general structure and characteristics. These features have marked and continue to mark the WTO's relationship with other rules of international law. Next, we focus more particularly on the legal nature of WTO obligations. The WTO agreement is, obviously, a *multilateral agreement*. It has 144 signatories. But what is the nature of WTO *obligations*? Are they of the *bilateral* (synallagmatic or reciprocal) type, in that WTO obligations can be reduced to a compilation of bilateral treaty relations, each

---

[89] Appellate Body report on *Japan – Alcoholic Beverages*, footnote 30.
[90] Panel report on *US – Section 301*, in particular at para. 7.118.
[91] This section draws on Joost Pauwelyn, 'The Nature of WTO Obligations', Jean Monnet Working Paper No. 1/2002, posted on the internet at http://www.jeanmonnetprogram.org.

of them detachable one from the other? Or are they of the *multilateral* (*erga omnes partes* or integral) type, in the sense that their binding effect is collective and the different relationships between WTO members cannot be separated into bilateral components?

Classifying WTO obligations in either of those two categories has major legal consequences. Crucially, for our topic of conflict of norms involving WTO rules, the distinction may determine the permissibility of certain *inter se* modifications to the WTO treaty, that is, agreements deviating from WTO rules that are concluded between a limited number of WTO members, not all WTO members. An *inter se* modification to a multilateral treaty is, in principle, only permissible when such modification relates to obligations *of the reciprocal type*. This is expressed in Art. 41 of the Vienna Convention, discussed at length in chapter 6 below. Article 41 renders illegal *inter se* modifications to a multilateral treaty which 'affect the enjoyment by the other parties of their rights under the treaty or the performance of their obligations' or relate to 'a provision, derogation from which is incompatible with the effective execution of the object and purpose of the treaty as a whole' (Art. 41(1)(b)(i) and (ii)). If either of these two conditions is met, the treaty rule modified must be seen as one of an integral nature and no *inter se* deviations from it are allowed.[92]

Secondly, the distinction between reciprocal and integral obligations is important also in terms of countermeasures or suspension of obligations in response to breach. The taking of countermeasures as a remedy in the field of state responsibility as against a defaulting state cannot be in the form of a suspension of obligations *of the integral type*. Indeed, suspending such obligations would not only affect the defaulting state, but all other state parties to the multilateral treaty in question. Article 49.2 of the 2001 Draft Articles on State Responsibility makes clear that '[c]ountermeasures are limited to the non-performance for the time being of international obligations of the State taking the measures *towards the responsible State*' (emphasis added). Moreover, Art. 50 explicitly prohibits the suspension of certain obligations, most of which are integral in nature. In the field of the law of treaties as well, Art. 60(5) of the Vienna Convention prohibits the termination and suspension of treaty obligations, as a result of material breach, in case of 'provisions

---

[92] Art. 58 provides for similar rules in respect of the *inter se* suspension of multilateral treaties. In the same vein, Art. 19(c) of the Vienna Convention prohibits reservations to a treaty that are 'incompatible with the object and purpose of the treaty'.

relating to the protection of the human person contained in treaties of a humanitarian character, in particular provisions prohibiting any form of reprisals against persons protected by such treaties'. Moreover, Art. 60(2)(c) of the Vienna Convention provides that, in case of material breach by one party, any other party to the multilateral treaty (not just the party specially affected by the breach) may suspend the treaty, in whole or in part, 'if the treaty is of such a character that a material breach of its provisions by one party radically changes the position of every party with respect to the further performance of its obligations under the treaty'. In other words, in case of breach of a multilateral treaty *of the integral type*, each and every party to that treaty can suspend the treaty, in whole or in part. Breach of a treaty *of the reciprocal type* will enable only the 'specially affected' party, i.e., the party at the other end of the bilateral relationship, to suspend the treaty.

Thirdly, a decision on whether WTO obligations are reciprocal or integral has its influence also on the rules on standing to bring a complaint before a WTO panel. In principle, legal standing to invoke the responsibility for breach *of a reciprocal obligation* is limited only to the state at the other end of the bilateral relationship. Breach *of an integral obligation*, in contrast, can be invoked by each and every one of the other parties to the multilateral treaty (albeit sometimes to a lesser extent, e.g., limited to claims of cessation only). This is reflected in Arts. 42 and 48 of the 2001 Draft Articles on State Responsibility.

In sum, and generally speaking, in case WTO obligations were of the multilateral or *erga omnes partes* type, *inter se* modifications to the WTO treaty and the suspension of WTO obligations as against a wrongdoing state would *not* be acceptable, whereas standing to bring a WTO complaint would, in principle, be granted to all WTO members, irrespective of the breach. In contrast, if WTO obligations were seen as bilateral or reciprocal obligations, *inter se* modifications and suspension in response to breach would, in theory, be *permissible*, whereas standing would normally be limited to those WTO members at the other end of the (compilation of) bilateral relationship(s) allegedly breached.

At the outset it must be stressed that drawing a clear line between reciprocal and integral obligations may not always be possible. As Oscar Schachter noted, '[t]he distinction is, of course, a familiar one, although the line between the two categories is sometimes blurred'.[93] A degree of discretion thus remains and it would be wrong to overformalise the

---

[93] Schachter, 'Entangled', 735.

distinction. The distinction is, nonetheless, very instructive. Although the words 'reciprocal' and 'integral' do not appear in any codified rule of international law, the distinction is prominent in a series of provisions in the Vienna Convention on the Law of Treaties and, in particular, in the recently adopted Draft Articles on the Responsibility of States for Internationally Wrongful Acts. The difference between reciprocal and integral obligations is, therefore, far from an invention of this author. The only novel element proposed here is the attempt to bring together the different features and consequences of the distinction as it plays out in different fields of international law.

One other caveat must be made. As will soon become clear, when examining whether an obligation is of a reciprocal or an integral nature, it is often difficult to separate possible *causes* or *reasons why* the obligation is, for example, reciprocal in nature, from the *consequences* attached to the obligation being of that particular nature. For example, the fact that for certain treaty obligations standing to bring a claim of breach is limited to the state(s) individually affected – and not available *erga omnes partes*, that is, to all states party to the treaty – can be seen, first, as a strong indication or *reason why* the obligations in question are of a bilateral or reciprocal nature. However, this fact could also be construed as a *consequence* of these obligations being of a bilateral or reciprocal nature. Since state parties to a particular treaty are free to neutralise, in explicit treaty provisions, one or more of the *consequences* attached to the distinction, the problem of separating cause from effect, and thus of identifying whether an obligation is reciprocal or integral, is further complicated. Indeed, even if certain treaty obligations are, for example, by their very nature reciprocal, the parties to the treaty may, nonetheless, decide that standing to bring complaints will be available to all parties, for all breaches. In principle, such *actio popularis* – where one state is explicitly allowed to exercise the rights of another – though hinting at the presence of integral obligations, does not, in and of itself, alter the nature of the treaty obligations from reciprocal to integral. They remain reciprocal in nature, but one of the consequences attached to this has been deactivated. What remains important, though, is that in case an obligation is, for example, determined to be of a reciprocal nature and the treaty in question remains silent on issues such as standing, *inter se* modifications and suspensions, the normal consequences attached to reciprocal obligations – that is, limited standing and the permissibility of *inter se* modifications and suspensions – will, given the silence of the treaty, be activated. It, therefore, becomes a matter of 'presumed consequences' only, that is, consequences that will flow from, say, obligations being of a reciprocal nature, but only in case the parties to the treaty left the particular consequence untouched.

Background to the distinction
Early PCIJ and ICJ cases

In the *Reservations to the Genocide Convention* case (1951), the ICJ gave particular importance to the 'objects' of the Convention. It noted that

> [t]he Convention was manifestly adopted for a purely humanitarian and civilizing purpose. It is indeed difficult to imagine a convention that might have this dual character to a greater degree, since its object on the one hand is to safeguard the very existence of certain human groups and on the other to confirm and endorse the most elementary principles of morality.[94]

With reference to these 'objects', the ICJ lay the foundation of what was to become the distinction between reciprocal and integral obligations:

> In such a Convention [as the Genocide Convention] the contracting States do not have any interests of their own; they merely have, one and all, a common interest, namely, the accomplishment of those high purposes which are the *raison d'être* of the convention. Consequently, in a convention of this type one cannot speak of individual advantages to States, or of the maintenance of a perfect contractual balance between rights and duties. The high ideals which inspired the Convention provide, by virtue of the common will of the parties, the foundation and measure of all its provisions.[95]

It was with reference, *inter alia*, to these 'objects' that the Court made its main finding:

> The object and purpose of the Convention thus limit both the freedom of making reservations and that of objecting to them. It follows that it is the compatibility of a reservation with the object and purpose of the Convention that must furnish the criterion for the attitude of a State in making the reservation on accession as well as for the appraisal by a State in objecting to the reservation.[96]

The ICJ's approach to treaty reservations was incorporated subsequently in Art. 19(c) of the Vienna Convention, prohibiting reservations

---

[94] ICJ Reports 1951, 23.
[95] *Ibid*. In his Dissenting Opinion, Judge Alvarez went even further, classifying treaties like the Genocide Convention as follows: 'To begin with, they have a universal character; they are, in a sense, the *Constitution* of international society, the *new international constitutional law*. They are not established for the benefit of private interests but for that of the general interest' (*ibid*., 51, emphasis in the original).
[96] *Ibid*., 24.

to a treaty that are 'incompatible with the object and purpose of the treaty'.

In earlier opinions by individual PCIJ judges, other hints at a distinction between reciprocal and integral treaties were made. In the *Customs Regime Between Germany and Austria* case, Judge Anzilotti questioned whether the parties to the 1922 Geneva Protocol

> were in a position to modify *inter se* the provisions of Article 88 [of the Treaty of Saint-Germain], which provisions... form an essential part of the peace settlement and were adopted not in the interests of any given State, but in the higher interest of the European political system and with a view to the maintenance of peace.[97]

Another reference can be found in the dissenting opinions of judges Van Eysinga and Schücking in the *Oscar Chinn* case. In contrast to the majority of the PCIJ, judges Van Eysinga and Schücking expressed the view that the 1919 Convention of St Germain relating to the Congo Basin was void between its signatories on the ground that it modified the earlier General Act of Berlin of 1885 without the assent of all the signatories thereto. Judge Van Eysinga expressed it thus:

> the Berlin Act presents a case in which a large number of States, which were territorially or otherwise interested in a vast region, endowed it [the Congo Basin] with a highly internationalized statute, or rather a constitution established by treaty, by means of which the interests of peace, those of 'all nations' as well as those of natives, appeared to be most satisfactorily guaranteed... [It] does not create a number of contractual relations between a number of States, relations which may be replaced as regards some of these States by other contractual relations... This régime, which forms an indivisible whole, may be modified, but for this agreement of all contracting Powers is required.[98]

---

[97] PCIJ, Series A/B, No. 41, 64 (1931).
[98] PCIJ, Series A/B, No. 63, 132–4 (1934). For other cases where a treaty was characterised as transcending the interests of the parties directly concerned and as constituting a so-called objective regime, binding even on non-parties, see the *Wimbledon* case, where the PCIJ found that the international regime for the Kiel Canal (set out in the Versailles Peace Treaty) was binding also on Germany, even though Germany was not a party to the treaty (PCIJ, Series A, No. 1 (1923)) and the *Dispute on the Regime of Demilitarization for the Aaland Islands*, where an *ad hoc* Committee of Jurists decided that the Paris peace settlement of 1856 setting out international obligations on demilitarisation was binding also on, and could be invoked by, Sweden and Finland, even though they were not parties to the settlement (see report of the International Committee of Jurists entrusted by the Council of the League of Nations with the task of giving an advisory opinion upon the legal aspects of the Aaland Islands Question, *League of Nations Official Journal*, Special Supplement No. 3, October 1920).

The ILC Reports on the Law of Treaties by Sir Gerald Fitzmaurice

Fitzmaurice refined the distinction between treaties referred to in the previous section and rephrased it as one between 'reciprocal' or 'concessionary' obligations, on the one hand, and 'integral' obligations, on the other. Multilateral treaties of the 'reciprocating type' are those 'providing for a mutual interchange of benefits between the parties, with rights and obligations for each involving specific treatment at the hands of and towards each of the others individually',[99] whereas multilateral treaties of the 'integral type' are those 'where the force of the obligation is self-existent, absolute and inherent for each party'.[100] In other words, 'integral obligations' are those 'towards all the world rather than towards particular parties'[101] and 'do not lend themselves to differential application, but must be applied integrally'.[102]

The standard example given by Fitzmaurice of a treaty of the reciprocating type was the 1961 Vienna Convention on Diplomatic Relations; that of the integral type, the 1948 Genocide Convention.

Fitzmaurice attached two important legal consequences to this distinction, one in the field of termination/suspension of treaties, the other in the field of conflict between treaties. Treaties of the reciprocating type could, in Fitzmaurice's view, be suspended or terminated as a result of fundamental breach.[103] Moreover, later treaties conflicting with previous ones of the reciprocal type were, in his view, *not* null and void (instead, priority rules applied).[104] Integral treaties, in contrast, could, under Fitzmaurice's draft, *not* be terminated or suspended by the other parties as a result of breach ('the juridical force of the obligation is inherent, and not dependent on a corresponding performance by the other parties to the treaty').[105] In addition, any subsequent treaty concluded *inter se* by the parties to such integral treaty which 'conflicts directly in a material particular with the earlier [integral] treaty will, to the extent of the conflict, be null and void'.[106]

Fitzmaurice also added a third type of multilateral treaties, namely those of an 'interdependent nature', where 'the participation of all the

---

[99] Third Report on the Law of Treaties by Sir Gerald Fitzmaurice, UN doc. A/CN.4/115, YBILC 1958, vol. 2, 20 (hereafter 'Fitzmaurice, Third Report'), 27, Art. 18, para. 2.
[100] *Ibid.*, 27, Art. 19.
[101] Second Report on the Law of Treaties by Sir Gerald Fitzmaurice, UN doc. A/CN.4/107, YBILC 1957, vol. 2, 16 (hereafter, 'Fitzmaurice, Second Report'), 54.
[102] *Ibid.*, 55.   [103] *Ibid.*, Art. 19.   [104] Fitzmaurice, Third Report, Art. 18.
[105] Fitzmaurice, Second Report, Art. 19(iv).   [106] Fitzmaurice, Third Report, Art. 19.

parties is a condition of the obligatory force of the treaty'.[107] He gave treaties on disarmament as an example of interdependent treaties. In terms of termination/suspension as a result of breach, interdependent treaties could, in Fitzmaurice's view, be terminated in their entirety by the other parties in case of fundamental breach (not just suspended or terminated partly as was the case for reciprocal treaties), since for these treaties 'performance by any party is necessarily dependent on an equal or corresponding performance by all the other parties'.[108] However, much like 'integral treaties' (and unlike 'reciprocal treaties'), a later *inter se* treaty which 'conflicts directly in a material particular with the earlier [interdependent] treaty will, to the extent of the conflict, be null and void'.[109] This notion of 'interdependent treaties' will not be further referred to here. Unlike the notions of reciprocal and integral treaties, the concept of interdependent treaties has not been generally used as a distinct category subsequently to Fitzmaurice's reports.[110] For purposes of conflict of norms (essentially, the legality of *inter se* modifications), these interdependent treaties can, indeed, be equated with integral treaties.

The Vienna Convention on the Law of Treaties

Fitzmaurice's distinction between reciprocal, integral and interdependent treaties was not, in so many words, maintained in the Vienna Convention as it was finally concluded. Nonetheless, it left manifest traces in not less than six different provisions. The Convention deals with termination/suspension as a result of 'material breach' in its Art. 60 and conflict with earlier treaties in its Arts. 30, 41, 53, 58 and 64.

First, under Art. 60(5) termination/suspension as a result of material breach is *not* allowed in case of 'provisions relating to the protection of the human person contained in treaties of a humanitarian character, in particular provisions prohibiting any form of reprisals against

---

[107] Fitzmaurice, Second Report, Art. 29.1(iii).
[108] *Ibid.*, Art. 19.1(ii)(b). Or, as he noted in respect of the example of disarmament treaties: 'the obligation of each party to disarm...is necessarily dependent on a corresponding performance of the same thing by all the other parties, since it is of the essence of such a treaty that the undertaking of each party is given in return for a similar undertaking by the others' (*ibid.*, 54).
[109] Fitzmaurice, Third Report, Art. 19.
[110] James Crawford, in his Third Report on State Responsibility (UN doc. A/CN.4/507, 10 March 2000, paras. 99–108, hereafter 'Crawford, Third Report') talks about reciprocal and integral obligations, not about interdependent ones.

persons protected by such treaties'. These treaties can, indeed, be seen as an example of integral treaties in respect of which Fitzmaurice precluded termination and suspension[111] (although not *all* integral treaties have been kept outside the scope of Art. 60, contrary to what Fitzmaurice originally proposed). Second, Art. 60.2(c) allows any other party (not just the party specially affected by the breach) to suspend the treaty, in whole or in part, with respect to itself 'if the treaty is of such a character that a material breach of its provisions by one party radically changes the position of every party with respect to the further performance of its obligations under the treaty'.[112] This provision resembles what Fitzmaurice wanted to see in respect of interdependent treaties (e.g., disarmament treaties).[113] Third and fourth, the reference in Arts. 53 and 64 to 'peremptory norms', conflict with which invalidates other treaties, is reminiscent of Fitzmaurice's proposal to invalidate treaties in conflict with *any* treaty of an integral or interdependent nature. However, Arts. 53 and 64 do not cover *all* conflicts with integral treaties, only conflicts with integral treaties of a particular type, namely those of *jus cogens*. Fifth and sixth, Arts. 41 and 58 recall Fitzmaurice's proposal to invalidate *inter se* agreements in conflict with integral or interdependent treaties. Article 41 outlaws (though not invalidates) *inter se* modifications to a multilateral treaty that 'affect the enjoyment by the other parties of their rights under the treaty or the performance of their obligations' or relate to 'a provision, derogation from which is incompatible with the effective execution of the object and purpose of the treaty as a whole' (Art. 41(1)(b)(i) and (ii)). Article 58 provides for similar rules in respect of the *inter se* suspension of multilateral treaties.

---

[111] In the same vein, the 2001 Draft Articles on State Responsibility (Art. 50(1)) prohibit the taking of countermeasures affecting: '(a) The obligation to refrain from the threat or use of force as embodied in the Charter of the United Nations; (b) Obligations for the protection of fundamental human rights; (c) Obligations of a humanitarian character prohibiting reprisals; (d) Other obligations under peremptory norms of general international law.'

[112] For an analogy in the law on state responsibility, see note 129 below.

[113] In contrast, for integral treaties, Fitzmaurice wanted to outlaw any termination or suspension. Hence, it is incorrect for the ILC in its commentary to Art. 40 (para. 19) of the 1996 Draft Articles (Draft Articles on State Responsibility adopted by the ILC on first reading, ILC 48th session, 1996) and James Crawford in his Third Report (at para. 91) to refer to Art. 60.2(c) as an expression of Fitzmaurice's theory on 'integral obligations'. The consequences in Art. 60.2(c) are rather those Fitzmaurice wanted to see in respect of 'interdependent' treaties.

The 2001 Draft Articles on State Responsibility

Aligned with Fitzmaurice's distinction between reciprocal and integral/interdependent obligations, James Crawford in his Third Report to the ILC on state responsibility distinguishes between 'bilateral' obligations and 'multilateral' obligations. In his view, 'bilateral obligations can arise from a variety of sources, including general international law, bilateral or multilateral treaties or unilateral acts'. Crawford, like Fitzmaurice, refers to the Vienna Convention on Diplomatic Relations as an example of a multilateral treaty setting out legal relations that are essentially bilateral in character. As opposed to bilateral obligations, Crawford posits the notion of multilateral obligations. Such multilateral obligations are subdivided into two classes.

First, multilateral obligations of the *erga omnes* type, 'owed to the international community as a whole, with the consequence that all States in the world have a legal interest in the compliance with the obligation'.[114] This is the type of obligation *erga omnes* referred to by the ICJ in the *Barcelona Traction* case. The Court distinguished between reciprocal/bilateral obligations and integral/*erga omnes* obligations, taking diplomatic relations as the standard example of the former type of obligations: 'an essential distinction should be drawn between the obligations of a State towards the international community as a whole, and those arising vis-à-vis another State in the field of diplomatic protection. By their very nature the former are the concern of all States.'[115]

Erga omnes obligations are, in Crawford's view, 'virtually coexistensive with peremptory obligations (arising under norms of *jus cogens*)'.[116]

In the final 2001 Draft Articles on State Responsibility, multilateral obligations of the *erga omnes* type are referred to as obligations 'owed to the international community as a whole'.[117] The Commentary to the final Draft Articles states that it is not its function to provide a list of those obligations. It refers instead to (i) the *Barcelona Traction* case in

---

[114] Crawford, Third Report, para. 106(a).
[115] *Barcelona Traction* case (Second Phase), ICJ Reports 1970 at pp. 32-3 (paras. 33-4). For other ICJ pronouncements in respect of *erga omnes* obligations, see *Namibia* Opinion, ICJ Reports 1971, p. 16 at p. 56 (para. 126); *Case concerning East Timor*, ICJ Reports 1995, p. 90 at p. 102 (para. 29); and *Application of the Convention on the Prevention and Punishment of the Crime of Genocide. Bosnia and Herzegovina v. Yugoslavia* (Preliminary Objections), ICJ Reports 1996, p. 625 at p. 626 (para. 4), p. 628 (para. 6).
[116] Crawford, Third Report, para. 106(a).   [117] 2001 Draft Articles, Art. 48(1)(b).

which the ICJ gave the following examples: 'the outlawing of acts of aggression, and of Genocide' and 'the principles and rules concerning the basic rights of the human person, including protection from slavery and racial discrimination',[118] and (ii) the *East Timor* case, where the ICJ added the right of self-determination of peoples to this list.[119]

The second class of multilateral (or integral) obligations identified in the ILC's work on state responsibility are those owed *erga omnes partes*, i.e., owed not to all states, but to all the parties to a particular regime (e.g., a multilateral treaty). In Crawford's view, this class concerns 'obligations which are expressed (or necessarily implied) to relate to matters of the common interest of the parties'. In other words, the performance of the obligations of each and every state party is recognised as being in the common interest of all state parties, common interest being defined as an interest 'over and above any individual interest that may exist in a given case'.[120] As examples he refers to obligations that arise 'in the fields of the environment (for example, in relation to biodiversity or global warming) and disarmament (for example, a regional nuclear free zone treaty or a test ban treaty)'.[121] Elsewhere Crawford rightly points out that 'human rights obligations are not the only class of international obligations whose performance cannot be considered as affecting any "particular State" considered alone. This is also true of some obligations in such fields as human development, world heritage and environmental protection.'[122]

In the final 2001 Draft Articles, multilateral obligations of the *erga omnes partes* type are referred to as obligations 'owed to a group of States...and...established for the protection of a collective interest of the group'.[123] Pursuant to the Commentary to the 2001 Draft Articles, multilateral obligations *erga omnes partes*

---

[118] *Barcelona Traction* (Second Phase), ICJ Reports 1970, p. 3 at p. 32, para. 34.
[119] ICJ Reports 1995, p. 90 at p. 102, para. 29.   [120] Crawford, Third Report, para. 92.
[121] *Ibid.*, para. 106(b). In note 195, Crawford submits that 'integral obligations' are a sub-category of obligations *erga omnes partes*. As noted earlier (note 113 above), he seems to be incorrect when referring to the treaties mentioned in Art. 60(2)(c) of the Vienna Convention as 'integral treaties'. Rather, they are what Fitzmaurice called 'interdependent treaties'. The way Fitzmaurice saw 'integral treaties' should classify them rather as both obligations *erga omnes* (Fitzmaurice's prime example of an integral treaty was, after all, the Genocide Convention) and obligations *erga omnes partes* (such as most human rights and environmental provisions).
[122] *Ibid.*, para. 88. On that basis, Crawford rightly criticises the ILC 1996 Draft Articles for singling out 'human rights and fundamental freedoms' in its Art. 40.2(e)(iii).
[123] 2001 Draft Articles, Art. 48(1)(a).

must apply between a group of States and have been established in some collective interest. They might concern, for example, the environment or security of a region (e.g. a regional nuclear free zone treaty or a regional system for the protection of human rights). They are not limited to arrangements established only in the interest of the member States but would extend to agreements established by a group of States in some wider common interest.[124]

The Commentary explicitly states that it is not its function to provide an enumeration of collective interests giving rise to multilateral obligations *erga omnes partes*. It states, though, that 'their principal purpose will be to foster a common interest, over and above any interests of the States concerned individually'.[125]

The distinction between bilateral and multilateral obligations (in particular those of the *erga omnes partes* type) may not always be easily discerned. The Commentary to the 2001 Draft Articles states that '[i]t will be a matter for the interpretation and application of the primary rule to determine into which of the categories an obligation comes' and stresses that it only offers an 'illustrative' discussion.[126]

The consequences attached to the distinction between bilateral and multilateral obligations in the Final Draft Articles relate to the question of standing.[127] Legal standing to invoke responsibility for breach of a *bilateral* (or reciprocal) obligation is limited to the state at the other end of the bilateral relationship (that is, the 'injured State').[128] Breach of a *multilateral* (or integral) obligation, in contrast, can be invoked either (i) by each and every one of the other parties to the multilateral treaty, in case of multilateral obligations *erga omnes partes*, or (ii) by any state, in case of obligations *erga omnes*, that is, obligations binding on all states of the international community. For breach of *multilateral obligations*, two types of standing are, however, introduced. Only those states that are 'specially affected' by the breach (so-called 'injured States') are granted full standing, that is, standing to claim all of the remedies related to breach (cessation, non-repetition, reparation and countermeasures).[129]

---

[124] Commentary, pp. 320–1, para. 7.   [125] Ibid.   [126] Commentary, p. 297, para. 6.
[127] For related consequences see Art. 50, quoted in note 111 above, prohibiting countermeasures that affect certain multilateral obligations.
[128] Art. 42(a) of the 2001 Draft Articles provides: 'A State is entitled as an injured State to invoke the responsibility of another State if the obligation breached is owed to: (a) That State individually...'
[129] Art. 42(b) states: 'A State is entitled as an injured State to invoke the responsibility of another State if the obligation breached is owed to...(b) A group of States including that State, or the international community as a whole, and the breach of the obligation: (i) Specially affects that State; or (ii) Is of such a character as radically to

All other, not 'specially affected' (i.e., not 'injured') states party to, or bound by, the multilateral obligation have standing only to claim cessation of the wrongful act and assurances and guarantees of non-repetition *in the collective interest*.[130] They can also claim reparation, but only in the interest of the 'injured State'. The Commentary to the Final Draft Articles leaves it open as to whether these 'non-injured' states can impose countermeasures.[131] In any event, for those states to impose countermeasures, if at all possible, will be more difficult than for 'injured States' to do so.

The distinction generalised

As already noted, the word 'reciprocal' versus the word 'integral' cannot be found in any codified rule of international law. In each of the provisions that reflect the distinction, such as Art. 41 of the Vienna Convention or Arts. 42 and 48 of the 2001 Draft Articles on State Responsibility, more precise wording is used or explicit examples are given. For an application of the distinction in a particular area to a given dispute one must, therefore, examine the precise terms of these provisions. It is useful, however, to transcend these specific provisions and to attempt to generalise the definition of reciprocal versus integral obligations and the consequences attached to it. These consequences are relevant mainly for rules deriving from multilateral treaties or rules otherwise binding on more than two states. This means, *a priori*, that not all norms set out in a *multilateral* treaty are of an integral nature. The very distinction is there to make a classification *as between* multilateral treaty norms, some being of a reciprocal nature, others of an integral nature.

We next develop the general criterion, proposed here, to distinguish reciprocal from integral obligations. The criterion suggested is, of course,

---

change the position of all the other States to which the obligation is owed with respect to the further performance of the obligation.' The obligations referred to in Art. 42(b)(ii) are those that Fitzmaurice termed 'interdependent' obligations, discussed earlier. The Commentary to the 2001 Draft Articles (p. 300, para. 13) defines them as 'obligations, breach of which must be considered as affecting per se every other State to which the obligation is owed' and makes the analogy with Art. 60(2)(c) of the Vienna Convention. According to the Commentary, '[e]xamples include a disarmament treaty, a nuclear free zone treaty, or any other treaty where each party's performance is effectively conditioned upon and requires the performance of each of the others' (*ibid.*). It is stated to be 'desirable that this subparagraph be narrow in its scope' (p. 301, para. 15). Like James Crawford (see notes 113 and 121 above), the Commentary wrongly equates 'integral' to 'interdependent' obligations on p. 296, para. 5 and in footnote 706.

[130] Art. 48(2).   [131] See Commentary, para. 8 on pp. 327–8.

not a scientific test. Crucially, it demonstrates that it is impossible to define a treaty in its entirety as reciprocal or integral in nature. One must look at every provision and every obligation individually.

Under reciprocal obligations set out, for example, in a multilateral treaty binding equally on all state parties, a promise is made towards each and every state *individually*. Integral obligations, in contrast, imply a promise not towards individual states, but towards the *collectivity* of all state parties *taken together*. Or, in the words of James Crawford, integral obligations concern 'obligations which are expressed (or necessarily implied) to relate to matters of the common interest of the parties', common interest being defined as an interest 'over and above any individual interest that may exist in a given case'.[132] Looked at from the other end – that is, not the *origins* of the obligation, but its eventual *breach* – when a reciprocal obligation is breached, it is not necessarily breached as against all other state parties, but only as against the one or more states towards whom the particular promise, allegedly breached, is owed. Breach of an integral obligation, in contrast, necessarily implies breach as against *all* state parties: the obligation constitutes a promise made to all state parties, collectively, hence its breach is necessarily a breach against all of them.

To give an example: human rights obligations that are held by states at the international level constitute, not a promise to one or more other states taken individually, but a promise to the collectivity or common conscience of all states involved. The objective of human rights obligations is essentially to prevent states mistreating *their own nationals*. To safeguard this objective states bind themselves not to other states taken individually, but to the collectivity of states involved. In the same way, breach of human rights obligations, that is, one government mistreating some of its own nationals, does not, in principle, affect one other state more than another. The breach is one towards the collective conscience of all states taken together. As a result, standing to invoke such breach is given to all contracting states.

It is suggested, in contrast, that most trade obligations – pursuant to which a state makes market access promises to another state, a promise which is then multilateralised through the obligation of MFN treatment – remain a collection of reciprocal or bilateral obligations, that is, obligations of a synallagmatic nature. Unlike human rights obligations, a trade or market access obligation is not a promise made

---

[132] Crawford, Third Report, para. 92.

to the collectivity or common conscience of all WTO members taken together. It is rather a promise made to each and every WTO member individually, multilaterally enshrined under the WTO umbrella of non-discrimination. If, for example, Canada in negotiations with the European Communities has bound its tariffs on computers at a ceiling of 5 per cent, this binding can, of course, be relied upon by all WTO members pursuant to the MFN obligation in Art. I of GATT 1994. However, notwithstanding the multilateral character of this binding, the Canadian promise remains a collection of bilateral promises towards each WTO member not to impose tariffs on computers above 5 per cent. If Canada were now to decide to impose 10 per cent for computers imported from Brazil, but 5 per cent for computers from all other countries, then Brazil can surely lodge a complaint against Canada. Brazil's right to 5 per cent in its relationship with Canada would be violated. However, it is not, for example, for China, the United States or the European Communities to complain about this breach. Their bilateral relationship of rights and obligations with Canada has not been affected. This results, it is suggested, from the reciprocal or synallagmatic nature of trade obligations.

Whereas the distinction between reciprocal and integral obligations is not as such based on values, but rather on the structure and origin of the promise made, it is not an entirely subjective distinction. Indirectly, integral obligations are those made towards the collectivity or common conscience of states, that is, they are often obligations involving so-called 'global commons'. To define what 'global commons' are may, however, involve a subjective value judgement. Coming back to the distinction made earlier between international law of co-existence and international law of co-operation, it could be argued – with the risk of oversimplification – that, whereas most international law of co-existence is constituted by reciprocal obligations, the modern law of co-operation has an increasing number of integral or *erga omnes (partes)* obligations. In the same vein, it could be submitted that international law striving at the harmonisation of legislation and rules in a collectivity of states, that is, a structure of so-called 'positive integration', tends to impose more integral or *erga omnes (partes)* obligations, whereas international law merely prohibiting states, for example, from discriminating without imposing common or harmonised standards, that is, a structure of so-called 'negative integration' (such as, for example, the majority of WTO law), is constituted mostly by reciprocal or bilateral obligations. In sum, whereas reciprocal obligations can be looked at more as a 'contract' or combination of bilateral contracts, integral obligations are reminiscent rather of legislation or statutes in domestic law.

Finally, given the inter-state matrix of international law and its relative state-to-state nature, the starting point or presumption must be that obligations are of a bilateral or reciprocal nature. It is, therefore, for those claiming that, for example, WTO obligations are *erga omnes partes* or integral obligations, to prove it. If they fail to do so, the presumed consequences related to reciprocal obligations will flow, unless, of course, explicit WTO provisions were to change or neutralise these consequences.

What the distinction is not about

First of all, the problem of identifying whether an obligation is of a reciprocal or an integral nature is not linked to the source of the obligation concerned. It is, in particular, not sufficient that an obligation derives from a *multilateral treaty*, for that obligation to be of the integral type (e.g., for all parties to that treaty to have standing to invoke breach of the treaty). The issue is to distinguish between different types of obligations all of which derive from a multilateral treaty.[133] Hence, the fact that WTO rules derive from a multilateral treaty is not enough for WTO obligations to be of the integral type.

Second, the notion of integral obligations should not be equated with obligations that are binding on states *without their consent*. Some integral obligations are binding on all states, irrespective of their consent, namely obligations deriving from norms of *jus cogens*. However, most integral obligations (such as those in the field of environmental protection) are binding only *erga omnes partes*, that is, binding only on the state parties to the treaty. They do not bind third states. We will discuss further below the allegation that some of these norms are 'public interest norms' binding even on third states.[134]

Third, to say that obligations are reciprocal in nature does not necessarily mean that they are affecting only two *governments* in their bilateral relations. They may well also affect individuals or economic operators other than public authorities. The fact that obligations have a direct or indirect effect on individuals does not make them integral (although

---

[133] Moreover, technically speaking, an obligation deriving from a bilateral treaty could also be of the integral type. Imagine, for example, that at the origin of the 1948 Genocide Convention, two states had first concluded a bilateral treaty outlawing genocide.

[134] See chapter 3 below, pp. 101–6.

most integral obligations, being obligations 'in the collective interest', will have a beneficial effect on individuals also). WTO rules are a perfect example of rules of a mainly reciprocal type that nonetheless have a clear effect on individual economic operators. Ever more precise and expanding WTO rules increasingly affect not only WTO members as governments, but also individuals, consumers and other economic operators in domestic and global marketplaces. The idea that GATT rules affect economic operators and not just states was already acknowledged in GATT case law.[135] But with the advent of new WTO agreements (such as the TBT, SPS and TRIPS agreements) it has been accentuated and expanded so as to include prominently not only private traders, but also consumers and private right-holders. As acknowledged by the panel on *US – Section 301*, WTO obligations have not so far been interpreted by GATT/WTO institutions as 'creating legally enforceable rights and obligations for individuals' or 'a legal order producing direct effect'.[136] Consequently, the WTO 'did *not* create a new legal order the subjects of which comprise both contracting parties or Members and their nationals'.[137] But as the panel on *US – Section 301* added:

it would be entirely wrong to consider that the position of individuals is of no relevance to the GATT/WTO legal matrix. Many of the benefits to Members which are meant to flow as a result of the acceptance of various disciplines under the GATT/WTO depend on the activity of individual economic operators in the national and global market places. The purpose of many of these disciplines, indeed one of the primary objects of the GATT/WTO as a whole, is to produce certain market conditions which would allow this individual activity to flourish.[138]

The panel continued as follows:

Trade is conducted most often and increasingly by private operators. It is through improved conditions for these private operators that Members benefit from WTO disciplines. The denial of benefits to a Member which flows from a breach is often indirect and results from the impact of the breach on the market place and the activities of individuals within it ... It may, thus, be convenient in the GATT/WTO legal order to speak not of the principle of direct effect but of the principle of indirect effect.[139]

Nonetheless, as noted before, this 'indirect effect' of WTO law does not stand in the way of WTO obligations being mainly of a reciprocal nature.

---

[135] See, for example, the panel report on *US – Taxes on Petroleum and Certain Imported Substances*, adopted on 17 June 1987, BISD 34S/136, para. 5.2.2.
[136] Panel report on *US – Section 301*, para. 7.72.   [137] *Ibid.*
[138] *Ibid.*, para. 7.73.   [139] *Ibid.*, paras. 7.77 and 7.78.

Fourth, obligations of the reciprocal type should not be confused with obligations the performance of which is inherently conditional on reciprocity. Although reciprocal in nature, reciprocal obligations may well be (and mostly are) *unconditional*, objective and self-existent in the sense that they must be complied with irrespective of compliance by other state parties (unless, of course, non-performance is justified as a suspension under Art. 60 of the Vienna Convention or as a countermeasure). Here again, WTO rules are a perfect example. The WTO obligation to accord MFN treatment is an unconditional one: a WTO member must grant MFN status to imports from all other WTO members irrespective of how these other WTO members treat its own exports. MFN is, in that sense, not conditional on reciprocity. Nonetheless, although certain breaches of the MFN obligation may well affect a large number of other WTO members, the MFN obligation is not as such an obligation of an integral type. A breach of the MFN principle – to revert to our earlier example: Canada imposing a 10 per cent tariff, over and above its 5 per cent binding, only on computers imported from Brazil – does not necessarily affect the rights of all WTO members; the discrimination may well be targeted at only one state, in our example, Brazil. MFN is essentially a collection of equivalent bilateral legal relationships in respect of which no discrimination is allowed to take place. It is, in other words, an obligation of the reciprocal type.

Fifth, to depict WTO obligations as mainly reciprocal obligations does not affect the binding nature of WTO obligations. Reciprocal and integral obligations are equally binding. By characterising an obligation as reciprocal, we do not in any way imply that the obligation is not legally binding or that one breach can always be excused by another. To take the example of WTO rules, the fact that WTO obligations are reciprocal does not mean that findings of WTO violations can simply be balanced by an equivalent suspension of obligations on the other side. Whether an obligation is reciprocal or integral, its breach always calls for cessation and, unless there is an explicit treaty provision to the contrary, suspension or compensation does not take away the obligation to comply with the rules, that is, to cease the breach, *even if it is a breach of a reciprocal obligation*.

Why are most WTO obligations reciprocal in nature?

Under the general criterion set out earlier, we suggested that most WTO obligations are of the reciprocal type. They are not integral in nature. WTO rules constitute a promise to each and every WTO member individually, not to the collectivity or common conscience of WTO members taken together, in pursuit of some collective interest 'over and above any individual interest that may exist in a given case'.[140] A breach of WTO obligations does not necessarily affect the rights of all other WTO members. More than one, and in some instances all, WTO members may see their rights affected. But often only their economic interests, not their rights, will be affected. This is a consequence rather of WTO obligations being trade-related and trade restrictions, in turn, being capable of affecting the economic interests – not necessarily the rights – of many WTO members.

That WTO obligations remain reciprocal and are not integral is, however, not always clearly discerned. The one author who, to my knowledge, examined this issue came to the same conclusion as we do here. Michael Hahn, after considering the hypothesis that GATT obligations are to be fulfilled *erga omnes partes* (and could, hence, be qualified as integral) reaches the conclusion that the basic structure of these obligations is against such qualification. He is also of the view that both GATT and the WTO treaty remain treaties establishing bilateral right–obligation relationships between WTO members.[141] Oscar Schachter, in addition, noted more generally that '[m]any trade treaties or agreements on foreign investment (even if multilateral) fall into this category [of reciprocal or synallagmatic treaties]'.[142]

Nonetheless, it must be recalled that the reciprocal versus integral distinction does not normally apply to treaties in their entirety. Indeed, even some rules in the WTO treaty are of the integral type, not because they are substantively more important than others, but for internal procedural/institutional reasons. The WTO integral rules in question are those relating to the operation of WTO bodies. When it comes to WTO rules setting out, for example, voting procedures, procedures on accession, the nomination of chairpersons or composition of certain WTO bodies, such rules must necessarily apply equally to all WTO members. The very nature of these procedural rules implies that their breach or *inter se* deviation would necessarily constitute breach towards all other WTO members (irrespective of trade or trade potential). As Schermers pointed out: 'An organization can have only one constitutional structure. An amendment, for example, which expands the Executive Board of the organization from 18 to 24 members cannot be applied for

---

[140] Crawford, Third Report, para. 92.
[141] Michael Hahn, *Die einseitige Aussetzung von Gatt-Verpflichtungen als Repressalie* (Berlin: Springer, 1995), 396 and Part 3.
[142] Schachter, 'Entangled', 735.

some member States only.'¹⁴³ Hence, *inter se* modification of such institutional/procedural provisions cannot be tolerated, nor can state-to-state suspension of the obligations deriving from these provisions be legal as a form of countermeasure. However, the importance of these provisions being of the integral type is theoretical only (why would WTO members, *inter se*, want to change, for example, the election procedure of chairpersons?). What counts is that the substantive trade provisions in the WTO treaty are reciprocal in nature.

Another potential class of WTO rules that may be integral in nature are some of the rules calling for harmonisation of intellectual property protection standards in the TRIPS agreement. These rules impose an element of 'positive integration'. It could be argued that they are there, not so much as a compilation of bilateral trade obligations, but as obligations in pursuit of common interests of all WTO members *taken together* (such as technological advancement and transfer of technology), that is, collective interests over and above the individual interests of the WTO members involved in a particular case. If so, these TRIPS obligations could be portrayed as integral obligations, in respect of which, for example, *inter se* deviations or suspensions should not be tolerated.

Having applied the general criterion to WTO obligations, we next elaborate on the main, underlying reasons why most WTO obligations are reciprocal. In a subsequent section, we then attempt to explain why it is sometimes (mistakenly) thought that they are integral.

The object of trade: state-to-state

First, and most importantly, trade is and remains a bilateral happening. Goods or services from one country are exported or transferred to one other country.¹⁴⁴ The rights and obligations negotiated in the WTO are aimed at ensuring market access for a given product from member A into the market of member B. In that sense, the WTO treaty is not all that different from the Vienna Convention on Diplomatic Relations (the standard example, referred to earlier, of a multilateral treaty imposing

---

[143] Henry Schermers, 'The Legal Basis of International Organization Action', in René-Jean Dupuy (ed.), *A Handbook on International Organizations* (Dordrecht: Nijhoff, 1998), 401 at 409.

[144] Several countries may, of course, have been involved in the production of a particular good, but rules of origin are there precisely to determine *the* origin of each and every particular good. The fact that a good can, legally speaking, originate only in one country confirms the bilateral nature of trade.

obligations of a bilateral/reciprocal nature): in the Vienna Convention, rights and obligations relate to diplomats sent from one country to another; the WTO treaty is about market access for goods from one country into another country. In the end, all WTO members may have similar market access rights (because of the MFN principle), but the rights thereby obtained remain trade-related, hence bilateral, in nature. Equally, a breach of WTO trade liberalisation obligations may have economic effects on more than one WTO member, because of the increased economic interdependence between states. But this is not the same as saying that a breach of WTO obligations *necessarily* affects the *rights* of *all* other WTO members, the way, for example, that human rights or certain environmental law breaches do. A breach of WTO trade rules may affect a number of members individually, but it does not amount to an offence of the collective right or conscience of *all* state parties, the way that a human rights breach does.

Trade (and hence WTO obligations) is *international par excellence*. A state cannot trade with itself. All WTO obligations relate, indeed, to foreign goods, foreign services or foreign service suppliers. Necessarily international, trade is also inherently *bilateral*. It takes the form of a physical or economic transfer of a unit from one country to another country. The benefits of WTO market access rights, as well as the welfare effects of compliance with WTO obligations, are spread over all WTO members (respectively, because of the MFN principle and a more efficient allocation of resources worldwide). But this collective *effect* does not negate the inherently bilateral character of trade and trade obligations.

The object and implementation of human rights and environmental treaties are, in contrast, a *national* matter. In particular, respect for human rights is a matter between the public authorities of a state and *its own nationals*. Steps taken to protect the environment are also national: laws and regulations are passed that set internal environmental standards within the territory of a particular state. Obviously, although human rights and environmental obligations are, in terms of object and implementation, a national or domestic matter, they are *international and collective* in terms of the values they protect and the effects they want to avoid. Respect for human rights has been elevated to the international level mainly because of the collective/universal values it seeks to achieve. Protection of the environment has been 'internationalised' for reasons of effectiveness: environmental pollution knows no borders, hence for a country to protect its environment effectively it must co-operate with other countries.¹⁴⁵ As a result, breach of environmental and, especially, human rights obligations becomes of international interest, but this interest is essentially collective. Quite often (as will be the case of, for example, violations of the Kyoto Protocol) one particular state will not be more affected than another. The interest protected is collective, not bilateral.

In sum, although trade is inherently *international*, its obligations are *bilateral*; whereas human rights and environmental protection are inherently *national*, most of their obligations are *collective*.

The objective of trade: an instrument, not a value

Second, unlike, for example, the prohibition of genocide or the protection of human rights or the environment, trade and the liberalisation of trade *is not a value*. It is not sought after for the achievement of some 'global common' that transcends the sum total of individual state interests. Trade is not a value, it is only an instrument. It is an instrument to increase the *economic* welfare of all states. But the increase in welfare thus created by trade does not exceed the sum of economic welfare experienced by its composite members. Of course, it can be expected that higher economic welfare will translate itself also into social and other benefits, but this would be the result mainly of what states or private operators themselves decide to do with their welfare, not a direct consequence of trade or WTO rules. Also, in many countries economic freedoms, such as the right to set up an enterprise, are characterised as human rights and hence as a special 'value' to be protected on an individual basis. WTO rules could then be seen as part of a wider framework in pursuit of economic freedoms. Indirectly, this may well be true.¹⁴⁶ But be that as it may, with the possible exception of the TRIPS agreement, WTO rules are currently not framed in terms of 'freedom to trade', but rather in terms of specific market access that is provided as between governments on a negotiated basis and obligations of 'negative integration' such as non-discrimination and 'least-trade restrictiveness' tests.

---

¹⁴⁵ Often a triple distinction is made between multilateral environmental agreements: they may seek to regulate trade in a particular category of products (such as wildlife), to protect states from substances harmful to their domestic environment (such as hazardous waste) or to protect so-called global commons such as the ozone layer or the global climate system. All three types require co-operation across borders. Especially the third type must be classified as being of an integral nature (protecting global commons).

¹⁴⁶ See Ernst-Ulrich Petersmann, 'Human Rights and International Economic Law in the 21st Century – The Need to Clarify their Interrelationships' (2001) 4 JIEL 3.

Moreover, as WTO rules now stand – and although, as the panel on *Section 301* recognised, they surely have an 'indirect effect' on individuals – they do not protect the rights of individuals, let alone their human right to trade.

Trade and WTO provisions seeking to enhance trade are not like, for example, the Genocide Convention where, in the words of the ICJ:

> the contracting States do not have any interests of their own; they merely have, one and all, a common interest, namely, the accomplishment of those high purposes which are the *raison d'être* of the convention. Consequently, in a convention of this type one cannot speak of individual advantages to States, or of the maintenance of a perfect contractual balance between rights and duties.[147]

The same has been said in respect of human rights treaties. As the Inter-American Court of Human Rights pointed out: 'human rights treaties... "are not multilateral treaties of the traditional type concluded to accomplish the reciprocal exchange of rights for the mutual benefit of the contracting States"; rather "their object and purpose is the protection of the basic rights of individual human beings, irrespective of their nationality, both against the State of their nationality and all other contracting States"'.[148] Or as the ECtHR noted:

> the purpose of the High Contracting Parties in concluding the Convention was not to concede to each other reciprocal rights and obligations in pursuance of their individual national interests but to realise the aims and ideals of the Council of Europe, as expressed in its Statute, and to establish a common public order... [I]t follows that the obligations undertaken by the High Contracting Parties in the Convention are essentially of an objective character, being designed rather to protect the fundamental rights of individual human beings from infringement by any of the High Contracting Parties than to create subjective and reciprocal rights for the High Contracting Parties themselves.[149]

The same objective or 'integral' nature has been attributed to EC treaties. This was done not so much because of the 'higher values' protected by EC treaties, but because EC law was construed as setting up a 'common market' and 'new legal order' that confers rights on individuals

---

[147] ICJ Reports 1951, 23.
[148] Inter-American Court of Human Rights, Advisory Opinion of 8 September 1983, quoted in Rudolf Bernhardt, 'Thoughts on the Interpretation of Human-Rights Treaties', in F. Matscher and H. Petzold (eds.), *Protecting Human Rights: The European Dimension, Studies in Honour of G. J. Wiarda* (Cologne: Heymanns, 1988), 65 at 68–9.
[149] *Decision of the Commission as to the Admissibility of Application No. 788/60 lodged by the Government of the Republic of Italy* (1961) 4 Yearbook of the ECHR 116 at 140.

and is superior to national law.¹⁵⁰ In addition, under EC law elements of exclusive competence have been granted to EC institutions (e.g., to regulate areas such as external trade).¹⁵¹ In that sense, EC treaties have become a form of domestic law, in respect of which Member States (much like individuals in internal law) have no competence to deviate *inter se*. To that extent, obligations under EC law – and especially those pursuing 'positive integration' – can, indeed, be characterised as integral in nature.

WTO obligations, in contrast, give states an instrument to achieve other 'nobler' goals. Since, therefore, the WTO treaty is only an instrument to achieve certain other goals, agreements modifying the WTO treaty *inter se* in pursuit of these other goals must, generally speaking, be accepted as long as they do not affect the rights of third parties.¹⁵² This is one of the major consequences of characterising WTO obligations as bilateral/reciprocal in nature and we come back to it later in chapter 6.

The negotiation, renegotiation and enforcement of WTO obligations

Third, the fact that WTO obligations are reciprocal in nature can be deduced from the way in which they are negotiated and renegotiated and, in particular, with reference as to how they are enforced.

WTO obligations, especially those set out in country-specific schedules of concessions, were negotiated first state-to-state, on a bilateral level: state A gives and takes; state B does the same. This bilateral and mutual reduction in trade restrictions is then multilateralised and applied, respectively, by state A and state B in their bilateral relationships with all

---

[150] See Case 26/62 *Van Gend en Loos* [1963] ECR 1. The importance of the new legal order in separating the EC from other international organisations was reiterated in the ECJ's *Opinion on the Draft Agreement on a European Economic Area*, Opinion 1/91, [1991] ECR I-6079, [1992] 1 CMLR 245.

[151] See Case 6/64 [1964] ECR 585, at pp. 593–4 (*Costa v. ENEL*): 'By creating a Community of unlimited duration, having its own institutions, its own personality, its own legal capacity and capacity of representation on the international plane and, more particularly, real powers stemming from a limitation of sovereignty or a transfer of powers from the States to the Community, the Member States have limited their sovereign rights, albeit within limited fields, and have thus created a body of law which binds both their nationals and themselves. The integration into the laws of each Member State of provisions which derive from the Community, and more generally the terms and the spirit of the Treaty, make it impossible, as a corollary, to accord precedence to a unilateral and subsequent measure over a legal system accepted by them on a basis of reciprocity.'

[152] See Arts. 41 and 58 of the Vienna Convention.

other WTO members. As the Appellate Body remarked: 'Tariff negotiations are a process of reciprocal demands and concessions, of "give and take".'[153] The ultimate aim of this 'give and take' exercise is to achieve an appropriate balance of trade concessions. Or, as the third paragraph of the preamble to the Marrakesh Agreement put it, the underlying objectives of the WTO are to be achieved by 'entering into reciprocal and mutually advantageous arrangements'.

In addition, the way GATT and GATS concessions are renegotiated under GATT Art. XXVIII and GATS Art. XXI proves the reciprocal nature of WTO obligations. Essentially, only other WTO members with a substantial trade interest must be involved and agree to the renegotiated list of concessions. Renegotiation, once again, happens largely on a bilateral level.

Crucially, however, the proof of the pudding comes with the eating: the way WTO obligations are enforced is exclusively bilateral. WTO dispute settlement does not, in the first place, tackle *breach*, but rather nullification of benefits *that accrue to a particular member*.[154] Panel and Appellate Body proceedings only examine claims made by one WTO member against one other WTO member. Most importantly, in case the defendant loses and does not comply within a reasonable period of time, the winning state will be authorised to impose *state-to-state countermeasures against the losing state* (DSU Art. 22). This exclusively bilateral modality of enforcement of WTO rules is an important indication that most WTO obligations are reciprocal in nature. In particular, the fact that the WTO treaty allows one member to *suspend its WTO obligations* as a form of countermeasure towards *one other member* provides a strong signal that WTO obligations are not of the integral type. *If WTO obligations were of the integral type*, their inter se *suspension would necessarily affect the rights of all other WTO members* and thus fall afoul of the *pacta tertiis* principle (according to which two states may in their dealings not affect the rights of third states),[155] as well as the general rule that countermeasures may suspend

---

[153] Appellate Body report on *EC – Computer Equipment*, complaint by the United States (WT/DS62/AB/R), adopted on 22 June 1998, para. 109.

[154] See Art. XXIII.1 of GATT 1994, setting out the requirement that 'any benefit accruing to it directly or indirectly under this Agreement is being nullified or impaired'. The other avenue in Art. XXIII.1 to start a WTO complaint, 'that the attainment of any objective of the Agreement is being impeded', one that is arguably of a less explicit bilateral nature, has not been utilised in practice.

[155] Confirmed in Art. 58 of the Vienna Convention.

only rights of the violating state, not of any third state.[156] Although third states may well feel an *economic effect* of the retaliation (an effect that may be positive or negative), their WTO *rights* will not normally be affected. In respect of integral obligations the situation is different: their *inter se* suspension or modification cannot be tolerated. The obligation, in those cases, is of an 'integral' type in that it ought to be respected in all circumstances (unless, of course, exceptions are provided for), irrespective of the conduct of other states.[157] This explains, for example, why fundamental human rights obligations (which are obligations of the integral type) cannot be suspended in response to breach:[158] their suspension towards the wrongdoing state would not only affect that state, but also breach the rights of all other contracting parties.

Of course, the general bilateral mode of enforcement of WTO rules cannot as such be seen as conclusive proof that all WTO obligations are reciprocal in nature. Human rights and environmental obligations (most of which are accepted as being of an integral nature) can also be enforced on a purely bilateral, state-to-state basis (although under these regimes a collective non-compliance mechanism is more common). What such integral obligations would, nonetheless, not allow for is the suspension of obligations as a form of retaliation, the way WTO suspension works. In that sense, WTO suspension as a form of countermeasures could, in and of itself, be seen as sufficient proof that WTO obligations are *not* integral in nature. The fact that such state-to-state suspension is also available under the TRIPS agreement – an agreement that may well also include integral obligations – could then be criticised.[159] At the same time, although WTO obligations are reciprocal in nature, nothing

---

[156] See Art. 49(1) of the 2001 Draft Articles ('An injured State may only take countermeasures against a State which is responsible for an internationally wrongful act').

[157] Recall, however, the special situation of so-called 'interdependent' obligations where breach or suspension by one state party may well make compliance by the other states impossible and allow all of the other state parties to suspend the treaty. The classic example is a disarmament treaty. See Art. 60(2)(c) of the Vienna Convention and Art. 42(b)(ii) of the 2001 Draft Articles.

[158] See Art. 50(1)(b) of the 2001 Draft Articles, quoted in note 111 above. See also Art. 60(5) of the Vienna Convention.

[159] In *EC – Bananas*, for example, Ecuador obtained authorisation to suspend its obligations vis-à-vis the European Communities under the TRIPS agreement. Although this enables developing countries to have some clout in enforcing DSB decisions, it risks undermining the 'regulatory' nature of WTO treaty provisions, in particular those TRIPS provisions that may be of an integral nature. WTO members should, hence, reconsider whether trade retaliation can be taken under all possible

prevents WTO members from setting up a collective non-compliance mechanism along the lines of certain environmental treaties (to some extent, the trade policy review mechanism does exactly that).[160] Such a collective non-compliance mechanism would not alter the character of WTO obligations and somehow transform them into integral obligations simply because they are *enforced* collectively (as noted earlier, explicit treaty provisions may neutralise or alter the consequences that normally flow from an obligation being reciprocal in nature). The efficient implementation of WTO rules may, indeed, be well (if not better) served by a collective compliance mechanism, instead of the current bilateral, state-to-state litigation system centred around breach and bilateral countermeasures.[161]

Three features of WTO obligations which could mistakenly lead to the conclusion that they are integral in nature

Trade liberalisation is beneficial to all WTO members

A first confusion that could arise is to take the increase in global welfare that trade liberalisation (and thus most WTO obligations) brings about as evidence that WTO obligations are a 'global common', in the collective interest, and, for that reason, must be integral in nature. Trade liberalisation is, indeed, in the general interest in that it should increase overall global welfare as a result of a better allocation of the world's resources, including the welfare of the state making a particular trade 'concession'. Much like environmental obligations of a mostly integral nature, WTO rules are, therefore, in the 'general interest'. However, unlike environmental obligations, the interest achieved by WTO obligations remains a compilation of individual welfare increases, not the achievement of a 'global common', such as the preservation of the planet's climate system, which transcends the individual benefits of individual states. The fact that engaging in an obligation is to everyone's *individual* benefit, including the one engaging in the obligation, does not mean that it is in

---

WTO obligations, or whether it should, for example, be limited to commitments set out in country-specific schedules.

[160] Another avenue for collective enforcement may be the so-called 'situation complaints' under Art. XXIII.1(c) of GATT 1994, pursuant to which one or more WTO members can challenge 'the existence of any other situation' created by other WTO members.

[161] See M. Pinto, 'From Dispute Resolution to Dispute Avoidance: Some Thoughts on Collective Management of Treaty Performance', in Volkmar Götz et al. (eds.), *Liber Amicorum Gunther Jaenicke* (Berlin: Springer, 1998), 353–74; Thomas Gehring, 'International Environmental Regimes: Dynamic Sectoral Legal Systems' (1990) 1 YIEL 353; and Pauwelyn, 'Enforcement', 621–33.

the *collective* interest in the sense of 'a common interest, over and above any interests of the States concerned individually'.[162]

After all, the fact that the WTO treaty, with its trade-liberalising obligations, is in the interest of *all WTO members* may not be that special. Is not every international treaty concluded by states supposed to be in the mutual interest of those states? This point is best illustrated with reference to the Vienna Convention on Diplomatic Relations, generally accepted as setting out reciprocal obligations. There as well, the fact that the provisions of this Convention are undoubtedly in the 'general interest' of all states (as confirmed by the ICJ in the *Diplomatic and Consular Staff* case),[163] does not alter the bilateral/reciprocal nature of the obligations they set out.

Finally, to state that *trade liberalisation* is, generally speaking, beneficial to all WTO members is one thing, to say that each and every WTO *rule* is of this 'public interest' nature, is quite another. As Benedek pointed out: 'the relevance of the "legal economics" in international economic law is questioned in view of the often strong political element involved in international economic relations which makes it unrealistic to regard the GATT rules from the perspective of a kind of "economic law of nature".[164] Witness, for example, WTO rules on anti-dumping which for many do not make economic sense and the GATT/WTO's reluctant incorporation of the agricultural and textiles sector into mainstream trade liberalisation rules, both as a result of strong political lobbying by developed country interests.

MFN 'multilateralises' all trade advantages, but it does not transform these advantages into a 'global common'

The multiple MFN obligations set out in the WTO treaty, the cornerstone of the multilateral trading system, ensure that any trade advantage a country gives to another must be 'multilateralised' and granted to all WTO members. As a result, MFN surely makes bilateral concessions collective in the sense that they must be given to all other WTO members. But in substance, this 'collectivisation' is nothing more than multiplying the original bilateral concession by the number of WTO members of the original bilateral concession. The bilateral concession is thereby granted

---

[162] Commentary to the 2001 Draft Articles, pp. 320–1, para. 7. See also Crawford, Third Report, para. 92.
[163] *United States Diplomatic and Consular Staff in Tehran*, ICJ Reports 1980, p. 3 at p. 43, para. 92.
[164] Benedek, *Rechtsordnung*, 468.

from state to state to all other WTO members. It does not, by means of MFN, transcend into some 'global common', more valuable than the sum total of the individual benefits it procures for each WTO member. Looked at from a different angle, MFN is, of course, an obligation owed towards all WTO members, but when member A discriminates against only member B – for example, by banning all imports coming from B or by imposing a higher tariff, above the set binding, only on imports from B – this MFN breach can hardly be said to affect the MFN right of members C, D and E (who can continue to export to member A, arguably even more so than before given that the ban or tariff hike has stopped or reduced the supply coming from member B).

Breach of a WTO obligation by one member is likely to affect many other WTO members

Finally, given that (i) compliance with WTO rules normally achieves an increase in welfare worldwide and (ii) the economic interdependence of states is ever increasing, a breach of WTO obligations by one member is likely to affect, directly or indirectly, the economic interests of many, sometimes all, other WTO members. This may wrongly be interpreted as granting a form of *actio popularis* to all WTO members for each and every breach of WTO rules, irrespective of the states involved. In turn, given that all WTO members could then (under this wrong assumption) complain about any WTO breach, this element could be mistakenly seen as proof that WTO obligations are of an *erga omnes partes* or integral nature.

In *EC – Bananas* the Appellate Body decided that the United States could bring a case under GATT even though it hardly produces any bananas and has not yet exported any. The Appellate Body quoted with approval the following remark from the panel report: 'with the increased interdependence of the global economy...members have a greater stake in enforcing WTO rules than in the past since any deviation from the negotiated balance of rights and obligations is more likely than ever to affect them, directly or indirectly'.[165]

One must, however, distinguish three issues: firstly, when does a WTO member have legal standing to bring a WTO complaint (the matter at issue in *EC – Bananas*)?; secondly, what is required for a WTO complaint to

---

[165] Appellate Body report on *EC – Bananas*, WT/DS27/AB/R, adopted on 25 September 1997, para. 136.

Standing

On the issue of standing, the Appellate Body in *EC – Bananas* made the rather astonishing finding that in order to bring a case under the DSU, no 'legal interest' is required. In particular, it did 'not read any of [the PCIJ/ICJ] judgements [referred to by the EC] as establishing a general rule that in all international litigation, a complaining party must have a "legal interest" in order to bring a case'.[166]

Looking at the cited international case law[167] and the 2001 Draft Articles on State Responsibility, it may be so that not much reference is made there to 'legal interest' (in the sense of an interest to see the law abided by), but this is so because *normally more than a 'legal interest' is needed for a state to have standing, namely one must prove the existence of a 'legal right'*. Any breach of international law could be said to affect the *legal interest* of all other states, that is, the interest of states in seeing respect for the rule of law in general (even if these states draw no individual rights from this law).[168] But this 'legal interest' is not normally enough for a state to invoke responsibility for breach.[169] Even if Art. 48 of the 2001 Draft Articles grants certain rights to enforce state responsibility to states that are not 'injured States', but merely have a legal interest, this occurs only for international norms of a certain nature, e.g., obligations *erga omnes* or *erga omnes partes*, not for obligations of a reciprocal nature, such as most WTO obligations. As Crawford noted in his Third Report: 'outside the field of "integral" obligations, or obligations *erga omnes partes*,... it is doubtful that States have a right or even a legally protected interest, for the purposes of State responsibility, in the legal relations of third States *inter se*'.[170]

Hence, even for those breaches of international law in respect of which the most lenient rules on standing apply (say, *erga omnes* or *jus cogens*

---

[166] *Ibid.*, para. 133. [167] *Ibid.*, footnote 66.
[168] In support of such argument, see Philip Jessup, *A Modern Law of Nations* (New York: Macmillan, 1948), note 2, and 154.
[169] Nor is it the way that the Vienna Convention has been drawn up (i.e., it has been drawn up on the basis of bilateral state relations, not in light of community interests). See Shabtai Rosenne, 'Bilateralism and Community Interest in the Codified Law of Treaties', in W. Friedmann, L. Henkin and O. Lissitzyn (eds.), *Transnational Law in a Changing Society, Essays in Honor of Philip C. Jessup* (New York: Columbia University Press, 1972), 203–27.
[170] Crawford, Third Report, para. 104.

obligations), standing is granted *because of the existence of a 'legal interest'*. Thus, in all cases where standing is acknowledged, *at least* a 'legal interest' must be pointed to. Therefore, the only way to make sense of the Appellate Body finding that no 'legal interest' is required is to assume that the Appellate Body did not mean to refer to 'legal interest' in its usual sense of 'interest to see the law abided by', but understood this term to mean, for example, a requirement of proof of actual damage or trade diversion.

It is important to recall what the Appellate Body did *not* state in *EC – Bananas*. It did not say that a purely 'legal interest' to see WTO rules abided by is sufficient for any WTO member to have standing in respect of all possible breaches of WTO law. On the contrary, it stated that there is *no* requirement of 'legal interest'. Of course, like any WTO member (and arguably even non-WTO members) the United States did have a 'legal interest' to see GATT rules abided by. In addition, however, the Appellate Body was careful enough to base its conclusion that the United States did have standing under GATT on other factors as well (not related to purely 'legal interest'): the United States was a producer of bananas and hence a potential exporter, the US market for bananas was potentially affected by the EC regime in terms of world supplies and prices and the GATT claims were inextricably interwoven with those under GATS for which the United States did unmistakably have standing.[171] The Appellate Body stressed that 'taken together, these reasons are sufficient justification...This does not mean, though, that one or more of the factors...would necessarily be dispositive in another case'.[172]

The Appellate Body forgot, however, to mention one other obvious but crucially important factor for standing to be granted, namely the fact that the EC import regime for bananas, if found to be discriminatory in the way the United States claimed it to be, was favouring certain former European colonies and hence, at least in theory, discriminating against *all other WTO members, including the United States*. The United States was, in that sense, one of the victims of the WTO inconsistent measure. The situation would have been different in case the measure would not have discriminated against the United States but only, for example, Ecuador; or in case the measure was otherwise not applicable to US exports (not even potential exports), the way an anti-dumping duty imposed by the EC on cement from Mexico would have nothing to do with US rights under the WTO. In those instances, where the measure does not apply

---

[171] Appellate Body report on *EC – Bananas*, paras. 136–7.   [172] *Ibid.*, para. 138.

to trade from the US, the US should not have standing to bring a WTO complaint.

In sum, based on a close reading of the Appellate Body decision in *EC – Bananas*, the mere fact that a WTO member breaches WTO rules does not suffice for all other WTO members to have standing to seek redress for this breach. A purely 'legal interest' is not enough.[173] For a member to have standing the inconsistent measure must, at least in theory, *apply to the trade of that member* (first condition of standing). An anti-dumping duty imposed by the United States only on steel from Japan cannot be challenged by the EC; nor can the United States complain about Zambia discriminating against exports only from Nigeria. In addition, even if the measure does *de jure* apply to the trade from that other member, some proof must be provided that either actual or *potential* trade flows may be restricted and/or that the member is otherwise economically affected (e.g., by an increase in world prices, as referred to in *EC – Bananas*) (second condition of standing).[174] The first condition will, in effect, constitute a bigger hurdle than the second. Indeed, if the measure does, on the books, apply to the complainant, trade potential or missed trade opportunities will be easily proven, in particular given the economic interdependence of WTO members.

The fact that these two conditions for standing do exist, and that, therefore, the WTO does *not* know an *actio popularis*, is an indication that WTO obligations are, indeed, reciprocal in nature, not integral or binding *erga omnes partes*. Hence, absent provisions in the WTO treaty to the contrary, the general rule in Art. 42(a) of the 2001 Draft Articles applies.[175] That is, a WTO member can only bring a complaint against another WTO member in case the obligation allegedly breached is owed to it 'individually'.

Here again, the traditional example of reciprocal/bilateral obligations, namely those in the Vienna Convention on Diplomatic Relations, is

---

[173] In support of the need for a *locus standi* doctrine in WTO dispute settlement, see: Rodrigo Bustamante, 'The Need for a GATT Doctrine of Locus Standi: Why the United States Cannot Stand the European Community's Banana Import Regime' (1997) 6 *Minnesota Journal of Global Trade* 533; William Davey, 'Has the WTO Dispute Settlement System Exceeded its Authority?' (2001) 4 JIEL 95 at 97–9; and Martha Rutsel, 'The Duty to Exercise Judgment on the Fruitfulness of Actions in World Trade Law' (2001) 35 JWT 1035.

[174] One additional hurdle for WTO members to bring a case is set out in Art. 3.7 of the DSU, stipulating that '[b]efore bringing a case, a Member shall exercise its judgement as to whether action under these procedures would be fruitful'. On how this could limit standing and interest to sue in the WTO, see Rutsel, 'Duty', 1035–59.

[175] See note 128 above.

instructive. As is the case for breach of WTO obligations, breach of obligations under the Vienna Convention is most likely to affect also other state parties.[176] However, this does not necessarily give those other states standing to invoke responsibility for the breach, nor does it detract from the bilateral/reciprocal nature of Vienna Convention obligations. Only in case the breach is one of an obligation owed to the state 'individually' – say, only in case the alleged wrongdoer has violated diplomatic law *as against diplomats of the complainant state* – will the complainant state have standing.

Nonetheless, two recent Appellate Body decisions could be regarded as going in the direction of giving wider standing to WTO members. In *US – Section 211 Appropriations Act*, the Appellate Body upheld a claim made by the European Communities as against the United States based on discrimination between original owners of intellectual property rights which are nationals of, on the one hand, Cuba and, on the other hand, the United States.[177] Although less favourable treatment was accorded to *Cuban* nationals, not to *European Community* nationals, the European Communities succeeded in their claim under Art. 3.1 of the TRIPS agreement. In *US – Line Pipe* too, Korea was allowed to make a claim under Art. 9.1 of the Safeguards agreement on the ground that the United States treated *developing countries* the same as all other suppliers, even though Art. 9.1 requires that safeguard measures 'not be applied against a product originating in a developing country Member as long as its share of imports of the product concerned in the importing Member does not exceed 3 per cent'.[178] Even though Korea is *not* generally regarded as a developing country, it succeeded under this claim. Crucially, however, in neither of these two cases did the defendant, *in casu* the United States, object to the European Communities and Korea, respectively, making such claims on behalf of *other* WTO members. Hence, it is fair to say that the Appellate Body, which was not faced with an objection of lack

---

[176] As the Commentary to the 2001 Draft Articles put it (with reference to the case on *United States Diplomatic and Consular Staff in Tehran*, ICJ Reports 1980, p. 3 at p. 43, para. 92): 'The identification of one particular State as injured by a breach of an obligation under the Vienna Convention on Diplomatic Relations does not exclude that all States parties may have an interest of a general character in compliance with international law and in the continuation of international institutions and arrangements which have been built up over the years' (Commentary, p. 298, para. 9).

[177] Appellate Body report, *United States – Section 211 Omnibus Appropriations Act of 1998*, WT/DS176/AB/R, adopted 1 February 2002, paras. 273–96.

[178] Appellate Body report, *United States – Definitive Safeguard Measures on Imports of Circular Welded Carbon Quality Line Pipe from Korea* ('*US – Line Pipe*'), WT/DS202/AB/R, adopted 8 March 2002, paras. 120–33.

of standing so that the United States could arguably be presumed to have accepted jurisdiction in this respect, has not yet expressed judgement on whether one WTO member can bring a claim on behalf of another. In any event, even if this were accepted, it must be recalled that such would only mean that WTO members can, in certain circumstances, exercise the *rights of other members*, not that breach of any WTO rule by any WTO member creates an *individual right for each and every other WTO member*. In other words, it would amount to granting wider standing to WTO members, not necessarily to declaring WTO obligations to be integral obligations binding *erga omnes partes*.

As pointed out, nothing prevents states, when concluding a bilateral/reciprocal treaty like the WTO treaty, from 'contracting out' of those general international law rules on standing. Hence, WTO members (or, for that matter, the Appellate Body) could well decide that, for whatever policy reason, it is desirable to make breach of WTO law challengeable by all WTO members, irrespective of the breach.[179] Such would not, in and of itself, change the nature of WTO obligations as reciprocal obligations. However, a strong argument against giving standing to all WTO members, based on a general legal interest to see the treaty abided by, is the risk of effectively appointing a number of powerful states as public prosecutors or policemen, with the result that especially (or only) obligations in the particular national interest of those states would be enforced. In the WTO, granting such *actio popularis* could mean that WTO agreements on, say, intellectual property or trade in services are more often judicially enforced than, for example, the agreements on agriculture or textiles and clothing.[180]

Breach
The second condition for a member to have standing (proof of trade effects or, at least, trade potential or opportunities) is directly related

---

[179] Arguably, such is already the case for breaches of the GATS, which in Art. XXIII.1 provides: 'If any Member should consider that any other Member fails to carry out its obligations or specific commitments under this Agreement, it may...have recourse to the DSU.'

[180] Another reason not to allow complaints against a measure that does not cause nullification to the complainant in question is that otherwise a claim could succeed on purely legal grounds but once implementation does not follow, the complainant (having a legal interest only) would not be able to retaliate since retaliation must be 'equivalent' to the nullification caused (DSU Art. 22.4). If there is no nullification, the complainant could not then suspend any concessions in retaliation. In these circumstances it could even be questioned whether bringing a case would be 'fruitful' in the sense referred to in Art. 3.7 of the DSU. See note 174 above.

to the conditions for a breach of WTO obligations to be established. Since standing essentially depends on the existence of a legal right, proof of a legal right will be inextricably linked to proof of breach. Now, for a breach of WTO rules to be established, it is generally accepted in GATT/WTO case law that a complainant is not required to prove that actual trade flows have been diverted.[181] Proof of trade opportunities being affected will be enough. This explains, at the same time, why proof of trade effects should not be a requirement either in terms of standing.

Nonetheless, as pointed out earlier, for a complainant to prove that a measure violates WTO rules is not enough for that measure to be condemned by a panel. In addition, the complainant must point to nullification or impairment of benefits *accruing to it*.[182] As noted above, this element supports the view that WTO obligations are reciprocal in nature. However, DSU Art. 3.8 provides for a presumption to the effect that breach 'is considered *prima facie* to constitute a case of nullification and impairment'. This is further explained to mean that 'there is normally a presumption that a breach of the rules has an adverse impact on other Members'. However, as the Appellate Body noted, Art. 3.8 is about 'what happens *after* a violation is established'.[183] It does not relate to the issue of standing required in order to be allowed to *invoke breach*. In other words, to say that nullification of benefits is presumed once breach is established (as Art. 3.8 does) is not the same as saying that all WTO members have a right to complain about any WTO breach.

Consequences of breach

Although breach of WTO rules may be successfully invoked by a number of WTO members (meeting, first, the two rather lenient conditions for standing and, second, the relatively wide definition of breach, both referring to trade opportunities, not trade effects), a finding of breach of WTO rules is a purely bilateral matter. Quite often, whether or not there is breach will actually be dependent on the complainant (are its exports, for example, 'like products' as compared to the domestic products

---

[181] See, for example, the panel report on *US – Taxes on Petroleum and Certain Imported Substances*, adopted on 17 June 1987, BISD 34S/136, para. 5.2.2, referring to GATT Art. III as a provision 'not only to protect current trade but also to create the predictability needed to plan future trade'.

[182] See GATT Art. XXIII. Note, in this respect, that the Appellate Body found also that for procedural objections in respect of a panel ruling to be upheld, the member invoking them must show prejudice (Appellate Body report on *EC – Hormones*, footnote 138).

[183] Appellate Body report on *US – Shirts and Blouses*, p. 13.

allegedly protected in breach of, say, GATT Art. III:4?). A finding of WTO breach is bilateral also in the sense that only the complainant, not other WTO members, may directly rely on it. Only the complainant may suspend concessions if no implementation follows, not other WTO members. In addition, the fact that other WTO members have exactly the same measure in place as the one found to be in breach does not give other WTO members any rights to suspend concessions. A new state-to-state complaint must be lodged against these equivalent measures for their WTO illegality to be conclusively established.

These bilateral consequences of breach, combined with the requirements for standing set out above and the state-to-state definition of breach (including the condition of member-specific nullification), are important indicators that WTO obligations are not integral, but reciprocal.

Conclusion on WTO obligations as bilateral obligations (focusing on inter se *modifications pursuant to Art. 41 of the Vienna Convention on the Law of Treaties)*

That most WTO obligations must be qualified as reciprocal in nature bears crucially important consequences for the topic assessed in this work. The fact that they are not integral obligations puts them in perspective. It stresses their relative importance as obligations of an essentially contractual type that can, in principle, be deviated from *inter se*. They are not integral in the sense of being immutable obligations to be respected at all times and as between all WTO members, irrespective of other norms of international law. WTO obligations are, in this sense, framework obligations only or *lex generalis* that can, at times, be supplemented or deviated from as between some or all WTO members, by other rules of international law (especially rules that are of an integral type).

WTO law is but a branch of public international law. Given its reciprocal nature, WTO law will, moreover, have to allow for and give way to a number of other rules of international law. The fact that some WTO members agree to deviate from WTO obligations in their *inter se* relations only – e.g., by mutually agreeing to condition their trade on respect for human rights *without affecting the rights of third parties* – must, in principle, be accepted, given the reciprocal nature of WTO obligations. Below, in chapter 6, we further examine the conditions for valid *inter se* deviations. As long as their rights are not affected, other WTO members, not party to such *inter se* deviation, cannot complain about these purely *inter se* contractual changes. The requirements for other members to have standing to challenge such *inter se* deviations will then, indeed, not be met (on the books, the measure does not even apply to their trade, nor even their potential trade). If WTO obligations were, however, of the integral type, no such *inter se* modifications could have been tolerated.

3 Hierarchy of sources

> [T]he system of international law consists of erratic parts and elements which are differently structured so that one can hardly speak of a homogeneous nature of international law. This system is full of universal, regional or even bilateral systems, subsystems and sub-subsystems of different levels of legal integration.[1]

We start this chapter with a description of some of the features of the sources of international law that may complicate an examination of conflict of norms in public international law. We then ask whether there are any *a priori* hierarchies in international law and, thereafter, examine the principal sources of international law as they may play out in a conflict of norms. We conclude the chapter by redefining international law as constituted by, first, general international law and, second, particular international law.

The continuing uncertainty as to the sources of international law

The problem of identifying the sources of international law

It is generally recognised that norms of international law may derive from the following five sources: treaties; custom; general principles of law; unilateral acts of states; and acts of international organisations. Obviously, a distinction must be made between these five 'sources' of law and the infinite number of 'norms' they may produce.

The first three of these sources – treaties, customary law and general principles of law – are explicitly confirmed in Art. 38(1)(a)–(c) of the

---

[1] Gerhard Hafner, 'Risk Ensuing from Fragmentation of International Law', ILC, Report on the Work of its 52nd Session, General Assembly, Official Records, 55th Session, Supplement No. 10 (A/55/10), 321.

ICJ Statute as part of the 'applicable law' before the ICJ. Based on Art. 38(1)(d), it is equally accepted that judicial decisions and teachings of publicists are *not* sources of international law, at least not in the strict sense of themselves creating new norms.[2]

Article 38 is, of course, but a treaty provision focusing on one given, although crucially important, court. It is in that sense *part* of international law and does not *define* international law. Article. 38 could, for example, be amended. Hence, Art. 38 has *not* been viewed as an exhaustive statement, valid for all times, on all possible sources of international law. State practice, confirmed by the ICJ itself, shows that new sources of international law have since arisen, in particular unilateral acts of states and acts of international organisations. The direction in Art. 38 itself that the ICJ's function is to 'decide in accordance with international law' confirms the dynamic potential and non-exhaustive character of Art. 38.[3] Consequently, Art. 38 is exhaustive neither within the ICJ's precinct nor *a fortiori* outside the ICJ as a general statement on the sources of international law.[4]

This open character of the sources of international law, in contrast to the clearly defined number of sources in domestic law, is a first element of uncertainty of which one should be aware when conducting this study. Indeed, uncertainty as to what the sources of law are necessarily reflects on the completeness of any theory on conflict of norms derived from these sources.

In addition, any attempt to sum up the sources of international law implies taking a position on the very nature of international law, its normative concept and the reason why international law is binding. As Bos has remarked: 'it is the normative concept of law which decides about the need for, and the number of, "sources" of law...no single normative concept of law exists for international relations, but a plurality of such concepts leading to different theories on "sources"'.[5]

---

[2] See below, pp. 109–10.
[3] This phrase is the only element that was added in 1945 with the establishment of the ICJ. For the rest, Art. 38 of the ICJ Statute copies what was Art. 38 of the Statute of the PCIJ.
[4] Of the same view, see, for example: Gerald Fitzmaurice, 'Some Problems Regarding the Formal Sources of International Law', in *Symbolae Verzijl* (The Hague: Nijhoff, 1958), 153 at 160; Clive Parry, *The Sources and Evidences of International Law* (Manchester: Manchester University Press, 1965), 15; Maarten Bos, 'The Recognized Manifestations of International Law' (1977) 20 GYIL 9 at 18; and Georges Abi-Saab, 'Les Sources du Droit International: Essai de Déconstruction', in *Le Droit International dans un Monde en Mutation, Melanges E. J. De Arechaga* (Montevideo: Fundación de Cultura Universitaria, 1994), 29 at 36.
[5] Bos, 'The Recognized', 14.

From the 'consumer's' or law-taker's perspective that we adopted[6] – that is, with reference to the question of 'what is the law that an international tribunal will apply to a given case?' – it is of crucial importance to know the law one is subject to. As put by Jennings: 'although lawyers know that the quality of certainty of law is one on which there must be much compromise, not least in the interest of justice, it is a desideratum of any strong law that there is reasonable certainty about where one should look to find it'.[7] In the specific field of WTO law, for example, it is of crucial importance for WTO members, as well as their producers, traders and consumers generally, to know what WTO law consists of and for what norms and obligations they can be held liable.[8] In this respect, it is important for WTO panels and the Appellate Body to pay close attention to identifying clearly the legal or other basis for referring to certain instruments, acts or statements as sources of WTO law in support of their decisions.

Uncertainty as to the normativity threshold

A second element of uncertainty in respect of sources – besides the problem of summing them up – stems from the difficulty of identifying exactly when the sources of international law that have to date been recognised create legally binding norms. This raises the question of the 'normativity threshold' for each of the sources of international law. This difficulty of knowing when something becomes part of international law, or *how* international law is created and what formal steps or procedures are required for international law to exist as law, relates to what most authors refer to as the '*formal* sources of international law'. They contrast these 'formal sources' to '*material* sources', the latter relating to *where* the law can be found in its material form and the instruments or acts in which international law finds its expression.[9]

No problems arise in identifying treaty norms. The same could be said of acts of international organisations. In contrast, identifying when

---

[6] See chapter 1 above, pp. 7–8.
[7] Robert Jennings, 'What Is International Law and How Do We Tell It When We See It?' (1981) 37 ASDI 59. Van Hoof starts his book on sources with the following sentence: 'As law is primarily a device for regulating and ordering relations in society, any system of law should be able to answer clearly the question of what the law is or where it can be found' (D. Van Hoof, *Rethinking the Sources of International Law* (Deventer: Kluwer, 1983), 1).
[8] On the sources of WTO law, see chapter 2 above.
[9] See, for example, Nguyen Quoc Dinh, P. Daillier and A. Pellet, *Droit International Public* (Montreal: Wilson & Lafleur, 1999), paras. 58 ff. and Ian Brownlie, *Principles of Public International Law* (Oxford: Clarendon, 1998), 1–2 (who questions the usefulness of this distinction).

something becomes a norm part of customary law or general principles of law is a much more difficult task. This is so because the criteria for recognition of these norms are less clear. Identifying unilateral acts of states which create binding obligations may be equally difficult as it may depend on factual circumstances that may not always be clear: for example, was there an intention to be bound and was the statement made publicly? In this sense, the ILC's decision in 1997 to put the topic of 'unilateral acts of states' on its agenda can only be applauded. Codification of how customary international law is created and revised could also be very useful.

In domestic legal systems, recognising when a norm is validly created is much easier. It can be done with reference to constitutional law: defining, for example, how new constitutional rules can be enacted, how statutes are made and by whom, and what else the law of the land is composed of, such as governmental decrees, local decisions, etc. In international law, in contrast, the question of what the law consists of is much more difficult to answer. In international law, there is no centralised legislator nor any division of powers between different organs or institutions that fit within an overall hierarchy. As remarked by Abi-Saab in the context of his view of international law as a 'long processus de transformation progressive à travers la zone grise qui sépare la valeur sociale émergente de la règle du droit bien établie': 'le seuil du droit positif (ou la frontière entre le droit et le pré-droit, la *lex lata* et la *lex ferenda*) ne peut pas toujours être clairement défini'.[10] The distinction between *lex lata* and *lex ferenda* is particularly blurred in respect of customary law. The following statement made in 1938 by Lazar Kopelmanas is still very much pertinent today. He remarked that the creation of customary law 'qui ne permet pas de préciser nettement le moment où une règle sociale devient règle de droit, ne remplit que partiellement les fonctions de source formelle, puisque la fonction essentielle des sources formelles est de servir de critère de distinction – pour le juge – entre les règles juridiques et les autres règles sociales'.[11]

The resulting difficulties for conducting this study are obvious. Indeed, when faced, for example, with an alleged conflict between instrument A and instrument B, how can one decide whether there *is* conflict

---

[10] Abi-Saab, 'Les Sources', 48. On the distinction between *lex lata* and *lex ferenda*, see Antonio Cassese and Joseph Weiler (eds.), *Change and Stability in International Law-Making* (Berlin: De Gruyter, 1988), 66–72 (presentation by Ian Brownlie) and 72–92 (discussion).
[11] Lazar Kopelmanas, 'Essai d'une Théorie des Sources Formelles de Droit International' (1938) *Revue de Droit International* 101 at 119–20.

and, if so, how can one *resolve* that conflict if it is not even clear whether instrument A and/or B is a norm of international law to which the parties in question can be held?

The often vague content of norms of international law

Finally, a third element of uncertainty, inherent in all legal norms, including those of domestic law, arises when trying to define the exact *content* of an instrument, act or series of acts that have been recognised as constituting a legally binding norm. This problem arises in respect of all sources of international law, including treaties, and more so, it would seem, in international law than in domestic law. Given the high number of participants and the widely divergent interests that each state negotiating a treaty may have, treaty norms are often left vague and ambiguous. Their adoption requires a *consensus of all states* involved, not a simple majority as is the case for most domestic laws. To circumscribe clearly the rights and obligations that derive from sources of international law other than treaties, in particular custom and general principles of law, and to apply them to a given case may even be more difficult.

In that sense, norms of international law are seldom 'finished products',[12] simply requiring implementation. The function of the international adjudicator in 'completing' the norm as it applies in a particular dispute – to be conducted, of course, within certain limits – should not be underestimated. As noted earlier, international law is not composed only of rules, it is a continuing process in which international adjudication plays an important role. As Jennings remarked in respect of both judicial decisions and commentators: 'it is these two sources which are most likely to bring certainty and clarity in the places where the mass of material evidences is so large and confused as to obscure the basic distinction between law and proposal'.[13] Or, as it was put by Fastenrath: 'According to modern legal theory, each judicial decision involves further development and, thereby, also the creation of law. Each decision defines the normative content of a legal rule and thus has far-reaching effects on the general interpretation of the rule, regardless of the limited binding force of the specific decision.'[14]

---

[12] Maarten Bos, *A Methodology of International Law* (Amsterdam: Elsevier, 1984), 22, referred to in Ulrich Fastenrath, 'Relative Normativity in International Law' (1993) 4 EJIL 305 at 308.
[13] Jennings, 'International Law', 79.
[14] Ulrich Fastenrath, *Lücken im Völkerrecht: zu Rechtscharakter, Quellen, Systemzusammenhang, Methodenlehre und Funktionen des Völkerrechts* (Berlin: Duncker & Humblot, 1991), English

For the topic of conflict of norms, the often vague nature of norms of international law cuts both ways. On the one hand, it makes the task of defining the exact content of each norm, as well as the question of whether they really conflict, more difficult. On the other hand, if norms are ambiguous, a harmonious interpretation of what may seem at first sight contradictory norms could be facilitated.[15]

Are there any *a priori* hierarchies in international law?

There is no formal 'hierarchy of sources' in international law

It seems to be generally accepted that there is no inherent hierarchy of the sources of international law. Unlike most hierarchies established in domestic law, a norm derived from one source of international law is *not a priori* of a higher value than a norm formed under another source based, for example, on the organ creating the norm or the procedure followed.[16] The enumeration of the traditional sources of international law in paragraphs 1(a) to (c) of Art. 38 of the ICJ Statute – treaty, customary law and general principles of law – is not regarded as setting out any *a priori* hierarchy. As Brownlie noted, the sources in Art. 38 'are not stated to represent a hierarchy, but the draftsmen intended to give an order and in one draft the word "successively" appeared'.[17] This 'intended

---

summary, 291, German text, 108–9. In the same sense: Abi-Saab, 'Les Sources', 34 ('c'est du pur formalisme artificiel que de dire que [la jurisprudence] ne fait qu'interpréter la matière normative déjà existante, sans ajouter en ce faisant à sa substance'); and Ian Brownlie, 'General Course on Public International Law' (1995) 255 *Recueil des Cours* 21 ('My general outlook is that of the objective positivist...However, my positivism is supplemented by an awareness of the significant role of international tribunals in making law').

[15] See chapter 5 below, pp. 244–74.

[16] There is wide support for this proposition. See, for example, Nancy Kontou, *The Termination and Revision of Treaties in the Light of New Customary International Law* (Oxford: Clarendon, 1994), 21 ('it is accepted that the binding force of conventional and customary rules is the same'); Quoc Dinh, *Droit*, para. 60 ('pour les sources, il n'existe pas de hiérarchie en droit international'); Brownlie, *Principles*, 3; Mark Villiger, *Customary International Law and Treaties, A Manual on the Theory and Practice of the Interrelation of Sources* (The Hague: Kluwer, 1997), para. 84 ('an *a priori* hierarchy of sources is an alien concept' to the structure of the international legal order); Michael Akehurst, 'The Hierarchy of the Sources of International Law' (1974–5) 47 BYIL 273 at 274–5; Emmanuel Roucounas, 'Engagements Parallèles Contradictoires' (1987-VI) 206 *Recueil des Cours* 9, para. 72 ('le système est fondé largement sur l'égalité entre les deux sources formelles (traités et coutume)'); and W. Czaplinski and G. Danilenko, 'Conflict of Norms in International Law' (1990) 21 NYIL 3 at 7 ('[t]he predominant majority of authors...reject every formal hierarchy of international law').

[17] Brownlie, *Principles*, 3.

order' seems to reflect the logical sequence in which the rules would occur to the judge's mind, rather than to establish a definite hierarchy of sources.[18]

International law, unlike domestic legal systems, is 'decentralised' in that it has no central legislator creating the rules. On the contrary, the prime *creators* of international law are also the main *subjects* of international law, namely states. States as *subjects* of international law, unlike individuals in domestic law, do not elect an 'international legislator' which is then mandated to make law on their behalf, binding on all states. Moreover, states as *creators* of law are complete equals. The law created by state A and state B has the same legal value as that created by state C and state D. International law is a law of co-operation, not subordination.[19] Its creation depends essentially on the consent of states, be it explicit or only implicit.[20] The lack of such consent by a given state generally means that it cannot be held to the rule in question (*pacta tertiis nec nocent nec prosunt*).[21] The absence of formal hierarchy in international law is a direct consequence of the assumption that all international norms, in one way or another, derive from state consent. Since, therefore, all norms essentially derive from the same source (state consent), it is presumed that they have the same binding value.

As a result, the fact that a norm derives from a treaty does not *necessarily* mean that it prevails over customary law and general principles of law. Nor does customary law *necessarily* prevail over general principles of law. A conflict of norms in international law cannot, therefore, be decided simply by reference to the respective *source* from which the norms originate, that is, the way a conflict of norms is generally resolved in domestic law.

In addition, formal elements other than the *source* of the norms in question do not play a role either. In terms of hierarchy, it does not in

---

[18] On the drafting history of Art. 38, see Akehurst, 'Hierarchy', 274.

[19] See Charles Rousseau, 'De la Compatibilité des Normes Juridiques Contradictoires dans l'Ordre International' (1932) 39 RGDIP 133 at 150 ('Le droit des gens est un droit de cooperation et non de subordination. L'accord des sujets de droit y est la seule source de droit et les normes qui résultent de cet accord de volontés sont d'égale valeur juridique').

[20] This consensual or positivist assumption is, indeed, one made throughout this work. As Michael Byers noted, however, 'this consent may take the form of a general consent to the process of customary law, of a diffuse consensus rather than a specific consent to individual rules' (Michael Byers, *Custom, Power and the Power of Rules* (Cambridge: Cambridge University Press, 1999), 14 and 142–6).

[21] See, for example, Arts. 34–8 of the Vienna Convention on treaties and third parties.

principle matter, for example, where or in what context or international organisation a norm has been created (be it the WTO or WIPO or under an MEA). Moreover, a treaty originally concluded by a head of state does not carry more weight than one concluded by an ambassador.[22] Similarly, a norm (say, an act of an international organisation) validly adopted by majority voting must not necessarily give way to one adopted by unanimity. Nor must oral or implied consent necessarily give way to written or explicit consent (say, consent implied from subsequent practice, as opposed to a written treaty provision).

In domestic law, in contrast, the hierarchy of norms is determined by *by whom* and *how* the norm was enacted: for example, was it enacted by constitutional procedure, the federal legislature or the local commune? The situation is different under international law, where a centralised legislature is lacking and formal sources of law are not as clearly defined as in domestic law. As we shall see below, what matters in international law is not so much by whom or how the norm was created, but rather what the norm is about, what the norm itself says about its hierarchical status and when it was established. An exception to this rule is the hierarchy of norms created *within* an international organisation – so-called acts of international organisations – where the organ which created the norm will normally, as in domestic law, determine the hierarchical status of that norm.

Given the absence of inherent hierarchies: lex posterior derogat legi priori

Since, in principle, all rules of international law have, as an expression of state will, the same legal status, a later expression of state will must logically prevail over an earlier one. This rule, related to the contractual freedom of states, corresponds to the adage *lex posterior derogat legi priori*. We come back to this rule in detail in chapter 7 below, but already at this stage some aspects of it are worth highlighting. In respect of treaty norms, the *lex posterior* rule is set out in Art. 30 of the Vienna Convention.[23] However, in respect of other conflicts (such as conflict between treaty and custom) the *lex posterior* rule applies equally. This is so because all rules of international law – be they set out in a treaty or in custom – are, in principle, of the same binding force. As a result,

---

[22] See Arnold McNair, *The Law of Treaties* (Oxford: Clarendon, 1961), 64.
[23] Art. 30(3) provides the core of the *lex posterior* rule: 'When all the parties to the earlier treaty are parties also to the later treaty...*the earlier treaty applies only to the extent that its provisions are compatible with those of the later treaty.*'

any later rule, that is, any later expression of state consent, normally overrules an earlier contradictory rule. The theory of *acte contraire*, by which a norm could only be modified by another norm originating *from the same source*, is not known in international law.[24]

Nonetheless, whereas treaties and acts of international organisations may have a precise date on which they were concluded (on which there will be more below in chapter 7), it is virtually impossible to point to the precise date on which a general principle of law or custom emerged. The same argument could be made in respect of unilateral acts of states which may consist of a series of events which, only taken together, constitute a binding undertaking. All of these norms of international law other than treaties and acts of international organisations do not, like most rules of domestic law from which the *lex posterior* rule is borrowed, come into being at a fixed point in time. They emerge over time and change gradually. They are, in this sense, more a 'process' in which other norms of international law may play a role, rather than a definite 'rule' with which other norms may conflict. The main result of this 'process' is that genuine conflicts between treaty, on the one hand, and custom or general principles of law, on the other, will be rather exceptional.

Another reason why the *lex posterior* rule does not work well in respect of most sources other than treaties – and, as we shall see, even among certain treaty-norms[25] – is that the *lex posterior* rule assumes that the two conflicting norms emanate from the *same* law-maker in that a later expression of that law-maker should prevail over an earlier one. However, in international law divergent law-making processes exist and overlap. Some of them are based explicitly on consent, others only implicitly; some emerge with reference to a wide range of actors in the international arena (such as custom), others only with reference to state conduct at the highest level (such as treaties). To rely, in this context, on a later expression overruling an earlier one, when the forms, characteristics and even authors of the expression are so divergent, is rather awkward. *Lex posterior* is copied from domestic law where the sources of law are formally organised and clearly defined. To transpose *lex posterior* by analogy to international law, with its decentralised features and divergent sources of law, may not always meet with success.

---

[24] See, for example, Quoc Dinh, *Droit*, para. 185. An exception to the absence of *acte contraire* in international law is *jus cogens*. Article 53 of the Vienna Convention states that a rule of *jus cogens* 'can be modified only by a subsequent norm of general international law having the same character'.

[25] See chapter 7 below, pp. 367–80.

The absolute priority of jus cogens

The only instance of *a priori* hierarchy between norms of international law is when one norm – derived from any source – contradicts another norm part of *jus cogens*. We come back to the hierarchical supremacy of *jus cogens* in chapter 6 below. The Vienna Convention defines a norm of *jus cogens*, that is, 'a peremptory norm of general international law', as one 'accepted and recognized by the international community of States as a whole as a norm from which no derogation is permitted and which can be modified only by a subsequent norm of general international law having the same character' (Art. 53). Nowhere does the Vienna Convention refer to, let alone restrict, the *source* of either, on the one hand, norms of *jus cogens* or, on the other, contradictory norms which may not derogate from *jus cogens*. In other words, the higher value of a norm of *jus cogens* is not based on its source, that is, with reference to how it was created or by whom, but rather based on its acceptance and recognition as a norm from which no derogation is permitted. The latter relates to the substantive content of the norm – is it of such fundamental value that no derogation from it can be tolerated? – rather than the formal creation or source of the norm. As the ILC noted: 'It is not the form of a general rule of international law, but the particular nature of the subject-matter with which it deals that may...give it the character of *jus cogens*...pre-eminence of [certain] obligations over others is determined by their content, not by the process by which they were created.'[26]

Views as to what sources of international law may create *jus cogens* are widely divergent.[27] Most authors acknowledge that customary law can create *jus cogens*. Some maintain that *only* custom can give rise to *jus cogens*.[28] Others give a role also to treaties and general principles of law as possible sources of *jus cogens*.[29]

We come back to the theory of *jus cogens* as a conflict rule in chapter 6 below. Note that norms of *jus cogens* are, as James Crawford noted, 'virtually coextensive'[30] with obligations of the international community as

---

[26] Quoted in Prosper Weil, 'Towards Relative Normativity in International Law?' (1983) 77 AJIL 413 at 425.
[27] For an overview of doctrinal positions on the issue, see Akehurst, 'Hierarchy', 282.
[28] For reasoning in this direction, see V. Degan, *Sources of International Law* (The Hague: Nijhoff 1997), 83.
[29] See, for example, H. Mosler, 'General Principles of Law', in R. Bernhardt (ed.), *Encyclopedia of Public International Law* (Amsterdam: North-Holland, 1984), VII, 89.
[30] James Crawford, Special Rapporteur to the ILC on State Responsibility, Third Report (With addenda), UN doc. A/CN.4/507 (2000), para. 106(a).

a whole or *erga omnes* obligations.[31] In the notion of *jus cogens*, the focus is on the higher hierarchical status of certain norms; in the notion of *erga omnes* obligations, the focus is on who can invoke responsibility for breach.

Other norms that are allegedly 'more important'

There are norms of international law, other than those of *jus cogens*, which are, in one way or the other, also given a higher legal status. Their increased importance is generally *not* related to their source (UN Charter obligations being the exception), nor does their higher status necessarily lead to these norms prevailing over all other norms. Nonetheless, since these norms are generally distinguished from other norms, they are briefly surveyed in this section on whether there are *a priori* hierarchies in international law. Some of these norms are dealt with in more detail in subsequent chapters. In a seminal piece, Prosper Weil expressed the view that this tendency towards what he calls 'graduated normativity' threatens the ideological neutrality of international law, a neutrality which he considers to be 'necessary to guarantee the coexistence of heterogeneous entities in a pluralistic society'.[32]

UN Charter obligations

As further explained in chapter 7 below, Art. 103 of the UN Charter results in 'obligations of the members of the United Nations under the [UN] Charter' prevailing over all other obligations 'under any other international agreement'. To that extent, some part of international law, namely 'UN Charter law', could be said to be of higher legal standing *based on its source*, namely the UN Charter. This is a consequence of an explicit conflict clause in the UN Charter itself. As a result, one cannot equate UN Charter obligations with norms of *jus cogens*. Whereas *jus cogens* cannot be derogated from (it can only be modified by a subsequent norm of *jus cogens*),[33] the UN Charter can be amended and so can UN Charter obligations, for example, by means of the UN Security Council reviewing its resolutions.

Crucially, however, in so far as the fifteen members of the UN Security Council can overrule the obligations of any UN member under any other earlier or later international agreement, the UN Security Council can be

---
[31] On the notion of *erga omnes* obligations, see Maurizio Ragazzi, *The Concept of International Obligations* Erga Omnes (Oxford: Clarendon, 2000).
[32] Weil, 'Normativity', 20–1.   [33] Art. 53 of the Vienna Convention.

portrayed as a type of 'global executive' which, within its limited sphere of competence, has the power to enact law on behalf of all other UN members not having a seat on the Security Council. For that reason, it is crucial to define clearly the limits of the Security Council's mandate, in particular its 'primary responsibility for the maintenance of international peace and security' (Art. 24(1) of the UN Charter). Some may argue, for example, that the Security Council's establishment of war crimes tribunals or authorisation of military action against human rights violators is at the outer limits of this mandate.

Obligations *erga omnes* and obligations *erga omnes partes* (integral obligations)

The 2001 Draft Articles on State Responsibility refer to two other types of norms that are given increased importance. First, Art. 48(1)(b) of the 2001 Draft Articles talks of obligations 'owed to the international community as a whole'. These obligations are so-called obligations *erga omnes* and, as noted earlier, are 'virtually coextensive'[34] with obligations of *jus cogens*. It is interesting to note that the previous version of the ILC Draft Articles, adopted on second reading in 2000, referred instead to obligations 'owed to the international community as a whole *and essential for the protection of its fundamental interests*' (Art. 41, emphasis added). Crucially, the notion of 'international crimes of states' that was to be found in Art. 19 and Chapter IV (Arts. 51 to 53) of the Draft Articles adopted by the ILC on first reading in 1996 was not maintained in the final 2001 Draft Articles.[35]

Second, Art. 48(1)(a) of the 2001 Draft Articles refers to obligations 'owed to a group of States...established for the protection of a collective interest of the group'. These obligations are so-called obligations *erga omnes partes* or integral obligations, discussed earlier in chapter 2. Chapter 6 below elaborates on how such integral obligations can be more important than other obligations and prevail, for example, over certain other norms (in particular, norms constituting *inter se* modifications to the integral obligation) on the ground of their substantive content or nature. Whereas obligations of *jus cogens* are virtually co-extensive with obligations *erga omnes*, obligations *erga omnes* (and thus *jus cogens*) can

---

[34] Crawford, Third Report, para. 106(a).
[35] For recent discussions on the concept of international crimes, see the First Report on State Responsibility by Special Rapporteur James Crawford, Addenda 1 and 2, UN doc. A/CN.4/490/Add. 1 and Add. 2 (1998) and Alain Pellet, 'Can a State Commit a Crime? Definitely, Yes!' (1999) 10 EJIL 425.

be seen as a sub-category of obligations *erga omnes partes*, a sub-catgeory which is, of course, of particular importance.

The 2001 Draft Articles give special prominence to obligations *erga omnes* and obligations *erga omnes partes* in that responsibility for breach of those obligations can also be invoked by states other than an injured state. Although these provisions may not relate directly to conflict of norms, they indicate that the international community of states is gradually recognising that some norms of international law are more important than others.

So-called 'public interest norms'

Some authors have argued in favour of giving *erga omnes* effect to so-called 'public interest' norms even though those norms are not part of *jus cogens*. The idea is to make those norms binding on all states, even without their consent, on the ground that they serve a 'public interest' and should hence be seen as benefiting also non-parties. This approach is essentially proposed as a way out of the free-riders problem faced in many fields of international relations.

The problem of free-riders was addressed in the *Genocide Convention* case: how could one ensure that as many states as possible signed up to the Convention? Indeed, if certain states kept out, the objective of eradicating genocide, something that required universal co-operation, was unlikely to be achieved. In order to promote universal adherence to the Genocide Convention, the Court accepted reservations to the Convention that were not incompatible with its object and purpose. A similar free-riders problem arises in the WTO: how can one ensure that trade liberalisation moves on, but at the same time avoid non-participating parties 'free-riding' too much on increased liberalisation agreed upon by others, an increased liberalisation which must, in principle, be extended also to all other WTO members pursuant to the MFN principle?[36] In the field of environmental protection the free-riders problem is even more prominent: given that, for example, global warming knows no borders, how can one ensure that as many states as possible sign up to the treaty that limits certain emissions? The very object and purpose of the treaty may be completely undermined by some free-riders who keep polluting. This free-rider problem explains, for example, why many MEAs include obligations in respect of non-parties.

---

[36] With the exception, of course, of regional arrangements meeting the requirements in GATT Art. XXIV.

Jost Delbrück defends the position that 'the *erga omnes* effect of particular norms is based on the special character of such norms; they articulate basic interests and needs as well as fundamental values of the international community as a whole'.[37] This may be so in respect of norms of *jus cogens*, but he takes it one step further so as to cover also other obligations:

> the core principle of the international regime created for the protection of the ozone layer and the regime created by the [1995 Fish Stocks] Agreement...give rise to obligations *erga omnes*. The *ratio legis* is that the common interest in protecting the ozone layer, protecting the environment from grave pollution, for instance, intentional oil spills as a means of warfare, and protecting endangered species is so overwhelming that no State may be permitted not to comply with the protective regimes regardless of whether or not it has consented to the creation of the regime.[38]

Such an approach, in so far as it steps beyond the boundaries of *jus cogens*, is both risky and unfounded. First, it brings an inherently subjective element into the binding nature of international law. Indeed, when is a norm in everyone's 'public interest' and who decides this matter? Prosper Weil warned against importing such subjective value judgements into international law, as, in his view, they would threaten its very function of providing a neutral framework for co-operation. His critique may not have been convincing in respect of *jus cogens*, but it seems convincing for 'lower' so-called 'public interest norms'. The cultural, social and economic diversity of states makes it impossible to proclaim a convention negotiated by some states as reflecting the 'public interest' of all, particularly when it comes to the detailed technical provisions.[39] All states may have an interest in the environment and an orderly regulation of fisheries, but they may want to go about achieving these interests in different ways. To recognise protection of the environment as a 'global common' is one thing, to impose detailed treaty obligations on non-parties to achieve that 'global common' is quite another.

---

[37] Jost Delbrück, 'Laws in the Public Interest – Some Observations on the Foundations and Identification of Erga Omnes Norms in International Law', in Volkmar Götz et al. (eds.), *Liber Amicorum Gunther Jaenicke* (Berlin: Springer, 1998) 17, 18.

[38] *Ibid.*, 26–7. Delbrück characterises these obligations as follows: 'They are not conceived in terms of traditional rights and duties in the national interest of the parties involved but they are meant to constitute objective guidelines or norms in the public interest of the international community as a whole' (*ibid.*, 28).

[39] On this issue of diversity, see Robert Jennings, 'Universal International Law in a Multicultural World', in TMC Institute (ed.), *International Law and the Grotian Heritage* (The Hague, 1985), 187–97.

Second, there is not only the problem of subjective value judgements. The principle *pacta tertiis* constitutes the main legal obstacle to recognising that certain treaty norms – other than those part of *jus cogens* or those that have developed into custom – are binding also on non-parties. Delbrück refers to the existence of so-called objective regimes, which were considered in certain cases to be binding also on non-parties.[40] However, the Vienna Convention did not incorporate this idea of objective regimes[41] and categorically confirmed the principle of *pacta tertiis*.[42] Much has been written about the allegedly binding nature on third parties of certain provisions of the 1995 Fish Stocks Agreement. However, this cannot be so under the *pacta tertiis* principle.[43] The Convention introduces, for example, the principle that access to the fishery resources in a particular region of the high seas is restricted to states which are members of the competent subregional or regional fisheries management organisation, or which agree to apply the conservation and management measures established by such organisation, or, in the absence of such regional organisation, which participate in conservation and management

---

[40] See, for example, the *Wimbledon case*, where the PCIJ found that the international regime for the Kiel Canal (set out in the Versailles Peace Treaty) was binding also on Germany, even though Germany was not a party to the treaty (PCIJ, Series A, No. 1 (1923)) and the *Dispute on the Regime of Demilitarization for the Aaland Islands*, where an *ad hoc* Committee of Jurists decided that the Paris peace settlement of 1856 setting out international obligations on demilitarisation was binding also on, and could be invoked by, Sweden and Finland, even though they were not parties to the settlement (see report of the International Committee of Jurists entrusted by the Council of the League of Nations with the task of giving an advisory opinion upon the legal aspects of the Aaland Islands Question, *League of Nations Official Journal*, Special Supplement No. 3, October 1920).

[41] It is reflected only in Art. 41, but then in the sense of *inter se* agreements not being allowed to deviate from multilateral treaties *that are binding on both parties*. Hence, the idea of certain multilateral treaties being more important than *inter se* treaties (notwithstanding the contractual freedom of states) was confirmed, but only in respect of treaties binding on both parties.

[42] As Rosenne remarked: 'It might be thought, and indeed not without reason, that... [Arts. 34–8] constitute an emphatic reassertion of the individual sovereignty of states vis-à-vis the law of treaties and negate any suggestion that the post-World War II codification of the law of treaties went any distance in acknowledging even the existence of community interest in the law' (Shabtai Rosenne, 'Bilateralism and Community Interest in the Codified Law of Treaties', in W. Friedmann, L. Henkin and O. Lissitzyn (eds.), *Transnational Law in a Changing Society, Essays in Honor of Philip C. Jessup* (New York: Columbia University Press, 1972), 203 at 204).

[43] For an overview and, in my view, correct conclusion on this matter, see Erik Franckx, 'Pacta Tertiis and the Agreement for the Implementation of the Straddling and Highly Migratory Fish Stocks Provisions of the United Nations Convention on the Law of the Sea' (2000) 8 *Tulane Journal of International and Comparative Law* 49.

arrangements directly entered into by the interested parties.⁴⁴ Important as it may be, this provision must remain ineffective for states not parties to the 1995 agreement. The same applies in respect of the Convention's principle that ships may be boarded and inspected on the high seas by member states of an existing subregional or regional organisation or arrangement, whether or not the flag state of the boarded or inspected vessel is a member of that organisation or is a participant in such an arrangement.⁴⁵ Here again, this principle can only apply to fishing vessels flying the flag of parties to the 1995 agreement. Other vessels can continue to invoke the customary law principle which provides that on the high seas only the flag state is competent.⁴⁶

The same problem arises under certain MEAs. The fact that an MEA imposes an obligation on parties to, for example, restrict trade with non-parties⁴⁷ does not make the agreement binding on non-parties. If, for example, parties to the MEA are obliged under the agreement to restrict trade with *non-parties* and this trade restriction goes against other norms (e.g., WTO rules), the parties to the MEA cannot invoke the agreement in and of itself as a legal justification for breach. Non-parties to the MEA cannot be held by the provisions of the MEA. Of course, parties could then still justify their action under exceptions in the WTO treaty itself (such as GATT Art. XX).

Arguing that 'public interest norms' ought to bind also non-parties amounts to reverting to a legal–technical means to solve an essentially political question: namely, how to induce more states to sign a treaty so as to avoid the free-riders problem. This political question ought to be resolved rather by political means, that is, through negotiation and attempts to convince non-parties that the 'public interest norm' is really also in their interest. It does not suffice for certain states to agree on something and to declare that something *they* agreed on is in the interest of all states so as to make it legally binding on these other states.

---

⁴⁴ Art. 8(4) of the 1995 Fish Stocks Agreement.   ⁴⁵ *Ibid.*, Art. 21.

⁴⁶ As codified in Art. 6(1) of UNCLOS. The *pacta tertiis* rule must apply also in respect of Art. 23(1) and (2) imposing an obligation on port states to take measures to promote the effectiveness of subregional, regional and global conservation and management measures.

⁴⁷ For examples of MEA provisions imposing obligations in respect of non-parties, see the WTO document entitled 'Matrix on Trade Measures Pursuant to Selected MEAs', WT/CTE/W/160/Rev.1, 14 June 2001, which has a separate column for 'Provisions for non-parties', including: Art. XVIII of the International Plant Protection Convention; Art. X of CITES; Art. 4(8) of the Montreal Protocol; Art. 11 of the Basel Convention; Art. 24(1) of the Cartagena Protocol on Biosafety; Art. 10.9(a) of the Rotterdam Convention; and Art. 3.2(b)(i) of the Stockholm Convention on Persistent Organic Pollutants.

Non-parties, especially developing countries, should be allowed to reap some benefits from their entry into, for example, an MEA as a result of political negotiations. These benefits could take the form of compensatory market access in exchange for commitments to environmental or labour standards. As Fidler noted in respect of the International Convention on Civil Aviation (mentioned elsewhere as being an example of a convention in 'the public interest', binding also on non-parties):

> The example of the International Convention on Civil Aviation was brought up, and it was noted that the states that really matter have adopted these rules, so everybody else has to fall into place. That is a matter of the exercise of power; it is not necessarily a matter of obeying law out of a sense of legal obligation. Weaker states really do not have any choice. That is a matter of power, not of law.[48]

Certain norms do become binding on states independent of their direct consent. *Jus cogens* is one example. Decisions taken by organs of international organisations, not requiring the consent of all member states (e.g., by majority voting), are another. States must have agreed to set up the organisation and to grant it this decision-making power in the first place, but this can result in the creation of norms of international law to which they are strongly opposed. Think, in this respect, of Security Council resolutions (as discussed in the *Lockerbie* cases). A third vehicle by which norms can be imposed on states independent of their explicit consent is custom. As Charney pointed out,[49] there may be a tendency towards more easily accepting the existence of custom, based mainly on treaties adopted by a large majority of states, without there necessarily being a great amount of state practice. This tendency may lend some support to the existence of 'public interest norms'. However, such norms can only become binding on non-parties by means of their transformation into custom. The notion of 'public interest norms' cannot operate independently to bind non-parties.[50]

---

[48] Jost Delbrück, *New Trends in International Lawmaking – International 'Legislation' in the Public Interest* (Berlin: Duncker & Humblot, 1997), 118, comment by Fidler, 131.

[49] Jonathan Charney, 'International Lawmaking – Article 38 of the ICJ Statute Reconsidered', in Delbrück, *Trends*, 171 at 174–5.

[50] Charney made this point (*ibid.*, 124) in respect of the Antarctic Treaty and the question of whether it is binding also on non-parties as some 'objective regime': 'I do not think that the party status of the most important state actors in Antarctica or the states that surround Antarctica makes this system binding as general international law. Rather, I think it is the fact that this system has become accepted by the international community as a whole. There was, of course, resistance to the idea that this club

Finally, it should be noted that attempts to make so-called 'public interest norms' binding also on non-parties may go further than simply breaching *pacta tertiis*. Following in the footsteps of *jus cogens*, it seems to imply also a certain higher hierarchical status for these norms vis-à-vis norms not in the public interest.[51] This risks creating a further erosion of the binding nature of these other norms, along the following lines: 'these other norms are not of *jus cogens* nor in the public interest, so one can easily derogate from them, and since one can do this, they are not really binding'. Although such reasoning is, of course, legally unsound, in practice it is often heard.

Norms that cannot be suspended or deviated from *inter se*

Another instance where a norm is – like *jus cogens* – given priority over other norms because of its 'fundamental' substantive content may occur in the event of suspension of obligations as a result of breach. This 'suspension' can take the form either of suspension/termination of a norm as a result of its material breach pursuant to Art. 60 of the Vienna Convention or of countermeasures under the law of state responsibility taken in response to breach of another norm. Certain norms may have a special status in that they cannot be suspended. Unlike *jus cogens*, it does not mean, however, that these norms always prevail over other norms. It simply means that the stability and enforcement of these norms is so important that they cannot be suspended.

To begin with, certain norms cannot be suspended by one party even if there was a prior material breach of the norm by another, or even if the taking of countermeasures in response to breach would generally be justified. Under Art. 60 of the Vienna Convention – suspension or termination because of material breach – this prohibition arises in case of 'provisions relating to the protection of the human person contained in treaties of a humanitarian character, in particular provisions prohibiting any form of reprisals against persons protected by such treaties'. Hence, even if a material breach of a provision within a humanitarian

---

would make Antarctic law. But it has become generally accepted internationally that this group of states really does create norms for Antarctica because of the acceptance by the general international community of the norms emanating from that group.'

[51] As Oxman noted (in Delbrück, *Trends*, 21): 'Those positing the idea of public interest norms presumably intend to distinguish them from other norms. But they presumably do not intend to suggest that other norms of international law are not in the public interest. Yet they cannot escape the possible consequences not only of being taken literally, but of suggesting a hierarchical relationship between some obligations and others.'

treaty were established, other state parties to this treaty are not allowed to suspend, in turn, the operation of such humanitarian obligation.

Moreover, under the law on countermeasures, set out in Art. 51(1) of the 2001 Draft Articles on State Responsibility, the taking of countermeasures is prohibited in respect of the following obligations: (a) 'The obligation to refrain from the threat or use of force as embodied in the Charter of the United Nations'; (b) 'Obligations for the protection of fundamental human rights'; (c) 'Obligations of a humanitarian character prohibiting any form of reprisals against persons protected thereby'; (d) 'Other obligations under peremptory norms of general international law'; and (e) 'Obligations to respect the inviolability of diplomatic or consular agents, premises, archives and documents'.

The special status given under Art. 51(1)(e) to elements of diplomatic law finds reflection also in the *Teheran Hostages* case where Iran tried to justify the occupation of the US embassy and detention of US diplomatic staff in Teheran as a legitimate response to alleged criminal activities of the United States in Iran. The ICJ refused to accept this argument and noted the following:

> the principle of the inviolability of the persons of diplomatic agents and the premises of diplomatic missions is one of the very foundations of this long-established régime [of diplomatic law]...The fundamental character of the principle of inviolability is, moreover, strongly underlined by the provisions of Articles 44 and 45 of the Convention of 1961 [Vienna Convention on Diplomatic Relations]...Even in the case of armed conflict or in the case of a breach in diplomatic relations those provisions require that both the inviolability of the members of a diplomatic mission and of the premises, property and archives of the mission must be respected by the receiving State.[52]

Elsewhere, the Court reiterated the fundamental nature of diplomatic law:

> In recalling yet again the extreme importance of the principles of law which it is called upon to apply in the present case, the Court considers it to be its duty to draw the attention of the entire international community...to the irreparable harm that may be caused by events of the kind now before the Court. Such events cannot fail to undermine the edifice of law carefully constructed by mankind over a period of centuries, the maintenance of which is vital for the security and well-being of the complex international community of the present day, to which it is more essential than ever that the rules developed to ensure the ordered progress of relations between its members should be constantly and scrupulously respected.[53]

---

[52] ICJ Reports 1980, 3 at 41 (para. 86).   [53] *Ibid.*, 42–3, para. 92.

On that basis, some authors have characterised all international treaties relating to international communications as setting out norms of a 'fundamental nature'.[54]

Within this category of norms that are allegedly more important on the ground that they cannot be 'suspended', one could refer also to so-called non-derogable human rights obligations, that is, the kind of obligations in many human rights treaties that cannot be suspended even in situations of national emergency.[55]

A different application of norms when 'vital interests' are at stake

Finally, certain norms have been applied or enforced in a different manner because the case at hand involved 'vital interests'. In such cases, the norm does not, as such, defend 'public interests' (the way so-called 'public interest norms' allegedly do). Rather it is applied as against the states bound by the norm in a way that is different, based on the 'vital interests' involved in a specific case. In the WTO context, for example, the Appellate Body in *EC – Asbestos* stressed that, in an evaluation of the 'necessity' requirement under GATT Art. XX,

'[t]he more vital or important [the] common interests or values' pursued, the easier it would be to accept as 'necessary' measures designed to achieve those ends. In this case, the objective pursued by the measure is the preservation of human life and health through the elimination, or reduction, of the well-known, and life-threatening, health risk posed by asbestos fibres. The value pursued is both vital and important in the highest degree.[56]

Against this background, the Appellate Body found that the measure at issue was, indeed, 'necessary' to protect human health.

In contrast, in *Korea – Beef*, where the interest at stake, i.e., to avoid consumers confusing imported with domestic beef, was not as vital, the measure was *not* found to be 'necessary' under GATT Art. XX(d). Under the SPS agreement as well, the Appellate Body applied the requirement that there be a reasonable relationship between a risk assessment and an SPS measure, in a way that is more lenient in case 'the risk involved

---

[54] See J.-A. Salmon, 'Les Antinomies en Droit International Public', in Chaim Perelman (ed.), *Les Antinomies en Droit* (Brussels: Bruylant, 1965), 285 at 290.
[55] See Ian Seiderman, *Hierarchy in International law – The Human Rights Dimension* (Antwerp, 2001), 67–99 and Koji Teraya, 'Emerging Hierarchy in International Human Rights and Beyond: From the Perspective of Non-derogable Rights' (2001) 12 EJIL 917.
[56] Appellate Body report on *EC – Asbestos*, para. 172, quoting from Appellate Body report on *Korea – Beef*, para. 162.

is life-threatening in character and is perceived to constitute a clear and imminent threat to public health or safety'.[57] In the SPS context too, the Appellate Body applied WTO rules more deferentially in case 'vital interests' related to human health were at stake, as opposed to, for example, trade restrictions imposed for the protection of animal or plant health.[58]

A similar approach, focused this time on the *circumstances of the breach*, not the gravity of the interests protected by the measure at issue, was taken recently by the ICJ in the *La Grand* case. There, the Court found that in case a state does not inform foreign detainees of their right to contact consular officers of their state of nationality, in breach of Art. 36 of the Vienna Convention on Consular Relations, 'an apology would not suffice in cases where the individuals concerned have been subjected to prolonged detention or convicted or sentenced to severe penalties'. In those cases, the defaulting state must 'allow the review and reconsideration of the conviction and sentence by taking account of the violation of the rights set forth in the Convention'.[59]

In all of these cases involving 'vital interests', the adjudicator has applied or enforced the norm differently and this even though the norm itself does not provide for such distinction. This form of giving more weight to certain interests is hence a largely judge-made process.

Judicial decisions and doctrine

Having highlighted some of the problems related to the sources of international law and having examined, in turn, the question of whether there are any *a priori* hierarchies in international law, we next address the relative importance of the main sources of international law and how they may play out in a conflict of norms. We start with judicial decisions and doctrine.

The relative legal value of judicial decisions/doctrine

Since neither judicial decisions nor doctrine are, in and of themselves, norms of international law, they cannot be at play in a conflict of norms.

---

[57] Appellate Body report on *EC – Hormones*, para. 194.
[58] The Appellate Body was, indeed, far stricter in its reports on *Australia – Salmon* (involving animal health) and *Japan – Varietals* (on plant health) than it was in *EC – Hormones* (addressing human health).
[59] *Germany v. United States of America*, Judgment of 27 June 2001, posted on the internet at http://www.icj-cij.org/icjwww/idocket.

Hence, in explaining, first, the relative importance of doctrine, one can only state the obvious, namely that in case a doctrinal writing contradicts a norm – be it a treaty norm, custom or any other norm – the norm is more important. In fact, the norm is then the only element regulating the conduct of states.

More interesting is the case of judicial decisions. Unlike doctrine, they must be *presumed* to be an accurate statement of what the law is, based on genuine sources of law, such as treaties or custom, as between two parties and as applied to a particular set of circumstances, at a particular point in time. Hence, at that point in time, and as between those states, there can, in theory, be no conflict between the judicial decision and the applicable norms of law *since the judicial decision is presumed to apply those norms*, not to contradict them.

This presumption is confirmed by the fact that, as between the parties to the particular dispute, the judicial decision is legally binding or *res judicata*. This binding nature of judicial decisions is, in turn, a result of the fact that both disputing parties have conferred jurisdiction on the adjudicator to state what the law is in a particular set of circumstances.

Res judicata

According to one much-quoted authority, there are three conditions for the application of the principle of *res judicata*: identity of parties; identity of object (or subject matter); and identity of cause (or legal basis of the action).[60] The third condition implies, for example, that the doctrine of *res judicata* does not preclude a party from advancing a legally distinct cause of action arising from the same facts.[61] As noted earlier, in the WTO as well, the principle of *res judicata* has been confirmed. In *Japan – Alcoholic Beverages* the Appellate Body found that adopted panel reports 'are not binding, *except with respect to resolving the particular dispute between the parties to that dispute*'.[62] In its report on *US – Shrimp (Article 21.5)*, the Appellate Body confirmed that 'Appellate Body Reports

---

[60] Judge Anzilotti, *Chorzów Factory*, PCIJ, Series A, No. 13, at 23–7, referred to in Vaughan Lowe, 'Res Judicata and the Rule of Law in International Arbitration' (1996) 8 *African Journal of International Law* 38 at 38–9. In favour of *res judicata* being a general principle of law, see: B. Cheng, *General Principles of Law as Applied by International Courts and Tribunals* (London: Stevens, 1953), 336–64 and the ICJ Advisory Opinion on *Effect of Awards of Compensation Made by the UN Administrative Tribunal*, ICJ Reports 1954, 47 at 61; contra, at least in certain circumstances: Willem Riphagen, in Cassese and Weiler, *Change*, 35 and 37.
[61] Lowe, 'Res Judicata', 40.
[62] Appellate Body report on *Japan – Alcoholic Beverages*, p. 14, emphasis added, confirmed in the Appellate Body report on *US – FSC*, para. 108.

that are adopted by the DSB are, as Article 17.14 provides, "... unconditionally accepted by the parties to the dispute", and, therefore, must be treated by the parties to a particular dispute as a final resolution to that dispute'.[63]

Obviously, as between other states, in other circumstances or at a different point in time, the law may be different or have changed as compared to what it was stated to be in a first judicial decision. Then, of course, the applicable norms are more important than the old judicial decision which, in these circumstances, no longer carries the weight of *res judicata*. There is then, once again, no conflict of norms since the original judicial decision is not a norm, nor an application of the allegedly contradictory norm. It is then simply a statement of what the law is (or was) in *another* factual circumstance. As a result, in the WTO as well, complaints by *different* members can be brought against one and the same measure. Since the dispute then involves different parties, the principle of *res judicata* does not apply.

Another reason to deactivate the doctrine of *res judicata* – other than lack of identity of parties, object or cause – may be the discovery of new facts which, had the judge known them, would have resulted in a different judgment. This presupposes that 'the fact must have existed prior to the award, even though discovered subsequently and, of course, that the lack of knowledge prior to the award was not due to negligence'.[64] In its report on *Canada – Aircraft*, for example, the Appellate Body implied that even if, in the case at hand, it had not been convinced of the WTO inconsistency of a Canadian measure, Brazil could always bring a new case against that measure, based on facts that it might discover in the future.[65] This approach seems to be in line with Art. 61 of the ICJ Statute on the revision of ICJ judgments in case of 'discovery of some fact of such a nature as to be a decisive factor, which fact was, when the judgement was given, unknown to the Court and also to the party claiming revision, always provided that such ignorance was not due to negligence'.

The binding nature of judicial decisions can also be undone with the consent of both parties involved.[66] For an interesting example in the

---

[63] Appellate Body report on *US – Shrimp (Article 21.5)*, para. 97. For a more detailed, but inconclusive, discussion of the principle of *res judicata* as it operates in the WTO, see panel report on *India – Autos*, paras. 7.42 ff.

[64] D. W. Bowett, 'Res Judicata and the Limits of Rectification of Decisions by International Tribunals' (1996) 8 *African Journal of International Law* 577 at 589.

[65] Appellate Body report on *Canada – Aircraft*, para. 206.

[66] See DSB decision in WTO doc. WT/DSB/M/90, acting on a US request in WT/DS108/11 of 2 October 2000.

WTO context, see the DSB decision in the *US – FSC* dispute to extend the deadline for withdrawal of the FSC subsidies from 1 October 2000 (as determined by the panel) to 1 November 2000. Both the United States and the European Communities agreed to this extension, but in effect it changed the judicial findings of the panel. In contrast, the binding nature of a judicial decision cannot, of course, be affected by a unilateral act of the state against whom the decision was rendered. In addition, the organs of the international organisation that are bound by a judicial decision cannot change or overrule such judicial decision. This remains the case even if the international organ itself created the judicial body that made the decision.[67]

Judicial decisions versus authoritative interpretations (the example of the WTO)

In the WTO context, the WTO Ministerial Conference or General Council can adopt 'authoritative interpretations' of WTO agreements by a three-quarters majority decision.[68] Such interpretations may contradict previous panel and/or Appellate Body interpretations in particular disputes. Article 3.9 of the DSU explicitly provides that WTO dispute settlement is 'without prejudice to the rights of Members to seek authoritative interpretation of provisions of a covered agreement through decision-making under the WTO Agreement'. But can such authoritative interpretation by an act of the WTO as an international organisation overrule an earlier WTO panel or Appellate Body decision?

It must be recalled, at this juncture, that a judicial decision is not a norm but an application of the law to a particular case. The authoritative interpretation, in contrast, is an act of the WTO as an international organisation that, in effect, 'changes' the law as opposed to what it was according to the prior judicial decision.[69] There is hence no conflict of norms, but a change in one and the same norm, namely the norm as

---

[67] See, in this respect, the ICJ Advisory Opinions on *Effect of Awards of Compensation Made by the UN Administrative Tribunal*, ICJ Reports 1954, 47 at 53, and on *Request for Revision of Judgement n. 273 of the UN Administrative Tribunal (Mortished)*, ICJ Reports 1982, 321.

[68] Pursuant to Article IX:2 of the Marrakesh Agreement.

[69] As the Appellate Body stated in footnote 127 in its report on *US – FSC*: 'The distinction between an authoritative interpretation and an interpretation made in dispute settlement proceedings is made clear in the *WTO Agreement*. Under the *WTO Agreement*, an authoritative interpretation by the Members of the WTO, under Article IX:2 of that Agreement, is to be distinguished from the rulings and recommendations of the DSB, made on the basis of panel and Appellate Body Reports. In terms of Article 3.2 of the DSU, the rulings and recommendations of the DSB serve only "to clarify the existing provisions of those agreements" and "cannot add to or diminish the rights and obligations provided in the covered agreements".'

interpreted by the judiciary as opposed to the norm as interpreted by the WTO membership in the authoritative interpretation.

If, in the authoritative interpretation, both disputing parties agree to change the law retroactively so as to apply it also to their dispute, the judicial decision, in so far as it relies on the old law, would lose its practical effect: if the complainant had won the dispute on the basis of the 'old law', that party, having agreed to the 'new law', would no longer seek (nor, it would seem, be allowed to seek) the implementation of the judicial decision; if, in contrast, the defendant had won the original dispute, the complainant would need to seek a new panel decision for it to see the 'new law' applied to its case.

Crucially, however, an authoritative interpretation is part and parcel of the norm in question. It is not a judicial decision, nor an application of the law to a particular case. As a result, unlike DSB rulings and recommendations, it cannot be used as an independent basis to obtain implementation. If the new interpretation favours the complainant, the complainant will need to seek a new panel decision for it to see the new law applied to its particular case.

But what if the disputing parties disagree and the three-quarters majority in favour of the contradictory 'authoritative interpretation' is nonetheless obtained and stated to be of retroactive effect? It could be submitted that since one of the disputing parties does not agree to overrule the law as stated in the judicial decision, the law that is reflected in that decision cannot be changed retroactively, without the consent of that state. However, the WTO member concerned agreed *ex ante* to the WTO provision on authoritative interpretations as well as to the DSU provision stating that WTO dispute settlement is 'without prejudice to the rights of Members to seek authoritative interpretation of [WTO] provisions'. Thus, if, but only if, the authoritative interpretation validly obtained under the WTO agreement were to state explicitly that it applies retroactively, including to the situation covered by the judicial decision, then this interpretation must prevail over the law as stated in the earlier judicial decision, even if the disputing party harmed by such retroactive effect did not agree to applying the authoritative interpretation retroactively. If the authoritative interpretation is silent on the matter of timing, it must, however, be presumed that it applies only prospectively. In such cases, an analogy with the principle of non-retroactivity of treaties[70] could be made and applied also to acts of international organisations such as WTO authoritative interpretations.

---

[70] Set out in Art. 28 of the Vienna Convention.

Conflict between judicial decisions

Although judicial decisions (not being norms) cannot be part of a conflict of norms, one could imagine that two distinct judicial decisions emerge as between the same parties on the same matter – both in terms of object or subject matter *and* legal cause of action – which are in conflict. With the increasing number of international tribunals, there is, indeed, a risk that two judicial decisions may contradict each other. One decision may find that no breach of international law occurred. Another may come to the opposite conclusion, as between the same parties on the same matter. Moreover, although judicial decisions do not themselves create new norms, they may, or may not, activate certain secondary rules of international law, such as an obligation to cease the breach or to pay reparation. If one decision activates such secondary obligations of international law and another does not (or does so differently), how should the defending state react?

No clear rules seem to exist in this respect, mainly because this situation of conflicting judicial decisions has not yet arisen and is, indeed, not likely to arise in the near future. Several reasons can be found in support.

First, in most cases where there is overlapping jurisdiction in two international tribunals, the risk of conflicting judgments can be avoided by simply applying the rules on conflict of norms that will be set out later in this book. Such conflict rules would then determine, for example, which of two treaty provisions granting jurisdiction to the respective tribunals prevails. In those cases, the problem of jurisdictional overlap is reduced to a normal conflict of norms. As Lowe put it, the tribunal first seized of a dispute 'must consider whether the effect of the jurisdictional provisions in the treaty that appear to establish its jurisdiction may have been modified by the treaty that purports to bestow jurisdiction upon the other tribunal'.[71] States may, for example, give preference to one dispute settlement mechanism over another in a conflict clause explicitly deciding situations of overlapping jurisdictions. Article 2005 of NAFTA, for example, gives preference to dispute settlement in NAFTA

---

[71] Vaughan Lowe, 'Overlapping Jurisdictions in International Tribunals' (2000) 20 *Australian Yearbook of International Law* 1 at 4. See also Gabrielle Marceau, 'Conflicts of Norms and Conflicts of Jurisdictions, The Relationship between the WTO Agreement and MEAs and other Treaties' (2001) 35 JWT 1081 at 1110. On the question more generally, see Jan Neumann, 'Die Koordination des WTO-Rechts mit anderen völkerrechtlichen Ordnungen – Konflikte des Materiellen Rechts und Konkurrenzen der Streitbeilegung', unpublished doctoral thesis (Münster, 2001).

over that in GATT in the areas of sanitary and phytosanitary measures, the environment and other standard-related disputes. It obliges a NAFTA complainant state to withdraw from a GATT dispute, involving two NAFTA parties, if the defending NAFTA state prefers to settle the dispute under NAFTA.[72] In addition, the principle of *lex posterior* or *lex specialis* may also solve the overlap. In respect of *lex specialis*, for example, Lowe has submitted the following:

> In circumstances where the parties have made special provisions for a certain category of disputes, in the absence of any indication to the contrary it must be supposed that they intended that it is this special provision, and not some more general acceptance of the jurisdiction of another tribunal, that they intended should be applied to disputes in that category.

In this respect, one could refer also to the statement by the WTO's Committee on Trade and Environment expressing a preference for trade disputes that arise in connection with an MEA to be resolved through the mechanisms established by such agreement.[73] In sum, even if there may at first sight seem to be a possibility of states engaging in 'forum shopping', quite often the rules on conflict of norms will decide in favour of only one tribunal having jurisdiction over a certain dispute. In that event, the risk of conflicting judgments is averted.

Second, as noted earlier, a correct application of the principle of *res judicata* should avoid the situation where a second tribunal decides the same dispute, as between the same parties, on the same object and cause, for a second time. Consequently, since there would then not even be a second judgment, *a priori* a conflict of judicial decisions would be avoided. Indeed, the very rationale behind the doctrine of *res judicata* is that legal relations should be homogenous, or unified, in the sense that they should appear the same no matter how they are looked at, or by whom. As Lowe expressed it, 'inconsistent findings by different tribunals on the same facts deprive the law of its predictability and hence of its ability to provide effective guidance'.[74]

Third, in addition to the doctrine of *res judicata*, conflicting judgments could also be averted through recourse to other general principles of law, in particular those of *lis alibi pendens* and abuse of process.[75] The doctrine

---

[72] See Marceau, 'Conflicts', 1116–18.   [73] WTO doc. WT/CTE/1, para. 171 (1996).
[74] Lowe, '*Res Judicata*', 48.
[75] Lowe, 'Overlapping', 12–13 and Marceau, 'Conflicts', 1112–14. Both authors argue, convincingly, against applying the principle *forum non conveniens* in situations of overlap between international tribunals.

of *lis alibi pendens* indicates that if a substantially identical case is already pending before a competent tribunal, a second forum may decline to exercise its own jurisdiction.[76] The doctrine of abuse of process, in turn, indicates that a tribunal should decline to exercise jurisdiction in a range of circumstances where the purpose of the litigation is to harass the defendant, or the claim is frivolous or manifestly groundless, or the claim is one which could and should have been raised in an earlier proceeding.[77] The doctrine of abuse of process seems confirmed, at least partly, in Art. 3.7 of the DSU, which provides that '[b]efore bringing a case, a Member shall exercise its judgement as to whether action under these procedures would be fruitful'.[78]

Fourth, in instances where there may be two judgments, most often those judgments, even if they are between the same parties on the same general dispute, will not address the same cause of action or claims. Although different international tribunals (such as WTO panels and ITLOS) may exist where parties could submit one and the same general dispute, this does not necessarily mean that two tribunals will have jurisdiction to decide on the exact same subject matter and, in particular, on the same legal cause of action, as between the same parties. Although a dispute may be submitted to two tribunals, the legal claims before each tribunal may be very different (for example, claims of violation under the WTO treaty, as opposed to claims of violation under UNCLOS).[79] In that case, two judicial decisions may, indeed, emerge, but they will not necessarily conflict since they address different legal claims. For the same reason, the judgment of the first tribunal will then not carry the weight of *res judicata* for the second tribunal.

Fifth, as just noted, there may be instances where two tribunals have to decide one and the same general dispute, but under a different cause

---

[76] Lowe, 'Overlapping', 12, referring to the *Polish Upper Silesia* case, PCIJ, Series A, No. 6, 20.
[77] Lowe, 'Overlapping', 13.
[78] See Martha Rutsel, 'The Duty to Exercise Judgment on the Fruitfulness of Actions in World Trade Law' (2001) 35 JWT 1035.
[79] See the WTO dispute on *Chile – Measures Affecting the Transit and Importation of Swordfish*, WT/DS193 (panel suspended on 23 March 2001) (hereafter *Chile – Swordfish*), brought also before the International Tribunal for the Law of the Sea (now suspended, on the basis of a provisional arrangement, by Order of 15 March 2001, http://www.un.org/Depts/los/ITLOS/Order1-2001). On this issue see: Jan Neumann, 'Die materielle und prozessuale Koordination völkerrechtlicher Ordnungen, Die Problematik paralleler Streitbeilegungsverfahren am Beispiel des *Schwertfisch*-Falls' (2001) 61 *Zeitschrift für ausländisches öffentliches Recht und Völkerrecht* 529.

of action (say, claims under the WTO treaty, as opposed to claims under UNCLOS). Crucially, in those circumstances, the claims each tribunal is asked to decide upon (be they WTO or UNCLOS claims) should then be examined in the context of all other rules of international law, both general international law and other treaties. This is one of the main tenets of this book which is, in respect of the applicable law before WTO panels, further developed in chapter 8 below. Hence, in cases where two tribunals have to decide on the same general dispute, they will have to do so on the basis of the *same legal rules* and this even if their mandate covers different claims. Consequently, conflict between judicial decisions should arise only as a result of different interpretations of the same law. As further explained in chapter 8, claims under the WTO treaty, for example, cannot be enforced in isolation. A WTO panel must take account also of other rules of international law, such as a defence under an MEA or human rights treaty binding on both disputing parties. It is on the basis of this entire universe of legal norms applicable to the case at hand that the validity of a WTO claim must be assessed. In case another, non-WTO, tribunal would have to address the same dispute (most likely, though, through examining different legal claims), that other tribunal would need to go through the same exercise: when examining, for example, whether an MEA or any other treaty was violated, it should look at possible defences under WTO law. In other words, the approach suggested below – of allowing all relevant international law to be part of the applicable law before a WTO panel – is not only crucial for WTO dispute settlement. It is, more generally, one of the main instruments that *all* tribunals should use so as to avoid contradictions between judicial decisions. Although different tribunals may be dealing with different claims, the applicable law to examine those claims should be the same no matter where the case is brought. Not to accept this proposition, as many authors seem to do[80] – arguing that in, for example, ITLOS only UNCLOS rules can be applied or in the WTO only WTO rules can be applied – necessarily results in the creation of small isolated pockets of international law, delinked from other branches of the wider corpus of international law. It goes against the unity of international law as well as the principle of *pacta sunt servanda* since it implies that whatever other rules of international law exist, that were concluded outside, for

---

[80] See Marceau, 'Conflicts', 1116 ('the applicable law before WTO adjudicating bodies is only WTO law'); Hafner, 'Risk', 332 ('most mechanisms, in particular the treaty bodies, are restricted only to their own substantive law as a legal basis for the legal evaluation of the dispute)'.

example, the WTO, they are not applicable within the safe haven of WTO dispute settlement. This isolationist approach would, finally, make the emergence of conflicting judicial decisions inevitable.

In contrast, when following the proposition put here – that the applicable law for a particular set of facts should be the same no matter where the case is brought – conflict between judicial decisions should arise only in case two tribunals interpret the exact same 'applicable law' in different ways. One way to streamline opinions and to avoid this conflict is for different tribunals to refer to, and take account of, each other's judgments and decisions. Focusing on the WTO, for example, panel and Appellate Body reports often refer to judgments of other international tribunals (especially the PCIJ and ICJ, but also the European Court of Justice). Conversely, other international tribunals have been faced with references to WTO panel and Appellate Body reports.[81]

In addition, and going slightly further, different international tribunals could ask for each other's opinion, or the opinion of the political branch of the treaty regime in question or that of its secretariat. Thomas Schoenbaum refers to the possibility of asking for an ICJ advisory opinion in case a WTO panel must decide a matter of non-WTO law, something that in his view 'would be extremely cumbersome'.[82] In making their assessment of non-WTO rules panels could, however, be assisted by other international tribunals or organisations through the operation of DSU Art. 13.1 allowing panels to 'seek information and technical advice from any individual or body which it deems appropriate'.[83] The panel on *US – Copyright*, for example, requested information from WIPO before coming to a conclusion on claims under the TRIPS agreement which incorporates certain WIPO rules (*in casu*, the Berne Convention).[84] The panel on *US – Section 211 Appropriations Act* made a similar move. In response to a request for information from the panel, the Director-General

---

[81] In the pleadings before the Arbitral Tribunal in the *Southern Bluefin Tuna* case (*Australia and New Zealand v. Japan*, Jurisdiction and Admissibility), for example, Japan referred to the Appellate Body report on *EC – Bananas* in support of its arguments on *lex specialis* (Hearing of 7 May 2000, statement by E. Lauterpacht). In reply, Australia and New Zealand submitted their views on the *EC – Bananas* report and added references to the panel reports on *Turkey – Textile* and *Indonesia – Autos* (Hearing of 8 May 2000, statement by J. Crawford). Transcripts of these hearings can be found on the internet (www.worldbank.org/icsid/bluefintuna/main.htm).

[82] Thomas Schoenbaum, 'WTO Dispute Settlement: Praise and Suggestions for Reform' (1998) 47 ICLQ 647 at note 43.

[83] On experts in the WTO, see Joost Pauwelyn, 'The Use of Experts in WTO Dispute Settlement' (2002) 51 ICLQ 325.

[84] See Attachment 4 to the panel report on *US – Copyright*.

of the International Bureau of WIPO stated that 'no provision [of the Paris Convention (1967), largely incorporated into the TRIPS agreement] addresses the question how the owner of a trademark has to be determined under the domestic law of States party to the Paris Convention'.[85] Moreover, in respect of IMF matters, GATT Art. XV:2 provides that '[i]n all cases in which the CONTRACTING PARTIES are called upon to consider or deal with problems concerning monetary reserves, balances of payments or foreign exchange arrangements, they shall consult fully with the [IMF]'.[86] The panel on *India – Quantitative Restrictions*, for example, asked for the opinion of the IMF in respect of certain balance of payments matters (with reference to DSU Art. 13, not GATT Art. XV:2) and based its final decision on that opinion.[87] The 1996 Agreement between the IMF and the WTO has amplified WTO–IMF co-operation, including in respect of dispute settlement.[88]

The Appellate Body, in addition, should not hesitate to ask the 'expert' opinion of other international organisations, including other international tribunals. It already now receives 'expert' legal advice set out in so-called *amicus curiae* briefs. In the *amicus curiae* procedures it adopted in the *EC – Asbestos* dispute, the Appellate Body made clear that such briefs must be 'strictly limited to legal arguments'.[89] If the Appellate Body is authorised to receive unsolicited briefs on legal matters from NGOs or individual law professors, why would it not be authorised to receive or even seek the opinion of other international organisations or tribunals (presumably more knowledgeable on the matter)? As is the case for panels, two important reasons should prompt the Appellate Body to

---

[85] Appellate Body report, *US – Section 211 Appropriations Act*, para. 189.
[86] GATT Art. XV:2 continues: 'In such consultations, the CONTRACTING PARTIES shall accept all findings of statistical and other facts presented by the Fund ... and shall accept the determination of the Fund as to whether action by a contracting party in exchange matters is in accordance with the Articles of Agreement of the [IMF], or with the terms of a special exchange agreement between the contracting party and the CONTRACTING PARTIES.'
[87] Panel report on *India – Quantitative Restrictions*, pp. 133 ff.
[88] Paragraph 6 of that agreement provides: 'The WTO shall invite the Fund to send a member of its staff as an observer to meetings of the WTO Dispute Settlement Body where matters of jurisdictional relevance to the Fund are to be considered. The WTO shall also invite the Fund to send a member of its staff to other meetings of the Dispute Settlement Body as well as of other WTO bodies for which attendance is not provided above (excluding the Committee on Budget, Finance and Administration, and dispute settlement panels), when the WTO, after consultation between the WTO Secretariat and the staff of the Fund, finds that such a presence would be of particular common interest to both organizations.'
[89] Appellate Body Report on *EC – Asbestos*, para. 7(c).

do so: first, other institutions or individuals may be more knowledgeable (i.e., 'epistemically superior');[90] second, streamlining the position of different institutions would be highly beneficial for the unity of international law.

As with other expert advice, the panel or Appellate Body would then not be bound by the legal information thus provided, but it would need to give deference to it. This would be particularly so in case the request for expert advice were directed at another international *tribunal*, say, the ICJ or the ITLOS (even if, as the law stands today, these other tribunals could arguably not respond, their power to issue advisory opinions could be extended so as to include also opinions at the request of WTO bodies).[91] For a panel or the Appellate Body to request the opinion of other courts or tribunals may be borderline between, on the one hand, transferring jurisdiction to another body without the agreement of the parties (something that cannot be done) and, on the other hand, seeking advice from an 'epistemically superior' institution (something that ought to enhance the legitimacy of the WTO process). In the end, the main argument in favour of WTO panels and the Appellate Body entering into a dialogue with other international tribunals remains that it would enhance the co-ordination between different branches of international law and decrease the risk of conflicting judgments being issued by different tribunals. In short, even if these non-WTO tribunals

---

[90] This notion is borrowed from Scott Brewer, 'Scientific Expert Testimony and Intellectual Due Process' (1998) 107 *Yale Law Journal* 1535 at 1589. Brewer characterises experts as 'epistemically superior beings' and rightly argues that 'the nonexpert practical reasoner [*in casu*, the panel/Appellate Body] must defer epistemically to the theoretical expert to reach the practical judgment' (ibid., at 1578).

[91] See, for example, the statements by President Chirac of France in a February 2000 speech at the ICJ, where he called for the ICJ to be invested with a 'regulatory role, advising the international organizations' ('When international law on the environment, trade, and labour standards conflict, we need a place where they can be reconciled. Why not request advisory opinions from your Court in such cases?') He also suggested that 'treaties containing dispute-settlement mechanisms ought to establish an explicit linkage with the Court...When these treaties set up a new jurisdiction, would it not be desirable for that jurisdiction to be able to refer questions to the Court for preliminary ruling, for guidance on points of law of general interest?' (Report of the ICJ, 1 August 1999 – 31 July 2000, para. 320 (http://www.icj-cij.org/icjwww/igeneralinformation/igeninf_Annual_Reports/iICJ_Annual_Report_1999-2000.htm). In the same sense, see Gilbert Guillaume, 'The Proliferation of International Judicial Bodies: The Outlook for the International Legal Order', Speech to the Sixth Committee of the General Assembly of the United Nations, 27 October 2000, posted on the internet at http://www.icj-cij.org/icjwww/ipresscom/SPEECHES/iSpeechPresident_Guillaume_SixthCommittee_20001027.htm, p. 5.

are not necessarily more knowledgeable on the matter, seeking their advice could constitute an important catalyst towards the unity of international law notwithstanding its fragmented enforcement by a series of different courts and tribunals. To formalise this dialogue further one could even oblige panels and/or the Appellate Body to send certain matters of non-WTO law to other, more specialised international tribunals for a binding preliminary ruling.[92]

If, notwithstanding the five reasons set out above, a conflict of judicial decisions nonetheless arises, and it involves an ICJ judgment, the argument could be made that a judgment by the ICJ, after all the principal judicial organ of the UN, carries more weight than decisions by other courts or tribunals. Pursuant to Article 92 of the UN Charter, the ICJ Statute forms an integral part of the UN Charter. Article 59 of the Statute states that decisions of the ICJ have binding force as between the parties and in respect of the particular case. Hence, the obligations derived from an ICJ judgment are legally binding and could be said to be 'obligations of the Members of the United Nations under the present Charter' in the sense referred to by Art. 103 of the UN Charter. In the *Lockerbie* cases[93] the ICJ decided that UN Security Council resolutions give rise to UN Charter obligations in the sense of Art. 103. The same could arguably be said about decisions of other organs of the UN, *in casu* the ICJ. Now, Art. 103 provides that in the event of conflict between such UN Charter obligations and 'obligations under any other international agreement', say, WTO Appellate Body reports adopted pursuant to the WTO treaty, the UN Charter obligations prevail. Article 103, further discussed in chapter 7 below, could thus constitute a legal ground to give preference to an ICJ judgment in the event of conflict with another judicial decision.

In the WTO context, another problem of potentially inconsistent judicial decisions may arise, not as between two decisions in respect of the *same* parties, but as between two decisions on the same measure as a result of complaints brought by two *different* WTO members. This situation was addressed in the panel report on *India – Patent* (complaint by the EC). There, the panel allowed the EC to bring the same claims, against the same Indian measure, as those that had already been decided by a previous panel at the request of the United States. The panel allowed for such 'repeat claims' on the ground of Article 9 of the DSU,[94]

---

[92] See speeches by Chirac and Guillaume, *ibid.*   [93] ICJ Reports 1992.
[94] Article 9 of the DSU provides as follows: '1. Where more than one Member requests the establishment of a panel related to the same matter, a single panel may be

but noted India's concern 'that an unmitigated right to bring successive complaints by different parties based on the same facts and legal claims would entail serious risks for the multilateral trade order because of the possibility of inconsistent rulings, as well as problems of waste of resources and unwarranted harassment'.[95] The panel stated that 'while we recognize that these are serious concerns, this Panel is not an appropriate forum to address these issues'.[96]

The urge to bring the same complaint as another WTO member did previously is inspired mainly by reasons of securing the right to suspend concessions or other obligations as against the losing party. This is so because suspension in the WTO remains a bilateral exercise, to be engaged in only by those WTO members that won the dispute as complaining parties.[97] In practice, however, with the existence of the Appellate Body, which is a standing body and operates on a collegial basis,[98] any inconsistencies between panel reports on the same measure, but as a result of different complaints, are most likely to be wiped out on appeal. The need for a WTO member to bring its own 'repeat' complaint for it to be able to join in putting pressure on the defaulting member highlights the bilateral, state-to-state nature of the WTO treaty and, in particular, its dispute settlement system. Thought ought to be given to making this system more collective, at least in respect of securing compliance with WTO rules in case the particular breach affects a number of WTO members and even if not all of these members have brought their own complaint.[99]

The risk of divergent case law

Crucially, the problem of conflicting judicial decisions *as between the same parties on the same subject matter*, examined in the previous section, must be distinguished from the more general risk, related to the proliferation of international tribunals, of two tribunals making contradictory

---

established to examine these complaints ... A single panel should be established to examine such complaints whenever feasible ... 3. If more than one panel is established to examine the complaints related to the same matter, to the greatest extent possible the same persons shall serve as panelists on each of the separate panels ...'

[95] Panel report on *India – Patent* (EC complaint), para. 7.22.
[96] *Ibid.*   [97] DSU Art. 22.2.
[98] DSU Art. 17.1 and Working Procedures of the Appellate Body, Rule 4 (WTO doc. WT/AB/WP/3, dated 28 February 1997).
[99] See Joost Pauwelyn, 'Enforcement and Countermeasures in the WTO: Rules are Rules – Toward a More Collective Approach' (2000) 94 AJIL 335.

statements – in *two completely different disputes* and/or at *two very different points in time* – on what a certain norm of international law means. After a detailed examination of the risk posed by multiple international tribunals, Charney concludes that 'the coherence of international law does not appear to be significantly threatened by the increasing number of international tribunals'.[100] He finds that '[o]n the basis of the available evidence, no substantial breakdown in the unity of central norms of general international law has developed'.[101] For Charney, the most promising strategy for success would 'rely on the ICJ itself to make optimal use of the historical, financial, intellectual, and reputational strengths it now holds, as well as efforts by all tribunals that address international legal matters to recognize their common enterprise and to engage in greater international dialogue'.[102] Kingsbury, in a foreword to a series of papers on the same topic, concludes along the same lines:

If a hierarchical judicial system for international law is not to be established, two factors will work as counter-forces against those centrifugal forces. First, the ICJ must continue to maintain its intellectual leadership role in the field. If it does so, the other tribunals will be under pressure to abide by the ICJ's determinations on international law. Second, the other tribunals and the ICJ should be encouraged to increase the dialogue that already exists among them. The idea that all of these tribunals are engaged in a common endeavour would be emphasized. This might provide strong pressures against the centrifugal forces at work, while still permitting the independence of these specialized tribunals.[103]

Other authors are less optimistic.[104] Gilbert Guillaume, president of the ICJ at the time of writing, refers to divergent case law on the rules for the interpretation of treaties – in particular, in respect of territorial reservations in declarations of compulsory jurisdiction – in the European

---

[100] Jonathan Charney, 'Is International Law Threatened by Multiple International Tribunals?' (1998) 271 *Recueil des Cours* 101 at 373.
[101] *Ibid.*   [102] *Ibid.*
[103] Benedict Kingsbury, 'Foreword: Is the Proliferation of International Courts and Tribunals a Systemic Problem?' (1999) 31 *New York Journal of International Law and Politics* 679 at 707. On the same topic, see also the papers and discussions in 'Implications of the Proliferation of International Adjudicatory Bodies for Dispute Resolution' (1995) 9 *ASIL Bulletin*.
[104] In particular, current or former judges of the ICJ. See, for example, Guillaume, 'Proliferation'; Gilbert Guillaume, 'The Future of International Judicial Institutions' (1995) 44 ICLQ 848; Robert Jennings, 'The Proliferation of Adjudicatory Bodies: Dangers and Possible Answers', in (1995) 9 *ASIL Bulletin*; and, in particular, S. Oda, 'The International Court of Justice from the Bench' (1993) 244 *Recueil des Cours* 9 at 139–55.

Court of Human Rights, as opposed to the ICJ.[105] Shane Spelliscy[106] addresses another instance of divergent case law. In her view,[107] the ICTY Appeals Chamber in the 1995 *Tadić* case contradicted the ICJ's judgment in the 1986 *Nicaragua* case on the question of when a state can be held liable for acts committed by individuals not officially agents of the state (finding in favour of, respectively, a rather lenient 'demonstrable link' test[108] and a stricter 'effective control' test).[109] Especially in the latter case, however, it may be difficult to distinguish a real divergence in case law from a further development of the law. Given the almost ten-years time lag between the two judgments, one could, indeed, argue that the law on state responsibility has developed towards a more lenient test and that, as a result, in case the ICJ were asked to decide on this matter again *today*, it would find the same test as that set out in the *Tadić* case. In any event, both Guillaume and Spelliscy seem justified in sending out a warning signal that the proliferation of international tribunals is a problem that needs attention. Both call for a more structured and institutionalised relationship between various courts, a 'constant inter-judicial dialogue'.[110] The suggestions made earlier, that WTO panels and the Appellate Body should refer to, and seek the advice of, other international tribunals, would be a step in that direction.

General principles of law

Having examined the role of judicial decisions and doctrine, we next assess the status of general principles of law in a conflict of norms. As pointed out recently by Degan, 'general principles of law have become one of the most difficult doctrinal problems since they were promulgated in 1920[111] as a distinct source of international law'.[112] Although certain authors, in particular in Soviet doctrine, refused to accept 'general principles of law' as a distinct source of international

---

[105] Guillaume, 'Proliferation', 4.
[106] Shane Spelliscy, 'The Proliferation of International Tribunals: A Chink in the Armor' (2001) 40 *Columbia Journal of Transnational Law* 143 at 159–68.
[107] Confirmed in Guillaume, 'Proliferation', 4.
[108] *Prosecutor v. Dusko Tadić*, International Criminal Tribunal for the Former Yugoslavia: Appeals Chamber, Decision of 2 October 1995, IT-94-1-AR72, at paras. 103–4.
[109] *Nicaragua case (Case concerning Military and Paramilitary Activities in and against Nicaragua)* (Merits), ICJ Reports 1986, 14, at paras. 110–15.
[110] Guillaume, 'Proliferation', 5.
[111] Part of the list of sources in Art. 38 of the PCIJ Statute.
[112] Degan, *Sources*, 17.

law,[113] in recent times at least one point of convergence seems to have emerged, namely that general principles of law constitute a genuine source of positive international law. Since they are, therefore, in and of themselves norms, they can be at play in a conflict of norms.

Four categories of 'general principles of law'

Broadly speaking, and acknowledging the risk of overlaps, four types of 'general principles of law' can be detected when reviewing judicial decisions and doctrine.[114] Although these four categories do not constitute watertight compartments, the classification is helpful. First, there are the so-called 'meta-principles'[115] or 'necessary principles', that is, 'rules of law that have an inherent and necessary validity, in whose absence no system of law at all can exist or be originated'.[116] The principle of *pacta sunt servanda* is the most-cited example.[117] Second, reference is made to legal principles derived from, or evidenced by, the consistent provisions of various municipal legal systems – principles *in foro domestico* – which can be validly transposed to international law. A major part of these domestic law principles relates to the conduct of judicial proceedings, such as principles on jurisdiction, burden of proof or

---

[113] This mainly Soviet view of general principles of law was based largely on the amendment consisting of the words 'whose function it is to decide in accordance with international law such disputes as are submitted to it', which were inserted into the opening phrase of Art. 38 when the ICJ Statute was adopted in 1945 (the phrase was not included in Art. 38 of the Statute of the PCIJ). As a result, Soviet lawyers argued, Art. 38 now requires that the principles in question are common to all national legal systems and applicable to international relations. Therefore they must enter international law either through treaty or custom (see G. Tunkin, 'General Principles of Law in International Law', in R. Marcic et al. (eds.), *Internationale Festschrift für Alfred Verdross* (Munich: Fink, 1971) 523 at 531; and Géza Herczegh (a member of the ICJ at the time of writing), *General Principles of Law and the International Legal Order* (Budapest: Akadémiai Kiadó, 1969), 97–100).

[114] For an overview of PCIJ and ICJ judgments in the field of 'general principles of law', see Degan, *Sources*, 53–68. For an overview of doctrine, see B. Vitanyi, 'Les Positions Doctrinales Concernant le Sens de la Notion de "Principes Généraux de Droit Reconnus par les Nations Civilisées"' (1982) 86 RGDIP 46. For a more progressive view, see Peter Hulsroj, 'Three Sources – No River, A Hard Look at the Sources of Public International Law with Particular Emphasis on Custom and "General Principles of Law"', (1999) 54 *Zeitschrift für öffentliches Recht* 219 at 245–6.

[115] Martti Koskenniemi, 'General Principles: Reflections on Constructionist Thinking in International Law' (1985) 18 *Oikevstiede-Jurisprudentia* 133.

[116] Fitzmaurice, 'Some Problems', 164.

[117] *Ibid*. For other examples, see Bos, 'The Recognized', 38; Mosler, 'General Principles', 90–1; and R. Monaco, 'Sources of International Law', in R. Bernhardt (ed.), *Encyclopedia of Public International Law* (Amsterdam: North-Holland, 1984), VII, 424 at 426.

the doctrine of *res judicata*. Other domestic law principles transposed to international law are of a more substantive nature, such as general principles related to responsibility and contracts. To this, one could add also fundamental human rights recognised in every organised society. Third, many authors, and particularly international adjudicators, have referred to legal principles of *international* law produced mainly through a process of induction from other positive rules of international law. Examples are the right of states to existence or preservation (including rights of self-defence and self-help), the right to independence or sovereignty and the principle of equality of states. Some have placed the principle of respect for human rights in this category.[118] These general principles are derived from more precise rules which are part of treaty or customary law but take on an importance of their own as broad-ranging 'principles' of *international* law. Fourth, many authors refer to principles of legal logic, that is, instruments in legal reasoning providing for logical consequences. These principles are said to form part of the technical skeleton of law. Examples of such logical principles given by certain authors are: *lex specialis derogat legi generali*, *lex posterior derogat legi priori* and *expressio unius est exclusio alterius*.[119] Sometimes the so-called 'equitable principles' invoked by the ICJ in its practice on maritime delimitations (to the extent they amount to equity *infra legem*) are mentioned under this heading.[120] In the *Continental Shelf (Tunisia/Libyan Arab Jamahiriya)* case, the ICJ confirmed that 'the legal concept of equity is a general principle directly applicable as law'.[121] One could, finally, include in this fourth category of principles of legal logic the so-called canons of treaty interpretation, often considered to be logical devices to be weighed against each other rather than absolute legal rules.[122]

---

[118] For example, Cassese (in Cassese and Weiler, *Change*, 170), who takes Art. 38(1)(c) to mean 'those fundamental principles of international law which govern international relations (substantially, the seven principles embodied in the 1970 Declaration on Friendly Relations, plus the principle of respect for human rights)'.

[119] On the role of *lex specialis* and *lex posterior* as logical consequences of the principle of contractual freedom of states, see chapter 7 below.

[120] See Degan, *Sources*, 89–99. Note, however, that a decision in application of equity is not the same thing as a decision *ex aequo et bono*, contemplated by Art. 38(2) of the ICJ Statute, which is possible only with the agreement of the parties. The former is basically 'within the law', whereas the latter is 'outside the law'. See Hugh Thirlway, 'The Law and Procedure of the International Court of Justice 1960–1989 (Part One)' (1989) 60 BYIL 1 at 49–62 and R. Lapidoth, 'Equity in International Law' (1987) 81 *ASIL Proceedings* 138.

[121] ICJ Reports 1982, 60, para. 71.

[122] See, for example, D. P. O'Connell, *International Law* (London: Stevens, 1970), I, 252–3.

General principles of law as a 'secondary' source but one with an important systemic role

The 'secondary' role of general principles of law

Having made the above distinctions (acknowledging, though, that no sharp delineation is feasible), what can be said about the hierarchical status of general principles of law as against other norms of international law?

First, the so-called 'necessary' principles – the first category referred to above – could, from an institutional point of view, be said to be of a higher value than all other norms of international law. Indeed, without these 'necessary' principles (think, for example, of the *pacta sunt servanda* principle), there would be no such other norms at all. As noted by Cheng: 'From the juridical point of view, the superior value of general principles of law over customs and treaties cannot be denied; for these principles furnish the juridical basis of treaties and customs and govern their interpretation and application.'[123] In this sense, some of those 'necessary' principles could even be described as norms part of *jus cogens*.[124]

Second, however, from an operational point of view, the hierarchical order between general principles of law and other norms is reversed. Unless the general principle of law is one of *jus cogens*, when an international adjudicator is faced with a treaty or customary norm in derogation of a general principle of law the treaty or customary norm will prevail. In that operational sense, general principles of law are, indeed, a 'secondary' source of international law. This operational order applies

---

[123] Cheng, *General Principles*, 393. In EC law, 'general principles' possess this higher standing both from a theoretical and an operational point of view. In the *Defrenne* case (ECJ, 8 April 1976, Case 43/75 [1976] ECR 455 at 475), for example, the ECJ responded to the argument that the notion of 'principle' implies a vague normative value in the following categorical way: 'dans le langage du traité, cette expression est précisément utilisée pour marquer le caractère fondamental de certaines dispositions', so that 'qu'en atténuant cette notion, au point de la réduire au rang d'une indication vague, on toucherait ainsi indirectement aux fondements mêmes de la Communauté et à la cohérence de ses relations extérieures' (quoted in Olivier Jacot-Guillarmod, 'La Hiérarchie des Règles dans l'Ordre Constitutionnel de l'Union Européenne', in Piermarco Zen-Ruffinen and Andreas Auer (eds.), *De la Constitution, Etudes en l'honneur de J.-F. Aubert* (Basle: Helbing & Lichtenhahn, 1996), note 52).

[124] For views which consider that general principles of law may be of *jus cogens* character, see: *Right of Passage* case, per Judge ad hoc Fernandes dissenting, ICJ Reports 1960, 6 at 139–40, and *South West Africa* (Second Phase), per Judge Tanaka dissenting, ICJ Reports 1966, 6 at 298. Brownlie also refers to 'a general principle part of the *jus cogens*' (Brownlie, *Principles*, 4).

in respect of all four categories of general principles of law (including the 'necessary' principles, except those part of *jus cogens*).¹²⁵

Support for the proposition that general principles of law have to give way to customary law can be found in the *Right of Passage* case. In that case, the ICJ established the right of transit through Indian territory of private persons, civil officials and goods on the basis of a local custom.¹²⁶ Portugal also invoked general international custom, as well as general principles of law, in support of its claims of a right of passage. The ICJ did not consider it necessary to examine whether these legal rules of general character led to the same result. It observed: 'Where therefore the Court finds a practice clearly established between two States which was accepted by the Parties as governing the relations between them, the Court must attribute decisive effect to that practice for the purpose of determining their specific rights and obligations. *Such a particular practice must prevail over any general rules.*'¹²⁷

The secondary or subsidiary nature of general principles of law is based on their broad character and main function of 'filling gaps' left open by treaty and custom; it is not, as noted earlier, based on their source or inherent legal quality or binding force which would, somehow, be of lesser value.

General principles of law are denominated 'principles' instead of 'rules' with reason. Although they are legally binding just like other

---

¹²⁵ In this sense, see: Cheng, *General Principles*, 393 ('From the operative point of view, however, the hierarchical order is reversed. Rules of law though in derogation of general principles of law are binding'). See also Akehurst, 'Hierarchy', 279 ('Case law and, with few exceptions, writers are unanimous that treaties and custom override general principles of law in the event of conflict'); Quoc Dinh, *Droit*, para. 60 ('Il est vrai, cependant, que certains sources, à défaut d'être secondaires, ont un caractère second: c'est le cas des principes généraux de droit. L'interprète n'y recourt qu'à défaut d'autre sources pertinentes. Le conflit potentiel est alors contourné') and para. 220 at 340 ('La contradiction éventuelle entre une règle coutumière, et un principe général de droit *stricto sensu* se résout nécessairement par la mise en œuvre de la règle coutumière'); Mosler, 'General Principles', 97; and Abi-Saab, 'Les Sources', 33–4.
¹²⁶ ICJ Reports 1960, 40.
¹²⁷ *Ibid.*, 44, emphasis added. Quoc Dinh, *Droit*, para. 220, is, on the basis of this judgment, of the view that '[l]a contradiction éventuelle entre une règle coutumière et un principe général de droit *stricto sensu* se résout nécessairement par la mise en œuvre de la règle coutumière'. The view expressed by Degan in this respect seems more accurate: 'specific rights and obligations of parties were at stake, not the hierarchy of sources of international law as such ... The Court simply established the existence of the Portuguese right on the basis of a local custom, presuming that no potentially existing general legal rule would be violated by this' (Degan, *Sources*, 520).

norms of international law, they are inherently broad and open-textured. They did not emerge, as treaties or custom normally do, in order to regulate a concrete situation at a given time. As a result, they leave ample room for specification by other norms of international law. In that sense, general principles of law are *lex generalis*, treaties and custom being *lex specialis*.[128]

Because of the vague nature of general principles of law, cases of genuine conflict between these principles and other norms of international law are rare. Where they arise, treaty and custom must prevail as *lex specialis* (unless, of course, *jus cogens* is involved). We come back to this particular application of the *lex specialis* rule in chapter 7 below.

From a practical perspective it is, however, quite unlikely that states decide one day that, for example, under a given treaty the principle of good faith or, before an international tribunal, the principle of due process is not to be applied. As noted by Cheng, 'the possibility of establishing rules in derogation of general principles of law must not be exaggerated. It may be compared to the theoretical omnipotence of the British Parliament to legislate except in order to make a woman a man, and a man a woman.'[129]

The secondary nature of general principles of law derives also from their intended function, namely that of filling gaps left open by treaty and custom with the objective of avoiding a *non liquet*. As noted by Baron Descamps during the preparation of Art. 38 of the ICJ Statute, 'If two States concluded a treaty in which the solution of the dispute could be found, the Court must not apply the international custom and neglect the treaty. If a well known custom exists, there is no occasion to resort to a general principle of law.'[130] Such a step-by-step 'default' approach is very much in line also with Art. 7 of the unratified Twelfth Hague Convention Relative to the Creation of an International Prize Court (1907):

If a question of law to be decided was covered by a convention in force between the belligerent captor and the Power which was itself, or whose subject was, a party to the proceedings, the Court has to apply the provisions of that Convention. In the absence of such provisions, the Court shall apply the rules of international law. If there are no rules generally recognized, the Court will decide according to the general principles of justice and equity.

---

[128] See chapter 7 below, p. 394.   [129] Cheng, *General Principles*, 393.
[130] PCIJ, Advisory Committee of Jurists, *Procès-Verbaux* of the Proceedings of the Committee, 16 June–24 July 1920, with Annexes, 1920, 337.

The potential importance of general principles of law, in particular in international organisations

The role reserved for general principles to fill gaps left open by other norms confirms that general principles of law are a distinct source of international law. This type of 'fall-back' on general international law, including general principles of law, is further discussed in chapter 4 below. In that capacity, the importance of general principles of law as norms cannot be overestimated. They provide international law with 'a most welcome possibility for growth'.[131] They extend 'the concept of the sources of international law beyond the limit of legal positivism according to which, the States being bound only by their own will, international law is nothing but the law of the consent and auto-limitation of States'.[132]

Whereas during the cold war, and until very recently, authors predicted 'a decline of this source'[133] because of vast ideological differences and a growing reliance on individual state consent in international law, the post-war era may well hold a brighter future for general principles of law, in particular general principles of *international* law. This may be so, particularly, within international organisations, especially those with compulsory dispute settlement like the WTO.

In that context, general principles of law may fulfil the important role of (i) go-between and converging factor between the law of the international organisation and the wider corpus of public international law; and (ii) a welcome tool for the judicial function within the organisation to construe the law of the organisation in a dynamic fashion responsive to today's problems. As Brierly opined in 1963, Art. 38(1)(c) of the ICJ

---

[131] Bos, 'The Recognized', 42.
[132] Dissenting Opinion, Judge Tanaka, *South West Africa* cases (Second Phase), ICJ Reports 1966, 298. In the same sense, see J. L. Brierly, *The Law of Nations* (Oxford: Clarendon, 1963), 63. Taking this line of thought one step further, Professor Albert de Lapradelle, during the preparation of Art. 38(1)(c) of the ICJ Statute, expressed the view that 'the tasks of the Court would be limited to registering the acts of the powerful' unless the Court were obliged to apply more than treaties and custom alone (PCIJ, Advisory Committee of Jurists, *Procès-Verbaux* of the Proceedings of the Committee, 16 June–24 July 1920, with Annexes, 1920, 319–20).
[133] Cassese and Weiler, *Change*, 170 (*per* Riphagen, Abi-Saab, Cassese, de Fiumel, Gaja). In the same sense, see: Czaplinski and Danilenko, 'Conflict', 6: '[e]ven if the general principles [of law] could play a certain role in international law (mostly a moderate one), the notion is too indefinite and disputable for their inclusion in the elaboration of a theory for the purposes of this paper'.

Statute, referring to general principles of law, is 'an authoritative recognition of a dynamic element in international law, and of the creative function of the courts which may administer it'.[134] Or as Jenks stated one year earlier:

> Neither agreement nor practice, even in the widest sense, can, however, provide sufficiently vigorous seeds of growth to enable the law to cope with new problems pressing for solution as the result of the activities of the international organisations. Legal principle therefore has an indispensable part to play in the development of the proper law of international organisations and its assimilation into the general body of international law.[135]

Custom and treaties

After judicial decisions, doctrine and general principles of law, we now turn to the question of how custom and treaties may play out in a conflict of norms.

How to distinguish custom from general principles of law

While the distinction between custom and treaty is obvious, it may not always be easy to distinguish custom from general principles of law. According to some authors, a norm may be both part of general customary international law and a general principle of law.[136] Others maintain that the sources of international law are mutually exclusive: if a norm becomes part of customary law, it can no longer be a general principle of law.[137] In any event, given the secondary nature of general principles of law as opposed to custom and treaty, the party invoking the norm will have an interest in defending the norm as part of customary law, not as a general principle of law, that is, a norm of a normally lower

---

[134] Brierly, *Law*, 63.
[135] Wilfred Jenks, *The Proper Law of International Organisations* (London: Stevens, 1962), 259–60.
[136] See Degan, *Sources*, 74.
[137] Charles De Visscher, 'Cours Général de Droit International Public' (1972) 136 *Recueil des Cours* 116 ('il faudrait exclure de la catégorie des principes généraux ceux d'entre eux qui se sont mués en coutume par l'effet d'une pratique subséquente, constante et générale assortie de l'*opinio juris*') and Hulsroj, 'Three Sources', 234 ('a source of law must be self-contained – [it] cannot in its norm-creative function rely on another source of law. If it does it has lost its raison d'être').

status which risks being less persuasive.[138] This is, for example, what the European Communities did in the WTO dispute on *EC – Hormones*, where they invoked the 'precautionary principle' as one part of customary law or 'at least' as being a general principle of law.[139] Another illustration of this point can be found in the *Southern Bluefin Tuna* case. When Japan, in its pleadings, relied on general principles of law such as *lex specialis* and *lex posterior*, Australia and New Zealand responded that such reliance by Japan on general principles was required for want of better legal arguments in treaty or custom.

The difference between 'principle' and 'rule' may also be recalled here: a rule is essentially practical, more clearly defined, whereas a principle, though legally binding, expresses a more general truth which is broadly defined. Mosler put it thus: 'many general principles form part of customary law; however, the two concepts are not identical: principles can be more general and less precisely determined than customary rules; in a given case the authority which has to apply them, in particular courts and arbitral tribunals, has a somewhat wider scope to determine their concrete form'.[140] Or as Hulsroj put it more succinctly, 'Custom does not elevate broad principles to law but makes patterns of specific behaviour law.'[141]

In addition, the conditions to be fulfilled for a norm to be a 'general principle of law' and a customary rule are different. As Cheng noted, custom is

confined to what is a general practice among States accepted by them as law. General practice among nations, as well as the recognition of its legal character, is therefore required... In the definition of ['general principles of law recognized by civilised nations']... there is also the element of recognition on the part of civilised peoples but the requirement of a general practice is absent. The object of recognition is, therefore, no longer the legal character of the rule implied in an international usage, but the existence of certain principles intrinsically legal in nature.[142]

In Hulsroj's view 'custom should be a predominantly state practice oriented source', whereas general principles of law 'should be the source creating rules based on the common legal consciousness of states'.[143]

---

[138] See above, pp. 127–9.   [139] Appellate Body report, para. 121.
[140] Mosler, 'General Principles', 91.   [141] Hulsroj, 'Three Sources', 229.
[142] Cheng, *General Principles*, 24.   [143] Hulsroj, 'Three Sources', 220.

No a priori *hierarchy between treaty and custom*

Turning to the relationship between treaty and custom, it is generally accepted that no inherent hierarchy exists between them.[144] As was the case in respect of general principles of law as opposed to other norms of international law, it would be unsound to state that custom, as a source of law, *always* has to give way to treaty.

Given the absence of a centralised 'legislator' in international relations and the basic role of state consent in all sources of international law, treaty and custom are viewed as being of equal binding value. Both types of norms rest on the consent of states (albeit tacit or implicit consent only in the case of custom). Hence, one form of consent can logically prevail over another. Recall also that the theory of *acte contraire* – by which a norm could only be modified by another norm originating in the same source – is not known in international law.[145] As a result, both treaty and custom have the same binding force.

This is also what the Institute of International Law found in its Resolution of 1 September 1995 on 'Problems arising from a succession of codification conventions on a particular subject'. In 'Conclusion 11: Hierarchy of sources', first sentence, it stated: 'There is no *a priori* hierarchy between treaty and custom as sources of international law.'[146]

In practice a treaty normally prevails over custom (with notable exceptions)

Having noted that, in theory, there is no *a priori* hierarchy between treaty and custom, in practice most cases of apparent, as well as genuine, contradiction between treaty and custom must be decided in favour of the treaty norm.[147] This general rule is confirmed in the 1995 Resolution of the Institute of International Law. The second sentence of Conclusion 11 of that Resolution reads: 'However, in the application of international

---

[144] See note 24 above. On the particular conflict between custom and treaties, see Sheila Weinberger, 'The Wimbledon Paradox and the World Court: Confronting Inevitable Conflicts between Conventional and Customary International Law' (1996) 10 *Emory International Law Review* 397.

[145] See note 23 above.

[146] (1995-I) 66 *Yearbook of the Institute of International Law* 245 at 248.

[147] Thirlway goes so far as saying that 'it is universally accepted that... as between the parties to a treaty the rules of the treaty displace any rules of customary law on the same subject' (Thirlway, 'Law (Part One)', 144). He thereby ignores, however, the possibility that new custom may alter the content of, or even terminate, an earlier treaty, as well as the possibility that custom is part of *jus cogens* and thus prevails over all treaty norms.

law, relevant norms deriving from a treaty will prevail between the parties over norms deriving from customary law.'[148]

The main exception to this rule is conflict between a treaty norm and a customary norm part of *jus cogens*. In that event, the custom not only prevails over the treaty, but actually terminates the treaty norm or renders it invalid.[149] Conclusion 4 of the 1995 Resolution of the Institute of International Law confirms this exception as it includes a caveat in respect of *jus cogens*, stating: 'These Conclusions are without prejudice to the application of Articles 53 and 64 of the Vienna Convention on the Law of Treaties of 1969', that is, the Vienna Convention provisions giving preference to rules of *jus cogens* over treaty norms.

The other exception to the general rule that normally treaty prevails over custom is that subsequent custom may terminate or revise an earlier treaty so that, in effect, the later custom prevails over the earlier treaty. We come back to this second exception below (pp. 137–43), but first attempt to explain the general rule further.

The general rule that normally treaties will prevail over custom can be readily explained. Treaty norms, being written rules, are easier to prove and identify. They are, in addition, an explicit expression of state intent at the highest level of government, mostly ratified also by parliament. Moreover, treaties (other than treaties codifying custom)[150] often constitute norms regulating a special field. They can, in that sense, be labelled as *lex specialis*.[151] Custom, on the other hand, lays down unwritten rules which are often vague and difficult to express in clear terms. They derive, moreover, from implicit consent only (or less than that). In addition, this 'consent', being based on state practice and *opinio juris*, must not necessarily be expressed by the highest levels of government (let alone parliament). Lower-ranking officials (as well as judges, academics and international civil servants) may also influence and shape custom.

According to Schachter, the prominence normally given to treaties over custom also conforms to the currently prevailing liberal approach to societal problems:

The liberal approach, reflecting faith in reason and progress, tends to favour the treaty process because it involves deliberate and rational effort to meet perceived needs by general rules applicable to all. Written text brings clarity and precision in place of the obscurity and uncertainty of past precedents. In addition,

---

[148] (1995-I) 66 *Yearbook of the Institute of International Law* 245 at 248.
[149] Pursuant to Arts. 53 and 64 of the Vienna Convention.
[150] Such as the Vienna Convention.   [151] See chapter 7 below.

multilateral treaty negotiations allow all governments the chance to participate and to express their consent in accordance with their constitutional processes. The treaty conferences generally are democratic in form, the participants are on an equal footing and the main decisions are taken openly and publicly. They are in keeping with the liberal idea.[152]

Echoing this approach, Hulsroj expressed the following, in favour of treaties over custom:

> International lawyers have surely felt very unconstrained in the area of custom and have superimposed their own political ideals. But these ideals did not always correspond to the political will – and politicians saw, felt, that political decisions were taken away from them. This is, to me, one of the reasons why there is, in general, a movement away from international law as a regulatory mechanism – and why only treaty law is effective.[153]

Schachter contrasts this 'liberal ideal', in favour of treaties, to a more conservative approach which, in his view, would tend to prefer custom over treaty:

> Customary law, in contrast, tends to appeal to the conservative. Its case-by-case gradualism reflects particular needs in concrete situations. It avoids grand formulas and abstract ideas. The law that evolves is more malleable and more responsive to each State's individual interest. Not least in the minds of some of its supporters is that custom gives weight to effective power and responsibility whereas multilateral treaty-making unrealistically and unwisely, in their view, treats all States as equally capable.[154]

In any event, given the often vague wording of custom, cases of genuine conflict between treaty and custom are rather exceptional. (Nonetheless, as elaborated in chapter 5 below, custom may play an important role in the *interpretation* of treaties.)[155] In most cases the treaty will simply be more explicit than the custom and hence be found to be the applicable rule. As Wolfke noted, after acknowledging that no inherent hierarchy between treaty and custom exists,

> [f]or the judge, however, the difference in application of conventional and customary rules is enormous. Suffice it to mention, for instance, the much greater

---

[152] Oscar Schachter, 'Entangled Treaty and Custom', in Yoram Dinstein and Mala Tabory (eds.), *International Law at a Time of Perplexity – Essays in Honour of Shabtai Rosenne* (Dordrecht: Nijhoff, 1998), 720.
[153] Hulsroj, 'Three Sources', 227.
[154] Schachter, 'Entangled', 721. On the role of power in the formation of custom, see Byers, *Custom*.
[155] See Philippe Sands, 'Treaty, Custom and the Cross-fertilization of International Law' (1998) 10 *Yale Human Rights and Development Law Journal* 3.

precision and ease of determination of content and range of validity in the case of conventional rules and, in consequence, the much stronger, by comparison with other rules, persuasive impact for the Court and the parties.[156]

A later treaty may modify an earlier custom

Given the dynamic features of customary law – continuously dependent on both state practice and *opinio juris* – and the gradual nature of its emergence, cases of genuine conflict between, on the one hand, a treaty norm that is still in existence and intact and, on the other hand, a rule of customary law recognised as validly established notwithstanding the continuing existence of a contradictory treaty norm, are quite exceptional.

In many cases of *alleged* conflict between treaty and custom, the question is not which of two valid norms should prevail, but rather what is currently the norm: in particular, is the custom still the same given the new treaty? This raises the question of whether a treaty can change custom. The issue there is most often not one of *conflict* between two predetermined norms, but one of determining a norm *in evolution* (such as the length of the territorial sea which, in the twentieth century, moved from three, to twelve and then 200 miles from the shore, by means of both conventions and custom[157]).

For present purposes, it suffices, first, to point out that the conclusion and operation of a contradictory treaty, in particular one that was adopted by many states, may gradually change customary law on the same subject matter so as to conform to the new treaty. In this sense, treaties may modify custom.[158] Villiger's conclusion on the issue of subsequent treaties changing pre-existing customary law is that 'a convention cannot directly impair customary law on the same subject matter'.[159] He admits, however, that

> the more States parties adhere to the convention, the less States will engage in practice upon the customary rule which will eventually – and gradually – cease to attract the required widespread practice. As a result, the original customary

---

[156] Karol Wolfke, *Custom in Present International Law* (Wroclaw, 1964), 93. See also Max Sørenson, *Les Sources du Droit International* (Copenhagen: E. Munksgaard, 1946), 249 and Hulsroj, 'Three Sources', note 16 ('one must recognize that argumentation by one party demonstrating that the other party has explicitly consented to the norm stands a far better chance of success than justice based arguments...This is, however, not to be understood as though different classes of normativity exist').
[157] See Kontou, *Termination*, chapter 3.
[158] See Villiger, *Customary* and Schachter, 'Entangled'.
[159] Villiger, *Customary*, para. 244.

rule may either be reduced to a special customary rule, or it may pass out of use – for instance, if it is modified by a new general customary rule which developed on the basis of a conventional rule.[160]

It is important to point out, in this respect, that a customary rule 'does not vanish only because it is under attack from a group of countries without enough strength to give birth to a different international law norm'.[161] To this extent, custom does know a certain theory of *acte contraire*: it only ceases to exist if replaced by another rule or by desuetude. In contrast, the same does not apply to general principles of law where a 'now consideration' is decisive. If *at the time of adjudication* not enough support can be found in favour of the existence of a general principle of law, no such principle can be applied.[162]

Second, though mostly a question of *law in evolution*, the relationship between pre-existing custom and a later treaty may also present itself as a genuine *conflict* of norms. This will be the case when a specific treaty norm aims at 'contracting out' of a norm of customary law which is, in one way or the other, more general in nature than the treaty norm. An example is WTO treaty norms in the DSU on suspension of concessions which 'contract out' of certain general international law rules on countermeasures. In this situation of conflict of norms, the later treaty norm – both as the *lex posterior* and as the *lex specialis* – prevails over the pre-existing custom. The customary norm thus 'contracted out' from will mostly be one of general customary international law, both in terms of parties bound by it and subject matter (such as custom on the law of treaties or state responsibility). But it may also be a norm of special customary international law, either in terms of parties bound by it (say, a bilateral treaty norm 'contracting out' of a local or regional custom binding also on the parties to the treaty) or in terms of subject matter (say, a treaty norm 'contracting out' of a norm of customary international environmental law). We come back to the situation of treaty norms 'contracting out' of general international law, including custom, in chapter 4 (distinguishing 'contracting out' from 'accumulation' of norms) and chapter 7.

A later custom may change an earlier treaty

At the same time, but much more controversially, it has been submitted that a pre-existing treaty can be terminated or revised by means

---

[160] *Ibid.*, para. 245.   [161] Hulsroj, 'Three Sources', 255.   [162] *Ibid.*, 257.

of the establishment of new customary law.[163] In such cases one can speak of a genuine conflict between an earlier, pre-existing treaty and a subsequently established custom: the earlier treaty still exists, but is contradicted by a later custom.

That modification of treaty norms by subsequent custom is a controversial matter is reflected in the negotiating history of the Vienna Convention itself. The 1964 ILC Draft on the law of treaties contained a provision on treaty modification 'by the subsequent emergence of a new rule of customary law relating to matters dealt with in the treaty and binding upon all the parties' (Art. 68(c)).[164] This provision was subsequently deleted and, as it was finally concluded, the Vienna Convention does not mention supervening custom as a ground for termination or revision of prior incompatible treaties.

More recently, it was confirmed that termination or revision of treaties by supervening custom remains a delicate question. The Institute of International Law in its final 1995 Resolution, referred to earlier, does *not* confirm the possibility of new custom modifying pre-existing treaty norms. However, in an earlier set of draft conclusions, dated December 1994, the second sentence of what is now Conclusion 11 (then Conclusion 12) read as follows: 'However, as a matter of the application of international law, relevant norms deriving from a treaty binding upon the parties to the dispute will prevail over norms deriving from customary law, save where the norm deriving from a treaty contravenes a rule of *jus cogens, or has been subsequently modified by a later norm of customary law.*'[165] A proposal (made by Rosalyn Higgins) to delete the last phrase in italics, confirming the possibility of subsequent custom modifying an earlier treaty norm, was originally rejected by twenty-two votes to fifteen, with thirteen abstentions.[166] Higgins expressed the view that 'this was a very

---

[163] In favour: Kontou, *Termination*; Villiger, *Customary*, paras. 302–52; Quoc Dinh, *Droit*, para. 201; and Separate Opinion of Judge Schwebel, *Maritime Delimitation in the Area between Greenland and Jan Mayen*, ICJ Reports 1993, 38. Contra: the position of the United Kingdom, criticising Art. 68(c) of the 1964 ILC Draft on the law of treaties ('treaties ought not to be modified without the consent of the parties'), YBILC 1966, vol. 2, p. 345; and less categorically: Hugh Thirlway, *International Customary Law and Codification* (Leiden: Sijthoff, 1972), 133 and Akehurst, 'Hierarchy', 276.
[164] YBILC 1964, vol. 2, p. 198.
[165] (1995-I) 66 *Yearbook of the Institute of International Law* 245 at 248 (emphasis added).
[166] *Ibid.*, Part II, 210. The controversial phrase originates in a comment made by Crawford, stating that an earlier draft of what is now Conclusion 11 (then Conclusion 12), not including any reference to custom modifying treaty, 'ignores the possibility that a treaty norm will have been modified in subsequent practice by a later rule of customary international law' (*ibid.*, Part I, 227).

complicated issue' and 'considered it inappropriate for the Institute to deal with such an important issue as an ancillary point at the end of a Conclusion'.[167] Feliciano, in contrast, noted that 'if the second sentence were to be retained as formulated by Mrs Higgins, so as to exclude the modification of a treaty by subsequent customary international law, this itself could be seen as endorsing a hierarchy of sources'.[168] In a later draft the phrase was nonetheless left out and a subsequent proposal to delete the *entire* second sentence of what is now Conclusion 11 was avoided only by twelve votes to eleven, with seven abstentions.

Kontou, in her monograph on the matter of custom changing an earlier treaty, and after careful examination of both judicial decisions and state practice, concludes as follows:

New customary law may be invoked as a ground for the termination or revision of a prior treaty if: (i) it is incompatible with the treaty provisions; (ii) it is different from the customary international law in force at the time of the conclusion of the treaty; and (iii) it is binding upon all parties to the treaty, unless (iv) the parties intended that the treaty should continue applying as special law.[169]

In respect of the fourth condition, Kontou adds that '[t]he intention of the parties to create a special regime may be expressly provided in the treaty or result from the interpretation of time clauses or other provisions'.[170] She acknowledges, however, that

it can at least be said that tribunals are reluctant to accept that supervening custom automatically abrogates or modifies prior incompatible treaties, unless this is what the treaty partners intended. The parties' consent to be bound by the new customary law is not in this respect sufficient, because it does not prove their intent to terminate or revise a prior treaty.[171]

Although she is not always clear on the matter, it seems, therefore, that, according to Kontou, for custom to revise treaty, more is needed

---

[167] *Ibid.*, Part I, 207. [168] *Ibid.*, Part I, 208.
[169] Kontou, *Termination*, 146. In support she refers, *inter alia*, to the *Spanish Fishermen's* cases of the European Court of Justice (for example, Case 812/79, *A.-G. v. Burgoa*, [1980] ECR 2787), the *La Bretagne* arbitration ((1986) 90 RGDIP 716), the *Fisheries Jurisdiction* case (*United Kingdom v. Iceland*), Jurisdiction of the Court (ICJ Reports 1973, 3) and Merits (ICJ Reports 1974, 3) and the *UK–France Continental Shelf Arbitration* ((1979) 18 ILM 397). In the latter case, for example, the Tribunal acknowledged 'both the importance of the evolution of the law of the sea which is now in progress and the possibility that a development in customary law may, under certain conditions, evidence the assent of the States concerned to the modification, or even termination, of previously existing treaty rights and obligations' (*ibid.*, para. 47).
[170] Kontou, *Termination*, 147. [171] *Ibid.*, 145–6.

than the existence of the custom *per se*. The party relying on the revision must prove in addition that the parties to the earlier treaty rule no longer want to apply that rule.[172]

Villiger is equally of the view that subsequent custom can revise or even terminate treaty rules. He seems to go one step further than Kontou, however, when submitting that 'inherent in the formation of a new customary rule is the obligation that the incompatible conventional rule is no longer applied and, hence, ceases to exist. But then, if the conventional rule is not in force, there is no conflict, and the customary rule alone remains applicable.'[173] For Villiger, the emergence of the custom *per se* is, therefore, enough for the contradictory rule to be revised. In his view, such revision is even a necessary consequence of the custom being created.

To start with Villiger, it seems that his approach overlooks the not uncommon situation of prior treaty rules that continue to exist as *lex specialis*, notwithstanding the emergence of subsequent contradictory custom. In other words, he seems to neglect the potential for genuine conflict between a treaty rule and a subsequent custom whereby both rules validly exist, but where the custom must be disapplied in favour of the treaty, the treaty being *lex specialis*. Villiger acknowledges, however, that 'there is certainly room for a small conventional subsystem as a *lex prior specialis* alongside a general (incompatible) customary rule, if this is the intention of the parties'.[174] It must, indeed, be possible that a new custom arises but that a prior conflicting treaty rule nevertheless continues to exist (on this 'contracting out' from custom by treaty, see more in chapters 4 and 7 below). As Waldock noted in his observations on Art. 68(c) of the 1964 ILC Draft on the law of treaties (addressing the modification of a treaty by 'the subsequent emergence of a new rule of customary law'):

The very object of a bilateral treaty or of a treaty between a small group of States is not infrequently to set up a special legal régime between the States concerned and sometimes a régime which derogates from the existing customary law. Accordingly, to say that the emergence of a new rule of customary law,

---

[172] In the same sense, see: Akehurst, 'Hierarchy', 275–6 ('subsequent custom can terminate a treaty only when there is clear evidence that that is what the parties intend...In the absence of express statements concerning termination...evidence can only be provided by abundant and consistent practice').
[173] Villiger, *Customary*, para. 324.   [174] *Ibid.*, para. 328.

binding on the parties as a general rule, is necessarily to modify the particular relations which they have set up between them may defeat their intention.[175]

Turning now to Kontou's approach, she does not seem to take the absence of hierarchy between custom and treaty seriously. If it is, indeed, so that subsequent custom can overrule an earlier treaty as a later expression of state consent, then there must be a *presumption that a later custom prevails over an earlier treaty norm*. For the earlier treaty rule to apply nonetheless, it is then up to the party relying on the earlier treaty to prove that the parties to that treaty intended to *continue applying* the treaty rule as *lex specialis*. Contrary to what Kontou implies, with reference especially to case law (where the judge seems to have a bias in favour of the more explicit treaty rule), it should *not* be up to the party relying on the later custom to show that the parties to the earlier treaty intended to change or even terminate the treaty. This would amount to a form of *acte contraire* under which custom can only revise treaty if the parties to the treaty themselves first express an intention to revise or terminate the treaty. In other words, when an international adjudicator is faced with a claim that new custom has terminated or revised an earlier treaty norm, and once the new custom is validly established, *it is for the party relying on the treaty norm to prove that this earlier treaty norm was intended to continue applying as special law*. If it cannot meet this burden of proof, the later custom should prevail.

Although the above-suggested approach is of great systemic importance – in particular, in recognition of custom being of the same hierarchical status as treaties – in practice it will often be relatively easy to prove that the prior treaty was intended to continue applying as *lex specialis*, either as between a limited number of states only (say, the EC treaty) or in a special field of application (say, trade under the WTO treaty). This will especially be so in case the original treaty contracted out of (an earlier version of) the customary rule and/or in case the treaty can be seen as a 'continuing treaty' (a notion we explain in chapter 7 below). Cases where an earlier, more special, treaty norm is found to prevail over a later, more general, custom would also be supported by the principle *generalia specialibus non derogant*, that is, a later more general rule does not change an earlier more specific rule (although this

---

[175] Dietrich Rauschning, *The Vienna Convention on the Law of Treaties, Travaux Préparatoires* (Frankfurt: Metzner, 1978), 308.

principle is arguably of questionable value, as discussed in chapter 7 below).

The following is a case in point. Article 5.7 of the SPS agreement allows for the imposition of provisional trade restrictions in instances where there is not sufficient scientific evidence *as long as certain conditions are met*. In addition to Art. 5.7, there is the so-called precautionary principle allowing for provisional health protection measures, which is, in the view of some, part of customary international law. If it were, indeed, so that Art. 5.7 is *incompatible* with this precautionary principle – in that the precautionary principle allows for trade restrictions where the conditions under Art. 5.7 for the imposition of trade restrictions are not met (something that is far from clear!) – nothing should prevent (or has prevented) this principle from becoming one of general customary international law. If it were established *by the WTO member invoking the precautionary principle* – that is, the defendant invoking the principle as a justification for breach of other SPS provisions – that this principle is, indeed, part of customary international law (another open question), a WTO panel ought to take cognisance of this new custom *even if it is incompatible with WTO rules*. Given the fact that supervening custom can revise a treaty (*in casu*, the SPS agreement), it would then be up to the other WTO member – that is, the complainant alleging breach of the SPS agreement – to prove that the SPS agreement (and Art. 5.7 in particular) continues to apply as *lex specialis, notwithstanding the fact that this new custom has emerged*. If such proof of *lex specialis* cannot be put forward, a WTO panel ought to acknowledge that the SPS agreement has been revised by subsequent custom. It may then, depending on the factual circumstances, accept this principle as a valid justification for an alleged breach of the SPS agreement (on the invocation of a defence found outside the WTO treaty, see chapter 8 below).

Importantly, even if a later custom revises an earlier treaty, the customary norm does not become part and parcel of the treaty. It leads a separate existence, although it has become the applicable law for the matter at issue. This explains why, for example, a later custom revising the WTO treaty cannot form the basis of a claim for breach before a WTO panel. The new custom does not become part of WTO covered agreements. Since a WTO panel's substantive jurisdiction stretches only as far as claims under these agreements, a claim under the new custom would fall outside a WTO panel's substantive jurisdiction.[176]

---

[176] See chapter 8 below.

Finally, a distinction must be made between, on the one hand, treaty termination or revision as a result of new customary law and, on the other, desuetude or modification of treaties by subsequent practice (only the former can involve a conflict of norms, not the latter). It is, indeed, generally considered that a treaty falls into desuetude when its non-application by the parties over a period of time establishes their consent to let it lapse.[177] Desuetude can hence be described as treaty termination based on the parties' *implied consent*.[178] Treaty modification by subsequent practice can also be seen as a form of modification by *implied consent*.[179] Such modification is not included in the Vienna Convention, but is generally understood to be a rule of customary law.[180] Termination or revision of a treaty based on new custom, in contrast, is based not so much on implied consent to terminate or revise the treaty, but on the emergence of new customary law as such.

Unilateral acts of states and acts of international organisations

Unilateral acts of states creating legally binding obligations

Unilateral acts[181] are only binding on the state making them if they evidence an intention to be bound. In the WTO context, for example, a panel attributed 'international legal significance'[182] to official, repeated and unconditional unilateral statements made by the United States in the proceedings before the panel. In doing so, the panel made reference

---

[177] For ICJ cases where a claim of desuetude was made, see the *Nuclear Tests* case, ICJ Reports 1973, 99 at 102, and the *Aegean Sea Continental Shelf* case, ICJ Reports 1978, 1 at 17 and 37. In neither of these two cases did the ICJ examine the claim.

[178] Kontou, *Termination*, 25.

[179] For an example of treaty modification by subsequent practice, see the 1963 *United States v. France Air Transport Services Agreement* arbitration, (1969) 38 ILR 182 at 249. For another prominent example, see the *Namibia Advisory Opinion*, ICJ Reports 1971, 22, where Art. 27(3) of the UN Charter, which requires the 'affirmative vote' of all Permanent Members of the Security Council, was, on the basis of subsequent practice, construed as meaning that the voluntary abstention of Permanent Members does not render invalid the resolution in question ('this procedure has been generally accepted by Members of the United Nations and evidences a general practice of that Organization').

[180] This rule was included in Art. 68 of the 1964 ILC Draft and Art. 38 of the 1966 ILC Draft (see Rauschning, *Travaux*, 304 and 309). For the view that it is part of customary law, see Wolfram Karl, *Vertrag und Spätere Praxis im Völkerrecht* (Berlin; Springer, 1983).

[181] For a comprehensive overview of the role of unilateral acts of states and acts of international organisations as sources of international law, see Quoc Dinh, *Droit*, paras. 235–49.

[182] Panel report on *US – Section 301*, para. 7.118.

to several PCIJ and ICJ cases, including the *Eastern Greenland* and *Nuclear Tests* cases.[183] Taken together with the US statement of administrative action that accompanied the US legislation at issue, the panel found that the United States was, on these grounds, under a duty, under both domestic and international law, to exercise the discretion given to it by the statutory language of the legislation in a way consistent with WTO obligations.[184] Given this legally binding undertaking, the panel concluded that the legislation at issue was *not* inconsistent with WTO rules.[185]

Turning to the hierarchical status of unilateral acts of states, their very nature confirms that they can only give rise to *additional obligations*. As Salmon noted, unilateral acts 'sont l'expression de la volonté d'un seul Etat et doivent par conséquent être compatibles avec toutes autres règles du droit international. Ils ont par nature un caractère subsidiaire.'[186] A unilateral act by a state aimed at *detracting* from *existing* obligations cannot as such constitute a new norm of international law which would somehow supersede an earlier obligation. Hence, in case a unilateral act is contradictory to any other norm of international law, it cannot, in and of itself, become a legally binding right or undertaking, let alone prevail over that other norm. Nonetheless, it may well be that a unilateral act of a state, in conflict with customary law, is the beginning of, and even a necessary condition for, changing that customary law.[187]

In addition, in case a new norm of international law emerges subsequently to the unilateral act and the new norm is binding also on the state which made the unilateral act but contradicts this act, then the new norm, as the latest expression of sovereign will and the only consensual norm at issue, prevails over the earlier unilateral act. The unilateral act could only prevail over the later norm if it were to impose *stricter* obligations on the state in question than the later norm, *and* the unilateral act were repeated or continued subsequently to the emergence of that later norm (or it can somehow be shown that there was an intention that the unilateral act is to continue applying as the special and more burdensome law for the state in question).

Legally binding acts of international organisations

Two major types of legally binding acts or 'decisions' of international organisations can be detected. First, there are decisions related to the

---

[183] *Ibid.*, footnote 692.   [184] *Ibid.*, paras. 7.117–126.
[185] *Ibid.*, para. 7.126.   [186] Salmon, 'Antinomies', 286–7.
[187] See the statement by Weiler, in Cassese and Weiler, *Change*, 8.

internal operation of the organisation, such as nominations of agents or judges, creation of subsidiary bodies or financial decisions, but also decisions with a more general scope such as the adoption of rules of procedure for the conduct of meetings or judicial proceedings. Second, there are decisions which *directly create or affect rights or obligations* of member states of the international organisation, such as certain decisions adopted by the UN Security Council (e.g., pursuant to Chapter VII of the UN Charter)[188] or, in the WTO context, waivers granted by the Ministerial Conference to a certain WTO member,[189] authoritative interpretations adopted by the Ministerial Conference or General Council[190] or decisions by the Dispute Settlement Body to establish a panel[191] or to authorise the suspension of concessions or other obligations.[192]

A clear distinction must, moreover, be made between decisions taken by organs of the international organisation itself and agreements concluded by states under the auspices of the international organisation. The latter are created by means of acts of the member states (not the international organisation), the former by the organs of the organisation itself (even if those organs are composed of delegates of member states). As pointed out in chapter 2 above, p. 45, in the WTO it is not always realised that there is this distinction.

Internal validity and ranking of the decision

The legal status of binding decisions of international organisations is to be determined first and foremost with reference to the normative system of the organisation itself. As such, these decisions can only bind organs and/or states *within* the organisation, not states that are not members of or parties to the organisation. Decisions of international organisations may be instrumental in the creation of customary law binding also on states that are not members of the organisation, but in and of themselves such decisions do not bind non-parties. As against non-parties, decisions of international organisations can hence not be invoked, let alone be invoked as prevailing over other norms of international law such as treaties or customary law.

---

[188] Article 25 of the UN Charter provides that '[t]he Members of the United Nations agree to accept and carry out the decisions of the Security Council in accordance with the present Charter'.
[189] By three-quarters majority, pursuant to Article IX:3 of the Marrakesh Agreement.
[190] By three-quarters majority, pursuant to Article IX:2 of the Marrakesh Agreement.
[191] By negative consensus (in other words, quasi-automatically) pursuant to DSU Art. 6.1.
[192] *Ibid.*, pursuant to DSU Art. 22.6.

As between parties to the organisation, decisions taken by organs of the organisation must, first of all, be consistent with the treaty or other legal instrument establishing the organ. They must, in particular, be within the competence attributed to the organ. We come back to this in chapter 6 below (pp. 285–90). In the UN context, for example, UN Security Council decisions must be consistent with the provisions of the UN Charter. In the WTO context as well, decisions by WTO organs must be consistent with the Marrakesh Agreement as well as any other WTO agreements granting them specific powers to act.

Once it is established that the decision of the international organisation is a valid one,[193] within most (if not all) international organisations the decision acquires a hierarchical status that corresponds to the organ that adopted the decision, or according to the procedure followed in its elaboration. In the WTO, for example, the highest authority is the Ministerial Conference, followed by the General Council which, in turn, is superior to the more specific Councils and Committees on, for example, Trade in Goods or Services or Agriculture.

How does the decision relate to norms outside the international organisation?

Like all other norms of international law, decisions of international organisations must be consistent with *jus cogens*. If not, they are invalid or terminate. Such decisions, like treaty and custom, should, however, at least from an operational point of view, prevail over general principles of law (other than those of *jus cogens*) as well as unilateral acts of states. As noted earlier, the latter can only add to, not detract from, existing obligations.

But what if a decision of an international organisation is in conflict with a treaty norm that finds its source *outside* the organisation? For example, what if, in the WTO context, the DSB grants authorisation to a WTO member to suspend obligations under the TRIPS agreement, but the resulting suspension is in conflict with that member's obligations under WIPO conventions? In these circumstances, the decision (*in casu*, the DSB authorisation to retaliate) can best be compared to a treaty norm adopted under the auspices of the organisation in question. In other words, the rules to be applied when one treaty norm is in conflict with another should apply also to conflicts between a decision of an international organisation and a treaty norm enacted outside that

---

[193] We briefly address the 'legality' of acts of international organisations (as opposed to their validity) in chapter 6 below.

organisation. Hence, in the absence of an explicit conflict clause, the starting point should be that the later norm in time (*in casu*, the DSB authorisation) prevails. We come back to this type of conflict in chapter 7 below (p. 384).

The same can be said about conflicts between two decisions of different international organisations, that is, two decisions that impose contradictory rights or obligations on states that are members of both organisations: the conflict ought to be treated like a conflict of treaty norms. In other words, if both parties concerned are bound by both of the decisions, the starting point must be that – absent an explicit conflict clause – the later decision in time, as the latest expression of state consent, prevails. If the two decisions are binding only on one of the two states, a conflict of the type AB/AC (A being a state with conflicting obligations vis-à-vis B and C), discussed in chapter 7 below (pp. 422–36), arises.

To resolve a conflict between a decision of the organisation and a norm of customary law, the same rules apply as those in respect of conflicts between treaty norms and norms of customary law, discussed earlier in this chapter. That is, there is no inherent hierarchy between the decision and the custom, but in practice, as between states bound by both, the decision prevails. Exceptions to this rule are: custom that is part of *jus cogens* or a decision that can be said to be modified or even terminated by subsequent custom (for this to happen, though, the decision must not be intended to continue applying as *lex specialis*).

From 'sources' of international law to 'general' versus 'particular' international law

In the previous sub-sections of this chapter, the point was made that, in principle, no hierarchy exists as between the different sources of international law. Although, in operational terms, a certain hierarchy between the sources can be detected – treaties normally prevailing over custom which should, in turn, prevail over general principles of law – this hierarchy cannot be generalised. Therefore, to build a theory of conflict of norms *with reference solely to the source of these norms* is unworkable. There would be too many exceptions and uncertainties, essentially because hierarchies in international law (unlike domestic law) are not based on form but on substance.

For purposes of understanding the existing hierarchies in international law, a more instructive manner of depicting the universe of that law may be to distinguish between 'general international law' and 'particular international law'.

General international law

Norms of general international law

On the edge of the international law universe, there are a number of norms that bind *all* states. Although international law does not have a central *legislator* it does, indeed, include an element with features of international *legislation*, namely *general international law*. The rules of this general international law are, by their very nature, binding on *all* states. Each new state, as well as each new treaty, is automatically born into it.[194]

With reference to the sources of international law discussed earlier, this corpus of general international law consists of:

1. *General customary international law (in terms of membership)* Prominent examples are rules on state responsibility, the law of treaties, interplay of norms and settlement of disputes as well as more substantive norms on, for example, the use of force, genocide or human rights. This class of norms also includes special customary international law *in terms of subject matter*, such as customary international *environmental* law, as long as it is binding on all states (i.e., as long as it is general customary international law in terms of membership). We make abstraction here of the possibility for states to be 'persistent objectors' to a rule of general customary law. Even if such rule would, as a result, not be binding on 'persistent objectors', it is still one that is part of general international law *unless* persistently objected to. Such persistent objection is, in fact, not much different in character from the 'contracting out' of general international law by treaty, discussed below, the major difference being that in the case of persistent objectors the 'contracting out' is based on unilateral state conduct.
2. *General principles of law* These principles are, by their very nature, binding on all states.
3. Jus cogens This is included in so far as a particular norm of *jus cogens* might not yet be covered under 1. or 2. Like general principles of law, norms of *jus cogens* are, by their very nature, binding on all states.

General international law: the 'highest' *and* the 'lowest' law

General international law performs two crucially important roles within the system of international law.

---

[194] This does not mean, of course, that states cannot 'contract out' of general international law: see chapter 4 below.

First, in so far as it includes all the rules of *jus cogens*, general international law sets out the highest law to which all other norms of international law must conform. Pursuant to the Vienna Convention, rules of *jus cogens* prevail over all – past and future – treaty norms.[195]

Second, in so far as it sets out what one could call 'secondary rules' of international law or rules that impose rights and obligations on states only *indirectly through other (primary) rules of law*,[196] general international law ensures the existence of international law as a legal system. These secondary rules include rules on the law of treaties, state responsibility, interplay of norms and settlement of disputes. Together they constitute international law's 'toolbox' for the creation, operation, interplay and enforcement of rules of international law. The fact that the contents of this 'toolbox' are, generally speaking, the same for all rules of international law is an important element of convergence in the decentralised system of international law. Importantly, however, and quite the opposite of *jus cogens*, these secondary rules of general international law (as well as all other general international law that is not *jus cogens*) are residual law only (or *droit supplétif*): that is, law on which one must 'fall back' only in case a treaty is silent on the matter.[197] Treaties and other rules of particular international law can freely 'contract out' of general international law (other than *jus cogens*).

Looked at from a certain angle, general international law does resemble domestic legislation. It is, indeed, the only international law that is binding on all states. In so far as, for example, Belgian law applies to all Belgians, general international law is the only international law that can be said to apply to all states. Some have even gone as far as saying that general international law is the only international 'law' in the strict sense of the word 'law'.[198] All other international law (*in casu*, particular international law and especially treaties) would then be nothing but

---

[195] See Arts. 53 and 64 of the Vienna Convention, discussed further in chapter 6 below.
[196] The distinction between primary and secondary rules was made prominently by H. L. A. Hart in *The Concept of Law* (Oxford: Clarendon, 1961) 92: 'secondary rules are all concerned with the primary rules themselves. They specify the ways in which the primary rules may be conclusively ascertained, introduced, eliminated, varied and the fact of their violation conclusively determined.' The scope of the 'secondary rules' referred to here (as well as by Hart) is much wider than the notion of 'secondary rules' used by the ILC in its discussions on Draft Articles on State Responsibility (where it is limited to the definition and consequences of *breach* of 'primary rules', excluding 'secondary rules' such as those on the creation, application, revision or termination of 'primary rules'). See, for example, Crawford, First Report, 4.
[197] This type of 'fall-back' is further discussed in chapter 4 below.
[198] See Fitzmaurice, 'Some Problems', 160.

'contracts' as between some states only (or, to complete the domestic law analogy, contracts binding on some Belgians only). To the extent that general international law coincides with *jus cogens* one could even compare it to domestic constitutional law. However, contrary to much of domestic legislation (and all domestic constitutions), general international law other than *jus cogens* does *not* have an inherent legal value that is superior to other rules of law (in domestic law, sub-federal law, administrative regulations and contracts; in international law, treaties). On the contrary, general customary international law and general principles of law are, as we saw earlier, often characterised as being vague and imprecise, treaties being much more explicit and specific. As a result, in the event of conflict, particular international law will normally prevail over general international law.

In sum, general international law includes at the same time (i) the weakest form of international law in the sense of norms that are a 'fallback' option only from which treaties can contract out as they wish; and (ii) the strongest form of international law, namely rules of *jus cogens*.

Is international law a 'complete' system (or can there be a *non liquet*)?

Finally, two remarks related to the scope and nature of general international law must be made. In this section we address the doctrinal discussion as to whether international law can be seen as a 'complete' system of law. Some argue that it must be so regarded either because of the 'residual negative principle' set forth in the *Lotus* case[199] decided by the PCIJ (further discussed below) or on the ground that general principles of law automatically fill all gaps in case no other international law exists (in other words, international law, from its very beginnings as general international law before the conclusion of treaties, was already

---

[199] *SS Lotus (France v. Turkey)*, PCIJ, Series A, No. 10 (1927): that is, the principle that 'everything which is not expressly prohibited is allowed'. In support, see, for example, Julius Stone, 'Non Liquet and the Function of Law in the International Community' (1959) 35 BYIL 135 and the Dissenting Opinion of Judge Shahabuddeen (Part I, para. 6, (1996) 35 ILM 866), as well as, apparently, the Individual Opinion of Judge Guillaume (para. 9, (1996) 35 ILM 1353) in the 1996 ICJ Advisory Opinion on *Legality of the Threat or Use of Nuclear Weapons*. *Contra*: Sir Gerald Fitzmaurice, 'The Law and Procedure of the ICJ, 1951–54: General Principles and Sources of Law' (1953) 30 BYIL 1 at 8; Hulsroj, 'Three Sources', 220; and the Declaration of President Bedjaoui (para. 16, (1996) 35 ILM 1347) in the 1996 ICJ Advisory Opinion on *Legality of the Threat or Use of Nuclear Weapons*.

'complete').²⁰⁰ The 'completeness' of international law is, for these authors, the reason why an international adjudicator cannot pronounce a *non liquet*.²⁰¹

Other authors do not consider international law to be a 'complete system' and regard it instead as a relatively primitive system of law which is, at times, incomplete or unclear. These authors do not shy away from a declaration of *non liquet*.²⁰² In its 1996 *Advisory Opinion on the Legality of the Threat or Use of Nuclear Weapons*, the ICJ found, according to many authors, a *non liquet* when stating that 'in view of the current state of international law, and of the elements at its disposal, the Court cannot conclude definitively whether the threat or use of nuclear weapons would be lawful or unlawful in an extreme circumstance of self-defence, in which the very survival of a State would be at stake'.²⁰³ Reacting to this ICJ judgment, Prosper Weil makes a distinction between contentious procedures (where, in his view, *non liquet* is prohibited) and advisory procedures (where a *non liquet* may be pronounced).²⁰⁴

As we shall see below, *non liquet* may, indeed, be the only solution in certain exceptional cases of conflict of norms, where it is impossible for the adjudicator to find a decision in the law as to which of two contradictory norms must be applied. In yet other exceptional cases there may simply be no applicable law so that, in the words of Martti Koskenniemi, '[f]or the voice of justice to be heard, law must sometimes

---

[200] See, for example, the Dissenting Opinion of Vice-President Schwebel (at p. 9) in the 1996 ICJ Advisory Opinion on *Legality of the Threat or Use of Nuclear Weapons*.

[201] See Prosper Weil, 'The Court Cannot Conclude Definitively... *Non Liquet* Revisited' (1997) 36 *Columbia Journal of Transnational Law* 109; Sir Hersch Lauterpacht, 'Some Observations on the Prohibition of "Non Liquet" and the Completeness of the Law', in *Symbolae Verzijl* (The Hague: Nijhoff, 1958), 196; Fitzmaurice, 'ICJ, 1951–54'; and Hersch Lauterpacht, 'Restrictive Interpretation and the Principle of Effectiveness in the Interpretation of Treaties' (1949) 26 BYIL 48 at 78. For case law against *non liquet* (which is rare since courts do not normally acknowledge that the law has lacunae or is unclear, they simply fill the gap or provide their own interpretation), see the *Lighthouses between France and Greece* case, PCIJ, Series A/B, No. 62, 14, 20 and the *Employment of Women during the Night* case, PCIJ, Series A/B, No. 50, 377.

[202] See, for example, Hulsroj, 'Three Sources', 220–8 and Fastenrath, *Lücken*.

[203] *Legality of the Threat or Use of Nuclear Weapons*, ICJ Reports 1996, para. 105. But see the Dissenting Opinion of, for example, Rosalyn Higgins, ICJ Reports 1996, 583 (stating that this part of the ICJ *dispositif* is inconsistent with the prohibition of *non liquet*) and H. Lauterpacht, 'Some Observations', 213 and note 2 (concluding that the prohibition of *non liquet* applies to both contentious and advisory jurisdiction).

[204] Weil, 'Non Liquet', 119 ('In advisory proceedings, *non liquet* is an expression of the principles of self-interpretation and polynormativity that are characteristic of the international legal system').

remain silent'.²⁰⁵ Daniel Bodansky refers to the example of 'what was the international rule concerning the continental shelf as of January 1945?' and the issue of expropriation in the 1970s.²⁰⁶ In both instances, there was, in his view, no norm one way or the other so that a *non liquet*, vindicating neither side's legal position, would have been justified at the time, thus leaving the issue to the normal process of international law-making.²⁰⁷ In those exceptional cases where there is simply no applicable law (or too much applicable law in that there is an unresolvable conflict) the judge may either pronounce a *non liquet* or himself *create* the law. Much will depend on the lacuna in question (e.g., is it one of detail that can be easily filled by analogy or would filling the lacuna really amount to creating an entirely new norm?) as well as, prominently, the role generally attributed to the judge concerned, in particular the extent of his law-creating function²⁰⁸ (to be weighed against the incentive that a *non liquet* may provide for *states* to fill the gap by normal law-making processes). Court activism may be more readily expected, for example, from the European Court of Justice than from the ICJ. The WTO judiciary could posit itself somewhere in between, although the diversity among WTO members as well as the prevailing 'member-driven' character of the WTO as a legal system is likely to tip the balance *against* court activism on many an occasion.

Note that in WTO dispute settlement the matter of *non liquet* is somewhat simplified because of the limited substantive jurisdiction of panels and the Appellate Body.²⁰⁹ This jurisdiction is limited to deciding whether or not there is a violation under *specific treaty provisions*, namely those of WTO covered agreements.²¹⁰ If there is no WTO law on the question, then there is no WTO claim to be made and hence not even

---

²⁰⁵ Martti Koskenniemi, 'The Silence of Law/The Voice of Justice', in Laurence Boisson de Chazournes and Philippe Sands (eds.), *International Law, the International Court of Justice and Nuclear Weapons* (Cambridge: Cambridge University Press, 1999), 488 at 489. Also in support of there being cases where a *non liquet* may be justified, see Daniel Bodansky, '*Non Liquet* and the Incompleteness of International Law', in Boisson de Chazournes and Sands, *Nuclear Weapons*, 153–70.

²⁰⁶ Bodansky, '*Non Liquet*', respectively at 157 and 158.   ²⁰⁷ *Ibid.*

²⁰⁸ Or, as Martti Koskenniemi put it: 'The question is not so much whether or not international law is a "complete system", but whether we can trust the lawyers who manage it always to do the right thing' (Koskenniemi, 'Silence', 507).

²⁰⁹ See Joost Pauwelyn, 'Cross-agreement Complaints before the Appellate Body: A Case Study of the *EC – Asbestos* Dispute' (2002) 1 *World Trade Review* 63 and Lorand Bartels, '*Non Liquet* in the WTO Dispute Settlement System', paper on file with the author.

²¹⁰ DSU Art. 1.1. See chapter 8 below.

jurisdiction to declare a *non liquet*. In case a WTO panel finds that the WTO provision invoked by the complainant does not prohibit the defendant's measure or conduct, the defendant wins and the panel cannot, for example, find violations of non-WTO law.[211] Since, therefore, the only state conduct that can be condemned at the WTO must necessarily be prohibited in WTO treaty provisions, the rules on treaty interpretation and the adage *jura novit curia* must normally be enough for the WTO judiciary to make up its mind as to whether a measure is prohibited under the WTO treaty.

Hence, a *non liquet* in the WTO based on the fact that there is no applicable law seems to be out of the question (in the absence of WTO law, there is simply no WTO claim, hence no jurisdiction for a WTO panel). The possibility of there not being any applicable law for a particular matter was, however, hinted at also in WTO law in the recent Appellate Body report on *US – Hot-Rolled Steel*.[212] There, the Appellate Body found what it called a 'lacuna' in the Anti-Dumping agreement, more particularly Art. 9.4 thereof, 'because, while Article 9.4 *prohibits* the use of certain margins in the calculation of the ceiling for the "all others" rate, it does not expressly address the issue of *how* that ceiling should be calculated in the event that *all* margins are to be *excluded* from the calculation, under the prohibitions'.[213] The Appellate Body refrained from dealing with this lacuna on the following ground: 'This appeal does not raise the issue of how that *lacuna* might be overcome on the basis of the present text of the *Anti-Dumping Agreement*. Accordingly, it is not necessary for us to address that question.' In this instance, as the Appellate Body seemed to imply, a *non liquet* could well be avoided (i.e., the '*lacuna* might be overcome') by the adjudicator with reference to related provisions in the Anti-Dumping agreement.

In contrast, the other situation of *non liquet*, referred to earlier, may still arise, even in the WTO, namely: a WTO panel may be faced with a conflict of norms (be it as between WTO norms, or between a WTO norm and another norm) and be unable to find a decision in the law as

---

[211] As Sir Gerald Fitzmaurice pointed out (although he opposed the view of international law being 'complete': see note 198 above): 'where the offence consists, and can only consist, in the violation of a specific prohibition, it must obviously be a sufficient defence to show that the act concerned did not involve such a violation, and was therefore "not contrary to international law"' (Fitzmaurice, 'ICJ, 1951–54', 14).

[212] Appellate Body Report, *US – Hot-Rolled Steel*, paras. 125–6.

[213] *Ibid.*, para. 126, emphasis in the original.

to which of the two contradictory norms must be applied (see chapter 7 below, pp. 419–22).

Is what is not prohibited *per* definition allowed?

Second, there is also a discussion as to whether the 'residual negative principle', i.e., the principle of 'what is not prohibited is allowed', lies at the origin of international law. Proponents of this principle, allegedly recognised in the PCIJ *Lotus* case,[214] claim that it is part of general international law and means that states, as sovereigns, have a complete freedom of action that is limited only by international law explicitly prohibiting them from engaging in certain conduct. Strong arguments have been put forward against this approach to international law.[215] Indeed, the right or freedom of one state, especially when exercised outside its territorial jurisdiction, often implies a corresponding restriction of sovereignty of another state. The right or freedom of one state and the obligation or restriction of sovereignty of another state are, in that sense, but two sides of the same coin. Moreover, in international adjudication, if a state can place itself on the defendant side, the principle means that it will be up to the complainant to prove a rule of international law that *restricts the defendant's sovereignty*. If the complainant is not able to do so, the defendant wins. If, however, the roles are reversed and the same state is put on the complainant side (for example, in a dispute over sovereignty over a certain piece of land), it will be *up to that state, as complainant, to prove that a rule of international law exists which restricts the complete freedom (at origin) of the opposing state*. For these reasons, it is difficult to accept the principle of 'what is not prohibited is allowed' as one that is part of general international law. It may be relevant in limited contexts such as WTO dispute settlement where only claims under WTO covered agreements can be made so that what is not prohibited *by the WTO treaty* must, at least for purposes of WTO dispute settlement, be considered as allowed. The complete freedom of states can, however, no longer be seen as a valid starting point for all international law questions, especially now that modern international law is increasingly a law of co-operation, with certain matters, such as the high seas and fundamental human rights, being classified as 'global commons'.

---

[214] See note 198 above.
[215] Especially by Fitzmaurice, 'ICJ, 1951–54'. See also Hulsroj, 'Three Sources', 220–8 and the authors referred to in note 205 above.

Particular international law

Whereas general international law is, by its very nature, binding on *all* states, particular international law is binding only on *some* states. With reference to the sources of international law discussed earlier, the diverse corpus of particular international law consists of:

1. *Treaties*, be they bilateral or multilateral;
2. *Special customary international law (in terms of membership)*, that is, local or regional custom binding as between a number of states only;
3. *Unilateral acts of states* creating additional obligations binding on those states only, as well as unilateral conduct of states that can be classified as *persistent objectors* to a norm of general customary international law;
4. *Acts of international organisations*, binding on the member states of the organisation only.

As noted earlier, this particular international law can 'contract out' of general international law other than rules of *jus cogens*. We further examine this 'contracting out' of general international law, especially by treaties, in chapter 4 (pp. 212–18) and chapter 7 (pp. 391–2).

However, particular international law can also confirm or add to rights and obligations set out in general international law. To that extent, particular international law simply confirms or complements general international law. Both can apply simultaneously and no situation of conflict arises. From this perspective, international law is a law of accumulation, not of exclusion (see chapter 4 below). In this context, states can, for example, conclude a treaty (particular international law) which simply confirms or 'codifies' customary law (general international law). Importantly, however, in that circumstance (treaty codifying custom), the customary rules underlying the treaty *continue to exist and lead a separate life that is distinct from that of the treaty rules*, including as between parties to the codifying treaty. This approach was confirmed by both the ICJ and the Institute of International Law. In the *Nicaragua* case (Jurisdiction and Admissibility) the ICJ stated: 'The fact that the above-mentioned principles, recognized as such, have been codified or embodied in multilateral conventions does not mean that they cease to exist and to apply as principles of customary law, even as regards countries that are parties to such conventions.'[216] This is also what the Institute of International Law concluded in its Resolution of 1 September 1995 on 'Problems arising from a succession of codification conventions on a particular subject'.

---

[216] ICJ Reports 1984, 424, para. 73. See, in this respect, Villiger, *Customary*, paras. 228–42 and Thirlway, *International*.

In Conclusion 11 it is stated: 'Treaty and custom form distinct, interrelated, sources of international law. A norm deriving from one of these two sources may have an impact upon the content and interpretation of norms deriving from the other source. In principle, however, each retains its separate existence as norm of treaty law or of customary law respectively.'[217]

Finally, it should be noted that norms of *particular* international law may 'graduate' to norms of *general* international law. Most commonly, a treaty norm may, for example, transform into a norm of *general customary* international law. It is then not just binding on the parties to the treaty but becomes binding on *all* states. Article 38 of the Vienna Convention provides, indeed, that '[n]othing in articles 34 to 37 [on treaties and third states, essentially setting out the *pacta tertiis* rule] precludes a rule set forth in a treaty from becoming binding upon a third State as a customary rule of international law, recognized as such'. This has, however, not always been the prevailing view. Witness, for example, Maarten Bos' statement (of 1977): 'Treaty and custom are not only independent of each other, but mutually exclusive in this sense, that a rule valid between two States cannot be a treaty rule and a rule of customary law at the same time.'[218] Degan originally held a similar view on the evolution of international law as a law composed mainly of customary law that would 'graduate' to the somewhat higher treaty status (distinguishing between the alleged 'perfect' (written) and 'imperfect' (unwritten) sources).[219] However, in his 1997 book on sources, Degan acknowledges that '[t]he developments in [the] last thirty-five years contradicted these expectations, first of all in respect of [the] importance of customary law'.[220]

Indeed, viewed from the general versus particular international law perspective, it remains so that it is for treaties (particular law) to 'graduate' to custom (potentially even *jus cogens*) so as to become part of *general* international law binding on all states. It is not for general customary law (by nature, binding on all states) to be 'perfected' into treaty form (in practice, binding only on a certain number of states). This is one of

---

[217] 'Problems Arising from a Succession of Codification Conventions on a Particular Subject', Resolution of the Institute of International Law of 1 September 1995 (1995-I) 66 *Yearbook of the Institute of International Law* 245.
[218] Bos, 'The Recognized', 74.
[219] V. Degan, *L'Interprétation des Accords en Droit International* (The Hague: Nijhoff, 1963) 3–15.
[220] Degan, *Sources*, 12, note 20.

the dilemmas of international law: either one tries to identify and live with relatively vague and imprecise custom binding on *all* states, or one attempts to codify and further develop this vague custom into written treaty form which, as a consequence, is likely to become binding only on a limited number of states. This dilemma between treaty and custom is reminiscent also of the divide between civil law and common law. For lawyers with a civil law background (such as Bos and Degan), statutes (hence, in international law, treaties) form the core of a legal system. For common lawyers, on the contrary, the common law (hence, in international law, custom) is more important. For Fitzmaurice[221] and Parry,[222] for example, treaties are only a source of *obligations*, not of *law*, which in time may become genuine international *law*, i.e., general customary international law.

[221] Fitzmaurice, 'Some Problems', 157–60.   [222] Parry, *Sources*, 34 and 42–55.

4 Accumulation and conflict of norms

> Rather than attempt once again to decide what is 'in' or 'out of' the WTO, we should try to mould the rules and their interpretation to structure the *interaction* of the trading regime with other powers and authorities, both domestic and international, in a legitimate manner.[1]

In the previous chapter, the conclusion was reached that a theory on conflict of norms could not be established with reference only to the *sources* of norms. Instead, we focused on the norms themselves, distinguishing general from particular international law norms. In this chapter, we examine the different functions of norms of international law, how these norms may interact (contrasting accumulation versus conflict of norms) and what the outcome of such interaction can be (focusing, in particular, on the processes of 'fall-back' and 'contracting out' of general international law).

The function of norms

Most norms of international law have one of four functions:[2]

(i) They impose an *obligation* on states *to do something*, that is a COMMAND (so-called 'prescriptive norms', 'must do' or 'shall' norms or norms imposing a 'positive' obligation);
(ii) They impose an *obligation* on states *not to do something*, that is a PROHIBITION (so-called 'prohibitive norms', 'must *not* do' or 'shall *not*' norms or norms imposing a 'negative' obligation);

---

[1] Robert Howse, 'From Politics to Technocracy – and Back Again: The Fate of the Multilateral Trading Regime' (part of the Symposium: The Boundaries of the WTO) (2002) 96 AJIL 94 at 112.
[2] See Hans Kelsen, *Théorie Générale des Normes* (Paris: Presses Universitaires de France, 1996), 1.

(iii) They grant a *right* to states *not to do something*, that is an EXEMPTION (so-called 'exempting' norms or 'need not do' norms); or
(iv) They grant a *right* to states *to do something*, that is a PERMISSION (so-called 'permissive norms' or 'may do' norms);

In addition, norms of international law may also

(v) *empower* an organ, institution or individual (other than states, discussed in (i) to (iv) above) with legal capacity under international law;[3] or

(vi) *regulate other norms*,[4] that is, they may address the creation, application, interplay,[5] suspension, termination,[6] breach or enforcement of other norms of international law (although many of these norms also impose, directly or indirectly, certain obligations on states or grant them rights and may hence fall also under norms of types (i) to (iv) above). Since these norms regulate other norms, they can be referred to as 'secondary norms'.[7]

On the basis of norms of types (i) and (ii), that is, those that impose an *obligation* on states, other states (and/or, as the case may be, international bodies or individuals) derive rights. On the basis of norms of types (iii) and (iv), that is, those granting a *right* to states, other states (and/or, as the case may be, international bodies or individuals) derive obligations.

The obligations thus imposed, or the rights thus conferred, upon a state by any of these types of norms may also be imposed or conferred upon *other subjects* of international law, in particular international institutions (including international adjudicators or international bodies not part of an international organisation).[8] As noted earlier, however, this work focuses on states.

---

[3] Such as treaty provisions establishing an international organisation, committee or body and related provisions regulating their functions (e.g., Arts. I–IV of the Marrakesh Agreement and DSU Art. 2.1 providing that '[t]he Dispute Settlement Body is hereby established'). WTO committee decisions appointing a committee chairman also fall under this type of norms.

[4] As most norms in the Vienna Convention and the ILC Draft Articles on State Responsibility do. Norms of type (vi) may also include individual norms though, terminating, for example, one specific other norm or convention (see note 6 below).

[5] Such as the General Interpretative Note to Annex 1A or Art. 30 of the Vienna Convention.

[6] Such as the WTO General Council decisions to terminate the International Dairy Agreement and the International Bovine Meat Agreement.

[7] See chapter 3 above, p. 149 and note 196.

[8] Such as the Meeting of Contracting Parties under GATT 1947 (GATT did not constitute an international organisation) or most of the bodies under multilateral environmental agreements (see Robin Churchill and Geir Ulfstein, 'Autonomous Institutional Arrangements in Multilateral Environmental Agreements: A Little-Noticed Phenomenon in International Law' (2001) 94 AJIL 623).

A norm may be *individual* in that it applies in one predetermined circumstance (such as the building of a dam or the cession of territory) or *general* in that it regulates conduct whenever it occurs (such as the MFN obligation in the WTO treaty).

The *obligation* imposed by a norm may be *unconditional* in that it is automatically activated when certain factual circumstances are present or *conditional* in that it applies only in case a state exercises certain rights. For example, the obligation not to discriminate in GATT Art. III:4 is unconditional (it applies in respect of all internal measures referred to in that provision). The obligation under GATT Art. XX(b) to ensure that the measure is 'necessary' to protect health is conditional in that it applies only in case a WTO member decides to have resort to its right to impose certain trade restrictions for health protection purposes. The flip side of certain obligations being conditional upon the exercise of a right is that *many permissive and exempting norms are also conditional*, that is, the right granted by them can only be relied upon in case certain conditions are met. Most WTO permissions and exemptions, for example (such as GATT Art. XX(b)), grant conditional rights to be invoked only in the event certain requirements are met. In that sense they impose, indirectly, certain obligations. Hence, norms such as GATT Art. XX(b) have a *permissive* component (they grant a right to restrict trade for health reasons, notwithstanding other GATT obligations) as well as a *prescriptive* component (if the right to restrict trade for health reasons is exercised, certain obligations of 'necessity' and non-discrimination must be met). If this *prescriptive* component is not met, the *permissive* component cannot be relied upon and one must fall back on the initial negative obligation not to restrict trade (set out, for example, in GATT Arts. I, III or XI).

In the WTO context, examples of *commands* or positive obligations (that is, norms of type (i) above) are relatively rare. Many of them are included in the TRIPS agreement, such as TRIPS Art. 12 prescribing a term of protection of copyrights of no less than fifty years. Most WTO provisions are, however, *prohibitions*, that is norms imposing negative obligations (of type (ii) above). This is the case, for example, of the GATT's most favoured nation and national treatment provisions which prohibit WTO members, *inter alia*, from discriminating, respectively, between like products of different WTO members and between imported products and like domestic products. The fact that the WTO treaty hence includes mainly prohibitions, and relatively few commands, explains also why it is generally speaking a system of 'negative integration' ('thou shalt not...'), not one of 'positive integration' ('thou shalt...').

Importantly, when we refer here to norms granting a permission or right to states to do something (norms of type (iv) above), we do not include the, what one could call, 'negative permission', that is, 'what is not prohibited in international law is allowed'. This 'negative permission', discussed earlier,[9] is allegedly set out in the PCIJ *Lotus* case. That this right is one of general international law has been criticised. In contrast, the norms of type (iv) defined here are limited to identifiable norms granting a 'positive permission' to states. Type (iv) norms do not cover areas where conduct is left unregulated (absence of norms) and where one could, according to some, fall back on the 'what is not prohibited is allowed' or 'negative permission' principle.

How norms interact

Norms of international law, whatever their function, may interact in two ways. They either (i) accumulate, or (ii) conflict. If two norms do not conflict, they necessarily accumulate (and vice versa). Two norms accumulate when they can be applied together and without contradiction in all circumstances. Two norms conflict when this is not the case (the definition of conflict is further defined below).

Accumulation

Focusing on the norms of types (i) to (iv) set out above – imposing obligations on, or granting rights to, states – a norm may accumulate with other norms in two different ways. It may either

  (i) *add* rights or obligations to already existing rights or obligations (without contradicting any of these rights or obligations) and hence form a complement to other norms ('complementary' relationship); or
  (ii) *confirm* already existing rights or obligations, without either adding to or detracting from these rights or obligations.

Two norms accumulate in the first sense of being 'complementary' when they deal with completely different subject matters (such as DSU Art. 4 on consultations and GATT Art. I on most favoured nation treatment), that is in the absence of overlap *ratione materiae*. Norms are also

---

[9] See chapter 3 above, p. 154.

in a purely 'complementary' relationship when they have no state parties in common, that is, in the absence of overlap *ratione personae* (for example, treaty X concluded by states A and B 'complementing' treaty Y concluded by states C and D).

Norms may also complement each other even though they deal with the same subject matter and have one or more state parties in common. This will be the case if one norm simply adds rights or obligations to those in the other norm without contradiction. This would occur, for example, when one norm regulates trade in goods and another trade in services, both dealing with trade, but one simply adding rights and obligations to the other, without detracting from them. Accumulation would arise also if one norm were to state, for example, that when navigating on the high seas one may not dump oil and another norm adds to this that when navigating on the high seas one must also emit certain signals. The first norm (on trade in goods or oil dumping) does not detract from the second norm (on trade in services or the emission of signals), or vice versa. Implementing or relying on one norm cannot lead to breach of the other. Hence, both norms accumulate and must be complied with at the same time. In that sense, international law is a law of accumulation.

As opposed to 'complementing' each other, two norms may accumulate also by means of one norm simply 'confirming' a pre-existing norm. DSU Art. 3.2, for example, merely 'confirms' pre-existing rules of general international law when stating that WTO covered agreements must be interpreted 'in accordance with customary rules of interpretation of public international law'. Other examples of mere confirmation are GATT 1994 incorporating and hence confirming GATT 1947 and the TRIPS agreement incorporating and hence confirming parts of certain WIPO conventions.

Note also that a norm that explicitly *terminates* another norm, without replacing it by another (i.e., a norm of type (vi) above), accumulates with the norm it is terminating. Both can, indeed, be applied at the same time in all circumstances. More particularly, application of the terminating norm will mean the end of the first norm so that both norms will never apply at the same time and hence cannot ever conflict.

In addition, one norm that sets out a general rule and another norm that *explicitly provides for an exception* to that rule (be it a permission or an exemption) accumulate. An example is GATT Art. XX providing for an exception under, *inter alia*, GATT Art. III (Art. XX explicitly states that 'nothing in this Agreement shall be construed to prevent' Art. XX measures). At first sight there is always an apparent conflict between a rule and an explicit exception to that rule. However, in case the exception explicitly provides that the rule does not apply in the exceptional circumstances, the apparent conflict disappears. Then, pursuant to the principle of 'effective treaty interpretation',[10] the rule must simply be carved out to the extent required to give effect to the exception (the exception can then even be considered as a conditional right, delinked from the general rule).[11] As a result, since both norms have a different scope of application, they can in all circumstances be applied side by side. In each and every circumstance only one of the two norms applies. Hence, they accumulate and no conflict arises.

The same does not apply, however, in case the permission or exemption does *not* explicitly state that it is 'notwithstanding' the general rule or where the general rule does *not* explicitly state that it applies 'except for' situations dealt with under the permission/exemption. These situations do raise conflict and are further discussed below.[12] The general rule is then *not* carved out and continues to apply also in case the permission/exemption applies; the permission/exemption is then not stated as an 'exception' and a genuine conflict between the obligation, on the one hand, and the permission/exemption, on the other, can arise. As discussed below, one way to resolve such conflict is to consider the permission/exemption as *lex specialis* that must prevail over the general rule or *lex generalis*.

Finally, also in case one norm regulates a matter differently from another norm (for example, by imposing different obligations for a safeguard measure to be taken), but *one of the two norms explicitly refers to or incorporates the other norm*, both norms accumulate. In that circumstance, given that the norms refer to or incorporate each other, the different obligations must be applied cumulatively so that both norms accumulate. Only if the obligations under the two norms are mutually exclusive would a conflict arise in these circumstances. Such accumulation occurs, for example, in respect of safeguard measures allowed for under the Safeguards agreement which, in its Arts. 1 and 11.1(a), explicitly refers back to the conditions for imposition of safeguards in GATT Art. XIX, including the requirement of 'unforeseen

---

[10] See chapter 5 below, pp. 247–51.
[11] See the Appellate Body report on *EC – Hormones*, in particular the findings on SPS Art. 3.3.
[12] See chapter 7 below, pp. 396–7.

developments'.¹³ The fact that this condition of 'unforeseen developments' was not explicitly copied in the Safeguards agreement does not mean that it no longer applies. This was confirmed by the Appellate Body in *Korea – Safeguards*¹⁴ and *Argentina – Safeguards*¹⁵ (in both cases reversing the panel which had found that, since the Safeguards agreement itself does not refer to 'unforeseen developments', this condition under GATT Art. XIX no longer applies). In these circumstances, given the explicit reference in Arts. 1 and 11.1(a) to GATT Art. XIX, the obligations in the Safeguards agreement must be accumulated with those in GATT Art. XIX. Only if these obligations had been mutually exclusive would a conflict arise.¹⁶

Conflict

Preconditions for conflict to arise

Before entering the discussion of when exactly two norms can be said to be 'in conflict', we first set out certain preconditions that must be fulfilled for conflict to arise.¹⁷

---

¹³ Art. 1 provides: 'This Agreement establishes rules for the application of safeguard measures which shall be understood to mean *those measures provided for in Article XIX of GATT 1994*' (emphasis added). Art. 11.1(a) states: 'A Member shall not take or seek any emergency action on imports of particular products *as set forth in Article XIX of GATT 1994 unless such action conforms with the provisions of that Article applied in accordance with this Agreement*' (emphasis added).
¹⁴ Appellate Body report on *Korea – Safeguards*, para. 81.
¹⁵ Appellate Body report on *Argentina – Safeguards*, para. 84.
¹⁶ Hence, the fact that WTO members must comply with the obligations under both the Safeguards agreement and GATT Art. XIX does not, as the Appellate Body seemed to imply, so much derive from the fact that 'a treaty interpreter must read all applicable provisions of a treaty [*in casu*, the WTO treaty, including both GATT 1994 and the Safeguards agreement] in a way that gives meaning to *all* of them, harmoniously'. Rather, it derives from the fact that the Safeguards agreement explicitly incorporates also the additional obligation set out in GATT Art. XIX. In case such explicit incorporation had been absent, 'effective treaty interpretation' would not have been able to resolve the matter (see chapter 5 below). In that event, one would, indeed, need to have recognised the existence of a conflict between the different (though not mutually exclusive) obligations in the Safeguards agreement and GATT 1994, one agreement dealing with the exact same factual circumstances differently in such a way that one norm detracts from the other (under GATT the safeguard may be prohibited; while under the Safeguards agreement it may be allowed). Such conflict would then need to be resolved by the conflict clause in the General Interpretative Note to Annex 1A, discussed below, that is, in favour of the obligations in the Safeguards agreement.
¹⁷ This section on conflict owes a lot to stimulating discussions with Lothar Ehring.

Overlap ratione materiae, personae *and* temporis
First, it must be stressed that there can be no conflict if either the subject matter or the parties bound by the two norms are *completely* different. There must at least be some overlap in terms of subject matter and some overlap in terms of state parties. More particularly, *at least one party must be bound by both rules*. As Capotorti noted:

> Pour qu'il y ait interférence entre deux accords, *il faut qu'ils aient au moins un point de contact subjectif et un point de contact objectif*; subjectif, en ce sens qu'un ou plusieurs Etats sont parties à ces deux accords; objectif, en ce sens qu'une même matière ou des matières connexes sont réglées, dans les deux accords, par une ou plusieurs dispositions.[18]

To these requirements of overlap *ratione personae* and *ratione materiae*, one must add the need for overlap *ratione temporis*: only if two norms exist or interact *at one point in time* can there be conflict. Such interaction may continue over a long period of time, when it leads only to one norm being disapplied in favour of the other (as in 'conflicts in the applicable law', discussed in chapter 7). The interaction may also be short-lived in that it leads instantaneously to the invalidity or termination of one of the two norms (as in certain 'inherent normative conflicts', discussed in chapter 6). However, when two norms apply at completely *different* points in time, there can be no conflict. In such cases, the question may arise as to which of several norms prevailing at *different* moments in time should apply to a particular case. This is the problem of the so-called 'intertemporal law'. Although, in this situation, the two norms in question may be contradictory or deal with the same issue in different ways, they do not conflict since both norms have a different scope *ratione temporis*. Some elements of the inter-temporal law are further addressed below in chapter 5 (pp. 264–8).

Conflict arises for one state in its relationship with another state
Second, one must approach conflict *from the perspective of a given state* (or, as the case may be, a given international body, such as a WTO panel or a WTO committee on which conflicting obligations may be imposed, such as the issuance of reports within different time limits). This state (or body) must necessarily be *bound by both rules*. If it is bound only by one of the two rules, there can be no conflict, at least not from the

---

[18] F. Capotorti, 'Interférences dans l'Ordre Juridique Interne entre la Convention et d'autres Accords Internationaux', in *Les Droits de L'Homme en Droit Interne et en Droit International* (Brussels, 1968), 123 (emphasis added).

perspective of that particular state or body (which could then rely on the *pacta tertiis* principle).

In addition, one must assess conflict in terms of a legal relationship of that given state (or body) *with a given other state*. As further explained below, this second state must not necessarily be bound by both rules. This second state may, indeed, be bound by both rules or by only one of them (as in the case of what we refer to as AB/AC conflicts, A being a state with conflicting obligations vis-à-vis B and C; B and C being bound only by one of the two conflicting rules: see chapter 7 below).

All conflicts, not just conflicts in the 'strict' or 'technical' sense

Once it has been established that the above-mentioned preconditions are fulfilled, the question arises as to how to identify a 'conflict of norms'.

Conflict as defined in doctrinal writings
The definition of when two norms of international law are in 'conflict' has, surprisingly, attracted little attention. Most authors writing on the topic of interplay or hierarchy of norms do not even provide a definition.[19] In respect of these authors, one can only guess at what they consider to be norms in 'conflict' by looking at the examples they cite. Doing so leads to a rather broad view of conflict.[20] Other authors do give

---

[19] See, for example, Michael Akehurst, 'The Hierarchy of the Sources of International Law' (1974–5) 47 BYIL 273; V. Degan, *Sources of International Law* (The Hague: Nijhoff, 1997); and Nguyen Quoc Dinh, 'Evolution de la Jurisprudence de la Cour Internationale de La Haye Relative au Problème de la Hiérarchie des Normes Conventionnelles', in *Mélanges Offerts à Marcel Waline, Le Juge et le Droit Public* (Paris: Librairie générale de droit et de jurisprudence, 1974, 2 vols.) I, 215.

[20] Akehurst, 'Hierarchy', 279, for example, cites the interplay between the customary law principle of liberty of state action (allegedly based on *Lotus*) and the general principle of law imposing a duty to pay moratory interest on debt as a question of hierarchy and hence, presumably, conflict of norms. This goes much further than the strict definition of Jenks and Karl as well as the wider definition suggested here (only an obligation as opposed to an explicit right, not the fall-back 'negative permission' referred to by some as 'what is not prohibited is allowed', can, in my view, constitute conflict). Vierdag refers to a conflict between, on the one hand, Art. 19(2) of the UN Covenant on Civil and Political Rights of 1966 granting 'to everyone *inter alia* the freedom to impart information of all kinds, regardless of frontiers, through any media of his choice' and, on the other hand, Art. 428A of the International Radio Regulations of 1971, prescribing that 'television broadcasting through a direct broadcasting satellite licensed by a State, which can also be received in the territory of neighbouring States, shall be subject to previous agreements of the licensing State with these neighbouring States' (E. W. Vierdag, 'The Time of the "Conclusion" of a Multilateral Treaty' (1989) 60 BYIL 75 at 98 ff.). Here, we have a clear-cut case of an

a definition. Some give a very vague or general one. Others, in contrast, give a very strict or technical definition of 'conflict'.

Jenks, it seems, was the first to adopt the strict or technical approach to conflict in international law. In 1953 he expressed the view that '[a] conflict *in the strict sense of direct incompatibility* arises only where a party to the two treaties cannot simultaneously comply with its obligations under both treaties'.[21] Karl (writing in 1984) remarked that '*[t]echnically speaking*, there is a conflict between treaties when two (or more) treaty instruments contain obligations which cannot be complied with simultaneously'.[22] Kelsen,[23] Klein[24] and, much later, Wilting[25] adopted a similarly strict definition of 'conflict', covering only mutually exclusive obligations.

Other authors provide a broader definition of conflict. Rousseau (1932) refers generally to 'la compatibilité des normes', 'rapports juridiques...

explicit right (freedom under Art. 19(2)) conflicting with a positive obligation (requirement of prior consent under Art. 428A). This is the conflict situation 3 we discuss below, a situation that would not be accepted as one of conflict by authors such as Jenks and Karl.

[21] Wilfred Jenks, 'Conflict of Law-Making Treaties' (1953) 30 BYIL 401 at 426 (emphasis added); and *ibid.* at 451: 'A conflict of law-making treaties arises only where simultaneous compliance with the obligations of different instruments is impossible.'

[22] Wolfram Karl, 'Conflicts Between Treaties', in R. Bernhardt (ed.), *Encyclopedia of Public International Law* (Amsterdam: North-Holland, 1984), VII, 468.

[23] Kelsen, *Théorie Générale*, 161: 'Un conflit entre deux normes existe quand ce que l'une pose comme obligatoire est incompatible avec ce que l'autre pose comme obligatoire, et quand l'obéissance ou l'application de l'une des deux normes implique de façon *nécessaire* ou *possible* la violation de l'autre.' In Hans Kelsen, *Théorie Pure du Droit* (translation H. Thevenaz) (Neuchâtel: Editions de la Baconnière, 1988), 144, a somewhat wider definition (not centred around the notion of obligation) was provided: 'Quand on est en présence de deux normes simultanément valables, mais contradictoires, celui qui doit les appliquer (organe de l'Etat ou sujet de droit) ne peut se conformer à l'une sans violer l'autre.'

[24] Friedrich Klein, 'Vertragskonkurrenz', in Karl Strupp and H.-J. Schlochauer (eds.), *Wörterbuch des Völkerrechts* (Berlin: De Gruyter, 1962), 555: 'Das Rechtsproblem der Vertragskonkurrenz ist also dasjenige der Vereinbarkeit oder Unvereinbarkeit verschiedener Bestimmungen in Bezug auf denselben Sachverhalt in zwei oder mehreren völkerrechtlichen Verträgen. Praktisch bedeutsam sind nur diejenigen Vertragskonkurrenzen, in denen sich die Vertragsbestimmungen, insbesondere die Vertragsverpflichtungen, in zwei oder mehreren völkerrechtlichen Verträgen formal unauflösbar widersprechen (Kollisions- oder Konflikts-Vertragskonkurrenz).'

[25] Wilting makes a distinction between 'Konkurrenzsituation', 'Kollisionssituation' and 'Konflikt'. A 'Kollisionssituation' arises only when, as between two norms 'die Rechtsfolgen nicht miteinander vereinbar sind, und zwar derart, dass eine gleichzeitige Anwendung der konkurrierenden Normen ausscheidet'. 'Konflikt', in his view, arises only when two norms do, in actual fact, lead to mutual exclusiveness (Wilhelm Wilting, *Vertragskonkurrenz im Völkerrecht* (Cologne: Heymanns, 1996) 2, at 4).

antinomiques' or one treaty 'contredisant' another treaty.[26] Hersch Lauterpacht, writing in 1937, also seems to hold a rather broad view, defining the word 'inconsistency' as it was used in Art. 20 of the Covenant of the League of Nations as meaning 'not only patent inconsistency appearing on the face of the treaty...but also what may be called potential or latent inconsistency...[such treaties] may become inconsistent and therefore abrogated, as soon as it becomes clear that their continued validity or operation is incompatible with the negative or positive obligations of the Covenant'.[27] In 1952, Aufricht stated that '[a] conflict between an earlier and a later treaty arises if both deal with the same subject matter in a different manner'.[28] In 1965, Perelman (not limiting conflict to obligations) defined 'antinomie' as 'l'impossibilité d'appliquer simultanément, telles qu'elles sont énoncées, deux normes de droit positif qui sont assez précises pour être applicables en elles-mêmes et qui ne sont pas subordonnées l'une à l'autre par une disposition juridique impérative'.[29] Importantly, Sir Humphrey Waldock in the preparation of Art. 30 of the Vienna Convention also held a broad view of conflict, noting that '[t]he idea conveyed by that term [conflict] was that of a comparison between two treaties which revealed that their clauses, or some of them, could not be reconciled with one another'.[30] Capotorti focuses on 'incompatibilité' between norms, distinguishing between 'conflit entre clauses obligatoires' and 'divergences'.[31] More recently, Czaplinski and

---

[26] Charles Rousseau, 'De la Compatibilité des Normes Juridiques Contradictoires dans l'Ordre International' (1932) 39 RGDIP 133 at 135. In the same sense, see J.-A. Salmon, 'Les Antinomies en Droit International Public,' in Chaim Perelman (ed.), *Les Antinomies en Droit* (Brussels, Bruylant, 1965), 285: 'Par "antinomies" nous entendons l'existence, dans un système déterminé, de règles de droit incompatibles; de telle sorte que l'interprète ne peut appliquer les deux règles en même temps, qu'il doit choisir.'
[27] Hersch Lauterpacht, 'The Covenant as the "Higher Law"' (1936) 17 BYIL 54 at 58.
[28] Hans Aufricht, 'Supersession of Treaties in International Law' (1952) *Cornell Law Quarterly* 655 at 655–6.
[29] Chaim Perelman, 'Les Antinomies en Droit, Essai de Synthèse', in Perelman *Antinomies*, 392 at 399.
[30] YBILC 1964, vol. 1, p. 125.
[31] Capotorti's starting point is 'interférences' between norms. This notion includes, in his view, three possibilities: (1) 'conflit entre clauses obligatoires' (i.e., 'des engagements rigoureusement incompatibles, le respect de l'un comportant la violation de l'autre'); (2) 'divergences' ('si celles-ci sont totales, on se trouve ramené au cas de l'incompatibilité et, si elles ne sont que partielles, elles laissent une marge plus ou moins grande de compatibilité'); and (3) norms that are 'complémentaires' ('les cas où un accord a pour but d'en compléter un autre ou bien prévoit un comportement ou une situation entraînant l'application d'un autre accord') (Capotorti, 'Interférences', 123–4.

Danilenko also opted for a wider perspective on conflict,[32] an approach followed in 2001 by Neumann[33] and Kelly.[34]

The approach adopted in this study
In this work we shall approach the notion of 'conflict' in the most open and non-dogmatic way. Like most authors, we use the term 'conflict' of norms interchangeably with 'inconsistent', 'incompatible' or 'contradictory' norms (that is, as opposed to norms that complement or confirm each other). We do so even though some jurists have seen a difference between the notions of incompatibility (or inconsistency), on the one hand, and conflict, on the other.[35] We plan, moreover, to distinguish

---

[32] They state that 'conflicts arise at the stage of application of the agreements when the later treaty in a particular situation violates the rights of any other party to the earlier treaty, or when the provision of the later treaty seriously infringes provisions of the earlier treaty which are indispensable for the effective implementation of the object or aim of that treaty' (W. Czaplinski and G. Danilenko, 'Conflict of Norms in International Law' (1990) 21 NYIL 3 at 13). See also Fastenrath, defining 'Kollisionslücken' as situations where 'zwei oder mehr Rechtssätze für einen Sachverhalt miteinander nicht vereinbare Rechtfolgen anordnen' (Ulrich Fastenrath, *Lücken im Völkerrecht: zu Rechtscharakter, Quellen, Systemzusammenhang, Methodenlehre und Funktionen des Völkerrechts* (Berlin: Duncker & Humblot, 1991), 227). Or as Villiger noted in respect of a treaty in conflict with a later custom: 'the test will lie therein that the two rules cannot be applied simultaneously, and the gap cannot be bridged by a mode of interpretation or ascertainment which seeks to conform the customary to the conventional rule' (Mark Villiger, *Customary International Law and Treaties, A Manual on the Theory and Practice of the Interrelation of Sources* (The Hague: Kluwer, 1997), para. 322).
[33] Jan Neumann, 'Die Koordination des WTO-Rechts mit anderen völkerrechtlichen Ordnungen – Konflikte des materiellen Rechts und Konkurrenzen der Streitbeilegung', unpublished doctoral thesis (Münster, 2001), 16 ('ein Widerspruch [besteht] nicht nur, wenn ein *Gebot* mit einem Verbot kollidiert, wenn also nach einer Norm eine Handlung erfolgen *muß*, die eine andere Norm verbietet, sondern auch, wenn eine *Erlaubnis* mit einem Verbot kollidiert, also das Verbot die Inanspruchnahme einer *Möglichkeit* in Frage stellt'); referring, in support, to Theodor Schilling, *Rang und Geltung von Normen in gestuften Rechtsordnungen* (Berlin: Nomos, 1994), 380.
[34] Claire Kelly, 'The Value Vacuum: Self-enforcing Regimes and the Dilution of the Normative Feedback Loop' (2001) 23 *Michigan Journal of International Law* 673 at 699 ('Direct conflicts may arise as a result of conflicting directives on behavior', using the example of a conflict between a CITES prohibition on trade and a WTO right to trade).
[35] In the preparation of Art. 30 of the Vienna Convention, for example, the earlier drafts referred to 'conflict' (Second Report on the Law of Treaties by Sir Humphrey Waldock, Special Rapporteur, YBILC 1963, vol. 2, 36–94 (Doc. A/CN.4/156 and Add. 1–3) (Waldock Report II), Art. 14, entitled 'Conflict with a prior treaty'; and Third Report, YBILC 1964, vol. 2, 5–65 (Doc. A/CN.4/156 and Add. 1–3) (Waldock Report III), entitled 'Priority of conflicting treaty provisions' in Dietrich Rauschning, *The Vienna Convention on the Law of Treaties, Travaux Préparatoires* (Frankfurt: Metzner, 1978), 228). As of the ILC Draft 1964, however, the word 'conflict' was dropped and replaced by 'incompatibility' (*ibid.*, 229). This change was prompted by Roberto Ago. At the 742nd Meeting of the ILC (10 June

clearly between the *definition* of conflict and *how to solve* an alleged conflict. Our focus will be on the latter. Hence, we do not want to prejudice the question of *how to resolve* an alleged conflict by opting for one or the other technical *definition* of conflict.

This approach leads us to reject the narrow definition of conflict advocated, in particular, by Jenks, who limits the situation of conflict between norms to two norms imposing *mutually exclusive obligations*. It may happen that in a certain treaty context 'conflict' must be so defined, based on an explicit treaty provision, but to define it that strictly, generically and in isolation, is unwarranted.

Indeed, by refusing to recognise certain situations as conflicts – such as a contradiction between a *prohibition* to do X and a *permission* to do X – Jenks' strict definition of conflict indirectly *resolves* a number of contradictions in favour of the strictest norm, *in casu*, in favour of the *prohibition* to do X, since not invoking the right to do X under the permissive norm

1964), Ago (as chairman) is reported to have said that: 'he doubted whether it was advisable to use the term "conflict" [in Art. 65, now Art. 30]. In article 41 the Commission had referred to "a further treaty relating to the same subject-matter". Article 65 was concerned, *inter alia*, with the case in which all the parties to a treaty decided to conclude a new treaty to regulate the same matter in a different way. Whether the second treaty replaced the first entirely or only in part, it was not correct in that case to speak of a "conflict" between the two treaties' (YBILC 1964, vol. 1, p. 125). In response, Sir Humphrey Waldock (the special rapporteur who had selected the word 'conflict') noted that 'in his opinion, it was appropriate to use the term "conflict"; which was used in Article 103 of the Charter. The idea conveyed by that term was that of a comparison between two treaties which revealed that their clauses, or some of them, could not be reconciled with one another. The process of determining whether a conflict existed presupposed an element of interpretation. He did not believe that the fact that the parties to the two treaties might be the same made it inelegant to speak of a conflict; the point would be of interest only if the parties were in dispute as to the compatibility of the two treaties' (*ibid.*, 125). Ago, however, 'still believed that there could be no "conflict" between two successive treaties concluded by the same parties. Either the second treaty prevailed entirely over the first, or the provisions of the first treaty which were not replaced by those of the second remained in force' (*ibid.*). Waldock (subsequently supported by Yasseen) replied, in turn, that 'the problem with which article 65 attempted to deal was different. Even where the parties to the two treaties were the same, the case was not one of a desire to replace one treaty by another, but of a dispute in which one party claimed that the two treaties were incompatible' (*ibid.*). It was, finally, Amado who came up with a compromise. In support of Ago, he pointed out that in his view 'the word "conflict" suggested contemporary things and was less appropriate when applied to successive ones'. He then suggested that the terms 'compatible' and 'incompatibility' were used. 'Incompatible' and 'compatible' are also the terms that can now be found in, respectively, Arts. 30(2) and 30(3) of the Vienna Convention.

will avoid breaching the prohibition to do X in the prohibitive norm. In those situations, the alleged conflict is then not solved by a rule on *how to solve* conflict but by the *very definition* of conflict. And this is exactly what we want to avoid. Although it may well be that, in such a situation, the strictest norm (that is, the prohibition) prevails, this will not necessarily be so in all cases (the permission may, for example, be later in time or more specific).

Jenks himself acknowledged, for example, that

[a] difference which does not constitute a conflict [in the strict sense] may nevertheless defeat the object of one or both of the divergent instruments. Such a divergence may, for instance, prevent a party to both of the divergent instruments from taking advantage of certain provisions of one of them recourse to which would involve a violation of, or failure to comply with, certain requirements of the other. A divergence of this kind may in some cases, from a practical point of view, be as serious as a conflict.

However, Jenks does *not* propose solutions for how to solve such 'divergence'. For Jenks, they are not conflicts 'in the strict sense', hence they fall outside the (artificial and self-made) scope of 'conflict of norms'.

Carving out certain situations as not being conflicts 'in the strict sense' or 'technically speaking' (as Jenks and other authors do) is focusing on one type of conflict only, thereby ignoring the complexity of the potential forms of interplay between norms. Doing so, one essentially solves part of the problem by ignoring it.

That 'rights' under international norms (be they permissions or exemptions) are as important as 'obligations' finds confirmation also in the drafting history of Art. 30 of the Vienna Convention.[36] Art. 63(1) (now Art. 30(1)) of the ILC Draft 1964 referred to obligations only ('the obligations of States parties to treaties the provisions of which are incompatible, shall be determined in accordance with the following paragraphs').[37] Following a comment by Israel ('reference should be made to the rights as well as the obligations of States'),[38] Art. 26(1) (now Art. 30(1)) of the ILC Final Draft was changed to its current wording ('the *rights and obligations* of States parties to successive treaties relating to the same subject-matter shall be determined in accordance with the following

---

[36] For confirmation in statements made before the ICJ (in the *Lockerbie* case) that states regard a contradiction between rights and obligations as a situation of conflict, see chapter 7 below, pp. 340–2.
[37] Rauschning, *Travaux*, 229.   [38] *Ibid.*

paragraphs').³⁹ Art. 30(4)(b) also makes explicit reference to obligations *and rights*.

Why did some authors adopt a 'strict' or 'technical' definition of conflict?
But how then does one explain the strict approach to conflict, adhered to by a number of eminent authors?

Conflict is seen as an anomaly First, it seems that, for the authors defending a strict definition of conflict, conflict of norms in a legal system implies an imperfection or shortcoming of that system. For these authors, conflict has, in other words, a negative ring to it and must be avoided. Hence, it should be defined strictly and cover situations only where the legal system does not offer clear solutions to the apparent contradiction. Hans Kelsen, in his original writings, went even further and posited that a legal system *cannot* have conflict of norms. In his view, any legal system is founded on one *Grundnorm* which explains and justifies all other norms. For this *Grundnorm* to be the genuine foundation of the legal system, it cannot simultaneously accord validity to two norms which are contradictory without threatening the unity of the legal system.⁴⁰

However, by thus closing one's eyes to conflict and recognising conflict only when it cannot be resolved, one confuses the *definition* of conflict

---

³⁹ *Ibid.*, 231. Waldock, in his observations and proposals following governments' comments on the 1964 ILC Draft, noted the following in this respect: 'In paragraph 1, the Government of Israel's suggestion that mention should be made of rights as well as of obligations appears to be well founded, even although the emphasis on the article may be primarily on obligations' (*ibid.*, 230).

⁴⁰ Kelsen, *Théorie Pure*, 146. Kelsen subsequently changed his mind and acknowledged the existence of conflict of norms in a legal system. He did so because a conflict of norms is a conflict of will or intent, not a logical contradiction where only one of the propositions can be valid: 'les normes sont créées par des actes de volonté et... expriment le sense de tels actes. Ce ne sont donc pas des actes de connaissance du genre de ceux auxquels la logique s'applique... quand la science du droit se trouve en présence de deux normes contradictoires, elle peut seulement formuler deux propositions constatant que chacune de ces normes est une norme valable, il n'y a pas de contradiction logique entre elles, car une contradiction [logique] ne peut apparaître que dans le cas où une proposition étant vraie, l'autre est nécessairement fausse' (*ibid.*, 147). Indeed, a conflict of norms takes the form, for example, of state A being obliged to do and not to do X at the same time (as a result of different expressions of intent in two different norms), but state A can, in principle, do or not do X. In contrast, a logical contradiction takes the form of, for example, saying that the door is open and the same door is closed. Here, only one of the two can be correct.

with the tools available to *resolve* conflict.⁴¹ One conflict may, indeed, be solved much easier than another (for example, when an explicit conflict clause has been inserted). And, in contrast, there may be conflicts where it is impossible for a judge to decide in favour of one or the other norm (that is, conflicts which constitute a lacuna in the law). But these are different *types* of conflict, not situations where there is no conflict as opposed to situations where there is conflict.

The great majority of conflicts of norms have nothing abnormal or anomalous to them, that is, the legal system can cope with them. However, the fact that a conflict is readily solved does not mean that there is no conflict. In the event one treaty explicitly states that in case of conflict, another, earlier, treaty prevails, the solution to conflict is obvious: the earlier treaty prevails. But this easy *solution* to conflict does not mean that there *is* no conflict. In such cases, determining conflict will, indeed, be crucial to deciding exactly when and to what extent the earlier treaty prevails. The same applies in respect of the *lex posterior* rule in Art. 30(3) of the Vienna Convention: 'the earlier treaty applies only to the extent that its provisions are compatible with those of the later treaty'. Here as well the *solution* to any conflict or contradiction is clear: the later treaty prevails. But this does not do away with the problem of conflict, in particular, the problem of defining exactly when, and to what extent, one provision is not 'compatible' with another. The same can be said in respect of Arts. 53 and 64 of the Vienna Convention, giving an unambiguous preference to rules of *jus cogens* in the event a treaty 'conflicts' (Art. 53), or 'is in conflict with' (Art. 64) *jus cogens*.⁴²

In all these cases – that is, in situations where an explicit conflict clause in favour of the earlier treaty, the *lex posterior* rule in Art. 30 or *jus cogens* under Arts. 53/64 are at stake – to use Jenks' strict definition of 'conflict' would lead to absurd situations. Under this definition, a prohibition to do X, as opposed to a permission to do X, would not

---

⁴¹ As illustrated above, in note 35, Ago seems to make the same mistake. He refused to see a later treaty aimed at overruling an earlier one as two treaties 'in conflict', on the ground that it should clearly be the later treaty that prevails. In that situation the solution to the conflict may, indeed, be obvious (the later treaty prevails). And if the later treaty explicitly terminates the earlier one, there is, indeed, no conflict. But if the fact that the later treaty prevails is to be derived from the implicit intention to overrule the earlier treaty or the *lex posterior* rule in Art. 30, conflict must be acknowledged before one can solve it. The extent of the conflict will, indeed, determine the extent to which both the earlier and the later treaty applies.

⁴² Note, indeed, that here the word 'conflict' is used, in contrast to Art. 30 where the term 'incompatible' was chosen (see note 35 above).

constitute 'conflict' (since there is then a way to avoid breach under both norms by simply adhering to the prohibition and not invoking the permission). Hence, under Art. 30, for example, an earlier treaty imposing the prohibition would in all instances prevail over a later treaty granting the permission (both treaties are, in Jenks' view, not 'incompatible', hence there is no conflict and Art. 30 is not activated so that the earlier treaty continues to apply). But it may have been the very intention of the later treaty to detract from the earlier prohibition and to overrule that prohibition in certain circumstances by granting an explicit permission. Under Jenks' strict definition of conflict, granting such explicit right could then only be effective if the later treaty setting out the right explicitly states that it terminates or derogates from the earlier treaty.

Equally, under Arts. 53 and 64 of the Vienna Convention dealing with *jus cogens*, imagine a treaty between two states in which they grant each other permission to trade in slaves and impose certain regulations in respect of the slave trade (without *obliging* each other to trade in slaves). Under Jenks' strict definition of conflict, there would not be a conflict between this treaty and the *jus cogens* prohibition of trading in slaves. The states party to the treaty are not *obliged* to engage in the slave trade. Hence, there are no mutually exclusive obligations and not to exercise the permission under the treaty would, in Jenks' view, solve the apparent conflict. In other words, only if a treaty *obliges* the trade in slaves would there, according to Jenks, be a conflict and only then would the treaty be invalid under Arts. 53 and 64.

Conflict in domestic law Second, the authors adhering to a 'strict' or 'technical' definition of conflict seem to be influenced also by domestic law, where for individuals subject to national legislation (i) a prescription (or command) and prohibition imposed by the state prevail over individual freedom, and (ii) prohibitions prevail, at least according to some authors, over prescriptions (or commands). De Vattel embodies the clearest example of this transposition of domestic law principles into international law. He offered the following three conflict rules: 'Dans tout les cas où ce qui est seulement *permis* se trouve incompatible avec ce qui est *prescrit*; ce dernier l'emporte...de même, la Loi, ou le Traité qui *permet*, doit céder à la Loi, ou au Traité qui *défend*...Toutes choses d'ailleurs égales, la Loi ou le Traité qui *ordonne* cède à la Loi, ou au Traité qui *défend*.'[43]

---

[43] Emer De Vattel, *Le Droit des Gens ou Principes de la Loi Naturelle* (Lyons: Gauthier, 1802), book II, chapter XVII, paras. 312–13. See also Hugo Grotius, *Le Droit de la Guerre et de la*

Note, first of all, that de Vattel recognised all of these situations – some of which involve only rights or permissions, not obligations – as conflict situations. In that sense, he does *not* adhere to Jenks' strict definition of conflict, limited to mutually exclusive *obligations*. Nonetheless, to transpose de Vattel's solutions allegedly offered in domestic law to international law would be unsound. In many cases, the prohibition or prescription will prevail over the permission or exemption, but this is not necessarily so in all cases. Whereas, in domestic law, an individual cannot contract out of prohibitions or prescriptions by exercising his or her contractual freedom in favour of certain permissions or exemptions, in international law, states do have this power and can, with the consent of other states, detract from previous obligations by means of granting each other certain rights in the form of explicit permissions or exemptions. Equally, a negative obligation (prohibition) may prevail over a positive one (command), but this is not guaranteed. In international law, all of these situations must be recognised as conflicts. Their resolution will not so much depend on the prescriptive, prohibitive or permissive nature of the norm, but on other factors such as timing and material scope.[44]

In sum, it may be so that 'mutually exclusive obligations' are a particularly grave situation of conflict (that is, conflict in the 'strict' or 'technical' sense). But it is not the only one. To submit differently inevitably leads to predetermined solutions to conflict before one has even identified the conflict.

Having rejected Jenks' strict definition of conflict, we next attempt to provide a more accurate and neutral definition of conflict.

An appropriate definition of conflict

Notwithstanding the varying definitions of conflict set out earlier, adopted by different authors, it is difficult to find reasons why a conflict or inconsistency of one norm *with another norm* ought to be defined differently from a conflict or inconsistency of one norm *with other types of state conduct* (e.g., wrongful conduct not in the form of another norm). *Essentially, two norms are, therefore, in a relationship of conflict if one*

Paix (D. Alland and S. Goyard-Fabre, eds.) (Paris: Presses Universitaires de France, 1999), 413: 'Que ce qui permet cède à ce qui ordonne.'

[44] De Vattel himself recognised as an exception to his earlier three principles the fact that 'Si le conflit se trouve entre...deux Traités affirmatifs aussi conclus entre les mêmes...Etats; le dernier en date l'emporte sur le plus ancien' (de Vattel, *Droit des Gens*, para. 315).

constitutes, has led to, or may lead to, a breach of the other.[45] Such conflict or potential for breach is, however, not real when the relationship between two seemingly contradictory norms is explicitly regulated in the form of a rule–exception relationship. Then the rule must simply be carved out to the extent required to give effect to the exception so that one norm cannot constitute or lead to breach of the other and both norms accumulate (see above, pp. 162–3).

The suggested approach of equating conflict to breach may sound like a truism, but it moves the debate on 'what is conflict' from the abstract relationship between two norms of international law to the more concrete and common question of 'when is there a breach of a given norm?'. Another advantage of approaching conflict in terms of breach is that conflict thereby becomes an 'objective' question, based on the rights and obligations set out in the norms in question, to be determined by normal rules on, for example, treaty interpretation. The existence of conflict does not turn, then, on a question of contradictory subjective 'intentions' held by one or the other state.

Further specifying this definition of conflict, one norm of international law (as opposed to other state conduct) may breach another norm either

(i) *in and of itself*, by its mere conclusion or emergence. Examples would be a multilateral treaty explicitly prohibiting the conclusion of certain *inter se* agreements or a norm in breach of *jus cogens* (see chapter 6). Here, one norm constitutes an inherent breach of the other. We shall refer to this situation as *inherent conflict*; or

(ii) by granting certain rights or imposing certain obligations which, *once exercised or complied with*, will constitute a breach of the other norm. Here, one norm will, or may, lead to a breach of the other. In some cases, such breach will occur *necessarily*, whenever either of the two norms is complied with as required (as in cases of mutually exclusive obligations). We shall refer to this situation as *necessary conflict*. In other instances, there is a margin of discretion and only if a state actually decides to exercise a right (permission or exemption) will the breach materialise. We shall refer to this situation as *potential conflict*.

Whatever the nature of the conflict – inherent, necessary or potential – it should be recognised that all of these instances do raise questions of conflict. No situation should be excluded *a priori* from the field of conflict of norms. Otherwise one risks solving a conflict by not realising that there is one.

---

[45] The word 'breach' is used here interchangeably with 'violation', 'incompatibility' or 'inconsistency'.

The situation under point (ii) is the more common one since norms of international law rarely prohibit the conclusion or emergence of other *norms*, they rather prohibit other *state conduct*. Under point (ii), the question is essentially: if there are two norms, does the exercise of rights or compliance with obligations under one of these norms breach an obligation under the other norm?

Most conflicts that arise before an international tribunal are of type (ii) set out above, that is, they result from the *exercise or implementation* of one norm which is, allegedly, in breach of another norm.[46] Such conflict results then *from the application* by state A of a norm which, according to state B, breaches another norm. To put it differently, state B will sue state A for breach of norm 1 whereas state A will invoke norm 2 in defence of the alleged breach. This raises the question of *necessary or potential conflict* of norms. In chapter 7 below, when we attempt to resolve such conflicts, we refer to them as *conflicts in the applicable law*.

An international tribunal may also be faced with *inherent conflicts*, that is, situations where one norm is alleged to constitute, in and of itself, breach of another norm. In chapter 6 below, when we attempt to resolve such conflicts, we refer to them as *inherent normative conflict*. Inherent conflicts may arise in the abstract, that is, without there being a question of any state conduct other than the two conflicting norms,[47] or in a more concrete dispute on the legality of certain state behaviour (in which case the defendant could claim, for example, that the norm which it has allegedly breached is an 'illegal' one under another norm).[48]

Conflict of norms

Inherent normative conflict	Conflict in the applicable law
Conflict depends solely on the conditions for breach of the particular norm in question	(i) Necessary conflicts (ii) Potential conflicts

---

[46] As Sir Gerald Fitzmaurice noted: 'The whole question of what inconsistency between two treaties means is a difficult one. Two treaties may be inconsistent in the sense that they set up mutually discordant systems, but so long as these do not have to be applied to or between the same parties, it may be quite possible to apply both...In short, there may be a conflict between the treaties concerned, without this necessarily resulting in any conflict of *obligation* for any of these parties' (YBILC 1958, vol. 2, pp. 20 ff., 44).

[47] As in ICJ advisory procedures or under Art. 66 of the Vienna Convention (conflict with *jus cogens*).

[48] See chapter 6 below.

Below, we shall use one further distinction, namely that between 'apparent conflicts' and 'genuine conflicts' (a terminology that we have used already in previous chapters). An apparent conflict is then a situation where there is no real conflict since the divergence can, for example, be 'interpreted away'. A genuine conflict will then arise only in case all of the conflict-avoidance techniques set out in chapter 5 have proven to be unsuccessful.

Finally, it should be stressed, once again, that the wider *definition* of conflict suggested here does not, and should not, prejudice in any way how conflicts are *to be resolved*. In some cases it will, indeed, be the (stricter) obligation that prevails (the standard result under Jenks' and Karl's very *definition* of conflict), but, as we shall see below, this is not necessarily the case. In any event, if the (stricter) obligation does prevail, it is not because of the definition of conflict but because of the will or intention of the parties, expressed either explicitly or implicitly, in conflict rules.

'Inherent normative conflict' and the four conflict situations in case of 'conflict in the applicable law'

When faced with an inherent normative conflict, that is, an allegation that one norm constitutes, in and of itself, a breach of another norm, the definition of conflict and the question as to whether there is, indeed, genuine conflict depends exclusively on the requirements set out in the first norm. The content of the primary obligation in the first norm determines whether there is breach. If there is breach, there is normative conflict.

In respect of conflicts in the applicable law the situation is different and more complex. Here we are faced with an allegation that there is conflict of norms because compliance or invocation of one norm has led, or would lead, to breach of the other norm. Focusing on the four main functions of norms in international law (command, prohibition, exemption and permission), a conflict in the applicable law *from the perspective of state A in its legal relationship with state B* may then take one of the following four forms:

A norm granting a certain right, that is, allowing a state to do, or not to do, something (a permission or an exemption) cannot be breached. Hence no conflict can arise in case norm 1 (the norm allegedly breached) is an exemption or a permission. Conflict can arise only in case norm 1 is either a command or a prohibition.

The four situations of conflict

Conflict situation	Norm 1 (Obligation of state A vis-à-vis state B)	Norm 2 (Compliance with obligation, or exercise of right, by state A constituting a breach of Norm 1 vis-à-vis state B)
1	*Command*: in a given situation state A **'shall do'** X	*Command*: in the same situation state A **'shall do'** Y (Y being either *different from* or *mutually exclusive with* X)
2	*Command*: in a given situation state A **'shall do'** X	*Prohibition*: in the same situation state A **'shall not do'** X
3	*Command*: in a given situation state A **'shall do'** X	*Right (exemption)*: in the same situation state A **'need not do'** X (it may, for example, do Y)
4	*Prohibition*: in a given situation state A **'shall not do'** X	*Right (permission)*: in the same situation state A **'may do'** X

The four situations of conflict

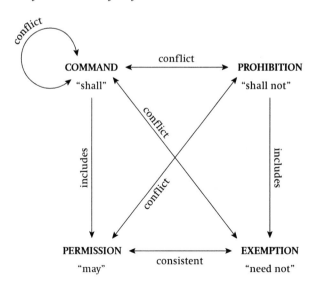

With one notable exception,[49] conflict situations 1 and 2 constitute what we referred to earlier as *necessary conflicts*, that is, whenever one norm is complied with as required, a breach or conflict with the other norm will necessarily arise. Conflict situations 3 and 4 constitute what we denominated *potential conflicts*. Here, a breach or conflict will emerge only in case the exemption or permission under norm 2 is actually exercised.

On that basis, all possible situations of conflict of norms can also be illustrated:

Let us give some examples under each of the four conflict situations sketched above: first, some drawn from the WTO context; second, some hypothetical examples illustrating the situation in more practical terms.

Conflict situation 1: *conflicting commands*
Conflicting positive obligations or commands may take the form of either

(i) two commands, covering the very same factual circumstances, that are 'merely different' but which may both be complied with at the same time ('conflicting commands that are *merely different*'); or
(ii) two commands that are mutually exclusive, that is, which cannot possibly be complied with at the same time ('conflicting commands that are *mutually exclusive*').

Conflicting commands that are merely different (but cover the very same factual circumstances) A conflict between commands that are simply *different* would arise when a WTO rule were to prescribe, for example, a minimum protection term of fifty years for copyrights, whereas a rule enacted in the WIPO context were to prescribe a minimum of forty years only. Mere compliance with the WIPO rule (norm 2) would constitute a breach of the WTO rule (norm 1). But in practice it is possible to comply with both norms, that is, by granting fifty years of protection (in that sense the conflict is a potential conflict only, not a necessary one).[50] The two obligations, covering the very same factual circumstances (term of protection for copyrights), are hence different but not mutually exclusive. The same type of conflict would arise in case a WTO member must, pursuant to a DSU rule, submit a written brief in a legal procedure within two weeks, whereas under a rule of the Subsidies agreement it must

---

[49] The exception is: conflict situations 1 where the contradictory commands or obligations are merely different, not mutually exclusive, as discussed below.
[50] See note 49 above.

submit such brief within one week.⁵¹ Mere compliance with the DSU rule (norm 2) would constitute a breach of the Subsidies rule (norm 1). But here again there is a way to comply with both norms, namely by submitting the brief within a week. Hence, the two obligations, covering the very same factual circumstances (deadline of submission of a brief), are different but not mutually exclusive.

Another example would be one norm prescribing that for a certain trade restriction to be validly imposed conditions A, B and C must be met, whereas another norm prescribes that for the same restriction to be imposed, in the same circumstances, it is sufficient that condition A be met. There may be a case, for example, where the conditions for a trade restriction to be justified under GATT Art. XX are *not* met, whereas the same trade restriction is justified under the TBT agreement (GATT Art. XX having a closed list of justifications, TBT Art. 2.2, referring to 'a legitimate objective' more generally, without providing an exhaustive list).

A more concrete example of conflicting commands that are merely different is one rule which prescribes that on Saturdays I must jog 10 km in the park, whereas another rule prescribes that on Saturdays I must jog 20 km in the park. Mere compliance with the first norm (jogging only 10 km) would mean violating the second (20 km). But once again it is possible to comply with both norms at the same time, namely by jogging 20 km. Nonetheless, a conflict arises in the mind of the jogger: what should I do now, jog 10 or 20 km?

Since, in those cases, it is *possible* to comply with both commands at the same time, the conflict is not a 'necessary conflict', but a 'potential conflict' only. Of all instances under conflict situations 1 and 2, this type of conflict (conflict between commands that are merely different) is, indeed, the only one raising potential and not necessary conflict. This conflict may arise, essentially, because one and the same situation is regulated differently in the two norms, even though complying with the most stringent norm would result in compliance also with the more lenient one.

Note, in addition, that situations of conflicting commands that are merely different may, in effect, overlap largely with conflict situations 3, further described below (command conflicting with an exemption).

---

⁵¹ An example in terms of conflicting commands resting on an international body would be a case where a WTO panel must issue its final report within six months under one rule, but within three months under another.

Of the two merely different commands, one will be more lenient than the other (say, the conditions in TBT Art. 2.2 being more lenient than those in GATT Art. XX; or forty years of protection being more lenient than fifty), so that mere compliance with the more lenient command (TBT Art. 2.2 or offering forty years of protection) could be construed as an exemption *not* to abide by the stricter command (GATT Art. XX or the command to offer fifty years of protection).[52] Although it may well be that, in those cases, the two commands should be complied with simultaneously, conflict rules ought to determine whether this is really the case (and whether, for example, it was not the intention of the parties that concluded the more lenient command to overrule the stricter command as between them).

Crucially, as pointed out before,[53] in case one norm simply adds rights or obligations to another norm on the same general subject matter, but does not cover the very same factual circumstances, that is, when there is no possibility that the implementation or reliance on one norm breaches the other norm, both norms accumulate (and must be complied with at the same time) and no conflict arises. This would be the case, for example, if norm 1 imposes an obligation not to dump oil on the high seas, while norm 2 prescribes that certain signals are emitted on the high seas. Although dealing with the same general subject matter (conduct on the high seas), the two norms do not cover the same factual circumstances (one deals with oil dumping, the other with signals). As a result, mere compliance with, or reliance on, one norm does not lead to breach of the other, and both obligations must simply be applied simultaneously.

When faced with conflicting commands that are merely different, one could submit (and Jenks and Karl would certainly do so under their strict definition of conflict) that since both obligations can be complied with at the same time, there is no conflict. Under our examples, one should just protect copyright for fifty years, submit the brief within a week or jog 20 km in the park. But this type of reasoning shows exactly why a strict definition of conflict not only is about *defining* conflict but actually

---

[52] Such conflict between two positive obligations would have arisen also in respect of safeguards had the Safeguards agreement not explicitly referred back to the conditions under GATT Art. XIX. Without such cross-reference, a safeguard could then be legal under the Safeguards agreement, but illegal under the GATT (since not meeting the 'unforeseen developments' condition set out only in GATT). As noted above, in note 16, such conflict would then have to be resolved by applying the General Interpretative Note to Annex 1A, giving preference to the Safeguards agreement.

[53] See above, p. 162.

resolves conflict. The result of Jenks' and Karl's strict definition here is, indeed, *an absolute preference for the strictest obligation*. It may well be so that the strictest obligation is to prevail, but this decision cannot be made with reference to some technical definition of conflict. Take, for example, our jogging in the park hypothesis. It may well be so that the rule prescribing 20 km was agreed upon in 1995 and subsequently it was thought that 20 km was too much so that in a later rule, enacted in 2000, only 10 km were called for. Following Jenks' and Karl's definition of conflict, there would not be a conflict and the 20 km rule would simply prevail (both obligations can be complied with at the same time). However, considering the contractual freedom of states, as confirmed in Art. 30(3) of the Vienna Convention, it must be possible for states to soften an obligation by means of a later norm in time. Although, in our hypothetical example, the two provisions are not 'mutually exclusive', they are clearly 'different' (20 as opposed to 10 km) and mere compliance with the later rule (10 km) means violating the earlier one (20 km). Both rules are hence 'incompatible' and, pursuant to Art. 30(3), the later rule in time (10 km) should, in principle, prevail (i.e., 'the earlier treaty applies only to the extent that its provisions are compatible with those of the later treaty').

Conflicting commands that are mutually exclusive A conflict between commands that are mutually exclusive arises, for example, when one rule prescribes that on Saturdays at 8 a.m. I must be jogging in the park, whereas another rule prescribes that at that very same time I must be working in the office. Here, complying with the former obligation necessarily means violating the latter, and vice versa. In other words, in this circumstance, the two norms are not only different; they are mutually exclusive. This is the type of conflict (a serious one, indeed) that even Jenks and Karl would recognise as 'conflict'. It is part of what we referred to above as 'necessary conflict'.

In the WTO context (where, as already noted, there are very few commands, but rather prohibitions), it is very difficult, if not impossible, to point to examples of this type of conflict. WTO rules, in particular procedural or institutional rules, may impose different commands (e.g., in terms of recommendations to be made by a panel and time-limits to be respected),[54] but this author has not been able to find any situation where one WTO rule prescribes a certain conduct whereas another WTO

---

[54] Compare, for example, DSU Art. 19.1 with Art. 4.7 of the Subsidies agreement.

rule prescribes other conduct *that cannot be complied with at the same time*. In most, if not all, situations, one of the two forms of conduct will simply be more demanding than the other, and complying with the stricter norm will mean compliance also with the other, more lenient, norm (which, of course, may create a situation of conflict between 'merely different' commands).

Conflict situation 2: *conflict between a command and a prohibition*
An example of one norm *prescribing* certain conduct and another norm *prohibiting* the same conduct in the same circumstance is: a rule in an environmental convention prescribing trade restrictions in respect of certain products (say, endangered species), as opposed to a WTO rule (say, GATT Art. XI in combination with GATT Art. XX) prohibiting trade restrictions in the same circumstances. As amongst WTO rules it is difficult to find this type of conflict, especially in respect of substantive trade provisions. As noted earlier, WTO rules mostly *prohibit* the imposition of trade restrictions, they do not impose positive obligations on WTO members to *restrict* trade (not even under agreements such as the SPS agreement). The WTO is essentially about negative integration, not positive harmonisation. A more concrete example of conflict between a command and a prohibition is: one rule prescribes that I go for a walk in the park on Saturdays, another rule prohibits me from walking in the park on Saturdays.

This type of conflict between positive and negative obligations also meets the strict definition of Jenks and Karl: compliance with one norm necessarily means violating the other (whether I walk in the park on Saturdays or do *not* walk in the park on Saturdays, I will, in any event, break a rule). It is part also of what we referred to as 'necessary conflict'.

Conflict situation 3: *conflict between a command and a right (exemption)*
The following are examples of conflict between a positive obligation and a right in the form of an exemption. One rule in an environmental convention prescribes an import ban on certain products (say, endangered species), as opposed to another rule in the same or another environmental convention which states that certain imports of endangered species are allowed as long as they carry the necessary documents and have been inspected (that is, a norm granting an explicit right to allow imports). One WTO rule prescribes copyright protection for a minimum of fifty years, whereas another WTO rule or a WIPO provision grants an explicit right not to protect certain copyrights or an exemption from

protecting certain copyrights. One rule may prescribe that I work in the office full time Mondays to Fridays, another rule may give me an explicit right to go for a walk in the park on Tuesdays and Thursdays. Under all these examples, exercising the right granted in the second norm (allowing inspected imports, not protecting copyright and going for a walk in the park on Tuesdays and Thursdays) necessarily results in breaching the obligation imposed in the first norm (the obligation to ban imports, to protect copyrights for fifty years or to work full time every weekday). Recall, however, that in these circumstances no conflict arises in case the second norm explicitly states that it derogates from, or is an exception to, the first norm. In that event, one norm simply carves out the scope of application of the other, and both norms accumulate. Conflict arises only when the question of whether the two norms are in a 'rule–exception' relationship is not explicitly regulated in either norm.

Here again, Jenks and Karl would deny the existence of conflict, since in these situations it is perfectly possible to comply with the command or positive obligation (to ban imports, to protect for fifty years or to work a full week) by simply not exercising the right granted in the other rule. In that sense, both norms are different, but not mutually exclusive. As a result, under Jenks' and Karl's definition, these examples would *not* constitute conflict and the positive *obligation* would simply prevail over the *right*.

However, as pointed out earlier, it may well be the case that the creators of the right wanted this right to prevail over the positive obligation, for example, in case they concluded the norm granting the right *subsequently* to the norm prescribing the positive obligation or in case they genuinely wanted the right to constitute an *exemption* to the positive obligation. To preclude that the explicit right prevails over the positive obligation simply because of some technical *definition* of conflict is unacceptable. One must, first, accept the *existence* of a conflict and only then, second, look for the parties' intentions or more objective rules so as to *resolve* the conflict. If not, one risks consistently elevating *obligations* in international law over and above *rights* in international law.

This preference for obligations over and above rights, inherent in Jenks' and Karl's strict definition of conflict, is, indeed, reminiscent of one very traditional view of international law where the starting point is 'complete freedom' for all states. Pursuant to this view, norms of international law simply impose 'complementary obligations' carving out of this freedom. In modern times, however, states are also granted certain rights which detract from earlier agreed obligations (say, an explicit right to restrict trade in certain 'non-green' products, whereas a previous obligation imposed a general prohibition on imposing trade restrictions).

Moreover, consistently to prefer obligations over and above explicit rights is at variance also with another principle of international law, of which the value has rightly been questioned,[55] namely that of *in dubio mitius*. Pursuant to this principle, explicitly confirmed by the Appellate Body in *EC – Hormones*, 'if the meaning of a term is ambiguous, that meaning is to be preferred which is less onerous to the party assuming an obligation, or which interferes less with the territorial and personal supremacy of a party, or involves less general restrictions upon a party'.[56] If in the *interpretation* of an obligation a somewhat deferential approach were required (something that is highly questionable),[57] then *a fortiori* an *explicit right* granted to a state in contradiction to another *obligation* should be taken seriously and should not consistently have to give way to such obligation.

In the *Lockerbie* case the ICJ confirmed the fact that a positive obligation incompatible with an explicit right constitutes 'conflict'. In that case, Libya invoked an explicit right granted to it under the Montreal Convention to keep the two Libyan suspects of the Lockerbie bombing in Libya so as to try them there (Art. 7 of the Convention).[58] Nonetheless, the United States and the United Kingdom invoked a UN Security Council resolution imposing an obligation on Libya to surrender its two nationals to the United States and the United Kingdom. In that situation, the ICJ, in its 1992 order on provisional measures, found *prima*

---

[55] For criticism that this principle is of doubtful value in international law, see Hersch Lauterpacht, 'Restrictive Interpretation and the Principle of Effectiveness in the Interpretation of Treaties' (1949) 26 BYIL 48 at 59–63; Hersch Lauterpacht, 'Report to the Institute of International Law', in *Yearbook of the Institute of International Law* (1950, Part I), 407–20; and Arnold McNair, *The Law of Treaties* (Oxford: Clarendon, 1961), 765–6.
[56] Appellate Body report on *EC – Hormones*, footnote 154, quoting from R. Jennings and A. Watts, *Oppenheim's International Law* (London: Longmans, 1992), I, 1278.
[57] Normally, the rules set out in Arts. 31 and 32 of the Vienna Convention should suffice to determine the meaning of a treaty norm. To interpret obligations for one state restrictively could, indeed, amount to not giving the intended effect to the rights of another state.
[58] Art. 7 provides: 'The Contracting State in the territory of which the alleged offender is found shall, if it does not extradite him, be obliged, without exception whatsoever and whether or not the offence was committed in its territory, to submit the case to its competent authorities for the purpose of prosecution.' In that sense, the Libyan right invoked under Art. 7 is (much like GATT Art. XX) a conditional one: it may refuse to extradite the suspects but then it must prosecute them (the way GATT Art. XX allows for trade restrictions if certain conditions, e.g., of necessity, are met).

facie that, pursuant to Art. 103, 'the obligations of the Parties in that respect [contained in UN Security Council resolution 748] prevail over their obligations under any other international agreement, including the Montreal Convention'.[59] For Art. 103 to be activated there must be conflict. Here, the ICJ did activate Art. 103 in the event of a command (to surrender the two suspects pursuant to the Security Council resolution) contradicting an explicit right (not to extradite the suspects on condition of trying them in Libya under the Montreal Convention). Hence, the ICJ also regards this situation (conflict situation 3) as one of conflict.

Conflict situation 4: *conflict between a prohibition and a right (permission)*
The same reasoning as that set out under conflict situation 3 applies also in respect of conflict situation 4. The following are examples of one norm prohibiting a state from doing something as opposed to another norm granting that state an explicit right or permission to do exactly that. A WTO rule prohibits the imposition of certain trade restrictions (say, GATT Art. III, prohibiting favouring domestic products over and above imports), whereas another WTO rule grants an explicit right to impose these trade restrictions in certain circumstances (such as Art. 27.3 of the Subsidies agreement granting a right to developing country members to provide subsidies contingent on the use of domestic products over and above imports until the year 2000). Alternatively, a WTO rule prohibits trade restrictions (say, GATT Arts. III or XI in combination with GATT Art. XX), as opposed to another rule in an environmental convention which grants an explicit right to impose trade restrictions on certain products (say, products harming the ozone layer). Or one rule prohibits me from going to the park, wheras another rule explicitly permits me to have a walk in the park on Tuesdays and Thursdays. Recall, once again, that in these circumstances no conflict arises in case the second norm explicitly states that it derogates from, or is an exception to, the first norm. In that event, one norm simply carves out the scope of application of the other, and both norms accumulate. Conflict arises only when the question of whether the two norms are in a 'rule–exception' relationship is not explicitly regulated in either norm.

In conflict situation 4, as well, exercising the explicit right or permission (to grant certain subsidies until the year 2000, to impose trade restrictions in respect of certain 'non-green' products or to go for a walk

---

[59] *Lockerbie* case (Provisional Measures), ICJ Reports 1992, para. 42.

in the park on Tuesdays) necessarily means breaching the other rule (prohibiting discrimination, the imposition of trade restrictions or walks in the park). For Jenks and Karl, however, these situations would not constitute conflict since complying with the prohibition is possible by simply not exercising the right. But this strict *definition* of conflict, once again, *resolves* the conflict. And it does so automatically in favour of *obligations* over and above *rights*.

The definition of conflict in WTO jurisprudence[60]

The notion of 'conflict' as it is found in different WTO provisions
Given the multitude of WTO agreements and rules, certain WTO provisions regulate what to do in the event of conflict between different WTO provisions (discussed in chapter 7 below). Two of these conflict clauses have attracted considerable attention and necessitated that panels and the Appellate Body define the notion of 'conflict'. The first of these clauses is set out in a General Interpretative Note to Annex 1A of the Marrakesh Agreement. It provides as follows: 'In the event of *conflict* between a provision of the [GATT 1994] and a provision of another agreement in Annex 1A to the [Marrakesh Agreement], the provision of the other agreement shall prevail *to the extent of the conflict*' (emphasis added). In other words, in the event of conflict between, for example, a GATT provision and a TBT, Subsidies or TRIMS provision, the TBT, Subsidies or TRIMS provision prevails over the GATT provision to the extent of the conflict.[61]

The second conflict rule that has been clarified through case law is found in DSU Art. 1.2: 'To the extent that there is a *difference* between the rules and procedures of this Understanding and the special or additional rules and procedures set forth in Appendix 2 [to the DSU], the special or additional rules and procedures in Appendix 2 shall prevail' (emphasis added). DSU Art. 1.2 also provides for the parties to agree on the applicable dispute settlement rules, or for the chairman of the DSB to determine such rules, 'if there is a *conflict* between special or additional rules and procedures' set out in different covered agreements. The DSB

---

[60] Parts of this section are taken from Joost Pauwelyn, 'Cross-agreement Complaints before the Appellate Body: A Case Study of the *EC – Asbestos* Dispute' (2002) 1 *World Trade Review* 63.
[61] A similar conflict rule is provided for in Art. XVI:3 of the Marrakesh Agreement: 'In the event of a *conflict* between a provision of this Agreement and a provision of any of the Multilateral Trade Agreements, the provision of this Agreement shall prevail *to the extent of the conflict*' (emphasis added). This provision has, however, not yet been interpreted in case law. It is further discussed in chapter 7 below.

chair must then be guided by 'the principle that the special or additional rules and procedures should be used wherever possible, and the rules and procedures set out in this Understanding should be used *to the extent necessary to avoid conflict*'.

We addressed the general international law definition of 'conflict' above. A specific treaty such as the WTO treaty may, of course, deviate from this definition. However, if no language to the contrary can be found, the general international law definition applies. Nowhere does the WTO treaty define the notion of 'conflict' or 'difference'. Recalling also that, pursuant to Art. 31(4) of the Vienna Convention, 'a special meaning shall be given to a term if it is established that the parties so intended', there is nothing in the WTO treaty itself to confirm that any such special meaning was given to the notions of 'conflict' or 'difference'.

In *Indonesia – Autos*, Japan referred to the *travaux préparatoires* of the General Interpretative Note in support of a strict definition of conflict, along the lines of conflict covering only 'mutually exclusive obligations'. Japan pointed to an earlier version of the Note, based on a Canadian proposal submitted on 14 October 1993 and entitled 'Conflict of Substantive Provisions'. This Canadian proposal read: 'In the event of a *conflict* between a provision of the GATT (1993) and a provision of another agreement in Annex 1A, the provision of the other agreement shall take precedence to the extent of the *inconsistency*.'[62] Subsequently, the delegation of Japan proposed to delete the term 'inconsistency' and to replace it with the term 'conflict', the way it now occurs in the General Interpretative Note. According to Japan,

[t]he delegations that addressed this amendment at the session generally concurred that it was intended to clarify the limited number of instances in which the Note would apply. Whereas 'inconsistency' was open to a broad interpretation, 'conflict' referred only to irreconcilable differences between an obligation under GATT 1994 and an obligation under another WTO agreement, such that the provisions of the two agreements were mutually exclusive and could not both be enforced at the same time.[63]

The United States and the EC, also complainants in the *Indonesia – Autos* case, neither confirmed nor denied the Japanese interpretation of this change from 'inconsistency' to 'conflict'. If the *travaux préparatoires* could be resorted to at all in order to give meaning to the word 'conflict' (i.e., if

---

[62] Canadian Proposal on 'Conflict of Substantive Provisions', dated 14 October 1993 (Japan Exhibit 64 in the *Indonesia – Autos* case).
[63] Panel report on *Indonesia – Autos*, para. 5.240.

it were considered that Art. 31 on treaty interpretation in the Vienna Convention leaves the meaning of 'conflict' ambiguous or obscure), it is difficult to see how a redrafting from 'inconsistency' to 'conflict' would support Japan's position that 'conflict' means 'mutually exclusive obligations only'. It seems rather that the change was necessary so as to streamline the General Interpretative Note itself: Canada's proposal first used 'conflict' (i.e., 'in the event of a conflict') but later on, in the same sentence, it referred to 'inconsistency' (i.e., 'to the extent of the inconsistency').

As we pointed out, when it comes to conflict of norms, 'conflict' and 'inconsistency' can be used interchangeably. Both can be reduced to one norm being, having led or potentially leading to a 'breach' of the other. Note, in this respect, that GATT Art. XXIII.1(b) also refers to the concept of 'conflict' in the sense of breach ('whether or not it *conflicts* with the provisions of this Agreement'). There is no reason why 'conflict' in the General Interpretative Note ought to be defined differently. Hence, it should include all four conflict situations set out earlier. Japan's argument that 'conflict' must be construed narrowly is correct to the extent it means that there is a *presumption* against conflict and that all conflict-avoidance techniques set out below (in chapter 5) must be resorted to before a genuine conflict arises. But it is, in my view, incorrect to the extent that it implies that conflict must be *defined* narrowly so as to include only 'mutually exclusive obligations'.

The panel on EC – Bananas
The first WTO panel confronted with the notion of 'conflict', as it is used in the General Interpretative Note, defined it as including the following two situations: '(i) clashes between obligations contained in GATT 1994 and obligations contained in agreements listed in Annex 1A, where those obligations are mutually exclusive in the sense that a Member cannot comply with both obligations at the same time, and (ii) the situation where a rule in one agreement prohibits what a rule in another agreement explicitly permits'.[64]

The first part of this definition of conflict in *EC – Bananas* covers conflict situations 1 and 2 set out above, with the exception of certain conflicts under conflict situation 1, namely conflicting commands that are merely *different*, but *not mutually exclusive* (such as an obligation in one rule to protect copyright for fifty years as opposed to forty years in

[64] Panel report on *EC – Bananas*, para. 7.159.

another rule). The second part of the definition covers conflict situation 4 described earlier (prohibition in conflict with a permission). The panel on *EC – Bananas* lost sight, however, of conflict situation 3, that is, conflict between a command and an exemption (most probably because, as we noted earlier, the WTO treaty includes so few positive obligations or commands).

Crucially, contrary to Jenks' and Karl's strict definition of conflict, the panel explicitly recognised the possibility of conflict between an obligation and a right (albeit only between a prohibition and a permission) as 'conflict' under the General Interpretative Note. In a footnote the reason why was aptly explained with reference to an example:

For instance, Article XI:1 of GATT 1994 prohibits the imposition of quantitative restrictions, while Article XI:2 of GATT 1994 contains a rather limited catalogue of exceptions. Article 2 of the Agreement on Textiles and Clothing ('ATC') authorizes the imposition of quantitative restrictions in the textiles and clothing sector, subject to conditions specified in Article 2:1–21 of the ATC. In other words, *Article XI:1 of GATT 1994 prohibits what Article 2 of the ATC permits in equally explicit terms*. It is true that Members could theoretically comply with Article XI:1 of GATT, as well as with Article 2 of the ATC, simply by refraining from invoking the right to impose quantitative restrictions in the textiles sector because Article 2 of the ATC authorizes rather than mandates the imposition of quantitative restrictions. However, *such an interpretation would render whole Articles or sections of Agreements covered by the WTO meaningless and run counter to the object and purpose of many agreements listed in Annex 1A which were negotiated with the intent to create rights and obligations which in parts differ substantially from those of the GATT 1994*. Therefore, in the case described above, we consider that the General Interpretative Note stipulates that an obligation or authorization embodied in the ATC or any other of the agreements listed in Annex 1A prevails over the conflicting obligation provided for by GATT 1994 (emphasis added).[65]

The same reasoning seems to apply, however, in respect of conflicts between two commands that are merely different but not mutually exclusive, and conflicts between a command and an explicit right in the form of an exemption (the two conflict situations *not* included in the panel's definition of conflict). Theoretically, one could then comply with both commands at the same time by simply complying with the strictest of the two (e.g., copyright protection for fifty years); or simply comply with the command by not exercising the exemption. But doing so may well 'run counter to the object and purpose of many agreements listed in Annex 1A which were negotiated with the intent to create rights and

---

[65] Ibid., footnote 728.

obligations which in parts differ substantially from those of the GATT 1994'. Systematically to prefer the strictest command or the prohibition, irrespective of whether it is set out in GATT 1994 or in one of the more special agreements on trade in goods, may, indeed, go against the drafters' intention to let these special agreements prevail over the more general GATT 1994. In sum, there is no *a priori* reason not to regard all four conflict situations set out earlier as falling within the definition of 'conflict' as it is used in the General Interpretative Note.

The panel explicitly refused to recognise as conflicts 'situations where rules contained in one of the Agreements listed in Annex 1A provide for *different or complementary obligations* in addition to those contained in GATT 1994'. But here the panel confused (i) the fact that different norms may, indeed, *complement* each other in case they deal with different factual circumstances so that implementation of, or reliance on, one norm cannot breach the other[66] or in case one norm explicitly refers to or incorporates the other norm[67] (in such cases one simply adds up the obligations), with (ii) the fact that two norms may also address the *exact same subject matter and circumstances* in a *different* way (say, fifty versus forty years of copyright protection) and this to such an extent that merely complying with one norm (forty years' protection) breaches the other norm (fifty years' protection). The former are situations of 'accumulation' (complementary obligations). The latter is a situation of 'conflict'.

It may be the case that the special agreements in Annex 1A are more likely to impose the *stricter* of the two obligations (the only hypothetical situation the panel itself referred to)[68] so that, in any event, when one applies the conflict rule in the General Interpretative Note, the stricter obligation in the special agreements will prevail over the more lenient obligation in the GATT 1994. But the panel overlooked the possibility that these special agreements may also set out *more lenient* obligations than GATT 1994 for exactly the same situation. For example, a trade restriction may *not* be justified under GATT Art. XX, but be valid under TBT Art. 2.2, the former referring to a closed list of policy exceptions, the latter accepting any 'legitimate objective', without providing an exhaustive list of such objectives. In that event, the existence of a conflict

---

[66] See above, pp. 161-2.
[67] As is the case for the relationship between the Safeguards agreement and GATT Art. XIX, discussed above, pp. 163-4.
[68] The panel did *not* refer to the possibility that GATT 1994 may impose stricter obligations as compared to the special Annex 1A agreement.

should be recognised and it should be the more lenient obligation in the special agreement that prevails.

The panel on Indonesia – Autos

The second panel which addressed the notion of 'conflict' (*Indonesia – Autos*) adopted a totally different position from the one espoused by the *EC – Bananas* panel. Instead of broadening the notion of conflict, as we suggested above, the panel restricted conflict to include only what Jenks and Karl consider as conflict 'in the strict' or 'technical' sense. In *Indonesia – Autos*, the complainants invoked a violation of, *inter alia*, GATT Art. III:2. In defence, Indonesia referred, *inter alia*, to its developing country rights under Art. 27.3 of the Subsidies agreement (explicitly permitting it to maintain subsidies contingent on the use of domestic over imported goods until the year 2000). The panel found a violation under GATT Art. III:2. It concluded that 'the obligations of the SCM Agreement and Article III:2 are not mutually exclusive. It is possible for Indonesia to respect its obligations under the SCM Agreement without violating Article III:2.'[69] Consequently, the panel did not even examine whether the Subsidies agreement would have provided Indonesia with a *right* or *permission* to maintain certain of its measures. In other words, the panel did not consider a situation of an obligation contradicting a right to be a conflict. In its view, the (strictest) obligation simply prevails. In the panel's opinion, 'under public international law a conflict exists in the narrow situation of mutually exclusive obligations for provisions that cover the same type of subject matter'.[70] Conflict situations 3 and 4 were hence excluded from the notion of conflict. In support, the panel referred to Jenks' and Karl's strict definition of conflict, the definition we criticised earlier.

This case shows that the very definition of conflict may, indeed, influence the outcome of a dispute. Had Indonesia's right to maintain certain of its measures under SCM Art. 27.3 been established, in my view, following the wider definition of conflict defended here, there would have been a 'conflict', namely between a GATT obligation and an explicit SCM right or permission. Pursuant to the General Interpretative Note to Annex 1A (giving preference to the Subsidies agreement over GATT in the event of conflict), Indonesia's permission under the SCM agreement

---

[69] Panel report on *Indonesia – Autos*, para. 14.99.
[70] *Ibid.*, para. 14.49. In a footnote, the panel remarked that 'the provisions must conflict, in the sense that the provisions must impose mutually exclusive obligations...which cannot be complied with simultaneously' (footnote 649).

would then have justified its violation of GATT Art. III:2, at least to the extent necessary to give effect to this SCM permission. In other words, had the correct definition of conflict been followed in *Indonesia – Autos*, Indonesia might have won part of the dispute.

The Appellate Body on Guatemala – Cement
In *Guatemala – Cement*, the Appellate Body interpreted the conflict rule in DSU Art. 1.2, more particularly, the term 'different' used therein. Unfortunately, it did so in line with the panel on *Indonesia – Autos* and Jenks' and Karl's strict definition of conflict. The Appellate Body defined conflict as: 'a situation where adherence to the one provision will lead to a violation of the other provision'.[71] The relevant finding deserves full quotation:

> In our view, it is only where the provisions of the DSU and the specific or additional rules and procedures of a covered agreement *cannot* be read as *complementing* each other that the special or additional provisions are to *prevail*. A special or additional provision should only be found to *prevail* over a provision of the DSU in *a situation where adherence to the one provision will lead to a violation of the other provision* [emphasis added], that is, in the case of a *conflict* between them.[72]

In other words, much like Jenks and Karl, the Appellate Body seemed to recognise as 'conflict' only a situation where 'mutually exclusive obligations' arise, that is, only part of conflict situation 1 (conflicting commands that are mutually exclusive) and conflict situation 2 (conflict between a command and a prohibition).[73] The Appellate Body seemingly refused to consider contradiction between an obligation and a right, be it a permission or an exemption (conflict situations 3 and 4), as 'conflict'. This strict definition was adopted even though DSU Art. 1.2 refers to a

---

[71] *Guatemala – Cement*, para. 65. In support of this definition, see: Elisabetta Montaguti and Maurits Lugard, 'The GATT 1994 and Other Annex 1A Agreements: Four Different Relationships? (2000) 3 JIEL 473 at 476.

[72] *Guatemala – Cement*, para. 65. This finding was recently quoted with approval in the Appellate Body report on *US – Steel*, para. 51, addressing the potential for 'conflict' between Article 17.6 of the Anti-Dumping Agreement and Art. 11 of the DSU. The Appellate Body added (*ibid.*, para. 52): 'Thus, we must consider the extent to which Article 17.6 of the *Anti-Dumping Agreement* can properly be read as "complementing" the rules and procedures of the DSU or, conversely, the extent to which Article 17.6 "conflicts" with the DSU.'

[73] Gabrielle Marceau, 'Conflicts of Norms and Conflicts of Jurisdictions, The Relationship between the WTO Agreement and MEAs and other Treaties' (2001) 35 JWT 1081 at 1085, confirms the view that the Appellate Body adopted Jenks' strict definition of conflict in *Guatemala – Cement*.

'difference' between provisions (it does not use the word 'conflict'). The Appellate Body used the terms 'difference', 'conflict' and 'inconsistency' interchangeably.

An assessment of Guatemala Cement
Importantly, however, even though the Appellate Body at first sight opted for a strict definition of 'conflict' in one sentence, in another sentence it equated 'difference' or 'conflict' with a situation where two provisions '*cannot* be read as *complementing* each other'. Depending on how one interprets the word 'complementing', it could be argued that in that other sentence a wider definition of conflict can be found.

In addition, the words '*adherence* to the one provision' which must lead to 'violation' of the other can be interpreted otherwise than as referring only to 'mutually exclusive *obligations*'. Could it not be said that complying with the explicit conditions set out under a *permissive* provision (say, GATT Art. XX) or exemption amounts to 'adherence' to that provision (albeit in the exercise of an explicit right)? One could go even further and argue that the simple invocation of, or reliance on, a 'right' (be it a permission or an exemption) set out in a provision also amounts to 'adherence to' that provision. Such 'adherence to the one provision', or exercise of an explicit right, may then violate an obligation (be it a command or a prohibition) in the other provision. The relevant phrase does, indeed, refer to adherence to *provisions*, not adherence to *obligations*. If so, conflict situations 3 and 4 would nonetheless be covered as 'conflict' (especially in so far as the exercise of the explicit right under norm 2 requires the 'adherence' to certain obligations).[74]

Further evidence that the Appellate Body may nonetheless recognise a contradiction between an obligation and an explicit right as constituting 'conflict' can be found in subsequent case law on DSU Art. 1.2. In the *Brazil – Aircraft* case, for example, the Appellate Body stated that

Article 4.7 [of the Subsidies Agreement] contains several elements which are *different* [emphasis added] from the provisions of Articles 19 and 21 of the DSU...For example, Article 19 of the DSU requires a panel to recommend that the Member concerned bring its measure 'into conformity' with the covered agreements. In contrast, Article 4.7 of the [Subsidies agreement] requires a panel to recommend that the subsidizing Member *withdraw* the subsidy. In addition,

---

[74] Of the same view are Neumann, 'Die Koordination', 18 and Dirk Falke, 'Vertragskonkurrenz und Vertragskonflikt im Recht der WTO' (2000) 3 *Zeitschrift für Europarechtlicher Studien* 307.

paragraph 1 of Article 21 of the DSU requires 'prompt compliance with recommendations or rulings', and paragraph 3 of that Article allows an implementing Member 'a reasonable period of time' to implement the recommendations or rulings of the DSB, where it is impracticable to comply immediately. In contrast, Article 4.7 of the [Subsidies agreement] requires a panel to recommend that a subsidy be withdrawn 'without delay'.[75]

Surely, all of these comparisons between the DSU and the Subsidies agreement should, indeed, be recognised as 'conflicting' obligations. They call for *different* implementation obligations to be imposed on the losing member in the same factual circumstances, that is, conflicting commands that are 'merely different' (part of conflict situation 1 above). But these 'different' obligations are in no way mutually exclusive, as would be required under the strict definition of conflict that most commentators read into the Appellate Body report on *Guatemala – Cement*.[76] A panel could well recommend that the member both (i) bring the measure 'into conformity' with the covered agreements, and (ii) withdraw the subsidy. Moreover, 'prompt compliance', 'within a reasonable period of time', on the one hand, and withdrawal 'without delay', on the other, are not mutually exclusive obligations either. The losing member could well comply with both sets of obligations at the same time (the same way, under our hypothetical example, one could jog 20 km in case one is subject to conflicting obligations of jogging 10 and 20 km).

The Appellate Body took the same approach in *US – FSC* when dealing with the relationship between GATT Art. XVI:4 and Arts. 3, 8, 9 and 10 of the Agreement on Agriculture. It noted, first of all, that '[i]t is clear from even a cursory examination of Article XVI:4 of the GATT 1994 that it *differs very substantially* [emphasis added] from the subsidy provisions of the *SCM Agreement*, and, in particular from the export subsidy provisions of both the *SCM Agreement* and the *Agreement on Agriculture*'.[77]

The Appellate Body found, in particular, that

Article XVI:4 of the GATT 1994 does not apply to 'primary products', which include agricultural products. *Unquestionably* [emphasis added], the explicit export subsidy disciplines, relating to agricultural products, contained in Articles 3, 8, 9 and 10 of the *Agreement on Agriculture* must *clearly* [emphasis added] take precedence over the *exemption* of primary products from export subsidy disciplines in Article XVI:4 of the GATT 1994.[78]

---

[75] Appellate Body report on *Brazil – Aircraft*, para. 191.   [76] See note 73 above.
[77] Appellate Body report on *US – FSC*, para. 117.   [78] *Ibid*.

Hence, the Appellate Body accepted that one provision setting out an exemption or permissive rule (GATT Art. XVI:4) as opposed to another imposing a prohibition (not to grant certain export subsidies in the Agreement on Agriculture) does amount to 'very substantial differences'. Recalling its equation between 'difference' and 'conflict',[79] this must hence amount also to a 'conflict'. When the Appellate Body concluded that 'unquestionably' and 'clearly' the Agriculture provisions must prevail in this conflict, it did not refer to any conflict rule in support. It should have referred to the General Interpretative Note, confirming that in the event of conflict, the SCM and Agriculture provisions prevail over those of GATT 1994.

The fact that the Appellate Body did recognise the examples in *Brazil – Aircraft* and *US – FSC* as 'differences', and hence 'conflict', means that the door is left open for the Appellate Body explicitly to recognise a situation of one obligation contradicting an explicit right as 'conflict'. This, combined with the interpretative flexibility offered by the phrases 'cannot be read as complementing' and 'adherence to the one provision' in the Appellate Body definition in *Guatemala – Cement* itself, demonstrates that the last word on how the Appellate Body defines 'conflict' has not yet been said. There remains, therefore, sufficient room for the Appellate Body to recognise that conflict includes all four situations set out above.

Specific reasons why a broader definition of conflict in the WTO is called for: taking WTO rights seriously

The reasons why in general international law as well as WTO law the broader definition of conflict suggested here ought to be adopted were set out in earlier sections. Some of those reasons take on added significance in the WTO context. In particular, to stick to the strict definition of conflict (mutually exclusive obligations only) would mean that the WTO systematically elevates the *obligations* of WTO members over and above the *rights* of WTO members. However, as the Appellate Body stressed twice in respect of Art. 6 of the Textiles agreement (but a statement that applies to the entire WTO treaty), Art. 6 is 'carefully negotiated language...which reflects an equally carefully drawn balance of *rights and obligations* of Members'.[80]

---

[79] Recall that in *Guatemala – Cement* it equated 'difference' with 'conflict': see above, p. 194.

[80] Appellate Body report on *US – Underwear*, p. 15 (emphasis added) and explicitly confirmed in *US – Shirts and Blouses*, p. 16.

The WTO can no longer be seen as the proverbial cyclist who needs to move on (i.e., *add* trade liberalising *obligations*, in particular tariff concessions) in order not to fall over. The WTO is an international treaty with *obligations* and equally important *rights*. It must take account of both interests *in favour of trade liberalisation* (leading to WTO obligations to liberalise trade) and legitimate interests *justifying trade restrictions* (leading to WTO rights to restrict trade). The obligations of WTO members to liberalise trade cannot systematically prevail over the rights of WTO members to restrict trade.

New WTO provisions (such as the TBT, SPS or Subsidies agreements) cannot only add *obligations* to liberalise trade,[81] they may also create new *rights* to restrict trade. The prevailing strict definition of conflict, on the contrary, creates the untenable situation that WTO obligations to liberalise trade can only be *accumulated* by adding other obligations to liberalise trade (much the way human rights agreements can, pursuant to standard human rights conflict clauses, only provide additional freedoms to individuals and not detract from freedoms granted earlier).[82] Under this strict definition, WTO prohibitions to restrict trade can only be *detracted from* or *overruled* by contradictory *obligations* to *restrict* trade (something that is hardly feasible in the WTO) or by provisions *explicitly stating* that the earlier prohibition no longer applies; not by WTO provisions granting a *right* to restrict trade *tout court*.[83]

In this context, the statement by Montaguti and Lugard that 'since the notion of *conflict* is being interpreted so narrowly, it allows each of the different legal terms set out in either the GATT 1994 or in the Annex 1A agreement to have their full meaning'[84] is only partly correct. Yes, all WTO *obligations* are given their 'full meaning' under the current (strict) definition of conflict. But what about explicit WTO *rights* (say, Indonesia's right to maintain certain measures under Art. 27.3 of the Subsidies agreement)? Surely, these *rights* are *not* given their full

---

[81] The Appellate Body in *EC – Asbestos* (at para. 80) made this mistake very explicitly, stating, in my view wrongly, that 'the *TBT Agreement* imposes obligations on Members that seem to be *different* from, and *additional to* [emphasis added], the obligations imposed on Members under GATT 1994'. The Appellate Body thereby lost sight of the fact that TBT provisions may also grant certain new rights to WTO members to impose, for example, specific trade restrictions.

[82] See chapter 7 below.

[83] See, for example, the sweeping statement made by the panel on *Turkey – Textile*, para. 9.92: 'As a general principle, WTO obligations are cumulative and Members must comply with all of them at all times unless there is a formal "conflict" between them.'

[84] Montaguti and Lugard, 'Relationships', 476.

meaning. They are then consistently overruled by contradictory obligations, however general these obligations and specific the rights may be (there is no conflict anyhow).

In addition, in the particular context of DSU Art. 1.2 and, especially, the General Interpretative Note, a broader view of conflict is required to give *some* effect to these two conflict clauses. Although the insertion of a conflict clause does not necessarily imply the existence of conflict, one can presume that if states insert such clause, they must at least have considered that there was potential for conflict to arise. Under the strict definition of 'mutually exclusive obligations only', this potential seems annihilated. Indeed, under this strict definition of conflict it is hard to see when these conflict clauses would ever be activated. A *right* to trade restriction under, say, TBT, would not 'conflict' with an *obligation* to liberalise trade under GATT (or vice versa): the obligation simply prevails. Nor would an *obligation* under GATT to liberalise trade *less* than a liberalising obligation under, say, TBT (or vice versa) 'conflict': the stricter obligation simply prevails. There would only be a conflict if one provision imposes an *obligation to liberalise trade* whereas another *obligates members to restrict trade*. But does the WTO ever impose an *obligation* on its members to *restrict* trade? Not so, it would seem, in the area of trade in goods or services.[85] Hence, the fact that the General Interpretative Note must be given some meaning (pursuant to the principle of 'effective treaty interpretation') supports the wider definition of the term 'conflict' set out in this work.

In addition, in respect of the non-trade related *procedural* or *institutional* provisions in GATT, the DSU or the more special Annex 1A agreements, it is difficult to find *mutually exclusive* obligations to be fulfilled at the same time, in the same circumstances. To give some meaning to DSU Art. 1.2 and the General Interpretative Note, conflict cannot, therefore, be limited to 'mutually exclusive obligations'.

Conclusion on the definition of conflict

In this section, we defined 'conflict' of norms as a situation where one norm breaches, has led to or may lead to breach of, another norm. On that basis, we subdivided conflict of norms into 'inherent normative conflicts' (one norm breaching, in and of itself, another norm) and 'conflicts in the applicable law' (where the implementation or reliance on a norm

---

[85] The TRIPS agreement does impose certain obligations to restrict trade, i.e., in reaction to infringement of intellectual property rights (see TRIPS Art. 44).

leads to conflict with another norm). The wider approach to conflict adopted here led us to recognise four types of conflicts in the applicable law. In conflict situations 1 and 2 (also referred to as 'necessary conflicts') an obligation under one norm leads to breach of an obligation under another norm. In conflict situations 3 and 4 the exercise of an explicit right under one norm breaches an obligation under another norm (also referred to as 'potential conflicts' given that they arise only in case a right, be it a permission or an exemption, is actually exercised).

The Appellate Body in *Guatemala – Cement* has apparently opted for the so-called 'strict' or 'technical' definition of conflict defended by authors such as Jenks and Karl. This definition covers only 'mutually exclusive obligations' or what we referred to as 'necessary conflicts'. However, in another panel report (*EC – Bananas*) and even in other Appellate Body reports (*Brazil – Aircraft* and *US – FSC*) other situations were also recognised as constituting 'conflict'. Moreover, even the definition of conflict in *Guatemala – Cement* itself seems broad enough to cover also situations of obligations contradicting rights. It seems therefore that the door is still open for the Appellate Body to bring its definition of conflict into line with the approach suggested here.

Let it be clear once again that by recognising a situation as one of conflict, we do not want to prejudice in any way the *solution* to the particular interplay of norms. For example, when arguing that an obligation (be it a command or a prohibition) can conflict with an exemption or permission, we do not in any way imply that the exemption or permission should always prevail. Rather, we want to leave it to the relative conflict rule to solve the issue. The question of defining conflict must be distinguished from that of what the outcome may be of an interplay between norms. The latter is what we examine next. It must, *a fortiori*, be separated from the question of how to resolve conflict (a question examined in chapters 6 and 7).

Accumulation and conflict with general international law

In the previous section, we discussed how norms of international law either accumulate or conflict. In this section we elaborate on one specific form of accumulation of norms ('fall-back' on general international law) and one specific form of conflict of norms ('contracting out' of general international law). Both examples highlight the crucial role of general international law as an instrument to bolster the unity of the international legal system. Both processes ('fall-back' and 'contracting out') also

Accumulation: 'fall-back' on other norms of international law

'Fall-back' on other law: *interpretation* with reference to other law versus *application* of law together with other law

When two norms accumulate, both of them continue to exist and have their full intended effect. In any given situation both norms can be applied at the same time.

All norms are created in the background of already existing norms, in particular norms of general international law. To the extent that the new norm (say, a new treaty)[86] does not contradict or 'contract out' of this general international law, general international law applies also to this new norm. To put it differently, for all issues not explicitly regulated by the new treaty (in provisions either adding, confirming or contracting out of rights or obligations), pre-existing norms of international law continue to apply and a 'fall-back' to, especially, general international law is required. There is no need for an explicit *renvoi* in the new treaty for rules of general international law to apply to the new treaty. In addition, new law is not only created in the context of *general* international law, but in the context of *all* rules of international law, including other treaties. If the new law does not contradict pre-existing treaties, the latter continue to apply.[87]

The so-called fall-back by a treaty on other norms of international law may take two forms:

> (i) *Interpretation of the treaty norm with reference to other norms of international law* (pursuant to Art. 31(3)(c) of the Vienna Convention, discussed in chapter 5 below). In other words, to the extent the terms in the treaty norm are ambiguous enough, general international law definitions as well as certain other rules should be injected in the treaty norm. As pointed out below, this 'fall-back' through interpretation must, however, respect the inherent limits of treaty interpretation (in particular the fact that the other norms to be relied

---

[86] We shall hereafter refer only to *treaties* contracting out of general international law. But recall that all particular international law (as set out in chapter 3 above) may contract out of general international law and that the same rules apply for these other forms of particular international law.

[87] See chapter 5 below, pp. 240–1.

on reflect the 'common intentions' of all parties to the treaty and that interpretations *contra legem* are prohibited).
(ii) *Application of the treaty in the context of other norms of international law.* For example, for those areas on which the treaty remains silent, other norms of international law (in particular, general international law) continue to apply. As a result, the treaty cannot be applied in isolation. It must be applied together with those other norms of international law.

The first type of fall-back is based on the process of *interpretation* of the treaty norm in question; the second type of fall-back (application) on the very fact that the treaty is part of the wider context of international law. The second type of fall-back is not restricted by the limits of treaty interpretation (such as the prohibition on interpreting *beyond* the clear meaning of the terms). It is not the result of interpreting a particular treaty term. It is the necessary consequence of that treaty being part of international law.

The distinction between *interpreting* the terms of a treaty with reference to other law and *applying* a treaty together with other law – be it other law to fill gaps left open by the treaty or other law that may overrule the treaty – was made clear by Sir Humphrey Waldock in his Third Report on the Law of Treaties. Article 56 of his draft, on intertemporal law, read as follows:

1. A treaty is to be *interpreted* in the light of the law in force *at the time when the treaty was drawn up*.
2. Subject to paragraph 1, the *application* of a treaty shall be governed by the rules of international law in force *at the time when the treaty is applied*.[88]

The second paragraph was meant to apply, for instance, to cases of conflict between rules of international law, such as a treaty rule and a subsequent rule of *jus cogens*.[89] The article was subsequently left out, not because it was thought to reflect bad law, but because the ILC rightly pointed out that the second paragraph was not strictly speaking a question of intertemporal law (we come back to the question of contemporaneous versus evolutionary interpretation in chapter 5 below).[90]

---

[88] YBILC 1964, vol. 2, p. 8, emphasis added.   [89] *Ibid.*, 9.
[90] It raised, instead, issues of modification of one rule by another. Intertemporal law, in contrast, specifies which of several rules prevailing *at different moments in time* should apply to a particular case (YBILC 1964, vol. 1, p. 33).

The same distinction was made by the International Law Institute in its 1975 Resolution on the Intertemporal Problem in Public International Law. Paragraph 4 of this Resolution provides in a first sentence:

Wherever a provision of a treaty refers to a legal or other concept without defining it, it is appropriate to have recourse to the usual methods of interpretation in order to determine whether the concept concerned is to be interpreted as understood at the time when the provision was drawn up or as understood at the time of its application.[91]

This first sentence addresses *interpretation*, in the sense of giving meaning to the *terms of a particular norm*. The second sentence of paragraph 4 continues as follows: 'Any interpretation of a treaty *must* take into account all relevant rules of international law which apply between the parties at the time of application.'[92] At first sight, this seems to contradict the first part of the first sentence (interpretation of a concept 'as understood at the time when the provision was drawn up'). However, it seems, rather, that the term 'interpretation of a treaty', as it is used in this second sentence, does not address *interpretation* in the sense of *giving meaning to particular terms*, but rather the *application* of a treaty in the wider context of international law at the time the treaty is being applied.

That a treaty must be applied in the context and together with other relevant law – independent of the process of treaty interpretation – was confirmed recently by the ICJ in the *Case Concerning the Gabcíkovo–Nagymaros Project (Hungary v. Slovakia)*. There, the Court noted: 'new [environmental] norms and standards have been developed, set forth in a great number of instruments during the last two decades. Such new norms have to be taken into consideration, and such new standards given proper weight, not only when States contemplate new activities but also when continuing with activities begun in the past.'[93]

In the *Lockerbie* case as well, the ICJ applied the 1971 Montreal Convention, but it did so taking account of other rules of international law applicable to the case at hand, *in casu*, UN Security Council resolution 748, dated 31 March 1992. This resolution was not resorted to as an element to *interpret* the Montreal Convention. Rather, it was actually

---

[91] '1975 Resolution of the Institute of International Law', *Yearbook of the Institute of International Law* (1975), 537.
[92] *Ibid*.
[93] *Case Concerning the Gabcíkovo–Nagymaros Project (Hungary v. Slovakia)*, ICJ Reports 1997, para. 140.

applied by the Court as a possible defence for an alleged breach under that Convention. The resolution was not only adopted *after* the Montreal Convention, it was actually taken three days after the close of the ICJ hearings on Libya's request for provisional measures.[94]

The distinction between *interpreting* a treaty in the light of new law and *applying* a treaty in the context of new law was also made in the *La Bretagne* arbitration. There, the tribunal held that the expression 'fishery regulations' in Art. 6 of a 1972 bilateral agreement between France and Canada should be interpreted in accordance with its original and ordinary meaning, which related only to the capture of fish and not to filleting. However, in view of the alleged developments in the law regarding the rights of the coastal state in its exclusive economic zone, the tribunal further examined whether an adjustment of the ordinary meaning of Art. 6 was required. But as the tribunal noted, this was no longer a question of interpretation of the 1972 Agreement, but a question of its 'application over time', which could, *in casu*, result in supervening custom prevailing over an earlier treaty provision.[95]

Many authors have ignored this distinction between *interpreting* a norm *with reference to* another norm, and *applying* a norm *together with* another norm.[96] And, indeed, when it comes to rules of *general international law*, it may be difficult to distinguish between the first and the second type of fall-back. For example, if a WTO panel makes reference to Art. 27 (internal law is not a justification for breach) or Art. 28 (non-retroactivity of treaties) of the Vienna Convention when deciding on whether a specific WTO rule has been breached, does it do so in the process of giving meaning to the terms of this WTO rule (first type of fall-back, interpretation) or in the process of applying general international law where the treaty is silent (second type of fall-back, application)? It seems that the latter view is more appropriate: possible justifications for breach and the question of retroactive application of a rule do not so much *give meaning to the specific terms* of the rule, rather they are part of the decision as to *when and to what extent the rule applies* with reference to other rules.[97]

---

[94] *Lockerbie* case, ICJ Reports 1992, para. 42; further discussed in chapter 8 below.
[95] *La Bretagne*, Arbitration Decision (1986) 90 RGDIP 716, at para. 58.
[96] See, for example, Eric Canal-Forgues, 'Sur l'Interprétation dans le Droit de L'OMC' (2001) 105 RGDIP 1 at 7 and 11 and Marceau, 'Conflicts'. On the related distinction between jurisdiction, applicable law and interpretation, see chapter 8 below.
[97] *Contra*: Canal-Forgues, 'Interprétation', 7.

We assess the first type of fall-back – *interpretation* with reference to other law – in chapter 5 below (pp. 251–74). In this section, we focus on the second type of fall-back, *application* of a norm together with other norms. We do so in the particular context of the WTO treaty and focus on fall-back on rules of *general international law*.

'Fall-back' on general international law in the application of the WTO treaty

Fall-back on other norms of international law for areas not covered by a treaty on the ground that the treaty is part of international law finds confirmation in both judgments of the PCIJ/ICJ and WTO dispute settlement reports. As one early source put it: 'Every international convention must be deemed tacitly to refer to general principles of international law for all questions which it does not itself resolve in express terms and in a different way.'[98] Given that there is a presumption against conflict or 'contracting out' (see chapter 5 below), it is, moreover, for the party claiming that general international law does *not* apply to a treaty to prove it.

PCIJ/ICJ jurisprudence
Both the PCIJ and the ICJ confirmed that in case a treaty remains silent on an issue – more particularly, in case it has not regulated the issue differently or 'contracted out' of pre-existing law – the rules of general international law regulating the issue continue to apply. In the *Chorzów Factory* case, the PCIJ confirmed it in respect of the obligation to make reparation for a breach of international law: 'Reparation is the indispensable complement of a failure to apply a convention, and there is no necessity for this to be stated in the convention itself.' It is, indeed, 'a general conception of law, that any breach of an engagement involves an obligation to make reparation'.[99]

---

[98] *Georges Pinson* case, Franco-Mexican Commission (Verzijl, President), AD 1927–8, No. 292, para. 50. Or, as McNair stated: 'Treaties must be applied and interpreted against the background of the general principles of international law' (McNair, *Law of Treaties*, 466). See also H. Lauterpacht, 'Restrictive Interpretation', 76: 'It is the treaty as a whole which is law. The treaty as a whole transcends any of its individual provisions or even the sum total of its provisions. For the treaty, once signed and ratified, is more than the expression of the intention of the parties. It is part of international law and must be interpreted against the general background of its rules and principles.'

[99] *Chorzów Factory* (Merits), PCIJ, Series A, No. 17, 29 (1928). In the same sense, *Oder Commission*, PCIJ, Series A, No. 23, 20 (1929) and *German Interests in Polish Upper Silesia* (Merits), PCIJ, Ser. A, No. 7, 22 (1926).

The ICJ made similar statements in respect of rules on treaty termination for breach and exhaustion of local remedies.[100] In the 1971 *Advisory Opinion on South West Africa*, the ICJ confirmed the right of termination of a treaty for breach (*in casu*, the Mandate for South West Africa) and found that for this right *not* to be applicable to the Mandate

> it would be necessary to show that the mandates system...excluded the application of the general principle of law that a right of termination on account of breach must be presumed to exist in respect of all treaties...The silence of a treaty as to the existence of such a right cannot be interpreted as implying the exclusion of a right which has its source outside of the treaty, in general international law.[101]

This very point was also confirmed in the *Case Concerning the Gabcíkovo–Nagymaros Project (Hungary v. Slovakia)*:

> [t]he 1977 Treaty does not contain any provision regarding its termination. Nor is there any indication that the parties intended to admit the possibility of denunciation or withdrawal. On the contrary, the Treaty establishes a long-standing and durable régime of joint investment and joint operation. Consequently, the parties not having agreed otherwise, the Treaty could be terminated only on the limited grounds enumerated in the Vienna Convention.[102]

In the *ELSI* case the acting Chamber of the ICJ had

> no doubt that the parties to a treaty can therein either agree that the local remedies rule shall not apply to claims based on alleged breaches of that treaty; or confirm that it shall apply. Yet the Chamber finds itself unable to accept that an important principle of customary international law should be held to have been tacitly dispensed with, in the absence of any words making clear an intention to do so.[103]

The Iran–US Claims Tribunal also confirmed this approach.[104]

---

[100] See also: *Interpretation of Peace Treaties*, Advisory Opinion, ICJ Reports 1950, 221 at 277, and the Dissenting Opinion of Basdevant, Winiarsky, McNair and Read in the *Admissions* case, ICJ Reports 1948, 86.

[101] *Legal Consequences for States of the Continued Presence of South Africa in Namibia (South West Africa)*, Advisory Opinion, ICJ Reports 1971, 16, para. 96.

[102] ICJ Reports 1997, para. 100.

[103] *Elettronica Sicula SpA (ELSI)* case, ICJ Reports 1989, 42, para. 50.

[104] *Amoco Int. Finance Corp. v. Iran* (1987) 15 IRAN–US CTR 189, para. 112: 'As a *lex specialis* in the relations between the two countries, the Treaty supersedes the *lex generalis*, namely customary international law. This does not mean, however, that the latter is irrelevant in the instant Case. On the contrary, the rules of customary law may be useful in order to fill in possible lacunae of the law of the Treaty, to ascertain the meaning of undefined terms in its text or, more generally, to aid interpretation and implementation of its provisions.'

In sum, when new law is created there is a presumption in favour of continuity or against conflict, in the sense that if a treaty does *not* contract out of a pre-existing rule, the pre-existing rule – being of the same inherent value as the new one (unless the new one is of *jus cogens*) – continues to apply.[105] Only if it can be shown that the new treaty does, indeed, contradict a rule of general international law will that rule be disapplied in respect of the treaty in question.

WTO jurisprudence
The WTO judiciary has also followed the process of 'fall-back' on general international law for matters on which the WTO treaty remains silent.[106] Even in the GATT days, two panels[107] applied general international law rules, namely Arts. 27 and 28 of the Vienna Convention, respectively, on internal law not being a justification for breach and the principle of non-retroactivity of treaties.

In *US – Shirts and Blouses*, the Appellate Body applied rules on burden of proof pursuant to which 'the party who asserts a fact, whether the claimant or the respondent, is responsible for providing proof thereof' and 'the burden of proof rests upon the party, whether complaining or defending, who asserts the affirmative of a particular claim or defence'.[108] It did so since these rules have, respectively, been 'generally and consistently accepted and applied' by 'various international tribunals, including the International Court of Justice' and are 'generally-accepted canon[s] of evidence in civil law, common law and, in fact, most

---

[105] *Oppenheim's International Law* refers to a 'presumption that the parties intend something not inconsistent with generally recognised principles of international law, or with previous treaty obligations towards third states' (Jennings and Watts, *Oppenheim's*, 1275, with references to ICJ decisions). In respect of the right to reparation, Crawford refers to 'a presumption against the creation of wholly self-contained regimes in the field of reparation' (James Crawford, Special Rapporteur to the ILC on State Responsibility, Third Report, UN doc. A/CN.4/507 (2000), para. 147).

[106] That this was not always the case in the GATT days, witness the *Grey Portland Cement* panel report, GATT doc. ADP/82, para. 5.9. It was held there that, in the absence of an explicit provision confirming the rule of exhaustion of local remedies in GATT proceedings, this rule does *not* apply in GATT. Now, it may be so that on the basis of, for example, subsequent practice this rule was 'contracted out'. But to give the absence of explicit confirmation as the reason not to apply the rule is flawed. This rule, in so far as it is one of general international law, must apply also to GATT unless GATT contracted out of it.

[107] Respectively, panel report on *Canada – Measures Affecting the Sale of Gold Coins*, not adopted, report circulated on 17 September 1985, L/5863, para. 53, and panel report on *United States – Countervailing Duties on Non-Rubber Footwear from Brazil*, adopted 13 June 1995, BISD 42S/208, at 231, para. 4.10.

[108] Appellate Body report on *US – Shirts and Blouses*, p. 14.

jurisdictions'.[109] The DSU is silent on these issues of burden of proof. Hence, the Appellate Body 'fell back' on and applied general principles of international law.

Another example of the Appellate Body applying general international law is in its case law on the principle of judicial economy. Nowhere in any WTO rule is this principle set out. Still, it plays an important role in the fulfilment of a panel's legal mandate. The principle was referred to in *US – Shirts and Blouses* as one providing that 'a panel need only address those claims which must be addressed in order to resolve the matter at issue'.[110]

Similarly, in *EC – Bananas*, the Appellate Body, when examining whether the United States had a right to bring claims under GATT, found that in international law there is no 'general rule that in all international litigation, a complaining party must have a "legal interest" in order to bring a case'.[111] But had there been such a rule in general international law,[112] it seems that the Appellate Body would have 'fallen back' on it, and applied that rule, as long as the DSU would not have contracted out of it. In the same case, the Appellate Body followed a similar *a contrario* reasoning when finding that there is nothing in the WTO treaty 'nor in customary international law or the prevailing practice of international tribunals which prevents a WTO Member from determining the composition of its delegation in Appellate Body proceedings'.[113]

In *India – Patent* as well, the Appellate Body referred to public international law when assessing the role of Indian municipal law and the extent to which the panel had utilised it as a fact or had effectively interpreted it: 'In public international law, an international tribunal may treat municipal law in several ways. Municipal law may serve as evidence of facts and may provide evidence of state practice. However, municipal law may also constitute evidence of compliance or non-compliance with international obligations.'[114] Here again, the Appellate Body, in the

---

[109] *Ibid.*
[110] *Ibid.*, p. 19. In the Appellate Body report on *Australia – Salmon*, para. 223, this principle was further refined as meaning, in the WTO context, that '[a] panel has to address those claims on which a finding is necessary in order to enable the DSB to make sufficiently precise recommendations and rulings so as to allow for prompt compliance by a Member with those recommendations and rulings "in order to ensure effective resolution of disputes to the benefit of all Members"'.
[111] Appellate Body report on *EC – Bananas*, para. 133.
[112] On this, see chapter 2 above, pp. 81–5.
[113] Appellate Body report on *EC – Bananas*, para. 10.
[114] Appellate Body report on *India – Patent*, para. 65. See also Appellate Body report on *US – Section 211 Appropriations Act*, paras. 105–6.

absence of WTO rules on the issue, applied general principles of international law.

Following another *a contrario* reference to general international law (albeit an implicit one only), the Appellate Body in *US – Shrimp* decided that the panel had erred when it found that it *could not* accept *amicus curiae* briefs. The Appellate Body stated that 'authority to *seek* information is not properly equated with a *prohibition* on accepting information which has been submitted without having been requested by a panel'. Having identified the absence of a *prohibition* in the DSU on accepting information not requested by a panel, the Appellate Body then 'fell back' on what was argued to be a general rule of international law for international tribunals, finding that a panel 'has the discretionary authority either to accept and consider or to reject information and advice submitted to it, *whether requested by a panel or not*'.[115]

In *Canada – Aircraft* too, the Appellate Body referred to 'general practice and usage of international tribunals' to find that panels examining claims of prohibited export subsidies have the 'authority to draw adverse inferences from a Member's refusal to provide information'. It did so even though this authority is nowhere specified in WTO rules. The Appellate Body found that this authority 'seems to us an ordinary aspect of the task of all panels to determine the relevant facts of any dispute involving any covered agreement'.[116]

Staying within the area of procedural rules, in *US – Anti-dumping Act of 1916* the Appellate Body also applied the, in its view, 'widely accepted rule that an international tribunal is entitled to consider the issue of its own jurisdiction on its own initiative, and to satisfy itself that it has jurisdiction in any case that comes before it'.[117] It did so when rejecting an EC argument that the United States raised a jurisdictional objection before the panel in an untimely manner. The Appellate Body agreed with the panel that 'some issues of jurisdiction may be of such a nature that they have to be addressed by the Panel at any time'.[118] Nowhere does the DSU grant this mandate of the so-called *compétence de la compétence* to

---

[115] Appellate Body report on *US – Shrimp*, para. 107.
[116] Appellate Body report on *Canada – Aircraft*, para. 202.
[117] Appellate Body report on *US – Anti-Dumping Act of 1916*, footnote 30.
[118] *Ibid.*, para. 54. In *Mexico – Corn Syrup (Article 21.5 – US)*, para. 36, the Appellate Body clarified this *compétence de la compétence* as follows: 'panels have to address and dispose of certain issues of a fundamental nature, even if the parties to the dispute remain silent on those issues...For this reason, panels cannot simply ignore issues which go to the root of their jurisdiction...Rather, panels must deal with such issues – if necessary, on their own motion – in order to satisfy themselves that they have authority to proceed.'

WTO panels or the Appellate Body. Again, it is to be read into the DSU through application of general rules of international law.

Moving then to more substantive rules of general international law, in *Brazil – Coconut* the Appellate Body applied the general principle of international law concerning the non-retroactivity of treaties (reflected in Art. 28 of the Vienna Convention). It did so in its examination of the temporal application of the WTO agreement to Brazilian countervailing duties taken during the period of co-existence of, on the one hand, the GATT 1947 and the Tokyo Round SCM Code with, on the other hand, the WTO agreement.[119] The WTO agreement is not explicit on this question of timing. Hence, the Appellate Body applied general principles of international law. The Appellate Body 'endorsed this general principle of international law'[120] of non-retroactivity of treaties in two further cases: *EC – Bananas* (in respect of Arts. II and XVII of GATS)[121] and *Canada – Term of Patent Protection* (in respect of Art. 70 of the TRIPS agreement).[122] In the latter case, it found that '[a] treaty applies to existing rights, even when those rights result from "acts which occurred" before the treaty entered into force'.[123] Finally, the arbitrators in *Brazil – Aircraft* applied general international law rules on termination of treaties (Arts. 60 and 70 of the Vienna Convention) when examining the legal status of a bilateral agreement.[124] The same arbitrators referred to Art. 27 of the Vienna Convention when stating that '[o]bligations under internal law are no justification for not performing international obligations'.[125]

In terms of customary international law, this process of 'fall-back' on general international law where the WTO treaty does not contract out of it was confirmed in a, for present purposes, crucially important panel report (not appealed).[126] This is the very first report in which it is explained why the WTO judiciary can fall back on general international law and where some limits are set out on the extent to which this fall-back is permitted. The panel in question found as follows:

We take note that Article 3.2 of the DSU requires that we seek within the context of a particular dispute to clarify the existing provisions of the WTO agreements in accordance with customary rules of interpretation of public international law. However, the relationship of the WTO Agreements to customary international

---

[119] Appellate Body report on *Brazil – Coconut*, p. 15.
[120] The words used in *Canada – Term of Patent Protection*, footnote 49.
[121] Appellate Body report on *EC – Bananas*, para. 235.
[122] Appellate Body report on *Canada – Term of Patent Protection*, paras. 71–4.
[123] *Ibid.*, para. 70.   [124] *Brazil – Aircraft*, Arbitration under DSU Art. 22.6, paras. 3.6–3.10.
[125] *Ibid.*, para. 3.65 and footnote 61.   [126] Further discussed in chapter 8 below.

law is broader than this. *Customary international law applies generally to the economic relations between the WTO Members*. Such international law applies to the extent that the WTO treaty agreements do not 'contract out' from it. To put it another way, *to the extent there is no conflict or inconsistency, or an expression in a covered WTO agreement that implies differently, we are of the view that the customary rules of international law apply to the WTO treaties and to the process of treaty formation under the WTO*.[127]

On these grounds, the panel applied 'general rules of customary international law on good faith and error in treaty negotiations',[128] in particular Art. 48 of the Vienna Convention.[129] The panel rightly rejected the *a contrario* argument that the reference in DSU Art. 3.2 *only* to rules of treaty *interpretation* of customary international law means that all *other* international law is excluded.[130] The panel limited its reference to *customary* international law. It should, instead, have referred to the broader class of *general* international law including both general *customary* international law and general *principles* of law. To be entirely correct, the panel should have specified also that only *general* customary international law applies as between all WTO members; not *all* customary international law (not, in particular, special or local customary law between certain WTO members only).

The approach of the panel on *Korea – Government Procurement* finds reflection in a recent Appellate Body report where general international law rules on treaty interpretation were at issue. In its report on *US – Hot-Rolled Steel* the Appellate Body stated:

We observe that the rules of treaty interpretation in Articles 31 and 32 of the *Vienna Convention* apply to *any* treaty, in *any* field of public international law, and not just to the WTO agreements. These rules of treaty interpretation impose certain common disciplines upon treaty interpreters, irrespective of the content of the treaty provision being examined and irrespective of the field of international law concerned.[131]

In a footnote, the Appellate Body then addressed the possibility for states to 'contract out' of general international law:

---

[127] *Korea – Government Procurement*, para. 7.96, emphasis added.
[128] *Ibid.*, para. 7.101.   [129] *Ibid.*, paras. 7.123–7.126.
[130] *Ibid.*, footnote 753: 'We should also note that we can see no basis for an *a contrario* implication that rules of international law other than rules of interpretation do not apply. The language of 3.2 in this regard applies to a specific problem that had arisen under the GATT to the effect that, among other things, reliance on negotiating history was being utilised in a manner arguably inconsistent with the requirements of the rules of treaty interpretation of customary international law.'
[131] Appellate Body report on *US – Hot-Rolled Steel*, para. 60.

It might be possible for the parties to a treaty expressly to agree that the rules of treaty interpretation in Articles 31 and 32 of the *Vienna Convention* do not apply, either in whole or in part, to the interpretation of a particular treaty. Likewise, the parties to a particular treaty might agree upon rules of interpretation for that treaty which differ from those rules of interpretation in Articles 31 and 32 of the *Vienna Convention*. But this is not the case here.[132]

Conflict: 'contracting out' of general international law

In the previous section we examined a particularly important instance of 'accumulation' of norms, namely treaties accumulating with general international law or, put differently, 'fall-back' on general international law for areas not regulated in the treaty. In this section we elaborate on a crucial form of 'conflict' of norms, namely treaties in conflict with, or 'contracting out' of, general international law. In many ways, this 'contracting out' is the flip side of the 'fall-back' discussed in the previous section. Indeed, only if a treaty does not 'contract out' of a particular rule of general international law is 'fall-back' on this rule called for.

The 'fall-back' on pre-existing law is limited only by the extent to which the new law conflicts or 'contracts out' of pre-existing law. To find out whether a new treaty 'contracts out' of general international law, the definition of conflict set out earlier should apply. The question then is: does the mere conclusion of the treaty norm breach a norm of general international law or, more importantly, if a state complies with the obligation set out in the treaty norm or exercises an explicit right (be it an exemption or a permission) under this treaty norm, would it breach the allegedly conflicting norm of general international law (or vice versa, if one were to exercise rights or comply with obligations under general international law, would one breach the treaty norm)? If so, the two norms are in conflict,[133] that is, the treaty norm 'contracts out' of the general international law norm.

Crucially, the extent of this 'contracting out' or conflict determines the extent to which the treaty norm does *not* fall back on pre-existing law, that is, the extent to which the treaty is *lex specialis* vis-à-vis general international law. Finally, given the presumption against conflict (discussed in chapter 5 below) and, hence, against 'contracting out', it

---

[132] *Ibid.*, footnote 40.
[133] Unless the treaty provision explicitly states that it is an exception or derogates from general international law, in which case the two norms enter a 'rule–exception' relationship and, as discussed earlier, simply accumulate without there being a conflict.

is for the party claiming that a treaty has 'contracted out' of general international law to prove it. In other words, the party claiming that there should *not* be a 'fall-back' on general international law bears the burden of proof.

'Contracting out' is a question of degree

The need to examine provision by provision
The question of contracting out, or determining the extent to which a treaty is *lex specialis* vis-à-vis general international law (say, most parts of the Vienna Convention on the Law of Treaties and the law on state responsibility), is one of degree. It is not one of black and white, everything 'in' or everything 'out'. As noted in chapter 2, the WTO treaty is *not* a self-contained regime in the sense that it was created *outside* the system of international law. Nor has the WTO treaty contracted out of *entire fields* of international law such as the law of treaties or state responsibility. All fields of general international law, to the extent relevant to the WTO treaty, continue to play a role. The extent of this role cannot be determined without looking at each and every WTO provision in detail. Only this type of detailed treaty interpretation can determine the extent to which the WTO treaty 'contracted out'. It is of no use to say: the WTO is *lex specialis* in terms of the law on treaties, state responsibility or the settlement of disputes. Of course it is. But the question is: *to what extent?* Nor is it really enlightening to say: WTO law is part of international law. Of course it is. But the question is: *to what extent* is this international law relevant in the WTO?

As Art. 55 of the 2001 Draft Articles on State Responsibility (entitled '*lex specialis*') provides, in respect of treaties contracting out of general international law on state responsibility: 'These articles do not apply where and *to the extent that* the conditions for the existence of an internationally wrongful act or the content or implementation of the international responsibility of a State are *governed by special rules* of international law.'[134]

To discover the 'extent' to which a treaty has contracted out of general international law, each and every treaty norm must be examined pursuant to normal rules of treaty interpretation and each time the extent of conflict and contracting out must be determined. For that reason, the statement made at the Sixth Committee of the UN General Assembly that the ILC Draft Articles on State Responsibility 'would not apply to

---

[134] See also Art. 5 of the Vienna Convention.

self-contained regimes, such as those on the environment, human rights and international trade, which had been developed in recent years'[135] is too categorical, misleading and, as a matter of fact, erroneous. Of course these regimes offer some *lex specialis*, but this does not mean that therefore the entire Draft Articles no longer apply.

Contracting out in one field does not mean contracting out of everything
Similarly, the fact that there is some 'contracting out' of general international law or some deviation by one treaty norm from another treaty norm (e.g., by means of *lex specialis*) does not mean that general international law or the other treaty norm have been disapplied lock, stock and barrel. It is not so that a *lex specialis* totally eclipses or supplants the *lex generalis*.[136] As was noted in a recent Arbitration Award under UNCLOS:

it is a commonplace of international law and State practice for more than one treaty to bear upon a particular dispute...there is frequently a parallelism of treaties, both in their substantive content and in their provisions for settlement of disputes arising thereunder. *The current range of international legal obligations benefits from a process of accretion and cumulation*; in the practice of States, the conclusion of an implementing convention does not necessarily vacate the obligations imposed by the framework convention [emphasis added].[137]

Explicitly confirming one rule does not mean contracting out of all other rules
One other trap to be avoided (but one often fallen into by authors and WTO negotiators alike)[138] is to take the explicit confirmation of *some* pre-existing rules of international law in, for example, the WTO treaty – such as DSU Art. 3.2 confirming customary international law rules on interpretation – as proof that the treaty has contracted out of all *other* rules of international law (pursuant to the adage *expressio unius est exclusio alterius*). As noted earlier, rather than explicitly *confirm* (or make a *renvoi* to) pre-existing rules of general international law for those rules to apply to it, the WTO treaty had to *exclude* those rules that were not to apply. As a result, any explicit confirmation of rules of general international law in the WTO treaty must be seen as made *ex abundante cautela*. Hence, even without DSU Art. 3.2, customary international law rules on treaty

---

[135] Report of the ILC on the work of its 51st session (1999). Topical summary of the discussion held at the Sixth Committee of the General Assembly during its 54th session prepared by the Secretariat, A/CN.4/504, 9, para. 15.
[136] See chapter 7 below, pp. 412–13.   [137] *Southern Bluefin Tuna* case, para. 52.
[138] See, for example, Joel Trachtman, 'The Domain of WTO Dispute Resolution' (1999) 40 *Harvard International Law Journal* 333 at 342–3.

interpretation would have applied to the WTO treaty. As the Appellate Body noted in *US – Hot-Rolled Steel*: 'the rules of treaty interpretation in Arts. 31 and 32 of the *Vienna Convention* apply to *any* treaty, in *any* field of public international law'.[139] For these rules not to apply to the WTO treaty, that treaty should have explicitly 'contracted out' of them.[140]

'Explicit' versus 'implicit' contracting out
As noted before, 'contracting out' of general international law by treaty must take place explicitly in the sense that silence means 'contracting in'.[141] However, this explicitness has graduations. Contracting out may occur by the very words of the treaty, read in isolation. It may occur also in a more implicit form, as a result of an interpretation of the treaty terms in their context and/or with reference to the object and purpose of the treaty or subsequent practice. The presumption against conflict – that is, the presumption that what was not contracted out still applies – means that one has to be careful when accepting these more implicit forms of contracting out. As noted by Simma: 'the burden of proving the "self-contained" character of a subsystem lies with those who allege such a detachment of primary rules from the normal regime'.[142] After all, however, the extent of the contracting out must be determined by the normal rules of treaty interpretation, in particular by determining the ordinary meaning of the treaty terms, in good faith, in their context and with reference to the object and purpose of the treaty. These different elements must express sufficiently the intention of the parties as to whether or not they wanted to contract out of pre-existing rules.

Under Art. 55 of the 2001 Draft Articles (quoted above on p. 213), for example, the question is: when can particular international law, especially treaty norms, be said to 'govern' a certain issue to the exclusion of general international law? That is what we examine next.

[139] Appellate Body report on *US – Hot-Rolled Steel*, para. 60. Discussed above, p. 211.
[140] This was explicitly acknowledged by the Appellate Body in its report on *US – Hot-Rolled Steel*, footnote 40, quoted above, p. 212.
[141] This is further discussed in chapter 5 below, pp. 240–4.
[142] Bruno Simma, 'Self-Contained Regimes' (1985) 16 NYIL 115 at 135. Subsequently however, he states: 'the exclusion or modification through a "self-contained regime" of "normal" secondary rules which leads to a "softening" of the legal consequences of wrongful acts should not be easily presumed' (*ibid.*). Here Simma seems to forget, though, that (as he noted on p. 135) there is actually a presumption *against* contracting out (not the reverse). Moreover, whether the special treaty rules soften or strengthen the 'normal' rules should not, in my view, influence the decision as to whether and to what extent there is contracting out. In both instances the normal rules of treaty interpretation must be applied.

'Explicit' contracting out

By explicit contracting out we mean here treaty provisions which either (i) explicitly state that they derogate from general international law (in that case, there is not even a conflict of norms);[143] or (ii) in explicit terms cover a specific subject matter differently from a given norm of general international law (so much so that if the treaty norm is exercised, the general international law norm would be breached, or vice versa). Examples of the former are rare. Examples of the latter are Art. IX:2 of the Marrakesh Agreement providing that authoritative interpretations can be adopted by a three-quarters majority instead of by agreement of all WTO members (contracting out of Vienna Convention Art. 31.3(a)) and Art. X of the Marrakesh Agreement providing for certain amendments by a two-thirds majority instead of by agreement of all WTO members (contracting out of Vienna Convention Art. 40). Equally, in terms of state responsibility, DSU Arts. 22.6 and 23.2(c) explicitly contract out of general international law rules on countermeasures (reflected in Arts. 50–3 of the ILC Draft 2001) by requiring, for example, multilateral authorisation and monitoring of countermeasures.

As noted by Arangio-Ruiz, special rapporteur to the ILC on state responsibility:

for a true derogation from the general rules to take effect, the parties to the instrument must *expressly indicate* that by entering the treaty-based regime they *exclude* the application of certain or of all the general rules of international law on the consequences of internationally wrongful acts, rather than confining themselves to *dealing globally with the consequences of the violation of the regime*.[144]

One author has taken this quote to mean that only 'explicit derogations' as we have construed them here – that is, only contracting out by the very terms of a treaty read in isolation – can amount to contracting out, not 'implicit derogations' based on treaty interpretation.[145] It seems, however, that Arangio-Ruiz was contrasting 'dealing globally

---

[143] As is the case of a norm explicitly providing for an exception to another norm. The derogating treaty norm then carves out the scope of application of the general international law norm as between the parties to the treaty.

[144] Emphasis added, quoted in Garcia Rubio, 'Unilateral Measures', 23. Or as the Commentary to Art. 55 of the 2001 Draft Articles states: 'For the *lex specialis* principle to apply it is not enough that the same subject matter is dealt with by two provisions; there must be some actual inconsistency between them, or else a discernible intention that one provision is to exclude the other' (Commentary, p. 358).

[145] Mariano Garcia Rubio, *Unilateral Measures as a Means of Enforcement of WTO Recommendations and Decisions* (The Hague: Academy of International Law, 2001), 23.

with the consequences of the violation regime' with 'expressly indicating' that certain rules are excluded. In other words, he was confirming the presumption in favour of general international law applying unless it is contracted out from in the treaty. He was not, the way I read it, limiting the form of this contracting out to explicit treaty terms taken in isolation only.

'Implicit' contracting out

A treaty norm may not contract out of general international law by means of its very terms. But it may still do so when these terms are interpreted in context and/or with reference to the object and purpose of the treaty. Elements extraneous to the treaty may also support contracting out, in particular subsequent treaty practice (pursuant to Art. 31(3)(b) of the Vienna Convention or international institutional law).

In the area of state responsibility, special rapporteur Riphagen recognised that '[a] rule of international law, whether customary, conventional or other origin, imposing an obligation on a State, may *explicitly or implicitly* determine also the legal consequences of the breach of such obligation'.[146] Riphagen referred to 'the object and purpose of the subsystem' as an element to decide on whether there was implicit derogation.[147]

In the *Case Concerning the Gabcíkovo–Nagymaros Project (Hungary v. Slovakia)* too, the ICJ checked indications of intentions of a not purely textual nature to decide on whether a treaty had 'contracted out' of rules on treaty termination:

[t]he 1977 Treaty does not contain any provision regarding its termination. *Nor is there any indication that the parties intended to admit the possibility of denunciation or withdrawal.* On the contrary, the Treaty establishes a long-standing and durable régime of joint investment and joint operation. Consequently, the parties not having agreed otherwise, the Treaty could be terminated only on the limited grounds enumerated in the Vienna Convention.[148]

By 'implicit' contracting out we do not mean, however, contracting out derived from elements other than those that can be referred to under the normal rules of treaty interpretation (such as the *travaux préparatoires* where treaty interpretation under the general rule of Art. 31 does not

---

[146] Emphasis added, W. Riphagen, Special Rapporteur to the ILC on State Responsibility, Third Report on the Content, Forms and Degrees of International Responsibility, YBILC 1982, vol. 2, part 1, para. 9.
[147] *Ibid.*, para. 75.   [148] Emphasis added, ICJ Reports 1997, para. 100.

leave the meaning ambiguous or obscure; or the subjective intention or legitimate expectation of only one or a few WTO members). Such cannot amount to contracting out.

As James Crawford noted, the question of the extent to which contracting out occurred 'is always a question of interpretation in each case, which no provision such as article 37 [now Art. 55 on *lex specialis*] can prejudice'.[149] This interpretation is bound by the customary rules of interpretation reflected in Arts. 31 and 32 of the Vienna Convention. If these rules lead to a conclusion that there is indeed contracting out, there is indeed contracting out. And in the end it does not make a difference whether the contracting out occurred explicitly or implicitly. If these rules do not lead to a finding of conflict or contracting out, the presumption in favour of general international law applying has not been rebutted.

'Contracting out': the example of WTO remedies versus general international law remedies

Let us apply what was said above on 'contracting out' to the question of the extent to which the WTO treaty contracted out of general international law rules on remedies (cessation, reparation and countermeasures).[150]

If the WTO treaty had only confirmed cessation as a remedy under the WTO treaty and added some special rules on how to obtain cessation, would this have meant that the other two remedies (reparation and countermeasures) were excluded as 'contracted out'? No. In and of itself, a mere confirmation of one rule of general international law does not exclude other rules. As noted earlier, the presumption in favour of general international law applying stands in the way and trumps the adage *expressio unius est exclusio alterius*.

But what then in case the WTO treaty, as it does in the DSU, deals with remedies more extensively, i.e., does not confine itself to cessation

---

[149] In the same sense, see Simma: 'the wording "except where and to the extent..." [in what is now Art. 55 of the ILC Draft] allows for the question of conditions for a fall-back on the normal consequences of international wrongs to be answered in each individual case' (Simma, 'Self-Contained', 131).

[150] 2001 Draft Articles, Arts. 28 ff. On remedies in the WTO, see: Petros Mavroidis, 'Remedies in the WTO Legal System: Between a Rock and a Hard Place' (2000) 11 EJIL 763; Joost Pauwelyn, 'Enforcement and Countermeasures in the WTO: Rules are Rules – Toward a More Collective Approach' (2000) 94 AJIL 335; Chi Carmody, 'Remedies and Conformity under the *WTO Agreement*' (2002) 5 JIEL 307; Patricio Grané, 'Remedies Under WTO Law' (2001) 4 JIEL 755.

and some modalities on how to obtain it? The DSU does, indeed, *oblige* panels and the Appellate Body, in case they have found a breach of WTO law, to recommend that 'the Member concerned bring the measure into conformity with' the relevant WTO agreement (DSU Art. 19.1). In other words, the general international law remedy of cessation is explicitly confirmed in the WTO treaty. No other types of recommendations are explicitly called for.[151]

On top of that, however, DSU Art. 22 also provides for 'compensation' and the 'suspension of concessions or other obligations'. Art. 22.1 provides: 'Compensation and the suspension of concessions or other obligations are temporary measures available in the event that the recommendations and rulings are not implemented within a reasonable period of time.' Compensation is 'voluntary' and must be 'consistent with the covered agreements' (DSU Art. 22.1). Compensation, in the DSU sense, is, indeed, not the compensation known in general international law. It is not the granting of monetary compensation to make good past injury. Rather, it is the granting of additional trade concessions to make good the continuation of the breach (it is, in a way, a temporary renegotiation of the WTO treaty).

Suspension of concessions also has a different background and is of a different scope to countermeasures in general international law (although WTO suspension is, these days, generally referred to as 're-taliation' or 'countermeasures'). In the GATT/WTO, suspension has, indeed, its roots more in the law on treaties (more particularly, Art. 60 of the Vienna Convention allowing for suspension in case of material breach) than in the law on state responsibility (i.e., countermeasures).[152] The amount of suspension authorised under the DSU ('equivalent to the level of the nullification and impairment' of the inconsistent measure, DSU Art. 22.4) supports the view of WTO 'countermeasures' merely being a tit for tat (one breach made good by another) and not an effective tool to induce compliance (as countermeasures are supposed to be under general international law).

---

[151] Other than those for specific WTO violations, such as prohibited subsidies where the recommendation must be that the member concerned 'withdraw the subsidy' (SCM Art. 4.7), or for cases of non-violation: see DSU Art. 26. In addition, panels and the Appellate Body are granted the explicit authority to make 'suggestions' as to how the member concerned could implement the recommendation to 'bring the measure into conformity' (DSU Art. 19.2).

[152] On the interplay between suspension of treaty and countermeasures, see Linos-Alexander Sicilianos, 'The Relationship between Reprisals and Denunciation or Suspension of a Treaty' (1993) 4 EJIL 341.

In these circumstances, what about the general international law remedies of reparation and countermeasures? Has the DSU contracted out of them by providing 'compensation' and 'suspension' as it is set out in the DSU?

James Crawford answers this question in the affirmative. For him, the DSU is an example where it is 'clear from the language of a treaty or other text that only the consequences specified flow'[153] (a statement repeated in the commentary to Art. 55 of the 2001 Draft Articles).[154] Crawford refers to the DSU's focus 'which is firmly on cessation rather than reparation'. In contrast, Petros Mavroidis answers the question in the negative. In support, he refers to DSU Art. 19.1 which obliges panels to recommend that the member concerned 'bring the measure into conformity' but leaves it open as to what this recommendation may require. Mavroidis points to the fact that Art. 19.1 'does not prejudge the form of remedies that the WTO adjudicating bodies can suggest' as ways in which conformity can be achieved so that '[t]o the extent...that the WTO regime does not provide for specific remedies, the ILC codification is relevant'.[155] The truth may lie somewhere in between.

In support of Crawford, the DSU does provide *lex specialis* and at least some contracting out when it comes to, for example, countermeasures. The DSU 'suspension of concessions' is now generally recognised as a form of countermeasures[156] and, in terms of multilateral authorisation and monitoring, DSU Art. 22.6 contracts out of general international law. In support of Mavroidis, however, there remains room for input by general international law in the field of WTO remedies, either as a fallback for particular issues not regulated in the DSU (the second type of fall-back we referred to earlier) or as a reference in the interpretation of the remedies that the DSU does explicitly provide for (the first type of fall-back discussed above).

As noted earlier, an examination of the extent to which contracting out occurred must be made separately for each particular rule, not for

---

[153] Crawford, Third Report, para. 420.
[154] Commentary to the 2001 Draft Articles, p. 357.   [155] Mavroidis, 'Remedies', 765.
[156] See, for example, the arbitrators' decision in *EC – Bananas* (US suspension request), at para. 6.3, addressing suspension of concessions under the DSU as 'countermeasures to *induce compliance*' and this even if, in principle, treaty 'suspension' is a remedy under the law of treaties rather than state responsibility (confirmed by the arbitrators in *EC – Hormones*, US suspension request, para. 40 and *Brazil – Aircraft*, para. 3.44). On the evolution of GATT suspension from a tit-for-tat to being a sanction or countermeasure, see Steve Charnovitz, 'Rethinking WTO Trade Sanctions' (2001) 95 AJIL 792.

'the field of remedies' generally, as both Crawford and Mavroidis seem to do. Let us focus, first, on whether the obligation of reparation for past damage has been contracted out. We shall then examine the same question in respect of general international law on countermeasures.

Reparation for past damage in the WTO

In support of the WTO treaty having contracted out of the general international law obligation of reparation for past damage, reference could be made to DSU Arts. 3.7 and 22.1. The latter was quoted earlier.[157] The former states: 'The provision of compensation should be resorted to *only* if the immediate withdrawal of the measure is impracticable and as a temporary measure pending the withdrawal of the measure' (emphasis added). An interpretation of these provisions in favour of 'contracting out' could refer also to what is allegedly a GATT 'subsequent practice' of *not* awarding reparation for past damage (with the exception of six panel reports, only three of which were adopted, in the areas of dumping and subsidies).[158] This alleged 'practice' was also echoed by some WTO members in recent DSB meetings.[159] DSU Art. 3.1 provides that 'Members affirm their adherence to the *principles for the management of disputes heretofore applied* under Articles XXII and XXIII of GATT 1947, and the rules and procedures as further elaborated and modified herein' (emphasis added). In addition, Art. XVI:2 of the Marrakesh Agreement provides: 'Except as otherwise provided... the WTO shall be guided by the decisions, procedures and *customary practices* followed by the CONTRACTING PARTIES to GATT 1947 and the bodies established in the framework of GATT 1947' (emphasis added). Finally, Art. 31(3)(b) of the Vienna Convention also directs that a treaty must be interpreted taking account of 'any *subsequent practice* in the application of the treaty which establishes the agreement of the parties regarding its interpretation' (emphasis added). An (in my view less convincing) argument in support of 'contracting out' could, furthermore, be that the object and purpose of the GATT (as well as, for some,[160] the WTO) was (and, for some, still is) to 'maintain a general level of reciprocal and mutually advantageous concessions' (GATT

---

[157] See p. 219 above.
[158] Cases summed up in Pauwelyn, 'Enforcement', note 21. See also Mavroidis, 'Remedies', 774–7.
[159] See, for example, statements made at the DSB by Australia, the United States, the EC and Canada when the *Australia – Leather* Art. 21.5 panel report was adopted (WTO doc. WT/DSB/M/75, 5 ff.).
[160] See Judith Bello, 'The WTO Dispute Settlement Understanding: Less is More' (1996) 90 AJIL 416.

Art. XXVIII:2), i.e., a certain general level of market access, not necessarily compliance with specific rules. To put it differently, the object and purpose of the GATT was to *allow for a certain level of trade*, not so much to have *trade policies in accordance with the rules per se*. A breach of the rules could, from this viewpoint, be made good by an additional concession elsewhere, or a reciprocal withdrawal of concessions by the victim state. There was no need, nor expectation, within this framework actually to hold the violator state 'responsible' for past damage. Although in today's context this argument is not convincing – given, especially, the clear DSU requirement of ultimate compliance with the rules – this traditionalist GATT view may play a role in the reconstruction of what WTO members had in mind when negotiating the WTO treaty.

The arguments above could lead to the interpretation that the DSU did contract out of the general international law obligation of reparation. However, if this were the case, this should not prevent panels from *interpreting* whatever *other remedies* the WTO does provide for in the light of general international law (pursuant to the first type of fall-back we referred to). For example, the remedy of 'compensation' in DSU Art. 22 could be interpreted so as to cover also elements of past damage. If not, it could be argued, the 'compensation' is not 'satisfactory' in terms of DSU Art. 22.2. In addition, WTO 'suspension of concessions' could be interpreted so as to cover past damage, for example, by means of assessing the level of suspension allowed for as including not only prospective nullification (for as long as the breach continues) but also past nullification.

In contrast, strong arguments can also be found in support of the obligation of reparation *not* being contracted out in the WTO treaty. First, DSU Arts. 3.7 and 22.1 may, indeed, limit the availability of 'compensation' to situations of non-compliance with panel recommendations (hence excluding that compensation be awarded in the panel report itself). However, this 'compensation' has, as noted earlier, little to do with the general international law remedy of reparation. DSU 'compensation' is a treaty-based remedy. It is essentially a temporary renegotiation of the treaty, requiring the consent of both parties, for as long as the breach continues. International law 'reparation', in contrast, is an automatic consequence of state responsibility.[161] It requires neither renegotiation of the treaty nor consent of the parties.

---

[161] See 2001 Draft Articles, Art. 31 and, as to the automaticity of reparation, *Chorzów Factory* (Merits), PCIJ, Series A, No. 17, 29 (1928).

Second, the GATT 'practice' of not awarding reparation for past damage may not amount to genuine 'subsequent practice'. There are notable exceptions to this practice (albeit in the areas of dumping and subsidies only).[162] What is more important, this 'practice' is not one where GATT panels have consistently rejected requests for reparation. Rather, it is one where GATT contracting parties have simply not made such requests. Hence, when GATT panels did not award reparation for past damage they did so because of the *non ultra petita* rule, not on the ground of a legal finding that such reparation was not available. The same is true for WTO panels. Consequently, this alleged GATT/WTO practice, being one of silence rather than rejected requests, does arguably not qualify as a 'principle for the management of disputes heretofore *applied*', nor as a 'customary practice *followed*' by GATT parties or a 'subsequent practice... which establishes the *agreement of the parties* regarding its interpretation' (respectively, in the sense of DSU Art. 3.1, Art. XVI:1 of the Marrakesh Agreement and Art. 31(3)(b) of the Vienna Convention (emphases added)). As the Appellate Body pointed out:

> Generally, in international law, the essence of subsequent practice in interpreting a treaty has been recognized as a 'concordant, common and consistent' sequence of acts or pronouncements which is sufficient to establish a discernible pattern implying the agreement of the parties regarding its interpretation. An isolated act is generally not sufficient to establish subsequent practice; it is a sequence of acts establishing the agreement of the parties that is relevant.[163]

In addition, as much as some WTO members have recently confirmed the absence of reparation for past damage, others have pleaded in favour of reparation.[164] Furthermore, there is one WTO panel report, albeit once again in the area of subsidies, that explicitly called for some form of reparation for past damage. It did so by finding that for a member to 'withdraw' a one-time past subsidy (as required in Art. 4.7 of the Subsidies agreement), the beneficiary of the subsidy must repay the entire sum of the subsidy to the government.[165] Finally, as already hinted

---

[162] See note 158 above. [163] Appellate Body report on *Japan – Alcoholic Beverages*, 12–13.
[164] At a DSB meeting Ecuador, in the context of the *EC – Bananas* dispute, stated: 'A careful reading of Article 3.2 of the DSU in conjunction with Article 31.3 of the [Vienna Convention] confirmed that the general principles of international law on state responsibilities were applicable in this case... Articles 19 and 22 of the DSU did not exclude the general principle of international law on reparation of injury caused by a violation of international law... it might be appropriate to initiate a new legal action in order to determine whether Ecuador had the right to compensation' (WT/DSB/M/89, para. 8).
[165] Panel report (pursuant to DSU Art. 21.5) on *Australia – Leather*, conclusion in para. 6.48.

at, the argument that the object and purpose of the WTO is a general balance of trade concessions safeguarded by treaty-based remedies, not compliance with specific rules enforced by state responsibility, may have been true in the early GATT days. It is not today.[166]

These arguments plead in favour of the fact that the WTO treaty has *not* contracted out of the general international law remedy of reparation. How then could this reparation be awarded?

First, reparation could be awarded by a panel, under the current DSU, by means of recommending that the violator make reparation in a separate 'recommendation', on top of the recommendation to 'bring the measure into conformity'. DSU Art. 19.1 *obliges* panels to make the latter recommendation. Nothing in DSU Art. 19 prohibits them from making other recommendations. As further explained in chapter 8 below, and recently confirmed by the ICJ in the *LaGrand* case, the power of a tribunal to award remedies, including reparation, is part of the implied or incidental jurisdiction of panels, that is, a competence inherent in the exercise of the judicial function.[167] There is no need for WTO members explicitly to confer this power on WTO panels, i.e., to make it explicit that they may 'recommend' also reparation. Making an explicit recommendation that reparation must be made would be the most obvious and open track. An ordinary reading of the recommendation to 'bring the measure into conformity' seems, indeed, to imply only cessation, either by removing the inconsistent measure altogether or by changing the measure so that it conforms to WTO rules.[168] In addition and

---

[166] See Philip Pierros and Mariusz Maciejewski, 'Specific Performance or Compensation and Countermeasures – Are These Alternative Means of Compliance Under the WTO Dispute Settlement System?' (2001) 6 *International Trade Law Review* 167.

[167] Unless, of course, the treaty enforced has contracted out of reparation. The panels on *Guatemala – Cement I* (at para. 8.3) and *US – Hot-Rolled Steel* (at para. 8.11), in my view, wrongly considered that for additional recommendations to be made by a panel, explicit DSU provisions to that effect should have been inserted. What then about, for example, preliminary rulings by WTO panels on procedural objections? No DSU provision allows for such rulings. But this does not mean that panels have no power to make them. They have this power as part of their judicial function to settle a dispute.

[168] The Appellate Body implicitly limited the recommendation to 'bring into conformity' to cessation only. In *US – Certain Products*, it reversed the panel's recommendation to 'bring the measure into conformity' on the ground that the measure that was found to be WTO inconsistent was no longer in existence. Hence, since the breach had stopped, it was no use recommending cessation. As the Appellate Body put it (at para. 81): 'there is an obvious inconsistency between the finding of the Panel that "the 3 March Measure is no longer in existence" and the subsequent recommendation of the Panel that the DSB request that the United States bring its 3 March Measure into

distinct from this recommendation of cessation, a clear recommendation of reparation could then be made.

Second, and in the alternative, a panel could restrict itself to recommending that the measure be brought 'into conformity' or, as required in the event of prohibited subsidies, to a recommendation to 'withdraw the subsidy'.[169] What is required to obtain this 'conformity' could then be said to include reparation for past damage. A panel could make a 'suggestion' in this direction pursuant to DSU Art. 19.2, i.e., suggest that, in its view, for the measure to be brought 'into conformity' (or, for the subsidy to be 'withdrawn') reparation is required. This is what the panel on *Australia – Leather* decided in respect of a past, one-time, non-recurring prohibited subsidy where 'withdraw the subsidy' was read as requiring reimbursement of the entire subsidy, not just repayment of that part of the subsidy that continued to affect the competitiveness of its beneficiary in the future. There seem to be no reasons why the same could not be done in similar circumstances in respect of other WTO breaches (interpreting 'bring into conformity' so as to include retrospective reparation also). This is what the panel on *Guatemala – Cement II* seemed to imply when stating that 'repayment might be justifiable in circumstances such as these' in response to a Mexican request that the panel 'suggest' that for 'conformity' to occur Guatemala ought to refund the anti-dumping duties so far collected. The panel nonetheless refrained from making such suggestion.[170]

This second track of widely interpreting 'bring the measure into conformity' is the one that will most likely be followed in the near future.[171] It is the one that rocks the boat the least, as opposed to a clear-cut

---

conformity with its WTO obligations'. In that case, although the measure was found to be WTO inconsistent, no recommendation was made (*ibid*., para. 129).

[169] Art. 4.7 of the Subsidies agreement.

[170] The panel's conclusion in this respect is arguably a form of *non liquet*. The reason for refusing the suggestion was basically that Mexico's request 'raises important systemic issues regarding the nature of the actions necessary to implement recommendations under Article 19.1 of the DSU, issues which have not been fully explored in this dispute' (panel report on *Guatemala – Cement II*, at para. 9.7). The same excuse was made *verbatim* in *US – Hot-Rolled Steel* (at para. 8.13). Given the *jura novit curia* principle, it was for the panel to 'fully explore' these 'important systemic issues' and, if need be, to question the parties in this respect. The fact that the panel did not do so could be seen as a denial of justice or *non liquet* (see Pauwelyn, 'Cross-agreement').

[171] But see the Appellate Body report on *US – Certain Products* where the Appellate Body found that making a recommendation to 'bring the measure into conformity' in case the measure is no longer in existence is inappropriate. This seems to imply that, in the eyes of the Appellate Body, 'bring into conformity' means cessation only. See note 168 above.

and separate recommendation to make reparation. It can be adapted also to the particular circumstances of each case, some breaches or circumstances requiring reparation, others not. The risk related to this approach is, however, that it creates a two-class society of breaches, in particular completed breaches (such as the one in *Australia – Leather*) as opposed to continuing breaches (such as most WTO breaches, by legislative or administrative measures of a continuing nature). The ironic result could then well be that for WTO members to avoid paying reparation for past damage (as Australia was forced to do in the *Leather* case) they should simply *continue the breach*, as a result of which cessation may still offer some remedy and reparation for past damage becomes less compelling.[172] To avoid this absurdity one could then award reparation also for continuing breaches.

On balance, it seems that the arguments *against* contracting out of the obligation of reparation are likely to prevail in the medium-term future. Nonetheless, for reparation to become a standard remedy in WTO law will take time.[173] This gradual shift may well start with some awards of reparation in special circumstances (such as protracted non-compliance), special fields (such as subsidies and dumping) or to certain WTO members (say, only developing countries).[174] WTO panels could also limit reparation for past damage to breaches that occur *subsequent* to the first finding that such reparation is, indeed, a remedy available in WTO law.[175] There do not seem to be any compelling legal reasons, however, to draw

---

[172] On the other hand, for the WTO not to award any remedy for completed breaches (as was done in *US – Certain Products*) is equally absurd. It would make a mockery of the DSU: if the breach is repealed during panel proceedings, nothing in terms of remedies could then be obtained. On the contrary, members could start engaging in so-called 'hit-and-run practices', enacting and repealing breaches at the appropriate time so as to avoid any responsibility. In those cases, the remedy of 'assurances and guarantees of non-repetition' referred to in Art. 30(b) of the 2001 Draft Articles and recently confirmed by the ICJ in the *LaGrand* case (Judgment of 27 June 2001 on Jurisdiction and Admissibility, at paras. 46–8 and 117–27, posted on the ICJ webpage at http:/www.icj-cij.org/icjwww/idocket) could offer some redress. Once again, even if the DSU does not explicitly set out this remedy, it could be awarded by panels as part of their inherent judicial function, the way the ICJ awarded the remedy of non-repetition under the Vienna Convention on Consular Relations in the *LaGrand* case.

[173] Unless the WTO members were to inject it explicitly into the treaty by authoritative interpretation or amendment or, in contrast, exclude it explicitly from WTO law.

[174] In support, see: Victor Mosoti, 'In Our Own Image, Not Theirs: Damages as an Antidote to the Remedial Deficiencies in the WTO Dispute Settlement Process; A View from Sub-Saharan Africa' (2001) 19 *Boston University International Law Journal* 231.

[175] Note, in this respect, the ICJ consideration in the *LaGrand* case that had Germany requested reparation for the US non-compliance with the Court's provisional

strict lines between different types of violations (such as breaches in the fields of subsidies and dumping versus breaches in other fields of WTO law). WTO breaches, as well as the suspension of WTO obligations in response to breach, have a direct impact on individual operators. Whereas a balancing act of trade concessions without reparation for past damage may be acceptable to governments, legal rules affecting individuals call for greater predictability and stability. They must be respected as international obligations whose breach leads to state responsibility – including some form of reparation for past damage – not as some political compromise that can be withdrawn or exchanged for another. However, as I noted elsewhere,[176] it would be wrong to take these important steps precipitously and without extensive discussion; doing so could threaten the political support and legitimacy of the WTO in general, and of its dispute settlement decisions in particular.[177]

>
> measure, the Court would have taken account of the fact that when the US breach occurred 'the question of the binding character of orders indicating provisional measures had been extensively discussed in the literature, but had not been settled by its jurisprudence'. The Court noted that it 'would have taken these factors into consideration had Germany's submission included a claim for indemnification' (at para. 116). This approach of not granting (full) reparation for breaches that occurred at a time when the law, as interpreted by the court, was not entirely 'clear' was adopted more openly by the ECJ in *Defrenne v. SABENA*. There, the Court decided for the first time that Article 141 (ex 119) had direct effect in relation to direct and overt discrimination in violation of the principle of equal pay for equal work for men and women. The Court specified, however, that its judgment could not be relied on to support claims relating to pay periods prior to the date of the judgment except as regarded those workers who had already brought legal proceedings or made an equivalent claim (Case 43/75 [1976] ECR 455).
>
> [176] Pauwelyn, 'Enforcement', 347. At the same time, and as noted earlier, it could well be so that two types of WTO obligations become distinguishable: those that set out mere concessions that can be traded (e.g., under GATT Art. XXVIII or as part of a suspension of concessions) and those containing genuine legal obligations (the breach of which is followed by state responsibility and which cannot be made subject to suspensions nor be exchanged).
>
> [177] What, indeed, if a WTO member refuses to pay reparation? If reparation becomes generally available, the risk could arise, moreover, that WTO members might want to scale down the substantive content of WTO rules and create less stringent new WTO rules. The fact that no reparation is available may have been one of the reasons why rather strict agreements such as the SPS agreement saw the light of day. Should it, one could submit, in the context of health and consumer information/protection issues, not be possible for WTO members, in certain extreme circumstances, to 'buy their way out' of certain SPS violations (by means of trade compensations or suspensions instead of compliance)? Or, on the contrary, should WTO members not have agreed to SPS rules in the first place if they wanted to reserve this right to 'buy' violations?

Countermeasures under general international law in the WTO

Given the remedies explicitly provided for in the DSU, outlined above, has the WTO treaty contracted out of general international law on countermeasures? In the GATT days this question attracted a lot of scholarly attention.[178] In the GATT context, the question was essentially whether a GATT contracting party could resort to unilateral countermeasures in case another GATT contracting party blocked the establishment of a panel or the adoption of a panel report (both required a consensus of all GATT contracting parties). Many authors (as well as, prominently, the United States) submitted that such fall-back on general international law was justified in case the WTO enforcement mechanism was thus blocked. Other GATT contracting parties, in particular the European Communities, maintained that this fall-back was not allowed on the ground that the GATT had contracted out of this aspect of general international law.[179]

We shall not here enter into this historical debate. The one aspect which it may be useful to clarify though is that the enforcement mechanism explicitly set out in GATT 1947 (Arts. XXII–XXIII) was largely, if not exclusively, a mechanism based *on the law of treaties*, namely: in the event of breach and in case the breach is not put to an end, the breach may be rectified by means of either (i) a renegotiation of the treaty (trade compensation by the violator) or (ii) in cases where 'the circumstances are serious enough to justify such action' (GATT Art. XXIII:2), a suspension of treaty obligations by the injured state vis-à-vis the violator. The latter, in particular, is a treaty-based remedy along the lines of Art. 60 of the Vienna Convention (suspension of treaty obligations in case of 'material breach') and the *exceptio inadimpleti contractus*. Both the GATT suspension, as originally conceived, and a suspension under Art. 60 bring, at least in theory, an end to the matter (although the obligations are only 'suspended', no doubt out of a desire to leave open the possibility of a resumption of treaty relations notwithstanding the breach). The original GATT breach then no longer constitutes a breach, nor does the

---

[178] For an excellent overview, see: Javier Fernandez Pons, 'Self-Help and the World Trade Organization', in Paolo Mengozzi (ed.), *International Trade Law on the 50th Anniversary of the Multilateral Trade System* (Milan: A. Giuffrè, 1999), 67–74. See also Michael Hahn, *Die einseitige Aussetzung von Gatt-Verpflichtungen als Repressalie* (Berlin: Springer, 1995).

[179] See Pieter Jan Kuijper, 'The Law of GATT as a Special Field of International Law, Ignorance, Further Refinement or Self-Contained System of International Law?' (1994) 25 NYIL 227 at 251.

suspension in response to that breach. The relevant treaty obligations have, indeed, been suspended so that they can, *a fortiori*, no longer be breached (*inadimpleti non est adimplendum*). If, in these circumstances, a fall-back on general international law rules on countermeasures would, indeed, have been appropriate (a question we leave open here), this would not so much have been because a GATT panel or GATT suspension had been previously blocked by the violator state, but rather because the GATT had, arguably, not contracted out of the law on *state responsibility*, including the law on countermeasures (GATT having provided *lex specialis* only in terms of the *law of treaties*).[180]

Countermeasures under the law of state responsibility are, indeed, of a different nature to suspension under Art. 60.[181] Countermeasures can be taken for any breach, not just material breaches. Moreover, countermeasures do not as such put an end to the breach (no treaty obligations are suspended). Rather, the original breach continues to exist and the countermeasure – in principle illegal, but justified as a response to the original breach – is there to induce compliance. It is not, as treaty suspension is, the end of the matter. Hence, if a fall-back would have been allowed for, it was, indeed, necessary for GATT contracting parties first to exhaust the treaty-based remedies provided for in GATT Arts. XXII–XXIII, but once this was done, and to the extent still necessary, they could then arguably have invoked also rules on state responsibility, including

---

[180] Rosenne, for example, makes a distinction between 'the law of the instrument' (i.e., the treaty) and 'the law of obligation' (i.e., the obligations derived from a treaty). He submits that the Vienna Convention focuses on 'the instrument in which an international obligation is expressed and not the obligation itself' (Shabtai Rosenne, *Breach of Treaty* (Cambridge: Grotius, 1985), 3–4). The 'law of obligations' is, then, what is currently examined by the ILC in the field of state responsibility. In this light, Art. 60 relates to the treaty as *instrument* and provides an opportunity to invoke suspension or termination in case the *instrument* has been, so to speak, endangered by a breach (only 'material breaches' can lead to suspension or termination). When it comes to the consequences of breach for the treaty *obligations* (as opposed to the treaty as an instrument), the law on state responsibility applies. See also Bruno Simma, 'Reflections on Article 60 of the Vienna Convention on the Law of Treaties and its Background in General International Law' (1970) 20 *Österreichische Zeitschrift für öffentliches Recht* 5 at 83.

[181] See Hahn, *Einseitige Aussetzung*, 396 (describing the law of treaties and the law of state responsibility as parallel bodies of law). In the same sense, see James Crawford, Special Rapporteur to the ILC on State Responsibility, Second Report, UN doc. A/CN.4/498 (1999), Add. 2, paras. 314–29 (comparing and distinguishing the *exceptio inadimpleti contractus* from the regime of countermeasures and treaty suspension under Art. 60) and Third Report, para. 60 (making a categorical distinction between Art. 60 of the Vienna Convention and state responsibility).

countermeasures.¹⁸² This was not primarily because the GATT treaty-based remedies were ineffective, but because remedies under treaty law and remedies under state responsibility are different. The old GATT situation was, indeed, similar to what we see now under many environmental treaties. These treaties provide for special enforcement mechanisms (in the case of MEAs, so-called collective compliance procedures) that have little to do with state responsibility. In these circumstances (and given the silence of these treaties on issues of state responsibility) it is, indeed, defensible to argue that a fall-back on general international law rules on state responsibility remains an option.¹⁸³ Again, this is not so much because of the ineffectiveness of the treaty-based mechanism, but because of the absence of contracting out of the law on state responsibility.

This situation has changed dramatically with the conclusion and subsequent interpretation of the WTO treaty, in particular the DSU. Suspension in the WTO is now generally equated with countermeasures.¹⁸⁴ In the Subsidies agreement the word 'countermeasures' is even used explicitly. WTO suspension is no longer seen as a suspension of treaty obligations (à la Art. 60 of the Vienna Convention) that rebalances the overall level of concessions and hence brings an end to the matter. The explicit 'temporal' nature of trade compensation and suspension as a solution to a dispute (DSU Arts. 3.7 and 22.1), as well as the clear-cut obligation that the DSU imposes on violators to bring their measures *into compliance* with WTO rules (DSU Arts. 3.7, 19.1 and 22.1), have made it very difficult to portray WTO suspension as anything other than countermeasures: that is, action taken, not as a tit for tat or to rebalance the situation, but *with the objective to induce compliance*.¹⁸⁵ Within this context, the provisions in the WTO treaty on suspension of treaty obligations have shifted into the area of state responsibility. Given their special nature – e.g., the requirement first to have a multilateral decision in support of breach¹⁸⁶ and the condition of 'equivalence' to nullification¹⁸⁷ – they must be seen as a form of *lex specialis* in the area of countermeasures. Consequently,

---

¹⁸² As Crawford noted in his Third Report (at para. 93): 'Suspension of treaty relations is no substitute for an adequate regime of State responsibility.'
¹⁸³ See Martti Koskenniemi, 'Breach of Treaty or Non-Compliance? Reflections on the Enforcement of the Montreal Protocol' (1992) 3 *Yearbook of International Environmental Law* 123.
¹⁸⁴ In support, see Pons, 'Self-Help', 63 and the reference to a long series of authors in his note 17. See also note 156 above.
¹⁸⁵ See note 156 above.   ¹⁸⁶ DSU Arts. 22.6 and 23.2(c).   ¹⁸⁷ DSU Art. 22.4.

they contract out, at least to some extent, of general international law rules on countermeasures.[188]

The situation under the WTO treaty, providing *lex specialis* on countermeasures,[189] is thus quite different from that under the GATT where, arguably, only treaty-based remedies were explicitly referred to. Moreover, since authorisation of WTO countermeasures can now only be blocked by a consensus of all WTO members (including the member seeking the countermeasures) and since DSU Art. 23 made it explicit that when a member seeks redress under WTO obligations, DSU procedures *must* be followed, the question of fall-back has, in practice, been narrowed down to this: can a WTO member take general international law countermeasures if WTO countermeasures turn out to be ineffective?

Answering this question in the affirmative, as some have done,[190] is, to say the least, problematic. If it is, indeed, so that WTO suspension is a form of countermeasures, and hence the WTO treaty provides for a special regime on countermeasures, this special regime must be taken as the explicit choice of WTO members. They decided to contract out of general international law rules in this respect. For a WTO member unilaterally to 'contract back in' on the ground that the special regime is not to its liking or ineffective cannot be accepted. Contracting out of general international law does not necessarily mean improving or making general international law *more* effective.[191] The way in which

---

[188] Pursuant to Art. 55 of the 2001 Draft Articles. *Contra*: Garcia Rubio, *Unilateral Measures*, 29: 'Nothing in article 23 of the DSU, according to which WTO Member States shall have recourse to the DSU and abide by its rules, amounts to an express derogation from the right to adopt countermeasures when a losing party fails to implement a decision of the dispute settlement organs and the remedies provided for in the treaty have been exhausted without any positive result.' If WTO suspension is, indeed, a countermeasure, it is difficult to see how the DSU does not provide *lex specialis* in the field of countermeasures. The DSU confirms that countermeasures can be taken but it makes this subject to a series of conditions, explicitly set out in the DSU.

[189] Even if the text of GATT Arts. XXII–XXIII has not been changed and the DSU still talks about 'suspension', the context in which these provisions now stand make it, as pointed out earlier, untenable to argue that WTO 'suspension' provisions have nothing to do with (and hence provide no *lex specialis* for) state responsibility. Recall also that the Subsidies agreement does mention the term 'countermeasures' explicitly in its Art. 4.11.

[190] See note 188 above.

[191] If contracting out were only permitted to make international law more effective, it would be impossible for states to agree on so-called 'soft law', in the sense of law to be enforced only through consultations or reporting (that this should be possible, see James Crawford, Special Rapporteur to the ILC on State Responsibility, First Report, UN doc. A/CN.4/490, 4 (1998), para. 27; implicitly *contra*, see Simma, 'Self-Contained', as discussed in note 142 above).

this contracting out is done – more effective or less effective remedies – is completely open and left to the contractual freedom of states, subject only to rules of *jus cogens*. As the Commentary to Art. 55 of the 2001 Draft Articles states: 'Article 55 is designed to cover both "strong" forms of *lex specialis*, including what are often referred to as self-contained regimes, as well as "weaker" forms such as specific treaty provisions on a single point, for example, a specific treaty provision excluding restitution.'[192] If the parties to a treaty decide to contract out of something, one party to such treaty cannot unilaterally contract in again (*pacta tertiis*). If it is unhappy with the contracting out, it must convince the other parties to the treaty to change the treaty. Or would it be possible for a state to fall back on the general international law obligation of reparation, even if a treaty has contracted out of it, on the mere ground that that state considers that the treaty's enforcement mechanism, and its contracting out of reparation, is ineffective?

Nonetheless, the fact that the WTO treaty did, therefore, contract out of some elements of general international law on countermeasures does not mean that this general law is irrelevant for the WTO treaty.

First, the contracting out is only in respect of countermeasures taken in response to a breach *under WTO agreements*. The DSU does not say anything on countermeasures taken in response to *non-WTO breaches* (say, countermeasures, including those in the field of trade, in response to breach under a human rights treaty). The non-WTO treaty that is breached may, of course, provide for *lex specialis*. But in case of breach of a *non-WTO norm* and in the event a countermeasure in the form of *suspension of WTO obligations* were taken in response to that breach – *in full respect of the particular treaty in question and general international law* – such suspension of WTO obligations, valid under international law, ought to be recognised also as valid in the WTO, including before a WTO panel (in the event, for example, the alleged violator under the human rights treaty were to challenge the WTO consistency of the trade sanctions imposed against it).[193] An important caveat is, however, that, for example, trade sanctions in response to breach under a human rights treaty or an MEA could then only be validly taken under general international law as against states *that are bound by the human rights treaty or the MEA*.

---

[192] Commentary, 358.
[193] *Contra*: Laurence Boisson de Chazournes, *Les Contre-Mesures en Droit International Economique* (Paris: Pedone, 1992), 184; Pons, 'Self-Help', 102; and Hahn, *Einseitige Aussetzung*, pt 5, 284 ff.

Non-parties to those treaties cannot see their rights under the WTO treaty affected by treaties they did not agree to in the first place. We come back to this in chapter 8 below when we address the 'applicable law' before WTO panels.

Second, the WTO treaty sets out *lex specialis* in respect of the timing, authorisation, nature and level of countermeasures that may be taken in order to induce compliance with WTO rules. But the terms used in this *lex specialis* are often open-textured enough to allow an interpretation with reference to general international law (the first type of fall-back referred to earlier). The ICJ explicitly supported this method of interpreting the *lex specialis* in the light of more general law in its Advisory Opinion on *the Threat or Use of Nuclear Weapons*.[194] All WTO arbitrators who have had to decide on countermeasures so far have made reference to the ILC Draft Articles on countermeasures, e.g., in support of the fact that countermeasures have the objective of inducing compliance.[195] Such reference could reach further and include also a broader interpretation of the 'equivalence' standard in DSU Art. 22.4, i.e., one that is more in line with the 'proportionality' standard in the ILC Draft.

In addition, a further fall-back on general international law may be required for matters such as the effect of countermeasures on third parties and individuals, that is, matters on which the WTO treaty itself remains silent. According to general international law, the rights of third parties may not be affected by countermeasures.[196] Hence, a suspension of, for example, transparency obligations under GATT Art. X as a form of WTO suspension should not normally be permitted. Such suspension vis-à-vis one state only would, indeed, seem quite difficult since non-publication is most likely to affect the rights of all WTO members, not just the member refusing to comply. Moreover, based on Art. 50(1) of the 2001 Draft Articles, a WTO suspension that were to go against fundamental human rights or certain provisions of humanitarian law

---

[194] ICJ Reports 1996, para. 30. Discussed in chapter 7 below.
[195] See the arbitrators' decision in *EC – Bananas* (US suspension request), at para. 6.3, addressing suspension of concessions under the DSU as 'countermeasures to *induce compliance*', confirmed by the arbitrators in *EC – Hormones*, US suspension request, para. 40 and *Brazil – Aircraft*, para. 3.44.
[196] 2001 Draft Articles, Art. 49(2) ('Countermeasures are limited to the non-performance for the time being of international obligations of the State taking the measures towards the responsible State'), confirmed in the arbitrators' decision in *EC – Bananas* (US suspension request).

should not be permitted either.[197] This does not mean, however, that every time individuals are affected by a WTO suspension such WTO suspension is to be regarded as inconsistent with international law.[198]

The question as to whether or not one can fall back on general international law countermeasures, notwithstanding the suspension/countermeasures provided for in the WTO treaty itself, is, after all, most likely to be of little practical interest. First, what can be obtained under general international law is not much more than what one now gets under the WTO treaty, especially if 'equivalence' were to be interpreted more in line with the general international law standard of 'proportionality'.[199] Also in terms of treaty-based remedies, the WTO offers remedies that are as good as those under general international law. Pursuant to Art. XV of the Marrakesh Agreement, a WTO member can withdraw from the WTO (e.g., in response to breach by others) on the mere condition of six months' notice. If a WTO breach were, moreover, so fundamental as to affect all other WTO members or the very object and purpose of the WTO and/or were to continue for a very long time, suspension of an increasing number of obligations by an increasing number of WTO members – under the banner of suspension 'equivalent' to nullification – should be allowed. Second, the question of fall-back on general international law countermeasures is likely to remain of academic interest only because states mostly prefer to take countermeasures in the area of trade. This is so, in particular, in response to breaches that are

---

[197] Art. 50(1) reads: 'Countermeasures shall not affect:...(b) Obligations for the protection of fundamental human rights; (c) Obligations of a humanitarian character prohibiting reprisals; (d) Other obligations under peremptory norms of general international law...' See also Art. 60(5) of the Vienna Convention: 'Paragraphs 1 to 3 do not apply to provisions relating to the protection of the human person contained in treaties of a humanitarian character, in particular to provisions prohibiting any form of reprisals against persons protected by such treaties.'

[198] Even if a WTO suspension affects property rights of individuals, it would be going quite far to submit that this affects 'fundamental human rights'. Art. 60(5), for example, is explicitly limited to 'provisions relating to the protection of the human *person*', not his or her property. In the end, any form of countermeasures, as well as WTO suspension, will affect, and is actually aimed at affecting, individuals in some form. How else would one 'hurt' a state so as to induce it to comply? Even to break off diplomatic relations with a state as a form of retorsion (not even countermeasures) affects individuals (e.g., the diplomats involved and the person renting out the embassy, etc.).

[199] This is acknowledged even by authors arguing in favour of such fall-back: Garcia Rubio, *Unilateral Measures*, 35–6, and Pons, 'Self-Help', 88 (that Pons is, indeed, in favour of such fall-back in the event WTO countermeasures are ineffective, can be seen in his note 80).

themselves in the area of trade, but also in response to other types of breaches, e.g., under human rights or environmental treaties. If countermeasures are to be effective at all, to take them in the field of commerce is often considered to be the best way to 'hurt' the opposing state (unless, of course, one starts to think of using force). Moreover, retort measures – that is, measures that are, unlike countermeasures, not illegal, such as the refusal to sign or ratify certain treaties, or blocking development aid – can now be taken. Unless such retort measures are explicitly linked to non-compliance with WTO rules,[200] the target state of such 'legal' measures has no redress against them.

So far the real problem has, indeed, been the timing and level of countermeasures *as they are explicitly provided for in the WTO treaty* (not countermeasures under general international law). And here WTO jurisprudence has made it clear that 'the DSU imposes a general obligation of Members to redress a violation of obligations or other nullification or impairment of benefits under the covered agreements *only by recourse to the rules and procedures of the DSU, and not through unilateral action*'.[201] Hence, suspension by the United States before multilateral DSB authorisation had been obtained was condemned[202] and even US legislation, on the basis of its text, leaving room for the US trade representative to impose countermeasures inconsistent with the DSU was found to constitute a *prima facie* violation of the DSU.[203]

It can, in other words, no longer be contested that WTO members (i) are obliged to establish a WTO violation exclusively by going through DSU procedures, and (ii) can only impose WTO countermeasures after such procedures have been completed and DSB authorisation has been obtained. Moreover, the Appellate Body language, as well as the examination above, seems to leave little doubt either that WTO members, in their search for redress of WTO violations, cannot (iii) operate unilaterally,

---

[200] If explicitly linked to an alleged violation of WTO rules, even retort measures (i.e., measures that are legal) could be seen as a form of 'seeking redress' for a violation of WTO rules in respect of which DSU Art. 23.1 explicitly provides that WTO members must have recourse to, and abide by, the DSU mechanism (instead of imposing retort measures on the basis of a unilateral determination that WTO rules have been violated). Once a member has obtained a DSU determination that WTO rules have, indeed, been violated, imposing retort measures may then, however, be justifiable.

[201] Appellate Body report on *US – Certain Products*, para. 111 (emphasis added). Note that this language excludes all types of unilateral action in response to an alleged WTO violation, even countermeasures under non-WTO rules. See also the panel report on *US – Section 301* (at para. 7.43) referring to DSU Art. 23.1 as an 'exclusive dispute resolution clause'.

[202] Appellate Body report on *US – Certain Products*.   [203] Panel report on *US – Section 301*.

outside the DSU, by means of taking countermeasures *in non-WTO obligations*, either *before* or *after* DSU procedures have been completed.[204]

Conclusion on 'contracting out'

Understanding the need for a treaty to 'contract out' of general international law for this general international law to be disapplied in respect of the treaty is crucial. Such 'contracting out' is a particularly important instance of conflict of norms, but, at the same time, highlights the unity of the international legal system (since in the absence of 'contracting out', general international law continues to apply).

The example of whether the WTO treaty 'contracted out' of the general international law rules on reparation and countermeasures shows the difficulty of determining the extent to which particular law contracts out of general law. It is a matter of interpretation. The presumption is that there is *no* contracting out, but the normal rules of treaty interpretation – if and when they lead to the conclusion that the treaty did contract out – may rebut this presumption. If the presumption is thus rebutted for one aspect of general international law, other aspects may, however, continue to apply. Moreover, even if a rule of general international law has been disapplied by a particular treaty norm, a correct *interpretation* of the terms used in this treaty norm may still require reference to rules of general international law.

---

[204] Recall that the Appellate Body report on *US – Certain Products* (para. 111) excluded all types of unilateral action in response to an alleged WTO violation, including countermeasures under non-WTO rules. It is most probably in that context that Kuijper's statement, referred to in chapter 2 above, must be understood ('[t]he intention to move further towards a self-contained system certainly underlies the WTO Agreement and its Dispute Settlement Understanding, but it remains to be seen how the WTO Members will make it function', Kuijper, 'Law of GATT', 257). In that sense unilateral countermeasures, including countermeasures in non-WTO fields, are no longer tolerated as a means of seeking redress for breach of the WTO treaty.

5 Conflict-avoidance techniques

In the previous chapter, we examined how norms of international law may either accumulate or conflict. Before entering the discussion of how the different conflict situations set out in that chapter might be resolved, this chapter highlights the relatively exceptional nature of conflict, that is, at least, as compared to the absolute number of norms in existence. That conflict can in many cases be avoided is based, first, on the presumption against conflict and, second, on the process of treaty interpretation pursuant to which many apparent conflicts can be resolved. In addition, states should also be advised to engage in conflict prevention when they negotiate new norms.

Co-ordination *ex ante* (conflict prevention)

Conflict of norms may, first of all, be avoided at the negotiation stage of new norms, that is, *ex ante*. Conflict may then be prevented by one norm explicitly stating that it derogates from, or is an exception to, another norm. One norm can also make an explicit reference to, or incorporate the conditions of, another norm. In those cases, the two norms simply accumulate and conflict is prevented from arising *ex ante*.

Conflict may further be avoided by drafting treaties more clearly (thereby avoiding especially inadvertent conflicts) or negotiating new treaties with other treaties in mind. As Jenks pointed out, when different treaties are negotiated by different people, negotiators are often tempted 'to secure fuller satisfaction for their own views on debatable questions of detail at the price of conflict between different instruments and incoherence in the body of related instruments'.[1] Here again, Jenks'

---

[1] Wilfred Jenks, 'Conflict of Law-Making Treaties' (1953) 30 BYIL 401 at 452.

call for negotiators to 'form the habit of regarding proposed new instruments from the standpoint of their effect on the international statute book as a whole'[2] must be repeated. To this end, it is important for states to collect and make use of reliable data on what they have previously agreed on. Access to this data should be available for all international negotiators within the state (not just the officials in the Foreign Ministry) as well as other states, allowing those other states to check beforehand whether a proposed new norm would conflict with obligations already held by the state on the other side of the negotiating table. The treaty series maintained by the United Nations, pursuant to the obligation in Art. 102 of the UN Charter to register all treaties with the UN Secretariat, may be of great help in this respect.

Co-operation and information sharing between international organisations may further assist in avoiding conflicts, both in the sense that each organisation stays within its area of competence and in the sense that newly created rules in an organisation take account of existing rules in other regimes. Recall, in this respect, the role of the UN Economic and Social Council to 'co-ordinate the activities of the specialised agencies through consultation with and recommendations to such agencies and through recommendations to the General Assembly and to the Members of the United Nations' (Art. 63.2 of the UN Charter). The WTO also has a range of co-operation agreements with other international organisations (such as the World Bank, the IMF, the International Plant Protection Agency, etc.).[3] These agreements were concluded on the basis of Art. V of the Marrakesh Agreement and with reference to, in particular, the Declaration on the Contribution of the WTO to Achieving Greater Coherence in Global Economic Policymaking, part of the 1994 Final Act. This declaration recognises that

[t]he interlinkages between the different aspects of economic policy require that the international institutions with responsibilities in each of these areas follow consistent and mutually supportive policies. The [WTO] should therefore pursue and develop cooperation with the international organizations responsible for monetary and financial matters, while respecting the mandate... and

---

[2] Ibid.
[3] See Art. V of the Marrakesh Agreement and Art. XXVI of GATS for the legal basis allowing WTO organs to conclude such arrangements. For the Agreements with the IMF and the World Bank, as well as a report on their implementation, see *Report by the Director-General on Implementation of the Agreements between the WTO and the IMF and the World Bank*, WT/GC/W/68, 13 November 1997 (for a text of the agreements, see WTO doc. WT/GC/W/43).

the necessary autonomy in decision-making procedures of each institution... Ministers further invite the Director-General of the WTO to review with the Managing Director of the [IMF] and the President of the World Bank, the implications of the WTO's responsibility for its cooperation with the Bretton Woods institutions, as well as the forms such cooperation might take, with a view to achieving greater coherence in global economic policymaking.[4]

These are conflict prevention methods focused at the time of *negotiation* of new norms. In addition, conflict can be avoided at the stage where the *enforcement* of, or *reliance* on, a particular norm is being considered (the enforcement/reliance stage). As noted earlier, many conflicts are 'potential conflicts' only, that is, they arise only in case a state decides to rely on a particular right, be it a permission or an exemption, or decides merely to comply with the more lenient of two conflicting commands. At that stage, states may negotiate with each other, at the international level, so as to avoid the potential conflict. In addition, such 'potential conflicts' may also be averted – or, in contrast, be activated – by means of domestic consultations or domestic expressions of preference against or in favour of relying on a particular right, or enforcing a particular obligation. This is part of what one author called the 'normative feedback loop' pursuant to which states decide, consistent with domestic constituency preferences, whether or not to promote a particular regime or rule. It was described as follows:

Nations, in response to regimes, balance the value of rule compliance against other interests they may have by means of the normative feedback loop. The normative feedback loop may take the form of a nation's decision to:

(i) comply with a regime rule which would require it to act (or not to act);
(ii) encourage another nation to comply (or not) with a regime rule;
(iii) enact (or refuse to enact) domestic legislation to promote regime values.[5]

This 'normative feedback loop' will, in most cases, determine whether a potential conflict of norms actually materialises. It may also provide the mechanisms by which a conflict is avoided. Many factors may play a role in the eventual outcome reached under this loop. It has been argued, for example, that regimes or norms which have a strong compliance mechanism – such as the WTO – are more likely to prevail in

---

[4] WTO Secretariat, *The Results of the Uruguay Round of Multilateral Trade Negotiations, The Legal Texts* (Geneva, 1995), 442 at 443 (para. 5).
[5] Claire Kelly, 'The Value Vacuum: Self-enforcing Regimes and the Dilution of the Normative Feedback Loop' (2001) 23 *Michigan Journal of International Law* 673 at 690.

this process than regimes or norms which do not impose direct costs on non-compliance (such as most MEA regimes).[6]

In the remaining sections of this chapter we assume that the conflict prevention techniques just mentioned – both at the negotiation stage and at the enforcement/reliance stage – did not work and led to a situation of apparent conflict that has been submitted to an international adjudicator. We examine, more particularly, the techniques to which an international adjudicator may resort in order to avoid a finding of conflict. This is where the distinction referred to above between 'apparent' and 'genuine' conflicts comes into play. If the conflict-avoidance technique works successfully, the alleged conflict will only be apparent. If it does not work, the conflict becomes a genuine one.

The presumption against conflict

The presumption and its consequences

The wide definition of conflict suggested in chapter 4 must be tempered by the generally accepted presumption against conflict.[7] Every new norm of international law is created within the context of pre-existing international law and the presumption is that this new norm, much like new legislation enacted by the same legislator, builds upon and further develops existing law.

This 'presumption' has three major consequences:

(i) For a new norm to deviate from existing law explicit language must be found. It cannot, in other words, be presumed that states 'changed their minds'. Evidence in support that this actually happened must be submitted in order to rebut the presumption of continuity, inherent in any legal system (see the discussion on 'contracting out' in chapter 4 above, pp. 212–18).

(ii) As a result, the state relying on a conflict of norms will have the burden of proving it.

(iii) When faced with two possible interpretations, one of which harmonises the meaning of the two norms in question, the meaning

---

[6] Ibid., 701 ff.
[7] See, for example, Jenks, 'Conflict', 427 ('It seems reasonable to start from a general presumption against conflict'); and Michael Akehurst, 'The Hierarchy of the Sources of International Law' (1974–5) 47 BYIL 273 at 275 ('just as there is a presumption against the establishment of new customary rules which conflict with pre-existing customary rules, so there is a presumption against the replacement of customary rules by treaties and vice versa'). See also the panel report on *Indonesia – Autos*, para. 14.28 ('in public international law there is a presumption against conflict') and footnote 649.

that allows for harmonisation of the two norms – and hence avoids conflict – ought to be preferred.[8] As the ICJ noted in the *Right of Passage* case: '[i]t is a rule of interpretation that a text emanating from a Government must, in principle, be interpreted as producing and as intended to produce effects in accordance with existing law and not in violation of it'.[9]

The presumption that new law is consistent with pre-existing law, that is, the presumption against conflict, is of the same nature as the presumption that any state conduct – not just the conclusion of new law – complies with the law.[10] In *EC – Hormones*, for example, WTO arbitrators made it clear that 'WTO Members, as sovereign entities, can be *presumed* to act in conformity with their WTO obligations. A party claiming that a Member has acted *inconsistently* with WTO rules bears the burden of proving that inconsistency.'[11] The same presumption of legality exists in respect of acts of international organisations. As the ICJ noted in the *Certain Expenses* case: 'when the Organization takes action which warrants the assertion that it was appropriate for the fulfilment of one of the stated purposes of the United Nations, the presumption is that such action is not *ultra vires* the Organization'.[12]

---

[8] As noted by Max Srenson, *Les Sources du Droit International* (Copenhagen: E. Munksgaard, 1946), 226–7: 'Le texte est considéré comme partie du système global du droit international et l'interprétation se propose de la mettre en harmonie avec la réglementation générale de celui-ci. La présomption sur laquelle se base cette méthode d'interprétation est que les contractants, en rédigeant le traité, sont partis de certaines données qu'il n'était pas besoin de reproduire dans le texte, et auxquelles ils se sont référés tacitement.'

[9] *Right of Passage over Indian Territory* (Preliminary Objections), ICJ Reports 1957, 142.

[10] See Jacques-Michel Grossen, *Les Présomptions en Droit International Public*, thesis (Neuchâtel, 1954), 60–3 (referring to the 'présomption de respect par les Etats, du droit en général, et du droit international en particulier', also expressed in the form of the Latin adage *omnia rite praesumuntur esse acta*); 114–17 ('les parties sont présumées n'avoir pas voulu adopter des dispositions contraires aux traités conclu par elles avec des Etats Tiers'); and 115–17 ('les traités sont présumés ne pas déroger au droit coutumier').

[11] Decision of the arbitrators under DSU Art. 22 in *EC – Hormones (US request for suspension)*, para. 9.

[12] ICJ Reports 1962, 168, continuing as follows: 'If the Security Council, for example, adopts a resolution purportedly for the maintenance of international peace and security and if, in accordance with a mandate or authorization in such resolution, the Secretary-General incurs financial obligations, these amounts must be presumed to constitute "expenses of the Organization".' See, in the same sense, *Lockerbie* case (Provisional Measures), ICJ Reports 1992, para. 42 (presuming the validity of Security Council resolution 748).

The limits of the presumption against conflict

At the same time, the effects of this presumption against conflict must not be exaggerated. First, it does not say anything about how conflict should be defined. Whatever conflict means, there is an initial presumption against it. But this presumption should not form an excuse to *define* conflict narrowly, the way Jenks and Karl have done, in much the same way that the presumption that state conduct is consistent with international law (until proved to the contrary) does not mean that breach of international law ought to be construed narrowly.

Second, in many cases, a new norm will be enacted with the very purpose of changing existing law. If this is the case, the presumption against conflict cannot stand in the way of this happening. The presumption against conflict is a presumption in favour of continuity, not a prohibition of change. It ought not to lead to a restrictive interpretation of the new, allegedly conflicting, norm (the same way the presumption of consistency of state conduct should not lead to a restrictive interpretation of the international law obligation allegedly breached).[13]

To put it differently, the presumption against conflict – and in favour of stability – must be balanced carefully with the need for change and evolution of the law. Or, as the Institute of International Law put it in the limited context of the problem of intertemporal law: 'it is necessary to promote the development of the international legal system whilst preserving the principle of legal stability which is an essential part of any judicial system...any solution of an intertemporal problem in the international field must take account of the dual requirement of development and stability'.[14]

Third, the presumption against conflict requires that an effort be made to interpret the new norm in a harmonious manner with existing law. If the new norm, as well as the potentially conflicting norm already in existence, is ambiguous enough, such harmonious interpretation may well be possible. But if reconciliation between the two norms is not feasible, that is where the presumption ends. The presumption is one against the *existence* of conflict, it is not a presumption *in favour of the earlier rule* in the event there is a real conflict. To put it differently, the presumption against conflict may show that an *apparent* conflict is

---

[13] As pointed out before, the principle *in dubio mitius* is of very questionable value. See chapter 4 above. *Contra* (confirming the principle): Appellate Body report on *EC – Hormones*, footnote 154.

[14] '1975 Resolution of the Institute of International Law', *Yearbook of the Institute of International Law* (1975), 537, preambles 2 and 3.

not real. It cannot, however, *solve* a real conflict once such conflict has been established. It may be possible to interpret the terms of norm 1 in a way that avoids conflict with norm 2 (or vice versa). *But once norm 1 and norm 2 are found to be in conflict, an interpretation of either norm cannot solve the conflict.* As Jenks put it, the presumption against conflict 'will not suffice to reconcile clearly unreconcilable provisions...[it] may eliminate certain potential conflicts; it cannot eliminate the problem of conflict'.[15] The conflict must then be resolved by a third norm (such as a conflict clause in either treaty or a rule of general international law, such as Art. 30 of the Vienna Convention).

Finally, with Grossen, one could question whether this so-called 'presumption against conflict' is a genuine presumption.[16] The typical example of a presumption provided by Grossen is the English law rule that when one has no news from a person for more than seven years, that person is presumed dead. In other words, on the basis of one fact (seven years no news), one presumes the existence of another fact (death).[17] Or, as Art. 1349 of the French Civil Code states: 'Les présomptions sont des conséquences que la loi ou le magistrat tire d'un fait connu à un fait inconnu.'[18] As a result, genuine presumptions are of a positive nature. They do not constitute simple *evidence* (or 'mode de preuve'), but amount to conclusive *proof* (or 'dispense de preuve') unless the presumption can and has been rebutted. Establishing a presumption *positively* discharges one's burden of proof: for someone to prove under English law that a person is dead, it will suffice to prove that no news has been received from that person for more than seven years. This proven fact (seven years no news) will then be positively accepted as sufficient proof of an unknown fact (namely, that the person is, indeed, dead).

The presumption against conflict, in contrast, is of a negative nature only. This is so because it amounts essentially to a restatement of the basic rule on burden of proof: it is for the party invoking something to prove it (*ei qui dicit incumbit probatio*). In other words, it is for the party relying on the conflict of norms to prove that there is such conflict. The starting point is that there is no conflict, and this will remain so up to the point that proof to the contrary can be provided. The consequence of this presumption against conflict is purely negative: if the party invoking

---

[15] Jenks, 'Conflict', 429.
[16] Grossen, *Présomptions*, 63 and 117. In the same sense, see: J.-A. Salmon, 'Les Antinomies en Droit International Public', in Chaim Perelman (ed.), *Les Antinomies en Droit* (Brussels: Bruylant, 1965), 285 at 299.
[17] Grossen, *Présomptions*, 16.   [18] *Ibid.*, 18.

conflict does not succeed in establishing its existence (including in situations of doubt), that party will lose. The presumption against conflict cannot produce the positive effects normally linked to a presumption. It will, for example, not be enough to rely on this presumption to counter a *prima facie* case raised by the opposing party that there *is* conflict.[19]

In sum, the presumption against conflict exists, but its importance ought not to be overstated. In essence, it means that the starting point is that new law is consistent with existing law and it is for the party claiming the opposite to prove it. Without this rule as to who bears the burden of proof, one could, indeed, imagine a situation where one party invokes the old law (claiming that it remains unaffected), whereas the other party relies on the new law (claiming that there is conflict and that the new law ought to prevail). In theory, each party must prove what it alleges (continuing existence of the old law versus prominence of the new law). Without the presumption against conflict, the party relying on the conflict could then argue that the other party relying on the old law must prove its continuing existence (and that it is not up to it to prove conflict and prevalence of the new law). The presumption against conflict solves this impasse *in favour of the party relying on the old law.*

Treaty interpretation as a conflict-avoidance tool

The inherent limits of treaty interpretation

Before examining the role of treaty interpretation as a conflict-avoidance technique[20] – that is, the extent to which interpreting one norm in the

---

[19] Grossen stated the following on the alleged presumption of consistency of state acts with international law: 'il n'y avait pas véritablement déplacement du fardeau de la preuve. En fait le juge, en "présumant" la licéité des actes étatiques, ne faisait que décider que la partie invoquant l'illicéité ne l'avait pas démontrée à suffisance. Cet aspect négatif de la règle ne se double d'aucun aspect positif susceptible d'en faire une présomption, c'est-à-dire que devant un commencement de preuve de l'illicéité, l'Etat poursuivi en responsabilité ne saurait se contenter d'invoquer à sa décharge la présomption de licéité des actes étatiques. Il faut donc conclure à l'inexistence d'une présomption de conformité des actes étatiques au droit international' (*ibid.*, 63). In that sense, the presumption or *prima facie* case referred to in WTO jurisprudence under rules on burden of proof (i.e., the 'commencement de preuve' established by the complainant) is a genuine presumption: if the opposing party does not submit anything in response, the complainant wins. See Joost Pauwelyn, 'Evidence, Proof and Persuasion in WTO Dispute Settlement, Who Bears the Burden?' (1998) 1 JIEL 227.

[20] For an excellent overview of the interpretative methods used in the WTO, see Michael Lennard, 'Navigating by the Stars: Interpreting the WTO Agreements' (2002) 5 JIEL 17,

light of the other norm may dissolve an apparent conflict – the inherent limitations of 'interpretation' must be recalled.

First, interpretation, at least in the relatively strict sense referred to in Arts. 31 and 32 of the Vienna Convention[21] (not in the wider sense it is sometimes given with reference to all possible actions that a judge can take), is about giving meaning to the terms of a treaty. It is a matter of definition.[22] In the WTO context, for example, for a WTO rule to be interpreted with reference to another, allegedly conflicting, rule, the WTO provision must, first of all, include terms that are broad and ambiguous enough to allow for input by other rules. In addition, the other rule must say something about what the WTO term should mean, that is, there must be a hook-up with the WTO term for the other rule to impart meaning in the process of interpretation. The other rule must, in other words, be relevant to the WTO rule. This was the case, for example, in *US – Shrimp* where the Appellate Body interpreted the WTO term 'exhaustible natural resources' in GATT Art. XX(g) with reference to, *inter alia*, UNCLOS, the Convention on Biological Diversity and CITES.[23]

Second, interpretation must be limited to giving meaning to rules of law. It cannot extend to creating new rules. *Within the process of treaty interpretation*, other rules cannot add meaning to WTO rules that goes either *beyond* or *against* the 'clear meaning of the terms' of the WTO rule in question. Interpretations *contra legem* are prohibited. Interpretation thus allows, for example, reading the WTO term 'exhaustible natural resources' to include *certain living species* with reference to international environmental law (such inclusion does not run counter to the 'clear meaning of the terms'). Interpretation would, however, prohibit this term being read so as to include also resources which are 'clearly' not

---

and Peter Maki, 'Interpreting GATT Using the Vienna Convention on the Law of Treaties: A Method to Increase the Legitimacy of the Dispute Settlement System' (2000) 9 *Minnesota Journal of Global Trade* 343.

[21] That Arts. 31 and 32 reflect general customary international law, see the ICJ *Case Concerning the Arbitral Award of 31 July 1989 (Guinea-Bissau v. Senegal)*, ICJ Reports 1991; the *LaGrand* case, at para. 99; and Appellate Body reports on *US – Gasoline* and *Japan – Alcoholic Beverages*.

[22] As the ICJ stated in the *Fisheries Jurisdiction* case (*Spain v. Canada*) in respect of interpretation: 'It is one thing to seek to determine whether a concept is known to a system of law, in this case international law...the question of the existence and content of the concept within the system is a matter of definition. It is quite another matter to seek to determine whether a specific act falling within the scope of a concept...violates the normative rules of that system: the question of the conformity of the act with the system is a question of legality' (ICJ Reports 1998, para. 68).

[23] Appellate Body report on *US – Shrimp*, paras. 128–32.

exhaustible (such as tomatoes) or resources that are 'clearly' *not* natural (such as plastic). Even 'evolutionary interpretation', further discussed below – that is, interpretation of treaty terms in the light of supervening law – is bound by this inherent limitation of treaty interpretation. New law may influence the meaning of pre-existing treaty terms. However, it cannot go either *beyond* or *against* the 'clear meaning' of these terms. This was confirmed in the *Guinea-Bissau/Senegal Maritime Boundary Arbitration*.[24] As noted by Bowett in another context: 'The cardinal principle is that interpretation as a procedure seeks to clarify what has already been decided, with binding force. It must stop short of changing what has been decided, for that involves *revision* which is a quite separate procedure governed by separate rules.'[25]

Interpretation is sometimes seen as a solution under domestic law for conflict between national law and international law.[26] National law

---

[24] Award of 31 July 1989 (1990) 83 ILR 1, at para. 85, where the tribunal did interpret notions such as continental shelf expressly mentioned in a 1960 bilateral agreement in the light of new law, existing in 1989, but made it clear, at the same time, that notions not mentioned in the 1960 treaty, such as 'exclusive economic zone', could not, by means of treaty interpretation, be incorporated *ex post facto* into the treaty: 'To interpret an agreement concluded in 1960 so as to cover also the delimitation of areas such as the "exclusive economic zone" would involve a real modification of its text and, in accordance with a well-known dictum of the International Court of Justice, it is the duty of a court to interpret treaties, not to revise them.'

[25] D. W. Bowett, '*Res Judicata* and the Limits of Rectification of Decisions by International Tribunals' (1996) 8 *African Journal of International Law* 577 at 586 (a statement made in the context of subsequent interpretations of *judgments* by the same court that rendered the original judgment, not in the context of interpretation of norms; but this 'cardinal principle' must apply in both contexts).

[26] See, in the United States, the Charming Betsy doctrine: 'an act of congress ought never to be construed to violate the law of nations if any other possible construction remains' (*Murray v. Schooner Charming Betsy*, 6 US (2 Branch) 64, 118 (1804)) and 'ambiguous statutory provisions . . . [should] be construed, where possible, to be consistent with international obligations of the United States (*Footwear Distributors and Retailers of America v. United States*, 852 F. Supp. 1078, 1088 (CIT), appeal dismissed, 43 F.3d 1486 (Table) (Fed. Cir. 1994), citing *DeBartolo Corp. v. Florida Gulf Coast Building and Trades Council*, 485 US 568 (1988)). In the EC, EC legislation must comply with international law, the latter being the 'higher law'. (See, for example, *A. Racke GmbH v. Hauptzollamt Mainz*, Case C-162/96 [1998] ECR I-3655, paras. 45–6.) If not, EC legislation can be annulled or set aside on condition that the international law is 'directly effective' pursuant to EC standards. However, even if the international law is not 'directly effective', the legislation must still be construed, as far as possible, consistent with international law (see *Hermès International v. FHT Marketing Choice BV*, Case C-53/96 [1998] ECR I-3603, para. 28). This may necessitate reading 'explicit rights' out of EC law (i.e., solving conflict situations 3 and 4 in favour of international law). The same applies in respect of national law alleged to be illegal under EC law. On EC law being the supreme law, see *Costa v. ENEL*, Case 6/64 [1964] ECR 585. On the requirement to

must then be interpreted so as to comply with international law. This may imply that certain rights granted under domestic law cannot be exercised (if not, international law would be breached).[27] In international law, interpretation as a conflict-avoidance technique cannot go that far since it would require a decision as to which of the two norms prevails, that is, something that can only be done once conflict is acknowledged. In domestic law this can be done because it is acknowledged *ex ante* that international law is the 'higher law'. In that sense, under domestic law, to 'interpret' the domestic law in line with international law is *a way of giving preference to international law*, not a technique to avoid conflict between domestic law and international law.

Having made these caveats, we next assess the different means by which treaty *interpretation* may avoid conflict.

Interpretation 'in the context' of all other treaty provisions

The terms of a treaty norm must, first of all, be interpreted 'in their context' (Art. 31(1) of the Vienna Convention). This context includes, particularly, all the other provisions of the treaty in which the norm is set out. Given the fact that all WTO treaty provisions constitute one single treaty, any WTO rule must, therefore, be interpreted in the context of all other WTO rules. Hence, in the event of an alleged conflict *between two WTO rules*, only if an interpretation of these two rules in the light of each other cannot lead to a harmonious result can conflict arise. In other words, only if one of the two norms explicitly goes against the other norm is the presumption against conflict rebutted. To the extent either or both of these norms includes terms that are open-textured or ambiguous and an interpretation of these terms consistent with the meaning of the opposing norm is feasible, such interpretation, harmonising the two norms, must be preferred. In that sense, contextual interpretation is but a confirmation of the presumption against conflict.

The principle of effective treaty interpretation

The principle of effectiveness in treaty interpretation (*ut res magis valeat quam pereat*) may also be useful in solving apparent conflicts. However, as in the case for the presumption against conflict, its importance as a conflict-avoidance tool should not be overestimated.

'interpret' national law consistently with EC law, even if that EC law has no 'direct effect', see *Von Colson and Kamann v. Land Nordrhein-Westfalen*, Case 14/83 [1984] ECR 1891.

[27] This was found to be the case, for example, by the panel on *US – Section 301*.

The tension between 'effective' and 'textual' treaty interpretation

The principle of effectiveness, in general, has certain limitations. It is not explicitly acknowledged in Arts. 31-2 of the Vienna Convention, but the Commentary to the final ILC Draft deals with it *in extenso*. This commentary draws attention to the usefulness of the principle in certain circumstances but rightly points out its limitations linked to the traditional 'textual' approach to treaty interpretation. It deserves full quotation:

> Nor did it [the ILC] consider that the principle expressed in the maxim *ut res magis valeat quam pereat* should not be included as one of the general rules [of treaty interpretation]. It recognized that in certain circumstances recourse to the principle may be appropriate and that it has sometimes been invoked by the [ICJ]. In the *Corfu Channel* case,[28] for example, in interpreting a Special Agreement the Court said:
>
>> It would indeed be incompatible with the generally accepted rules of interpretation to admit that a provision of this sort occurring in a Special Agreement should be devoid of purport or effect.
>
> ...The Commission, however, took the view that, in so far as the maxim *ut res magis valeat quam pereat* reflects a true general rule of interpretation, it is embodied in [what is now Art. 31(1)] which requires that a treaty shall be interpreted in *good faith* in accordance with the ordinary meaning to be given to its terms in the context of the treaty *and in the light of its object and purpose*. *When a treaty is open to two interpretations one of which does and the other does not enable the treaty to have appropriate effects, good faith and the objects and purposes of the treaty demand that the former interpretation should be adopted* [emphasis added]. Properly limited and applied, the maxim does not call for an 'extensive' or 'liberal' interpretation in the sense of an interpretation going beyond what is expressed or necessarily to be implied in the terms of the treaty. Accordingly, it did not seem to the Commission that there was any need to include a separate provision on this point. Moreover to do so might encourage attempts to extend the meaning of treaties illegitimately on the basis of the so-called principle of 'effective interpretation'. The Court, which has by no means adopted a narrow view of the extent to which it is proper to imply terms in treaties, has nevertheless insisted that there are definite limits to the use which may be made of the principle *ut res magis valeat* for this purpose. In the *Interpretation of Peace Treaties* Advisory Opinion[29] it said:
>
>> The principle of interpretation expressed in the maxim: *ut res magis valeat quam pereat*, often referred to as the rule of effectiveness, cannot justify the Court in attributing to the provisions for the settlement of disputes in the Peace Treaties a meaning which...would be contrary to their letter and spirit.

---

[28] (Merits) ICJ Reports 1949, 4 at 24.   [29] ICJ Reports 1950, 229.

And it emphasized that *to adopt an interpretation which ran counter to the clear meaning of the terms would not be to interpret but to revise the treaty* [emphasis added].[30]

The WTO's Appellate Body adopted the exact same approach. It confirmed that 'an interpreter is not free to adopt a reading that would result in reducing whole clauses or paragraphs of a treaty to redundancy or inutility'.[31] On the other side of the spectrum, the Appellate Body stated also that the Vienna Convention 'principles of interpretation neither require nor condone the imputation into a treaty of words that are not there or the importation into a treaty of concepts that were not intended'.[32] Therefore, as much as words cannot be *interpreted 'out of'* WTO provisions, new words that are not there or were not intended cannot either be *interpreted 'into'* WTO provisions.

The principle of effectiveness as a conflict-avoidance tool

How then could this principle of effectiveness solve apparent conflicts? Giving the intended effect to each of the – at first sight – contradictory norms may, indeed, solve an apparent conflict. This will be the case, for example, when one norm explicitly derogates from another or makes it otherwise clear that the scope of one norm must be restricted or carved out so as to give effect to another norm. As between two WTO treaty norms, it could, for example, be submitted that GATT Arts. III and XX constitute an apparent conflict, the former prohibiting certain trade restrictions which the latter explicitly allows for. However, this apparent conflict can be solved readily by 'effective treaty interpretation' along the lines that for the GATT Art. XX right to have its desired effect, the scope of GATT Art. III prohibitions must be narrowed down or carved out. Art. XX provides, indeed, explicitly that 'nothing in this Agreement shall be construed to prevent the adoption or enforcement' of the measures specified in Art. XX. Much the same happened in *EC – Hormones* where the Appellate Body reversed the panel's finding that Arts. 3.1 and 3.3 of the SPS agreement are in a 'general rule–exception' relationship. In that case, the Appellate Body stated that 'Article 3.1...simply excludes from its scope of application the kinds of situations covered by Article 3.3...Article 3.3 recognizes the autonomous right of a Member to establish'

---

[30] Dietrich Rauschning, *The Vienna Convention on the Law of Treaties, Travaux Préparatoires* (Frankfurt: Metzner, 1978), 251.
[31] Appellate Body reports on *US – Gasoline*, p. 23, confirmed in, inter alia, *Japan – Alcoholic Beverages*, p. 12.
[32] Appellate Body report on *India – Patent*, para. 46.

its own level of protection.[33] Here as well, Art. 3.1 explicitly allows for Art. 3.3 to 'deviate' from Art. 3.1. Art. 3.1 states that it applies 'except as otherwise provided for in this Agreement, and in particular in paragraph 3'. In both instances – GATT Arts. III and XX as well as SPS Arts. 3.1 and 3.3[34] – an apparent conflict is resolved by means of effective treaty interpretation, in particular by giving effect to wording making clear that one provision (GATT Art. III or SPS Art. 3.1) is derogated from by another.

It should, in this context, be pointed out that Arts. 31–2 of the Vienna Convention do not call for a restrictive interpretation of derogating norms or exceptions. Whereas under GATT 1947 panels stated that exceptions (in particular GATT Art. XX) are to be interpreted narrowly,[35] the Appellate Body has rightly pointed out that 'merely characterizing a treaty provision as an "exception" does not by itself justify a "stricter" or "narrower" interpretation of that provision than would be warranted... by applying the normal rules of treaty interpretation'.[36]

The limits of effectiveness

In other circumstances, however, a reading that harmonises both norms will not be possible. Not to acknowledge conflict in that event would go *against* the principle of effectiveness. To restrict the meaning of one norm with reference to the other would then, indeed, *not* give the required effect to the first norm. To put it differently, in the absence of explicit wording stating that one provision applies notwithstanding another, 'effective treaty interpretation' can work both ways: in favour of the first norm (giving 'full effect' to the first norm) or in favour of the second norm (giving 'full effect' to the second norm).

---

[33] Appellate Body report on *EC – Hormones*, para. 104.
[34] This similarity is a strong argument in favour of revisiting also the 'general rule–exception' relationship between GATT Arts. III and XX. As much as SPS Art. 3.3, GATT Art. XX should be seen as an autonomous right, carving out certain situations from the prohibition in GATT Art. III. Art. XX provides, indeed, that 'nothing in this Agreement shall be construed to prevent the adoption or enforcement' of certain types of measures. Consequently, under GATT Art. XX (as is the case under SPS Art. 3.3) the burden of proof should rest on the complainant.
[35] See, for example, the GATT panel report on *US – Countervailing Duties on Fresh, Chilled and Frozen Pork from Canada* (BISD 38S/30, adopted on 11 July 1991, at para. 4.4): 'an exception to basic principles of the General Agreement had to be interpreted narrowly'. See also the GATT panel report on *Canada – Import Restrictions on Ice Cream and Yoghurt* (BISD 36S/68, adopted on 4 December 1989, at para. 59), where the panel 'noted, as had previous panels, that exceptions were to be narrowly interpreted'.
[36] Appellate Body report on *EC – Hormones*, para. 104.

Let us take the hypothetical example of a measure being *GATT inconsistent* (say, not conforming to GATT Art. XX) but *TBT consistent* (say, justified as pursuing 'a legitimate objective', not mentioned in GATT Art. XX, but acceptable under TBT Art. 2.2). Neither GATT Art. XX nor TBT Art. 2.2 explicitly derogate from one another. It could then be argued that for the TBT *right* to be given effect, the GATT *prohibition* must be interpreted as carved out. But one could equally submit that for the GATT *obligation* to have its effect, the TBT *right* must be interpreted narrowly. To put it differently, effective interpretation of a WTO prohibition may require neutralising a WTO right, the same way effective interpretation of a WTO right may require deactivation of a WTO prohibition. In such instances, effective treaty interpretation alone cannot provide the solution. It must be accepted that in that event a genuine conflict has arisen (more particularly, between a prohibition and a permission) and the appropriate conflict rules must be applied (in this case, the General Interpretative Note to Annex 1A).

In that sense, the principle of effectiveness puts a limitation on the presumption against conflict. If a harmonious reading of the two norms is *not* feasible within the realm of treaty interpretation, the presumption must be seen as rebutted and the existence of conflict acknowledged. Refusing to do so would result in *not* giving the intended effect to at least one of the norms in question.

Interpretation with reference to norms outside the treaty

A treaty norm must also be interpreted in the light of certain other norms of international law *not* set out in the treaty in question. This process too can prevent a genuine conflict from arising. There are four provisions in Arts. 31 and 32 of the Vienna Convention that may require a reference to rules of international law other than those set out in the treaty itself or in agreements or instruments signed in connection with its conclusion:

- 'any *subsequent agreement* between the parties regarding the interpretation of the treaty or the application of its provisions' (Art. 31(3)(a));[37]
- 'any *subsequent practice* in the application of the treaty which establishes the agreement of the parties regarding its interpretation' (Art. 31(3)(b));

---

[37] Article IX of the WTO agreement has contracted out of Art. 31(3)(a) on subsequent agreements 'between the parties' regarding interpretation. It suffices, in the WTO, that three quarters of WTO members agree to an interpretation of the WTO treaty for that interpretation to be authoritative.

- 'any *relevant rules of international law* applicable in the relations between the parties' (Art. 31(3)(c)); and
- the non-exhaustive category of '*supplementary means* of interpretation' of Art. 32, in particular other norms part of the 'historical background' of the treaty under interpretation.

In the event of an apparent conflict between a WTO treaty rule and a non-WTO rule, the WTO rule must, therefore, be interpreted in the light of and, to the extent possible, consistently with the non-WTO rule *whenever this non-WTO rule falls under one of these four categories*. Equally, in the event the non-WTO rule is a treaty rule, this treaty rule must be interpreted in the light of and, to the extent possible, consistently with the WTO rule *whenever this WTO rule falls under one of these four categories*. In an alleged conflict of norms there are necessarily two norms and each of these two norms may need interpretation. If there is room for an interpretation under either of these norms that is consistent with the other norm, such interpretation must be preferred.

'Subsequent agreement' and 'subsequent practice'

As far as the WTO treaty is concerned, the first two provisions – subsequent agreement and subsequent practice – are essentially limited to *agreements in the specific WTO context*. This is the case given the large membership of the WTO. Note, indeed, the strict requirement, also in respect of subsequent practice, that *agreement* between the parties on interpretation or application of WTO rules must be established. In chapter 2 above we discussed the importance of 'subsequent practice' as a source of WTO law.

Historical background

In respect of the fourth provision – 'supplementary means of interpretation' – the Appellate Body in *EC – Poultry* made a reference to the bilateral Oilseeds Agreement between the EC and Brazil as 'a part of the historical background of the concessions of the European Communities for frozen poultry meat'.[38] This reference to 'historical background' limits the relevance of non-WTO rules under Article 32 to those existing *at the time of conclusion* of the WTO treaty (15 April 1994). It should be pointed out, in this context, that the importance of 'historical background' or *travaux préparatoires* as reference material to interpret a treaty dwindled quite dramatically in the course of the twentieth century. Under GATT 1947

---

[38] Appellate Body report on *EC – Poultry*, para. 83.

this element was, for example, given a high degree of importance. In the WTO, in contrast, *travaux préparatoires* are generally not referred to, with the notable exception of interpretation of concessions set out in the country-specific schedules of WTO members.[39] In the recent *LaGrand* case too, the ICJ based its interpretation that provisional measures (under Art. 41 of the ICJ Statute) are, indeed, legally binding exclusively on the elements referred to in Art. 31 of the Vienna Convention. The ICJ noted: 'Given the conclusions reached by the Court above in interpreting the text of Article 41 of the Statute in the light of its object and purpose, it does not consider it necessary to resort to the preparatory work in order to determine the meaning of that Article.'[40] It adopted the same approach when deciding that Art. 36(1) of the 1963 Vienna Convention on Consular Relations creates rights not only for state parties but also for individuals. The Court noted: 'The clarity of these provisions, viewed in their context, admits of no doubt. It follows, as has been held on a number of occasions, that the Court must apply these as they stand.'[41]

Other 'relevant rules of international law'

The third provision set out above – when interpreting a treaty, account must be taken of 'any relevant rules of international law applicable in the relations between the parties' (Art. 31(3)(c)) – is the most interesting one for present purposes. As Sands noted, 'Article 31.3(c) reflects a "principle of integration". It emphasizes both the "unity of international law" and the sense in which rules should not be considered in isolation of general international law.'[42] For the WTO, this means that there is

a presumption that the WTO system...is to be interpreted consistently with general international law, and that the customary rule is to apply unless it can be shown that such an application would undermine the object and purpose of the WTO system [I would say, rather, unless the WTO treaty has 'contracted out'

---

[39] See, for example, the Appellate Body reports on *EC – Computer Equipment* and *Canada – Dairy Products*.

[40] *LaGrand* case, para. 104. The Court added, nonetheless, that 'the preparatory work of the Statute does not preclude the conclusion that orders under Article 41 have binding force' (*ibid.*).

[41] *Ibid.*, para. 77. In his Separate Opinion, Vice-President Shi criticised the Court's refusal to examine also the *travaux préparatoires* of Art. 36. In his view, it is not possible to conclude from the negotiating history that Art. 36(1)(b) was intended by the negotiators to create individual rights.

[42] Philippe Sands, 'Treaty, Custom and the Cross-fertilization of International Law' (1998) 10 *Yale Human Rights and Development Law Journal* 3 at 8, para. 25.

of this general rule]. The burden should therefore be on the party opposing the interpretation compatible with the customary rule to explain why it should not be applied.[43]

This allocation of burden of proof results from the presumption against conflict or 'contracting out' set out earlier.

Importantly, however, not in every situation of alleged conflict must one norm be interpreted with reference to the other, pursuant to Art. 31(3)(c). There are limitations *ratione materiae* as well as limitations *ratione temporis*. We examine them in turn (pp. 254–64 and 264–8).

Finally, also under Art. 31(3)(c) the most important limitation on the process of treaty *interpretation* (as opposed to *applying* a treaty) remains relevant: 'outside rules' to be referred to pursuant to Art. 31(3)(c) can only assist in *giving meaning* to the terms used in, for example, the WTO treaty; they cannot change or overrule those terms. As Sands noted, 'under 31(3)(c), the treaty being interpreted retains a primary role. The customary norm [to be referred to under Art. 31(3)(c)] has a secondary role, in the sense that there can be no question of the customary norm displacing the treaty norm, either partly or wholly.'[44]

The material scope of rules to be referred to pursuant to Art. 31(3)(c)

In so far as the material scope of Art. 31(3)(c) is concerned, three questions arise. First, what type of rules of international law can be referred to? Does Art. 31(3)(c) cover, for example, only general principles of international law, or can reference be made also to other *treaty* rules? Second, what is meant by rules 'applicable in the relations between the parties'? More particularly, can reference be made only to rules binding on *all* WTO members, or is it sufficient that a rule is binding as between the *disputing parties* involved in a particular case? Third, what is meant by 'relevant' rules of international law? We deal with these three questions in turn.

What type of rules can be referred to?

The rules of international law referred to in Art. 31(3)(c) do not seem to be limited to any particular sources of international law. Art. 31(3)(c) refers to 'relevant rules of international law' without restriction as to their source. Hence, in the interpretation of WTO provisions, Art. 31(3)(c) directs panels and the Appellate Body to take account of treaty

---

[43] *Ibid.*, p. 12, para. 41.   [44] *Ibid.*, p. 12, para. 39.

provisions, customary international law and general principles of law that meet certain conditions.⁴⁵

In the *Golder* case, decided by the European Court of Human Rights (ECtHR) in 1975, it was held, for example, that the reference to 'relevant rules of international law' in Art. 31(3)(c) includes 'general principles of law and especially "general principles of law recognized by civilized nations" (Article 38 para. 1(c) of the Statute of the International Court of Justice)'.⁴⁶ The Iran–US Claims Tribunal, in turn, interpreted provisions of the Claims Settlement Declaration with reference to other rules of international law, pursuant to Art. 31(3)(c). The 'other rule' in question was one related to nationality, namely the rule of 'dominant and effective nationality'.⁴⁷ The tribunal did not specify whether this rule was a general principle of (international) law or a rule of general customary international law. It did find, however, that it was a rule falling within the scope of Art. 31(3)(c) of the Vienna Convention.

In *US – Shrimp* too, the Appellate Body's reference to Art. 31(3)(c) was focused on 'general principles of international law', namely the principle of good faith and the related doctrine of *abus de droit*.⁴⁸ In what is so far the only case where the Appellate Body explicitly used Art. 31(3)(c), it stated that: 'our task here is to interpret the language of the chapeau [of Art. XX of GATT 1994], seeking additional interpretative guidance, as appropriate, from the general principles of international law'.⁴⁹

Nonetheless, it must be remembered that Art. 31(3)(c) may cover also rules of customary international law and even certain treaty provisions. According to Sir Ian Sinclair, for example, Art. 31(3)(c) 'may be taken to include not only the general rules of international law but also treaty obligations existing for the parties'.⁵⁰ This approach was followed in the recent *Al-Adsani* case, decided by the ECtHR. In that case, the Court

---

⁴⁵ In support: Gabrielle Marceau, 'Conflicts of Norms and Conflicts of Jurisdictions, The Relationship between the WTO Agreement and MEAs and other Treaties' (2001) 35 JWT 1081 at 1087.
⁴⁶ *Golder v. the United Kingdom*, judgment of 21 February 1975, Series A no. 18, p. 14, para. 29, published in 57 ILR 201. See also *Johnston and Others v. Ireland*, judgment of 18 December 1986, Series A no. 112, p. 24, para. 51 and *Loizidou v. Turkey* (Preliminary Objections), p. 27, para. 73.
⁴⁷ *Espahanian v. Bank Tejarat* (1983 I) 2 IRAN–US CTR 157. See also *Iran v. United States (Case A18)* (1984 I) 5 IRAN–US CTR 251.
⁴⁸ Appellate Body report on *US – Shrimp*, para. 158 and footnote 157.
⁴⁹ *Ibid*. A footnote to this sentence states: 'Vienna Convention, Article 31(3)(c)'.
⁵⁰ Ian Sinclair, *The Vienna Convention on the Law of Treaties* (Manchester: Manchester University Press, 2nd edn, 1984), 119. *Contra*: Sands, 'Cross-fertilization', 11, para. 38, who seems to limit the rules referred to in Art. 31(3)(c) to general customary

first expressed its established position that the Convention 'cannot be interpreted in a vacuum' and that the ECtHR 'must also take the relevant rules of international law into account'.[51] The 'other rules' at issue in this dispute were 'generally recognised rules of public international law on State immunity', more particularly, as they apply in a civil suit brought in one state for damages in respect of acts of torture committed in another state. The ECtHR established those rules on the basis of certain treaties (1972 Basel Convention, Universal Declaration of Human Rights, International Covenant on Civil and Political Rights and UN Convention against Torture). It also referred to judgments of other courts, in particular the International Criminal Tribunal for the Former Yugoslavia and the House of Lords.

This trend of taking account not only of general principles of law but also of other treaties finds reflection in the Appellate Body report on *US – Shrimp*, where the words 'exhaustible natural resources' in Art. XX(g) of GATT 1994 were interpreted with reference to a number of non-WTO treaties (such as UNCLOS and the Convention on Biological Diversity).[52] In doing so, the Appellate Body did not refer, however, to Art. 31(3)(c). It, therefore, remains unclear whether these references to non-WTO treaties were made pursuant to Art. 31(3)(c) or, for example, pursuant to Art. 31(1) of the Vienna Convention, calling for an interpretation of treaties 'in good faith in accordance with the ordinary meaning to be given to the terms of the treaty'.

Finally, in the *Loizidou* case, the ECtHR made reference also to certain acts of international organisations, another generally recognised source of international law. More particularly, pursuant to Art. 31(3)(c), the ECtHR took account of two UN Security Council Resolutions and decisions of the Committee of Ministers of the Council of Europe, the European Community and the Commonwealth Heads of State, in coming to its decision that 'the international community does not regard the [Turkish Republic of Northern Cyprus] as a State under international law'.[53] It would seem, therefore, that also WTO panels and the Appellate Body could be empowered, pursuant to Art. 31(3)(c), to refer to certain acts of international organisations, in particular of the United Nations, in the interpretation of the WTO treaty.

international law (they 'must be legally binding (other than *qua* treaty) upon the parties disputing the interpretation to be given to a particular treaty').
[51] *Al-Adsani v. The United Kingdom*, judgment of 21 November 2001, para. 55.
[52] Appellate Body Report, *US – Shrimp*, para. 130.
[53] *Loizidou v. Turkey*, judgment of 18 December 1996, Reports 1996-VI, para. 44.

Rules 'applicable in the relations between the parties'

Article 31(3)(c) refers to rules 'applicable in the relations *between the parties*' (emphasis added). Article 2(1)(g) of the Vienna Convention defines 'party' as 'a State which has consented to be bound by the treaty and for which the treaty is in force'. Hence, it would seem, Art. 31(3)(c) refers to parties *to the treaty*, not parties *to a particular dispute under that treaty*.[54]

That a treaty can, in principle, only be interpreted with reference to elements that reflect the *common* intentions of all parties to the treaty, not a few of them, finds support in the Appellate Body report on *EC – Computer Equipment*: 'The purpose of treaty interpretation under Article 31 of the *Vienna Convention* is to ascertain the *common* intentions of the parties. These *common* intentions cannot be ascertained on the basis of the subjective and unilaterally determined "expectations" of *one* of the parties to a treaty.'[55] The same approach was adopted by the ICJ in, for example, the *Case Concerning Maritime Delimitation and Territorial Questions between Qatar and Bahrain*.[56]

This approach is mandated by the principle of *pacta tertiis*: a state cannot be held by a treaty it did not agree to, nor can it see the interpretation of a treaty to which it *is* bound affected by a treaty it refused to sign. This principle is, in terms of treaty interpretation, aptly expressed also in the adage *ejus est interpretare legem cujus condere*, or as the PCIJ stated in its Advisory Opinion on the *Question of Jaworzina*: 'it is an established principle that the right of giving an authoritative interpretation of a legal rule belongs solely to the person or body who has the power to modify or suppress it'.[57] In *Oppenheim's International Law* the rationale behind this principle was formulated thus: 'An interpretation agreed between some only of the parties to a multilateral treaty may, however, not be conclusive, since the interests and intentions of the other parties may have to be taken into consideration.'[58]

---

[54] In support: Sands, 'Cross-fertilization', 11, para. 38, who goes even further and seems to limit the rules referred to in Art. 31(3)(c) to customary international law (see note 50 above).

[55] Appellate Body Report on *EC – Computer Equipment*, para. 84 (emphasis in the original).

[56] Jurisdiction and Admissibility, ICJ Reports 1995, 6 at 22: 'whatever may have been the motives of each of the Parties, the Court can only confine itself to the actual terms of the Minutes as the expression of their *common intention*, and to the interpretation of them which it has already given' (emphasis added).

[57] *Delimitation of the Polish–Czechoslovakian Frontier (Question of Jaworzina)*, PCIJ, Advisory Opinion, Series B, No. 8 (1923).

[58] R. Jennings and A. Watts, *Oppenheim's International Law* (London: Longmans, 1992), I, 1268.

Such interpretation of Art. 31(3)(c) – that 'other rules' can only be referred to under Art. 31(3)(c) if they reflect the 'common intentions' of all parties to the treaty under interpretation – seems to be called for also by the context in which Art. 31(3)(c) is set. In particular, Arts. 31(3)(a) and (b) provide, respectively, that account must be taken of 'any *subsequent agreement* between *the parties* regarding the interpretation of the treaty or the application of its provisions' and 'any *subsequent practice* in the application of the treaty which establishes the agreement of *the parties* regarding its interpretation'. Examining the preparatory work of these provisions it seems, indeed, that the 'subsequent agreements' and 'subsequent practice' referred to are only agreements and practice reflecting the common intentions of all parties to the treaty. As Sir Humphrey Waldock noted in his observations on the 1964 ILC Draft on the law of treaties in respect of 'subsequent practice':

> Under [what is now Art. 31(3)(b)] it is only subsequent practice which clearly establishes the understanding of all the parties regarding the meaning of the treaty which is recognized as equivalent to an interpretative agreement and the reason is, of course, that *two parties or even a group of parties cannot, by their interpretation of the treaty, bind the other parties as to its correct interpretation* [emphasis added].[59]

The same approach was followed by the (unadopted) GATT panel on *United States – Restrictions on Imports of Tuna* in respect of Art. 31(3)(a). This panel read Art. 31(3)(a) as allowing reference only to treaty provisions other than those in the GATT that had been accepted by *all* GATT contracting parties. Since the Convention on International Trade in Endangered Species (CITES) was not so accepted, the panel refused to take it into account.[60]

If this were correct – and only a 'subsequent agreement' or 'subsequent practice' *within* the WTO context that reflects the common intentions of all WTO members can be taken into account under Arts. 31(3)(a) and (b) – it would, indeed, seem difficult to argue that, pursuant to Art. 31(3)(c), a bilateral agreement between the disputing parties concluded *outside* the WTO context can play a role in the interpretation of the *WTO agreement*.

Further support for the proposition that bilateral treaties between the disputing parties cannot be taken into account in the interpretation of WTO provisions pursuant to Art. 31(3)(c) can be found in Art. IX of the

---

[59] Rauschning, *Travaux*, 307.
[60] Panel report, *United States – Restrictions on Imports of Tuna ('US – Tuna (EEC)')*, 16 June 1994, unadopted, DS29/R, para. 5.19.

WTO agreement. Article IX:2 provides that the 'Ministerial Conference and the General Council shall have the exclusive authority to adopt interpretations of this Agreement and of the Multilateral Trade Agreement' and that the decision to adopt such interpretation 'shall be taken by a three-fourths majority of the Members'. Now, if Art. IX explicitly provides that a three-quarters majority of WTO members is required for an authoritative interpretation, could it not be argued that this excludes a bilateral treaty, concluded between only two WTO members, from being referred to as an interpretative resource under Art. 31(3)(c)?

Nonetheless, some commentators have suggested that Art. 31(3)(c) covers also treaties that are binding only as between the disputing WTO members in a particular case.[61] Mavroidis and Palmeter criticised the above-mentioned finding of the (unadopted) GATT panel on *United States – Restrictions on Imports of Tuna*. They argued that this finding, focused though on Art. 31(3)(a), is inconsistent with Art. 31(3)(c) and that

[a]n interpretation of this language [of Art. 31(3)(c)] to mean only any subsequent agreement among all of the parties to the GATT – and not simply to an agreement among the parties to the dispute – does not seem supportable by the text of Article 31(3)(c). The word 'parties', as used in Article 31(3)(c), would seem to refer to the parties to the particular dispute, not to the parties to the multilateral agreement.[62]

A similar focus on whether the *disputing parties* – not all WTO members – are bound by a particular treaty can be found in the panel report on *US – Shrimp (Article 21.5 – Malaysia)*. The panel found as follows:

Finally, we note that the Appellate Body, like the Original Panel, referred to a number of international agreements, many of which have been ratified or otherwise accepted *by the parties to this dispute*. Article 31.3(c) provides that, in interpreting a treaty, there shall be taken into account, together with the context, 'any relevant rule of international law applicable to the relations between the parties'. We note that, with the exception of the Bonn Convention on the Conservation of Migratory Species of Wild Animals (CMS), *Malaysia and the United*

---

[61] David Palmeter and Petros Mavroidis, *Dispute Settlement in the WTO, Practice and Procedure* (The Hague: Kluwer, 1999), 57; and Marceau, 'Conflicts', 1087 ('The requirement that any such rule be "applicable to the relations between the parties" in the WTO/MEA debate, implies that the *two WTO Members* must be parties to the MEA for it to be used in the interpretation of the WTO provision' (emphasis added); later, at 1107, she seems to go even further, implying that it is sufficient that only one of the disputing parties is bound by the non-WTO rule: 'when interpreting WTO provisions, *all international obligations and rights of WTO Members* must be taken into account' (emphasis added)).

[62] Palmeter and Mavroidis, *Dispute*, 57.

States have accepted or are committed to comply with all of the international instruments referred to by the Appellate Body.[63]

The panel never examined whether these agreements can also be said to reflect the 'common intentions' of WTO members other than Malaysia and the United States. Instead, it focused on the question of whether *the two WTO members in dispute* (Malaysia and the United States) were bound by the non-WTO rules to be taken into account pursuant to Art. 31(3)(c). The more recent panel on *Chile – Price Band System*, in contrast, explicitly stated that it was 'leaving aside the question of whether such a rule of international law [referred to in Art. 31(3)(c)] should be applicable between *all* parties to the WTO Agreement'.[64]

It should be pointed out, however, that although Art. 31(3)(c) may not permit reference to treaties that do *not* reflect the common intentions of all WTO members, such treaties may still play a role as part of the historical background of the WTO treaty to be taken into account under the supplementary rules of interpretation of Art. 32 of the Vienna Convention.[65]

In addition, even though a particular treaty provision may not be legally binding on all WTO members, or not even on all disputing parties in a particular case, such treaty may still play a role under Art. 31(3)(c) if it can be said to reflect the 'common intentions' of WTO members, or under Art. 31(1) if it can be said to reflect the 'ordinary meaning' of a WTO treaty term. This was arguably the case when the Appellate Body in *US – Shrimp* referred to certain treaties that were not binding even on the disputing parties, let alone on all WTO members.[66] Although the Appellate Body remained silent as to the legal basis for this reference to non-WTO treaties, it could be submitted that the non-WTO treaties it referred to, though not legally binding on all WTO members, reflected the 'common intentions' of all WTO members and/or the 'ordinary meaning' of the term 'exhaustible natural resources' as it is used in Art. XX(g) of GATT 1994. The same could be said about the double taxation treaties and domestic taxation rules referred to by the Appellate Body in *US – FSC (Article 21.5 – EC)* when it was interpreting the term 'foreign-source income' in footnote 59 of the Subsidies agreement.[67] Those treaties and domestic

---

[63] Panel report on *US – Shrimp (Article 21.5 – Malaysia)*, para. 5.57 (emphasis added).
[64] Panel report on *Chile – Price Band System*, para. 7.85.
[65] See, for example, Appellate Body Report on *EC – Poultry*, para. 82.
[66] Appellate Body Report on *US – Shrimp*, para. 130.
[67] Appellate Body report on *US – FSC (Article 21.5 – EC)*, paras. 141–5.

rules are, obviously, not binding on all WTO members. Nonetheless, the Appellate Body found that 'certain widely recognized principles of taxation emerge from them' and that 'it is appropriate... to derive assistance' from these principles when giving meaning to the WTO term 'foreign-source income'.[68] Although the Appellate Body remained silent on the reason why this was appropriate, it could be said that these principles reflect the 'common intentions' of all WTO members and/or the 'ordinary meaning' of the term 'foreign-source income' to be taken into account, respectively, pursuant to Art. 31(3)(c) and Art. 31(1).

Article 31(3)(c) refers to 'the parties', not '*all* the parties'.[69] As a result, and particularly in the light of the ILC commentary to Art. 31(3)(b),[70] it could be argued that the requirement is not that *all* the parties to the WTO agreement have, one after the other, formally and explicitly agreed with the non-WTO rule, nor even that this rule is otherwise *legally binding* on *all* WTO members. It could be submitted that the criterion is rather that the rule can be said to be at least *implicitly* accepted or tolerated by all WTO members, in the sense that the rule can reasonably be said to express the common intentions or understanding of all members as to what the particular WTO term means.[71] This could also be what the panel on *Chile – Price Band System* had in mind when it stated that it was leaving aside the question of whether rules that can be referred to

---

[68] Ibid., para. 142.

[69] Article 31(2)(a), for example, uses the expression '*all* the parties' when it comes to agreements relating to the treaty made in connection with the conclusion of the treaty.

[70] The commentary to Art. 31(3)(b) states as follows: 'The text provisionally adopted in 1964 spoke of a practice which "establishes the understanding of all the parties". By omitting the word "all" the Commission did not intend to change the rule. It considered that the phrase "the understanding of the parties" necessarily means "the parties as a whole". It omitted the word "all" merely to avoid any possible misconception that every party must individually have engaged in the practice where it suffices that it should have accepted the practice' (Rauschning, *Travaux*, 254).

As a result, if 'the parties' in Art. 31(3)(b) means *all* the parties *without* requiring that all of them have explicitly agreed with (or actually conducted) the practice, it could be argued that the same meaning should be given to 'the parties' as the term is used in Art. 31(3)(c). In that context as well, it could then mean: rules accepted (or tolerated) by all the parties to the treaty, either explicitly or by some form of implied or tacit consent.

[71] See Joost Pauwelyn, 'The Role of Public International Law in the WTO: How Far Can We Go?' (2001) 95 AJIL 535 at 575–6, and Gabrielle Marceau, 'WTO Dispute Settlement and Human Rights' (2002) 13 EJIL 753 ('it could be argued that the use, without... qualifications, of "the parties" in Article 31(3)(b) and (c) allows consideration of treaties signed by a subset of the WTO membership that is less than all the parties, but more than one of the parties, that is *accepted* by the other parties').

under Art. 31(3)(c) 'should be applicable between *all* parties to the WTO Agreement'.[72] Instead of leaving open the possibility for bilateral treaties to be referred to, it may have been thinking more about certain treaty provisions, not accepted by *all* WTO members, that nevertheless express the 'common intentions' of all WTO members.[73]

Recall, indeed, that the input of other rules of international law in the interpretation of a treaty norm is limited to giving meaning to explicit treaty terms. It is a question of definition and importing meaning, not one of incorporating legal rights or obligations set out in the foreign rule which are not included under the 'clear meaning of the terms' of the treaty norm under interpretation. Indeed, when it comes to defining a term in the exercise of treaty interpretation, why should, for example, the *Oxford English Dictionary* play an uncontested role in giving meaning to the terms 'exhaustible national resources' in GATT Art. XX(g) and, in contrast, a series of MEAs with large membership *a priori* be excluded even if these agreements are not binding on *all* WTO members? Like the *Oxford English Dictionary*, these other agreements may reflect the common understanding of all WTO members.

Consequently, not in every alleged conflict of norms must one norm be interpreted in the light of the other. Of course, in the event of an apparent conflict between two bilateral treaty norms binding on both of the parties in question, one norm must necessarily be interpreted with reference to the other. The same applies in respect of two norms derived from multilateral treaties with exactly the same parties. In these situations, both norms *express the same combination of state intentions* and one expression of intent must be assessed in the light of the other. There can be no doubt either that, in the event of an alleged conflict between a treaty norm and a norm of general international law, the treaty norm must be interpreted with reference to the norm of general international law. Since general international law is, in principle, binding on all states, the latter must be a rule 'of international law applicable in the relations between the parties'. The situation is different when either of the two

---

[72] Panel report on *Chile – Price Band System*, para. 7.85.
[73] Note in this respect the Separate Opinion of Judge Jiménez de Aréchaga in the *Continental Shelf (Tunisia/Libya)* case: 'even if a new accepted trend does not yet qualify as a rule of customary law, it may still have a bearing on the decision of the Court, not as part of the applicable law, but as an element in the existing rules or an indication of the direction in which such rules should be interpreted' (ICJ Reports 1982, 108 ff., para. 33). See also Ulrich Fastenrath, *Lücken im Völkerrecht: zu Rechtscharakter, Quellen, Systemzusammenhang, Methodenlehre und Funktionen des Völkerrechts* (Berlin: Duncker & Humblot, 1991), 338–9.

norms that are allegedly in conflict derives from a multilateral treaty that is binding on both states in question, but includes also third states not bound by the second norm. In that event, the norm derived from the *broader* multilateral treaty may *not* normally be interpreted with reference to the norm derived from the more *limited* treaty, and this even though both parties involved in the conflict are themselves bound by the two norms. An example would be a norm in an MEA, not binding on all WTO members, which is allegedly in conflict with a WTO norm. In that event the WTO norm may not normally be interpreted with reference to the MEA norm. However, if all parties to the environmental norm are also WTO members, the environmental norm must be interpreted with reference to the WTO norm. Nonetheless, the MEA norm, though not legally binding on all WTO members, could still influence the meaning of the WTO norm if it can be shown that the MEA norm is an expression of the 'common intentions' or 'understanding' of all WTO members.

Finally, and of crucial importance, even if it may be the case that in the process of *interpreting* WTO treaty terms, it is not appropriate to refer to non-WTO treaty provisions that do not reflect the common intentions of all WTO members, such non-WTO treaty provisions, say, a bilateral agreement between the disputing parties, could still play a role before a WTO panel or the Appellate Body as part of the law to be *directly applied* by them (a point further discussed in chapter 8 below). The direct application of such a bilateral treaty as between the disputing parties only (always, of course, as part of the examination of certain WTO claims) would then not influence the meaning or interpretation of WTO treaty terms as they apply to other WTO members. Such a bilateral treaty could then, for example, be invoked as a defence under a claim of violation of WTO law as it applies between the disputing parties, or as proof that the disputing parties agreed to deviate from certain DSU procedures in the particular case, say, in respect of time-limits or sequencing of Arts. 21.5 and 22 of the DSU.

'Relevant' rules of international law

Finally, Art. 31(3)(c) is limited to any 'relevant' rules of international law applicable in the relations between the parties. It would seem that the subject matter of the WTO term to be interpreted and that of the 'other rule' to be referred to pursuant to Art. 31(3)(c) will be decisive.[74] If this

---

[74] In support: Sands, 'Cross-fertilization', 11, para. 38; and Marceau, 'Conflicts', 1087.

'other rule' sheds light on the meaning of the WTO term, it is 'relevant'. If it has no bearing on it, it is not 'relevant'.

The panel on *Chile – Price Band System* gave added value to the term 'relevant'. It found that Art. 24 of the agreement between Chile and MERCOSUR (ECA 35) was *not* 'relevant' to the interpretation of Art. 4.2 of the WTO Agreement on Agriculture, not because of its unrelated subject matter, but because of certain specific wording in Art. 24:

> First, the Preamble [to ECA 35] states that the commercial policies and compromises of ECA 35 shall 'adjust to' the WTO framework of rights and obligations. *A fortiori*, Article 24 of ECA 35 cannot influence the interpretation of the WTO Agreement. Second, Chile's commitment regarding its PBS [Price Band System] in Article 24 of ECA 35 has been explicitly made 'within the framework of' ECA 35. Such language suggests that the parties to ECA 35 did not intend to exclude the possibility that different commitments regarding the Chilean PBS may have been or will be made in the context of other international agreements.[75]

The temporal scope of Art. 31(3)(c): 'contemporaneous' or 'evolutionary' interpretation?

Article 31(3)(c) of the Vienna Convention refers to 'any relevant rules of international law applicable in the relations between the parties' without restriction as to the timing of these rules. At first sight, Art. 31(3)(c) directs, therefore, that in the interpretation of, for example, WTO provisions account must be taken of both (i) relevant rules of international law that existed *at the time of conclusion* of the WTO agreement, that is, on 15 April 1994; and (ii) relevant rules of international law that emerged *subsequently* and exist *at the time of interpretation*.

However, the text in Article 31(3)(c) originally read: 'rules of international law in force *at the time of conclusion of the treaty*'.[76] As it was then drafted, the provision thus allowed for reference only to rules of international law that existed *at the time the treaty was concluded*. This reflected the so-called 'principle of contemporaneity'. This principle is the first part of the intertemporal law according to which a juridical fact must be appreciated in the light of the law contemporary with it.[77] For example, when the International Court of Justice interpreted the provisions of Art. 20 of the treaties between the United States and Morocco of 1787 and 1836 (substantially identical in terms) in the *United States Nationals*

---

[75] Panel report on *Chile – Price Band System*, para. 7.85.
[76] Article 70.1(b) of the Waldock Report III, quoted in Rauschning, *Travaux*, 238.
[77] This was first expressed by Judge Huber in the *Island of Palmas* arbitration (*Netherlands v. United States*) (1928) 2 RIAA 831 at 845.

in Morocco case, it stated that 'it is necessary to take into account the meaning of the word "dispute" at the times when the two treaties were concluded'.[78]

Notwithstanding the final text of Art. 31(3)(c) – which no longer refers to 'time of conclusion' – it seems that this principle of contemporaneity remains the rule.[79] This would mean that in interpreting terms in the WTO agreement, in principle, reference is to be had to the meaning of these terms in international law on 15 April 1994, the date of conclusion of the WTO agreement.

On that basis, it would seem that the reference to the Berne, Paris and Rome Conventions in the TRIPS agreement[80] is a reference to these agreements *as they stood in April 1994*, i.e., at the time of conclusion of the WTO treaty. The incorporation of these WIPO conventions into the WTO treaty would only be a dynamic one – automatically incorporating also modifications brought to these conventions in WIPO – if there were a clear indication on behalf of the drafters of the TRIPS agreement to that effect.[81] Such indication can be found, for example, in the second paragraph of item (k) in Annex I to the Subsidies agreement, referring to 'an international undertaking on official export credits to which at least twelve original Members to this Agreement are parties as of 1 January 1979 *(or a successor undertaking which has been adopted by those original Members)*' (emphasis added). As the panel on *Brazil – Aircraft (Article 21.5 – Canada II)* found, 'the "successor undertaking" at issue in the second paragraph of item (k) is the most recent successor undertaking which has been adopted prior to the time that the second paragraph

---

[78] ICJ Reports 1951, 189.
[79] See *Guinea-Bissau/Senegal Maritime Boundary Arbitration* (Award of 31 July 1989 (1990)) 83 ILR 1, at para. 85: 'the 1960 Agreement must be interpreted in the light of the law in force at the date of its conclusion. It is a well established general principle that a legal event must be assessed in the light of the law in force at the time of its occurrence and the application of that aspect of intertemporal law to cases such as the present one is confirmed by case-law in the realm of the law of the sea.' See also the Individual Opinion of Judge Bedjaoui, in the *Case Concerning the Gabčíkovo–Nagymaros Project (Hungary v. Slovakia)*, ICJ Reports 1997 (in his view evolutionary interpretation is then the exception, if proof of intention to that effect can be pointed to).
[80] Footnote 2 in the TRIPS agreement.
[81] David Palmeter and Petros Mavroidis, 'The WTO Legal System: Sources of Law' (1998) 92 AJIL 398 at 410, hold the same view. See, in contrast, the final report of the Arbitration Panel Established Pursuant to Article 2008 of the North American Free Trade Agreement (NAFTA), in the matter of *Tariffs Applied by Canada to Certain US-Origin Agricultural Products*, 2 December 1996, where it was found that the use of the term 'GATT' in the cross-reference provisions of the FTA and NAFTA had to be interpreted to mean GATT as it evolved into the WTO agreement.

is considered. For purposes of these proceedings, we conclude that the most recent successor undertaking which has been adopted is the 1998 OECD Arrangement.'[82] In other words, because of the explicit reference to 'successor undertakings', the reference to the OECD Arrangement in item (k) is not a static one (limited to arrangements existing at the time of conclusion of the WTO treaty), but a dynamic one.

There is, however, ample scope for exception to the principle of contemporaneity. Indeed, already in the preparation of the Vienna Convention itself, it was realised that 'the content of a word, e.g. "bay" or "territorial waters", may change with the evolution of the law if the parties used it in the treaty as a general concept and not as a word of fixed content'.[83]

This reflects the so-called 'evolutionary approach' to treaty interpretation. It is the second part of the intertemporal law. This interpretative rule has been confirmed in three subsequent ICJ judgments, interpreting, for example, the term 'territorial status'.[84] It was confirmed also by the Appellate Body in US – Shrimp, where it was found that the term

---

[82] Panel report on *Brazil – Aircraft (Article 21.5 – Canada II)*, para. 5.83.

[83] Observations and Proposals of the Special Rapporteur, quoted in Rauschning, *Travaux*, 244.

[84] *Namibia (Legal Consequences)* Advisory Opinion, ICJ Reports 1971, 31: 'the concepts embodied in Article 22 of the Covenant...were not static, but were by definition evolutionary...The parties to the Covenant must consequently be deemed to have accepted them as such.'

See also the *Aegean Sea Continental Shelf* case, ICJ Reports 1978, 3; the more recent *La Bretagne* arbitration decision ((1986) 90 RGDIP 716, at para. 49, explicitly referring to Art. 31(3)(c) and, on that basis, taking account of developments in the international law of the sea for purposes of interpreting a 1972 bilateral agreement); the *Guinea-Bissau/Senegal Maritime Boundary Arbitration* (Award of 31 July 1989 (1990) 83 ILR 1, at para. 85, interpreting the notions of territorial sea, contiguous zone and continental shelf, expressly mentioned in a 1960 bilateral agreement, as defined in 1989, i.e., with reference to UNCLOS III); and the ICJ *Case Concerning the Gabčíkovo–Nagymaros Project (Hungary v. Slovakia)*, ICJ Reports 1997, although in that case the evolutionary aspect was explicitly incorporated in the 1977 treaty (Arts. 15, 19 and 20 of that treaty obliged the parties jointly to take, on a continuous basis, appropriate measures necessary for the protection of water quality, nature and fishing interests (*ibid.*, para. 106)). On that basis, the ICJ noted that 'the Treaty is not static, and is open to adapt to emerging norms of international law' (*ibid.*, para. 112). It found also: 'In order to evaluate the environmental risks, current standards must be taken into consideration. This is not only allowed by the wording of Articles 15 and 19, but even prescribed, to the extent that these articles impose a continuing – and thus necessarily evolving – obligation on the parties to maintain the quality of the water of the Danube and to protect nature' (*ibid.*, para. 140). See, in this respect, the dissertation by S. Aly, 'L'Interprétation Evolutive en Droit International Public' (1997), on file at the library of the Institut des Hautes Etudes Internationales, Geneva, Ref. HEIDS 576.

'exhaustible natural resources' in GATT Art. XX 'must be read by a treaty interpreter in the light of contemporary concerns of the community of nations about the protection and conservation of the environment [not as it was understood in 1947]'.[85]

In doing so, the Appellate Body did not refer, however, either to the first part of the intertemporal law (the principle of contemporaneity) or to Art. 31(3)(c) of the Vienna Convention.

Given these two, seemingly contradictory, parts of the intertemporal law – the principle of contemporaneity and the evolutionary approach – the question may arise as to which interpretative method to apply in respect of a particular WTO provision. The answer to this question, it has been argued, should depend on the intention of the drafters of the WTO agreement.[86] As the commentary to Art. 31(3)(c) has put it: 'the relevance of international law for the interpretation of treaties in any given case was dependent on the intentions of the parties' and 'would normally be indicated by interpretation of the term in good faith'.[87] In 1975 the Institute of International Law adopted a resolution in the same sense.[88]

As a result, it could be submitted that the use of broad, unspecified terms – such as 'exhaustible natural resources', 'public morals' or 'essential security interests' in GATT Arts. XX and XXI – is an indication that the drafters intended these terms to be interpreted in an 'evolutionary' manner. It may, indeed, be an indication that WTO members *wanted* these terms to evolve with society and international law or, at least, *should have realised* that the vagueness of these terms would result in their meaning being open to discussion and variation depending on the context and times.

In sum, as far as the temporal scope of Art. 31(3)(c) is concerned, it would seem that, for example, a WTO term, if intended by the drafters to be evolutionary in nature (not static), needs to be interpreted with

---

[85] Appellate Body report on *US – Shrimp*, paras. 128–32.
[86] See Rosalyn Higgins, 'Some Observations on the Inter-Temporal Rule in International Law', in Jerzey Makarcyk (ed.), *Theory of International Law, Essays in Honour of K. Skubiszewski* (The Hague: Kluwer, 1999), 173.
[87] Rauschning, *Travaux*, 240.
[88] 1975 Resolution of the Institute of International Law, paragraph 4, first sentence: 'Wherever a provision of a treaty refers to a legal or other concept without defining it, it is appropriate to have recourse to the usual methods of interpretation in order to determine whether the concept concerned is to be interpreted as understood at the time when the provision was drawn up or as understood at the time of its application' (*Yearbook of the Institute of International Law* (1975), 537 at 539).

reference to 'relevant rules of international law applicable in the relations between the parties', not at the time of *conclusion* of the WTO agreement, but at the time that agreement is being *interpreted*. Given the regulatory nature of many WTO provisions, often using rather broad terms, it may well be that, on these grounds, the two parts of the intertemporal law are reversed so that in the WTO, evolutionary interpretation becomes the rule, contemporaneous interpretation the exception.[89] Note, in this respect, that when construing the 'ordinary meaning' of WTO terms, both panels and the Appellate Body consistently resort to the most recent version of, for example, the *Oxford English Dictionary*, not the version as it existed in 1994.

WTO jurisprudence where WTO norms have been interpreted with reference to rules of general international law

Based on the theory explained above – that is, the need to interpret treaty norms with reference also to other norms outside the treaty (in particular on the basis of Art. 31(3)(c)) – panels and the Appellate Body have referred to a number of non-WTO rules in the interpretation of the WTO treaty. Earlier, we mentioned certain cases where non-WTO *treaties* were taken into account.[90] In this section we focus on the longer list of cases where the Appellate Body made reference to rules of *general international law*.[91] Above, we set out the limitations for such references to be made pursuant to Art. 31(3)(c) of the Vienna Convention.

---

[89] In support: Fastenrath, *Lücken*, 295; M. McDougal, H. Lasswel and J. Miller, *The Interpretation of International Agreements and World Public Order* (Dordrecht: Nijhoff, 1967), 99 ('the principal aim of an interpreter should be to give effect to the continuing consensus of the parties – that is, their contemporary shared expectations concerning problems of the type being disputed'); Denys Simon, *L'Interprétation Judiciaire des Traités d'Organisations Internationales* (Paris: Pedone, 1981), 373 ('la fonction de l'interprète est...de donner effet au consensus continu des parties plutôt qu'à des volontés cristallisées à la date de signature'); and Tetsuo Sato, *Evolving Constitutions of International Organizations* (Dordrecht: Kluwer, 1996). See also the Individual Opinion of Judge Lauterpacht in *South West Africa* (Voting Procedure) ICJ Reports 1955, 67 at 106 and Jennings and Watts, *Oppenheim's*, 1268 ('There is however room for the view that a treaty of a "constitutional" character should be subject to somewhat different rules of interpretation so as to allow for the intrinsically evolutionary nature of a constitution.')

[90] See Appellate Body report on *EC – Poultry*, para. 83; panel report on *US – Tuna (EEC)*, para. 5.19; panel report on *US – Shrimp (Article 21.5 – Malaysia)*, para. 5.57; panel report on *Chile – Price Band System*, para. 7.85.

[91] We do not generally refer in this section to references made by *panels* to rules of general international law, focusing instead on what the Appellate Body, as the highest judicial body in the WTO, has found.

It should be recalled, however, that in only one of these disputes was reference made to Art. 31(3)(c).[92] Crucially, referring to non-WTO rules in the interpretation of WTO provisions is something a WTO panel can, and should, do *on its own initiative*, as part of its own legal reasoning (*jura novit curia*).[93] There is no need for the parties to invoke such non-WTO rules. As Sands pointed out, Art. 31(3)(c) states that certain outside rules 'shall be taken into account', which means that 'an adjudicatory body is not entitled to exercise discretion. It must "take account" of those outside rules.[94] WTO panels and the Appellate Body should, indeed, foster a built-in reflex to look also outside the 'four corners' of the WTO treaty for guidance on how to interpret WTO treaty terms. In contrast, for a panel to refer to non-WTO rules as *facts* – for example, to refer to an MEA regulating trade in genetically modified organisms as factual evidence that such organisms constitute a health risk (or to refer to a multilateral convention on the protection of turtles as a 'factual reference' in an examination of whether there has been discrimination in the sense of the *chapeau* of GATT Art. XX)[95] – one of the parties must first raise these non-WTO rules. That party has then also the burden of proof in this respect.

In *US – Shrimp* the Appellate Body referred to the principle of good faith and the doctrine of *abus de droit* as general principles of international law in the process of interpreting the *chapeau* of GATT Art. XX. The Appellate Body acknowledged that its 'task here is to interpret the language of the chapeau [of GATT Art. XX], seeking additional interpretative guidance, as appropriate, from the general principles of international law'.[96] In doing so, the Appellate Body made reference for the very first (and until today, last) time to Art. 31(3)(c) of the Vienna Convention, albeit in a footnote only.[97]

In *US – FSC*, the Appellate Body confirmed that the principle of good faith is 'at once a general principle of law and a principle of general

---

[92] Appellate Body report on *US – Shrimp*, para. 158 and footnote 157.
[93] This explains why the Appellate Body in *EC – Computer Equipment* (at paras. 89–90) chastised the panel for not having looked at certain non-WTO rules (legal instruments created in the context of the World Customs Organization), obviously related to the WTO rules under interpretation, even though the parties to the dispute had not invoked these non-WTO rules.
[94] Sands, 'Cross-fertilization', 12, para. 39.
[95] Appellate Body report on *US – Shrimp (Article 21.5)*, para. 130.
[96] Appellate Body report on *US – Shrimp*, para. 158.   [97] *Ibid.*, footnote 157.

international law'.⁹⁸ Applying it in the area of procedural DSU rules, the Appellate Body added:

This pervasive principle requires both complaining and responding Members to comply with the requirements of the DSU (and related requirements in other covered agreements) in good faith. By good faith compliance, complaining Members accord to the responding Members the full measure of protection and opportunity to defend, contemplated by the letter and spirit of the procedural rules. The same principle of good faith requires that responding Members seasonably and promptly bring claimed procedural deficiencies to the attention of the complaining Member, and to the DSB or the Panel, so that corrections, if needed, can be made to resolve disputes.⁹⁹

In *US – Hot-Rolled Steel*, the Appellate Body noted that the general principle of good faith 'informs the provisions of the *Anti-Dumping* Agreement, as well as the other covered agreements'.¹⁰⁰ In *Brazil – Aircraft*, the arbitrators also made reference to the principle of good faith (albeit in a different guise) when applying 'a presumption of good faith to statements and evidence originating in subjects of international law'.¹⁰¹ In *US – Cotton Yarn*, the Appellate Body referred to 'the "pervasive" general principle of *good faith* that underlies all treaties'¹⁰² when it mentioned a potential obligation to withdraw a safeguard measure in case certain errors are proven.

In *EC – Computer Equipment*,¹⁰³ the Appellate Body referred to 'the fundamental rule of due process' in its interpretation of Art. 6.2 of the DSU (specificity of panel requests).¹⁰⁴ In *EC – Hormones*,¹⁰⁵ the Appellate Body made reference to 'fundamental fairness, or what in many jurisdictions is known as due process of law or natural justice' in setting out the meaning of 'an objective assessment' which panels have to conduct pursuant to Art. 11 of the DSU. On that basis, the Appellate Body found that Art. 11 sets out a standard prohibiting (only) 'egregious error [by panels] that calls into question the good faith of a panel'. In the same report, the Appellate Body again referred to 'due process' in order to find that

---

⁹⁸ Appellate Body report on *US – FSC*, para. 166.   ⁹⁹ Ibid.
¹⁰⁰ Appellate Body report on *US – Hot-Rolled Steel*, para. 101, footnote 40.
¹⁰¹ *Brazil – Aircraft*, arbitration report under DSU Art. 22.6, paras. 2.10–2.11 and footnote 15.
¹⁰² Appellate Body report on *US – Cotton Yarn*, para. 81.
¹⁰³ Appellate Body report on *EC – Computer Equipment*, para. 70.
¹⁰⁴ In its report on *US – Underwear*, 15, the Appellate Body had already referred to 'due process considerations' in support of its finding that the backdating of restraint measures would 'diminish the utility and significance of prior consultations'.
¹⁰⁵ Appellate Body report on *EC – Hormones*, para. 133.

'an appellant requesting the Appellate Body to reverse a panel's procedural ruling on matters of procedure must demonstrate the prejudice generated by such legal ruling'.[106]

Also in WTO arbitrations on the question of retaliation, reference has been made to general international law in the field of countermeasures. This was done in order to answer the question of whether a proposal for 'suspension of concessions or other obligations' under DSU Art. 22.2 meets DSU requirements, in particular that of 'equivalence' with the level of nullification and impairment caused by the WTO inconsistent measure still in place. In *EC – Bananas (US suspension request)*, the arbitrators invoked, for example, 'the general international law principle of proportionality of countermeasures'.[107] In *Brazil – Aircraft*, an arbitration on the 'appropriateness' of 'countermeasures' under the Subsidies agreement, the arbitrators referred to the meaning and objective of 'countermeasures' in general international law (in particular the work of the ILC in this field)[108] to give meaning to the term 'countermeasures' as it is used in the Subsidies agreement.[109] The Appellate Body has also referred to general international law rules on countermeasures in its interpretation of the Safeguards agreement. In *US – Cotton Yarn*, it noted that one of its conclusions 'is further supported by the rules of general international law on state responsibility, which require that countermeasures in response to breaches by states of their international obligations be commensurate with the injury suffered'.[110] In *US – Line Pipe*, the Appellate Body also took note of 'the customary international law rules on state responsibility', recalling that 'the rules of general international law on state responsibility require that countermeasures in response to breaches by States of their international obligations be proportionate to such breaches'.[111] The Appellate Body referred explicitly to Art. 51 of the 2001 Draft Articles on State Responsibility, specifying that '[a]lthough Article 51 is part of the International Law Commission's Draft Articles,

---

[106] Ibid., footnote 138.
[107] *EC – Bananas*, arbitration report under DSU Art. 22.6 (US suspension request), para. 6.16.
[108] The arbitrators considered the ILC Draft Articles on State Responsibility, setting out certain rules on countermeasures, to be 'an indication of the agreed meaning of certain terms in general international law' and this even though Canada objected to these rules being part of customary international law (*Brazil – Aircraft*, arbitration report under DSU Art. 22.6, footnote 48).
[109] Ibid., para. 3.44 and footnote 45.
[110] Appellate Body report on *US – Cotton Yarn*, para. 129.
[111] Appellate Body report on *US – Line Pipe*, para. 259.

which do not constitute a binding legal instrument as such, this provision sets out a recognized principle of customary international law'.[112]

In another dispute (*EC – Poultry*),[113] the Appellate Body referred to 'customary usage in international trade' to conclude that the term 'c.i.f. import price' in Art. 5(1)(b) of the Agreement on Agriculture refers simply to the cost-insurance-freight (c.i.f.) price *without* customs duties and taxes. In doing so, the Appellate Body did not further elaborate on where this 'customary usage in international trade' can be found, nor did it explain why such usage is to play a role in treaty interpretation pursuant to customary international law.

A word of caution on the role of interpretation with reference to other norms as a conflict-avoidance technique

Interpretation may solve apparent conflicts; it cannot solve genuine conflicts

Interpretation of one norm with reference to another, allegedly conflicting, norm – if at all permissible under the limitations regarding membership and time, set out earlier – may lead to a harmonious reading of both norms, that is, it may lead to the conclusion that there is, after all, no conflict. However, if interpretation leads to the conclusion that one norm in and of itself, or as it is implemented or relied on by a state, *does* constitute a breach of another norm, that is where the role of interpretation of treaty terms as a conflict-avoidance technique stops. To put it differently, interpretation of the terms in question may resolve apparent conflicts; it cannot resolve genuine conflicts.

We set out above some of the inherent limitations of the process of interpretation: the need for open-textured terms as well as a hook-up between the two norms and the prohibition on interpretations *contra legem*. These restrictions linked to the process of treaty interpretation make it clear that the role of non-WTO rules in the *interpretation* of WTO covered agreements must be rather limited (in particular because of the requirement that the non-WTO rules reflect the 'common intentions' of all 144 WTO members). Hence, contrary to what certain authors seem to imply,[114] treaty interpretation with reference to other rules of

---

[112] *Ibid.* [113] Appellate Body report on *EC – Poultry*, para. 146.
[114] See, for example, Joel Trachtman, 'The Domain of WTO Dispute Resolution' (1999) 40 *Harvard International Law Journal* 333 at 343; Gabrielle Marceau, 'A Call for Coherence in International Law – Praises for the Prohibition Against "Clinical Isolation" in WTO Dispute Settlement' (1999) 33 JWT 87; Gabrielle Marceau, untitled, World Bank

international law is *not* a panacea for all problems of interplay between WTO and other rules of international law.

In contrast, it may be easier for WTO rules to impart meaning to non-WTO rules, given that the latter often have a more limited membership. Indeed, even if *WTO rules* may not be interpreted with reference to such non-WTO rules, say, certain MEAs (because of questions of membership), when interpreting these *non-WTO rules* reference to WTO rules may still be called for. This reference may facilitate an interpretation of the non-WTO rule that is in line with the WTO treaty and thereby resolve an apparent conflict. But if such harmonious interpretation is not feasible, a genuine conflict arises and treaty interpretation in and of itself is incapable of resolving it.

Interpretation of the treaty with reference to other law versus *application* of the treaty together with other law

It is of crucial importance to recall here the distinction made earlier (in chapter 4) between the two types of 'fall-back' on other rules of international law: first, interpretation of specific treaty terms with reference to other law; second, application of the treaty in the context of other law.

Fall-back by means of *interpretation* with reference to other rules of international law is subject to many limitations: it is definitional in nature, it cannot go beyond the clear meaning of the terms and it is bound to norms expressing the 'common intentions' of all parties to the treaty.

Fall-back because of a 'gap' in the treaty, that is, because of the presumption that international law continues to apply to the treaty unless there is contracting out, is much broader in scope. There, the influence of other norms is not linked nor limited to giving meaning to explicit terms in the treaty. The other norms, by their very nature – they fill a 'gap' – *add* to the treaty terms as a fully fledged part of the applicable law in case of judicial disputes. They are not bound either by temporal limitations: the gap is filled by international law rules *as they stand at*

Seminar on International Trade Law, 24–25 October 2000, 3, on file with the author; Jonathan Charney, 'Is International Law Threatened by Multiple International Tribunals?' (1998) 271 *Recueil des Cours* 101 at 219; and Eric Canal-Forgues, 'Sur l'Interprétation dans le Droit de l'OMC' (2001) 105 RGDIP 1 at 11 ('Cette formulation générale [in Art. 31(3)(c)] a pu être considérée comme *la seule* à pouvoir prendre en compte l'enlacement et l'interconnexion des branches du droit international tout en permettant de réconcilier les normes conventionnelles et coutumières issues de branches différentes.')

the time of application of the treaty, not as they stood at the time of its conclusion. Moreover, as we shall see in chapter 8 below, this second type of fall-back on international law is, unlike that of interpretation, not limited to rules of international law reflecting the 'common intentions' of all parties to the treaty. It extends also to any rule of international law binding as between the *two disputing parties*. Since the WTO treaty was created and continues to exist in the context of international law, all rules of international law binding on the parties are potentially relevant in a decision on whether or not WTO law applies and has been breached.

6 Resolving 'inherent normative conflict'

Preliminary classifications for conflict resolution

Solutions in the law of treaties, the law of state responsibility and international institutional law

The conflict-avoidance techniques set out in the previous chapter may fail. An apparent conflict then becomes a genuine conflict. Having validly established it as a genuine conflict, resolution of a conflict of norms may involve different disciplines of public international law. The law of treaties, including the provisions of particular treaties, provides the bulk of all conflict rules. Nonetheless, state responsibility is highly relevant. When it comes to acts of international organisations, international institutional law must also be referred to.

'Inherent normative conflict' versus 'conflict in the applicable law'

As pointed out in chapter 4, a conflict of norms may take one of two forms:

(i) One of the two norms constitutes, in and of itself, breach of the other norm. This is what we called an 'inherent normative conflict'. An inherent normative conflict will arise, for example, when a norm conflicts with another norm of *jus cogens* or when an *inter se* agreement is concluded by some parties to a multilateral treaty, in breach of an explicit prohibition to conclude such agreement. We examine the resolution of inherent normative conflicts in this chapter.

(ii) Compliance with, or the exercise of rights under, one of the two norms constitutes breach under the other norm. This is what we referred to as 'conflict in the applicable law'. Conflict in the applicable law includes what we called earlier *necessary* conflicts and *potential* conflicts, where one norm, in and of itself, is not in conflict with another norm, but where the implementation of an obligation, or the exercise of a right, under one of the norms constitutes breach of the other. We examine the resolution of conflict in the applicable law in the next chapter (chapter 7).

When faced with an inherent normative conflict, one norm constitutes breach of the other. In other words, one norm is 'illegal', that is, constitutes wrongful conduct, under the other norm. Inherent normative conflict, therefore, gives rise to state responsibility. In addition, rules on the law of treaties or of international institutional law may apply and result, for example, in the 'invalidity' of the norm constituting breach. We come back to the distinction between 'illegality' and 'invalidity' below. Moreover, apart from state responsibility incurred for the very conclusion of one of the two norms, inherent normative conflicts may also give rise to state responsibility because of *specific state conduct* performed in compliance with the 'illegal' (or, as the case may be, 'invalid') norm.

In contrast, when faced with conflict in the applicable law, the question of 'illegality' or 'invalidity' of one of the two norms vis-à-vis the other norm does not arise. The question is rather: a state has acted in a certain way, two norms apply to the act in question, under one norm the act is 'illegal', under the other it is not; which of the two norms must be applied?

Conflict in the applicable law may arise, therefore, when a state, before acting, is confronted with two contradictory norms and decides to comply with obligations or exercise rights under one of the two norms, thereby breaching the other norm. If this other norm, which has been breached, is the one that prevails in the conflict, then the state in question, by its unilateral conduct, will have breached the prevailing norm so that its responsibility can be invoked. If, in contrast, the norm breached has to give way to the norm complied with, then the state in question made the right choice and it incurs no responsibility. To put it differently, a WTO member, having imposed a specific trade restriction, may be challenged before a WTO panel for breach of GATT Art. XI (prohibition on imposing quantitative restrictions) and invoke in its defence an MEA rule (explicitly prescribing or permitting certain trade restrictions). If it convinces the panel that the MEA rule prevails over the GATT rule in this conflict, then the state made the right choice and incurs no responsibility. If, in contrast, the WTO member concerned fails to convince the panel that the MEA rule prevails over the GATT rule, then the panel may find that the specific trade restriction is in violation of the GATT so that state responsibility is incurred. Such responsibility is then incurred, not by the very conclusion of the MEA, but by other state conduct (here, a specific trade restriction) that allegedly relied on the MEA, but in effect constitutes a breach of the GATT rule.

'Invalidity' distinguished from 'illegality'

In inherent normative conflicts and conflicts in the applicable law, rules on state responsibility may lead to one of the two norms, or other state conduct, respectively, being 'illegal', that is, it may constitute wrongful conduct under the other norm. In addition, but limited to inherent normative conflicts, the law on treaties and international institutional law may also result in the 'invalidity' of one of the two norms because of conflict with the other norm. 'Illegality' must hence be distinguished from 'invalidity', first of all, on the basis of the rules leading to it (the law on state responsibility versus the law on treaties or international organisations).

Secondly, 'invalidity' as a sanction is explained on the ground of lack of competence, contracting power or other anomalies related to the consent given to be bound *by the norm in question*, such as error, fraud, corruption or coercion. 'Illegality', in contrast, is a somewhat lesser sanction in that, looked at in isolation, the norm was validly *created*. However, it is or becomes 'illegal' because it constitutes conduct that is defined as wrongful under *another norm*. In that sense, invalidity is normally a sanction that applies *ab initio* or *ex tunc* (except for supervening invalidity, as a result of, for example, supervening *jus cogens*).[1] It cannot be rectified, except by concluding a new norm (this time not taken *ultra vires* or created without error, fraud, corruption or coercion). 'Illegality', on the other hand, can be cured or rectified without changing the norm affected by it. It can, for example, be cured by altering the norm with which it is in conflict.

Finally, and linked to the fact that invalidity, as opposed to illegality, cannot normally be cured, 'invalidity' should be a matter to be discovered and decided upon by an international adjudicator *on its own initiative*.[2] 'Illegality', in contrast, will normally be pronounced by an adjudicator only if so asked by one of the parties (here, the principle of *non ultra petita* applies).

---

[1] Nonetheless, pursuant to Art. 69 of the Vienna Convention, 'acts performed in good faith before the invalidity was invoked are not rendered unlawful by reason of the invalidity of the treaty' (in situations other than fraud, corruption or coercion).

[2] See, in this respect, the statement by Judge Schücking in his Dissenting Opinion in the *Oscar Chinn* case: 'It is an essential principle of any court, whether national or international, that the judges may only recognize legal rules which they hold to be valid' (PCIJ Reports, Series A/B, No. 63, 149 (1934)).

Hierarchy among conflict rules

In this chapter and the next, we classify the different types of solutions to a conflict of norms according to their outcome: (i) one of the two norms disappears; (ii) one of the two norms is 'illegal'; (iii) one of the two norms 'prevails' (but is not 'illegal'); (iv) both norms are complete equals (and state responsibility may provide the solution). The first two solutions are solutions for inherent normative conflict; the last two, for conflict in the applicable law.

When faced with a particular conflict between two norms, this is also the hierarchical order one ought to follow. Each time one should ask

(i) whether either of the two norms is 'invalid' or 'terminated' (section below, pp. 278–98);
(ii) if not, whether one of them is 'illegal' (section below, pp. 298–327);
(iii) if this is not the case either, the question must be: which of the two norms 'prevails', i.e., must be applied according to the priority rules of international law (discussed in chapter 7, pp. 327–418);
(iv) if these priority rules do not solve the conflict either, one must resort to the solutions offered in chapter 7, pp. 418–36: both norms are complete equals and state responsibility may offer the way out, or the conflict constitutes a genuine lacuna in the law.

One of the two norms ceases to exist

A conflict of norms, when constituting an inherent normative conflict as defined above, may result in the disappearance of one of the two norms. The question is then one of 'survival', or: which of the two norms remains? A norm may disappear as a result of conflict either through (i) invalidity; or (ii) termination.

If that is the case, the invalid or terminated norm can (no longer) be breached so that no state responsibility can be incurred under this norm. Of course, breach of the prevailing norm – either by the very conclusion of the 'invalid' norm or by state conduct adopted pursuant to this norm – does result in state responsibility.

Invalidity of a norm because of conflict with jus cogens

In international law, invalidity of a norm because of conflict with another norm is limited to the extreme, namely to cases where a norm is in conflict with *jus cogens*. If that is the case, the conflicting norm is, or becomes, void so that only one of the two conflicting norms (the norm of *jus cogens*) continues to exist (Arts. 53 and 64 of the Vienna Convention).

Note, in this respect, Art. 71 of the Vienna Convention. If a treaty is void because of a conflict with *existing jus cogens* (pursuant to Art. 53), the parties must: '(a) eliminate as far as possible the consequences of any act performed in reliance on any provision which conflicts with the peremptory norm of general international law; and (b) bring their mutual relations into conformity with the peremptory norm of general international law'. In contrast, if a treaty becomes void and terminates because of *supervening jus cogens* (pursuant to Art. 64), 'the termination of the treaty: (a) releases the parties from any obligation further to perform the treaty; (b) does not affect any right, obligation or legal situation of the parties created through the execution of the treaty prior to its termination; provided that those rights, obligations or situations may thereafter be maintained only to the extent that their maintenance is not itself in conflict with the new peremptory norm of general international law'.

Given that the treaty norm is then invalid, some have questioned whether there was a genuine conflict of norms in the first place. Waldock noted, for example: 'where a treaty was invalid for conflict with a rule of *jus cogens*, it was not a treaty for legal purposes and no question of a conflict between two treaties arose'.[3] He used this as a reason not to mention *jus cogens* in what is now Art. 30 of the Vienna Convention. However, from all other angles one must see Arts. 53 and 64 as raising a problem of 'conflict' of norms. After all, these provisions include the very word 'conflict' and the invalidity is a *consequence* of *conflict*, even if this consequence of conflict means that the conflict disappears.

For those states bound by the Vienna Convention, Art. 66 accords compulsory jurisdiction to the ICJ for disputes 'concerning the application or the interpretation of articles 53 and 64' (unless the parties by common consent agree to submit the dispute to arbitration). However, so far no single case has been brought pursuant to this provision.

Invalidity may arise only in one other instance of conflict, namely a conflict between an act of an international organisation and the constituent instrument of that organisation (discussed below, pp. 285–98).

Background to the limitation of 'invalidity' to conflicts with *jus cogens*

That invalidity of norms of international law ought to occur only in case of conflict with *jus cogens* has, however, not always been the

---
[3] YBILC 1964, vol. 1, 742nd Meeting, 121, para. 23.

prevailing view. Witness, for example, the preparatory works of the Vienna Convention and the quite dramatic shift that occurred there, from 'invalidity' as a solution to conflict between treaties, to 'priority' of one treaty provision over the other.[4]

Indeed, Sir Hersch Lauterpacht, the first rapporteur to the ILC, originally proposed as a general rule that a treaty should automatically be *void* 'if its performance involves a breach of a treaty obligation previously undertaken by one or more of the contracting parties'.[5] Sir Gerald Fitzmaurice, the second rapporteur, on the other hand, proposed a draft based on the view that in general the question is one of reconciling conflicting legal provisions. In his view, only in certain types of cases may the later treaty be invalid (in particular in the event of conflict with an earlier treaty of an 'interdependent' or 'integral' type).[6] The third, and probably most influential rapporteur, Sir Humphrey Waldock, sided with Fitzmaurice and even took it a step further. In his view, invalidity occurred only in the event of conflict with *jus cogens* (and in certain cases of inconsistency with the constituent instrument of international organisations, an exception he later dropped).

Waldock, as well as the Vienna Convention as it was finally adopted, focuses not on 'invalidity' but on 'opposability' and 'priority' of treaty norms, combined with state responsibility (not nullity), in case of breach of one treaty by another. Consequently, *invalidity* of a norm of international law is a rare sanction. It occurs only in the event of conflict with *jus cogens*. This conflict is seen as so serious that the conflicting norm should not only give way to the norm of *jus cogens*, but should actually be declared invalid or, in case of supervening *jus cogens*, become void and terminate. The invalidity of norms in conflict with *jus cogens* is explained, in theoretical terms, on the ground that states have no 'legal capacity' to conclude norms against *jus cogens*. The very fact of states being part of the international community invalidates their consent to such norms.

Below, we discuss the possibility of declaring 'invalid' acts of international organisations that are inconsistent with the constituent instrument of the organisation. We also explain that *inter se* modifications of

[4] Summarised in Waldock's Second Report, Commentary to Art. 14, YBILC 1964, vol. 2, 53–61.
[5] *Ibid.*, 55, referring to Art. 16 of Lauterpacht's draft (A/CN.4/63 and 87). Lauterpacht did, however, add a series of exceptions to this general rule (a list which increased in his second report).
[6] Waldock's Second Report, Commentary to Art. 14, YBILC 1964, vol. 2, 55–9.

a multilateral treaty that do not meet the conditions in Art. 41 of the Vienna Convention are not 'invalid' but 'illegal'. Finally, it will become clear also that conflicts of the type AB/AC (that is, situations where state A has conflicting obligations vis-à-vis B and C, while B and C are bound only by one of the two conflicting rules) do not lead to the invalidity of the AC norm, but that both the AB and the AC norms are, in principle, equally valid (see below, pp. 422–7).

Invalidity of the entire treaty or of the conflicting provisions only

In case a new treaty conflicts with *existing jus cogens* – the situation addressed in Art. 53 of the Vienna Convention – the conflict is regarded so seriously that the offending treaty provision becomes inseparable. As a result, the *whole treaty* is invalid, even if only one of its provisions is impugned. Article 44(5) of the Vienna Convention provides, indeed, explicitly that '[i]n cases falling under articles 51, 52 and 53, no separation of the provisions of the treaty is permitted'. In contrast, in the event of conflict between an existing treaty and *supervening jus cogens*, the existing treaty becomes, pursuant to Art. 63, 'void and terminates'. However, Art. 44 on 'separability of treaty provisions' remains applicable (and this even though Art. 63 provides that the '*treaty...becomes void and terminates*'). Hence, it may well be the case that only one provision in the earlier treaty becomes invalid because of the conflict with supervening *jus cogens*, not the entire treaty.[7]

The ILC, in its commentary to Art. 63 (then Art. 61), noted the following:

although the Commission did not think that the principle of separability is appropriate when a treaty is void *ab initio* under article 50 [now Art. 53] by reason of an existing rule of *jus cogens*, it felt that different considerations apply in the case of a treaty which was entirely valid when concluded but is now found with respect to some of its provisions to conflict with a newly established rule of *jus cogens*. If those provisions can properly be regarded as severable from the rest of the treaty, the Commission thought that the rest of the treaty ought to be regarded as still valid.[8]

It is difficult to see what these different considerations might be. There seem to be no valid reasons to make a distinction – *in terms of separability*

---

[7] *Contra*: James Crawford, Second Report, UN doc. A/CN.4/498 (1999), Annex 2, para. 306.
[8] Dietrich Rauschning, *The Vienna Convention on the Law of Treaties, Travaux Préparatoires* (Frankfurt: Metzner, 1978), 440.

of treaty provisions – between invalidity at the time of conclusion of a treaty and invalidity at a later stage. Of course, invalidity because of conflict with existing *jus cogens* results in invalidity *ab initio*, whereas invalidity because of supervening *jus cogens* operates only as of the establishment of the *jus cogens*. But this distinction relates to the timing of the invalidity, not to its material scope. In the latter sense, no distinction ought to be made. Either in both cases there is invalidity of the entire treaty or in both cases normal rules on separability apply. Given the exceptional nature of invalidity of a norm because of conflict with another norm, the continued application of separability rules in both instances seems more appropriate. The importance and superiority of *jus cogens* should not thereby be compromised. If it is, indeed, so that a non-respect for *jus cogens* underlies the entire treaty, the normal rules, in Art. 44, on separability would ensure the invalidity of the entire treaty.[9] As Capotorti remarked, after having rejected the distinction made in terms of separability between Art. 53 and Art. 64: 'il conviendra plutôt de distinguer entre les dispositions étroitement liées à la clause incompatible et les dispositions indépendantes, et de voir si l'accord conserve encore son objet une fois que le contenu se réduit à ces dernières dispositions'.[10]

In case somehow the WTO treaty, with its myriad of agreements (but legally constituting one single treaty), were to include one single provision in conflict with *jus cogens*, would it, indeed, not be going too far to say that because of this conflict with one WTO provision, the entire WTO treaty is invalid?

Termination of a treaty by means of concluding another, incompatible, treaty

A conflict between two norms may cause the 'disappearance' of one of the two norms in a way other than invalidity. The emergence of a new norm, in conflict with an earlier norm, may lead to the termination of the earlier norm. Pursuant to Art. 59 of the Vienna Convention, a later treaty may terminate an earlier one, either because 'it appears from the

---

[9] Art. 44(3) allows for invalidity of only the impugned provision in case (i) that provision is separable from the others 'with regard to their application'; (ii) the impugned provision 'was not an essential basis of the consent of the other party or parties to be bound by the treaty as a whole'; and (iii) the 'continued performance of the remainder of the treaty would not be unjust'.

[10] F. Capotorti, 'Interférences dans l'Ordre Juridique Interne entre La Convention et d'autres Accords Internationaux', in *Les Droits de L'Homme en Droit Interne et en Droit International* (Brussels, 1968), 123 at 131.

later treaty or is otherwise established that the parties intended that the matter should be governed by that treaty' or because the provisions of the later treaty are 'so far incompatible with those of the earlier one that the two treaties are not capable of being applied at the same time'.

The incompatibility or conflict required for the earlier treaty to be terminated must hence be of a rather serious nature: it must result in the impossibility of applying both *treaties* – not just two provisions of the two treaties – at the same time. Article 59(2) adds that '[t]he earlier treaty shall be considered as only *suspended* in operation if it appears from the later treaty or is otherwise established that such was the intention of the parties' (emphasis added).

Article 59 is based on the Dissenting Opinion of Judge Anzilotti in the *Electricity Company of Sofia and Bulgaria* case where he introduced the distinction between explicit and tacit abrogation.[11] In the *Free Zones of Upper Savoy and the District of Gex* case, the PCIJ refused to hold that the 1919 Treaty of Versailles had implicitly abrogated, or was intended to lead to the abrogation of, the provisions of the earlier 1815 Treaties of Paris and other supplementary acts regarding the customs and economic regime of the free zones of Upper Savoy and the District of Gex.[12] The Court interpreted the later Treaty of Versailles as requiring that France and Switzerland agree between themselves on a modification of the existing 1815 regime. Pending the conclusion of such agreement, 'this [1815] regime must continue in force so long as it has not been modified by agreement between the parties'.[13] In other words, in the view of the Court, the difference between the 1815 and the 1919 treaty was not such as to imply the termination of the earlier treaty.[14]

Importantly, as pointed out earlier, if one norm *explicitly* terminates or suspends another, no conflict of norms arises.[15] The operation of the second norm then simply means the end or suspension of the earlier norm and both norms can be applied side by side. Here, a situation of conflict arises only if the later treaty does not itself state that it terminates the earlier one and the termination must be implied instead from the degree of incompatibility between the two treaties. To put it differently, there is no conflict if norm 2 *itself* terminates norm 1. There is only a conflict in case norm 1 is terminated because of its very inconsistency with norm 2. That norm 1 is then terminated is not so much

---

[11] PCIJ, Series A/B, No. 77, 92 (1939).   [12] PCIJ, Series A/B, No. 46 (1932).
[13] *Ibid.*, 80.   [14] But see the Dissenting Opinion of Judge Dreyfus, *ibid.*, 110.
[15] See chapter 4 above, p. 162.

the result of norm 2, but the result of a third norm of international law resolving the inconsistency between the two norms by terminating the earlier one (*in casu*, Art. 59 of the Vienna Convention).

The *chapeau* of Art. 59(1) provides as follows: 'A *treaty* shall be considered as *terminated* if *all the parties* to it *conclude a later treaty* relating to the *same subject-matter*' (emphasis added). Hence, Art. 59 leads to the termination of the *entire* treaty, not just some of its *provisions*. This termination is a result of 'incompatibility' between the two treaties, that is, it occurs because there is a conflict between them. Given this 'incompatibility' – and recalling that for conflict to arise there must be overlap *ratione materiae* – it goes without saying that the two treaties must be 'relating to the same subject-matter'.[16]

Moreover, termination pursuant to Art. 59 requires that *all parties* to the first treaty are parties also to the second one. If some parties are missing, Arts. 30 and 41 of the Vienna Convention apply. However, nothing precludes that the later treaty which terminates the earlier one has additional parties, not bound by the earlier treaty. In that event, Art. 59 must have its full effect as between the parties to both treaties.

In order to determine which of two treaties is the 'later' one, the date of conclusion of the treaty (i.e., the date of its adoption) is decisive. However, as Vierdag remarked, Art. 59 does not apply in case either the earlier or the later treaty has not yet entered into force:

> [Article 59] speaks of 'parties', which indicates that the treaty to be terminated or suspended is a treaty in force (Article 2(1)(g) [pursuant to which a 'party' is a state bound by a treaty and for which the treaty is in force]). Consequently, it seems that the later treaty can only effectively terminate it or suspend its operation if it is itself in force. In theory, if only the text of a treaty has been adopted, this text can be replaced through the adoption of another text by all the negotiating States. But this is not the situation envisaged by Article 59 according to its terms. So 'conclude' in Article 59 refers to the whole process of treaty-making, including the entry into force of the later treaty.[17]

The fact that Art. 59 leads to the termination of the *entire treaty*, combined with the requirement that *all parties* to the earlier treaty also adopted the later one, means that Art. 59 will apply only in limited circumstances.[18] Nonetheless, before applying Arts. 30 and 41 of the Vienna Convention (discussed at length below), resort must always be

---

[16] Art. 30 includes the same condition: see chapter 7 below, pp. 364–7.
[17] E. W. Vierdag, 'The Time of the "Conclusion" of a Multilateral Treaty' (1989) 60 BYIL 75 at 92.
[18] *Ibid.*, 91.

had first to Art. 59. Only if termination or suspension does not follow under Art. 59 may Arts. 30 and 41 be applied. As Vierdag noted, 'in cases of termination or suspension Article 59 is *lex specialis*'.[19] Article 30(3) makes it explicit that it applies only in case 'the earlier treaty is not terminated or suspended in operation under article 59'.[20]

Acts of international organisations that are inconsistent with their constituent instruments

One other instance of 'invalidity' of a norm because of conflict with another norm is that where an act of an international organisation is inconsistent with the constituent instrument of that organisation. Here too we are faced with what we called an inherent normative conflict, not a conflict in the applicable law.

The validity of an act of an international organisation may be challenged by member states, or one organisation may challenge the validity of an act taken by another. In both instances the claim will be based on conflict between the act of the organisation and its constituent instrument. Also, *within an international organisation* discussion may arise as to the validity of an act taken by one organ in the light of the competence of another organ. These different organs may be distinct political organs or political versus judicial bodies.

In terms of conflicts *within* an organisation, in the EC, for example, the question often arises as to whether the competence of the European Commission, Parliament or Council has been respected.[21] In the UN the question has arisen as to whether the General Assembly or the Security Council is competent for a certain matter.[22] Prominently in the UN is

---

[19] Ibid.
[20] The ILC Commentary is also very clear in this respect: Art. 30 'comes into play only *after it has been determined under [Art. 59] that the parties did not intend to abrogate, or wholly to suspend the operation of, the earlier treaty*' (YBILC 1966, vol. 2, 253, emphasis in original).
[21] In this respect, the ECJ has introduced the principle of *institutional balance*: 'Observance of the institutional balance means that each of the institutions must exercise its powers with due regard for the powers of the other institutions. It also requires that it should be possible to penalize any breach of that rule which may occur... it is the Court's duty to ensure that the provisions of the Treaties concerning the institutional balance are fully applied and to see to it that the Parliament's prerogatives, like those of the other institutions, cannot be breached' (*Parliament v. Council*, Case C-70/88 [1990] ECR 2073).
[22] Schermers refers to the 1950 Uniting for Peace Resolution 377(V) of the UN General Assembly as a 'classical example of a decision of an organ which was considered to be *ultra vires* by a number of countries' on the ground that the resolution dealt with

also the question of attribution of powers between the Security Council and the ICJ in respect of threats to the peace, breach of the peace and acts of aggression.[23] In the WTO as well, questions have arisen as to the competence of panels to decide a dispute which has been examined, or is still under examination, by a particular WTO (political) committee.[24]

In the WTO these institutional limitations are sometimes overlooked and the distinction between acts taken by WTO members *as states* (say, the conclusion of a new agreement) as opposed to acts taken by *WTO organs* is not always respected.[25] WTO members can, of course, as the *Herren der Verträge*, always change WTO rules, including the institutional provisions. But when they act in the format of WTO organs, they must respect the existing rules. The WTO may be a member-driven organisation, but when members act within WTO organs, their decisions must respect WTO rules.

Invalidity because of lack of competence

International organisations have 'attributed competence' only
Unlike states, international organisations as well as their organs have limited powers in the sense that they can exercise competence only if this competence has been attributed to them (in particular, by the states setting up the organisation or organ). If they exceed this competence, the act by which this is done is 'invalid'. As Schermers and Blokker put it: 'while *states* are free to act as long as this is in accordance with international law...*international organizations* are competent to act only as far as powers have been attributed to them by the member states. Basically, international organizations may not generate their own powers.'[26]

This represents the so-called doctrine of attributed competence (*compétence d'attribution*) or 'principle of speciality' in terms of the competence of international organisations. As the ICJ put it in its Advisory Opinion on *Use of Nuclear Weapons* (at the request of the WHO):

> breaches of the peace or acts of aggression even though the primary responsibility for the maintenance of international peace and security rests on the Security Council pursuant to UN Charter Art. 24(1) (Henry Schermers and Niels Blokker, *International Institutional Law, Unity Within Diversity* (The Hague: Nijhoff, 1995), para. 208.

[23] On this question see, for example, the *Lockerbie* case, ICJ Reports 1992.
[24] See, on this issue, Frieder Roessler, 'The Institutional Balance between the Judicial and the Political Organs of the WTO', paper presented at the Center for Business and Government, Harvard University, June 2000, on file with the author.
[25] See chapter 2 above, pp. 44–7.   [26] Schermers and Blokker, *Institutional*, para. 209.

international organizations are subjects of international law which do not, unlike States, possess a general competence. International organizations are governed by the 'principle of speciality', that is to say, they are invested by the States which create them with powers, the limits of which are a function of the common interests whose promotion those States entrust to them.[27]

In the UN, the limits of the organisation are determined, *inter alia*, by Art. 2(7) of the UN Charter (precluding that the UN intervenes 'in matters which are essentially within the domestic jurisdiction' of states). The competence of UN organs, such as the General Assembly, the Security Council and the ICJ, are also set out in the UN Charter.

In the WTO, Arts. II and III of the Marrakesh Agreement set out the 'scope' and 'functions' of the WTO as an international organisation, and of its organs. This is done very broadly, referring, for example, to the WTO providing 'the common institutional framework for the conduct of trade relations among its Members in matters related to the agreements' (Art. II.1) as well as providing 'the forum for negotiations among its Members concerning their multilateral trade relations in matters dealt with under the agreements' (Art. III.2). As far as WTO *organs* are concerned, Art. IV of the Marrakesh Agreement sets out the competence of the Ministerial Conference, the General Council and other subsidiary bodies. Other WTO bodies are established by different agreements or even decisions of other WTO organs. Article 2 of the DSU, for example, establishes the DSB which has 'the authority to establish panels, adopt panel and Appellate Body reports, maintain the surveillance of implementation of rulings and recommendations, and authorize suspension of concessions'. Another example is the Understanding on the Balance-of-Payments Provisions of GATT 1994 which establishes the Committee for Balance-of-Payments Restrictions.

The theory of 'implied powers'
Notwithstanding the fact that international organisations have 'attributed competence' only, when it comes to interpreting the scope of this competence, a teleological and dynamic approach has been adopted. As a result, the competence of international organisations has often been interpreted broadly so as to include also certain 'implied powers' with reference to 'institutional effectiveness' and 'subsequent practice'. In the Advisory Opinion on *Reparations for Injuries*, the ICJ found: 'It

---

[27] Advisory Opinion on *Use of Nuclear Weapons* (WHO request), ICJ Reports 1996, 226, at para. 25.

must be acknowledged that its Members [that is, Members of the UN], by entrusting certain functions to it, with the attendant duties and responsibilities, have clothed it with the competence required to enable those functions to be effectively discharged.'[28]

The ICJ stated further that the 'rights and duties of an entity such as the Organization must depend upon its purposes and functions as specified or implied in its constituent document and developed in practice'.[29] This approach was more recently confirmed in the ICJ Advisory Opinion on *Use of Nuclear Weapons*: 'the necessities of international life may point to the need for organizations, in order to achieve their objectives, to possess subsidiary powers which are not expressly provided for in the basic instruments which govern their activities. It is generally accepted that international organizations can exercise such powers, known as "implied powers".'[30]

Thus, for an act of an international organisation to be invalid it will not suffice to point to the fact that no explicit competence has been conferred on the organisation for it to take the act. Implicit competence may be found so that the act is, nonetheless, valid.

Invalidity because of *ultra vires* exercise of competence

In addition to acting only pursuant to the competence that was attributed to them, international organisations and their organs must also *exercise* their limited competence in line with the conditions and restrictions that may have been imposed on this competence. In the UN context Art. 24(2) of the UN Charter makes it explicit that the Security Council 'shall act in accordance with the Purposes and Principles of the United Nations'.

One could refer here to voting procedures (must the decision be taken by consensus, majority voting or is there a veto to be respected?), but also to more substantive conditions, such as the requirement that there be a request for consultations before the DSB can establish a panel (DSU Art. 6.2) and requirements in respect of terms of reference or multiple complaints (DSU Arts. 7 and 9). Also, when the Ministerial Conference

---

[28] ICJ Reports 1949, 179. Along these lines, Reuter has referred to the 'functional' nature of the competence of international organisations (Paul Reuter, *Institutions Internationales* (Paris: Presses Universitaires, de France 1972), 214–16).

[29] ICJ Reports 1949, 180. See also the Advisory Opinion on the *Question of Certain Expenses of the United Nations*, ICJ Reports 1962, 168, and *Jurisdiction of the European Commission of the Danube*, Advisory Opinion, PCIJ, Series B, No. 14, 64 (1927). On this issue, see Tetsuo Sato, *Evolving Constitutions of International Organizations* (Dordrecht: Kluwer, 1996), 33–7.

[30] ICJ Reports 1996, para. 25.

grants, for example, a waiver, it must respect the conditions set out in Arts. IX:3 and IX: 4, both in terms of voting requirements and substantive conditions (such as the statement of 'exceptional circumstances justifying the decision' and an annual review of waivers granted for more than one year).[31]

In addition, acts or decisions taken by WTO panels or the Appellate Body could be 'invalid' on the ground that they are inconsistent with the DSU. If so, these judicial acts of WTO organs would be taken *ultra vires*, that is, outside the limited competence granted to them. This might occur, for example, if a panel or the Appellate Body were to adopt case-specific working procedures that are inconsistent with the DSU. Given that their competence derives from the DSU, both judicial organs must respect the DSU, they cannot deviate from it (unless they do so in compliance with an agreement between the disputing parties which constitutes a valid modification to the DSU for the dispute in question: see the discussion below, pp. 318–21).

In respect of the Appellate Body, Art. 16.1 of the Working Procedures for Appellate Review explicitly confirms this: 'In the interests of fairness and orderly procedure in the conduct of an appeal, where a procedural question arises that is not covered by these Rules, a division may adopt an appropriate procedure for the purposes of that appeal only, *provided that it is not inconsistent with the DSU, the other covered agreements and these Rules.*'[32] In respect of panels, DSU Art. 12.1 provides: 'Panels shall follow the Working Procedures in Appendix 3 unless the panel decides otherwise after consulting the parties to the dispute.' The first paragraph of the standard working procedures in Appendix 3 states: 'In its proceedings *the panel shall follow the relevant provisions of this Understanding.* In addition, the following working procedures shall apply' (emphasis added).

The same applies in respect of the general working procedures the Appellate Body was called to draw up in consultation with the Chairman of the DSB and the Director-General, pursuant to DSU Art. 12.9. These working procedures – which are not case-specific but apply to all appeals – are now set out in the Working Procedures for Appellate Review. They were, as called for by the DSU, drawn up by the Appellate

---

[31] It must be acknowledged that here the line between 'invalidity' because of *ultra vires* exercise of competence and 'illegality' on the ground of breach of other law that applies to the organ in question becomes thin. On the former issue of 'illegality', see below, pp. 324–6.

[32] WTO doc. WT/AB/WP/3, dated 28 February 1997, emphasis added.

Body itself, not the WTO membership. Hence, given the limited competence of the Appellate Body, these procedures could not possibly deviate from the DSU. If they did so, the procedural rule in question would be invalid. There is no need for an explicit DSU rule stating that WTO panels and the Appellate Body cannot adopt procedural rules inconsistent with the DSU. This rule automatically derives from the limited competence of WTO organs. The question as to whether WTO members may change the DSU, including by means of an *inter se* agreement applying to a particular case only, is an entirely different one. It is addressed below, pp. 315–24.

Judicial review of the validity of acts taken by international organisations

It is one thing to note that acts of international organisations must respect the limits of the competence attributed to them. It is quite another, however, to obtain a decision which determines this invalidity.

Acts of international organisations are often taken by decisions that do not require unanimity. As a result, one or more members in the minority may claim that a given act was taken in violation of the constituent instrument. Also, in a particular dispute between two states, one of them may rely on an act of the organisation wheras the other contests its validity. Finally, as between two organisations or two organs within one organisation, one of them may contest the validity of the act taken by the other on the ground, for example, that the act falls within its competence. In this respect, Schermers and Blokker noted the following:

> In the absence of agreement to the contrary, the international system has no tribunal competent to make a finding of nullity. It is the affected state itself which rejects the decision on the ground that it considers it null and void. Such a unilateral rejection of the validity of international decisions is, of course, antithetical to the implementation of the law of international organizations. To avoid leaving the decision on the validity of international acts to the states concerned, judicial organs may be established, especially in organizations empowered to take binding decisions.[33]

The presumption of validity of acts of international organisations
The ICJ has stated the following on the conformity of acts of international organisations with constituent instruments: 'when the Organization takes action which warrants the assertion that it was appropriate

---

[33] Schermers and Blokker, *Institutional*, para. 912.

for the fulfilment of one of the stated purposes of the United Nations, the presumption is that such action is not *ultra vires* the Organization'.[34] In the same case, the ICJ remarked: 'If the Security Council, for example, adopts a resolution purportedly for the maintenance of international peace and security and if, in accordance with a mandate or authorization in such resolution, the Secretary-General incurs financial obligations, these amounts must be presumed to constitute "expenses of the Organization".'[35] In other words, even if the competence of international organisations is limited, their acts nonetheless benefit from a presumption of validity, similar to the presumption that state conduct is consistent with international law, until proof to the contrary.

In the *Lockerbie* cases (Provisional Measures), the ICJ confirmed this presumption. It first recalled the obligation resting on the parties as UN members 'to accept and carry out the decisions of the Security Council in accordance with Article 25 of the Charter' and then considered that 'prima facie this obligation extends to the decision contained in resolution 748 (1992)'.[36]

Jurisdiction to review the validity of acts of international organisations
The situation in the EC and the UN The EC is one of the few international organisations where a proper action for the annulment of decisions by the organs of the international organisation is available. In the EC, such an action can be brought against binding acts of most Community institutions. Article 230 (ex 173) of the EC Treaty provides for an independent and direct cause of action to challenge the legality of these Community acts before the European Court of Justice.[37] Article 241 (ex 184) of the treaty also provides for a plea of illegality against EC regulations when an action is otherwise competently before the Court.[38]

---

[34] Advisory Opinion on the *Question of Certain Expenses of the United Nations*, ICJ Reports 1962, 168.
[35] *Ibid.*   [36] ICJ Reports 1992, Order of 14 April 1992, para. 42.
[37] Note that the EC action for annulment covers both invalidity and illegality. Art. 230 does not make a distinction between the two in terms of grounds for annulment (although 'lack of competence' undermines the validity of the act, whereas, for example, 'infringement of any rule relating to its application' would result in illegality as we defined it above). See below, pp. 324–6.
[38] In this respect, see Anthony Arnull, 'Private Applicants and the Action for Annulment under Article 173 of the EC Treaty' (1995) 32 *Common Market Law Review* 7, and Paul Craig, 'Legality, Standing and Substantive Review in Community Law' (1994) 14 *Oxford Journal of Legal Studies* 507.

As far as the UN is concerned, the ICJ may be faced with questions of validity of UN decisions in advisory procedures at the request of an organisation of the UN family. The ruling it can then provide is, however, merely advisory and does not annul the decision. It will, however, deprive the decision of its political force so that for all practical purposes it amounts to annulment. There is also a second route pursuant to which the validity of UN decisions could be brought to the attention of the ICJ, namely in contentious procedures where one of the parties relies on a UN decision and the other party contests the validity of this decision.

In two instances, however, the ICJ seemed to imply that it does not have the power to 'judicially review' UN decisions. In *Certain Expenses*, it remarked that: 'Proposals made during the drafting of the Charter to place the ultimate authority to interpret the Charter in the [ICJ] were not accepted;...As anticipated in 1945, therefore, each organ must, in the first place at least, determine its own jurisdiction.'

More categorically, in the 1971 *Namibia* case, the Court stated that: 'Undoubtedly, the Court does not possess powers of judicial review or appeal in respect of the decisions taken by the United Nations organs concerned.'[39]

The question arose again in the *Lockerbie* cases where the United States and the United Kingdom invoked a UN Security Council resolution in defence against Libyan allegations of breach of the 1971 Montreal Convention for the Suppression of Unlawful Acts Against the Safety of Civil Aviation. In response, Libya claimed that this Security Council resolution was inconsistent with the UN Charter and could hence not be invoked as a norm that, pursuant to Art. 103 of the Charter, should prevail over the Montreal Convention. The ICJ did not take a position on this important matter of judicial review either in its 1992 order on provisional measures or in its 1998 judgment on jurisdiction and admissibility.[40] The ICJ confirmed that UN members are under an obligation to accept and apply the decisions of the Security Council pursuant to Art. 25 of the UN Charter, but hesitated to confirm that it was empowered to review

---

[39] ICJ Reports 1971, 45.
[40] See, in this respect, L. B. Sohn, 'Enabling the United States to Contest "Illegal United Nations Acts"' (1975) 69 AJIL 852, and Krzysztof Skubiszewski, 'The International Court of Justice and the Security Council', in Vaughan Lowe and Malgosia Fitzmaurice (eds.), *Fifty Years of the International Court of Justice: Essays in Honour of Sir Robert Jennings* (Cambridge: Cambridge University Press, 1996), 606.

the conformity of these decisions with the UN Charter.[41] Some judges expressed clear opinions *against* the Court having the power to review Security Council resolutions, in particular those taken in the field of threat to the peace (Schwebel and Jennings). Others expressed opposing views (Rezek, Kooijmans).[42] However, even the judges expressing views against the ICJ's competence to review certain Security Council resolutions did accept that the Security Council must comply with the UN Charter and that in case it fails to do so its acts will be invalid. As Jennings stated:

The first principle of the applicable law is this: that all discretionary powers of lawful decision-making are necessarily derived from the law, and are therefore governed and qualified by the law. This must be so if only because the sole authority of such decisions flows itself from the law. It is not logically possible to claim to represent the power and authority of the law, and at the same time, claim to be above the law ... I therefore wholly agree with the Libyan argument that the Security Council decisions and actions should in no wise be regarded as enjoying some sort of 'immunity' from the jurisdiction of the principal organ of the United Nations.[43]

The situation in the WTO Unlike the EC, and much like the situation in the UN, in the WTO the judicial branch does not have direct and substantive jurisdiction to consider claims of invalidity of decisions or acts taken by WTO organs. WTO panels can only consider claims made by a WTO member against another WTO member for breach of that member's obligations under WTO covered agreements. WTO members cannot start a procedure against WTO organs. Nor can WTO organs ask for advisory opinions or challenge each other's competence before a WTO panel.

Nonetheless, the question of validity of acts taken by WTO organs could arise indirectly in a contentious case between two WTO members. Three situations could be thought of.

---

[41] Order on Provisional Measures, ICJ Reports 1992, 15 and 126.
[42] See the Opinions attached to the ICJ's judgment on Jurisdiction and Admissibility, ICJ Reports 1998.
[43] Dissenting Opinion of Judge Jennings, ICJ Reports 1998, 110. Jennings subsequently stated, however, that when 'the Security Council, exercising the discretionary competence given to it by Article 39 of the Charter, has decided that there exists a "threat to the peace", it is not for the principal judicial organ of the United Nations to question that decision much less so to substitute a decision of its own, but to state the plain meaning and intention of Article 39, and to *protect* the Security Council's exercise of that body's power and duty conferred upon it by the law' (*ibid.*).

First, a defendant could challenge the jurisdiction of a WTO panel and claim that, although the DSB established the panel, it did so in disregard of timing or consultation requirements. If a panel were, for example, established by the DSB without a prior request for consultations by the complainant, should the panel not decline jurisdiction and thereby indirectly state that the DSB's decision to establish the panel was an invalid one, to be set aside? It would seem so. By deciding that it has no jurisdiction, the panel would then, of course, not annul the DSB decision, but for practical purposes that decision would lose its effect. As further explained below, the jurisdiction to examine whether one has jurisdiction (*compétence de la compétence*) is a power inherent in the judicial function. It is a power to be exercised also by WTO panels, *even on their own initiative*.[44]

An analogy can be found in the *Tadić* case. There, the Appeals Chamber of the ICTY found that 'the International Tribunal has the jurisdiction to examine the plea against its jurisdiction based on the invalidity of its establishment by the Security Council'.[45] It did so even though the International Tribunal had not been granted any explicit authorisation to make such examination and after a finding by the Trial Chamber that the International Tribunal was *not* empowered to question the legality of the law which established it.[46] After a careful analysis of the powers granted to the Security Council under Chapter VII of the UN Charter, the Appeals Chamber concluded that the Security Council did have the power to set up the tribunal and that the tribunal had been created in conformity with the appropriate procedures of the UN Charter.[47]

Second, one could imagine also a situation where the WTO Committee on Balance-of-Payments (BOP) has taken a decision in respect of a WTO member's BOP restrictions, but nonetheless a claim is submitted by another WTO member for breach of WTO provisions on BOPs by that first member. The Appellate Body previously decided that both the political and the judicial track in respect of BOP measures do not exclude each other, so that a panel would have jurisdiction to decide the matter.[48]

---

[44] That WTO panels have *la compétence de la compétence* was explicitly confirmed by the Appellate Body in *US – Anti-Dumping Act of 1916* and *Mexico – Corn Syrup (Article 21.5 – US)*.
[45] Appeals Chamber, Decision of 2 October 1995, IT-94-1-AR72, para. 22.
[46] Trial Chamber, Decision of 10 August 1995, IT-94-I-T, para. 8.
[47] Appeals Chamber, Decision of 2 October 1995, IT-94-1-AR72, paras. 26–48.
[48] Appellate Body report on *India – Quantitative Restrictions*, para. 88, referring to the second sentence of footnote 1 to the BOP Understanding ('The provisions of Articles XXII and XXIII of GATT 1994 as elaborated and applied by the Dispute Settlement Understanding may be invoked with respect to *any matters arising from the application of*

But would a panel be able to review the Committee's decision that, for example, the BOP measure is WTO consistent?

It would seem that in this case, the panel would not review the Committee's decision as such, but rather make its own finding on the WTO consistency of the BOP measure in question, finding guidance in the Committee's decision. As the Appellate Body noted:

> We are cognisant of the competence of the BOP Committee and the General Council with respect to balance-of-payments restrictions under Article XVIII:12 of the GATT 1994 and the *BOP Understanding*. However, we see no conflict between that competence and the competence of panels. Moreover, we are convinced that, in considering the justification of balance-of-payments restrictions, panels should take into account the deliberations and conclusions of the BOP Committee, as did the panel in *Korea – Beef*.[49]

In other words, the panel would redo the exercise and take into account the Committee's evaluations. But nothing would prevent it from coming to a conclusion which is different from that reached by the Committee. Here as well the Committee decision would not be annulled, nor even be declared illegal. However, the practical result of the panel concluding differently would be that the Committee decision loses its effect.

A similar situation has arisen in terms of the competence of WTO panels versus that of the WTO Committee on Regional Trade Agreements which reviews regional trade agreements under GATT Art. XXIV. In *Turkey – Textile*, the Appellate Body implicitly held that panels have jurisdiction to examine the overall consistency of a regional integration agreement with relevant WTO rules, including GATT Art. XXIV:5, notwithstanding the competence in this field of the Committee on Regional Trade Agreements.[50] A comparable tension between the WTO

---

restrictive import measures taken for balance-of-payments purposes', emphasis added): 'In our opinion, this provision makes it clear that the dispute settlement procedures under Article XXIII, as elaborated and applied by the DSU, *are* available for disputes relating to *any* matters concerning balance-of-payments restrictions' (emphasis in the original text). For a critique on this finding, see Roessler, 'Institutional Balance'.

[49] Appellate Body report on *India – Quantitative Restrictions*, para. 103.

[50] The Appellate Body found, first of all, that for GATT Art. XXIV to constitute a defence 'the party claiming the benefit of this defence must demonstrate that the measure at issue is introduced upon the formation of a customs union that fully meets the requirements of sub-paragraphs 8(a) and 5(a) of Article XXIV' (Appellate Body report on *Turkey – Textile*, para. 58). In addition, it noted the following: 'The Panel maintained that "it is arguable" that panels do not have jurisdiction to assess the overall compatibility of a customs union with the requirements of Article XXIV. We are not called upon in this appeal to address this issue, but we note in this respect our ruling in [*India – Quantitative Restrictions*, referred to in note 48 above] on the jurisdiction of

judiciary and a WTO political organ arose also when the United States requested the establishment of a panel against the Philippines concerning trade-related investment measures applied by the Philippines in the automotive sector. The United States did so notwithstanding a pending request by the Philippines for an extension of the transition period under Art. 5.3 of the TRIMS agreement, a request that was being discussed by the Council for Trade in Goods.[51]

Third, one could imagine a claim under GATT Art. I (MFN) in defence of which a waiver under Art. IX of the Marrakesh Agreement is invoked. In turn, the complainant could argue, however, that the waiver was adopted inconsistently with the Marrakesh Agreement, e.g., that it does not state the 'exceptional circumstances justifying the decision', has not been reviewed annually or was taken inconsistently with the voting procedures in Art. IX. Should a panel be allowed to review such objections against a waiver decision? It would seem so. The same applies in respect of any decision taken by a WTO organ invoked by either party but in respect of which the opposing party raises claims of inconsistency with WTO agreements. The WTO holds *its members* to WTO rules, hence also WTO *organs* should respect the rules that apply to them. In such cases, a panel could, once again, *not* decide that the WTO decision is invalid or annulled. It could only find inconsistencies and on that basis refuse to apply the decision. The practical consequence of this would be that the decision loses its effect.

Finally, the question could be raised as to whether *all* inconsistencies with WTO rules – no matter how minor – ought to lead to the disapplication of the decision by the WTO organ. It could, indeed, be submitted that minor procedural mistakes should not lead to this result. In this respect, guidance could be found in the grounds for annulment of decisions taken by EC institutions, set out in Art. 230 (ex 173) of the EC Treaty. These are: 'lack of competence, infringement of an *essential procedural requirement*, infringement of this Treaty or of any rule of law relating to its application, or misuse of powers' (emphasis added).

Moreover, situations could arise where the member invoking the invalidity of a WTO decision has previously voted *in favour of* the decision or not objected to it, for example, at the DSB meeting when the decision was taken. Some negative inferences could be drawn from such conduct,

---

panels to review the justification of balance-of-payments restrictions under Article XVIII:B of the GATT 1994' (Appellate Body report on *Turkey – Textile*, para. 60).

[51] See the discussions at the DSB meeting of 17 November 2000, WT/DSB/M/92 (15 January 2001).

in particular if the ground for invalidity invoked is a procedural one. In the *US – FSC* case, for example, the United States made a preliminary objection to the EC's claim under Art. 3 of the Subsidies agreement on the ground that the EC's request for consultations at the origin of the panel did not include a 'statement of available evidence', as required by Art. 4.2 of that agreement. The United States argued that because of this procedural deficiency, the panel should dismiss the claim. Both the panel and the Appellate Body refused to do this (although they recognised that the procedural requirement in Art. 4.2 may well have been violated), *inter alia*, on the ground that the United States did not 'object to the allegedly deficient request for consultations during those DSB meetings when the European Communities' request for establishment of a panel was on the agenda of the DSB and the Panel was established'.[52] On that basis, the Appellate Body found that 'the United States acted as if it had accepted the establishment of the Panel in this dispute, as well as the consultations preceding such establishment'.[53] The Appellate Body derived this conclusion from the obligation to engage in dispute settlement procedures 'in good faith in an effort to resolve the dispute' (DSU Art. 3.10), noting that good faith

> requires that responding Members seasonably and promptly bring claimed procedural deficiencies to the attention of the complaining Member, and to the DSB or the Panel, so that corrections, if needed, can be made to resolve the disputes. The procedural rules of WTO dispute settlement are designed to promote, not the development of litigation techniques, but simply the fair, prompt and effective resolution of trade disputes.[54]

One can derive some aversion from this statement to dismissing a case on the basis of procedural deficiencies. This reasoning seems well founded, however, on principles of good faith, acquiescence, estoppel and *forum prorogatum*.

Nonetheless, in cases of breach of *essential* procedural requirements or *substantive* WTO rules applying to WTO organs, panels ought to be willing, in certain circumstances, to dismiss a dispute (or to disapply a decision of a WTO organ), and this even if the member raising the objection does so for the first time before the panel. It could even be argued

---

[52] Appellate Body report on *US – FSC*, para. 163.
[53] *Ibid.*, para. 165. See also the Appellate Body report on *Mexico – Corn Syrup (Article 21.5 – US)*, where Mexico was found to have waived its right to consultations (in case such right were to exist under DSU Art. 21.5, a question that was left open) through certain conduct before the panel.
[54] *US – FSC*, para. 166.

that, much like the matter of *compétence de la compétence*,⁵⁵ such fundamental inconsistencies with WTO rules ought to be raised by the panel *on its own initiative* (without there being a need for either party to do so). As the Appellate Body noted in *Mexico – Corn Syrup (Article 21.5 – US)*: 'panels have to address and dispose of certain issues of a fundamental nature, even if the parties to the dispute remain silent on those issues... panels cannot simply ignore issues which go to the root of their jurisdiction'.⁵⁶

In the WTO, the need for judicial review of decisions by WTO organs is all the more present (more so, for example, than in the UN):

(i) because most WTO organs, such as the DSB, take legally binding decisions (UN General Assembly resolutions, in contrast, are only 'recommended');

(ii) because the WTO (unlike the UN Charter) has a compulsory dispute settlement mechanism;

(iii) because the WTO treaty does not seem to reserve any area of competence under WTO covered agreements exclusively to the WTO's political branch (unlike, arguably, Art. 24.2 of the UN Charter reserving the 'primary responsibility for the maintenance of international peace and security' to the UN Security Council).

One of the two norms is 'illegal'

In the previous section, the conflict of norms was resolved by bringing an end to one of the two norms, either through invalidity or termination. In this section, we discuss the situation where one norm is 'illegal' under the other norm. As in the previous section, but unlike in the next chapter, we are faced here with 'inherent normative conflict'. An allegation that the very conclusion of a norm is 'illegal' under, or constitutes breach of, another norm implies that the other norm is earlier in time. The later norm then constitutes wrongful conduct under the earlier norm because either

(i) the later norm, in and of itself, is explicitly prohibited by the earlier norm; or

(ii) the later norm, in and of itself, is illegal pursuant to Arts. 41 or 58 of the Vienna Convention which prohibit certain *inter se* modifications and suspensions of an earlier multilateral agreement.

---

⁵⁵ See note 44 above.
⁵⁶ Appellate Body report on *Mexico – Corn Syrup (Article 21.5 – US)*, para. 36.

In those situations one of the two norms is clearly more important than the other, namely the earlier norm with reference to which the other norm is illegal. In both instances, the later norm may not only be a treaty norm. It can also be an act of an international organisation which is illegal under international law that applies to it, or is prohibited pursuant to principles equivalent to those set out in Arts. 41 and 58.

In the previous section, the question was mainly: which norm *survives*? In this section, the essential question is: does one norm *breach* the other? (In the next section it will be: which of the two norms *applies*?)

The solution to inherent normative conflicts set out in this section is based largely on the law of state responsibility (including responsibility of international organisations), leading to the 'illegality' of one of the norms. In terms of responsibility, if one norm does, indeed, constitute breach of the other (say, a regional arrangement in breach of GATT Art. XXIV), one of the secondary obligations resulting from this breach will be the obligation to cease the breach, that is, of doing away with the illegal *inter se* agreement. In that sense, the ultimate solution to the conflict is not that different from conflicts discussed in the previous section: it resides in the end of one of the two norms. In the previous section this end was achieved by means of invalidity or termination. In this section it will be induced by state responsibility and the secondary obligation of cessation. For acts of international organisations that are 'illegal' under the law applicable to them (to be distinguished from the situation where they are 'invalid', e.g., because of lack of competence), the responsibility of the particular organ may be invoked and that organ too will have to cease the illegal act. In practice, if an adjudicator has jurisdiction to determine the illegality, the illegal norm will then be set aside and as a result lose its practical effect.

Although, in practical terms, the distinction between 'invalidity' (under the previous section) and 'illegality' (see above, p. 277) may sometimes be minimal, as pointed out before, a major difference between 'invalidity' and 'illegality' is, however, that normally invalidity is something to be examined *ex officio* by an adjudicator, whereas illegality will, in principle, only be looked at if claimed by one of the parties to the dispute.

The conclusion of a norm is explicitly prohibited by another norm

Normative conflicts where one (later) norm is explicitly prohibited by another (earlier) norm, may take two forms:

(i) Not all of the parties to the later, 'illegal' norm are parties to the earlier norm. A conflict of the type AB/AC then arises (A being a state with conflicting obligations vis-à-vis B and C), where from the perspective of state A the very conclusion of the AC norm with state C constitutes breach of the earlier AB norm vis-à-vis state B.

(ii) The later, 'illegal' norm constitutes an *inter se* modification or suspension of an earlier multilateral treaty, explicitly prohibited by that treaty.

One state concluding a norm with another state in breach of a pre-existing norm with a third state (conflict of the type AB/AC)

Examples of a later AC norm constituting breach of an earlier AB norm can be found in the following case law. In the PCIJ Advisory Opinion on *Customs Regime Between Germany and Austria*, the Court found that a 1931 Protocol concluded between Austria and Germany setting up a customs union between the two countries was incompatible with an earlier 1922 Protocol concluded between Austria, France, Great Britain, Italy and Czechoslovakia, and subsequently acceded to by Belgium and Spain, in which Austria made a commitment not to violate her economic independence by granting to any state a special regime or exclusive advantages calculated to threaten this independence.[57] In other words, from the perspective of Austria (state A), the later 1931 norm between Austria and Germany (AC norm) was found to constitute, in and of itself, breach of an earlier 1922 norm binding on Austria and other states, but not on Germany (AB norm). As a result, Austria had to bring an end to this incompatible treaty (which in and of itself constituted wrongful conduct) so as to bring its conduct in line with the earlier 1922 Protocol. Nonetheless, Germany, not being bound by the 1922 Protocol, could not be held by this incompatibility based on the 1922 Protocol. Depending on the circumstances, it could then claim compensation from Austria for bringing an end to their customs union.[58]

Another example where a later norm (AC) was found to constitute breach of an earlier norm (AB), not binding on one of the parties (C) to

---

[57] PCIJ, Series A/B, No. 41, 5 September 1931.

[58] Note that the finding of illegality of the 1931 Protocol between Germany and Austria under the multilateral 1922 Protocol has nothing to do with *lex specialis* or the 1922 Protocol prevailing as an 'objective regime'. The finding is based on state responsibility, not on the law of treaties or priority rules to be resorted to in a conflict in the applicable law. Czaplinski and Danilenko missed this point, arguing that this PCIJ case rejects the *lex specialis* principle, giving preference to the more general 1922 Protocol on the basis of its substantive content as a peace treaty (W. Czaplinski and G. Danilenko, 'Conflict of Norms in International Law' (1990) 21 NYIL 3 at 20).

the later norm, can be found in the *Costa Rica v. Nicaragua* case.[59] There, the Central American Court of Justice declared that Nicaragua (state A) had violated its obligations towards Costa Rica, set out in the 1858 Canas–Jerez Treaty (AB norm), not to grant concessions to any other state, by concluding the 1914 Bryan–Chamorro Treaty (AC norm) in which Nicaragua did grant such concessions also to the United States. More particularly, the Central American Court of Justice held that Nicaragua was internationally responsible to Costa Rica for entering into a treaty with a third state, without first complying with the consultation requirements of an earlier treaty between Nicaragua and Costa Rica. In other words, from the perspective of Nicaragua, the later 1914 norm between Nicaragua and the United States (AC norm) was found to constitute, in and of itself, breach of an earlier 1858 norm binding on Nicaragua and Costa Rica, but not on the United States (AB norm).[60] Consequently, Nicaragua had to bring an end to this incompatible treaty so as to bring its conduct in line with the 1858 treaty. Nonetheless, the United States, not being bound by the 1858 treaty, could not be held by this incompatibility based on the 1858 treaty. Depending on the circumstances, it could then claim compensation from Nicaragua for not granting the concessions to it.

It must be stressed that the later (AC) norm – in the cases above, the 1931 Protocol between Austria and Germany and the Bryan–Chamorro Treaty between Nicaragua and the United States – is, in these circumstances, not 'invalid', but only 'illegal'.[61] Moreover, it is illegal only from the perspective of the state bound by both norms (that is, state A; in our examples, respectively, Austria and Nicaragua), not from the perspective of the party bound only by the later norm (that is, state C; in our examples, respectively, Germany and the United States). We come back to this in chapter 7 below, pp. 422–36. The extent to which state C can then invoke the responsibility of state A for bringing an end to, or not implementing, the later AC norm is also discussed there.

---

[59] Judgment of the Central American Court of Justice, reprinted in (1917) 11 AJIL 181–229.

[60] In the same sense, see the *El Salvador v. Nicaragua* case where the Central American Court found that the Bryan–Chamorro Treaty also violated rights of El Salvador set out in a 1907 treaty concluded between Central American states (reprinted in (1917) 11 AJIL 674–730).

[61] In the *Costa Rica v. Nicaragua* case, the Court did not go as far as saying that the Bryan–Chamorro Treaty is invalid, albeit mainly on the ground that the United States was not a party to the dispute. See chapter 7 below, pp. 422–7.

A later *inter se* modification or suspension that is explicitly prohibited by an earlier multilateral treaty

Articles 41 and 58 of the Vienna Convention confirm the illegality of *inter se* modifications or suspensions explicitly prohibited by an earlier multilateral treaty (that is, agreements concluded subsequent to the conclusion of a multilateral agreement between only a limited number of the parties to that multilateral agreement). Under Art. 41, one of the conditions for '[t]wo or more of the parties to a multilateral treaty [to] conclude an agreement to modify the treaty as between themselves alone' is that 'the modification in question is *not prohibited by the treaty*' (emphasis added). Under Art. 58, one of the conditions for '[t]wo or more parties to a multilateral treaty [to] conclude an agreement to suspend the operation of provisions of the treaty, temporarily and as between themselves alone' is that 'the suspension in question is *not prohibited by the treaty*' (emphasis added).

Instances where *inter se* modifications or suspensions are prohibited can be found, for example, in UNCLOS and GATT. Article 20(1) of the Covenant of the League of Nations provided another example: 'The members of the League...solemnly undertake that they will not hereafter enter into any engagements inconsistent with the terms thereof.'[62]

Article 311(3) of UNCLOS provides as follows:

> Two or more States Parties may conclude agreements modifying or suspending the operation of provisions of this Convention, applicable solely to the relations between them, provided that such agreements do not relate to a provision derogation from which is incompatible with the effective execution of the object and purpose of this Convention, and provided further that such agreements shall not affect the application of the basic principles embodied herein, and that the provisions of such agreements do not affect the enjoyment by other States Parties of their rights or the performance of their obligations under this Convention.

This provision largely confirms the conditions set out in Arts. 41 and 58 of the Vienna Convention for *inter se* modifications or suspensions to be legal under the general law of treaties. Article 311(5) adds that Art. 311 'does not affect international agreements expressly permitted or preserved by other articles of this Convention'. Article 311(6) provides for an additional instance where subsequent agreements are prohibited: 'States Parties agree that there shall be no amendments to the basic principle

---

[62] For other examples, see Art. 8 of the North Atlantic Treaty (UNTS, vol. 34, p. 243), Art. 7 of the Warsaw Treaty of 1955 (UNTS, vol. 219, p. 3) and the respective clauses of the Geneva Red Cross Conventions of 1949.

relating to the common heritage of mankind set forth in article 136 and that they shall not be party to any agreement in derogation thereof.'

In sum, if a state party to UNCLOS were to conclude any of these agreements prohibited under Art. 311 of UNCLOS, such agreement would, from its viewpoint, constitute a breach of its earlier UNCLOS obligations. For that state, the later norm would then be 'illegal' under the earlier norm.[63]

GATT also prohibits the conclusion of certain *inter se* agreements, namely regional trade arrangements in which trade concessions are granted only to regional partners and not to other WTO members, in violation of GATT Art. I (MFN), to the extent they do not meet the conditions set out in GATT Art. XXIV (e.g., that the *inter se* or regional arrangement covers 'substantially all the trade' between the regional partners).[64] GATT does so, arguably, in less explicit terms in that it prohibits rather the state conduct resulting from such *inter se* agreements (that is, the fact that trade concessions given to regional partners are not given to other WTO members), not the *inter se* agreement as such. Nonetheless, in *Turkey – Textile* the Appellate Body implied that panels have jurisdiction to review the overall compatibility of regional arrangements with GATT Art. XXIV in order to assess whether a particular state measure is justified under WTO rules. A panel could, hence, find that a regional arrangement does not meet GATT Art. XXIV and, although it could not declare that arrangement 'illegal', for all practical purposes the arrangement would need to be changed so as to conform to Art. XXIV. If not, the regional partners could no longer implement or rely on the regional arrangement, at least not in line with their WTO obligations.

---

[63] Note that, in addition to prohibiting *inter se* agreements deviating from Art. 136, Art. 311(6) prohibits even amendments to Art. 136 by *all* states parties. In other words, even if all parties to UNCLOS were to conclude an amendment to Art. 136, Art. 311(6) would prohibit such amendment. Such prohibition would make the amendment 'illegal' (Art. 40 of the Vienna Convention gives effect to any special provisions set out in treaties in terms of their amendment). However, unless Art. 136 (and thus Art. 311(6) were to be part of *jus cogens* (something that is not unthinkable), the contractual freedom of states parties to UNCLOS should allow them to amend Art. 311(6) *itself*, e.g., by concluding a deviation from Art. 136 and explicitly stating that this deviation is not subject to Art. 311(6). Moreover, Art. 311(6) also prohibits that UNCLOS parties conclude treaties with third states, not party to UNCLOS, in deviation from Art. 136. Any such deviation would be illegal looked at from the angle of the UNCLOS party. However, as against the third party, Arts. 136 and 311(6) are *res inter alios acta* (unless they were to be part of *jus cogens*). Pursuant to the *pacta tertiis* principle, one would then be faced with a conflict of the type AB/AC: A, the UNCLOS party, would have (i) obligations vis-à-vis other UNCLOS parties (B) under Arts. 136 and 311(6); and (ii) at the same time, be bound by conflicting obligations vis-à-vis the third party to UNCLOS (C).

[64] GATS Art. V has a similar provision.

Inter se *agreements prohibited under Art. 41 or Art. 58 of the Vienna Convention on the ground that they affect third party rights or the object and purpose of the treaty*

We noted earlier that a conflict of norms arises and must be examined as between *two states* (see chapter 4 above, pp. 165–6). We added that normally the fact that *other states* are also bound by either of the two norms does *not* play a role. The exception to this rule is the theory set out in Arts. 41 and 58 of the Vienna Convention. These provisions provide living testimony that it is no longer correct to state that 'every multilateral treaty can simply be divided up into a number of bilateral legal relationships leaving no remainder'.[65] The very idea behind Arts. 41 and 58 is that an earlier *multilateral* treaty limits the contractual freedom of states subsequently to change their *bilateral* relationships *inter se*. In that sense, the bilateral relationship between two states is not an isolated matter, it is influenced also by the relationship these two states have with third states under a multilateral treaty.

In respect of *inter se* agreements to modify a multilateral agreement, Art. 41(1) of the Vienna Convention provides as follows:

Two or more of the parties to a multilateral treaty may conclude an agreement to modify the treaty as between themselves alone if:

(a) the possibility of such modification is provided for by the treaty; or
(b) the modification in question is *not prohibited by the treaty* and:
  (i) *does not affect* the enjoyment by the *other parties* of their rights under the treaty or the performance of their obligations;
  (ii) does not relate to a provision, derogation from which is incompatible with the *effective execution of the object and purpose of the treaty* as a whole (emphasis added).

Article 41(2) provides that, unless the possibility of the *inter se* modification is provided for by the treaty itself and this without further notification, 'the parties shall notify the other parties of their intention to conclude the agreement and of the modification to the treaty for which it provides'.

Article 58 is an almost exact copy of Art. 41, but it applies, not to *inter se* modifications, but to *inter se* suspensions of an earlier multilateral treaty.[66] Note, however, that Art. 41(1)(b)(ii) refers to incompatibility with

---

[65] Comment by the Netherlands in the preparation of the Vienna Convention, in Rauschning, *Travaux*, 230.
[66] Art. 58(1) of the Vienna Convention provides as follows: 'Two or more parties to a multilateral treaty may conclude an agreement to suspend the operation of the

'*the effective execution of* the object and purpose of the treaty *as a whole*' (emphasis added), whereas Art. 58(1)(b)(ii) refers to incompatibility with 'the object and purpose of the treaty' *tout court*. Although there is this difference in wording, it is difficult to see what consequences it may have or even why different rules ought to apply in this respect as between *inter se* modification and *inter se* suspension.

While it can safely be said that Arts. 41(1) and 58(1) constitute general customary international law (they have, for example, been copied in Art. 311 of UNCLOS, quoted earlier), it is doubtful whether the more procedural obligation in Arts. 41(2) and 58(2) to notify other parties meets that standard.[67]

Inter se agreements under Arts. 41 and 58 can take the form of

(i) a bilateral or multilateral treaty where all parties are bound also by the original multilateral treaty (ABCD/AB or ABCD/ABC conflicts); or
(ii) a multilateral treaty which includes also parties not bound by the original multilateral treaty (ABCD/ABEF conflicts).

The three grounds of illegality set out in Arts. 41 and 58 (an application of the notion of 'integral obligations')

The three grounds

Articles 41 and 58 thus *prohibit inter se* agreements in three instances:

(i) in case the multilateral treaty itself prohibits the *inter se* agreement in question (the instance discussed above, pp. 302–3);
(ii) if the agreement affects the rights or obligations of third parties; or
(iii) if the agreement relates to a multilateral treaty provision derogation from which is incompatible with the (effective execution of the) object and purpose of the treaty (as a whole).

The first ground of illegality under Arts. 41 and 58 results from the specific multilateral treaty in question and was discussed earlier. As Waldock pointed out, this first ground is different from the other two

provisions of the treaty, temporarily and as between themselves alone, if: (a) the possibility of such a suspension is provided for by the treaty; or (b) the suspension in question is *not prohibited by the treaty* and: (i) *does not affect* the enjoyment by the *other parties* of their rights under the treaty or the performance of their obligations; (ii) is not incompatible with *the object and purpose of the treaty*' (emphasis added). Art. 58(2) provides that, unless the possibility of the *inter se* suspension is provided for by the treaty itself and this without further notification, 'the parties in question shall notify the other parties of their intention to conclude the agreement and of those provisions of the treaty the operation of which they intend to suspend'.

[67] See, however, for a similar provision: Art. 311(4) of UNCLOS.

(relating to third parties and object and purpose) in that 'it leaves no room for the subjective questions of interpretation which may arise under the other two conditions'.[68]

The second and third conditions are self-standing grounds of illegality and cannot be overestimated. They relate to the notion of integral obligations, discussed at length in chapter 2 above. We reduced this essentially 'value-based' and subjective matter of 'integral obligations' to one of checking whether a multilateral treaty obligation constitutes a promise towards each and every state party *individually* (reciprocal obligations) or towards the *collectivity* of all state parties *taken together* (integral obligations); in other words, whether breach of the multilateral treaty obligation in question *necessarily* constitutes breach vis-à-vis *all* parties to the multilateral treaty (integral obligations), or whether this obligation can also be breached as against only one or several (but not necessarily all) state parties to the treaty, that is, the state parties towards whom the particular promise, allegedly breached, is owed (reciprocal obligations).

If an obligation under international law is of the integral type, it receives a higher legal status in that the obligation cannot be deviated from *inter se*, without the agreement of all parties to the treaty. This is the case because Arts. 41 and 58 of the Vienna Convention prohibit the conclusion of *inter se* agreements which affect either: (i) rights or obligations of *third parties* (parties to the multilateral treaty but not parties to the *inter se* agreement), pursuant to the *pacta tertiis* principle; or (ii) the very *object and purpose* of the treaty as a whole, by derogating from a particularly important multilateral treaty provision. In other words, the *inter se* agreement, though not necessarily prohibited by the earlier treaty itself, is then prohibited because it undermines the 'integral nature' of the multilateral treaty (either by affecting third parties or the very object and purpose of the treaty).

It may, at first sight, be difficult and amount to a rather subjective exercise to decide whether an *inter se* agreement relates to a provision derogation from which is incompatible with the 'object and purpose' of a multilateral treaty. If the *inter se* agreement is prohibited by the treaty itself, with reference, *inter alia*, to the 'object and purpose' of the treaty (a reference required by rules on treaty interpretation),[69] then no problem of subjectively assessing whether the agreement goes against the 'object and purpose' in the sense of the 'spirit' of the treaty arises.

[68] Rauschning, *Travaux*, 302.   [69] See Art. 31(1) of the Vienna Convention.

Indeed, an *inter se* agreement incompatible with the very object and purpose of the treaty is most likely to be prohibited also by the treaty itself (that is, under the first ground of illegality set out above). As the ILC Commentary pointed out: 'an *inter se* agreement incompatible with the object and purpose of the treaty may be said to be impliedly prohibited by the treaty'. The ILC suggested even that incompatibility with object and purpose would be a particularly grave breach of the treaty itself when it wanted to keep the two grounds of illegality separate because 'it is always possible that the parties might explicitly forbid *any inter se* modifications, thus excluding even *minor modifications not caught by the second condition* [on object and purpose]'.[70]

Nonetheless, there may be instances also where the *inter se* agreement is not as such prohibited by the treaty, but nonetheless relates to a provision derogation from which is against the 'object and purpose' of the treaty. However, in my view, those cases would then fall also under the second ground of illegality under Arts. 41/58 (that is, illegality based on the *pacta tertiis* principle). Indeed, the notion of 'object and purpose' of the treaty as a whole is closely related also to the notion of integral treaties, discussed in chapter 2 above. Recall, for example, that the *Genocide Convention* case which introduced the idea of integral obligations did not refer to the term 'integral' as such, but to the 'objects' of the treaty. In respect of *inter se* modifications incompatible with the object and purpose of the treaty as such, the ILC commentary to Art. 41 notes that '[h]istory furnishes a number of instances of *inter se* agreements which substantially changed the régime of the treaty and which overrode the objections of interested States'. The one example provided is that of 'an *inter se* agreement modifying substantive provisions of a disarmament or neutralization treaty'.[71] Such *inter se* agreements are incompatible with the 'object and purpose' of the treaty, not because of some subjective evaluation of the 'spirit' of the treaty, but as a result of the fact that they necessarily affect also the rights of third parties, that is, because the obligations under the multilateral treaty deviated from are of an integral nature (as we defined them in chapter 2).

Hence, it can safely be said that the ground of illegality based on incompatibility with the object and purpose of the treaty as a whole (third ground) overlaps either with a prohibition in the treaty itself (first ground) or with the ground of illegality based on the effect on third party rights (second ground).

[70] Rauschning, *Travaux*, 303.   [71] *Ibid.*

Some examples

We noted earlier (in chapter 2) that the notion of integral obligations, and hence Arts. 41 and 58 of the Vienna Convention, finds its roots, *inter alia*, in the *Genocide Convention* case, where the ICJ addressed the legality of reservations to treaties and concluded that reservation 'incompatible with the object and purpose of the treaty' could not be tolerated (a finding incorporated now in Art. 19(c) of the Vienna Convention). More focused on the legality of *inter se* agreements deviating from an integral multilateral treaty are the Opinion of Judge Anzilotti in the *Customs Regime Between Germany and Austria* case and the Dissenting Opinions of Judges Van Eysinga and Schücking in the *Oscar Chinn* case. Judge Anzilotti questioned whether the parties to an *inter se* agreement, *in casu*, the 1922 Geneva Protocol,

> were in a position to modify *inter se* the provisions of Article 88 [of the Treaty of Saint-Germain], which provisions... form an essential part of the peace settlement and were adopted not in the interests of any given State, but in the higher interest of the European political system and with a view to the maintenance of peace.[72]

In contrast to the majority of the PCIJ in *Oscar Chinn*, Judges Van Eysinga and Schücking expressed the view that the 1919 Convention of St Germain relating to the Congo Basin, another form of *inter se* agreement, was void between its signatories on the ground that it modified the earlier General Act of Berlin of 1885 without the assent of all the signatories thereto. Judge Van Eysinga expressed it thus:

> the Berlin Act [from which the *inter se* agreement deviated] presents a case in which a large number of States, which were territorially or otherwise interested in a vast region, endowed it [the Congo Basin] with a highly internationalized statute, or rather a constitution established by treaty, by means of which the interests of peace, those of 'all nations' as well as those of natives, appeared to be most satisfactorily guaranteed... [It] does not create a number of contractual relations between a number of States, relations which may be replaced as regards some of these States by other contractual relations... This régime, which forms an indivisible whole, may be modified, but for this agreement of all contracting Powers is required.[73]

In Van Eysinga's view, the later *inter se* Convention of St Germain was, therefore, illegal – even void – because it deviated from an integral treaty (second/third ground of illegality in Arts. 41/58). In addition, in his

---

[72] PCIJ, Series A/B, No. 41, 64 (1931).   [73] PCIJ, Series A/B, No. 63, 132–4 (1934).

opinion, Art. 36 of the Berlin Act explicitly 'precludes any modification by some only of the contracting parties'[74] (first ground of illegality in Arts. 41/58). The majority of the Court decided not to examine whether the *inter se* agreement was invalid on the ground that 'the validity of this Act has not so far, to the knowledge of the Court, been challenged by any government'.[75] Judges Van Eysinga and Schücking, in contrast, were of the view that the invalidity at hand was one to be examined by the Court *ex officio*.[76]

When it comes to *inter se* agreements affecting the rights of third parties (second ground of illegality), one may think also of an *inter se* agreement as between two parties to an MEA in which the prior MEA obligation of 30 per cent reduction in emission of a certain substance is brought down *inter se* to only 20 per cent. Such *inter se* agreement necessarily affects third parties that are parties to the MEA, but not to the *inter se* agreement. Moreover, it would seem to affect also the very object and purpose of the MEA (third ground of illegality). Hence, on two grounds, the *inter se* agreement is illegal pursuant to Art. 41. In both instances, this is so because the MEA obligation is one of an integral nature. The *inter se* agreement would, in other words, be illegal even if the multilateral treaty itself does not explicitly say so. The illegality results then from Art. 41, more particularly, from the integral nature of the obligation deviated from *inter se*.

The same reasoning would apply in respect of an *inter se* agreement that detracts from substantive human rights or a so-called objective regime setting up, for example, an international regime for a certain territory (e.g., the Antarctic Treaty). Such *inter se* agreement would necessarily affect also the rights of parties to the human rights treaty or objective regime that are not parties to the *inter se* agreement (as well as arguably undermine the very object and purpose of those treaties). This is the case because human rights obligations or obligations under such an objective regime are mostly of an integral nature. Hence, the *inter se* agreements concerned are illegal under Art. 41 of the Vienna Convention. As the ILC Commentary noted:

> Some obligations contained in treaties are in the nature of things intended to apply generally to all the parties all the time. An obvious example is the Nuclear Test-Ban Treaty, and a subsequent agreement entered into by any individual party contracting out of its obligations under that Treaty would manifestly be

---

[74] PCIJ, Series A/B, No. 63, 133 (1934). [75] *Ibid.*, 80.
[76] *Ibid.*, respectively at 135 and 149.

incompatible with the Treaty. Other obligations may be of a purely reciprocal kind, so that a bilateral treaty modifying the application of the convention *inter se* the contracting States is compatible with its provisions.[77]

The consequence of an *inter se* agreement being prohibited under Arts. 41 or 58: illegality, not invalidity

In case any of the three conditions in Art. 41 or Art. 58 is met, it will be the *lex prior* (multilateral treaty) which prevails, not the *lex posterior* (*inter se* agreement). What is more, the *lex posterior* will then be illegal on the basis of the *lex prior*, i.e., it constitutes wrongful conduct under the earlier norm, either directly (explicit prohibition, first ground of illegality) or indirectly (through the operation of Arts. 41 and 58, second and third grounds of illegality).[78] Unlike, for example, Art. 30, Arts. 41 and 58 not only set out a 'priority rule'. The earlier multilateral treaty not only 'prevails over' the later *inter se* agreement, Arts. 41 and 58 go further and actually declare the *inter se* agreement impermissible or illegal. As the ILC Commentary notes, under Art. 41 'the main issue is the conditions under which *inter se* agreements may be regarded as *permissible*' (emphasis added).[79]

---

[77] Rauschning, *Travaux*, 234.

[78] It is interesting to note that at the Vienna Conference France proposed an amendment to what is now Art. 30(4)(a). France wanted to add an explicit reference to what are called *restricted multilateral treaties*, a notion that comes close to that of 'integral treaties'. France defined a 'restricted multilateral treaty' as 'a treaty which is intended to be binding only on the States referred to in the treaty and whose entry into force in its entirety with respect to all the negotiating States is an essential condition of the consent of each of them to be bound by it' (Documents of the Conference, 112, French proposal in UN doc. A/CONF.39/C.1/L.24). France would have rephrased Art. 30(4)(a) as follows: 'As between States parties to both treaties the same rule applies as in paragraph 3 [the later treaty prevails], *however, when the earlier treaty is a restricted multilateral treaty and the later treaty is concluded between certain of the parties only, the provisions of the earlier treaty shall prevail*' (Documents of the Conference, 148, French proposal in UN doc. A/CONF.39/C.1/L.44, emphasis added). France stated that the earlier treaty should thus prevail 'in the interests of the integrity of the treaty; that integrity was essential to the very existence of that type of treaty' (per de Bresson, Meetings of the Committee of the Whole, 166, para. 24). The proposal was not accepted. However, it is submitted here that Art. 41 has exactly the same effect and goes even further in that the later *inter se* agreement deviating from an integral obligation must not only give way to the earlier treaty, it also becomes illegal.

[79] Rauschning, *Travaux*, 303. Or, as noted in Nguyen Quoc Dinh, P. Daillier and A. Pellet, *Droit International Public* (Montreal: Wilson & Lafleur, 1999) para. 173 at 270: 'Dans les situations où les conditions posées par l'article 41 de la Convention de 1969 ne sont pas respectées, le traité restreint postérieur au traité général n'est pas licite. Il faut donc affirmer la primauté du traité antérieur et écarter l'application du traité postérieur. La solution est nettement affirmée en jurisprudence.'

On the other hand, although Arts. 41 and 58 go further than, for example, the priority rule in Art. 30, they do not go as far as, for example, Arts. 53 and 64 on *jus cogens*. Arts. 41 and 58 may lead to the *illegality* of an *inter se* agreement; they do not result in its *invalidity*.

This was made clear in the *travaux préparatoires* to Art. 41. Originally, as outlined before,[80] ILC drafts on the law of treaties (mainly Lauterpacht's report) provided for the 'invalidity' of later treaties (including *inter se* agreements) which are incompatible with an earlier treaty. This was founded on the argument that parties to the earlier treaty had limited their capacity to conclude later inconsistent treaties. This theory was rejected, first by Fitzmaurice, then more categorically by Waldock. The latter noted that the ILC 'felt bound to conclude that, as the law stands today, by entering into the earlier treaty the parties do not render themselves legally *incompetent* to enter into another inconsistent treaty and that the later treaty is *valid and effective* as between the States parties to it'.[81]

Karl too notes that 'Art. 41, which refers to these cases [of *inter se* agreements expressly or impliedly prohibited], governs only the question of their *legality*. The later treaty may therefore be *illegal* and cannot be invoked against States standing aloof, but it is *not invalid*.'[82]

Rosenne, in the context of Art. 311(4) of UNCLOS referred to earlier (basically a copy of Arts. 41 and 58), would nonetheless take it a step further and declare *inter se* agreements not meeting the standard of Art. 311(4) 'invalid'. He puts it thus:

the conclusion seems inescapable that if the law of the treaty-instrument contained in the 1969 Convention does not lead directly to the invalidity of the later treaty or impair the capacity of the States to conclude it (since article 6, on capacity, does not mention any limitation on the capacity of every State to conclude treaties) at the same time it does not exclude the possibility that another branch of law, whether the law of treaty-obligations or the law of State responsibility, could lead to that result in appropriate circumstances, especially if appropriate procedural provisions for determining the issue of breach exist

---

[80] See above, pp. 279–81. [81] Rauschning, *Travaux*, 303.
[82] Wolfram Karl, 'Conflicts Between Treaties', in R. Bernhardt (ed.), *Encyclopedia of Public International Law* (Amsterdam: North-Holland, 1984), VII, 468 at 471, emphasis added. See also Waldock, 742nd Meeting of the ILC, YBILC 1974, vol. 1, 121, para. 25: 'an undertaking not to contract out was implied in every treaty containing "integral" or "interdependent" obligations, but the consequences [sic] of the breach of any such undertaking, whether express or implied, was to raise an issue of *priority rather than validity*, except in cases of *jus cogens*' (emphasis added).

in a form binding the parties concerned. Article 311 of the [UNCLOS]...may be one of those.[83]

The illegality operates vis-à-vis third parties, but also as between the parties to the *inter se* agreement

However, the fact that a later *inter se* agreement which does not meet one of the conditions in Arts. 41 or 58 cannot be seen as 'void' or 'invalid' as between its parties does not do away with its 'illegal' nature.

As against third parties, all *inter se* agreements are, first of all, 'not opposable'. This is so because of the *pacta tertiis* principle which is implied in Arts. 41 and 58, and stated more generally in Art. 34 to mean: 'A treaty does not create either obligations or rights for a third State without its consent.' A third party – party to the multilateral agreement, but not to the *inter se* agreement – cannot, therefore, see its rights or obligations affected by an *inter se* agreement to which it did not consent. In respect of third parties, the *inter se* agreement is hence non-opposable. This is the effect of the *pacta tertiis* rule and Art. 34 of the Vienna Convention, in particular. However, an *inter se* agreement that does not meet the conditions set out in Arts. 41 or 58 takes it a step further and is not simply 'non-opposable' to third parties. In addition, it constitutes, in and of itself, *breach* of the rights of third parties under the multilateral agreement and this on the ground that the *inter se* agreement is either (i) explicitly prohibited by the multilateral treaty or (ii) violates third party rights under that treaty (as a result of which the second

---

[83] Shabtai Rosenne, *Breach of Treaty* (Cambridge: Grotius, 1985), 89. In support of a rather technical/procedural reasoning leading to acceptance of 'invalidity' of *inter se* agreements inconsistent with Art. 311(4) of UNCLOS, Rosenne refers in particular to Art. 319(2)(c) of UNCLOS imposing an obligation on the UN Secretary-General to 'notify States Parties of agreements in accordance with article 311, paragraph 4'. He also finds support in Arts. 76 and 77 of the Vienna Convention on the depository functions of the UN Secretary-General. On these grounds, he believes that 'it may be suggested that the action of the Secretary-General under the two sets of provisions, looked at in the light of the total structure of the final provisions (Part XVII) of the Convention, may be such as could set in motion a process by which breach of article 311 could be established and the later treaty found to be void because of a specific provision to that effect in the Convention' (*ibid.*, 92). If it comes to the *establishment of breach* of Art. 311(4) (i.e., of illegality under Art. 41), Rosenne's procedural approach is helpful. However, the *consequence of invalidity* once breach is established (instead of illegality) is not sufficiently explained, nor would it, as noted earlier (see text below, p. 299), in many cases seem to make much of a difference if the treaty were invalid, as opposed to only illegal (except for conflicts of the AB/AC type, discussed in chapter 7 below). Also in the latter instance the *inter se* agreement would most likely lose its practical effect.

or third condition of Arts. 41 or 58 was triggered). Hence, as against third parties bound by the multilateral treaty, the *inter se* agreement is both non-opposable and illegal. This is what Arts. 41 and 58 add to Art. 34.

On top of that, Arts. 41 and 58 affect more than the legal relationship between parties to the *inter se* agreement, on the one hand, and nonparties to that agreement, on the other hand. Indeed, these provisions mean also that an *inter se* agreement not permitted under Art. 41 or Art. 58 (and hence 'illegal') may not be invocable either *as between parties* to the *inter se* agreement. This goes much further than the *pacta tertiis* rule in Art. 34, a rule that applies in respect of third parties to a treaty, not *as between* the parties to a treaty.

The ILC, as well as Art. 30(5) of the Vienna Convention, made it very explicit that in the event of conflict of norms rules on state responsibility continue to apply. Now, if it is so that the *inter se* agreement is illegal, the responsibility of *all of the parties* to the *inter se* agreement is engaged and the agreement, constituting a breach under international law, must cease.[84] Hence, to allow one of the parties to enforce the *inter se* agreement as against another party to the *inter se* agreement would not only be giving effect to an illegal instrument from the point of view of both parties (something that could, in the circumstances, be enough for an adjudicator not to enforce the agreement), it would constitute, moreover, confirmation of breach vis-à-vis third parties, given that the implementation of the *inter se* agreement necessarily breaches the rights of third parties.

Thus, although the *inter se* agreement is not invalid or void under the law of treaties, as a result of its illegality grounded in Art. 41 or Art. 58 and the law of state responsibility, the *inter se* agreement must be ended and cannot, therefore, be enforced, *not even as between the parties to it*.

This explains why Arts. 41 and 58 provide for an exception to the contractual freedom of states. For an international tribunal to enforce the *inter se* agreement at the demand of either party would necessarily affect third parties. Thus, even if it is one of the parties to the *inter se* agreement that contests its legality under Art. 41 or Art. 58, that party should be allowed to do so and be successful if any of the three conditions for illegality are met. A different question is whether an adjudicator should, on

---

[84] This clearly distinguishes the situation from conflicts of type AB/AC discussed in chapter 7 below, where responsibility is incurred only by state A, not by states B or C.

his or her own initiative, examine the legality of the *inter se* agreement even if the parties in dispute do not make any claims in this respect. As pointed out earlier, whereas invalidity should be examined *ex officio*, illegality is normally subject to the *non ultra petita* rule so that the adjudicator should only decide on it if and when it is invoked by one of the parties.[85] In practice, however, one would expect that the illegality will be raised either (i) by the party to the *inter se* agreement in whose favour the illegality would work, or (ii) by the third parties affected by the *inter se* agreement. In that sense, the question of legality vis-à-vis parties to the *inter se* agreement may, after all, be a largely theoretical problem since it is most likely that *third states* will challenge the agreement, not states that agreed to it in the first place.

Especially if the multilateral agreement is administered and monitored in the context of an international organisation and/or can be enforced under a system of compulsory third party adjudication (as under the WTO treaty and, to a great extent, UNCLOS), the illegality of *inter se* agreements inconsistent with Art. 41 or Art. 58, *even as between parties to it*, ought to be accepted.

The fact that a state party could hence rely on the illegality of such *inter se* agreement, even if it originally agreed to it, does not mean that that state is no longer responsible for breach vis-à-vis third parties. Given that it was part of the *inter se* agreement, it should in principle bear collective responsibility together with the other parties to the *inter se* agreement vis-à-vis third parties. As against another state party to the *inter se* agreement, it could, of course, not claim damages. Since it is itself, together with other states, responsible for the conclusion of the *inter se* agreement, it should then only be able to obtain cessation of the illegal *inter se* agreement.

In these circumstances, the difference between 'invalidity' of the *inter se* agreement and 'illegality' of such agreement may be minor. For all practical purposes the illegal *inter se* agreement will lose its effect. The

---

[85] In case the parties to the *inter se* agreement do not contest the legality of their agreement and implement it, it will then be up to the third parties to challenge the legality of the agreement. If the parties to the *inter se* agreement by mutual consent ask the adjudicator to enforce that agreement (i.e., none of the parties contests its legality), the question may, indeed, arise as to whether the adjudicator should examine the legality of the *inter se* agreement on his or her own initiative. Since illegality in these circumstances is not only a matter as between the parties to the *inter se* agreement, but one affecting the rights of third states, there are strong reasons, in particular in the context of WTO law that is administered in the framework of an international organisation, in favour of the adjudicator assessing the issue *ex officio*.

inter se agreement would only continue to be relevant in case it is binding also on states which are not at the same time parties to the multilateral treaty.

The legality of inter se agreements deviating from the WTO treaty

The legal relationship between WTO members under the WTO treaty can be affected by amendments, interpretations or other decisions taken pursuant to the Marrakesh Agreement. In addition, Vienna Convention rules on the application of successive treaties (in particular Art. 30(4)(a)) and *inter se* agreements to modify a multilateral treaty (Art. 41) apply also to the WTO treaty. For most parts, the WTO treaty did not 'contract out' of these rules of general international law. As a result, they apply also to the WTO treaty to the extent they were not contracted out from.[86] Hence, the trade relationship between WTO members may be affected by bilateral agreements, as well as multilateral agreements, to which not all WTO members are a party and which do not necessarily constitute WTO norms. As noted by Hersch Lauterpacht as early as 1935: 'It is clearly impossible to accept the view that the provisions of a multilateral treaty can never be modified and its obligations limited by particular agreements unless with the consent of all other contracting parties.'[87]

Crucially – and this is a point that is missed by a number of authors[88] – the fact that the WTO treaty can, in effect, only be 'amended' by the consent of all WTO members (Art. X of the Marrakesh Agreement) does not preclude that a limited number of WTO members validly conclude *inter se* 'modifications' to the WTO treaty. The Vienna Convention makes a clear distinction between 'amendments' (governed in Arts. 39 and 40), on the one hand, and 'modifications' (governed in Art. 41), on the other. The same distinction must be made in respect of the WTO treaty: although, in most cases, it can be 'amended' only by consensus, its 'modification' as

---

[86] See chapter 4 above, pp. 201–11.
[87] Hersch Lauterpacht, 'The Chinn Case' (1935) 16 BYIL 162 at 166.
[88] For example, Joel Trachtman, 'The Domain of WTO Dispute Resolution' (1999) 40 *Harvard International Law Journal* 333, and Gabrielle Marceau, 'Conflicts of Norms and Conflicts of Jurisdictions, The Relationship between the WTO Agreement and MEAs and other Treaties' (2001) 35 JWT 1081 at 1104 ('the WTO Agreement contains specific rules for its amendment (Article X of the Agreement Establishing the WTO) excluding the application of bilateral amendments amending a multilateral treaty (Article 41.2 of the Vienna Convention)'; Marceau thereby clearly confuses 'amendment' of treaties, governed in Arts. 39 and 40 of the Vienna Convention and Art. X of the Marrakesh Agreement, with the *inter se* 'modification' of treaties, addressed in Art. 41 of the Vienna Convention and *not* excluded in Art. X of the Marrakesh Agreement).

between some WTO members only has, in most cases, *not* been excluded (that is, of course, as long as the conditions in Arts. 41 and 58 of the Vienna Convention are met). Unlike 'amendments', such 'modifications' would then not affect WTO members that did not agree to them. Nor would modifications necessarily result in a rewriting of specific WTO provisions, albeit as between the parties to the *inter se* agreement only. *Inter se* 'modifications', in the wide sense of the word, may also take the form of outside treaties whose very conclusion changes the legal relationship as between certain WTO members, without having explicitly changed this or that provision of the WTO treaty as it applies between them.

If such 'modifications' in the wide sense of the word were *per se* excluded, the legal relationships as between all WTO members set out in the WTO treaty would be written in stone, to be altered only by consensus. This would make change virtually impossible and impair the flexibility needed to keep abreast of changing international conditions. Moreover, such a 'status quo' would make it impossible also to reflect the diversity as between WTO members. If the WTO treaty could only be affected by WTO norms, in particular, by formal WTO *amendments*, it would become the alpha and omega of all trade relations as between all WTO members. No room would be made, for example, for more detailed or special rules, either in terms of subject matter (say, rules in the World Customs Organisation) or membership (say, the EC or NAFTA treaties).

It is one of the main purposes of this book to reject this 'self-contained' view of WTO law, expressed, for example, by Marceau when she argues that 'WTO obligations are always the same for all Members' so that bilateral modifications of WTO rights and obligations cannot be tolerated.[89] If this were true, no treaty could ever prevail over WTO rules, not even as between parties to both norms, and WTO law would, in effect, be supreme over all other norms of international law. In contrast, the view defended here is that *inter se* 'modifications' to the WTO treaty *must* be tolerated as long as (i) they are not explicitly prohibited in the WTO treaty (as are certain regional arrangements, not meeting the conditions in GATT Art. XXIV); and (ii) they do not affect the rights of other WTO members. This is the position we examine next in more detail.

For WTO purposes, a distinction should be made between two types of *inter se* agreements:

---

[89] Marceau, 'Conflicts', 1105.

(i) those *further liberalising trade* as between some WTO members only for which the WTO treaty has explicit rules; and
(ii) those *restricting trade* in contrast to trade flows called for under the WTO treaty (again, as between some WTO members only), on which the WTO treaty is silent.

An example of the former is a free trade arrangement. An example of the latter is an agreement between some WTO members only, say in an MEA, not to invoke GATT Arts. III and XI vis-à-vis certain trade restrictions they both consider to be justified (even though they are, in principle, contrary to GATT rules, including, for example, GATT Art. XX).[90] This second category of *inter se* agreements could also include *inter se* agreements concluded regarding a particular WTO dispute in which two WTO members agree not to invoke certain procedural rights granted to them in the DSU (say, the right to appeal pursuant to DSU Arts. 16.4 and 17[91] or the right to take retaliatory measures).

Inter se *agreements further liberalising trade*

The first type of *inter se* agreements – *further liberalisation* as between some WTO members only – is explicitly dealt with in the WTO treaty itself. It prohibits such agreements unless they

(i) extend the increased liberalisation to *all* WTO members (in accordance with WTO rules on most-favoured-nation treatment); *or*
(ii) conform with the conditions in GATT Art. XXIV (GATS Art. V) in respect of regional arrangements.

Being 'prohibited by the treaty' in the sense of Art. 41(1)(b) of the Vienna Convention, they are not permitted to modify WTO rules as between the WTO members that concluded the *inter se* agreement. A

---

[90] Another example is an *inter se* agreement between some WTO members only in which they agree that, as between themselves, an import ban on hormone-treated beef should be imposed (notwithstanding the Appellate Body report on *EC – Hormones*, declaring such a ban as inconsistent with the SPS agreement).

[91] In the *Australia – Leather* case, for example, Australia and the United States reached a bilateral agreement concerning the procedures to be applicable for proceedings pursuant to Arts. 21 and 22 of the DSU and Art. 4 of the SCM agreement. Paragraph 4 of that bilateral agreement stated: 'Both Australia and the United States will unconditionally accept the review panel report [pursuant to Art. 21.5] and there will be no appeal of that report' (agreement reproduced in WTO doc. WT/DS126/8). For another bilateral agreement on how to proceed under DSU Arts. 21.5 and 22.6, see the US–EC agreement in the *US – FSC* dispute, reproduced in WTO doc. WT/DS108/12.

fortiori, such *inter se* agreements cannot affect the WTO rights and obligations of WTO members which are *not* a party to the *inter se* agreement.

Apart from a regional arrangement not meeting the conditions in GATT Art. XXIV, one could imagine other 'illegal' *inter se* agreements aimed at further liberalisation *inter se*. An *inter se* agreement could, for example, further liberalise trade as between its parties only in the sense of narrowly defining 'injury' in the area of anti-dumping (hence *inter se* limiting the scope for trade restricting anti-dumping duties). Not to grant this trade advantage on an MFN basis to all WTO members is prohibited by the WTO treaty, hence illegal also under Art. 41 of the Vienna Convention.

Other *inter se* agreements deviating from or suspending WTO rules

In contrast, in respect of the second type of *inter se* agreements – *restricting trade* as between some WTO members only under an MEA or altering DSU procedural rights *inter se* – the WTO treaty itself does not provide for *lex specialis*. Indeed, nothing in the WTO treaty prevents a limited number of WTO members from agreeing in an MEA not to invoke, for example, GATT Arts. III or XI in respect of certain trade restrictions they both consider to be justified (but in respect of which they know or fear that, for example, GATT Art. XX is not met). The same can be said about a bilateral agreement as between two disputing WTO members setting out, for example, that contrary to DSU rules, for the particular dispute in question, no appeal shall be possible, an arbitration under DSU Art. 21.3 need not be completed within ninety days or retaliation under DSU Art. 22.6 will remain possible beyond the sixty-day period after the end of the reasonable period of time.[92]

Pursuant to Art. 41 of the Vienna Convention, WTO members have the contractual freedom to change their *inter se* relationships as long as (i) the WTO treaty does not explicitly prohibit the *inter se* agreement and (ii) they respect the rights of third parties. Indeed, since the *inter se* agreements referred to are 'not prohibited by the [WTO] treaty', only the two conditions in Art. 41(1)(b) of the Vienna Convention apply:

(i) the *inter se* agreement may not 'affect the enjoyment by the other parties [i.e., the other WTO members that are not parties to the *inter se* agreement] of their rights under the [WTO] treaty or the performance of their obligations'; and

[92] *Ibid.*

(ii) the *inter se* agreement may not relate to a WTO provision 'derogation from which is incompatible with the effective execution of the object and purpose of the [WTO] treaty as a whole'.

In respect of the first condition, although an *inter se* derogation from WTO rules – say, an *inter se* agreement to expand GATT Art. XX justifications for trade restrictions under an MEA – may well have an effect also on *trade flows* or *trade opportunities* with certain third parties, the WTO *rights and obligations* of these third parties remain unaffected by the *inter se* agreement. (Indeed, if such *inter se* trade restricting agreement does have an effect on trade flows with third parties, this is likely to be one to the benefit of these third parties: the trade that is restricted *inter se* is likely to lead to increased imports from third parties.)[93] The same applies in respect of an *inter se* agreement in which the DSU right to appeal or to have consultations in an Art. 21.5 procedure has been waived (the rights of third parties are not affected by such waiver). *In all of these cases the* inter se *agreement does not affect third party rights because, as we discussed in chapter 2, trade obligations under the WTO treaty are reciprocal in nature, not integral.* The expansion of GATT exceptions can, for example, only be invoked by and against parties to the *inter se* agreement, not by or vis-à-vis third parties. Such expansion, although deviating from WTO rules as between the parties to the *inter se* agreement, does not affect the rights of third states.

In particular, the MFN rights of third parties are not breached by such *inter se* agreements. To the contrary, the parties to the *inter se* agreement are those that will see their trade restricted. Third parties will continue to see trade flow and, as a result, *benefit from the* inter se *agreement rather than be discriminated against*. As a result, the MFN obligation in the WTO does not stand in the way of *inter se* agreements that restrict trade or waive DSU rights as between some WTO members only. The non-discrimination obligation under this MFN clause extends only to trade *advantages*: *inter se* trade advantages have to be granted to all WTO members, without discrimination. It does not extend to trade *restrictions*: when some WTO members agree on certain trade restrictions to be imposed only on their *inter se* trade, they are (fortunately for other WTO members!) not under an obligation to extend those restrictions to

---

[93] See, in contrast, *inter se* agreements allowed under GATT Art. XXIV, where the effect on trade flows from third parties is more likely to be negative: the increased trade between the parties to the *inter se* agreement is, indeed, likely to diminish imports from third states.

all WTO members (unless those other members explicitly agree to them). The WTO is about trade liberalisation and granting trade advantages on a non-discriminatory basis; not about spreading trade restrictions, to which some WTO members agreed, to all other WTO members without the agreement of these other WTO members.

Moreover, what counts under Art. 41 of the Vienna Convention is not whether there is a conflict with WTO rules *as concerns the parties to the inter se agreement* (when they decide to deviate from WTO rules *inter se*, such conflict will obviously be unavoidable; it is even the very purpose of the *inter se* agreement). Hence, the fact that there is derogation from, or conflict with, WTO rules as concerns the parties to the *inter se* agreement does not mean that the WTO treaty prohibits such *inter se* agreement. What counts under Art. 41 is rather whether the *inter se* agreement derogates from rights of third parties. And in respect of *inter se* agreements modifying WTO rules this is unlikely to be the case given the reciprocal nature of those rules. If an *inter se* agreement were, nonetheless, to breach the rights of third parties, then it would go against Art. 41(1)(b) and hence be illegal.

In respect of the second condition set out in Art. 41(1)(b), it is difficult to predict exactly which WTO rights are so important that 'giving them away' *inter se* (without affecting third parties) would nonetheless threaten the effective execution of the object and purpose of the WTO treaty *as a whole* (if any such rights exist at all). Indeed, since most substantive trade rights and obligations under the WTO can be reduced to reciprocal rights and obligations as between two WTO members, it is difficult to see how *inter se* modifications that are not prohibited by the WTO treaty itself, nor affect rights or obligations of third parties, could, nevertheless, prejudice 'the effective execution of the object and purpose of the treaty as a whole'. As explained earlier, if an *inter se* agreement is not prohibited by the treaty itself, nor affects the rights or obligations of third parties, it should not normally be found to be incompatible either with the very object and purpose of the treaty as a whole.[94] In that sense, the ground of incompatibility with object and purpose of the treaty overlaps with the two other grounds of illegality set out in Arts. 41 and 58.

If, but only if, *inter se* agreements modifying the WTO treaty meet the conditions set out above, will they 'legally' change the relationship

---

[94] See above, pp. 305–7.

between the WTO members party to the agreement. The effect of such changes in WTO dispute settlement is discussed in chapter 8 below. Once again, the *inter se* agreement cannot, however, alter the rights and obligations of third parties.

If an *inter se* agreement thus changes the relationship between certain WTO members, the conflict of norms – between the *inter se* agreement and the WTO rule deviated from *inter se* – is then not resolved by one norm being 'illegal' under the other. Rather, a conflict in the applicable law may then arise. That is, as between the WTO members party also to the *inter se* agreement, one state may invoke the WTO rule, the other the *inter se* agreement deviating from that rule. In that event, the conflict in the applicable law ought to be resolved by Art. 30(4)(a) of the Vienna Convention so that the norm to be applied by the adjudicator is the *lex posterior* set out in the *inter se* agreement (not the earlier WTO rule). We come back to Art. 30 in chapter 7 below.

In contrast, if *inter se* agreements do not meet the conditions in Arts. 41 or 58, an inherent normative conflict arises which must be decided in favour of the WTO treaty, the *inter se* agreement then being 'illegal' under the prior WTO treaty. The WTO treaty then not only prevails, it leads to the illegality of the *inter se* agreement to the extent of the conflict.

Inter se modifications in the form of another multilateral treaty concluded in an entirely different context

For Art. 41 to apply, it is not required that the *inter se* modification is concluded in the same functional or organisational context as that of the original multilateral treaty. As noted before (p. 305), a conflict under Art. 41 may take the form also of an ABCD norm deviated from *inter se* by A and B in an ABEF norm (that is, a norm to which states not bound by the original multilateral treaty are also parties). Nor does Art. 41 require that the parties to the *inter se* agreement explicitly acknowledge that their agreement is aimed at modifying another multilateral treaty. Art. 41 applies when 'two or more of the parties to a multilateral treaty...conclude an agreement to modify the treaty as between themselves alone'. Hence, two multilateral treaty norms stemming from entirely different contexts could also fall under the scope of Art. 41.

Indeed, WTO rules, on the one hand, and rules under MEAs or human rights treaties, on the other, could, in the event of conflict and depending on their membership, also be seen as a situation of *inter se* agreements deviating from an earlier multilateral treaty. Depending on which of the two can be defined as the *multilateral treaty earlier in time*, the other could then be characterised as a *subsequent* inter se *deviation* of the ABCD–ABEF type (in that event, however, states E and F are kept out of the operation of Art. 41 which would then only affect the relationships between states A, B, C and D, that is, the states party to the original multilateral treaty).

WTO rules constituting an inter se *modification of an earlier human rights treaty or MEA of an integral nature: the WTO rule is illegal to the extent of the conflict*
In chapter 2, we pointed out that many MEA and human rights obligations (but not necessarily all of them) are of an integral type, while trade obligations under the WTO are mostly reciprocal in nature. Hence, in case the *WTO rule* can be defined as the *later in time* (ABEF norm), it could be seen as an *inter se* agreement modifying *earlier integral human rights or MEA obligations* (ABCD norm). If this is the case – that is, if the WTO rule deviates from earlier human rights or MEA obligations as between WTO members only – then the WTO rule would not only affect WTO members but also third party rights (i.e., rights of non-WTO members, party to the human rights treaty or MEA, *in casu* states C and D). In addition, the later WTO rule could then even be seen as incompatible with 'the effective execution of the object and purpose of the [human rights or MEA] treaty as a whole'. Consequently, as between parties to the earlier MEA or human rights treaty (ABCD norm), the particular WTO provision (ABEF norm), to the extent of the conflict, would then be illegal pursuant to Arts. 41/58 of the Vienna Convention.

In other words, the inherent normative conflict should then be decided in favour of the earlier MEA or human rights provision, the later WTO rule being 'illegal' to the extent of the conflict. This would be the result of Arts. 41/58. The fact that the WTO rule is the *lex posterior* under Art. 30(4)(a) of the Vienna Convention does not alter this solution. As noted below, Art. 30(5) explicitly makes the operation of Art. 30(4) subject to Art. 41.

WTO rules subsequently modified inter se *by a human rights treaty or an MEA: WTO rules must give way as* lex prior
In contrast, if the *human rights treaty or MEA* would be the *later in time* (ABEF norm), it must be recalled that *inter se* agreements modifying reciprocal obligations, such as those set out in the WTO treaty, are more

easily accepted under Arts. 41/58 of the Vienna Convention. The human rights treaty or MEA (ABEF norm) could then be defined as an *inter se* agreement deviating from certain WTO rules (ABCD norm) as between some of the parties to the human rights treaty or MEA. Given the reciprocal nature of WTO obligations, this *inter se* agreement is unlikely to be illegal under Arts. 41/58 (unless it affects the rights of third parties, that is, WTO members not party to the later human rights treaty or MEA). Hence, in the event of conflict, the later human rights treaty or MEA would *not* be prohibited as an illegal *inter se* deviation. It should then prevail as the *lex posterior* pursuant to Art. 30(4) of the Vienna Convention (of course, only as between the parties to both norms). The earlier WTO rule is then, however, not illegal. It is simply the *lex prior* having to give way *inter se* to the later human rights treaty or MEA.

In summary, when integral obligations are involved, conflicting WTO rules must normally give way (irrespective of timing)
In sum, irrespective of the actual timing of the two norms, in the event of conflict between a WTO rule *of the reciprocal type* and a human rights or MEA rule *of an integral nature*, the human rights or MEA rule must, either pursuant to Arts. 41/58 or pursuant to Art. 30(4)(a) of the Vienna Convention, prevail in the relationship between two parties that are bound by both norms (*in casu*, states A and B).[95]

Take the example of conflict between a WTO prohibition to restrict trade in product X (assuming that GATT Art. XX does not allow for trade restrictions on product X) and an MEA obligation or command, of the integral type, to restrict trade in product X because product X is defined there (rightly or wrongly) as a harmful substance. As between states that are bound by both rules, the MEA rule could then be said to prevail, irrespective of whether it comes earlier or later in time. If it comes later in time, it prevails as the *lex posterior* under Art. 30(4)(a). If it is the earlier in time, it cannot, as an integral obligation, be validly deviated from *inter se* by the later WTO rule pursuant to Arts. 41/58.

Another example would be conflict between a human rights obligation or command to respect certain property rights and an explicit WTO right or exemption on infringing such human rights (say, certain property rights that may be violated by WTO countermeasures in the field

---

[95] However, in chapter 7 below, we point to certain difficulties in respect of determining the date of a treaty. The conclusions reached here are subject to these considerations.

of intellectual property, or against foreign service suppliers already established in the country taking the countermeasures). Here again, as between states that are bound by both rules, the human rights rule – in case it is one of an integral nature – could be said to prevail, irrespective of whether it comes earlier or later in time. If it comes later in time, it prevails as the *lex posterior* under Art. 30(4)(a). If it is the earlier in time (which is most likely, in case the conflicting WTO right derives from a DSB authorisation to impose sanctions), it cannot, as an integral obligation, be deviated from *inter se* by the later WTO rule. Once again, all of this applies only in case both norms are binding on both of the parties. The human rights rule cannot prevail over the WTO rule as against a WTO member which is not bound by the human rights rule.

Acts of international organisations that are 'illegal'

The responsibility of international organisations is a topic that has so far attracted little attention. Earlier, we set out the possibility that acts of international organisations could be 'invalid' because of a lack of competence or other breach of the constituent instruments of the organisation. This invalidity derived from international institutional law. In addition, acts of international organisations may also be inconsistent with norms of international law other than those set out in the constituent instruments of the organisation, that is, norms that do not directly relate to the competence of the organisation or its organs.

Acts of international organisations are, indeed, not taken in a legal vacuum nor within the context only of certain constituent instruments. They are, like new treaties, part of the corpus of international law. There is no inherent hierarchy of sources in international law. As a result, an act of an international organisation has the same hierarchical status as a treaty norm. However, such act must then abide also by the same rules on legality that apply to treaty norms.

Hence, there can be little doubt that acts of international organisations must also respect norms of *jus cogens*. If not, the consequences specified above (in particular, the invalidity of the act) must apply (by analogy to Arts. 53 and 64 of the Vienna Convention).

Moreover, international organisations and their organs, as subjects of international law, must also respect general principles of law and relevant rules of general customary international law, unless they decide to contract out of these rules and are competent to do so under their attributed powers. Schermers notes, for example, that

[it] can be safely submitted that international organizations are bound by international customary law, either on the ground that all subjects of international law are so bound, or on the ground that the member States were bound by international customary law when they created the organization and thus may be presumed to have created the organization as being so bound, or on the ground that the rules of international customary law are at the same time general principles of law to which international organizations are bound.[96]

Furthermore, it has been submitted that 'an international organization is bound to all international treaties to which all its member States were parties when the organization was established' (pursuant to the adage *nemo plus juris transferre potest quam ipse habet*) and that '[w]hen only some of the member States were bound by particular treaties when the organization was established one should still uphold the presumption that the organization must respect the treaty obligation of those States. In order to be allowed to ignore the obligation of some of its members the organization must bring convincing arguments.'[97]

Hence, depending on the law that is found to apply to them, acts of international organisations, when in conflict with another norm, may be found to be 'illegal' under that other norm.

Also, Arts. 41 and 58 would seem to apply by analogy to acts of international organisations. In other words, in case these acts constitute, in effect, an *inter se* deviation or suspension of an earlier multilateral treaty (say, a treaty to which not all members of the international organisation are parties) which either (i) is explicitly prohibited by that treaty or (ii) constitutes a breach of rights of third parties (not members of the organisation), such *inter se* deviation or suspension should be regarded as 'illegal' (not on the basis of Arts. 41 or 58, but on the basis of international institutional law).

Take the example of a decision by a WTO organ, say, a DSB authorisation to suspend certain WTO obligations as between two WTO members. Such suspension, if implemented, may be inconsistent with the obligations as between these two WTO members under a human rights treaty. The DSB authorisation could then, in effect, constitute an *inter se* suspension or modification of that human rights treaty. However, since human rights obligations are of an integral nature, such *inter se* suspension or modification could then be illegal on the ground that it affects also the

---

[96] Henry Schermers, 'The Legal Basis of International Organization Action', in René-Jean Dupuy (ed.), *A Handbook on International Organizations* (Dordrecht: Nijhoff, 1998), 401 at 402.
[97] *Ibid.*, 403.

rights of other parties to the human rights treaty (that are not WTO members). As a result, the DSB decision, to the extent it deviates from the human rights norm in a way that is inconsistent with the conditions set out in Arts. 41 or 58 of the Vienna Convention, would then be illegal and should not be implemented.[98]

In contrast, if the DSB decision were to allow for an *inter se* suspension or modification of obligations that are *not* of an integral nature, say, obligations under a WIPO convention whose breach remains bilateral and does not affect third parties, the DSB decision would then constitute a 'legal' *inter se* suspension or modification (not falling under any of the grounds of illegality set out in Arts. 41 or 58). The DSB decision should then, as the later norm in time, prevail over the inconsistent WIPO treaty rule, of course, as between the parties to the DSB suspension only.[99]

---

[98] On the limits of suspending human rights as a form of countermeasure, see also chapter 4 above, p. 234.

[99] See chapter 3 above, pp. 146–7, and chapter 7 below, pp. 346–7 and 384–5.

7 Resolving 'conflict in the applicable law'

One of the two norms 'prevails'

In the previous chapter, 'inherent normative conflict' was resolved rather categorically by effectively bringing to an end one of the two norms, either through invalidity or termination or through illegality. In most conflicts, however – that is, when faced with what we called 'conflicts in the applicable law' – both norms will continue to exist and international law will only offer what one could call 'priority rules'. In that event, both norms survive the conflict and are considered as valid and 'legal'. The conflict is then resolved in favour of one of the two rules because that rule has been, or can be, labelled as the more 'prominent' or 'relevant' one, or because it expresses the latest intention of the parties. The result of these 'priority rules' is that only one of the two rules applies to the particular situation at hand.

The initial question is hence not, as under the previous chapter, which of the two norms *survives*, but which of the two norms *applies*. In that sense, 'conflict in the applicable law' is a question of 'choice of law'; not one of validity or legality of one norm in the light of another norm.

In terms of state responsibility, under a conflict in the applicable law, obviously, only the rule that must finally be applied can be breached and result in responsibility. The discarded rule does not apply and can hence *a fortiori* not be breached. However, although this rule is disapplied in the particular circumstances, it is not declared invalid nor is it in any way seen as an 'illegal rule'. It is simply a rule that must give way to another one in the circumstances. In other circumstances, the discarded rule may continue to apply.

The priority rules to resolve a conflict in the applicable law are determined by three basic principles:

(i) the contractual freedom of states;
(ii) the *pacta sunt servanda* principle;[1] and
(iii) the principle of *pacta tertiis nec nocent nec prosunt*.[2]

In most instances, the contractual freedom of states will be decisive. In other words, the latest expression of the states' intentions will count and prevail. This latest expression of intention may, for example, be found in explicit conflict clauses set out in a treaty provision or be activated as a result of the *lex posterior* principle.

Nonetheless, the *pacta tertiis* rule is as important. States may, by mutual consent, change their minds. But they may not do so in a way that affects the rights or obligations of other states. If, by concluding a new norm, they affect third party rights, the resulting norm will be non-opposable to those third parties. Hence, the contractual freedom of states, as well as the *pacta sunt servanda* rule, is limited by the *pacta tertiis* principle.

Explicit conflict clauses

When states negotiate treaty norms they may not only express their intention as to what the content of the treaty norms should be, but also create rules as to what should happen in case of conflict with other norms. There are three types of explicit, treaty-based conflict clauses:

(i) those relating to *pre-existing* treaties;
(ii) those relating to *future* treaties; and
(iii) those regulating conflict of norms within the *same* treaty.

The expression of state intent in any of these conflict clauses must be accepted as valid and decisive by an international adjudicator unless

(i) the conflict clause results in conflicts with *jus cogens* (say, a treaty on slave trading explicitly states that it prevails over norms prohibiting the trade in slaves); or
(ii) the conflict clause goes against Art. 41 of the Vienna Convention, in particular, by violating third party rights (say, a plurilateral WTO agreement on the reduction of tariffs in information technology products explicitly states that the advantages accorded in it apply only *inter se* and that, in this respect, the *inter se* agreement prevails over MFN obligations in the WTO treaty); or

---

[1] In respect of treaty norms: 'Every treaty in force is binding upon the parties to it and must be performed by them in good faith' (Art. 26 of the Vienna Convention).
[2] In respect of treaty norms: 'A treaty does not create either obligations or rights for a third State without its consent' (Art. 34 of the Vienna Convention).

(iii) the conflict clause is overruled by a later expression of state intent (say, if states X, Y and Z agree in treaty A that this treaty A prevails over another treaty B, nothing prevents X, Y and Z from subsequently changing their minds and from agreeing in treaty C that it should, nonetheless, be treaty B that prevails over treaty A).

In cases under (ii), the conflict clause cannot be applied because of the *pacta tertiis* principle; under (iii) it cannot be invoked because of the contractual freedom of states.

These limitations on the effect of explicit conflict clauses are a reminder also of the hierarchy of conflict rules set out earlier. When faced with a conflict of norms, one must first examine whether there is 'inherent normative conflict' as a result of which either of the two norms ceases to exist or is illegal. Only if that is not the case must one resort to the rules set out in this chapter on resolving 'conflict in the applicable law'.

Conflict clauses may be straightforward in that they provide which norm prevails in the event of conflict. In that case, an adjudicator must decide only whether there is conflict and, if so, the extent of the conflict. Once conflict is found, he or she knows exactly which norm must prevail.

Recall, however, that the very strict definition of conflict defended by some authors should not be accepted.[3] Hence, adopting a proper definition of conflict is important also in the operation of conflict clauses. If one were to reject, for example, the fact that an obligation may conflict also with an explicit right, the obligation would always prevail, not as a result of the conflict clause but as a result of a strict definition of conflict. Because of the importance of both rights and obligations under other treaties, conflict clauses ought to be drafted also with reference to 'provisions' or 'rights and obligations' under other treaties, which are, for example, 'not affected by' the new treaty. To refer only to 'obligations' under other treaties would give a wrong signal as to the definition of conflict and could, indeed, be interpreted strictly so that the explicit conflict clause applies only to a certain type of conflict, namely those affecting obligations under other treaties, not those affecting rights. Art. 104 of NAFTA and Art. 103 of the UN Charter, for example, refer to *obligations*, not to 'rights and obligations' or 'provisions'.[4] In contrast,

---

[3] See chapter 4 above, pp. 175–88.
[4] See the discussion below in note 13 (Art. 104 of NAFTA) and on p. 337 (Art. 103 of the UN Charter).

following a proposal by Israel, Art. 30(1) of the Vienna Convention refers to both obligations *and rights*.[5]

There may also be clauses under which the adjudicator is required to decide more than the question of whether there is conflict. Under Art. 22(1) of the UN Convention on Biological Diversity, for example, the adjudicator must give way to rights and obligations under other treaties only if 'the exercise of those rights and obligations would not cause a serious damage or threat to biological diversity'. Art. 104 of NAFTA gives prominence to certain MEAs but it does so 'provided that where a Party has a choice among equally effective and reasonably available means of complying with such obligations, the Party chooses the alternative that is the least inconsistent with the other provisions of this Agreement'.

It should be recalled also that a treaty explicitly abrogating another one,[6] or a treaty provision explicitly deviating from another one (in the form of 'general rule–exception'), does not involve conflict of norms nor, *a fortiori*, the operation of conflict clauses.[7] In the event of one treaty explicitly abrogating another one, the two norms are never in operation at the same time so that there is no conflict. In case of one treaty norm explicitly carving out of the scope of application of another norm (say, GATT Art. XX carving out of all other GATT norms), the scopes of application of the two norms (mostly in a 'general rule–exception' relationship) are simply different and do not overlap. Hence, there is no conflict and the fact that the exceptional norm states that it deviates from the general rule cannot be seen as a conflict clause.

Finally, even in the absence of explicit conflict clauses, other more implicit expressions of intent on what to do in case of conflict may be found. These implicit indications as to the intentions of the parties will play a role, firstly, in the interpretation of the norms in question *so as to avoid conflict*. Here, elements such as the preambles to the treaties in question (part of the context in which interpretation must take place) and, in case of ambiguity, their *travaux préparatoires* may be important. However, these implicit elements may be influential also in the event

[5] See chapter 4 above, pp. 171–2.
[6] See, in this respect, Art. 20 of the 1919 Covenant of the League of Nations: '1. The Members of the League severally agree that this Covenant is accepted as abrogating all obligations or understandings *inter se* which are inconsistent with the terms thereof... 2. In case any Member of the League shall, before becoming a Member of the League, have undertaken any obligations inconsistent with the terms of this Covenant, it shall be the duty of such Member to take immediate steps to procure its release from such obligations.'
[7] See chapter 4 above, pp. 162–3.

of genuine conflict, i.e., where interpretation did not lead to a harmonious reading. This will be the case, in particular, in the absence of a clear-cut solution to the conflict, say, in the event of conflicts where no explicit conflict clause is available and the *lex posterior* principle is difficult to apply (e.g., in cases of 'continuing' treaties).[8] In that event, the search for 'current state consent' may be determined by other methods such as the *lex specialis* principle or other indications as to what the states in question would have done had they been faced with the conflict. As explained below, both the *lex posterior* and the *lex specialis* principles are, in effect, but two elements or methods of one and the same legal question, namely: following the principle of contractual freedom of states, what coincides with current state consent? Under this legal test other implicit expressions of intent may be important also. If they cannot provide a predictable solution either – that is, a solution where the judge is applying the law, not making it – a situation of conflict of norms constituting a lacuna may arise (discussed below, pp. 419–22).

We next deal with the three types of conflict clauses set out above – those related to pre-existing treaties, those related to subsequent treaties and those regulating conflicts within the treaty – using the particular example of the WTO treaty.

Conflict clauses in respect of pre-existing treaties

The new treaty states that it prevails over pre-existing ones

An example of a treaty providing that it is to prevail over pre-existing norms is Art. 311(1) of UNCLOS: 'This Convention shall prevail, as between States Parties, over the Geneva Convention on the Law of the Sea of 29 April 1958.' Another example is Art. 103 of NAFTA:

1. The Parties affirm their existing rights and obligations with respect to each other under the *General Agreement on Tariffs and Trade* and other agreements to which such Parties are party.
2. In the event of any inconsistency between this Agreement and such other agreements, this Agreement shall prevail to the extent of the inconsistency, except as otherwise provided in this Agreement.

A treaty clause stating that, in the event of conflict, the new treaty prevails over an earlier treaty *as between the parties to the new treaty* is simply confirming the contractual freedom of states, as it is expressed

---

[8] Discussed below, pp. 378–80.

in Art. 59 and Art. 30(3) of the Vienna Convention.[9] However, while such conflict clause confirms the obvious as between the parties to the new treaty, it cannot impose the new treaty on third parties without their consent. As the ILC Commentary to Art. 30 noted:

> When, on the other hand, the parties to a treaty containing a clause purporting to override an earlier treaty do not include all the parties to the earlier one, the rule *pacta tertiis non nocent* automatically restricts the legal effect of the clause. The later treaty, clause or no clause, cannot deprive a State which is not a party thereto of its rights under the earlier treaty [emphasis added].[10]

This would be the case, for example, in the event, referred to earlier, that a plurilateral WTO agreement on the reduction of tariffs in information technology products were to state that the advantages accorded in it apply only *inter se* and that, in this respect, the *inter se* agreement prevails over MFN obligations in the WTO treaty. Such *inter se* agreement cannot detract from the MFN rights of third parties under the WTO treaty. Equally, because of the *pacta tertiis* principle, Art. 311(1) of UNCLOS cannot lead to UNCLOS prevailing over the 1958 Convention on the Law of the Sea for states party *only to the 1958 Convention* and not party to UNCLOS. Article 311(1) makes this explicit by stating that the conflict clause applies only 'as between States Parties' to UNCLOS.

The new treaty states that it is subject to pre-existing ones
A new treaty may also state that, in the event of conflict with a pre-existing treaty, the earlier treaty prevails. This type of clause is mostly expressed, not in terms of 'conflict' and 'one treaty prevailing over the other', but in terms of the later treaty not derogating from, not being incompatible with, not affecting, or being subject to, the earlier treaty.

In so far as the clause relates to pre-existing treaties *with third states*, it only confirms the obvious. Because of the *pacta tertiis* principle, the new treaty is simply not capable of derogating from the rights or obligations of third states under pre-existing treaties. Pre-existing treaties may be treaties either (i) between *one or some* of the state parties to the new treaty and third states, or (ii) between *all* of the state parties to the new treaty and third states (an example of the latter would be a clause in a plurilateral WTO agreement stating that the plurilateral agreement

---

[9] See ILC Commentary to Art. 30, in Dietrich Rauschning, *The Vienna Convention on the Law of Treaties, Travaux Préparatoires* (Frankfurt: Metzner, 1978), 233.
[10] *Ibid.*

does not derogate from rights and obligations of other WTO members under the WTO treaty).

However, in so far as the clause gives priority to earlier treaties *as between the parties* to the new one, the clause deviates from the *lex posterior* principle set out in Arts. 59 and 30(3). This is why Art. 30(2) was needed. It explicitly permits conflict clauses in favour of pre-existing treaties, notwithstanding the *lex posterior* principle: 'When a treaty specifies that it is subject to, or that it is not to be considered as incompatible with, an earlier...treaty, the provisions of that other treaty prevail.'

Many examples of conflict clauses giving priority to earlier norms can be referred to. Article 22(1) of the UN Convention on Biological Diversity provides, for example: 'The provisions of this Convention shall not affect the rights and obligations of any Contracting Party deriving from any existing international agreement, except where the exercise of those rights or obligations would cause serious damage or threat to biological diversity.'[11]

Article 4 of the European Energy Charter Treaty, as amended, provides: 'Nothing in this Treaty shall derogate as between particular Contracting Parties which are members of the WTO, from the provisions of the WTO Agreement as they are applied between those Contracting Parties.'[12] Article 40 of the North American Agreement on Environmental Cooperation states: 'Nothing in this Agreement shall be construed to affect the existing rights and obligations of the Parties under other international environmental agreements, including conservation agreements, to which such Parties are party.' Article 104 of NAFTA provides:

1. In the event of any inconsistency between this Agreement and the specific trade obligations set out in: a) [CITES], b) [the Montreal Protocol on Substances that Deplete the Ozone Layer], c) [the Basel Convention], or d) the agreements set out in Annex 104.1, such obligations shall prevail to the extent of the inconsistency, provided that where a Party has a choice among equally effective and reasonably available means of complying with such obligations, the Party chooses the alternative that is the least inconsistent with the other provisions of this Agreement.[13]

---

[11] Done at Nairobi, 22 June 1992.
[12] Done at Lisbon, 17 December 1994, amended in 1998.
[13] Note that Art. 104 of NAFTA refers only to inconsistency with MEA trade *obligations*, not explicit rights granted therein that would allow parties to restrict trade. Nonetheless, it could be argued that for every 'explicit right' to restrict trade there is a corresponding 'trade obligation' to respect this right.

Article 60 of the European Convention on Human Rights also gives priority to prior treaties, but only to the extent that they *add* human rights or fundamental freedoms in favour of the individual: 'Nothing in this Convention shall be construed as limiting or derogating from any of the human rights and fundamental freedoms which may be ensured under the laws of any High Contracting Party or under any other agreement to which it is a Party.'[14]

Finally, the preamble to the Cartagena Biosafety Protocol provides: 'this Protocol shall not be interpreted as implying a change in the rights and obligations of a Party under any existing international agreements'. This clause would make the Protocol subject to pre-existing agreements. Nonetheless, it is followed by an '[u]nderstanding that the above recital is not intended to subordinate this Protocol to other international agreements'. These two preambular paragraphs seem to neutralise each other. In the end, it is difficult to speak of any remaining conflict clause so that it would seem warranted rather to revert to the conflict rules in general international law, such as *lex posterior* or *lex specialis* (discussed below).

A conflict clause stating that a norm ought not to be interpreted or considered in conflict with another norm is, in terms of result, little different from one stating that, in the event of conflict, the other norm prevails: in both cases, the other norm must be applied. However, in terms of legal technique there is a major difference. In the first instance, the very existence of conflict is precluded. In the second instance, the existence of conflict is acknowledged but solved in a certain way.[15] In the first case, the adjudicator is precluded from adopting an interpretation that conflicts with another norm. In the second case, he or she must follow normal rules on treaty interpretation, may find a conflict and must then give preference to the other norm. To avoid all confusion, and recalling that 'interpretation' covers only the definition of terms in a treaty provision (unless, of course, the parties to a treaty say differently),

---

[14] See Evert Alkema, 'The Enigmatic No-Pretext Clause: Article 60 of the European Convention on Human Rights', in J. Klabbers and R. Lefeber (eds.), *Essays in the Law of Treaties* (The Hague: Nijhoff, 1998), 41.

[15] This point was made by the delegate of Japan at the Vienna Conference itself, commenting on the phrase 'is not to be considered as incompatible with' part of what is now Art. 30(2) of the Vienna Convention: 'the case of a treaty that was not to be considered as inconsistent with an earlier treaty was different from the case of a treaty being subject to another. In the former case, the question of one treaty prevailing over the other should not arise' (Meetings of the Committee of the Whole, 164, para. 7, *per* Mr Fujisaki).

states should, however, be advised to use genuine conflict clauses in the treaties they negotiate, in the style of 'in the event of conflict between the provisions of (or rights or obligations under) treaty A and treaty B, those in treaty A shall prevail'.

Conflict clauses relating to future treaties

The treaty states that it will prevail over subsequent ones

The limited effect of clauses claiming priority over future treaties In so far as a clause claims priority over future treaties which would affect third party rights (say, future *inter se* agreements modifying the treaty in a way inconsistent with Arts. 41/58), such clause only confirms the principle of *pacta tertiis*. However, the few existing clauses which claim priority over future treaties are perceived as wider in scope and cover any future treaty, not just future treaties adversely affecting third parties. To that extent, the clause contradicts the contractual freedom of states pursuant to which a later treaty normally prevails over an earlier one, at least as between the parties to both treaties (Art. 30(3) of the Vienna Convention).

Generally speaking, however (and with the possible exception of Art. 103 of the UN Charter, discussed below), a conflict clause proclaiming its priority over future treaties *cannot* limit the contractual freedom of states. States can always change their minds in the future, by mutual consent (subject only to *jus cogens* and Arts. 41/58). Hence, a conflict clause claiming *ex ante* priority over all future treaties is severely limited by the continuing contractual freedom of states and the *pacta sunt servanda* principle that results from the future exercise of this contractual freedom. Article 30(2) does *not* sanction conflict clauses stating that the treaty *prevails over* future treaties. Article 30(2) only excludes from the application of Arts. 30(3) and 30(4) those cases where the treaty says that it is *subject to* other treaties. As the ILC Commentary to Art. 30 noted: 'Article 103 [of the UN Charter] apart, clauses in treaties which purport to give priority over another treaty, whether earlier or later in date, do not by themselves appear to alter the operation of the general rules of priority set out in paragraphs 3 and 4 of the article.'[16]

Put differently, with the exception of Art. 103 of the UN Charter, an explicit conflict clause claiming priority over future treaties must anyhow give way to the *lex posterior* principle (pursuant to which future treaties will anyhow prevail over the treaty containing the conflict clause). Hence, conflict clauses may well provide that the treaty prevails

---

[16] Rauschning, *Travaux*, 233.

over future treaties, but nothing prevents the parties to the first treaty from changing their minds and deciding in the later treaty that, notwithstanding the earlier conflict clause, the later treaty must prevail. Crucially, even if this later treaty does not include an explicit conflict clause that deactivates the first conflict clause, in the event of conflict between the two treaties, the later treaty, as between the parties to it, would still prevail pursuant to the *lex posterior* principle in Art. 30(3). Following Art. 30(4)(a), this later treaty would then prevail *even if it were concluded only as between some of the parties to the first treaty* (of course, as long as the conditions in Arts. 41/58 are met).

Take the example of an ABCD treaty X stating that it prevails over all future treaties as between A, B, C and D. According to one author, DSU Arts. 3.2 and 19.2 constitute such a conflict clause as between WTO members vis-à-vis post-1994 non-WTO treaties.[17] A later treaty Y is subsequently concluded as between A, B, C and D and conflicts with the earlier treaty X. Treaty Y will then, notwithstanding the conflict clause in treaty X, prevail *unless treaty Y explicitly states that it is subject to treaty X* (only in that case does Art. 30(2) apply and deactivate the *lex posterior* principle). Treaty Y will so prevail even if it does not explicitly reverse the conflict clause in treaty X. The mere incompatibility with the earlier treaty X activates Art. 30(3) and calls for preference for the later treaty Y. Even if states A and B, subsequent to treaty X between A, B, C and D, conclude an *inter se* agreement deviating from treaty X, this *inter se* agreement shall, as between A and B, prevail, once again, notwithstanding the conflict clause in treaty X (assuming, of course, that the conditions in Arts. 41/58 are met). The same reasoning should apply also in respect of DSU Arts. 3.2 and 19.2 in case they were to constitute a general conflict clause in favour of the WTO treaty (*quod non*).[18] They would be subject to any subsequent change of mind, both as between all WTO members and as between some WTO members only in *inter se* agreements. Hence, their effect would be extremely limited in terms of ensuring the priority of the WTO treaty.

In sum, as Karl rightly remarked: 'Clauses which claim priority over future treaty engagements are futile: They cannot be invoked against third States; they do not render later conflicting treaties void; and they can always be overcome by the common will of the parties.'[19]

---

[17] Lorand Bartels, 'Applicable Law in WTO Dispute Settlement Proceedings' (2001) 35 JWT 499.

[18] See below, pp. 352–5.

[19] Wolfram Karl, 'Conflicts Between Treaties', in R. Bernhardt (ed.), *Encyclopedia of Public International Law* (Amsterdam: North-Holland, 1984), VII, 468 at 471.

The exceptional case of Art. 103 of the UN Charter The most prominent example of a conflict clause claiming priority over future treaties is Art. 103 of the UN Charter. This clause represents a special case and is, indeed, far from 'futile'.[20] This provision states: 'In the event of a conflict between the obligations of the Members of the United Nations under the present Charter and their obligation under any other international agreement, their obligations under the present Charter shall prevail.'

We have already discussed the higher status of UN Charter obligations in chapter 3 above (pp. 99–100).

The term 'any other international agreement' in Art. 103 covers both past and future agreements. Hence, a conflict between a UN Charter obligation and a future agreement must be decided in favour of the UN Charter obligation. Article 30(1) of the Vienna Convention makes an explicit exception to the *lex posterior* principle for Art. 103 of the UN Charter, thereby making Art. 103 a special case among the conflict rules claiming priority in the future: '*Subject to Article 103 of the Charter of the United Nations*, the rights and obligations of States Parties to successive treaties relating to the same subject-matter shall be determined in accordance with the following paragraphs' (emphasis added).[21]

Four remarks are warranted which put the importance of Art. 103 in perspective.

First, even if Art. 103 represents a special case, it must be recalled that the contractual freedom of UN members does not prevent them from amending Art. 103, unless Art. 103 were to be seen as *jus cogens*. Thus, Art. 103 is also limited and subject to the contractual freedom of UN members. UN Charter obligations prevail over other agreements, not because they represent an inherently 'higher law', but because UN members have agreed to this priority rule in the UN Charter itself.

Second, although there has been a lot of discussion on this matter,[22] Art. 103 is not binding on states that are not UN members,[23] except

---

[20] *Ibid*. Note also in this respect Art. 20(1) of the 1919 Covenant of the League of Nations: 'The Members of the League... solemnly undertake that they will not hereafter enter into any engagements inconsistent with the terms thereof.'

[21] The ILC in its Commentary to Art. 30(1) explained this reference to Art. 103 as follows: 'the position of the Charter of the United Nations in modern international law is of such importance, and the States Members of the United Nations constitute so large a part of the international community, that it appeared to the Commission to be essential to give Article 103 of the Charter special attention and a special place in the present article' (Rauschning, *Travaux*, 232).

[22] For an overview, see W. Czaplinski and G. Danilenko, 'Conflict of Norms in International Law' (1990) 21 NYIL 3 at 15.

[23] In support see, for example, V. Degan, *Sources of International Law* (The Hague: Nijhoff, 1997), 428 and P. Cahier, 'Le Problème des Effets des Traités à l'Egard des Etats Tiers'

for that part of UN Charter obligations which is part of *jus cogens*. Non-UN members (such as, until recently, Switzerland) have not even signed up to UN Charter obligations: how could these obligations then prevail over their other obligations?[24] Even if certain provisions of the UN Charter can be said to be part of customary law binding also on non-UN members, as we saw earlier, custom does not have a legal status that is higher than other obligations. Hence, only if Art. 103 could itself be seen as custom would non-UN members be bound under customary law to give preference to UN Charter obligations *as expressed in custom*, over and above their other obligations. However, the higher standing of UN Charter obligations would then derive not from Art. 103 but from customary law.

Third, Art. 103 is phrased in terms of a priority rule. In the event of conflict, UN Charter obligations 'prevail' over other obligations. The norms setting out these other obligations do not, because of Art. 103 as such, become 'invalid'.[25] Article 103 does not speak of invalidity, nor do Vienna Convention rules on invalidity of treaties mention Art. 103 as a ground of invalidity. Invalidity because of conflict with UN Charter obligations may occur. But then it would be the result of these Charter obligations being part of *jus cogens* (not of Art. 103 as such).

Fourth, the obligations that prevail under Art. 103 are not just any UN obligations. Only obligations *under the UN Charter* are cloaked with this higher legal standing, not, for example, obligations under any agreement or act concluded *in the context of a UN body* (which would then prevail, for example, over WTO rules, the WTO not being a UN body).

With these limitations in mind, though, it must be stressed that Art. 103 does, indeed, go a step further than other conflict clauses

---

(1974) 143 *Recueil des Cours* 718. *Contra*: K. Dahl, 'The Application of Successive Treaties Dealing with the Same Subject-Matter' (1974) 17 *Indian Yearbook for World Affairs* 305. Some authors referred to the *travaux préparatoires* of the UN Charter which allegedly indicate that Art. 103 was intended to be applicable in relation to non-UN members (see, for example, Wilfred Jenks, 'Conflict of Law-Making Treaties' (1953) 30 BYIL 401 at 438). However, this intention would not as such seem enough to trump the *pacta tertiis* rule. It is not enough for A and B to agree in an AB treaty that the treaty must apply also to C for that to be the case. The situation may be different in respect of the UN Charter in so far as it is part of *jus cogens*. But then the priority of UN Charter obligations does not result from the UN Charter as such but from their *jus cogens* character.

[24] At the Vienna Conference on the law of treaties, Switzerland opposed the formula of Art. 30(1) which refers to Art. 103 of the UN Charter on the ground that Switzerland, being a non-UN member, could not recognize the priority of UN Charter obligations (Vienna Conference, *Official Records*, 1st Session, 31st Meeting, 165 (1986)).

[25] In support: Czaplinski and Danilenko, 'Conflict', 16. *Contra*: Karl, 'Conflicts', 470.

claiming priority over future treaties. The breadth of Art. 103 should not be underestimated either. In this respect, four remarks are called for.

First, whereas other conflict clauses claiming priority for the future (such as, according to some authors, DSU Arts. 3.2 and 19.2) will be overruled by any subsequent contradictory treaty as between the parties to this later treaty (unless this later treaty explicitly states that it is subject to the earlier treaty),[26] an agreement concluded by some or even all UN members, *without amending Art. 103*, would not prevail over the UN Charter. This is the case because Art. 30(1) explicitly disapplies the *lex posterior* rule (in Arts. 30(3) and 30(4)) in respect of Art. 103 (but not in respect of other conflict clauses claiming priority over future treaties).

Second, the *Lockerbie* cases confirmed that Security Council resolutions (not just UN Charter provisions themselves) prevail over all other (past and future) international agreements, *in casu* the 1971 Montreal Convention. In its Order on Provisional Measures, the ICJ found as follows:

Whereas both Libya and the United States, as Members of the United Nations, are obliged to accept and carry out the decisions of the Security Council in accordance with Article 25 of the Charter; whereas the Court...considers that prima facie this obligation extends to the decision contained in resolution 748 (1992); and whereas, *in accordance with Article 103 of the Charter, the obligations of the Parties in that respect prevail over their obligations under any other international agreement, including the Montreal Convention* [emphasis added].[27]

Or as Sir Andrew Hardie (United Kingdom) noted at the public sitting of the ICJ:

both the sense and the literal terms of Article 103 apply its effect to binding decisions of the Security Council as well as to the provisions of the Charter itself. The syllogism is simple: Member States are under a legal obligation to 'accept and carry out' the binding decisions of the Council; that obligation is an 'obligation under the Charter'; therefore that obligation prevails over 'Member States obligations under any other international agreement'.[28]

Following this line of reasoning, it could be argued also that decisions of the ICJ, the principal judicial organ of the UN, are obligations under the UN Charter which, pursuant to Art. 103, prevail over any other international agreement (possibly including even judgments of other international tribunals taken pursuant to such other international agreements,

---

[26] See above, pp. 335–6.   [27] ICJ Reports 1992, para. 42.
[28] UK statement (Sir Andrew Hardie) at the public sitting of the ICJ on 14 October 1997, 10 a.m., referring to the UK submission, at para. 5.39, posted on the internet at http://www.icj-cij.org/icjwww/idocket.

as we discussed in chapter 3 above, p. 121). Pursuant to Art. 92 of the UN Charter, the ICJ Statute forms an integral part of the UN Charter and Art. 59 of the ICJ Statute states that decisions of the ICJ have binding force as between the parties and in respect of the particular case. Hence, the obligations derived from an ICJ judgment are legally binding and could be said to be 'obligations of the Members of the United Nations under the present Charter' in the sense referred to by Art. 103 of the UN Charter.

Third, Art. 103 only gives priority to UN Charter obligations in the event of conflict with 'obligations under any other *international agreement*'. Should this mean that later acts of *international organisations* (other than those giving rise to UN Charter obligations) can deviate from Charter obligations? Not so, it would seem, since 'obligations under any other international agreement' could be interpreted broadly so as to include also obligations arising under an act of an international organisation, in particular one – like the WTO – not part of the UN family (say, a DSB decision to suspend concessions). Such obligations can, indeed, be said to arise, albeit indirectly only, from an 'international agreement', i.e., the agreement in which the states in question granted the authority to the international organisation to take the act in the first place. More problematic though is whether UN Charter obligations prevail also over *customary* international law: not so, it would seem, on the basis of Art. 103 which refers only to 'obligations under any other *international agreement*'.

Fourth, Art. 103 only addresses 'obligations' under both the UN Charter and other agreements. It does not explicitly refer to rights.[29] As noted earlier, however, conflict can arise also as between an obligation and an explicit right (be it a permission or an exemption).[30] Hence, Art. 103 would have been better drafted if it had referred also to rights. The drafting of Art. 103 caused discussion in the *Lockerbie* cases. Libya suggested that Art. 103, which speaks of obligations, may not extend also to rights under another treaty or under general international law.[31] In other words, in the eyes of Libya, the UN Charter prevails over other *obligations*, not over other *explicit rights*. In response, the United Kingdom (Mr Crook) stated thus:

---

[29] See, in contrast, Art. 30(1) of the Vienna Convention which was, following a proposal by Israel, extended so as to cover both obligations *and rights*. See above, p. 330.
[30] See chapter 4 above, pp. 175–88.
[31] UK statement (Mr Crook) at the public sitting of the ICJ on 15 October 1997, 10 a.m., para. 3.35, posted on the internet at http://www.icj-cij.org/icjwww/idocket.

The obligation to comply with Security Council decisions applies fully both to decisions affecting the *rights* and those affecting the *obligations* of States. The relevant provisions of the Charter are phrased broadly and are intended to be broad in effect. They must be in order to assure the effectiveness of the régime of Chapter VII and in interpreting this aspect of the Charter this Court has not recognized any distinction between 'rights' and 'obligations'... Moreover, this suggested limitation creates serious difficulties. Suppose a bilateral treaty gives the nationals of each party the right to invest in the territory of the other. Surely the Charter gives the Security Council the power in a Chapter VII situation to require that one party prohibit investments by its nationals in the territory of the other, notwithstanding these treaty provisions.[32]

The example referred to by Mr Crook is a clear case of conflict between an *obligation* and an *explicit right* or permission from the point of view of the state victim of the boycott, namely: a UN Security Council obligation to respect the boycott imposed on it by other states versus a bilateral treaty granting it an explicit right or permission to invest in another state.

Moreover, when viewed from the standpoint of *two parties*, one can always point to *two obligations*, even if the conflict, in the eyes of the party facing it, is one of an obligation versus an explicit right. The explicit right corresponds then to an obligation on the other party to respect the explicit right. Thus, looked at from this angle, there will always be opposing *obligations* involved. Article 103 itself seems to allow for an examination of conflict looked at from the angle of *several parties* (not only from the viewpoint of one UN member facing conflict, i.e., the way we have addressed conflict above). Article 103 refers, indeed, to 'conflict between the obligations of the *members* of the United Nations under the present Charter and *their* obligations under any other international

---

[32] Ibid. Note that the United Kingdom never argued that a UN Charter obligation versus an explicit (investment) right does *not* constitute conflict on the ground, for example, that the right could simply not be exercised so as to comply with the obligation. The United Kingdom implicitly recognised that there was conflict, explaining why Art. 103 should also apply to this type of conflict, even though strictly speaking it could be said not to apply on the ground that Art. 103 does not refer to 'rights'. Libya's argument implied, *a fortiori*, that an explicit right may constitute a conflict with an obligation and that it should not always be the obligation that prevails: in Libya's opinion, its explicit right in the Montreal Convention should even prevail over UN Charter obligations. The United States also recognised the existence of conflict between a Montreal Convention right and a UN Security Council obligation. As Prof. Schachter noted: 'it is more precisely and correctly a collision between rights that the State may have under treaties and the obligations imposed by the mandatory measures of the Council' (public sitting held on 15 October 1997, at 10 a.m., para. 4.4, referring to a statement by Judge Shahabuddeen).

agreement' (emphasis added). Thus, as the UK argued, the priority given to the UN Charter should apply in respect of both obligations and *explicit rights*. Moreover, the priority from which UN Charter provisions benefit should, in turn, cover UN Charter obligations as well as UN Charter *explicit rights*, at least in so far as these explicit rights correspond to obligations on behalf of other UN members.

The treaty states that it is subject to subsequent treaties
For a treaty to provide that it must give way to subsequent treaties as between its parties amounts to confirming the obvious. By mutual consent, states can change their mind and, as between parties to two treaties, the latest one prevails (Art. 30(3) of the Vienna Convention). Still, it may be useful for a treaty to clarify that it may be supplemented by other more specific treaties, in particular if these other treaties are *inter se* agreements. Arts. 41 and 30(4)(b) of the Vienna Convention permit that such *inter se* agreements change the legal relationship between the parties, as long as certain conditions are met and this even without any specific reference in the treaty to *inter se* agreements. But it does no harm to confirm or specify this possibility to conclude *inter se* agreements in the treaty itself, and/or the conditions that such *inter se* agreements must meet in order for them to be permissible. A good example is Art. 311(3) of UNCLOS (which is largely taken from Art. 41 of the Vienna Convention itself):

Two or more States Parties may conclude agreements modifying or suspending the operation of provisions of this Convention, applicable solely to the relations between them, provided that such agreements do not relate to a provision derogation from which is incompatible with the effective execution of the object and purpose of this Convention, and provided further that such agreements shall not affect the application of the basic principles embodied herein, and that the provisions of such agreements do not affect the enjoyment by other States Parties of their rights or the performance of their obligations under this Convention.

Another example of a conflict clause giving priority to future treaties is Art. 73(2) of the 1963 Vienna Convention on Consular Relations which explicitly recognises the right to *supplement* its provisions by bilateral agreements.[33] One could refer also to Art. 60 of the European

---

[33] This is the example referred to in the ILC Commentary to Art. 30(2) (Rauschning, *Travaux*, 232).

Convention on Human Rights which makes it explicit that it must not be 'construed as limiting or derogating from any of the human rights and fundamental freedoms which may be ensured...under any other agreement to which it [a High Contracting Party] is a Party', including future agreements. Much like Art. 60, Art. 19(8) of the Statute of the ILO and Art. 20 of the Berne Convention for the Protection of Literary and Artistic Works allow for future treaties to prevail but only in case they are more favourable to the rightholders (respectively, workers and copyright owners). Finally, Art. 52 of the UN Charter also explicitly allows for the conclusion of future regional arrangements.[34]

Although such conflict clauses confirm general rules (in particular, the *lex posterior* principle, but also the principle of *lex specialis*), Art. 30(2) nonetheless explicitly confirms their validity: 'When a treaty specifies that it is subject to, or that it is not to be considered as incompatible with, a...*later* treaty, the provisions of that other treaty prevail' (emphasis added).'

Conflict clauses in the WTO treaty on the relationship between WTO law and other norms of international law

Having set out the two types of conflict clauses that a treaty may contain to regulate its relationship with other norms of international law, we next examine how the WTO treaty has dealt with its relationship to other treaties.

The WTO treaty itself contains very little in terms of how it relates to other rules of international law. This is surprising, given the vast potential for interplay between WTO norms and other norms (discussed in chapter 1 above). It is probably explained because of (i) a lack of preoccupation with (and, for many, expertise in) public international law on behalf of the negotiators of the WTO treaty (recall that trade negotiators are often employed by a ministry of trade or the economy, delinked from that of foreign affairs); and (ii) political deadlock for those rules of international law WTO negotiators did have in mind (in particular, MEAs). Unlike, for example, UNCLOS, the WTO treaty does *not* include a general conflict clause setting out its relationship with pre-existing

---

[34] Art. 52 provides: 'Nothing in the present Charter precludes the existence of regional arrangements or agencies for dealing with such matters relating to the maintenance of international peace and security as are appropriate for regional action, provided that such arrangements or agencies and their activities are consistent with the Purposes and Principles of the United Nations.'

international law. The WTO treaty does not explicitly provide that it is to prevail over pre-existing law, nor does it state that it is without derogation from pre-existing law.[35] The WTO treaty does not include a general conflict clause in respect of future treaties either. One author has argued that DSU Arts. 3.2 and 19.2 – stating that 'the panel and Appellate Body' and '[r]ecommendations and rulings of the DSB cannot add to or diminish the rights and obligations provided in the [WTO] covered agreements' – constitute a general conflict clause in favour of WTO rules in all situations of conflict between WTO norms and other norms.[36] We refute this contention below in this section and have already pointed out the very limited effect such clause would have as against future conflicting treaties (see above, pp. 335–6).

WTO members could, of course, always clarify or change the relationship between WTO rules and other rules of international law. This could be done, for example, by providing authoritative interpretations of WTO rules, by granting certain waivers or by amending WTO rules (respectively, under Arts. IX:2, IX:3 or X of the Marrakesh Agreement). WTO organs, such as the Ministerial Council or General Council, on the advice of, for example, the Committee on Trade and Development, could also adopt certain guidelines. Several WTO rules explicitly allow for WTO organs to define more clearly the relationship between the WTO and other international organisations.

Art. V.1 of the Marrakesh Agreement on 'Relations with Other Organizations' provides: 'The General Council shall make appropriate arrangements for effective cooperation with other intergovernmental organizations that have responsibilities related to those of the WTO.' GATS Art. XXVI on 'Relationship with Other International Organizations' provides, in turn: 'The General Council shall make appropriate arrangements for consultations and cooperation with the United Nations and its specialized agencies as well as with other intergovernmental organizations concerned with services.'[37]

---

[35] Note, in contrast, the very elaborate Art. 311 of UNCLOS on 'Relation to Other Conventions and International Agreements'. See, in this respect, Emmanuel Roucounas, 'Engagements Parallèles et Contradictoires' (1987-VI) 206 *Recueil des Cours* 9.

[36] Bartels, 'Applicable Law'.

[37] From the other side of the spectrum, recall the powers of the UN Economic and Social Council to 'co-ordinate the activities of the specialised agencies through consultation with and recommendations to such agencies and through recommendations to the General Assembly and to the Members of the United Nations' (Art. 63(2) of the UN Charter: see chapter 5 above). Note, however, that the WTO is not part of the UN family.

Recall also the Declaration on the Contribution of the WTO to Achieving Greater Coherence in Global Economic Policymaking, part of the 1994 Final Act, discussed earlier in chapter 5.

Hence, further conflict rules may derive from WTO members as states (taking the form of treaty language) or from WTO organs acting as international organisations. In the former case, the conflict rule is likely to become a full part of WTO covered agreements. In the latter case, it would not, although it would clearly be part of WTO law in the wider sense used here, as well as part of the applicable law before a WTO panel.

As the WTO treaty stands today, there are, however, relatively limited exceptions where the WTO treaty does provide some rules on how to resolve conflict between the WTO treaty and certain other norms of international law. We examine them in turn.

GATT 1947 and related instruments

With reference to paragraph 1 of GATT 1994 – which sums up the legal instruments that are to be part of GATT 1994 – it can be presumed that all pre-1994 GATT related instruments that were *not* incorporated into the WTO treaty (in particular, into GATT 1994) have been terminated or at least have been superseded by the WTO treaty.

In *EC – Poultry*, the Appellate Body found that the so-called Oilseeds agreement concluded bilaterally between the EC and Brazil in the framework of GATT Art. XXVIII renegotiations (as part of the resolution of a previous 1990 oilseeds dispute) was *not* a 'covered agreement' subject to the DSU, nor part of the multilateral obligations accepted by Brazil and the EC pursuant to the WTO agreement. As a result, the Appellate Body concluded that 'it is Schedule LXXX [the relevant 1995 EC schedule of concessions attached to the WTO agreement into which only parts of the Oilseeds agreement had been incorporated], rather than the Oilseeds Agreement, which forms the legal basis for this dispute'.[38] The Appellate Body added that, in its view, 'it is not necessary to have recourse to either Article 59.1 [termination of a treaty by conclusion of a later treaty] or Article 30.3 [application of successive treaties] of the *Vienna Convention*, because the text of the *WTO Agreement* and the legal arrangements governing the transition from the GATT 1947 to the WTO resolve the issue of the relationship between Schedule LXXX and the Oilseeds Agreement in this case'.[39]

---

[38] Appellate Body report on *EC – Poultry*, para. 81.   [39] *Ibid.*

The WIPO conventions incorporated into the TRIPS agreement

Article 2.2 of the TRIPS agreement provides that '[n]othing in Parts I to IV of this Agreement shall derogate from existing obligations that Members may have to each other under the Paris Convention, the Berne Convention, the Rome Convention and the Treaty on Intellectual Property in Respect of Integrated Circuits'.

The arbitrators in *EC – Bananas*, assessing the request by Ecuador to suspend obligations vis-à-vis the EC under the TRIPS agreement, noted the following in respect of Art. 2.2:

> This provision can be understood to refer to the obligations that the contracting parties of the Paris, Berne and Rome Conventions and the IPIC Treaty, who are also WTO Members, have between themselves under these four treaties. This would mean that, by virtue of the conclusion of the WTO Agreement, e.g. Berne Union members cannot derogate from existing obligations between each other under the Berne Convention. For example, the fact that Article 9.1 of the TRIPS Agreement incorporates into that Agreement Articles 1–21 of the Berne Convention with the exception of Article 6*bis* does not mean that Berne Union members would henceforth be exonerated from this obligation to guarantee moral rights under the Berne Convention.[40]

It must be stressed, however, that the priority rule in Art. 2.2 only extends to *Parts I to IV* of the TRIPS agreement. Any rights or obligations that WTO members may obtain under *Parts V to VII* do not necessarily have to give way to WIPO conventions, at least not pursuant to Art. 2.2.[41] Importantly, Part V sets out the dispute settlement provisions that apply to the TRIPS agreement. Hence, any obligations or suspensions of rights that are imposed on a WTO member as a result of WTO dispute settlement, including as a result of DSB authorisations to suspend TRIPS obligations because of non-compliance with dispute settlement recommendations, may prevail over WIPO conventions. Indeed, as between state parties to the relevant WIPO convention that are also WTO members, the DSB authorisation, constituting an act of a WTO organ, should then normally prevail over the earlier WIPO convention as the *lex posterior*.[42] The conflict clause in Art. 2.2 of the TRIPS agreement – which covers only Parts I to IV of the TRIPS agreement – does not prevent this from happening. Recall that there is no inherent hierarchy between the

---

[40] Report of the arbitrators under DSU Art. 22.6 (Ecuador's request for suspension), para. 149. See also Art. 20 of the Berne Convention, referred to above, p. 343.
[41] Report of the arbitrators, para. 150.
[42] See the discussion in chapter 6 above, p. 326; chapter 3 above, pp. 146–7; and below, pp. 384–5.

sources of international law, *in casu*, between a treaty norm and an act of an international organisation. As a result, the latest expression of state intent, *in casu*, the DSB authorisation, must prevail. For treaty norms this is confirmed in Art. 30. For acts of international organisations, it must be seen as part of customary international law.

That Art. 2.2 does not prevent the suspension of TRIPS obligations, even if such suspension constitutes a suspension of WIPO obligations also, was confirmed by the same arbitrators in *EC – Bananas*:

> nothing in Article 64 or other Articles of the TRIPS Agreement provides specifically that Article 22 of the DSU does not apply to the TRIPS Agreement... Provided that Ecuador's request for the suspension of certain TRIPS obligations is consistent with all the requirements of Article 22 of the DSU, including paragraphs 3 and 4 thereof, neither Article 2.2 read in context with Article 64 of the TRIPS Agreement, nor any other provision of the WTO agreements indicate that an authorization by the DSB of that request would in theory be prohibited under WTO law.[43]

IMF rules

In respect of the relationship between the WTO treaty and IMF rules, the Declaration on the Relationship of the WTO with the IMF[44] states, in essence, that GATT 1994 and other Annex 1A agreements prevail over IMF rules unless otherwise provided for in these agreements:

> [u]nless otherwise provided for in the Final Act, the relationship of the WTO with the International Monetary Fund, with regard to the areas covered by the Multilateral Trade Agreements in Annex 1A of the WTO Agreement, will be based on the provisions that have governed the relationship of the CONTRACTING PARTIES to the GATT 1947 with the International Monetary Fund.

In *Argentina – Footwear*, the Appellate Body examined whether a 3 per cent statistical tax found by the panel to be in violation of GATT Art. VIII could be excused by means of an allegedly conflicting obligation imposed on Argentina in a Memorandum of Understanding between Argentina and the IMF. In this IMF Memorandum it was set out that the fiscal

---

[43] Report of the arbitrators under DSU Art. 22.6 (Ecuador's request for suspension), paras. 150–1. The arbitrators claimed not to have jurisdiction 'to pass judgment on whether Ecuador, by suspending, once authorized by the DSB, certain TRIPS obligations, would act inconsistently with its international obligations arising from treaties other than the agreements covered by the WTO (e.g. the Paris, Berne and Rome Conventions which Ecuador has ratified)' (*ibid.*, para. 152). See chapter 8 below, pp. 445–7.

[44] WTO Secretariat, *The Result of the Uruguay Round of Multilateral Trade Negotiations, The Legal Texts* (Geneva, 1995), 447.

measures to be adopted by Argentina included 'increases in import duties, including a temporary 3 per cent surcharge on imports'. Referring to the Declaration on the Relationship of the WTO with the IMF, the Appellate Body found, however, that since no IMF-related exceptions under GATT Art. VIII were to be found in GATT itself, independent IMF rules, such as the IMF Memorandum, could not justify Argentina's violation of GATT Art. VIII.[45]

In this respect, mention could also be made of the 1996 Agreement between the IMF and the WTO as well as the Declaration on the Contribution of the WTO to Achieving Greater Coherence in Global Economic Policymaking. Both were discussed earlier, in chapter 5. However, none of these instruments set out explicit conflict clauses.

OECD arrangements on export credits
Although not strictly speaking a conflict clause, reference could be made here also to the Subsidies agreement which provides that an export credit practice shall not be considered an export subsidy prohibited by the Subsidies agreement if it is in conformity with the interest rate provisions of 'an international undertaking on official export credits to which at least twelve original Members to this Agreement are parties as of 1 January 1979 (or a successor undertaking which has been adopted by those original Members)'.[46] Though not explicitly referred to, the 'undertaking' in mind is the OECD Arrangement on Guidelines for Officially Supported Export Credits (the 'OECD Arrangement'). This provision, in effect a 'safe-harbour' clause, explicitly permits certain export credit practices under conditions which conform to the OECD Arrangement. It thereby gives preference to certain rights under the OECD Arrangement, over and above certain obligations in the WTO Subsidies agreement. As noted earlier, the panel on *Brazil – Aircraft (Article 21.5 – Canada II)* found that the relevant OECD Arrangement is not limited to the one that existed when the WTO treaty was concluded, but is 'the most recent successor undertaking which has been adopted prior to the time that the second paragraph [providing for the 'safe harbour'] is considered'.[47] In that particular case, the most recent successor undertaking was the 1998 OECD Arrangement. Nonetheless, as the panel in *Canada – Aircraft (Article 21.5)* remarked:

---

[45] Appellate Body report on *Argentina – Footwear*, paras. 69–74.
[46] Second paragraph of item (k) in Annex I to the Subsidies agreement.
[47] Panel report on *Brazil – Aircraft (Article 21.5 – Canada II)*, para. 5.83.

the second paragraph of item (k) is quite unique in the sense that it creates an exemption from a prohibition in a WTO Agreement, the scope of which exemption is left in the hands of a certain *subgroup* of WTO Members – the Participants, all of which as of today are OECD Members – to define, and to change as and when they see fit.[48]

International standards referred to in the SPS and TBT agreements
Both the SPS and TBT agreements make reference to 'standards' adopted in other international organisations. In essence, they provide a general obligation for WTO members to base their own national measures on these international standards, unless they can provide a valid justification to deviate from those standards.[49] In addition – and this is where a certain hierarchy has been built in – if WTO members impose national measures that conform to those international standards, their national measures shall be presumed to be consistent also with the obligations set out in the SPS or TBT agreements.[50] The international standards referred to in the SPS agreement are, to date, limited to those established by the Codex Alimentarius Commission (for food safety), the International Office of Epizootics (for animal health and zoonoses) and the Secretariat of the International Plant Protection Convention (for plant health).[51] The international standards referred to in the TBT agreement are not as clearly defined. It suffices that they were established by an 'international body or system', defined, in turn, to mean a 'body or system whose membership is open to the relevant bodies of at least all Members'.[52]

Although most of these international standards are not legally binding within the organisation where they were created, they have gained prominence through this 'soft' incorporation into the WTO treaty. Although this 'soft' incorporation does not give absolute preference to

---

[48] Panel report on *Canada – Aircraft (Article 21.5)*, para. 5.132.
[49] SPS Art. 3 and TBT Art. 2.4. For case law on these provisions see, respectively, the Appellate Body report on *EC – Hormones* and the panel report on *EC – Sardines*.
[50] SPS Art. 3.2 (which includes, in addition, a presumption of consistency with GATT) and TBT Art. 2.5 (where the presumption is somewhat weaker since TBT Art. 2.2 must anyhow be complied with, even if one's measure is 'in accordance with' relevant international standards).
[51] Annex A, paragraph 3, to the SPS agreement, which adds that 'for matters not covered by the above organizations; appropriate standards, guidelines and recommendations promulgated by other relevant organizations open for membership to all Members, *as identified by the [SPS] Committee*' (emphasis added). So far, however, the SPS Committee has not identified any organisation other than the three explicitly mentioned in Annex A.
[52] Annex 1, paragraph 4, to the TBT agreement.

international standards over and above WTO rules, it does provide for a degree of deference to non-WTO rules through the presumption of consistency with certain WTO rules in case international standards are complied with.

Multilateral environmental agreements
As far as the relationship between the WTO treaty and MEAs is concerned, reference can be made to the Declaration on Trade and Environment, part of the 1994 Final Act.[53] However, rather than setting out a conflict clause itself, the merit of this declaration is that it establishes the WTO Committee on Trade and Environment (CTE). One of the major tasks of this Committee is to examine the relationship between the WTO treaty and MEAs. This mandate has, so far, not resulted in any explicit conflict rules. Importantly, the CTE did, however, endorse 'multilateral solutions based on international cooperation and consensus as the best and most effective way for governments to tackle environmental problems of a transboundary or global nature' and expressed a preference for trade disputes that arise in connection with a multilateral environmental agreement to be resolved through the mechanisms established by such agreement.[54]

Additional guidance for the resolution of conflict between the WTO treaty and MEAs – though, once again, not in the form of an 'explicit conflict clause' – can be found in the preamble to GATT 1994. This preamble provides guidance, both for interpretative purposes and in terms of what WTO members had in mind when concluding the WTO treaty. It explicitly calls for 'the optimal use of the world's resources in accordance with the objective of sustainable development, seeking both to protect and preserve the environment and to enhance the means for doing so in a manner consistent with their respective needs and concerns at different levels of economic development'. One could refer also to the *travaux préparatoires* of certain MEAs, where GATT officials had expressed the opinion that the draft MEAs were in conformity with GATT rules.[55] As a result, it seems, the drafters of the MEAs did not include a

---

[53] WTO Secretariat, *Legal Texts*, 469.
[54] WTO doc. WT/CTE/1, para. 171 (1996). For an interesting, though inconclusive, evaluation of the relationship between the WTO treaty and earlier MEAs, see Robert Housman and Don Goldberg, 'Legal Principles in Resolving Conflicts Between Multilateral Agreements and the GATT/WTO', in Robert Housman et al. (eds.), *The Use of Trade Measures in Select Multilateral Environmental Agreements* (Nairobi: UNEP, 1995), 297.
[55] For references, see Housman and Goldberg, 'Legal Principles', 303.

conflict clause. But this could be interpreted both ways: (i) the drafters wanted to make sure that the GATT was left unaffected, GATT officials confirmed that this was so: as a result, there was no need to include a savings clause for the GATT; or, in contrast, (ii) the drafters wanted to make sure that the new MEA would be effective and not be nullified by the earlier GATT: they heard a GATT opinion that this was so; as a result, they did not have to confirm that the later MEA prevails over the earlier GATT in the event of conflict. However, given the presumption that the later treaty in time prevails, it would seem that, in the absence of a conflict clause, the intention was to let Art. 30 and the *lex posterior* principle (to the extent it can be applied)[56] play their role. Hence, the most logical conclusion to be derived from the absence of a conflict clause in these MEAs is that, in case there is a conflict, these MEAs must prevail over earlier treaties (but see the concept of 'continuing' treaties below).[57]

UN Charter obligations for the maintenance of international peace and security
GATT Art. XXI(c) (entitled 'Security Exceptions') sets out an explicit conflict clause giving preference to certain obligations of WTO members under the UN Charter, over and above the WTO treaty. It provides as follows: 'Nothing in this Agreement shall be construed...to prevent any contracting party from taking any action in pursuance of its obligations under the United Nations Charter for the maintenance of international peace and security.'

GATS Art. XIV*bis*(c) sets out the exact same conflict clause in respect of GATS. These GATT/GATS clauses are a partial reflection of Art. 103 of the UN Charter. They are limited, indeed, to UN Charter obligations 'for the maintenance of international peace and security'. In practice, they make clear that whenever UN members are under an obligation to impose economic sanctions on another state (pursuant to a UN Security Council resolution), their WTO trade obligations vis-à-vis that state should not prevent them from doing so.

GATT Art. XXI(c) and GATS Art. XIV*bis*(c), as important as they are in terms of linking WTO law to UN law, only confirm a pre-existing conflict rule that already applied to WTO members that are also UN members. Indeed, even without these WTO clauses, WTO members should have given preference to their UN Charter obligations over and above those in the WTO treaty and this on the basis of Art. 103 of the UN Charter.

[56] See below, pp. 378–80.   [57] *Ibid.*

GATT Art. XXI(c) and GATS Art. XIV*bis*(c) merely confirm part of this rule. In this respect as well, it is crucial that before a WTO panel all relevant international law, including UN Charter law, must apply (even if the jurisdiction of WTO panels is limited to claims under WTO covered agreements: see chapter 8 below).

Consultation and dispute settlement provisions in the area of health
Article 11.3 of the SPS agreement provides that '[n]othing in this Agreement shall impair the rights of Members under other international agreements, including the right to resort to the good offices or dispute settlement mechanisms of other international organizations or established under any international agreement'.

One author submitted that this SPS provision should extend to other rules of international law *not related to consultations and dispute settlement*.[58] However, although the word 'including' is used, it seems to refer to a non-exhaustive list of *consultation and dispute settlement* provisions in other international agreements ('including the right to resort to the good offices or dispute settlement mechanisms'), not to any other type of provisions. This is confirmed by the context of Art. 11.2. Article 11 is entitled 'Consultations and Dispute Settlement'. It would hence be surprising to find that WTO members had subjected the SPS agreement to all other international agreements in this article dealing only with consultations and dispute settlement.

DSU Arts. 3.2 and 19.2 do not constitute a conflict clause
It has been submitted that DSU Art. 3.2, as confirmed in DSU Art. 19.2, is another, more general, conflict clause addressing the relationship between WTO law and other norms of international law.[59] The last sentence of Art. 3.2 provides: 'Recommendations and rulings of the DSB cannot add to or diminish the rights and obligations provided in the covered agreements.' Article 19.2 states: 'In accordance with paragraph 2 of Article 3, in their findings and recommendations, the panel and Appellate Body cannot add to or diminish the rights and obligations provided in the covered agreements.'

Should these provisions be read to mean that WTO panels and the Appellate Body as well as the DSB cannot ever add to, or diminish,

---

[58] Marc Iynedjian, 'L'Accord de l'Organisation Mondiale du Commerce sur l'Application des Mesures Sanitaires et Phytosanitaires, Une Analyse Juridique', doctoral thesis (University of Lausanne, 2000), 351–2.
[59] See Bartels, 'Applicable Law'.

the rights and obligations explicitly set out in WTO covered agreements? In other words, should these provisions be interpreted to mean that no other law, be it pre- or post-1994, can ever influence WTO covered agreements and that, in the event of conflict between WTO covered agreements and another rule of international law, the WTO rule must *always* prevail?

In my view, they cannot. DSU Arts. 3.2 and 19.2 do not address the *jurisdiction* of panels nor the *applicable law* that a panel can apply to a particular dispute. Nor do they proclaim that WTO covered agreements must necessarily and always prevail over all past and future law. These provisions deal rather with the inherent limits of a WTO panel as a judicial organ in *interpreting* WTO covered agreements.[60] In the exercise of this judicial function of interpretation, WTO panels may clarify and interpret what WTO covered agreements mean, but they may not 'add to or diminish the rights and obligations provided in the covered agreements'. The immediate context of this passage in Art. 3.2 confirms this reading. The sentence follows directly the instruction for panels to clarify WTO covered agreements 'in accordance with customary rules of interpretation of public international law'. This is a clear indication that also the last sentence of Art. 3.2 – the one scrutinised here – deals with the interpretative function of panels, not with the applicable law before a panel, nor with conflict of norms.

To put it differently, as judicial organs WTO panels may not create new rights and obligations, they must apply those that WTO members agreed to. This limitation on the interpretative function of WTO panels was made *ex abundante cautela*. Even without it, it would have applied to WTO panels as an inherent limitation of the judicial function prescribed in general international law. As the ICJ noted in the *Interpretation of Peace Treaties* Advisory Opinion: 'to adopt an interpretation which ran counter to the clear meaning of the terms would not be to interpret but to revise the treaty'.[61]

As for DSU Arts. 3.2 and 19.2 being a conflict clause automatically deciding all conflicts of norms in favour of WTO rules, there is a major difference between stating what the *judiciary* can do with the law and stating what the *legislature* (i.e., WTO *members*) have done, or can do with the law. DSU Arts. 3.2 and 19.2 direct that the WTO *judiciary*, like any

---

[60] On the crucial distinction between jurisdiction, applicable law and interpretation, see chapter 8 below, pp. 476–8.
[61] ICJ Reports 1950, 229. On the inherent limits of treaty interpretation see chapter 5 above, pp. 244–7.

other judiciary, cannot 'change' the WTO treaty at the time they are asked to apply that treaty. A conflict clause, in contrast, would

  (i) tell us that WTO *members*, when negotiating the treaty, did not want *any other* existing rules of international law to prevail over the WTO treaty, as well as
 (ii) direct WTO *members* that in their future dealings they *cannot* change or overrule the rights and obligations set out in the WTO treaty (except pursuant to the amendment and other provisions in the WTO treaty itself).

To interpret DSU Arts. 3.2 and 19.2 in this way would be erroneous. To make an analogy with the ICJ, the fact that the ICJ Statute prescribed in 1945 that the Court must 'decide in accordance with international law' – a phrase interpreted in the *South West Africa* cases to mean that the ICJ's 'duty is to apply the law as it finds it, not to make it'[62] – can hardly be interpreted to mean that the law the ICJ may look at is limited to that of 1945 nor can it mean that international law as it existed in 1945 must always and necessarily prevail over all subsequent rules of international law.

The drafters of the WTO treaty *could have* inserted a conflict clause stating that the WTO treaty is to prevail over *all past and future* international law, similar to the one in Art. 103 of the UN Charter.[63] Although such would have been with limited effect only,[64] the contractual freedom of WTO members would have allowed them to do so (within the limits of *jus cogens* and the principle of *pacta tertiis*). But in the event that the drafters of the WTO treaty had really wanted the WTO treaty to play this role of a second UN Charter, prevailing over all other law – something that is not only in legal terms questionable, but also in political terms highly unlikely – would they not have explicitly said so? Would they, for example, not have put a non-derogation clause in the Marrakesh Agreement itself, instead of twice inserting a sentence at the end of a provision on the function of WTO panels in the, after all, technical DSU?

Finally, even if DSU Arts. 3.2 and 19.2 were to amount to a conflict clause claiming priority for the WTO treaty over all other norms of international law (*quod non*), when it comes to *future* treaties in conflict with the WTO treaty, this conflict clause would have little effect. As

---

[62] ICJ Reports 1966, 48.
[63] See also, but in a much more limited way, Article 311(6) of UNCLOS.
[64] See above, pp. 335–6.

noted earlier,⁶⁵ the contractual freedom of WTO members allows them to deviate from the WTO treaty, *including the alleged conflict clause*. All WTO members could conclude a new treaty and, even without explicitly amending DSU Arts. 3.2 and 19.2, such new treaty would then, as the later in time, prevail over the old WTO treaty, notwithstanding the conflict clause. This would occur pursuant to Art. 30(3) of the Vienna Convention, unless the later treaty is explicitly made subject to the earlier WTO treaty (so that Art. 30(2) applies). As pointed out before, Art. 30 gives effect to only one conflict clause claiming priority over future treaties and this is Art. 103 of the UN Charter. For all other conflict clauses of the same type, the *lex posterior* principle is *not* deactivated. Also a *limited number* of WTO members could then conclude an *inter se* agreement that meets the conditions of Arts. 41/58 of the Vienna Convention. If they do so and thereby derogate from certain WTO rules, as between themselves, the later *inter se* agreement prevails pursuant to Art. 30(3)(a) and this notwithstanding the alleged conflict clause in DSU Arts. 3.2 and 19.2 (in that event Art. 30(2) does not apply, nor does the exception provided for in Art. 30(1) in respect of Art. 103 of the UN Charter).

In sum, even if DSU Arts. 3.2 and 19.2 were to constitute a conflict clause calling for automatic preference to be given to WTO rules over other rules (*quod non*), this conflict clause would have no effect in respect of post-1994 treaty norms as between the WTO members party to these norms. As conflict clauses related to future norms, DSU Arts. 3.2 and 19.2 would then be subject to any subsequent change of mind, both as between all WTO members and as between some WTO members only in *inter se* agreements. To that extent, DSU Arts. 3.2 and 19.2 would be an example of 'futile' conflict clauses referred to by Karl.⁶⁶

Conflict clauses resolving conflict within a treaty: the example of the WTO treaty

As noted in the introduction to this section on 'Explicit conflict clauses', apart from conflicts clauses that regulate the relationship of a treaty to other pre-existing or future treaties, a conflict clause may also address potential conflicts as between norms *within* the treaty in which it is set out. We next examine the example of conflicts of norms within the WTO treaty and how these may have been regulated by explicit conflict clauses.

---

⁶⁵ *Ibid.*   ⁶⁶ Karl, 'Conflicts', 471.

The WTO treaty includes a series of conflict clauses that address internal WTO conflicts, that is, conflicts between two norms both of which are part of WTO covered agreements.[67] Obviously, in the event that no explicit conflict clause can be found to resolve an internal WTO conflict, in the WTO treaty itself, the conflict rules which are part of general international law, discussed in this work, must be reverted to.

The Marrakesh Agreement prevails over all other multilateral trade agreements
In the event of conflict between a rule in the Marrakesh Agreement and another rule in any of the multilateral trade agreements (such as the GATT, GATS, TRIPS or DSU), the rule of the Marrakesh Agreement must prevail. Article XVI.3 of the Marrakesh Agreement provides: 'In the event of a conflict between a provision of this Agreement and a provision of any of the Multilateral Trade Agreements, the provision of this Agreement shall prevail to the extent of the conflict.'

GATT 1994 is subject to all other Annex 1A agreements on trade in goods
In the event of conflict between a provision of GATT 1994 and a provision of another agreement on trade in goods part of Annex 1A to the Marrakesh Agreement, the provision of the other Annex 1A agreement prevails. The General Interpretative Note to Annex 1A provides: 'In the event of conflict between a provision of the [GATT 1994] and a provision of another agreement in Annex 1A [to the Marrakesh Agreement]... the provision of the other agreement shall prevail to the extent of the conflict.'[68]

Schedules of concessions must give way to WTO treaty provisions as such
Article II:7 of GATT provides that '[t]he Schedules annexed to this Agreement are hereby made an integral part of Part I of this Agreement'. Member-specific commitments under the Agreement on Agriculture are also an integral part of the GATT. Article 3.1 of the Agreement on Agriculture provides: 'The domestic support and export subsidy commitments in Part IV of each Member's Schedule constitute commitments limiting subsidization and are hereby made an integral part of GATT

[67] On intra-WTO conflict more generally, see Elisabetta Montaguti and Maurits Lugard, 'The GATT 1994 and Other Annex 1A Agreements: Four Different Relationships?' (2000) 3 JIEL 473.
[68] For the case law on this provision, see chapter 4 above, pp. 188–94, and Joost Pauwelyn, 'Cross-agreement Complaints before the Appellate Body: A Case Study of the *EC – Asbestos* Dispute' (2002) / 1 *World Trade Review* 63. See also the discussion below, pp. 397–9.

1994.' Finally, specific commitments under the GATS set out in the GATS schedule of WTO members are an integral part also of the GATS pursuant to GATS Art. XX.3. On that basis, the Appellate Body found in *EC – Computer Equipment* that 'the concessions provided in that Schedule are part of the terms of the treaty. As such, the only rules which may be applied in interpreting the meaning of a concession are the general rules of treaty interpretation set out in the *Vienna Convention*.'[69]

However, even though the norms set out in WTO members' schedules are treaty language and an integral part of the WTO treaty, they do have an inherently lower legal standing than the provisions in the WTO treaty *stricto sensu*, i.e., those binding equally on all WTO members. In respect of concessions contained in the schedules annexed to GATT 1947, the panel on *US – Sugar Headnote* found that 'Article II permits contracting parties to incorporate into their Schedules acts yielding rights under the General Agreement but not acts diminishing obligations under that Agreement.'[70]

This approach was confirmed in respect of market access concessions and commitments for agricultural products contained in the schedules annexed to GATT 1994 by the Appellate Body in *EC – Bananas*:[71] 'The ordinary meaning of the term "concessions" suggests that a Member may yield rights and grant benefits, but it cannot diminish its obligations.'[72]

As the Appellate Body pointed out, this interpretation is supported by paragraph 3 of the Marrakesh Protocol (itself an integral part of GATT 1994 pursuant to paragraph 1(d) of GATT 1994), which provides: 'The implementation of the concessions and commitments contained in the schedules annexed to this Protocol shall, upon request, be subject to multilateral examination by the Members. This would be *without prejudice to the rights and obligations of members under Agreements in Annex 1A of the WTO Agreement*.'[73]

---

[69] Appellate Body report on *EC – Computer Equipment*, para. 84.
[70] GATT panel report on *United States – Restrictions on Importation of Sugar*, adopted on 22 June 1989, BISD 36S/331, at para. 5.2.
[71] In that case, the EC had argued that even if its tariff quota share allocation as a result of the Framework Agreement on Bananas (concluded by the EC with Colombia, Costa Rica, Venezuela and Nicaragua) were inconsistent with GATT Art. XIII, the fact that this quota allocation is included in the EC's schedule on agricultural products, an integral part of the WTO treaty, constitutes a valid defence against breach of GATT Art. XIII. In the EC's view, the schedule should then, as the more specific commitment, prevail over GATT Art. XIII (Appellate Body report on *EC – Bananas*, paras. 19–21).
[72] *Ibid.*, para. 154.
[73] *Ibid.*, emphasis added. The Marrakesh Protocol to the GATT 1994 is reprinted in WTO Secretariat, *Legal Texts*, 37.

The Appellate Body found that nothing in the Agreement on Agriculture allows market access concessions on agricultural products to deviate from GATT provisions, *in casu*, GATT Art. XIII.[74] It confirmed that a schedule must be consistent with the GATT itself in *EC – Poultry*, finding that 'the concessions contained in Schedule LXXX pertaining to the tariff-rate quota for frozen poultry must be consistent with Articles I and XIII of the GATT 1994'.[75]

In sum, in the event of conflict between a GATT schedule, on the one hand, and the provisions of GATT 1994, on the other, the provisions of GATT 1994 prevail. Pursuant to paragraph 3 of the Marrakesh Protocol, the same applies in respect of conflict between a GATT schedule, on the one hand, and any treaty provision in Annex 1A to the WTO treaty, that is, any treaty provision on trade in goods binding on all WTO members (such as the Agreement on Agriculture or the SPS agreement), on the other hand. This is supported by the ordinary meaning given to the words 'concessions' or 'commitments' in GATT Art. II and Arts. 3 and 4 of the Agreement on Agriculture.

The Marrakesh Protocol does not apply, however, in respect of conflicts between GATS schedules and provisions of the GATS as such. Here, the remaining reason for giving preference to the provisions in the GATS itself, over and above GATS schedules, is the ordinary meaning to be given to the terms 'concessions' and 'specific commitments' in Parts III and IV of GATS. Even though no conflict clause similar to that in the Marrakesh Protocol is provided for, it would seem inconsistent to let GATS schedules prevail over GATS, whereas GATT schedules must give way to GATT. Note, indeed, that in the *US – Sugar Headnote* case no conflict clause similar to paragraph 3 of the Marrakesh Protocol was available either, but this panel, on the basis of the ordinary meaning of the word 'concessions' in GATT Art. II, still came to the conclusion that GATT schedules must give way to provisions in GATT 1947 itself. On that basis, the priority of treaty provisions over schedules (including GATS schedules) could be said to be part of the 'customary practices followed by CONTRACTING PARTIES to the GATT 1947' by which the WTO

---

[74] Appellate Body report on *EC – Bananas*, paras. 155–8. The Appellate Body thereby overruled the EC argument (at paras. 19–21) that concessions on agricultural products are part of the Agreement on Agriculture and should hence, pursuant to Art. 21 of that Agreement (discussed above), prevail over GATT provisions. In support of the Appellate Body finding, it must be pointed out that Art. 3.1 incorporates agriculture schedules *into GATT 1994*, not into the Agreement on Agriculture as such (which pursuant to Art. 21 prevails over GATT 1994).

[75] Appellate Body report on *EC – Poultry*, para. 99.

must be guided (pursuant to Art. XVI.1 of the Marrakesh Agreement). It must be acknowledged, however, that, in the absence of this practice and the words 'concessions' or 'commitments' and, for GATT schedules, the Marrakesh Protocol, strong arguments would have been available to let WTO schedules *prevail* as *lex specialis* over other treaty provisions.[76] Schedules are an integral part of the WTO treaty, accepted as such *by all WTO members*, and address certain trade matters more specifically than other treaty provisions, both in terms of subject matter (e.g., tariff concessions for a particular product) and membership (that is, obligations applying to one WTO member only).[77]

The Agreement on Agriculture prevails over GATT 1994 and all other Annex 1A agreements
In the event of conflict between the Agreement on Agriculture, on the one hand, and GATT 1994 or any other Annex 1A agreement, on the other, the Agreement on Agriculture prevails. Art. 21 of the Agreement on Agriculture states: 'The provisions of GATT 1994 and of other Multilateral Trade Agreements in Annex 1A to the WTO Agreement shall apply subject to the provisions of this Agreement.'

Special or additional rules and procedures on dispute settlement prevail over the DSU
The special or additional rules and procedures on dispute settlement set out in Appendix 2 to the DSU prevail over the more general rules and procedures in the DSU itself, to the extent of the difference. Article 1.2 of the DSU states:

The rules and procedures of this Understanding shall apply subject to such special or additional rules and procedures on dispute settlement contained in the covered agreements as are identified in Appendix 2 to this Understanding. To the extent that there is a difference between the rules and procedures of this Understanding and the special or additional rules and procedures set forth in Appendix 2, the special or additional rules and procedures in Annex 2 shall prevail.

Article 1.2 also provides for a special procedure in case of 'disputes involving rules and procedures under more than one covered agreement,

---

[76] See the EC argument paraphrased above in note 71. On *lex specialis*, see below, pp. 385–418.
[77] In respect of post-1994 commitments in WTO schedules this *lex specialis* argument would find support also in the *lex posterior* principle.

if there is a conflict between special or additional rules and procedures of such agreements under review'; 'where the parties to the dispute cannot agree on rules and procedures within 20 days of the establishment of the panel, the Chairman of the [DSB]..., in consultation with the parties to the dispute, shall determine the rules and procedures to be followed within 10 days after a request by either Member'. In making such decision, 'the Chairman shall be guided by the principle that special or additional rules and procedures should be used where possible, and the rules and procedures set out in this Understanding should be used to the extent necessary to avoid conflict'.

Note that in the first part of Art. 1.2 there is talk of 'difference' (between DSU rules and special or additional rules), whereas in the second part reference is made to 'conflict' (between special or additional rules under different agreements). However, recalling the definition of conflict set out above, both notions ('difference' and 'conflict') should, in this context, be given the same meaning.

If the SPS agreement applies, the TBT agreement cannot apply
Although not strictly speaking a conflict clause but a rule defining the respective scope of application of two agreements, in case a measure falls under the SPS agreement, the TBT agreement does not apply. Article 1.5 of the TBT agreement provides: 'The provisions of this Agreement do not apply to sanitary and phytosanitary measures as defined in Annex A of the Agreement on the Application of Sanitary and Phytosanitary Measures.'

To put it differently, for those measures that, absent TBT Art. 1.5, would have fallen under both the SPS and the TBT agreements, the SPS agreement 'prevails' (pursuant to Art. 1.5 it is actually the only applicable agreement in the first place). Article 1.4 of the SPS agreement, *ex abundante cautela*, states that: 'Nothing in this Agreement shall affect the rights of Members under the Agreement on Technical Barriers to Trade with respect to measures not within the scope of this Agreement.' Obviously, an agreement (*in casu*, the SPS agreement) cannot affect measures not falling under its scope of application.

Note, however, the exclusive reference in SPS Art. 1.4 to 'rights' of WTO members under the TBT agreement, seemingly implying that the SPS agreement imposes more obligations than the TBT agreement does (the TBT agreement thus retaining more 'rights' to restrict trade). Nonetheless, it goes without saying that the SPS agreement cannot affect the *obligations* under the TBT agreement with respect to measures that do not even fall within the scope of the SPS agreement.

The DSU 'prevails over' panel and Appellate Body working procedures as well as the Rules of Conduct
Although not related to conflict clauses as such, it may be recalled here that the working procedures of both panels and the Appellate Body must be consistent with the DSU itself. WTO members may deviate from the DSU, including by means of *inter se* agreements that apply to one dispute only (as long as the conditions in Arts. 41/58 of the Vienna Convention, discussed in chapter 6 above, are met). Nonetheless, procedural decisions taken by WTO panels and the Appellate Body, being organs with a limited competence, are invalid if they are inconsistent with their constituent instrument, i.e., the DSU.[78]

The same applies in respect of the Rules of Conduct for the DSU.[79] These rules were adopted by the WTO's Dispute Settlement Body in 1996. Rule II explicitly provides: 'These Rules shall in no way modify the rights and obligations of Members under the DSU nor the rules and procedures therein.' In this sense, the DSU 'prevails' over the Rules of Conduct.

No conflict clauses for the relationship GATT–GATS–TRIPS
Surprisingly enough, however, the WTO treaty does not include conflict clauses to resolve contradictions between provisions in GATT, GATS or TRIPS. The GATT–GATS overlap is discussed below in the section on '*Lex specialis*'.

The conflict clauses referred to above to resolve internal WTO conflicts can be summarised in the table on the following page.

Lex posterior

Preliminaries

Article 30 of the Vienna Convention provides for the following conflict rules in respect of 'Application of successive treaties relating to the same subject-matter':

1. Subject to Article 103 of the Charter of the United Nations, the rights and obligations of States Parties to successive treaties relating to the same subject-matter shall be determined in accordance with the following paragraphs.

---

[78] See chapter 6 above, pp. 289–90.
[79] Rules of Conduct for the Understanding on Rules and Procedures Governing the Settlement of Disputes, WT/DSB/RC/1, adopted by the DSB on 11 December 1996.

Internal hierarchy as between WTO norms

Marrakesh Agreement			
Agreement on Agriculture			Special and additional rules and procedures on dispute settlement (App. 2 to DSU)
GATT 1994	GATS	TRIPS	DSU ...
Specific Annex 1A agreements on trade in goods			Rules of conduct/working procedures of panels and the Appellate Body
SPS agreement			
TBT agreement			
Member-specific schedules of concessions			

2. When a treaty specifies that it is subject to, or that it is not to be considered as incompatible with, an earlier treaty or later treaty, the provisions of that other treaty prevail.
3. When all the parties to the earlier treaty are parties also to the later treaty but the earlier treaty is not terminated or suspended in operation under article 59, *the earlier treaty applies only to the extent that its provisions are compatible with those of the later treaty.*
4. When the parties to the later treaty do not include all the parties to the earlier one:
   (a) as between States Parties to both treaties the same rule applies as in paragraph 3;
   (b) as between a State Party to both treaties and a State Party to only one of the treaties, *the treaty to which both States are parties governs* their mutual rights and obligations.
5. Paragraph 4 is without prejudice to article 41, or to any question of the termination or suspension of the operation of a treaty under article 60 or to any question of responsibility which may arise for a State from the conclusion or application of a treaty, the provisions of which are incompatible with its obligations towards another State under another treaty [emphasis added].

Articles 30(3) and 30(4)(a) are a confirmation in the law of treaties of the adage *lex posterior derogat legi priori*, that is, the contractual freedom of states according to which their latest expression of intent prevails.

This principle not only applies in respect of successive treaty norms (as Art. 30 does). As noted before in chapter 3 (pp. 96–7), it applies also in respect of other norms of international law, in particular custom and acts of international organisations. Nonetheless, whereas treaties and acts of international organisations may have a precise date on which they were concluded, it is virtually impossible to pinpoint the precise date on which a general principle of law or custom emerged.

Article 30(4)(b) confirms the *pacta tertiis* rule pursuant to which states can only be held by treaty norms they agreed to.

Resort may be had to Art. 30 only in case Art. 59 – on 'Termination or suspension of the operation of a treaty implied by conclusion of a later treaty' – has *not* led to the termination or suspension of the earlier treaty. Article 30(3) explicitly refers to Art. 59. More generally, as pointed out before, the conflict rules provided in Art. 30 are subject to those set out in earlier sections. To that extent, Art. 30 is of a residual nature only, subject to explicit conflict clauses in either treaty, *jus cogens*, termination or suspension pursuant to Arts. 59 or 60 as well as – crucially – illegality under Arts. 41/58. Article 30 makes explicit caveats for Arts. 41 and 60 as well as Art. 103 of the UN Charter.

The ILC Commentary on Art. 30 further clarified that the ILC wanted to 'avoid the risk of paragraph 4(c) [now Art. 30(4)(b)] being interpreted as sanctioning the conclusion of a treaty incompatible with obligations undertaken towards another State under another treaty'.[80] This reservation is important both for Arts. 41/58 illegality (vis-à-vis third parties not bound by an *inter se* agreement) and conflicts of the AB/AC type discussed below (A being a state with conflicting obligations vis-à-vis B and C).

Article 30(5) specifies further that Art. 30(4) is 'without prejudice... to any question of responsibility which may arise for a State from the conclusion or application of a treaty, the provisions of which are incompatible with its obligations towards another State under another treaty'. Note also that special rules applicable in the context of an international organisation may apply. These rules prevail over Art. 30(4)(b) pursuant to Art. 5 of the Vienna Convention.

As a last preliminary remark, it should be recalled that Art. 30 provides for *priority* rules as between specific *provisions* of successive treaties. It does not *invalidate* or *terminate* norms, nor does it give priority to (let alone does it invalidate or terminate) *entire treaties*. Consequently, if

---

[80] Rauschning, *Travaux*, 232; see also 235.

under Art. 30 the later treaty provision ceases to exist, the earlier provision with which it was in conflict will be reactivated. In contrast, if, under Art. 59, the later treaty is ended, the earlier treaty which was terminated by the later one does not revive.

We next examine the two conditions for Art. 30 to apply: (i) the treaties must be 'relating to the same subject-matter'; (ii) the treaties must be 'successive treaties'. Both conditions are set out in the title of Art. 30: 'Application of successive treaties relating to the same subject-matter'.

The treaties must be 'relating to the same subject-matter'

The conflict rules in Art. 30 apply only in the event that successive treaties relate to 'the same subject-matter'. This is made clear in the title of Art. 30 as well as in Art. 30(1).

If there is conflict, the two treaties necessarily relate to 'the same subject-matter'
At the Vienna Conference, Sir Ian Sinclair expressed doubts about the meaning of the phrase 'the same subject-matter': 'Did the United Nations Covenants on Human Rights relate to the same subject-matter as the European Convention on Human Rights or the ILO and UNESCO Conventions on certain specific aspects of human rights?'[81]

According to Sinclair, the phrase 'same subject-matter', 'should be construed strictly'.[82] The Expert Consultant agreed, saying 'that those words should not be held to cover cases where a general treaty impinged indirectly on the content of a particular provision of an earlier treaty; in such cases the question involved such principles as *generalia specialibus non derogat*'.[83]

As noted below, and further elaborated in the section on '*Lex specialis*', there should, indeed, be room to apply the *lex specialis* principle over and above the *lex posterior* rule in Art. 30. However, to base this priority rule on the requirement in Art. 30 that the two treaties must relate to 'the same subject-matter' is not convincing. To let *lex specialis* prevail over *lex posterior*, it is better to refer, for example, to the absence of 'successive treaties' (the second condition for Art. 30 to apply) with reference, in particular, to the notion of 'continuing treaties' developed below.

Indeed, if there is a genuine conflict between two treaty norms, the two treaty norms must necessarily deal with the same subject matter. If not, there would be no conflict in the first place since there would

---

[81] Meetings of the Committee of the Whole, 165, para. 13.
[82] *Official Records of the Vienna Conference*, vol. 2, 222.   [83] *Ibid.*, 253.

be no overlap *ratione materiae* (that is, one of the three preconditions for there to be conflict set out in chapter 4). As Vierdag pointed out:

> The requirement that the instruments must relate to the same subject-matter seems to raise extremely difficult problems in theory, but may turn out not to be so very difficult in practice. If an attempted simultaneous application of two rules to one set of facts or actions leads to incompatible results it can be safely assumed that the test of sameness is satisfied.[84]

Does this mean that the words 'relating to the same subject-matter' have no meaning (against the principle of effective treaty interpretation)? No. The words impose a requirement that there be a conflict or incompatibility. They limit the scope of application of Art. 30 to situations of conflict, thereby referring explicitly to one of the three overlaps required for there to be conflict (overlap *ratione personae, ratione temporis* and *ratione materiae*). In the two sentences where the phrase 'relating to the same subject-matter' is used, it constitutes the only reference to the existence of conflict or incompatibility as between the two successive treaties: in the title ('Application of successive treaties relating to the same subject-matter'); and in Art. 30(1) ('the rights and obligations of States Parties to successive treaties relating to the same subject-matter shall be determined in accordance with the following paragraphs'). In subsequent provisions, the phrase is no longer used. Instead, reference is made to 'incompatible' (Arts. 30(2) and 30(5)) and 'compatible' (Art. 30(3)). Hence, the words 'relating to the same subject-matter' are important in that they require the existence of a conflict. That is their ordinary meaning. They do not inject the *lex specialis* principle into Art. 30, nor, *a fortiori*, should they be read as implying an absolute preference for the *lex specialis* principle over and above the *lex posterior* rule.[85]

---

[84] E. W. Vierdag, 'The Time of the "Conclusion" of a Multilateral Treaty' (1989) 60 BYIL 75 at 100. Or, as noted in *Oppenheim's*: 'Article 30 of the Vienna Convention deals with successive treaties relating to "the same subject-matter": it is not clear what limitation this involves, since in a sense if a course of conduct is such as to attract the application of two different treaties they can be said to be related to the same subject matter' (R. Jennings and A. Watts, *Oppenheim's International Law* (London: Longmans, 1992), I, 1212, note 2). See also Philippe Sands, 'Treaty, Custom and the Cross-fertilization of International Law' (1998) / 10 *Yale Human Rights and Development Law Journal* 3 at 8, para. 22 ('Presumably, when two treaty rules do not address the same subject matter, no dispute is likely to arise regarding which prevails').

[85] Some authors nonetheless posit that the *lex posterior* rule in Art. 30 is subject, and must always give way, to the *lex specialis* principle. See Jan Neumann, 'Die Koordination des WTO-Rechts mit anderen völkerrechtlichen Ordnungen – Konflikte des materiellen Rechts und Konkurrenzen der Streitbeilegung', unpublished doctoral

Nonetheless, the statements by Sinclair and the Special Rapporteur on the existence of a *lex specialis* principle (made, without objection, at the Vienna Conference itself) remain important elements in support of *lex specialis* being either an element to be looked at in determining the 'current expression of state consent' or a principle of customary international law in its own right. These statements are crucial also as a form of recognition that in certain cases the *lex posterior* principle must, indeed, give way to the *lex specialis* rule (a proposition defended below).

'Same subject-matter' and the WTO panel on Indonesia – Autos
Another example of unjustified reliance on the phrase 'relating to the same subject-matter' can be found in the WTO panel report on *Indonesia – Autos*. This panel did not invoke 'same subject-matter' as a ground for applying the *lex specialis* principle, nor did it actually refer to Art. 30. It made reference to 'same subject-matter' in support of a strict definition of conflict.[86] The alleged conflict at issue was one between the Subsidies agreement and the TRIMS agreement (the latter confirming GATT Art. III in respect of certain investment measures). We noted earlier that the panel, in our view incorrectly, only accepted situations of 'mutually exclusive obligations' as situations constituting conflict.[87] To make its definition of conflict even stricter, the two provisions alleged to be in conflict ought, according to the panel, also to 'cover the same type of subject matter'.

Instead of looking at the particular provisions at issue and examining whether, *as invoked in the particular circumstances*, they would have led to conflicting results – i.e., under GATT Art. III/TRIMS the measure is a domestic content requirement in breach of national treatment, whereas under the Subsidies agreement it constitutes a subsidy which developing countries might grant up to the year 2000 – the panel examined 'same type of subject matter' *in the abstract*. On that ground, it refused to consider the situation as one of conflict:

With respect to the nature of obligations, we consider that, with regard to local content requirements, the SCM Agreement and the TRIMs Agreement are concerned with *different types of obligations and cover different subject matters*. In the

---

thesis (Münster, 2001), 35 (referring in support to Theodor Schilling, *Rang und Geltung von Normen in gestuften Rechtsordnungen* (Berlin: Nomos, 1994), 455–8); and Rüdiger Wolfrum and Nele Matz, 'The Interplay of the United Nations Convention on the Law of the Sea and the Convention on Biological Diversity' (2000) 4 *Max Planck Yearbook on United Nations Law* 445.

[86] Discussed in chapter 4 above, pp. 193–4.   [87] *Ibid.*

case of the SCM Agreement, what is prohibited is the grant of a subsidy contingent on use of domestic goods, not the requirement to use domestic goods as such. In the case of the TRIMs Agreement, what is prohibited are TRIMs in the form of local content requirements, not the grant of an advantage, such as a subsidy.[88]

But, of course, if *the grant* of a subsidy contingent on a domestic content requirement were *permitted* under the Subsidies agreement, would then not also, *a fortiori*, the *domestic content requirement* which is implied in this subsidy be allowed? As a result, would there then not be a conflict between the Subsidies agreement, *explicitly permitting* the grant of the subsidy, and the TRIMS agreement which *prohibits* the domestic content requirement? Obviously, norms that are in conflict are 'different' (if not, there would be no conflict) and may approach a subject matter from a different angle (subsidy contingent on a requirement versus the requirement as such). But this 'difference' between provisions does not mean that there can be no conflict. On the contrary, it is this very difference that leads to the conflict.[89]

In sum, the first condition for Art. 30 to apply – the treaties must relate to 'the same subject-matter' – cannot be used as an abstract criterion on which to base either a *lex specialis* principle that was supposedly injected into Art. 30 or a general decision as to whether there is conflict between two treaties. The requirement of 'same subject-matter' relates rather to whether there is a genuine conflict (i.e., a material overlap) *as between two specific treaty provisions in the particular circumstances of each case.*

The treaties must be 'successive'

The second condition for Art. 30 to apply – according to the title of Art. 30 itself – is that the treaties must be 'successive treaties', that is, successive in time.

---

[88] Panel report on *Indonesia – Autos*, para. 14.50, emphasis added.
[89] Hence, the three requirements for there to be conflict summed up by the *Indonesia – Autos* panel in footnote 649 of the report are all mistaken or at least erroneously interpreted. The panel stated: 'In international law for a conflict to exist between two treaties, three conditions have to be satisfied. First, the treaties concerned must have the same parties.' This is incorrect since it overlooks conflicts of type AB/AC (A being a state with conflicting obligations vis-à-vis B and C) discussed below. The panel continued: 'Second, the treaties must cover the same substantive subject matter.' Again, the way the panel interpreted this requirement, that is, *in the abstract*, not as a requirement of material overlap depending on the circumstances, was flawed (see this section). The panel then stated: 'Third, the provisions must conflict, in the sense that the provisions must impose mutually exclusive obligations.' We discarded this strict definition of conflict in chapter 4 above.

Treaties as instruments with a time-label
As Rosenne pointed out, the focus of the Vienna Convention is treaties as *instruments*, not *obligations* deriving from treaties. It is 'the instrument in which an international obligation is expressed not the obligation itself'.[90] The Vienna Convention addresses, indeed, issues such as the conclusion and validity *of treaties*, the application and interpretation *of treaties* and the modification, amendment and termination *of treaties*. Article 30, as well, deals with the application of 'successive treaties' and 'an earlier treaty' as opposed to 'a later treaty'. This seems to imply that the timing of treaties under Art. 30 is a question of putting a date on the treaty *as an abstract instrument*, not a question of defining when the treaty imposes a particular obligation as between two given states.

This approach of putting a time-label on treaties as instruments makes sense in case one is faced with a treaty that is clearly concluded in order to amend an earlier one and where the parties to both treaties are exactly the same. One may think here of a 1990 bilateral investment treaty between A and B which is subsequently amended in 2000 by a treaty between A and B; or a 1994 WTO agreement which is subsequently amended in 2000 by a treaty between all WTO members, pursuant to Art. X of the Marrakesh Agreement.

In those instances, the domestic law analogy with 'legislative intent' and 'the legislator' being able to change earlier legislation by later legislation may make sense. In those cases, one is, indeed, faced with one homogenous bloc of states, acting, arguably, as some kind of legislator in a particular field (albeit legislation applicable only as between the parties to the treaty).

The fiction of 'legislative intent' unfolded
However, the fiction of later 'legislative intent' overruling earlier 'legislative intent' loses its attraction as soon as the 'same context – same parties' constellation changes. Indeed, even in respect of two AB treaties, it becomes hard to refer to one and the same 'legislature' in case the earlier bilateral treaty was concluded in the context of an MEA and the later one in the context of, for example, the WTO. A state's consent must be seen as one and indivisible, irrespective of who negotiated the treaty, but the reality remains that in the context of an MEA a very different set of people and values are at work than those active in, for example,

---

[90] Shabtai Rosenne, *Breach of Treaty* (Cambridge: Grotius, 1985), 3–4. On that basis, Rosenne distinguishes 'the law of the instrument' from 'the law of the obligation'.

the WTO context. Hence, the position of one state in one context may, indeed, be diametrically opposed to that same state's position in another context.[91]

But it is not only the difference in context that may make the analogy with 'legislative intent' unworkable. In many instances – and especially in respect of the great regulatory treaties of modern times, such as certain MEAs, UNCLOS and the WTO – the two treaties will have a different membership. The two treaties are then clearly the result of a *different* 'legislature', i.e., a different composition of states. They will hence be the reflection of a different balance of interests and one state may well have been able to push through its interests more under one treaty than under another. This difference will be accentuated in case a norm in one treaty context is adopted by unanimity and a norm in another treaty context is adopted by majority voting, even as between states that are parties to both treaties. In that case, it may well be that one of the parties accepted the first norm but explicitly voted against adoption of the second norm. Such objection cannot mean that the state in question is not bound by the second norm since it agreed to the majority voting procedure in the first place. But it would make the comparison with one and the same 'legislator' simply changing its mind over time more difficult.

The above considerations highlight the diversity as between different treaties and the difficulty of making a domestic law analogy based on changing 'legislative intent'. Nonetheless, these difficulties must, as a general rule, be accepted as a reality of international law. Adopting a *lex posterior* rule in this context may, indeed, provide a strong incentive for states to streamline their positions across international organisations and irrespective of the membership of particular treaties. States must realise that, in principle, whatever they consent to now prevails over what they agreed on earlier, irrespective of the context in which the obligations were entered into.

Hence, the *lex posterior* rule may be an important instrument that creates some order in the chaos of international law. However, given its

---

[91] The example of the position of some developing countries in respect of genetically modified organisms (GMOs) is telling. In the WTO, they are very much opposed to trade restrictions in respect of GMOs (thus safeguarding trade rights in a WTO trade context). In contrast, during the negotiations of the Cartagena Biosafety Protocol they pleaded very much in favour of granting as much leeway as possible to states wanting to protect themselves against GMO imports (thus safeguarding environmental protection rights in the biosafety, environmental context).

shaky foundation of changing 'legislative intent', it cannot be seen as an absolute rule the way it is regarded, for example, in domestic law for interacting statutes. Exceptions to it must be allowed for in case the analogy with 'latest legislative intent' loses touch with reality.

The ambiguity inherent in any conflict rule of international law based purely on timing was aptly worded by Jenks as follows:

> Nor, unhappily, is it always reasonable, in view of the complexity of governmental organization in the modern State and the wide variations in the procedures whereby international obligations are now contracted, to assume, when conflicting networks of obligations have developed simultaneously or almost simultaneously, that the parties concerned knew, or must be deemed to have known, when undertaking an obligation of a specialized character, of the existence of a prior obligation of a similar character which may be inconsistent with it. In these circumstances one of the essential elements in the *lex prior* principle, the principle of good faith [and, one may add, in the *lex posterior* principle, the principle of subsequent legislative intent], ceases to be at issue. The principle may still be a reasonable and convenient one in so far as some rule for resolving the conflict is necessary; and priority of obligation, when it can be determined, is an intelligible criterion which tends to discourage the irresponsible conclusion of new law-making instruments with insufficient regard for their effect on other instruments, but it loses the absolute quality attributed to it when it is thought of as a necessary consequence of the principle of good faith [subsequent legislative intent] and it has to be weighed against, and reconciled with, other principles which may be relevant.[92]

The difficulty of putting a time-label on a treaty as 'instrument'
The *lex posterior* rule in Art. 30 may not only be put in doubt because of the shaky analogy it makes with changing 'legislative intent'. From a more practical point of view, it will in many cases also be difficult to 'put a time-label' on a treaty.

To begin with, it is generally accepted that the timing of a treaty is determined by the *date of its conclusion or adoption*. In the case of the WTO treaty, for example, this is 15 April 1994. It is *not* the date of entry into force that determines the timing of a treaty under Art. 30. This was made explicit by the Expert Consultant at the Vienna Conference: 'for purposes of determining which of two treaties was the later one, the relevant date should be that of the adoption of the treaty and not that

---

[92] Jenks, 'Conflict', 444–5.

of its entry into force. His own understanding of the intentions of the [ILC] confirmed that assumption.'[93]

The fact that the date of conclusion is decisive was explained with reference to the concept of 'legislative intent' elaborated earlier: 'when the second treaty was adopted, there was a new legislative intention; that intention, as expressed in the later instrument, should therefore be taken as intended to prevail over the intention expressed in the earlier instrument. That being so, it was inevitable that the date of the adoption should be the relevant one.'[94] That the date of conclusion counts to define a 'later treaty' under Art. 30 finds support also in Art. 59 where reference is made to 'conclusion of a later treaty' and 'conclude a later treaty'.[95]

Hence, it is not the difficulty of deciding between the date of conclusion, opening for signature, ratification or entry into force that makes it difficult to put a time-label on treaties. What counts is the date of conclusion, *irrespective of the fact that the treaty may have been ratified by, or entered into force for, different parties at different times.*

Utilising the date of conclusion does, indeed, make logical sense when faced with a conflict between two treaties *to which no parties acceded subsequently*: for example, as between a 1990 bilateral investment treaty between A and B and a subsequent 2000 bilateral investment treaty between the same states A and B. The situation is more complicated in the context of treaties to which additional states have acceded. This is the case in respect of all regulatory treaties with a universal calling (such as the WTO treaty, UNCLOS, most MEAs and most human rights treaties) as well as many regional arrangements (such as the EC, ECHR and NAFTA).

---

[93] *Official Records of the Vienna Conference*, vol. 2, 253, para. 39. The Expert Consultant was confirming an earlier statement to that effect by Sir Ian Sinclair, the UK representative: 'the decisive date should be that of the adoption of the treaty; it is based on paragraph 1 of Article 56 [now Art. 59], which referred to the conclusion of a later treaty' (ibid., vol. 2, 222). Before the vote on what is now Art. 30 was taken, the Ceylonese delegation once again confirmed this approach as follows: 'the crucial date...should be the date when the text of the new treaty had been finally and formally established' (ibid., vol. 2, 56, para. 50).

[94] *Ibid.*, vol. 2, 253, para. 39.

[95] See note 93 above. Consequently, one of the problems put forward by Sir Ian Sinclair at the Vienna Conference can be easily resolved. The problem was the following: 'Supposing that Convention A was signed in 1964 and came into force in 1966, whereas Convention B was signed and entered into force in 1965, which of them would be earlier?' (*Official Records of the Vienna Conference*, vol. 1, 165). The answer must be: Convention A since A was concluded in 1964 and B only later in 1965.

The underlying objective of these treaties is that an increasing number of states accede to them (with or without regional restrictions). When faced with such 'expanding' treaties, it often becomes untenable to stick to the date of original conclusion of the treaty as defining the time at which state consent was expressed. This problem had already been pointed out by Sir Ian Sinclair at the Vienna Conference itself:

> supposing a multilateral convention was opened for signature in 1960, State A ratified it in 1961, and the convention entered into force in 1962. Then State A and State B concluded a bilateral treaty on the same subject in 1963 which entered into force in 1964, after which State B acceded to the multilateral convention in 1965. Which of the treaties was the earlier and which was the later? In State A's view, the multilateral convention was the earlier [1960] but in State B's view it was the later [1965].[96]

The fact that the parties to a treaty did not 'conclude' the treaty at the same point in time makes it impossible to put a single time-label on the treaty in question. It necessitates a shift away from the treaty as *abstract instrument* to an assessment of the treaty as source of rights and obligations *resting on particular states*.[97] This fact is, moreover, a death blow to the fiction of each treaty being concluded by one and the same 'legislative intent', expressed at one point in time. This fiction must, in turn, be brought back to a genuine principle of international law, namely the contractual freedom of states. We next examine Art. 30 from this perspective of treaty provisions binding *on particular states* and contractual freedom *as between the two states in question*.

Treaties as a source of rights and obligations as between particular parties
Although the crucial date under Art. 30 is the *date of conclusion* of the treaty, Art. 30 can be activated only as between two parties for which the treaty has *entered into force*. If not, there could not be conflict.[98] This obvious importance of entry into force was highlighted by the Expert Consultant as follows:

---

[96] *Ibid.*, vol. 1, 165.
[97] In this respect, Vierdag refers to 'the distinction between abstract norms and concrete rights and obligations... "Abstract norms" refers here to treaty rules as such, irrespective of the legal position of signatories or States bound by the rules. "Concrete rights and obligations" refers to the specific position of a particular State with respect to one or more treaties' (Vierdag, 'Conclusion', 94).
[98] But note, however, Art. 18 of the Vienna Convention on 'Obligation not to defeat the object and purpose of a treaty prior to its entry into force'.

Another question, however, arose: that of the date at which the rules contained in article 26 [now 30] would have effect for each individual party. In that connexion, the date of entry into force of a treaty for a particular party was relevant for purposes of determining the moment at which that party would be bound by the obligations arising under article 26 [now 30]. The provisions of that article referred to 'States parties'; they therefore applied only when States had become parties to the two treaties.[99]

However, once the treaty has entered into force for the two states in question, i.e., once a conflict may arise, in order to put a time-label on the treaty it is not the date of entry into force that counts – that date may well be different for the parties involved – but the date of conclusion of the treaty.

But this leaves us with the situation referred to by Sinclair – that is, the situation that prompted us to examine Art. 30 in terms of *rights and obligations resting on particular states* – namely: treaty 1 to which state A is an *original member* and state B *acceded* at a later point in time, in conflict with a bilateral treaty 2 that was concluded by A and B *in between these two points of time*. One may think here of a conflict between a WTO rule and a provision in a bilateral treaty concluded in 2000 between two parties, one of which is an *original* WTO member (1994), the other being a state that *acceded* to the WTO only in 2001. For the original (WTO) member (state A) treaty 1 (the WTO treaty) is 'concluded' at the time of the treaty's original conclusion (15 April 1994). Hence, for A treaty 1 is the 'earlier treaty'. In contrast, for the acceding member (state B), treaty 1 (the WTO treaty) is 'concluded' at the time its accession was adopted (*in casu*, 2001).[100] Hence, for B the same treaty 1 is the 'later treaty'. The same situation would arise in case A and B are original WTO members, A concludes and becomes bound by a WTO amendment in 2000, whereas

---

[99] *Official Records of the Vienna Conference*, vol. 2, 253, para. 40. This is not entirely correct since Art. 30(4)(b) also covers situations where a party is bound by only one of the two treaties. See also Sir Ian Sinclair, *The Vienna Convention on the Law of Treaties* (Manchester: Manchester University Press, 2nd edn, 1984), 98.

[100] In the WTO, for example, this would be the date at which the Ministerial Conference approves 'the agreement on the terms of accession' pursuant to Art. XII:2 of the Marrakesh Agreement. Note that such approval can be adopted by a two-thirds majority of WTO members. Hence, here as well, the situation may arise that a WTO member does not agree to another state's accession but nonetheless that state can accede. As a result, earlier treaties between these two parties would, without the consent of the original WTO member, be overruled by the later WTO agreement. Art. XIII of the Marrakesh Agreement allows, however, for existing WTO members to decide not to apply the WTO treaty in their relationship with an acceding state. Moreover, the WTO practice is to approve accession only by consensus.

B only does so in 2002, and in 2001 A and B conclude a treaty in conflict with the WTO amendment. For A, the 2001 treaty is the later in time; for B the WTO amendment is the later in time. In those cases, as Vierdag pointed out,

> [p]aradoxically, as a result of the *lex posterior* rule laid down in paragraph 3 of Article 30, a treaty [or amendment] to which a State was quick to become a party will be set aside by an incompatible treaty to which it became a party at a later date, perhaps reluctantly. For States that were slow in adhering to a treaty [or amendment] the effect of paragraph 3 will be that this treaty will supersede an incompatible treaty they were quick to enter into at an earlier date.[101]

At this juncture, two approaches are possible. First, in application of Art. 30 one could search for the time of 'convergence of state consent' in respect of the particular treaty provision. Second, one could disapply Art. 30 altogether on the ground that the two treaties are not 'successive'. We next deal with these two alternatives in turn.

Look for the 'time of convergence of state consent' in respect of the treaty provision concerned
Cases where for one party the treaty is 'earlier in time', for the other it is 'later in time' First, one could submit that in circumstances where for one state a treaty is 'earlier' and for the other that same treaty is 'later', one ought to focus, not so much on the timing of the treaty as abstract instrument, but *on the date at which the consent of the two states in question converged*. Hence, instead of focusing on the date of 'legislative intent' underlying the treaty as abstract instrument, one would then focus on the date when the expression of contractual freedom of the particular states in question met. Under this first approach, the hypothetical conflict outlined above between the WTO treaty and a bilateral treaty (concluded *subsequently* in 2000 but *before* the second state acceded to the WTO in 2001) would then be resolved in favour of the WTO rule *since the consent of both parties to the WTO treaty arose subsequently to that underlying the bilateral agreement* (i.e., 2001, date of accession of the second state to the WTO, as opposed to 2000, date of conclusion of the bilateral treaty). In other words, when faced with two parties for which a treaty has different dates, the latest date should be adopted as the date reflecting the time at which both parties' consent around the treaty emerged.

---

[101] Vierdag, 'Conclusion', 101. He adds that in those cases '[t]he dates of adoption (or opening for signature) or entry into force of a treaty are of limited relevance in this connection, and the relevance of Article 30 is limited accordingly'.

In the context of a multilateral treaty in conflict with a bilateral treaty this approach may work. But if one applies it also to a similar type of conflict between *two multilateral* treaties, the solution may be problematic for it becomes difficult to talk of an earlier versus a later convergence of state consent. Take the example of the WTO treaty (1994) in conflict with the Cartagena Biosafety Protocol (1999). States A and B are original WTO members which adopted the Protocol in 1999. State C acceded to the WTO in 2000 after it had adopted the Protocol in 1999. State D acceded to the WTO in 2001 and subsequently adopted the Protocol. In that situation (and making abstraction of any conflict clauses that may be found in the Cartagena Protocol)[102] our first approach offers the following outcome:

- as between states A and B, the *Protocol prevails* as the later treaty;
- as between states A and B, on the one hand, and state C, on the other, the *WTO prevails* as the later treaty;
- as between states A, B and C, on the one hand, and state D, on the other, the *Protocol prevails* as the later treaty.

This differential approach would thus mean that for some states WTO rules prevail, for others the Protocol. Depending on the circumstances – i.e., is the Protocol obligation one of an integral nature? – the WTO rule may be 'illegal' pursuant to Art. 41 of the Vienna Convention as an *inter se* deviation from an integral obligation (see the discussion in chapter 6 above). But if no integral obligations are involved, can this 'balkanisation' of multilateral treaties be tolerated?

As between states that both participated in the conclusion of the two treaties (*in casu*, states A and B), to say that the 'later treaty' prevails as between them – *even if for other states this treaty may not be the later one* – seems to make sense. However, as soon as one of the treaties is the 'later' in time for one party and the 'earlier' in time for another party, the solution offered becomes shaky. Indeed, in terms of state practice, would states A and B (original parties to both the WTO and the Protocol) realise that when they let C accede to the WTO in 2000 *in their relationship with C, WTO rules prevail*; but when they subsequently let D accede to the WTO in 2001 *in their relationship with D, the Protocol prevails*?

Conflict involving treaties that are reconcluded, amended or regularly revised
The problem of whether the *lex posterior* rule in Art. 30 still reflects

---

[102] See above, p. 334.

'the later expression of state consent to prevail over earlier expressions' arises not only in case the treaty has a different date for the two parties involved. It may emerge also in the event of amendments to either treaty where the treaty as amended is 'concluded' once again *in its entirety*. The conclusion of the WTO treaty offers a good example. GATT 1947 was concluded in 1947 and continued to exist up to 1995. In 1994, however, GATT 1947 was incorporated into the WTO agreement (as part of GATT 1994) under whose umbrella also a number of new treaties were put. As a result, when the WTO agreement was concluded on 15 April 1994, also the provisions of GATT 1947 *as incorporated into the WTO agreement* were 'reconcluded'. The Appellate Body confirmed in, for example, *Argentina – Footwear* that all provisions of the WTO agreement 'entered into force... at the same time'.[103] However, as against treaties concluded between 1947 and 1994, did this reconclusion of GATT result in a complete *tabula rasa* in the sense that *whereas before 1994, these other treaties prevailed, as of 1994, it was again GATT that must prevail as the 'later treaty'*?[104]

Vierdag refers to another example of conflict involving 'amended treaties', namely alleged conflict between the Covenant on Civil and Political Rights (1966) and certain International Telecommunications Union Radio Regulations (1982):

the Radio Regulations are subject to regular revisions, and they are adopted and become binding again on member States in the revised form. The regular conclusion of revised Regulations means that in the end the Regulations will always become the later treaty *vis-à-vis* every other treaty that is not likewise regularly revised, such as the Covenant on Civil and Political Rights.[105]

In other words, treaties subject to regular revision, that is, in particular *technical treaties*, would then, through Art. 30, always prevail over

---

[103] Appellate Body report on *Argentina – Footwear*, para. 81: 'the provisions of Article XIX of the GATT 1994 *and* the provisions of the *Agreement on Safeguards* are *all* provisions of one treaty, the *WTO Agreement*. They entered into force as part of that treaty at the same time.'

[104] In contrast, if one were to take the singular *act of conclusion* of a multilateral treaty seriously, it could be argued that GATT 1947 (as incorporated without any change in GATT 1994) remains, pursuant to Article II:4 of the WTO agreement, a 'legally distinct' instrument *concluded* not in 1994, but in 1947. In terms of timing, *GATT would then remain the earlier treaty* vis-à-vis, for example, pre-1994 environmental treaties. At the same time, new WTO agreements (such as the 1994 SPS agreement) would then, however, be *later in time*. Thus, having to make a distinction between GATT and SPS rules demonstrates the sometimes absurd results obtained under the 'guillotine' rule of time of conclusion in respect of 'continuing treaties' (a notion discussed below).

[105] Vierdag, 'Conclusion', 101.

treaties not subject to revision (i.e., treaties of a more immutable or regulatory type such as GATT articles). It is highly questionable whether this result is still in line with the 'latest expression of state consent'.

Conflict between treaties with universal calling and regional treaties Another case where the principle of *lex posterior* may lead to an absurd outcome is that of conflict between a regional treaty (say, the ECHR or EC treaties) and a subsequent multilateral treaty with universal calling (say, a UN treaty on human rights or the WTO treaty) binding on all regional partners. Even if, for the two parties involved (say, two member states of the EC), the respective dates of the two treaties are the same (1991 for the Maastricht Treaty and 1994 for the WTO treaty), should *the later multilateral treaty prevail over the earlier regional one*, pursuant to Art. 30(3) providing that '[w]hen all the parties to the earlier [EC] treaty are parties also to the later [WTO] treaty...the earlier [EC] treaty applies only to the extent that its provisions are compatible with those of the later [WTO] treaty'? In the case of conflict between human rights treaties, explicit conflict clauses in either treaty may resolve the conflict. However, no such clauses can be found for conflict between an EC treaty and the WTO treaty. Nor could one invoke, in that instance, the fact that the EC treaty is of an objective or integral nature under Art. 41 so that no deviations from it are allowed. Article 41 applies only in the event of *inter se* modifications to the integral (EC) treaty, *not in case all EC member states have signed up to the later WTO treaty*.

More absurd still, did WTO rules, as between EC member states, prevail over the 1991 Maastricht Treaty simply because they were concluded later in time, and was this situation reversed again in 1997 with the conclusion of the Amsterdam Treaty, once again, simply because that treaty succeeded WTO rules *ratione temporis*?

Under the examples cited above – of conflict between multilateral treaties where a treaty has different dates for each of the parties, has been reconcluded or revised or comes subsequently to a regional treaty – it can be questioned whether Art. 30 still finds application. To use the words of Jenks, could it, in these circumstances, not be said that '[w]hen matters reach this degree of intricacy the *lex prior* [and *lex posterior*] principle ceases to have any rational bearing on the real questions at issue'?[106] Or, in the words of Vierdag: 'Article 30 rests on an assumption that will often appear not to be correct, as it fails to take account

[106] Jenks, 'Conflict', 444.

of the complication in time of multilateral treaty-making through complex procedures.'[107]

Disapply Art. 30 – the notion of 'continuing' or 'living' treaties
This brings us to a second approach. One could submit, indeed, that in situations where for one state a conflicting treaty is the earlier one, whereas for the other state it is the later one, it is impossible to define the treaty as either 'earlier' or 'later' in time as required in Art. 30 (for A it is 'earlier' and for B it is 'later'). Consequently, the conflict in question is not one of 'successive treaties'. Hence, Art. 30 does not apply and one must have resort to other conflict rules (in particular, *lex specialis* developed in the next section below).

A strong argument in support of this second approach can be made when faced with a multilateral treaty of what I term a 'continuing' or 'living' nature. Such multilateral treaty norms are part of a regulatory framework or legal system that was created at one point in time but continues to exist and evolve over a mostly indefinite period. Most rules of modern multilateral conventions are of this nature, including EC treaties, WTO rules, UNCLOS and many environmental conventions and human rights treaties. They are rules part of a framework or system which is continuously confirmed, implemented, adapted and expanded, for example, by means of judicial decisions, interpretations, new norms or the accession of new state parties (for which not only the consent of the new party is required, but also the reciprocal acceptance of all, or a majority of, existing parties). Such treaty norms were not only consented to when they originally emerged, but continue to be confirmed, either directly or indirectly, throughout their existence, in particular when monitored and evolving within the context of an international organisation (such as the WTO).[108] It would arguably be inconsistent with the genuine will of states to 'freeze' this type of rules into the mould

---

[107] Vierdag, 'Conclusion', 98. He explains elsewhere: 'there is an inadequacy and inconsistency in Article 30 with regard to the time of treaties and the time of rights and obligations: the occurrence of treaties (legal rules) in time does not necessarily correspond at all with the actual acquisition of rights and the incidence of obligations under treaties in force by particular States parties to them. It is one thing to adopt the text of a multilateral treaty, and to adopt the text of another treaty at a later moment of time; it is another thing to identify at a given moment the concrete rights and obligations of two or more States under two or more treaties in force' (*ibid.*, 97).

[108] See, for example, Denys Simon, *L'Interprétation Judiciaire des Traités d'Organisations Internationales* (Paris: Pedone, 1981), 372: 'l'accord de volontés qui a présidé à la conclusion de la convention ne s'est pas épuisé dans la rédaction d'un texte;

of time at which they were originally created and to label them as an expression of state consent limited to, say, 15 April 1994. This type of treaty norm derives from what I term 'continuing' or 'living' treaties, not reflections of a 'one-shot-end-all' expression of state consent.[109] As a result, when such a treaty norm conflicts with another treaty norm, in particular another continuing treaty norm, the 'guillotine' approach of time of conclusion (the later in time prevailing) may not make sense and may lead to arbitrary solutions.

This theory of 'continuing' or 'living' treaties is a logical consequence also of the obligation to interpret certain treaties in an 'evolutive' manner (discussed in chapter 5 above, pp. 264–8). Evolutive interpretation of a treaty and the difficulty of putting a single time-label on that treaty go hand in hand. Thus, in respect of the WTO treaty, for example, the Appellate Body's evolutive approach to interpreting certain WTO terms could arguably be matched with an acknowledgement that the WTO treaty is a 'continuing' or 'living' treaty in respect of which an application of the *lex posterior* principle in Art. 30 may not always be warranted.

Nonetheless, even 'continuing' or 'living' treaties do have a starting point, even if this starting point is not the beginning and the end of state consent to the treaty. As a result, there may be treaties that were concluded *before the starting point* of a continuing treaty. Consequently, there may still be conflicts involving a continuing treaty where the two treaties are 'successive' and the continuing treaty prevails as *later in time* under Art. 30. For example, the starting point of GATT is 1947, that of new WTO agreements, 1994. Thus, in case of a conflict between a GATT 1947/WTO norm and another norm (*not* of a continuing nature) which clearly predates the GATT 1947/WTO norm (say, a bilateral agreement concluded in, respectively, 1930 or 1980), Art. 30 should still find application given that the two treaties are then, indeed, 'successive' in time.

Especially in the event of conflict between *two* norms of the 'continuing' or 'living' type, it seems difficult to apply Art. 30 (except in case one norm is an explicit amendment of the other in the sense of Art. 40 of

---

l'application d'une telle convention suppose nécessairement le renouvellement permanent de l'adhésion des Etats membres au contenu de normes juridiques dont l'instrument signé ne constitue qu'une expression solennelle, mais, par essence, éphémère'. See also chapter 5 above, pp. 264–8.

[109] Such 'continuing treaties' are, indeed, 'continuing acts', as referred to in Art. 14(2) of the 2001 Draft Articles on State Responsibility. On this notion, see Joost Pauwelyn, 'The Concept of a "Continuing Violation" of an International Obligation: Selected Problems' (1995) 66 BYIL 415.

the Vienna Convention).[110] Even if the starting point of one of the two treaties may then predate that of the other, given that the norms are in conflict, at the time of the conflict both exist and 'continue' *at the same time*. Hence, it may be difficult to define the two treaties as 'successive' in time. They are rather 'parallel' in time. If so, Art. 30 cannot be applied and, most probably, the *lex specialis* principle should resolve the conflict.

In sum, the argument made here is that in certain situations, given the complexities of modern treaty-making, it will be difficult to define two conflicting treaties as 'successive in time'. If so, Art. 30 should not find application and resort should be had rather to other conflict rules which more appropriately reflect the principle that 'the current expression of state consent' ought to prevail. Whether and when Art. 30 and the *lex posterior* rule should thus be disapplied will depend on the particular conflict, as well as the norms and states involved. It requires a case-by-case examination.

Conclusion on the timing of treaties
The above examination shows that the analogy with 'latest legislative intent' underlying the *lex posterior* rule in Art. 30 may not always be convincing, in particular if the two norms stem from a different context or were created by a different set of states. Nonetheless, as a starting point, the *lex posterior* principle must be accepted in international law as the 'best available solution' that may well create order in the chaos of interplay between norms. The principle is confirmed in the Vienna Convention and is based on an objective criterion (time). Its outcome should, in most cases, be predictable. However, already at this stage it was noted that, given the sometimes shaky analogy with 'latest legislative intent', *lex posterior* in international law cannot be the absolute legal principle which it is in domestic law.

Having set out the two conditions for Art. 30 to apply – 'successive treaties', 'relating to the same subject-matter' – we next assess the substantive solutions offered by Art. 30. Two types of situations must be distinguished: (i) those where all the parties to the earlier treaty are party also to the later one (Art. 30(3)); and (ii) those where *not* all the parties to the earlier treaty are party also to the later one (Art. 30(4)).

---

[110] Art. 30 should continue to apply in case of amendments to a continuing treaty norm. There as well, there can be no doubt that the two norms are 'successive': the amendment comes later in time than the provision of the continuing treaty which is then no longer confirmed as of the date of the amendment. Hence the amendment must prevail as the later rule in time under Art. 30.

All the parties to the earlier treaty are party also to the later one (Art. 30(3))

Article 30(3) deals with conflicts where '*all the parties* to the earlier treaty are parties also to the later treaty', but where the later treaty was not terminated or suspended pursuant to Art. 59. Two conflict situations are covered by Art. 30(3):

(i) conflicts where the parties to the two treaties are *exactly the same* (conflicts of type ABC/ABC);
(ii) conflicts where the second treaty is binding on all parties to the first treaty, *plus a number of additional states*[111] (conflicts of type ABC/ABCD).

The solution offered in Art. 30(3) is straightforward: 'the earlier treaty applies only to the extent that its provisions are compatible with those of the later treaty'. To put it differently, *to the extent of the conflict, the later treaty prevails*. As the ILC noted in its Commentary, this is 'no more than an application of the general principle that a later expression of intention is to be presumed to prevail over an earlier one'.[112] In other words, the *lex posterior* rule in Art. 30(3) is nothing more than a logical consequence of states being their own law-makers, possessing the contractual freedom to 'change their minds': a later expression of consent prevails over an earlier one.

Obviously, in the second type of conflict covered by Art. 30(3) – conflicts of type ABC/ABCD – this solution applies only to the relationship between parties bound by both treaties, that is, as between states A, B and C. As far as the relationship with parties bound only by the later treaty is concerned (*in casu*, state D), the *pacta tertiis* rule expressed in Art. 34 applies: 'a treaty [*in casu*, the earlier treaty ABC] does not create either obligations or rights for a third State [*in casu*, state D] without its consent'.

Not all the parties to the earlier treaty are party also to the later one (Art. 30(4))

In contrast to Art. 30(3), Art. 30(4) covers conflicts where 'the parties to the later treaty do *not* include all the parties to the earlier one'. Three types of conflict fall under Art. 30(4):

---

[111] The ILC Commentary states explicitly that Art. 30(3) applies 'for cases where all the parties to a treaty (*whether without or with additional States*) conclude a later treaty relating to the same subject matter', Rauschning, *Travaux*, 234 (ILC Commentary to Art. 30, para. (9), emphasis added).
[112] Rauschning, *Travaux*, 234, para. (10).

(i) a later *inter se* agreement deviates from an earlier multilateral treaty (conflicts of type ABC/AB) – this is the first type of *inter se* agreement referred to in the section on Arts. 41/58 (see chapter 6 above, p. 305);
(ii) a later *inter se* agreement concluded *with a number of third parties* deviates from an earlier multilateral treaty (conflicts of type ABC/ABD) – this is the second type of *inter se* agreement referred to in the section on Arts. 41/58 (see chapter 6 above, p. 305);
(iii) a later agreement concluded by *only one of the parties to the earlier treaty* conflicts with the obligations of that party under the earlier treaty (conflicts of type AB/AC or ABC/AD).

In respect of the first two conflict situations (ABC/AB and ABC/ABD), resort must be had first to Art. 41. As noted before, the conflict rules in Art. 41 prevail over those in Art. 30(4) (Art. 30(5) makes this explicit). Hence, only in the event that the later *inter se* agreement is permissible under Art. 41 – that is, only if it is a 'legal' agreement – should Art. 30(4) be applied.[113] If the *inter se* agreement is illegal, it cannot be opposed as against third parties, nor, as we saw earlier, should it be opposable vis-à-vis states bound by the *inter se* agreement. As between parties to both the earlier and the later agreements, Art. 41 thus provides for an exception to the principle of contractual freedom. If the later *inter se* agreement is not permissible under Art. 41, it cannot prevail as the latest expression of state intent *even as between the parties to both treaties*.

If the later *inter se* agreement *is* permissible under Art. 41, the solutions offered by Art. 30(4) are, once again, straightforward:

(1) As between *parties bound by both* the earlier and the later treaty, the later treaty prevails to the extent of the conflict.

Art. 30(4)(a) states that in this situation the rules in Art. 30(3) apply. Hence 'the earlier treaty applies only to the extent that its provisions are compatible with those of the later treaty'. Or, to put it differently, the later treaty prevails to the extent of the conflict. Much like Art. 30(3), this first solution set out in Art. 30(4)(a) is 'no more than an application of the general principle that a later expression of intention is to be presumed to prevail over an earlier one'.[114] It finds application only under the

---

[113] It is interesting to note that at the Vienna Conference France proposed an amendment to what is now Art. 30(4)(a). France wanted to add an explicit reference to what it called 'restricted multilateral treaties', a notion that comes close to that of 'integral treaties', in respect of which it wanted to limit the application of the *lex posterior* principle. See chapter 6 above, note 78.

[114] Rauschning, *Travaux*, 234, para. (10).

first and second conflict situations set out above, that is, those of the ABC/AB and ABC/ABD types. Only in these instances is there a double overlap *ratione personae* (that is, only there are both A and B bound by the two treaties). In the third conflict situation (of the AB/AC type), only one of the parties is bound by both rules so that Art. 30(4)(a) does not find application.

> (2) As between a *party to both* treaties and a *party to one* of the treaties only (be it the earlier or the later one), 'the treaty to which both States are parties [respectively, the earlier and the later one] governs their mutual rights and obligations' (Art. 30(4)(b)).

In the first conflict situation (of the type ABC/AB), this means that A and B's relationship with C is governed only by the earlier ABC treaty. In the second conflict situation (of the type ABC/ABD), it means that (i) A and B's relationship with C is governed only by the earlier ABC treaty; and (ii) A and B's relationship with D is governed only by the later ABD treaty. In the third conflict situation (of the type AB/AC), the solution offered in Art. 30(4)(b) means that (i) A's relationship with B is governed only by the earlier AB treaty; and (ii) A's relationship with C is governed only by the later AC treaty.

Article 30(4)(b) is, in other words, a simple confirmation of the *pacta tertiis* rule in Art. 34. Indeed, as far as the first and second conflict situations are concerned, *Art. 30(4)(b) does not provide a solution to conflict* since the legal relationships it addresses are free of conflict: in the first situation, the relationship between AB and C; in the second, the relationship between AB and C and that between AB and D.[115]

Nonetheless, Art. 30(4)(b) is crucial as a conflict rule in the third type of conflict (of the type AB/AC). This conflict is one that arises for A which has obligations towards B (under an AB norm) that are contradictory with its obligations towards C (under an AC norm). Crucially, in this event, Art. 30(4)(b), *instead of giving priority to either of the two norms, simply confirms the validity of both of them*.

Recall, however, that in earlier ILC reports (especially that by Lauterpacht), a later treaty (AC) in conflict with an earlier one (AB) was said to be invalid.[116] Article 30(4)(b) does away with this theory. It confirms the

---

[115] As Vierdag noted: 'Paradoxically, [Art. 30(4)(b)], which can be regarded as crucial in terms of the subject-matter of Article 30, does not deal with "application of successive treaties" at all. This provision concerns only one treaty, namely the treaty to which both States are parties, only one of these States being party to two "successive" treaties' (Vierdag, 'Conclusion', 96).

[116] See chapter 6 above, pp. 279–81.

validity of both treaties but limits this validity as between the parties to those treaties. However, the fact that both treaties are hence valid does not mean that they are necessarily legal under Arts. 41/58. Here again, the conflict rules in Arts. 41/58 prevail over those in Art. 30(4)(b).

The situation of treaty norms in conflict with later acts of international organisations

Article 30 applies only in respect of successive *treaty norms*. However, as we noted above, Art. 30 is essentially but the logical consequence of a broader principle, namely that 'a later expression of intention is to be presumed to prevail over an earlier one' (already discussed in chapter 3 above).[117] This general principle applies also in respect of a treaty norm in conflict with supervening custom. It should apply, moreover, in respect of a treaty norm in conflict with a later act of an international organisation. A good example is the potential conflict between, on the one hand, WIPO conventions (setting out positive obligations to protect intellectual property rights) and, on the other hand, a subsequent DSB authorisation to suspend concessions under the TRIPS agreement (granting an explicit exemption not to protect certain intellectual property rights). In that event, which of the two norms should prevail, the earlier WIPO treaty norm or the later act of the DSB, being an organ of an international organisation other than WIPO?

As the *lex posterior*, the DSB authorisation ought to prevail (at least as between those states bound by both the relevant WIPO *and* WTO norms). In chapter 3, we noted that no *a priori* hierarchy exists as between the sources of international law, including as between treaties and acts of international organisations. We pointed out also that the fact that norms have been created in different contexts (WIPO or the WTO) does not normally say anything about their hierarchical relationship. Hence, as the latest expression of state intent, the later DSB authorisation must prevail. That is, of course, only as between states that are both WTO members and bound by the relevant WIPO convention, and only to the extent that the DSB authorisation is legal under both WTO rules (Arts. 41 and 58 of the Vienna Convention and in particular the DSU) and other applicable international law norms (e.g., Art. 51(1)(b) of the ILC Draft 2000, precluding countermeasures under obligations for the protection of fundamental human rights).[118] We noted earlier that the conflict clause in

---

[117] ILC Commentary on Art. 30, in Rauschning, *Travaux*, 234, para. (10).
[118] See chapter 3 above, p. 107.

TRIPS Art. 2.2 does not affect this solution.[119] If the suspension of TRIPS obligations meets these conditions of legality under WTO and other international law norms, the DSB decision authorising this suspension must prevail over the WIPO convention to the extent of the conflict. Of course, the relevant WIPO rule is not thereby rendered illegal. As soon as the DSB authorisation expires, the WIPO rule will be reactivated.

Lex specialis

In the event that the conflict rules set out earlier do not find application, or are unable to resolve the conflict of norms, resort must be had to the *lex specialis* principle. The principle of *lex specialis* is often referred to by authors, litigators and international tribunals alike. Nonetheless, many have expressed doubts as to the status of this principle under international law. Is it, for example, part of customary law? Any useful discussion of the principle of *lex specialis* must acknowledge, up front, that the principle is referred to in different contexts and may have a different meaning depending on its context. What is of interest to this study is, of course, the principle *lex specialis derogat legi generali*, that is, the principle of *lex specialis* as a rule to resolve a genuine conflict between two norms. Pursuant to this principle, in the event of conflict, the more special norm prevails over the more general norm.

It may not always be easy to determine whether a reference to *lex specialis* is meant to be one to *lex specialis* as a conflict rule. For example, in the *Case Concerning the Gabcíkovo–Nagymaros Project (Hungary v. Slovakia)*, the ICJ confirmed the notion of *lex specialis* as follows:

it is of cardinal importance that the Court has found that the 1977 Treaty is still in force and consequently governs the relationship between the Parties. That relationship is also determined by the rules of other relevant conventions to which the two States are party, by the rules of general international law and, in this particular case, by the rules of State responsibility; but it is governed, *above all*, by the applicable rules of the 1977 Treaty as a *lex specialis* [emphasis added].[120]

It is unclear from this statement whether the ICJ considered the 1977 treaty as a *lex specialis* simply in terms of more specific law supplementing other law or whether the ICJ intended to go further, implying also that 'above all' means that, in the event of conflict, the 1977 treaty must prevail.

---

[119] See above, pp. 346–7.   [120] ICJ Reports 1997, para. 132.

In the following subsections we examine *lex specialis* as a rule to resolve conflict in the applicable law. We then end this section on *lex specialis* with an assessment of certain other functions of the *lex specialis* principle.

It must be recalled, once again, that the conflict rules supplied below are subject to those set out in earlier sections of this chapter and in chapter 6, in particular *jus cogens*, Arts. 41/58 of the Vienna Convention and explicit conflict clauses. The relationship between the *lex posterior* and the *lex specialis* principle is further discussed below.

An interesting example of interplay between (i) the rules on validity of acts of international organisations (*in casu*, UN Security Council resolutions); (ii) an explicit conflict clause (*in casu*, Art. 103 of the UN Charter); (iii) the *lex posterior* principle; and (iv) the *lex specialis* rule, can be found in the *Lockerbie* cases. There, a conflict arose as between the rights of Libya under the 1971 Montreal Convention (i.e., Libya's right to keep and try the two suspects in Libya), on the one hand, and the obligations of Libya under a UN Security Council resolution (i.e., Libya's obligation to surrender the two suspects to the UK and the US), on the other. Libya, claiming that its Montreal Convention *right* ought to prevail, (i) relied on the invalidity of the Security Council resolution, claiming that it was taken in disregard of the UN Charter; (ii) submitted that because this resolution was invalid, Art. 103 did not find application;[121] and (iii) argued that the 1971 Montreal Convention as both *lex specialis* and *lex posterior* ought to prevail over the UN Charter system.[122] In defence, the UK and the US relied on the explicit conflict clause in Art. 103. In their view, any rights that Libya might have had under the Montreal Convention were now superseded by Libya's UN Charter obligations under the Security Council resolution. In its judgment on Provisional Measures, the ICJ seemed to support the UK and US positions, finding (i) that the obligation resting

---

[121] See Libya's Oral Statement, *per* Prof. Suy, public sitting held on 22 October 1997 (posted on the internet at http://www.icj-cij.org/icjwww/idocket): 'La primauté établie par cet article 103 *présuppose* une obligation établie conformément à la Charte. Il présuppose donc, dans la présente espèce, une décision du Conseil de sécurité respectant les limites que la Charte lui impose.'

[122] See Libya's Oral Statement, *per* Prof. David, public sitting held on 17 October 1997 (posted on the internet at http://www.icj-cij.org/icjwww/idocket): 'très naturellement le système de la convention de Montréal apparaît, par rapport au système de la Charte des Nations Unies, à la fois comme une *lex posterior* et comme une *lex specialis*; c'est pour cela aussi que dans les domaines qui relèvent de cette convention, celle-ci doit à priori l'emporter sur les systèmes prévus par la Charte, sauf application de l'article 103' (at para. 4.20).

on all UN members to accept and carry out the decisions of the UN Security Council in accordance with Article 25 of the Charter extended *prima facie* to the decision contained in resolution 748 (1992); and (ii) that 'in accordance with Article 103 of the Charter, the obligations of the Parties in that respect prevail over their obligations under any other international agreement, including the Montreal Convention'.[123]

Why should *lex specialis* prevail, and when is a norm more special than another?

An early reference to *lex specialis* as a conflict rule can be found in the writings of Grotius: 'Parmi les conventions...que l'on préfère ce qui est le plus particulier, et ce qui approche le plus de la chose! Car ce qui est spécial est ordinairement plus efficace que ce qui est général.'[124]

In the same sense, de Vattel stated: 'De deux Loix, ou de deux Conventions, toutes choses d'ailleurs égales, on doit préférer celle qui est la moins générale, & qui approche le plus de l'affaire dont il s'agit. Parce que ce qui est spécial souffre moins d'exceptions que ce qui est général; il est ordonné plus précisément, & il paraît qu'on l'a voulu plus fortement.'[125]

Pufendorf gave the following example in support: 'Une loi défend de paraître en public avec des armes, pendant les jours de fête, une autre Loi ordonne, de sortir en armes pour se rendre à son poste, dès qu'on entendra sonner le tocsin. On sonne le tocsin un jour de fête. Il faut obéir à la dernière Loi, qui forme une exception à la première.'[126]

Based, *inter alia*, on the rather prosaic references to *lex specialis* in the writings of Grotius, de Vattel and Pufendorf, the following two reasons for letting a more specific norm prevail over a more general norm can be given:

(i) the special norm is the more effective or precise norm, allowing for fewer exceptions (the *lex specialis*, if it prevails, is, indeed, already an exception to the *lex generalis*); and
(ii) because of this, the special norm reflects most closely, precisely and/or strongly the consent or expression of will of the states in question.

---

[123] ICJ Reports 1992, para. 42.
[124] Hugo Grotius, *Le Droit de la Guerre et de la Paix* (D. Alland and S. Goyard-Fabre, eds.) (Paris: Presses Universitaires de France, 1999), 413.
[125] Emer de Vattel, *Les Droit des Gens ou Principes de la Loi Naturelle* (Lyons: Gauthier, 1802), 511.
[126] Samuel von Pufendorf, *Droit de la Nation et des Gens*, book V, chapters XII–XXIII (quoted in de Vattel, *Droit des Gens*, 511).

Consequently, much like *lex posterior* – which is based on the view that the 'latest expression of state consent' ought to prevail – the principle of *lex specialis* is but a consequence of the contractual freedom of states, grounded in the idea that the 'most closest, detailed, precise or strongest expression of state consent', as it relates to a particular factual circumstance, ought to prevail. Both Art. 30 and the *lex specialis* principle thus attempt to answer one and the same question, namely: which of the two norms in conflict is the 'current expression of state consent'? Since both *lex posterior* and *lex specialis* derive from the principle of contractual freedom of states, both principles are 'subjective' conflict rules in the sense that it is the intention of the parties that counts, not some formal criterion such as source.

Looked at from this angle, it would be unwise to portray the *lex posterior* and *lex specialis* principles as absolute and self-standing legal norms. They are rather practical methods in the search for the 'current expression of state consent'. They deduce logical consequences from the fact that a norm is later in time or more specific so as to determine the 'current expression of state consent'.[127] In sum, they are more factual/subjective elements in the assessment of contractual freedom and state consent than absolute legal norms in their own right. Thus, if we suggest in this book that Art. 30 may not apply to certain conflicts and the *lex specialis* principle ought to be resorted to instead, this shift from Art. 30 to *lex specialis* is a shift in the methods used to assess one and the same question, namely what is the 'current expression of state consent'? It is not a shift in the underlying legal norm applied to resolve conflict. This norm remains the principle of contractual freedom of states.

Nonetheless, in terms of detecting a *lex posterior* and *lex specialis*, a major difference does persist. In the former case, the decisive element is *time*. In the latter, it is *speciality*. Now, time is generally seen as a criterion to be applied more easily than speciality and, in that sense, it is considered to be more explicit or objective than the sometimes implicit and subjective determination of what is more special. This appearance may, however, be misleading. First, as we saw above,[128] determining the relevant date of a treaty is often *not* as straightforward as noting that, for example, the WTO treaty was concluded on 15 April 1994. Second, a decision on which norm is more special or specific may be easier

---

[127] In that sense they are rather 'principles of legal logic', as we defined them in chapter 3 above, p. 126.
[128] See above, pp. 367–80.

than first thought. A norm may be *lex specialis* on one of two grounds: (i) subject matter; or (ii) membership.

Recall, in this respect, Art. 38(1)(a) of the ICJ Statute which refers also to 'international conventions, *whether general or particular*' and the broader discussion in chapter 3 above, where we rephrased international law in terms of general versus particular norms of international law.

Subject matter

A norm may, first of all, be more special than another one based on its more specific subject matter. Although necessarily dealing with the '*same* subject-matter' – if not, there would be no conflict[129] – one norm may then be *lex specialis* because it addresses the particular subject matter that a general law also addresses more directly or precisely. In that sense, the material scope of one norm can be more precise or limited than another. On that basis, a WTO rule dealing with countermeasures for *breach of WTO obligations* is *lex specialis* as opposed to general international law dealing with countermeasures generally, for *any breach* of international law. Equally, an obligation to do something *in events A to Z* is *less specific* than an obligation not to do this something *in the specific events A and B*. Or a WTO obligation *not* to restrict trade, *irrespective of the product involved*, must be seen as *less specific* than an obligation (or permission) to restrict trade *in the specific products A and B* (which are, for example, labelled as harmful).[130] In that sense, the WTO's SPS agreement, dealing generally with all sanitary and phytosanitary measures, *irrespective of the product or health concern*, could be seen as less specific than, for example, the Cartagena Protocol on Biosafety which addresses certain specific products, such as 'living modified organisms', and deals with a specific health concern, namely risks related to certain genetically modified organisms. NAFTA confirms the specificity of MEA trade provisions as compared to WTO/NAFTA rules when, in its Art. 104, it addresses 'inconsistency between this Agreement and the *specific* trade

---

[129] See chapter 4 above, p. 165, and this chapter, pp. 364–7.
[130] In a recent submission, the European Communities noted that to resolve conflict in the applicable law 'an important consideration could be not so much the application of the lex specialis test but which of the two sets of rules provides for a more specific regulation of the issue under dispute' (*Multilateral Environmental Agreements (MEAS): Implementation of the Doha Development Agenda*, Submission by the European Communities, paragraph 31(i), 21 March 2002, TN/TE/W/1, p. 7). However, the latter is exactly what is understood here as an application of the *lex specialis* principle. It is unclear on what basis the European Communities distinguish these two tests.

obligations set out in', *inter alia*, CITES, the Montreal Protocol and the Basel Convention.

Membership

A norm may also be more specific than another norm with reference to its membership. By this we do not mean that a treaty with fewer parties generally prevails over a treaty with more parties or that an *inter se* agreement always prevails over an earlier multilateral agreement.[131] Rather, some treaty norms must be seen as *lex specialis* because they deal with the same subject matter as the opposing *lex generalis* does, but in a way that goes further, *either in terms of detail or in terms of the objectives pursued under both treaties*.

As an example one could refer here to the WTO treaty (a treaty with universal calling) as opposed to EC treaties (of a regional nature). Both address trade matters and aim at trade liberalisation. However, the EC treaty does so in more detail and in a way that goes further in terms of trade liberalisation. On that basis, and depending on the particular provisions at issue, it should, therefore, be seen as *lex specialis* as between EC member states.[132] Hence, it should, for example, not be possible for an EC member in its relationship to other EC members to rely on an explicit WTO right (to restrict trade) that contradicts an EC treaty obligation (to free trade), even if the EC treaty is the earlier in time. The same could be said about *multilateral* trade agreements in the WTO (binding on all WTO members) as opposed to WTO *plurilateral* agreements, binding only on some WTO members, and intended to take trade liberalisation a step further. The same applies also in respect of regional human rights conventions (such as the ECHR) as opposed to universal human rights conventions (such as those concluded in the UN). In many respects, the regional human rights treaty will deal with the protection of human rights in more detail and go further in the shared aim of human rights protection. To that extent, these regional conventions ought to be seen as *lex specialis* that prevails over more general norms.[133] Another example

---

[131] See Arts. 41/58 of the Vienna Convention (discussed in chapter 6 above, pp. 304–15) for proof to the contrary.

[132] That is, of course, to the extent EC rules are not *explicitly prohibited* by WTO rules (such as GATT Art. XXIV, discussed in chapter 6 above, pp. 317–18, in which case it must be clear, at least under international law, that WTO rules 'prevail' over EC rules (the latter are then even 'illegal')).

[133] This is the example Sinclair referred to at the Vienna Conference: see above, p. 364. Note also that regional conventions themselves may include explicit conflict clauses to this effect.

can be found in the preference given by the ICJ to special customary international law binding as between some states only over and above general customary international law which is, in principle, binding on all states.[134]

Now that we have provided some clarifications as to how a *lex specialis* can be identified, in the four subsections below we examine when and to what extent the *lex specialis* principle applies, as a conflict rule, under current international law. We begin with the instance where it applies beyond doubt, namely: treaty provisions contracting out of general international law. We next examine cases where the prominence of *lex specialis* was accepted, but where the decision in favour of the *lex specialis* was made partly (if not largely) because it was at the same time the *lex posterior*. We then assess the 'hard cases' of conflict between provisions in the same treaty (should either of them prevail as *lex specialis*?) and conflict involving a *lex specialis* which is at the same time the *lex prior*.

Particular international law prevails over general international law

As hinted at in chapter 3 (pp. 155–7), in the event of conflict between, on the one hand, *particular* international law (say, a specific treaty norm or special customary international law) and, on the other hand, *general* international law (general customary international law or general principles of law), particular international law prevails (subject, of course, to *jus cogens*).

Treaties contracting out of general international law
As we explained earlier (in chapter 4, pp. 212–44), it is perfectly possible for a treaty norm to 'contract out' of general international law. In that event, the conflict between the treaty norm and the norm of general international law must be decided in favour of the treaty norm. It is then the treaty norm which prevails, although the norm of general international law continues to exist. This solution is based on the principle of *lex specialis*. As the Iran–US Claims Tribunal found:

As a *lex specialis* in the relations between the two countries, the Treaty supersedes the *lex generalis*, namely customary international law. This does not mean, however, that the latter is irrelevant in the instant Case. On the contrary, the

---

[134] *Right of Passage* case (Portugal v. India), ICJ Reports 1960, 6, quoted below on p. 394.

rules of customary law may be useful in order to fill in possible lacunae of the law of the Treaty, to ascertain the meaning of undefined terms in its text or, more generally, to aid interpretation and implementation of its provisions.[135]

This approach of allowing more specific treaty norms to prevail over general international law is explicitly confirmed in both the law of treaties and the 2001 Draft Articles on State Responsibility. Article 5 of the Vienna Convention states that it is 'without prejudice to any relevant rules of [international] organisations'. Moreover, on several occasions, Vienna Convention provisions are explicitly made subject to *lex specialis* that may be set out in particular treaties, using phrases such as 'unless the treaty so (or otherwise) provides' or 'unless it is prohibited by the treaty' (e.g., in Arts. 19(a), 20(1), 28, 29, 30(2), 40(1), etc.). In turn, Art. 55 of the 2001 Draft Articles, entitled '*Lex specialis*', states the following: 'These articles do not apply where and to the extent that the conditions for the existence of an internationally wrongful act or the content or implementation of the international responsibility of a State are governed by special rules of international law.'

In these instances, the treaty norm is mostly also the *lex posterior*. Even if, for example, the Vienna Convention was concluded only in 1969, it largely codified customary law predating 1969. As a result, there is a double reason to let the treaty norm prevail: it is at the same time *lex posterior* and *lex specialis*.

Supervening custom in conflict with an earlier treaty
Nonetheless, as explained in chapter 3 (pp. 137–43), in cases where it is established that the custom is later in time (something that may be difficult to prove), the custom must, in principle, prevail over the earlier treaty norm as *lex posterior unless it can be shown that the treaty norm continues applying as lex specialis*. Hence, in respect of conflict between a treaty norm and supervening custom, one first applies the *lex posterior* rule, which is then subject, however, to the principle of *lex specialis*. In other words, if it can be shown that the treaty norm still exists as particular international law (that is, it was intended to continue to exist as a *lex specialis*), the new general international custom must give way.

An example can be found in the *INA Corp. v. Iran* case, decided by the Iran–US Claims Tribunal, where INA Corp. had filed a compensation claim for the expropriation of certain shareholdings. It invoked the 1955

---

[135] *Amoco Int. Finance Corp. v. Iran* (1987) 15 IRAN–US CTR 189, para. 112.

Treaty of Amity concluded between the United States and Iran imposing a compensation standard of prompt, adequate and effective compensation. Iran claimed, however, that this treaty had been superseded by developments in general international law which, in its view, imposed less stringent compensation requirements. The Tribunal held that both norms prescribe the same standard and that, in any case, in the circumstances, the treaty had priority over the custom: 'for the purpose of this case we are in the presence of a *lex specialis*, in the form of the Treaty of Amity, which in principle prevails over general rules'.[136]

Another example is the WTO treaty contracting out of certain general customary international law rules on countermeasures.[137] In this respect, WTO rules prevail over general custom. If, over time, this general custom were to change, however, the general custom as amended would become the *lex posterior* prevailing over the WTO treaty. This would be the case unless it could be shown that the specific WTO treaty rules on countermeasures continue applying as *lex specialis*. It may also occur that the WTO treaty specifically addresses an issue (say, national treatment) which was, at the time of conclusion of the WTO treaty, not regulated in general custom. There is then, at the time of conclusion of the WTO treaty, no conflict or contracting out. However, if such general custom were, nonetheless, to develop subsequently and it conflicts with the earlier WTO rules, this general custom should, in principle, prevail over the earlier WTO treaty as *lex posterior*. But this again is subject to rebuttal in case it can be proven that the specific WTO rules on, say, national treatment continue applying as *lex specialis*.

These two situations of supervening custom in conflict with pre-existing treaty norms – i.e., treaty 'contracting out' of custom which then changes, or treaty regulating a matter dealt with in custom only subsequent to the treaty – must be distinguished from cases where (i) the treaty is silent on a matter (say, in respect of rules on burden of proof), (ii) there is general custom or a general principle of law at the time the treaty is concluded, but (iii) this custom or principle changes subsequently. In those cases, *there is no conflict* since the treaty is silent on the matter and the general custom or principle *as it evolves over time* continues to apply to the treaty pursuant to the process of 'fall-back' on general international law described in chapter 4.

---

[136] Award of 12 August 1985, 8 IRAN–US CTR 373 at 379. This was confirmed in *Phillips v. NIOC and Iran*, Case No. 39, Chamber Two, Award no. 425-39-2, 29 June 1989, para. 107.
[137] See chapter 4 above, pp. 228–36.

Treaties and custom as lex specialis *prevailing over general principles of law*
Earlier, in chapter 3, it was explained also that general principles of law, from an operational perspective, are only a 'secondary source of law'. As noted there, this is based partly on the principle of *lex specialis*. In particular *treaty norms* are most likely to be more specific than general principles of law. The same applies, but to a lesser extent, in respect of custom versus general principles of law. In both cases, the general principle of law is most likely also the *lex prior*. Hence, it will have to give way to, for example, a conflicting treaty norm on the ground of both the *lex specialis* and the *lex posterior* principles. It is most unlikely that a conflict would arise as between an existing treaty norm and a later general principle of law: either the treaty norm will have been terminated or have fallen into desuetude or the general principle will not have developed in the light of a conflicting treaty. Moreover, given the very function of general principles of law (fall-back in case there is no treaty or custom), any conflict between an existing treaty and a general principle of law should, indeed, be decided in favour of the treaty (with the exception of *jus cogens*).

Special customary law prevailing as lex specialis *over general customary law*
Finally, based also on the principle of *lex specialis*, we saw earlier that special customary international law (in terms of either subject matter or membership) prevails over general customary international law. This was confirmed in the *Right of Passage* case. There, the ICJ established the right of transit through Indian territory of private persons, civil officials and goods, on the basis of 'a constant and uniform practice' which 'was accepted as law by the Parties'.[138] Portugal had also invoked general international custom as well as general principles of law in support of its claim of a right of passage. The Court did not consider it necessary to examine whether these more general rules lead to the same result as that set out in the special custom. It simply observed: 'Where therefore the Court finds a practice clearly established between two States which was accepted by the Parties as governing the relations between them, the Court must attribute decisive effect to that practice for the purpose of determining their specific rights and obligations. Such a particular practice must prevail over any general rules.'[139]

It should be noted, however, that special custom can only prevail over general custom in case the general custom is not part of *jus cogens*. In

[138] ICJ Reports 1960, 40.   [139] *Ibid.*, 44.

addition, strong arguments exist in support of making an analogy with Arts. 41/58 of the Vienna Convention.[140] Special custom (much like an *inter se* agreement deviating from an earlier multilateral treaty) should then be allowed to prevail over general custom only in case it does not contract out of an integral obligation, i.e., in case the special custom does not affect third party rights under the general custom.

Cases where the *lex specialis* prevailed but where it was at the same time *lex posterior*

In the previous subsection, we addressed conflict between particular and general international law, the latter being either general customary international law or general principles of law. In what follows we shall focus mainly on conflict as between *two treaty norms*. Has the principle of *lex specialis* been applied so as to let a special treaty norm prevail over a conflicting, general treaty norm? In most cases where *lex specialis* was referred to as a rule to resolve conflict, the *lex specialis* was, at the same time, the *lex posterior*. Hence, on the ground of that case law it is difficult to conclude that the *lex specialis* principle prevails over the *lex posterior* rule. It is nonetheless useful to refer to some of these cases.

In the *Mavrommatis Palestine Concessions* (Jurisdiction) case, the PCIJ examined the relationship between Great Britain's 1922 Mandate over Palestine and a subsequent 1923 Protocol. The Court held that if there were a conflict between these two agreements (something that turned out not to be the case), the Protocol, being the special and more recent agreement, would prevail over the Mandate:

> It is certain that Protocol XII is an international instrument, quite distinct from and independent of the Mandate for Palestine. It deals specifically and in explicit terms with concessions such as those of M. Mavrommatis, whereas Article 11 of the Mandate deals with them only implicitly. Furthermore it is more recent in date than the Mandate. *All the conditions therefore are fulfilled which might make the clauses of the Protocol overrule those of the Mandate...in cases of doubt, the Protocol, being a special and more recent agreement, should prevail* [emphasis added].[141]

In the *Polish Postal Service in Danzig* case, the parties invoked the 1919 Treaty of Versailles and two bilateral treaties concluded between Poland and Danzig, one in 1920, the other in 1921. The PCIJ confirmed the *lex specialis* principle, stating that the more specific bilateral treaty prevails over the more general Treaty of Versailles pursuant to which the

---

[140] See chapter 6 above.   [141] PCIJ, Series A, No. 2, at 30, 31 (1924).

bilateral treaty was concluded.¹⁴² In *Jurisdiction of the European Commission of the Danube*, the PCIJ was faced with two legal instruments regulating the regime of the Danube, one general instrument, the 1919 Treaty of Versailles, and another more specific one, the 1923 Statute of the Danube. The Court applied the more specific treaty, which was at the same time the *lex posterior*.¹⁴³

Lex specialis as amongst provisions of the same treaty (or same date)

The widely acclaimed *lex specialis* principle is only really put to the test in case it is not at the same time the *lex posterior*. This may be the case, firstly, if both conflicting norms are set out in the same treaty (or, in the rather exceptional case of two norms deriving from different instruments concluded *at the same point in time*). This is what we examine in this subsection. In the next subsection we examine a second set of 'hard cases', namely where the *lex specialis* is also the *lex prior*. Importantly, whereas in the second type of cases, the *lex specialis* principle enters into conflict with Art. 30's *lex posterior* rule, in the first type of cases we discuss here (norms with the same date) there is no such conflict since Art. 30 does not apply in the first place (it applies only to 'successive treaties').

As far as conflict between treaty norms with the same date is concerned, *Case A/2* of the Iran–United States Claims Tribunal confirmed the *lex specialis* principle. There, the Tribunal examined the relationship between a 1981 Declaration referred to as 'the General Declaration' and another 1981 Declaration, of the same date, referred to as 'the Claims Settlement Declaration'. The Tribunal found as follows: 'if there were any inconsistency, it is a well recognised and universal principle of interpretation that a special provision overrides a general provision...Moreover, the terms of the Claims Settlement Declaration are so detailed and so clear that they must necessarily prevail over the purported intentions of the parties, whatever they could have been.'¹⁴⁴

That the *lex specialis* principle applies as between two instruments of the same date was also confirmed, albeit implicitly, by the ICJ in the

---

¹⁴² PCIJ, Series B, No. 11 (1925).
¹⁴³ PCIJ, Series B, No. 14, 24 (1927). For another example, see *Chemin de Fer Zeltweg (Austria v. Yugoslavia)* (1934) 3 RIAA 1795, 1803.
¹⁴⁴ *Iran–United States, Case A/2*, (1981) 1 IRAN–US CTR 101, at 104. Note, however, that *lex specialis* as referred to here by the Tribunal is not a rule of *interpretation*, but a rule on *how to resolve conflict* in case treaty interpretation does not do away with an apparent conflict.

Ambatielos case (Preliminary Objection) where the Court addressed the relationship between a 1926 treaty and an accompanying declaration of the same date. The Court held that the declaration formed an integral part of the treaty so that it had jurisdiction to decide any dispute as to the interpretation or application of the declaration pursuant to Art. 29 of the treaty. More particularly, it found that on that basis it had jurisdiction to decide whether there was a difference between the parties within the meaning of the declaration that must be referred to a Commission of Arbitration. If so, the Commission of Arbitration would decide on the merits of the difference. The Court then noted the following, and this is where the *lex specialis* principle comes into play:

> It may be contended that *because a special provision overrides a general provision*, the Declaration should override Article 29 of the Treaty...and, as it lays down a special arbitral procedure, it excludes the jurisdiction of the Court under Article 29. While it is true that the Declaration excludes the Court from functioning as the Commission of Arbitration, it is equally true that it lies with the Court to decide precisely whether there should be a reference to a Commission of Arbitration [emphasis added].[145]

Conflict between WTO treaty rules offers another example. The WTO treaty, including its approximately sixty different agreements, understandings and other legal instruments, was concluded as a 'single package' at one point in time.[146] Even GATT 1947 was reconcluded as part of GATT 1994, in turn an integral component of the Marrakesh Agreement. We saw earlier that a number of explicit conflict clauses are provided for in the WTO treaty itself, resolving conflict, for example, as between the Marrakesh Agreement and other multilateral WTO agreements.[147] For those internal WTO conflicts not resolved by explicit conflict clauses, resort must be had to the *lex specialis* principle (knowing that the *lex posterior* principle does not apply to treaty norms of the same date).

Lex specialis *and the General Interpretative Note to Annex 1A*
One of the explicit conflict clauses in the WTO treaty – the General Interpretative Note to Annex 1A – can, indeed, be seen as a confirmation of the *lex specialis* principle. This note prescribes that '[i]n the event of conflict between a provision of the [GATT] and a provision of another agreement in Annex 1A [e.g., the TBT or SPS agreement or the Agriculture or

---

[145] ICJ Reports 1952, 28 at 44.   [146] See above, p. 376.
[147] See above, pp. 355–61.

Subsidy agreement]...the provision of the other agreement shall prevail to the extent of the conflict'.

The note thereby gives a preference to *the more specific agreement*: GATT can be said to deal with trade in goods generally; the agreements in Annex 1A ('Multilateral Agreements on Trade in Goods') can be considered as dealing with particular issues or sectors of trade in goods (such as sanitary measures or textiles).

Note, however, that the General Interpretative Note gives preference to other Annex 1A agreements *as agreements*, i.e., irrespective of whether the particular provision in those agreements is actually more specific than the conflicting GATT provision. It is, indeed, not precluded that a conflict may arise with an Annex 1A provision that is *less specific* than the contradictory GATT provision. However, even in that case the Annex 1A provision must prevail. Consequently, the General Interpretative Note to Annex 1A does to a large extent confirm the *lex specialis* principle, but in certain circumstances it may contradict this principle.

Moreover, it should be recalled that the General Interpretative Note must not always result in giving preference to the most stringent obligation in terms of trade liberalisation.[148] Other Annex 1A agreements, such as the TBT agreement, may largely be more specific and place additional obligations on WTO members. But this is not *necessarily* so. They may also detract from GATT obligations in that they can provide for explicit rights or permissions to restrict trade, whereas GATT would have prohibited such restrictions. As noted before, the WTO is not the proverbial cyclist who needs to move on (i.e., further liberalise) in order to survive. New WTO rules, such as the other Annex 1A agreements, may not only further liberalise trade, they may also allow for certain new instances where trade restrictions are permitted. This is why the following statement by the Appellate Body in *EC – Asbestos* is far too categorical: 'the *TBT Agreement* imposes obligations on Members that seem to be *different* from, and *additional* to, the obligations imposed on Members under the GATT 1994'.

It may be the case that the TBT agreement only adds obligations to those in GATT, but this is not necessarily so. Nothing precludes the TBT agreement from detracting from previous GATT obligations. For example, GATT Art. XX provides for an exhaustive list of justifications, whereas TBT Art. 2.2 refers to *any* 'legitimate objective'. In that event as well, the TBT explicit rights or permissions to restrict trade must, pursuant to the

---

[148] See chapter 4 above, pp. 197–9.

conflict clause in the General Interpretative Note to Annex 1A, prevail over GATT obligations to liberalise trade.

The GATT–GATS overlap: no explicit conflict clause, but lex specialis *may resolve the conflict*
WTO treaty provisions have the same date and many internal conflicts are resolved by explicit conflict clauses. But what happens in case there is a conflict between two WTO rules and no such treaty-based conflict clause can be found? This may be the case in respect of a GATT rule in conflict with a GATS provision or a GATT/TRIPS or GATS/TRIPS conflict. *In respect of none of these conflicts does the WTO treaty provide for explicit conflict clauses.*[149] Hence, the conflict rules in general international law must be applied and resort may be had, in particular, to the *lex specialis* principle.

Let us take the GATT/GATS conflict as an example. It is the only conflict as between the three WTO pillars (GATT/GATS/TRIPS) that has received attention in WTO jurisprudence.[150]

GATT and GATS are not 'mutually exclusive' The GATT does not include a general provision that defines the material scope of application of the GATT agreement. To find out whether a GATT provision, such as GATT Art. III on national treatment, applies one must focus on the language of that particular provision. Although GATT is generally recognised to apply to trade *in goods* and is listed in Annex 1A entitled 'Multilateral Agreements on Trade *in Goods*', nowhere is the scope of GATT explicitly limited to trade in goods. On the contrary, many GATT provisions seem to have a rather broader scope. GATT Art. III:4, for example, explicitly provides that it applies to 'all laws, regulations and requirements *affecting* [the] internal sale, offering for sale, purchase, transportation, distribution or use [of products]' (emphasis added).

Hence, GATT Art. III, with its broad 'affecting' requirement and reference to 'offering for sale', 'transportation' and 'distribution', does seem to cover also elements of trade in services, in particular in the sectors of wholesale, transportation and distribution services *as long as the services measure has an effect on goods.*

---

[149] See above, p. 361.
[150] On the GATT/GATS overlap see John Gaffney, 'The GATT and the GATS: Should they be Mutually Exclusive Agreements?' (1999) 12 *Leiden Journal of International Law* 135, and, more generally, Werner Zdouc, 'The Triangle of GATT/GATS and TRIPS', in Thomas Cottier, Petros C. Mavroidis and Marion Panizzon (eds.), *Intellectual Property: Trade, Competition, and Sustainable Development: The World Trade Forum*, vol. III (University of Michigan Press, forthcoming).

The material scope of GATS, in contrast, is generally defined up front in GATS Art. I. GATS 'applies to measures...affecting trade in services' (GATS Art. I:1). Pursuant to GATS Art. XXVIII(c), such measures include measures in respect of (i) the purchase, payment or use of a service; (ii) the access to and use of, in connection with the supply of a service, services which are required by those Members to be offered to the public generally; (iii) the presence, including commercial presence, of persons of a Member for the supply of a service in the territory of another Member.

GATS Art. I:2 defines 'trade in services' as the supply of a service in one of four modes (cross-border supply, consumption abroad, commercial presence and movement of natural persons). Hence, although GATS (unlike GATT) does define its general scope of application, it does so in a very broad manner, using, in particular, a rather vague 'effects' criterion ('measures...*affecting* trade in services'), very much like, for example, GATT Art. III.

There is, of course, nothing wrong with broadly defining the scope of an agreement. It means only that many measures may fall under it. But if two equally broadly defined agreements deal with subject matters as closely related as measures 'affecting trade in goods' and measures 'affecting trade in services', the potential for overlap is vast. Indeed, whenever a measure restricts the supply of, for example, foreign distribution *services*, the measure will most likely 'affect' also the trade in the foreign *goods* normally supplied by these foreign distributors. Or, conversely, whenever a measure restricts the importation of particular *goods*, such restriction is very likely to lead also to less demand for, and hence a restriction in, the foreign *services* that may be needed to distribute and sell these imported goods. Where there is potential for overlap, there is, of course, potential for conflict, especially if the two regimes set out a number of substantially different obligations as GATT and GATS do[151] (unlike, for example, the goods versus services regime under the EC treaty).

When they overlap, GATT and GATS rules may simply accumulate (i.e., either confirm or complement each other), but they may also conflict. GATT and GATS may, first of all, set out mutually exclusive obligations (most of conflict situations 1 and 2 referred to in chapter 4

---

[151] In particular, the national treatment obligation in GATT Art. III applies across the board, whereas national treatment under GATS Art. XVI applies only in service sectors where explicit commitments by the member in question were made.

above). But they may also (and more likely) raise conflicts of the obligation versus explicit-right type (conflict situations 3 and 4 set out in chapter 4):

(i) a GATT norm may prohibit something which a GATS norm permits (say, a GATT Art. III prohibition on discriminating periodicals on the ground that they include certain advertising versus no national treatment commitments in the advertising sector under GATS Art. XVII);[152]
(ii) a GATT norm may permit something which a GATS norm prohibits (say, an anti-dumping duty on steel justified under the Anti-Dumping agreement versus the MFN obligation in GATS Art. II in respect of the distribution and wholesale of steel, not providing for exceptions in case of dumping).[153]

If any of these conflict situations arise, in favour of which norm must they be decided? WTO jurisprudence has, first of all, acknowledged the potential for *overlap* between GATT and GATS, thereby rejecting the argument that GATT and GATS are mutually exclusive. In *EC – Bananas* the Appellate Body found as follows:

Given the respective scope of application of the two agreements [GATT and GATS], they may or may not overlap, depending on the nature of the measures at issue. Certain measures could be found to fall exclusively within the scope of the GATT 1994, when they affect trade in goods as goods. Certain measures could be found to fall exclusively within the scope of the GATS, when they affect the supply of services as services. There is yet a third category of measures that could be found to fall within the scope of both the GATT 1994 and the GATS. These are measures that involve a service relating to a particular good or a service supplied in conjunction with a particular good. In all such cases in this third category, the measure in question could be scrutinized under both

---

[152] This was the situation in *Canada – Periodicals*, where the United States had invoked violations of GATT and Canada argued, in defence, that GATT did not apply since the measure was a GATS measure. The panel and the Appellate Body rejected Canada's argument on the rather narrow ground that the measure did fall under GATT, leaving it open as to whether it fell also under GATS. Instead, the panel should have examined whether both agreements applied, and, if so, whether a conflict between the two arose in the particular case. If there was such a conflict, it should then have decided which provision must prevail. This would have been most likely the GATT prohibition as *lex specialis*. See below, pp. 404–5.

[153] The anti-dumping duty on steel from one particular company or country could then be argued to violate the MFN rights of that country in particular service sectors. Indeed, if it can no longer export its steel because of the higher duties, that country's distributors as service suppliers may also be affected and thus be discriminated against in comparison to other foreign distributors whose steel is not subject to anti-dumping duties.

the GATT 1994 and the GATS. However, while the same measure could be scrutinized under both agreements, the specific aspects of that measure examined under each agreement could be different. Under the GATT 1994, the focus is on how the measure affects the goods involved. Under the GATS, the focus is on how the measure affects the supply of the service or the service suppliers involved. Whether a certain measure affecting the supply of a service related to a particular good is scrutinized under the GATT 1994 or the GATS, or both, is a matter that can only be determined on a case-by-case basis.

This conclusion that there are measures (i) falling only under GATT, (ii) falling only under GATS, and (iii) falling under both GATT and GATS, was unavoidable given the broadly defined scope of application of both GATT and GATS, referred to earlier. One could even go as far as saying that it will be difficult to find a measure that falls *only* under GATT or *only* under GATS (that is, measures of type (i) or (ii)), since, as noted above, most goods measures are likely to have some effect also on services, and vice versa.

In any event, it would have been legally unsound to 'interpret' the respective scopes of application of GATT and GATS in such a way as to *exclude* overlaps. If the measure at issue, on the basis of the 'clear meaning' of the two agreements, does, indeed, fall within the scope of both agreements, 'interpretation' cannot change this without effectively changing the content of the agreements.[154] In these circumstances, to 'interpret' the scope of application of one agreement narrowly so as to conclude that only the other applies would, indeed, go against the principle of 'effective treaty interpretation'. We are faced here with a situation, referred to earlier,[155] where 'effective treaty interpretation' works both ways. To find that only GATT applies – because, for example, the measure is 'essentially' a goods measure – would disregard the *effet utile* of GATS. To say that only GATS applies – because, for example, the measure is 'predominantly' a services measure – would disregard the *effet utile* of GATT.

GATT and GATS may accumulate As noted before, in the event of overlap between GATS and GATT, the provisions may, firstly, be *cumulative* in nature (discussed in chapter 4 above, pp. 161–2). This will be the case, for example, when a GATT obligation is simply *confirmed* from another (services) angle by a similar GATS obligation in respect of the same

---

[154] See chapter 5 above, pp. 245–6.   [155] See chapter 5 above, pp. 250–1.

measure. In case a breach is then found under these two obligations, bringing the measure in conformity with GATT will most likely imply also conformity with GATS. In other words, in case of GATT/GATS obligations which essentially confirm each other (albeit from a different perspective), it may not be of much use to find the additional GATS or GATT breach. The panel or Appellate Body could then even not examine the second agreement on the grounds of judicial economy.[156] This was arguably the case in the EC – Bananas dispute where the Appellate Body found that the EC import licensing regime for bananas violated MFN and national treatment under both GATT and GATS. This would arguably have been the case also had the Appellate Body confirmed the panel's finding in Canada – Autos that Canada's import duty exemption for certain motor vehicles violated the MFN obligation under both GATT and GATS.[157]

However, GATT and GATS may also accumulate in that the obligation under one agreement *adds to or complements* the obligation under the other (without contradiction). In that case, a panel *must* examine both agreements. Bringing the measure into compliance with, for example, GATT will then normally not mean compliance also with GATS.

GATT and GATS may conflict Instead of accumulating – in the sense of either confirming or complementing each other – a GATT/GATS overlap may also constitute conflict, as noted before, especially of the type obligation versus explicit right (conflict situations 3 and 4 in chapter 4). One and the same measure may fall under both GATT and GATS, but the solution offered by each agreement may be different. As noted by the Appellate Body in Canada – Autos: 'In cases where the same measure can be scrutinized under *both* the GATT 1994 and the GATS...the focus of the inquiry, and the specific aspects of the measure to be scrutinized,

---

[156] To find an additional breach under the other agreement may, indeed, not further 'solve the dispute' since it would, in terms of the implementation required, not have added value (see the criterion for exercise of judicial economy in the Appellate Body report on *Australia – Salmon*).

[157] The Appellate Body reversed the panel's finding of violation under GATS on the ground that the panel had not sufficiently explained why GATS applied in the first place (Appellate Body report on *Canada – Autos*, para. 167: 'The Panel did not show that the measure at issue affects wholesale trade services of motor vehicles, as services, or wholesale trade service suppliers of motor vehicles, *in their capacity as service suppliers*', emphasis in original).

under each agreement, will be different because the subjects of the two agreements are different.'[158]

Nonetheless both agreements apply to one and the same measure and may lead to a contradictory result (under one agreement the measure may be permitted, under the other it may be prohibited). If so, they deal with the 'same subject-matter' but differently.

In case of a GATT/GATS conflict, as noted before, 'interpretation' cannot resolve the conflict.[159] To resolve genuine conflict one must choose sides based on conflict rules, not interpretation. In GATT/GATS conflicts as well one must first acknowledge the existence of a conflict and then apply general international law rules on how to resolve conflict.

In *Canada – Periodicals*, for example, the potential for conflict was not even acknowledged. Canada's defence that under GATS it did not have obligations (amounting, allegedly, to an explicit right or permission to impose the measure at issue) was examined only in terms of an argument to interpret GATT in such a way that it would not apply in the first place. Of course, the measure *did* fall within the scope of GATT. But it arguably fell also within the scope of GATS. And if that were the case, there may have been a conflict and the GATS rule may have prevailed so that the GATT provision that must give way did, upon closer examination, *not* apply. If so, this would have been the result *not* of the *wording* of GATT Art. III but of *the conflict with GATS*. This aspect was not examined by the Appellate Body. Instead, it presumed that once a measure falls within the scope of GATT, GATT must necessarily apply irrespective of there being a conflicting GATS provision. Hence, in the view of the Appellate Body, *any GATT/GATS conflict of the type GATT prohibition/GATS explicit right must be decided in favour of GATT*. It noted, indeed, that '[t]he entry into force of the GATS...does not diminish the scope of application of the GATT 1994'.

But it gave this general preference to GATT without any textual reference, nor reference to any conflict rule. In the absence of an explicit conflict clause in favour of GATT and given that GATT and GATS are part of the same treaty (so that their date is the same), such *a priori* preference for GATT is not justified. It flows from a general misunderstanding that new WTO rules can only further liberalise trade. The WTO provides for a set of international law norms which may, like any other norms, be adapted or supplemented *either way*: towards further liberalisation or

---

[158] Appellate Body report on *Canada – Autos*, para. 160. See also, but less categorically, its report on *EC – Bananas*, para. 221: 'the specific aspects of [the] measure examined under each agreement could be different'.

[159] See chapter 5 above, pp. 250–1.

taking a step backwards, allowing for certain additional instances where trade restrictions may be imposed. Unlike the EC, the WTO's objective is not a 'single world market'.

Lex specialis *may resolve the conflict*   Given that the conflict rules set out in previous sections and in chapter 6 do not resolve GATT/GATS conflicts – there is, for example, no conflict clause and both GATT and GATS have the same date – in order to resolve GATT/GATS conflicts resort must be had to the *lex specialis* principle. The decisive question should then be: which of the two legal provisions covers the factual circumstances more closely and precisely? The detail in the respective GATT/GATS provision will count, but so too will the focus of the measure in question: is it 'essentially' or 'predominantly' a measure regulating goods or services (e.g., in terms of its structure and scope or economic effect)?

Under the examples of potential conflicts given above,[160] such examination should lead to the conclusion that (i) in the example of *Canada – Periodicals*, the GATT provision was the more specific one;[161] and (ii) in the example of anti-dumping duties permitted under GATT but prohibited under GATS, it is the anti-dumping agreement that deals more specifically with the measure at issue so that, there as well, GATT must prevail over GATS.

Does the *lex specialis* principle prevail over the *lex posterior* principle?

If the *lex specialis* norm is the later in time, should it still prevail? In other words, must the *lex posterior* principle give way to that of *lex specialis*? Some authors answer this question in the affirmative based solely on the adage *generalia specialibus non derogant*.[162] They do not refer to case

---

[160] See above, p. 401.
[161] See, for example, the Appellate Body report on *Canada – Periodicals* (at 17), explaining why the measure at issue (a provision in the Canadian Excise Tax Act) is a 'goods measure': 'First of all, the measure is an excise tax imposed on split-run editions of periodicals. We note that the title to Part V.1 of the Excise Tax Act reads, "TAX ON SPLIT-RUN PERIODICALS", not "tax on advertising"... Secondly, a periodical is a good comprised of two components: editorial content and advertising content. Both components can be viewed as having services attributes, but they combine to form a physical product – the periodical itself.'
[162] See, for example, Hans Aufricht, 'Supersession of Treaties in International Law' (1952) 37 *Cornell Law Quarterly* 655 at 698: 'if the scope of the later treaty provisions is broader than that of the earlier ones the maxim *lex posterior generalis non derogat priori specialis* applies'. See also Neumann, 'Die Koordination', 35 (referring in support to Schilling, *Rang*, 455–8) and Wolfrum and Matz, 'Interplay', 445–80.

law nor, more importantly, do they explain on what legal basis Art. 30 of the Vienna Convention can be set aside.

Earlier, we set out the difficulties that may arise in applying the *lex posterior* rule in Art. 30,[163] especially when it comes to multilateral treaties to which states may accede, which may be amended or regularly 'reconcluded'. In that respect, we noted also that it is difficult to identify many of today's regulatory treaties with one particular moment in time. These treaties could be seen rather as 'continuing treaties', to which the state parties regularly and on a continuous basis reaffirm their consent. In those 'hard cases' it may no longer be consonant with the intent of the parties in question to define either treaty as earlier or later. Looked at from the angle of the underlying rationale of Art. 30 (that is, preference must be given to the latest expression of state consent), it could then be concluded, on a case-by-case basis, that Art. 30 should not apply.

But, apart from the fact that Art. 30's objective would no longer be met, how can one legally justify this setting aside of Art. 30? There seem to be two ways.

First, as hinted at earlier, in those 'hard cases' one could conclude that there are no 'successive treaties' and hence decide that Art. 30 does *not* apply in the first place. One could then simply apply the *lex specialis* principle, even if from certain points of view the *lex specialis* is the earlier norm. There would then be no conflict between the *lex posterior* and the *lex specialis* rule since the former does not apply. The *lex specialis* principle would then offer the solution, either as a self-standing principle of customary law or a general principle of law, or as a particularly useful method to detect the 'current expression of state consent'. That Art. 30 of the Vienna Convention left room for application of the *lex specialis* principle, even if the more specific norm was the earlier in time, was confirmed in the *travaux préparatoires* of Art. 30, discussed above (p. 364) The 'residual nature' of Art. 30 is confirmed also in Art. 30(2) and the ILC Commentary, although the focus of those is on *explicit* conflict clauses.[164]

Second, it could be submitted that the adage *generalia specialibus non derogat* is part of customary international law or a general principle of law, pursuant to which the more specific law must *always* prevail over the more general law *even if the more general law is later in time*. Note that this would go a step further than claiming that customary law or general principles of law prescribe that a special law prevails over a more general

---

[163] See above, pp. 367–81. [164] See above, p. 363.

one. It would go as far as saying that even if the *lex posterior* principle in Art. 30 would apply and favour the later, more general law, the earlier *lex specialis* nonetheless prevails.¹⁶⁵ Paragraph 8 of the preamble to the Vienna Convention includes a safeguards clause in which it is affirmed 'that the rules of customary international law will continue to govern questions not regulated by the provisions of the present Convention'. But is not the question of successive treaties regulated in Art. 30 *without* mentioning the *lex specialis* principle so that if a norm is, indeed, later in time it prevails *even if the other norm is more special*? Or could it be said that the *lex specialis* principle continued to exist as custom (or a general principle of law) alongside the *lex posterior* rule and that, in the event of conflict between the two, the Vienna Convention does not 'govern the question' so that resort must be had to another custom (or general principle of law) – namely, *generalia specialibus non derogat* – to resolve that conflict? Some support for the latter proposition may be found in the *travaux préparatoires* of Art. 30,¹⁶⁶ but, as noted earlier, it is very difficult to find state practice or case law that supports the adage *generalia specialibus non derogat*. Hence, its value as a custom can be questioned.

The first of these two grounds for letting the *lex specialis* prevail – i.e., in certain circumstances Art. 30 does not apply in the first place – is the most convincing one. It is also the one that would protect legal security and predictability the most. An established *lex specialis* ought then to prevail over another norm, alleged to be *lex posterior*, only in case it is impossible or would be absurd to put one single or definite time-label on either of the two norms: that is, in the event that the two treaties in question, as between the states concerned, cannot be seen as 'successive' so that Art. 30 does not apply in the first place. Such examination must be made on a case-by-case basis, so that sometimes the *lex posterior* principle will prevail, other times, that of *lex specialis*.

As noted already, the second ground – based on the adage *generalia specialibus non derogant* being part of customary law or a general principle of law – is difficult to establish: if support can be found in state practice that a special law prevails over a more general one, it is hard to find instances where states acknowledged that a treaty which is clearly later in time must give way to an earlier one on the ground that the

---

[165] As is argued by the authors referred to in note 162 above.
[166] In support see the statements made by Sinclair and the Expert Consultant at the Vienna Conference, referred to in notes 81–3 above.

earlier treaty is more special. Moreover, under this second ground the *lex specialis* would *always* prevail over the other norm, even if it is perfectly possible (and would make logical sense) to determine their respective dates of conclusion. This would grant the *lex specialis* principle an absolute higher legal standing than the *lex posterior* rule and this *even though only the latter was codified in the Vienna Convention*. The absence of the *lex specialis* principle in the Vienna Convention must be given meaning and makes it very difficult, if not impossible, to justify the position that a *lex specialis* must *always* prevail over another norm validly identified under Art. 30 as the *lex posterior*.

In sum, the *lex posterior* rule in Art. 30 is and should remain the rule of first resort. It is for the party making the claim to prove that, although it could be said that one of the norms is, from certain viewpoints, later in time, this norm should nonetheless give way, essentially because Art. 30 does not apply. To give wider credence to the *lex specialis* principle (without further codification) would threaten legal security and predictability in the field of conflict of norms.

This being said, our examination above does attribute great importance to the *lex specialis* rule in case, for example, 'continuing treaties' are involved. In a number of cases involving multilateral treaties it will, indeed, be difficult to apply Art. 30 since there are no 'successive treaties' so that the conflict must be decided in favour of the more specific norm. This seems to be what the ICJ did in one of the few cases where an allegedly 'later norm' (environmental conventions) had to give way to a seemingly 'earlier', more specific norm (law on the use of force). Given the 'continuing' nature of the norms involved, it would have been difficult to put a single time-label on either of these norms and to define one of them as the 'later in time'. In respect of environmental norms that would allegedly be violated by the use of nuclear weapons, the Court did 'not consider that the treaties in question could have intended to deprive a State of the exercise of its right of self-defence under international law because of its obligations to protect the environment. Nonetheless, States must take environmental considerations into account when assessing what is necessary and proportionate in the pursuit of legitimate military objectives.'[167]

Here, we have an example of an earlier *lex specialis* (law on self-defence and armed conflict) contradicting a later, more general norm (environmental rules). In this instance, there is, indeed, a conflict since nowhere

---

[167] Advisory Opinion on *Threat or Use of Nuclear Weapons*, ICJ Reports 1996, para. 30.

does the environmental norm itself provide for an exception in armed conflict. Given the special character of the law on self-defence and armed conflict, it is this *lex specialis* that prevails. Nonetheless, this *lex specialis* (necessity and proportionality of use of force) must be *interpreted* with reference to the *lex generalis* (environmental norms).[168] The ICJ did not explicitly acknowledge conflict but did apply only the law on self-defence and armed conflict.

Conclusion on the principle of *lex specialis* as a conflict rule

In sum, the principle that the more specific norm prevails over the more general one must be accepted as a solution to conflict where none of the other conflict rules set out earlier applies and in case:

(i) the *lex specialis* is contracting out of general international law (hence Art. 30 on conflict between *treaty norms* does not apply);
(ii) the *lex specialis* is, at the same time, the *lex posterior* (hence, in the event of conflict between treaties, the principle *confirms* the result reached under Art. 30);
(iii) both treaty norms in question have the same date, e.g. because they are set out in one and the same treaty (hence Art. 30 on *successive* treaties does not apply); or
(iv) given, for example, the 'continuing' or 'living' nature of the treaties involved, the two conflicting treaties cannot be said to be 'successive' in time (hence Art. 30 on *successive* treaties does not apply).

However, in the event that Art. 30 on 'successive treaties' does apply, the fact that the earlier norm is *lex specialis* should not prevent the later *lex generalis* from prevailing.[169]

Thus, the *lex specialis* principle as conflict rule is both limited and broad. It is limited in the sense that it cannot, in my view, overrule the *lex posterior* principle in Art. 30. It is broad to the extent that it will, nonetheless, be the decisive criterion in many cases (especially where Art. 30 does not apply).

---

[168] *Ibid.*: 'Respect for the environment is one of the elements that go to assessing whether an action is in conformity with the principles of necessity and proportionality.'
[169] This is the conclusion reached also in Nguyen Quoc Dinh, P. Daillier and A. Pellet, *Droit International Public* (1999) Montreal: Wilson & Lafleur, para. 173, at 270: 'Si par contre le traité restreint est antérieur, et dans le silence du traité postérieur, le principe *lex posterior* l'emporte sur le principe *in toto jure*... [that is, *lex specialis*] (superiorité du traité postérieur), conformément à la volonté implicite des Etats.'

Lex specialis in forms other than as a rule to resolve conflict

Above, we examined the content and consequences of the *lex specialis* principle as a rule to resolve conflict in the applicable law. Nonetheless, *lex specialis* is often also referred to in different contexts, not involving conflict.

In those other cases, *lex specialis* is invoked as the more specific norm which supplements the more general one without contradiction. The *lex specialis* and the *lex generalis* then simply accumulate. This is often the case, for example, in respect of treaty or custom supplementing general principles of law (discussed in chapter 3). One could refer also to more specific treaties supplementing so-called framework treaties or *traités-cadres*, without conflict between the two.

A *lex specialis* supplementing a *lex generalis* must always be interpreted in the light of the *lex generalis*, and vice versa.[170] This interpretation may result in an apparent conflict being 'interpreted away' (discussed in chapter 5). For example, in its Advisory Opinion on *Threat or Use of Nuclear Weapons*, the ICJ, invoking elements of *lex specialis*, found that 'the most directly relevant applicable law...is that relating to the use of force enshrined in the United Nations Charter and the law applicable in armed conflict which regulates the conduct of hostilities, together with any specific treaties on nuclear weapons the Court might determine to be relevant'.[171] The Court considered that the right not to be arbitrarily deprived of one's life – guaranteed in Art. 6 of the International Covenant on Civil and Political Rights (in this case, the *lex generalis*) – applies also in hostilities. It noted, nonetheless, that '[t]he test of what is an arbitrary deprivation of life...then falls to be determined by the applicable *lex specialis*, namely, the law applicable in armed conflict'.

This is an instance where *lex specialis* is used to *interpret* the terms of another, more general norm (*in casu*, the words 'arbitrarily deprived'). It does not conflict with nor, *a fortiori*, overrule the other norm. Thus, in this case both the *lex specialis* and the *lex generalis* could be applied side by side, the *lex specialis* playing the greater role of the two.

In the first two subsections below we focus on two specific arguments based on *lex specialis* (other than *lex specialis* as a conflict rule): first, *lex specialis* as an argument for an adjudicator to examine a more specific norm *before* he or she examines a more general norm; second, *lex specialis*

---

[170] This is the case even if the *lex specialis* contracts out of the *lex generalis*. See chapter 4 above.

[171] ICJ Reports 1996, para. 34.

as an argument for an adjudicator to examine and apply *only* the more specific norm. The first argument is correct, the second one is difficult to sustain. Thereafter, we examine the use made of *lex specialis* as a rule of treaty interpretation, although there it largely coincides with the principle of effectiveness. In a last subsection we examine *lex specialis* elements that are at play in the principle of speciality that applies to the powers of international organisations.

Lex specialis *as a reason to examine the more specific norm first*
In the WTO context, *lex specialis* has been referred to on several occasions as a reason to *examine* the most specific WTO agreement *first*. Under this approach, a WTO panel should normally start its examination by assessing those claims under the WTO agreement or provision that is established as *lex specialis*. As the Appellate Body noted in *EC – Bananas*, after finding that both the GATT and the Licensing Agreement applied to the measure at issue: 'the Panel, in our view, should have applied the *Licensing Agreement* first, since this agreement deals specifically, and in detail, with the administration of import licensing procedures'.[172]

In *EC – Hormones* too, where claims of violation under both GATT and the SPS agreement were made, Canada argued that 'the SPS Agreement is the *lex specialis* for a review of sanitary measures and should, therefore, be addressed first'.[173] The panel followed this suggestion by first examining the complainants' SPS claims, *inter alia*, on the ground that '[t]he SPS Agreement specifically addresses the type of measure in dispute'.[174] In *Argentina – Footwear* as well, the Appellate Body, when faced with Arts. II:1(a) and II:1(b) of GATT, noted: 'Paragraph (b) prohibits a specific kind of practice that will always be inconsistent with paragraph (a)...Because the language of Article II:1(b), first sentence, is more specific and germane to the case at hand, our interpretative analysis begins with, and focuses on, that provision.'[175]

In *US – Shrimp*, the Appellate Body stressed that under GATT Art. XX a panel must first examine 'the specific exemptions provided for in Article XX' and only thereafter assess whether also the standards in the *chapeau*

---

[172] Appellate Body report on *EC – Bananas*, para. 204. For an example where the Appellate Body itself failed first to examine the most specific agreement (*in casu*, the TBT agreement) without apparent justification (other than a statement that it felt insecure about making findings under the TBT agreement for the very first time), see *EC – Asbestos* (discussed in Pauwelyn, 'Cross-agreement').
[173] Panel report on *EC – Hormones* (Canadian complaint), para. 8.37.
[174] *Ibid.*, para. 8.45.
[175] Appellate Body report on *Argentina – Footwear*, para. 45.

of Art. XX are met, standards that are 'necessarily broad in scope and reach'.[176]

Lex specialis as a reason to examine only the more specific norm
However, in a situation where *lex specialis* supplements the *lex generalis* (without conflict), to say that the *lex specialis* must be examined first does not amount to saying that the *lex generalis* no longer applies. Both norms apply and it makes logical sense to examine first the *lex specialis*. But nothing precludes that the *lex generalis* is still relevant and adds certain rights or obligations. Moroever, in case there is conflict between the two, the fact that a norm is *lex specialis* is not a guarantee that it will prevail. As pointed out earlier, the *lex specialis* may, for example, be the earlier in time that must, pursuant to Art. 30, give way to a later *lex generalis*.

The erroneous position that a *lex specialis* necessarily disapplies and eclipses the *lex generalis* has nonetheless been adopted by a number of states in recent disputes. In the WTO context, for example, Indonesia (in *Indonesia – Autos*)[177] submitted that GATT and the Subsidies agreement are mutually exclusive and that, as soon as the Subsidies agreement applies (the Subsidies agreement being *lex specialis*), GATT (as *lex generalis*) no longer applies. The argument was rejected by the panel. Indeed, assuming that agreements like the TBT or Subsidies agreements are *lex specialis* as opposed to the GATT, this does not mean that a given measure, once found to be subject to the TBT or Subsidies agreement, no longer falls under the GATT. To the contrary, both agreements continue to apply and, in the event of conflict, this conflict must be solved by the conflict rules set out above (such as the General Interpretative Note to Annex 1A).

In *Argentina – Safeguards*, the Appellate Body explicitly confirmed that a *lex specialis* does not vacate or subsume a *lex generalis*. The case involved the relationship between GATT Art. XIX and the more specific Safeguards agreement. The Appellate Body found as follows: 'We see nothing...that suggests an intention by the Uruguay Round negotiators to *subsume* the requirements of Article XIX of the GATT 1994 within the

---

[176] Appellate Body report on *US – Shrimp*, para. 120. See, in contrast, and against its normal line of reasoning first to examine the *lex specialis*, the Appellate Body finding in *EC – Hormones*, at para. 250: 'We are, of course, surprised by the fact that the Panel did not begin its analysis of this whole case by focusing on Article 2 that is captioned "Basic Rights and Obligations", an approach that appears logically attractive.'

[177] Panel report on *Indonesia – Autos*, paras. 5.129 ff.

Agreement of Safeguards and thus to render those requirements no longer applicable.'[178]

A similar submission to that made by Indonesia in *Indonesia – Autos* was made by Japan in the *Southern Bluefin Tuna* case.[179] There, Japan argued as follows: 'In accordance with generally accepted principles, the provisions of a *lex specialis* not only specify and implement the principles of an anterior framework agreement; they exhaust and supplant those principles as long as the implementing agreement remains in force.'[180] In response, New Zealand and Australia argued the following:

> The contention that the 1993 Convention [allegedly a *lex specialis*] 'covers' and thus eclipses the obligations in respect of...UNCLOS [allegedly the *lex generalis*] is wrong in fact, and the principle of 'coverage' is unknown to international law. The array of modern standards of international law has been achieved by a process of accretion and cumulation, not by erosion and reduction. Only where there is actual inconsistency between two treaties do questions of exclusion arise.[181]

The arbitrators sided with New Zealand and Australia, rejecting the Japanese argument that *lex specialis* eclipses *lex generalis* on the following grounds:

> [I]t is a commonplace of international law and State practice for more than one treaty to bear upon a particular dispute...[T]here is frequently a parallelism of treaties, both in their substantive content and in their provisions for settlement of disputes arising thereunder. The current range of international legal obligations benefits from a process of accretion and cumulation; in the practice of States, the conclusion of an implementing convention does not necessarily vacate the obligations imposed by the framework convention.[182]

This generally confirmed refusal to regard *lex specialis* as 'eclipsing' *lex generalis* is an element in support also of the thesis defended across this work, namely that WTO law (as a *lex specialis*) must be applied in the context of public international law more generally. WTO law does not 'eclipse' that other law.[183]

---

[178] Appellate Body report on *Argentina – Safeguards*, para. 83. Recall that in this situation the Safeguards agreement explicitly refers back to GATT Art. XIX, so that there is no conflict between the two (see chapter 4 above, pp. 163–4).

[179] *Australia and New Zealand v. Japan*, Award of 4 August 2000, posted on the internet at www.worldbank.org/icsid/bluefintuna/main.htm.

[180] *Ibid.*, para. 38, point (c).   [181] *Ibid.*, para. 41, point (g).

[182] *Ibid.*, para. 52.   [183] See chapter 2 above.

Lex specialis *as a rule of treaty interpretation*

Lex specialis considerations may play a role also when interpreting different treaty provisions. Nonetheless, when limiting treaty interpretation to its true sense, that is, giving meaning to terms in a treaty pursuant to Arts. 31 and 32 of the Vienna Convention, *lex specialis* offers little help. At best, it coincides with the principle of effectiveness. For example, if one treaty norm states that it is an exception to another norm, i.e., that it is a specific carve-out from this other norm, this first treaty norm or *lex specialis* must be given effect and 'prevail' over the general rule (the way GATT Art. XX 'prevails' over GATT Art. III in respect of measures 'necessary to protect human health').[184] In that case, as we saw earlier,[185] there is, however, no conflict of norms, since one norm explicitly delimits the scope of application of the other and in one given circumstance only one of two norms finds application (either the general rule or the exception, if the conditions for the latter are met). Based on the presumption against conflict and applying the conflict-avoidance techniques set out earlier, *lex specialis* may also be resorted to so as to give full effect to more special treaty provisions, notwithstanding other, more general ones.[186] Nonetheless, in the event that a genuine conflict arises between these two norms, the conflict rules set out earlier must apply and *lex specialis as a rule of treaty interpretation* cannot resolve the conflict. As pointed out above, the principle of effectiveness can then work both ways.[187] To give too much effect to the *lex specialis* risks reducing the *lex generalis* to a

---

[184] In the same sense, see the PCIJ *Case Concerning the Payment of Various Serbian Loans Issued in France*, PCIJ, Series A, Nos. 20/21, 30 (1929): 'The coupons in each of these issues either provide for payment in gold ... or carry the words " ... % Gold loan" ... It is argued that there is ambiguity because in other parts of the bonds, respectively, and in the documents preceding the several issues, mention is made of francs without specification of gold. As to this, it is sufficient to say that the mention of francs generally cannot be considered as detracting from the force of the specific provision for gold francs. The special words, according to elementary principles of interpretation, control the general expressions. The bond must be taken as a whole, and it cannot be so taken if the stipulation as to gold francs is disregarded.'

[185] See chapter 4 above, pp. 162–3.

[186] In this sense, see Peter Maxwell, *The Interpretation of Statutes* (Helsinki: Finnish Lawyers' Publishing Company, 1946), 183: 'where general words in a later Act are capable of reasonable and sensible application without extending them to subjects specially dealt with by earlier legislation ... that earlier and special legislation is not to be held indirectly repealed, altered or derogated from merely by force of such general words, without any indication of a particular intention to do so'. Nonetheless, if a genuine conflict arises, the later more general act will *not* be 'capable of reasonable and sensible application without extending them to subjects specially dealt with' in the earlier act. At that point, conflict rules must be applied, not rules of interpretation.

[187] See chapter 5 above, pp. 250–1.

nullity. In contrast, to focus too much on the *lex generalis* risks not giving the intended effect to the *lex specialis*. The PCIJ case on *Upper Silesia Minorities* illustrates that in some cases of treaty interpretation the focus must be on the *lex generalis*, rather than the *lex specialis*.[188]

The principle of 'speciality' governing international organisations
In chapter 6, we referred to the so-called 'principle of speciality' governing the competence of international organisations. As the ICJ put it in its Advisory Opinion on *Use of Nuclear Weapons* (at the request of the WHO):

international organizations are subjects of international law which do not, unlike States, possess a general competence. International organizations are governed by the 'principle of speciality', that is to say, they are invested by the States which create them with powers, the limits of which are a function of the common interests whose promotion those States entrust to them.[189]

This principle of 'limited' or 'special' competence of international organisations must be played out against the theory of 'implied powers' to be attributed to these organisations so as to enable them effectively to achieve their objectives.[190] In the *Use of Nuclear Weapons* case, this interplay led the Court to reject the WHO's request for an advisory opinion on the legality of the use of nuclear weapons for lack of jurisdiction under Art. 96(2) of the UN Charter. Pursuant to this provision, specialised UN agencies are only allowed to request an advisory opinion 'on legal questions arising *within the scope of their activities*'. The Court concluded that 'none of [the WHO's] functions has a sufficient connection with the question before it for that question to be capable of being considered as arising "within the scope of [the] activities" of the WHO'.[191] In the opinion of the ICJ:

---

[188] In that case, the Court found that a general clause whose overriding character is beyond dispute cannot validly be modified by a *lex specialis*: 'The Court in this respect recalls the fact that the provisions of Division I [of the third Part of the Geneva Convention] are provisions the terms of which were settled beforehand by the Conference of Ambassadors. They had to be accepted such as they were and subject to no modifications ... These provisions constitute a separate category among the provisions relating to the protection of minorities, *and subsequent provisions entered into between the contracting parties* [in casu, the more specific Division II of the third Part of the Geneva Convention] *cannot modify them or be construed as being contradictory and thus diminishing the extent of the protection provided*' (PCIJ, Series A, No. 15 at 30, 31 (1928), emphasis added).
[189] ICJ Reports 1996, para. 25.   [190] See chapter 6 above, pp. 286–8.
[191] ICJ Reports 1996, para. 22.

to ascribe to the WHO the competence to address the legality of the use of nuclear weapons – even in view of their health and environmental effects – would be tantamount to disregarding the principle of speciality; for such competence could not be deemed a necessary implication of the Constitution of the Organization in the light of the purposes assigned to it by its member States.[192]

Could this principle of 'speciality' be used as an argument to let, for example, a UNEP rule prevail over a WTO rule in case of a conflict of norms involving *environmental* issues *on the ground that the competence of UNEP covers environment, that of the WTO, trade?* To answer this question, a distinction must be made between (i) norms created by the state parties to either of these conventions *as states*; and (ii) norms created by the WTO or UNEP *as international organisations*. The principle of 'speciality' applies only in respect of the latter norms. Only these norms are acts taken by the WTO or UNEP as an international organisation for which it must have the necessary competence. Norms created by the states themselves, irrespective of the context in which these norms emerged (be it under the auspices of the WTO or UNEP), are not restricted by the principle of 'speciality'. The competence of *states* to conclude norms is a general one.

Acts of the international organisation

Only if, for example, the WTO norm in conflict with a UNEP norm were to be an act of the WTO (or any of its organs) as an international organisation would the principle of 'speciality' apply. However, given the broadly defined functions of the WTO (e.g., 'the forum for negotiations among its Members concerning their multilateral trade relations in matters dealt with under the agreements'),[193] it may be difficult to convince a judge that the WTO does *not* have competence to address certain environmental matters. Such argument may be successful, nonetheless, if the WTO *as an organisation* (say, the SPS or TBT Committee) were to start adopting decisions, not so much related to *trade* in allegedly harmful products, but addressing the very substantive environmental question of whether or not a particular product is harmful, or decisions in which specific maximum residue levels are specified or commitments are made to reduce emissions in certain harmful substances. These types of WTO decisions may then be 'invalid' for lack of competence on behalf of the WTO as an international organisation (see above, pp. 286–90) – and this even if these

[192] *Ibid.*, para. 25.   [193] Art. III.2 of the Marrakesh Agreement.

decisions were later confirmed by the General Council or the Ministerial Conference, since these organs *remain WTO organs*.

The allocation of competence within the UN system was illustrated by the ICJ in the *Use of Nuclear Weapons* case as follows:

> the Charter of the United Nations laid the basis of a 'system' designed to organize international co-operation in a coherent fashion by bringing the United Nations, invested with powers of general scope, into relationship with various autonomous and complementary organizations, invested with sectorial powers. The exercise of these powers by the organizations belonging to the 'United Nations system' is co-ordinated, notably, by the relationship agreements concluded between the United Nations and each of the specialized agencies.[194]

On that basis, the Court noted that the powers of specialised agencies must be interpreted taking account of 'the logic of the overall system contemplated by the Charter'. It even seemed to go as far as saying that the competence of the UN and those of particular specialised agencies are *mutually exclusive* when noting that WHO responsibilities 'are necessarily restricted to the sphere of public "health" and cannot encroach on the responsibilities of other parts of the United Nations system. And there is no doubt that questions concerning the use of force, the regulation of armaments and disarmament are within the competence of the United Nations and lie outside that of specialized agencies.'

In his Dissenting Opinion Judge Weeramantry warned about the dangers of such approach:

> The Court is of course anxious to ensure that there should not be an unnecessary confusion or overlapping of functions between the different organs and agencies of the United Nations. However, the principle of speciality does not mean that there can be no overlap. It is in the nature of a complex organization like the United Nations that there will be, owing to the multiplicity and complexity of its functions, some areas of overlap between the legitimate spheres of authority of its constituent entities.[195]

Referring to the example of overlap between the ICJ itself and the Security Council, Weeramantry referred instead to the 'principle of complementarity'. He rightly concluded as follows:

> The family of United Nations organizations was not set up in a fretwork pattern of neatly dovetailing components, each with a precisely carved outline of its own. These organizations deal with human activities and human interrelationships and it is of their very nature that they should have overlapping areas of concern.

[194] ICJ Reports 1996, para. 25.   [195] *Ibid.*, 150.

Their broad contours are of course defined, but different aspects of the self-same question may well fall within the ambit of two or more organizations.[196]

It must, in this context, be recalled that the WTO is not a specialised UN agency. Nonetheless, the principle of 'speciality' also applies to it, although not, perhaps, to the extent that account must be had of 'the logic of the overall [UN] system contemplated by the Charter'. Thus, whereas it may be so that no overlaps of competence are tolerated *within* the UN system (something which is, for the reasons set out by Weeramantry, highly questionable), overlaps could be acceptable as between a UN organisation (say, UNCTAD) and the WTO.

Acts of states

The situation is entirely different for WTO/UNEP norms created *by states themselves*. Here, no principle of 'speciality' applies in terms of competence. Thus, the fact that states adopt an agreement on substantive environmental matters (say, an agreement on GMOs) *in the context of the WTO* (but not acting in the form of a WTO organ) cannot be objected to on the ground of 'speciality' of the WTO *as an international organisation*. Such WTO norms are then of inherently equal value to UNEP norms, be the latter enacted by states as states in the context of UNEP or by UNEP organs pursuant to UNEP powers. However, even though 'speciality' in terms of WTO competence could then not be used as an argument to let UNEP rules prevail, UNEP rules may still cover the subject matter at issue more directly and precisely and on that ground prevail as the *lex specialis*.[197] But then the UNEP norm prevails, not on the ground of *lack of WTO competence*, but on the ground of a *substantive conflict rule* given preference to the more specific norm.

Both norms are 'equal'

There are, finally, cases where the conflict rules set out above do not provide a solution. A particular type of conflict for which international law generally does not provide a solution is that of the AB/AC type (that is, state A promising one thing to B, but another contradictory thing to C). This is essentially so because of the *pacta tertiis* principle. These conflicts are discussed in the second subsection. In addition, there may, in exceptional cases, be conflicts of the more traditional AB/AB type (that

[196] *Ibid.*, 151. [197] See above, pp. 387–90.

is, where the norms in conflict are binding on both parties) where none of the conflict rules in the previous sections lead to a clear result. These are discussed next.

Conflict of norms binding on both parties that cannot be resolved: conflict in the applicable law constituting a lacuna

Can there be conflicts of the traditional AB/AB type where none of the conflict rules above offer a solution? That is, can there be conflicts between treaty norms where Arts. 41/58 are irrelevant, no explicit conflict clauses are set out, the *lex posterior* principle does not apply and where the *lex specialis* principle does not make it possible to detect the 'more specific norm'? In very exceptional cases, this possibility must be acknowledged. Whatever the exact nature and source of conflict rules (be they derived from an explicit conflict clause or the general principle of contractual freedom of states), they must derive from norms of international law that are legally binding when the conditions for their application are fulfilled. A solution to conflict of norms must be found in the law. It is not for an adjudicator to decide arbitrarily which of two conflicting norms ought to apply. This means that in exceptional cases, where no conflict rule is available or where none of the applicable conflict rules leads to a result, an adjudicator may have to pronounce a *non liquet*, based on the absence of conflict rules.

An international adjudicator is assumed to know the law (*jura novit curia*) and, if two conflicting norms apply to the same situation, his or her function will be to apply conflict rules so as to enable only one of the two norms to apply. But if the law itself fails to offer the solution as to which of the two norms applies, it should not, normally, be for the judge him/herself to make that decision. In effect, and although there would then be a problem of 'too much law' (two norms apply and one cannot decide which one ought to prevail), one is faced with a lacuna in the law: international law offers no solution as to which norm must prevail. As a result, one may have to declare a *non liquet*.[198] This possibility is envisaged, for example, by Fastenrath who refers to 'Kollisionslücken'[199] and Salmon who speaks of 'lacune de règle de solution d'antinomie'.[200]

---

[198] On the question of *non liquet*, see chapter 3 above, pp. 150–4, and Pauwelyn, 'Cross-agreement'.
[199] Ulrich Fastenrath, *Lücken im Völkerrecht: zu Rechtscharakter, Quellen, Systemzusammenhang, Methodenlehre und Funktionen des Völkerrechts* (Berlin: Duncker & Humblot, 1991), 227.
[200] J.-A. Salmon, 'Les Antinomies en Droit International Public', in Chaim Perelman (ed.), *Les Antinomies en Droit* (Brussels: Bruylant, 1965), 449.

There may be contexts where the judge will take up a more proactive role and decide for him/herself which rule ought to prevail (as, for example, in the ECJ). But this should not be the general rule under public international law where it is generally acknowledged that the judge applies the law (and may thereby further develop the law), but does not create new law. If the judge decides nonetheless to create his or her own conflict rule, he or she is, moreover, unlikely to do so openly. A judge would then rather cover this solution under the all-embracing approach of, for example, 'teleological interpretation'.

This exceptional situation is most likely to arise as between two contradictory provisions in the same treaty. A potential example can be found in DSU Art. 21.5 versus DSU Art. 22.6. Article 21.5 provides, without time limitation, that '[w]here there is disagreement as to the existence or consistency with a covered agreement of measures taken to comply with the recommendations and rulings such dispute *shall be decided through recourse to these dispute settlement procedures*'. Article 22.6, in contrast, and without cross-reference to the Art. 21.5 panel procedure, states that 'the DSB, upon request, *shall grant authorization* to suspend consessions or other obligations *within 30 days* of the expiry of the reasonable period of time unless the DSB decides by consensus to reject the request'. In *US – Certain Products*, the Appellate Body seemed to realise the unavoidable contradiction between these two provisions, noting the following:

> we are cognizant of the important systematic issue of the relationship between Articles 21.5 and 22 of the DSU. As the United States correctly points out in its appellee's submission, the terms of Articles 21.5 and 22 are not a 'model of clarity' and the relationship between these two provisions of the DSU has been the subject of intensive and extensive discussion among Members of the WTO. We note that, on 10 October 2000, eleven Members of the WTO presented a proposal in the General Council to amend, *inter alia*, Articles 21 and 22 of the DSU. In so noting, we observe that it is certainly not the task of either panels or the Appellate Body to amend the DSU or to adopt interpretations within the meaning of Article IX:2 of the *WTO Agreement*. Only WTO Members have the authority to amend the DSU or to adopt such interpretations. Pursuant to Article 3.2 of the DSU, the task of panels and the Appellate Body in the dispute settlement system of the WTO is 'to preserve the rights and obligations of Members under the covered agreements, and to *clarify existing provisions* of those agreements in accordance with customary rules of interpretation of public international law' (emphasis added). Determining what the rules and procedures of the DSU ought to be is not our responsibility nor the responsibility of panels; it is clearly the responsibility solely of the Members of the WTO.[201]

---

[201] Appellate Body report on *US – Certain Products*, paras. 91–2.

In not less than three bananas-related disputes, the WTO judiciary has managed to avoid solving the Art. 21.5–Art. 22 dilemma (*EC – Bananas*, US request for suspension; *US – Section 301*; *US – Certain Products*). This sent a clear signal to the WTO membership that it was for them to resolve the conflict. The rather passive role taken by the WTO judiciary seems justified, in particular in the context of its rather strict 'interpretative mandate' under DSU Art. 3.2 ('not [to] add to or diminish from' WTO covered agreements). As noted before, in other contexts where the judiciary is granted a more creative role (as in the ECJ), the judge may have reacted differently and resolved the question him/herself.

There is, finally, one important benefit linked to declaring a *non liquet* in case of 'non-resolvable' conflict. States should then realise that it will not suffice to let potential conflicts linger without political solution. For negotiators to leave the interaction between treaty provisions ambiguous would hence imply a serious risk: if the conflict turns out to be an 'unresolvable' one, the international judge may declare a *non liquet* and simply apply neither of the two rules, thereby nullifying the effect of both treaties or both treaty provisions. For states in the position of defendant this may be the ideal solution. But in a context of compulsory dispute settlement, as in the WTO, one day a state is the defendant, another day it is the complainant. Hence, the risk of not seeing any law applied should constitute a serious incentive for states to provide more explicit solutions to potential conflicts, in the form, for example, of more clearly phrased provisions or explicit treaty-based conflict clauses.

The occurrence of 'unresolvable' conflicts of the traditional AB/AB type is not limited to two provisions in the same treaty. Two norms deriving from different treaties may raise the same problem, especially if either of the two is of a 'continuing' nature and the *lex posterior* principle cannot be applied. If it is, in these circumstances, not possible to determine which of the two is *lex specialis*, one may then be faced with a lacuna and be forced to declare a *non liquet*.

It is not inconceivable that such a lacuna might arise in the event of a conflict between a WTO rule and a rule under another multilateral agreement, say, an MEA. If the MEA were to set out general trade clauses (not limited to specific, harmful products), or the WTO rule were to include product-specific environmental exceptions (in open conflict with MEA rules), a conflict between these two 'continuing' norms might not be resolvable under the *lex specialis* principle. One might then again be forced to declare a *non liquet*. The likelihood of the WTO and MEAs regulating matters at this same level of specificity is small (after all, the WTO is about trade, MEAs about environment). But the possibility of such openly conflicting norms arising ought not to be precluded. Recall, in this respect, the often diametrically opposed positions adopted by states in different contexts (say, in the WTO as opposed to the biodiversity context).[202] If the same states were, indeed, to conclude in one context (say, the WTO) that genetically modified organisms (GMOs) are *not* harmful (e.g., in a new WTO agreement on GMOs) and, at the same time, to adopt the position that GMOs *are* harmful in another context (say, under the Cartagena Biosafety Protocol), the conflict would be one of two equally specific provisions. Such conflict, essentially the result of the schizophrenic behaviour of *states*, ought not to be resolved by an international *adjudicator*. It would be for the states themselves to bring their act together and solve the conflict at a law-making level. If not, some states (especially the most powerful ones) could well regard the potential for judges to decide difficult political questions as an incentive to leave these questions open, in the hope that they could then convince the judge, at the time of a dispute, of their position.[203]

Conflict of norms where only one party is bound by both rules: conflicts of the AB/AC type

As pointed out earlier, a conflict of norms may also arise even if the two states concerned are not both bound by the two conflicting norms in question, that is, from the point of view of state A in case it first promises one thing to state B in one norm (AB) and thereafter promises another, contradictory thing to state C in another norm (AC).

In the past, especially in the days of Grotius and de Vattel, but actually up to the end of the Second World War (i.e., up to the boom in so-called law-making treaties), AB/AC conflicts were of the greatest concern in international law, in particular in the field of the law of war and neutrality (for example, state A promising intervention to state B, but neutrality to state C for exactly the same situation). As of 1947, however, the risk and importance of AB/AB conflicts rose dramatically, not because of an increase in bilateral treaties reviewing earlier ones, but as a result of

---

[202] See note 91 above.
[203] Recall, in this respect, the two irreconcilable conflict clauses in the preamble to the Cartagena Biosafety Protocol (quoted above, p. 334). It provides an example of a treaty in respect of which the parties could not agree on whether the new norms ought to prevail over, or be subject to, WTO rules. Each side obtained its preambular paragraph but the result seems to be that they neutralise each other. In the end, an adjudicator would not have any guidance based on this preambular language. Nonetheless, in this case, it would seem that the *lex specialis* principle should work in favour of the Protocol (it being more specific in terms of subject matter than, for example, the SPS Agreement). See above, pp. 387–90.

a growing number of multilateral treaties being concluded in different contexts by the same states.

Inherent normative conflict of the AB/AC type versus conflict in the applicable law of the AB/AC type

We saw above that the very conclusion by A of a later norm AC may constitute breach of an earlier norm AB.[204] Such an event raises an 'inherent normative conflict' where one norm is, in and of itself, a breach of the other (not a conflict in the applicable law). Recall, in this respect, the *Customs Regime Between Germany and Austria* case and the *Costa Rica v. Nicaragua* (pp. 300–3) case involving the Bryan–Chamorro Treaty, discussed in chapter 6 above. If the later norm AC does, in and of itself, constitute breach of the earlier norm AB, then state B can challenge the legality of norm AC and obtain a ruling as against state A that the AC norm is illegal. From the point of view of state C, however, the AC norm is not illegal (C is not bound by the earlier norm AB) and C may then claim compensation from A for not implementing the AC norm.

In contrast, the conclusion of norm AB – being the earlier in time – cannot constitute breach of the later norm AC even if the two are in an inherent normative conflict. At the time of conclusion of norm AB, norm AC was not yet in existence.

A conflict of the AB/AC type may also give rise to conflict in the applicable law. This will be the case in the event that norm AC does not, in and of itself, constitute breach of the earlier norm AB (hence there is no inherent normative conflict), but compliance with either norm would constitute breach of the other. That is, in one set of circumstances state A is bound to do one thing under norm AB, but another, contradictory thing under norm AC. If A complies with the first norm vis-à-vis B it will necessarily breach the second norm vis-à-vis C. If A complies with the second norm vis-à-vis C it will necessarily breach the first norm vis-à-vis B.

This is the situation we shall examine further in this subsection. It may arise at two points in time:

(i) *after* A elects to comply with either norm (say, A decides to implement norm AC and B subsequently challenges this implementation as a breach of the AB norm); or
(ii) as a more abstract question *before* A decides to comply with either norm (say, A, B and C ask an adjudicator to determine which norm A should comply with).

---

[204] See chapter 6 above, pp. 300–3.

Conflict in the applicable law of the AB/AC type arises only in the event of mutually exclusive obligations imposed on A

From the above description, it is apparent that in respect of conflicts in the applicable law of the type AB/AC, conflict situations 3 and 4 outlined in chapter 4 (those involving explicit rights) do not find application. Indeed, where A has an explicit right (be it an exemption or a permission) to do X under the AB norm vis-à-vis B, but an obligation *not* to do X under the AC norm vis-à-vis C, *there is no conflict*. In that instance, the explicit right (vis-à-vis B) must always give way to the obligation (vis-à-vis C). Here, the right was granted *by B*, the obligation imposed *by C*. It is, therefore, impossible that the right (in AB) overrules the obligation (in AC). An AB right cannot replace an AC obligation. For C – the beneficiary of the obligation – the AB norm is *res inter alios acta*. Hence, C cannot see its right to compliance by A affected by this AB norm. B, in contrast, the state which gave the explicit right to A (and which is a third party to the AC norm), is *not* affected by state A not exercising the explicit right under the AB norm.

The same applies in case the later AC norm grants an explicit right to do something that is prohibited in the earlier AB norm. There is then no conflict and A is fully capable of complying with both norms, namely by not exercising its explicit right vis-à-vis C in a way that would breach its obligations towards B under the other norm. In sum, conflict in the applicable law of the AB/AC type arises only in case of mutually exclusive obligations imposed on A under the two norms in question.[205]

Conflict resolution in the law of treaties

The evolution from 'invalidity' of the later AC norm to no solution at all in the law of treaties

In doctrine a tendency has long prevailed in support of declaring the later AC norm *invalid* (on the ground that the earlier AB norm detracted from A's very 'legal capacity' to conclude the later AC norm) or, at least, to let, in these circumstances, the earlier AB norm *prevail* over the later, conflicting AC norm (*lex prior* principle or *prior in tempore potior in jus*). Witness, for example, the draft convention on the law of treaties of the Harvard Research in International Law: 'If a State assumes by a Treaty

---

[205] Conflict situation 1, in so far as it relates to conflicting positive obligations that are merely different but not mutually exclusive (see chapter 4 above), does not give rise to conflict either in an AB/AC constellation. A can then avoid breaching its obligations towards both B and C by simply complying with the stricter norm.

with another State an obligation which is in conflict with an obligation which it has assumed by an earlier treaty with a third State, the obligation assumed by the *earlier treaty takes priority* over the obligation assumed by the later treaty.'[206]

Lauterpacht, in Art. 16 of each of his Reports on the Law of Treaties prepared for the ILC went even a step further and started from the principle that a treaty is *void* if its performance involves a breach of a treaty obligation previously undertaken by one or more of the parties, subject to the right of an innocent party (*in casu*, state C) to damages for resulting loss.[207] We discussed earlier how this principle of invalidity of one of the two conflicting norms evolved into rules on priority of application (with reports by Fitzmaurice and Waldock).[208] For AB/AC conflicts, this culminated even in a complete absence of priority rules and an exclusive reliance on state responsibility in the Vienna Convention.

We saw earlier that in the *Costa Rica v. Nicaragua* case, the later Bryan–Chamorro Treaty was not invalidated for cause of breach with the earlier Canas–Jerez Treaty.[209] In a more recent dispute, the *Case Concerning East Timor (Portugal v. Australia)*, the ICJ was even more reticent to declare a treaty invalid on the ground that it violated an earlier one with another party. In that case, Portugal argued that Australia's entry into a treaty with Indonesia conflicted, *inter alia*, with the rights of Portugal under the UN Charter and gave rise to the international responsibility of Australia. Unlike Costa Rica in the Bryan–Chamorro dispute, Portugal expressly did not seek a determination that the later treaty which Australia had concluded with Indonesia was void. Rather, Portugal restricted itself to a claim of state responsibility. In this dispute, the ICJ declined to decide the case at all, on the ground that it could not do so without first pronouncing on the illegality of the conduct of Indonesia, a state not party to the proceeding. In these circumstances,

---

[206] Reprinted in (1935) 29 AJIL 1024, supplement.
[207] UN documents A/CN.4/63 of 24 March 1953, 198–208 and A/CN.4/87. This invalidity was conditional on whether the departure from the terms of the prior treaty was such as to interfere seriously with the interests of the other parties to that treaty, or seriously impair the original purpose of the treaty. In his second report this was slightly revised to refer specifically to a bilateral or a multilateral treaty or any provision thereof, while the last phrase of the condition was reworded to read 'to impair an essential aspect of [the prior treaty's] original purpose'. See also Hersch Lauterpacht, 'The Covenant as the "Higher Law"' (1936) 17 BYIL 54, and 'Contracts to Break a Contract', in E. Lauterpacht (ed.), *International Law, Being the Collected Papers of Hersch Lauterpacht* (Cambridge: Cambridge University Press, 1978), 341 at 374–5.
[208] See chapter 6 above, pp. 279–81.   [209] See chapter 6 above, pp. 300–1.

the ICJ concluded, it was not competent to determine Portugal's claim of state responsibility against Australia.[210]

The resolution provided for in the Vienna Convention
In order to resolve AB/AC conflicts under present international law, the three principles set out earlier (contractual freedom of states, *pacta sunt servanda* and *pacta tertiis*) must be resorted to.

Pursuant to the *pacta sunt servanda* principle, A is bound by the first norm vis-à-vis B, but at the same time A is bound also by the second, contradictory norm vis-à-vis state C.[211]

Moreover, pursuant to the *pacta tertiis* principle, C cannot be held by the earlier AB norm. Neither can it see its AC rights detracted from because of conflict with this AB norm to which it did not consent. The same applies for state B in respect of the AC norm to which state B did not consent.

Finally, the contractual freedom of state A allowed it to conclude the contradictory AC norm (assuming that the AB norm is not of *jus cogens*). International law does *not invalidate* the AC norm because it conflicts with the earlier AB norm. From the viewpoint of A, the AC norm can be *illegal* if it constitutes, in and of itself, breach of the earlier AB norm, but it cannot be *invalid*.

Crucially, in case the AC norm does *not*, in and of itself, constitute breach of the AB norm, international law does *not* offer a *priority* rule obliging A to comply with the AB norm over and above the AC norm or vice versa. Both norms are then valid and legal and can be invoked by A's contractual partners. This is the solution explicitly provided by Art. 30(4)(b) of the Vienna Convention (discussed above, pp. 383–4): 'When the parties to the later treaty [AC norm] do not include all the parties to the earlier one [AB norm]... as between a State Party to both

---

[210] Note that in the *Costa Rica v. Nicaragua* case, the Central American Court did declare the responsibility of Nicaragua (notwithstanding the absence of the United States), but that in that case it could do so without having to decide first on the legality of US conduct (whereas in the *East Timor* case both Australia and Indonesia were bound by the UN Charter, under which Portugal invoked the breach; in the *Costa Rica v. Nicaragua* case, the treaty invoked by Costa Rica (the Canas–Jerez Treaty) was binding only on Nicaragua, not on the United States).

[211] Or, as Crawford noted: 'if any of the parties to two inconsistent treaties is different, both treaties are considered to remain in force, with the consequence that State A (a party to both) may have one set of obligations to one group of States and another set of obligations to another... The Vienna Convention... does not contemplate that a treaty will be void for inconsistency with another treaty' (James Crawford, Second Report, UN doc. A/CN.4/498 (1999), para. 9, (c) and (d)).

treaties [A] and a State Party to only one of the treaties [B and C], the treaty to which both States are parties governs their mutual rights and obligations.' In other words, in case of conflict in the applicable law of the AB/AC type, A is bound towards B by the AB norm as much as it is bound towards C by the contradictory AC norm.

Hence, if an adjudicator were faced *ex ante* by a request of, for example, A, B and C to decide which norm A must comply with, the adjudicator would not be able to decide either way.[212] It is then up to A to make a political choice as to whether it will comply with the AB norm or with the AC norm. The law of treaties does not direct A either way. Or, as Karl put it: 'With the law stepping back, a principle of political decision takes its place whereby it is left to the party to the conflicting obligations to decide which treaty it prefers to fulfil.'[213]

It is interesting to note that an earlier version of what is now Art. 30(4)(b) made a reservation for conflicts of the AB/AC type. It provided for a priority rule in favour of the *earlier treaty* for cases where C 'was aware of the existence of the earlier treaty [AB norm] and that it was still in force with respect to the first State [A]'.[214] This proviso was later dropped.

Conflict resolution in the law of state responsibility

In sum, the law of treaties does not provide a solution for AB/AC conflicts in the sense that it does not direct state A to give preference to either one of the two norms. However, this lack of conflict rules in the law of treaties has left untouched normal international law rules on state responsibility.[215] This is, again, what Art. 30(5) of the Vienna Convention provides: 'Paragraph 4 is without prejudice to...any question of responsibility which may arise for a State from the *conclusion* or *application* of a treaty, the provisions of which are incompatible with its obligations towards another State under another treaty.'

---

[212] Unless, of course, the AC norm constitutes, in and of itself, breach of the earlier AB norm, but then we no longer have a conflict in the applicable law, but an inherent normative conflict (discussed above, pp. 300–3).

[213] Karl, 'Conflicts', 470–1. That this solution is 'sans doute guère satisfaisante', see Quoc Dinh, *Droit*, para. 175 at 274.

[214] Third Report on the Law of Treaties by Sir Humphrey Waldock, YBILC 1964, vol. 2, 5–65 (UN doc. A/CN.4/156 and Add. 1–3), Art. 65.4(c). Discussed, *inter alia*, at the 742nd Meeting of the ILC, YBILC 1964, vol. 1, 119 at 120 (where it is stated in para. 11 that the proviso had been suggested by McNair with reference to the principle of good faith).

[215] See Crawford, Second Report, para. 9.

As Crawford noted, the Vienna Convention 'seeks to resolve the difficulties of conflicting treaty obligations by expressly reserving [the rules of state responsibility]...Thus it is no excuse under international law for non-compliance with a subsisting treaty obligation to State A that the State was simultaneously complying with a treaty obligation to State B.'[216] This means also, as another author put it, that the conflict is not actually resolved: 'Il ne s'agit donc plus de résoudre un conflit de normes (problème objectif de compatibilité), mais de sanctionner (subjectivement) un comportement internationalement illicite.'[217]

We have already examined the instance of the later AC norm constituting, in and of itself, breach of the earlier AB norm.[218] To use the words of Art. 30(5), this relates to the 'question of responsibility which may arise for a State [A] from the *conclusion*...of a treaty [*in casu*, the AC norm], the provisions of which are incompatible with its obligations towards another State [B] under another treaty [*in casu*, the AB norm]'. In case of such inherent normative conflict, the law of state responsibility directs state A to stop the breach, i.e., *to cease the existence of the AC norm*. This, in turn, will activate state A's responsibility vis-à-vis state C.

In case of conflict in the applicable law of the type AB/AC (that is, two norms impose mutually exclusive obligations on state A, but one norm is not, in and of itself, breach under the other norm), as soon as state A executes either of the two norms it will engage its state responsibility. To use the words of Art. 30(5), this raises the 'question of responsibility which may arise for a State [A] from the *application*...of a treaty [*in casu*, either the AB or the AC norm], the provisions of which are incompatible with its obligations towards another State [respectively, C or B] under another treaty [respectively, the AC or the AB norm]'. If A complies with norm AB, it will engage its responsibility vis-à-vis state C. If it complies with norm AC, it will engage its responsibility vis-à-vis state B. Since not to execute either of the two norms is, in the event of mutually exclusive obligations, not an option that would avoid breach, for state A to sit still and not to execute either of the two norms would mean that it breaches at least one of them, perhaps even both. In the latter event, state A would engage its responsibility vis-à-vis both state B and state C. In sum, under the law of treaties state A is free to comply with either norm. Nonetheless, doing so will necessarily activate state A's responsibility under the other norm. It is then that the application of

---

[216] *Ibid.*, para. 9, (c) and (d).   [217] Quoc Dinh, *Droit*, para. 175 at 274.
[218] See chapter 6 above, pp. 300–3.

either norm (not the conclusion of the second norm as such) may lead to adjudication. If so, the adjudicator will have to find breach of the opposing norm which A did not implement and grant damages to the state wanting to rely on that opposing norm. Or, as Jiménez de Aréchaga phrased it at an ILC meeting:

> According to the principle of nullity, a treaty which conflicted with a prior treaty was void. According to the principle of State responsibility, it was valid, but the State which had assumed conflicting obligations was free to choose which of the treaties it would fulfil; so far as the unfulfilled treaty was concerned, it was required to pay an indemnity. The State which had assumed conflicting obligations thus 'bought' its choice.[219]

The problem then is, of course, that although A can pay *compensation* to its contracting partner towards whom it did not comply, it cannot *cease* the breach towards that state without in turn breaching the other norm. As we discuss below, this is why the only long-term solution to a conflict of the type AB/AC is to renegotiate either norm so as to end the conflict.

Nonetheless, in case of breach of either norm by state A, and in the event such breach constitutes a 'material breach', the state subject to the breach may then be allowed to invoke the termination or suspension of the treaty breached by state A pursuant to Art. 60 of the Vienna Convention. Article 30(5) explicitly reserves the operation of Art. 60. In most cases, however, the subject of the breach will be interested more in performance of the treaty rather than in its suspension or termination. The latter may well benefit more state A which would then be freed of its contradictory obligations.

Can state C be held responsible for breach by state A of the AB norm?

However, does this almost exclusive reliance on state responsibility in the Vienna Convention for AB/AC conflicts mean that states B and C are put in exactly the same position? Not necessarily so. Conclusion or implementation of the later AC norm, in conflict with the earlier AB norm, may not only engage the responsibility of state A. It could be

---

[219] YBILC 1964, vol. 1, 123, 742nd Meeting, para. 44. Degan (*Sources*, 435) criticised the Art. 30 solution to conflicts of the AB/AC type as follows: 'The solution from paragraph 5 of Article 30 seems to be insufficient, especially because it considers both incompatible treaties as equal. It does not protect the rights of the injured party from the earlier treaty', *in casu* state B. Nonetheless, as explained below, in some cases B should be able to claim compensation from both A and C.

argued that state C, by concluding the later AC norm, aided or assisted state A in the commission of the breach of norm AB. In other words, in the event state A decides to comply with the later AC norm, state B could invoke, not only the responsibility of state A, but also that of state C. Or, looked at from a different angle, state A could, in its defence, refer to the responsibility of state C, for example in order to reduce the amount of damages to be paid by state A to state B.

The ILC Draft 1996 on State Responsibility
Article 27 of the ILC Draft 1996, entitled 'Aid or assistance by a State to another State for the commission of an internationally wrongful act', addresses the issue of aid or assistance in breach as follows: 'Aid or assistance by a State to another State, if it is established that it is *rendered for the commission of an internationally wrongful act* carried out by the latter, itself constitutes an internationally wrongful act, *even if, taken alone, such aid or assistance would not constitute the breach* of an international obligation' (emphasis added).

As James Crawford remarked, 'article 27 posits a rather extensive principle of responsibility of one State for the acts of another'.[220] Three requirements for Art. 27 to be activated should be pointed at.

First, for present purposes, the exact degree of 'aid or assistance' required, i.e., the question of whether there is actual or material assistance by state C or only advice, encouragement or incitement, is not that important. For state C to conclude a treaty with state A which breaches another international obligation of state A (under norm AB), or will necessarily lead to such breach if complied with, undoubtedly amounts to actual and material aid and assistance. It could even be said that state C thereby 'becomes a co-perpetrator of an internationally wrongful act'.[221] Indeed, without state C, the treaty and hence the breach would not have materialised.

Second, the 'mental element' required for there to be liability of state C, i.e., the fact that the assistance must be given 'with the *intent* to facilitate the commission'[222] of the breach, does, in the circumstances, not raise serious difficulties either. As Crawford noted, '[i]gnorance of international law is not generally an excuse for wrongful conduct by States'. Thus, state C, when concluding the conflicting norm AC, must

---

[220] Crawford, Second Report, Add. 1, para. 167.
[221] ILC Commentary to Art. 27, para. (2).   [222] *Ibid.*, para. (16), emphasis in original.

normally have been aware that this new norm would breach or lead to breach of other obligations of state A. By effectively concluding the new norm, state C must, moreover, be presumed to have intended to facilitate the occurrence of this breach.

A potential third requirement is more problematic in the circumstances, that is, the question as to whether or not the assisting state, *in casu* state C, must also be bound by the obligation that state A breaches by concluding the norm AC. In other words, for state C to be responsible must it also be bound by the AB norm? Article 27 of the ILC Draft 1996 did not seem to impose this requirement. Nonetheless, most of the examples given in the Commentary to Art. 27 involve assistance by one state in the use of armed force by another, e.g., through allowing overflight or landing rights in the course of a military operation by another state which is said to constitute aggression or intervention. Indeed, all of the examples given involve breaches of obligations arising under rules by which the assisting state was itself bound.

The Reports of James Crawford and the ILC Draft 2001
The fact that the text of Art. 27 of the 1996 ILC Draft could, nonetheless, be read as including also breaches of rules *not* binding on the assisting state (that is, situations where state C was *not* itself bound also by the AB norm) was criticised by Crawford, who rightly remarked:

> Take the case of a bilateral treaty between State [A] and State [B] under which the two States agree not to export certain materials or technology to, or not to trade with, State [C]... State [C], the target State, is of course not bound by the treaty. Why should it be legally responsible if, knowing of the treaty, it assists State [A] in breaching? Article 27 could thereby become a vehicle by which the effect of well-published bilateral obligations was extended to the rest of the world.[223]

In support of his position, Crawford, in Addendum 3 to his Second Report, provided a comparative analysis of the concept of 'interference with contractual rights' in domestic law.[224] He concluded that while English, US, French and German law recognise that knowingly and intentionally inducing a breach of contract – even if the inducing party is not bound by the contract – is a civil wrong, they approach the matter in different ways. These differences are accentuated if one brings into

---

[223] Second Report, Add. 1, para. 184. The denomination of states in the example has been adapted to conform to the hypotheses used here.
[224] UN document A/CN.4/498/Add. 3.

account a wider range of comparisons, such as, for example, Islamic or Russian law. Under Islamic law, for example, no such liability seems to be recognised. He concluded that the statement of a general principle that any knowing interference with the performance of any contract constitutes a delict or tort is an oversimplification of a more complex situation.[225]

In his remarks under Art. 27, Crawford then continues as follows:

even if the support to be drawn from the domestic analogies such as inducing breach of contract were less equivocal than it is, there are difficulties in applying such a general principle to international relations. Treaties reflect the particular policies of the States entering into them, and international law has a strict doctrine of privity in relation to treaties. Moreover, treaties have proliferated, and many obligations to provide finance, materials or technology are incorporated in treaties. National legal systems have more rigorous controls on the legality of contracts than international law currently has for treaties, and there are ways under national law by which third parties can challenge the legality of contracts adversely affecting them which do not yet exist for treaties.

On that basis, Crawford proposed to replace Art. 27 by the following (now Art. 16 of the 2001 Draft Articles):

A State which aids or assists another State in the commission of an internationally wrongful act by the latter is internationally responsible for doing so if:

(a) That State does so with knowledge of the circumstances of the internationally wrongful act; and
(b) *The act would be internationally wrongful if committed by that State* [emphasis added].

Hence, under the third point discussed earlier, it is now made clear that the assisting state (*in casu*, state C) can only be held liable for assisting state A in its breach of norm AB if state C itself is bound by the

---

[225] French law is the most open in principle to such liability (but subject to limitations in practice such as a strict burden of proof), German law least so, since it requires something over and above knowing assistance or inducement, amounting to improper conduct. English and United States law take an intermediate position; there is liability in principle for deliberate and knowing inducement, but this is subject to the defence of justification and the proof of actual damage arising from the breach. Whether there is sufficient justification depends on a number of factors but, in English law, for example, to justify an inducement it is not enough to show that one was acting in good faith in the pursuit of a legitimate interest, there has to be something in the nature of a moral duty, or a distinct legal right to act.

obligation set out in norm AB. Moreover, under the second point discussed earlier, the 'mental element' required in the 1996 Draft for there to be liability of state C, i.e., the fact that the assistance must be given 'with the *intent* to facilitate the commission', has now been deleted.

Some examples: WTO obligations (AB norm) versus MEA obligations imposed in respect of non-parties (AC norm)
Where does this leave us under the example of the 1914 Bryan–Chamorro Treaty concluded by Nicaragua and the United States in breach of Nicaragua's earlier obligations vis-à-vis Costa Rica under the 1858 Canas–Jerez Treaty (the *Costa Rica v. Nicaragua* case)? Under Art. 16 of the 2001 Draft Articles, with its requirement that the assisting state must be bound also by the norm breached, the United States (allegedly the state which assisted Nicaragua in its breach of the earlier treaty with Costa Rica) could not be held responsible for its assistance provided to Nicaragua in the form of concluding the Bryan–Chamorro Treaty. The United States was, indeed, not itself bound by the Canas–Jerez Treaty.

But what in respect of other examples? Take a WTO rule between state A and state B, obliging state A not to restrict trade from state B in conflict with a subsequent MEA rule concluded by state A with state C under which state A is obliged to restrict trade of certain products *even if these products come from non-parties*, including state B (not bound by the MEA). Many MEAs include such obligations in respect of non-parties.[226]

Under the law of treaties, the AB/AC conflict (the earlier AB norm being a WTO rule; the later AC norm an MEA rule obliging state A to restrict trade with state B) would not result in the invalidity of the later MEA norm, nor does the law of treaties provide for a priority rule. The obligation of state A vis-à-vis state B not to restrict trade is of equal standing with the obligation of state A vis-à-vis state C to restrict trade. But what about state responsibility? If state A executes the WTO norm (norm AB), it breaches the MEA norm and engages its responsibility vis-à-vis state C in the MEA. If state A executes the MEA norm (norm AC),

---

[226] For an overview, see *Matrix on Trade Measures Pursuant to Selected MEAs*, WTO doc. WT/CTE/W/160/Rev.1, dated 14 June 2001. See, *inter alia*, Art. X of CITES, Art. 4(8) of the Montreal Protocol, Art. 11 of the Basel Convention, Art. 24(1) of the Cartagena Protocol on Biosafety, Arts. 8(4), 17 and 33 of the UN Fish Stocks Agreement, Art. 10(9)(a) of the Rotterdam Convention and Art. 3(2)(b)(i) of the Stockholm Convention.

it breaches the WTO norm and engages its responsibility vis-à-vis state B in the WTO.

However, in the second instance (compliance with the MEA, breach of the WTO), would state B (or for that matter state A) be able to invoke also the responsibility of state C and this *on the ground that state C assisted state A in committing the breach*, i.e., in concluding the MEA? If state C is, like states A and B, a WTO member the answer should be yes (at least under Art. 16 of the 2001 Draft Articles). In that event, state C has, indeed, assisted in the commission of wrongful conduct by state A vis-à-vis state B and this wrongful conduct, in case it had been committed by state C, would also have constituted a breach of the WTO obligations of state C. If, on the other hand, state C is only a party to the MEA and not a WTO member, it cannot be held responsible pursuant to Art. 16 for assistance to breach since state C is not itself bound by the WTO norm breached by state A.

Importantly, although the legal value of the WTO and the MEA norms are then equal from the point of view of A, the compulsory dispute settlement system available for breach of WTO norms may provide an incentive for state A to comply with the WTO norm, rather than the MEA norm.

On the other hand, the fact that all MEA parties that are also WTO members could be held 'co-responsible' for the breach of WTO norms by any of these MEA parties vis-à-vis a third party to the MEA which is nonetheless a WTO member could provide a strong enough safety net for WTO members (not party to the MEA) who see their trade restricted by the implementation of MEA norms they did not consent to in the first place. Such WTO members may then see their trade restricted, but they would be allowed to claim compensation for such restrictions in breach of WTO rules from all WTO members that are party also to the MEA.

The only long-term solution: renegotiate either norm so as to end the conflict

In the end, the optimal (and actually, the only genuine) resolution of AB/AC conflicts ought to be found in a renegotiation of either of the two norms. Also from a democratic legitimacy point of view, this makes sense: it should not be for a judge to decide such conflicts 'among equals', but for the states involved themselves. Such renegotiation could take the form of

(i) the termination of either norm by common consent and compensation (say, the termination of norm AC by agreement between A and C, with C being compensated); or
(ii) making the two norms binding on all three parties involved, e.g., by means of the accession of B to the AC norm (*in casu*, the MEA) with B being compensated for it in the context of the AB norm (say, by means of the original MEA parties granting increased market access to B in the WTO).[227]

Invoking the responsibility of C for the breach by A of the earlier AB norm (*in casu*, the WTO rule) may provide some pressure either to change the AC norm (*in casu*, the MEA rule) or to offer compensation to B on condition that B joins the AC norm.

If neither of the two norms is changed, there is an impasse. As noted earlier, the responsibility of A is necessarily incurred, whatever A does. Moreover, restitution under the violated norm is materially impossible. It requires the co-operation of the state not party to the norm breached. In addition, cessation of the norm breached is not an option either since it would necessarily lead to a violation of the other norm. To put it differently, without renegotiating either norm, state A would be in a continuing situation of breach, for which it would need to pay compensation, without being able to stop the breach. If it were to do so, it would engage in another breach.

The fact that renegotiation of either norm will be required in the long term leads to another consideration. Measures taken by WTO members under the AC norm (be it an MEA or a labour standards agreement), to which B is not bound, should not be too easily accepted under WTO exceptions (say, GATT Art. XX). Often it is mistakenly thought that not to offer such exception under explicit WTO rules necessarily condemns the measure in question. As explained below (pp. 456–72), the defendant should be allowed also to invoke defences or exceptions under non-WTO rules. If both parties are bound by these rules, defendants should be able to justify breach of WTO rules, depending on the applicable conflict rules. If the complainant is *not* bound by these non-WTO rules, such rules should not be invocable[228] and cannot justify an established breach of WTO law. However, to find on that basis that the measure is WTO

---

[227] Along these lines, see Kyle Bagwell, Petros Mavroidis and Robert Staiger, 'It's a Question of Market Access' (2002) 96 AJIL 56.
[228] Except perhaps for purposes of *interpretation* of WTO rules if these non-WTO rules reflect a 'common understanding' of all WTO members. See chapter 5 above, p. 273.

inconsistent is not necessarily the end of the matter. B should not be held bound by rules it did not agree to, but once the WTO inconsistency is established, states A and C would do well in renegotiating their WTO relationship with B so as to induce B to sign up to the MEA or labour standards agreement. In short, WTO dispute settlement should not be used as a fall-back in case B refuses to sign an MEA so as to get B bound by that MEA anyhow. B should be offered equal opportunities to negotiate its entry (and related benefits) to the MEA.

Conclusion on conflict resolution

To sum up chapters 6 and 7 on how to resolve conflict of norms, the starting point for resolving any conflict of norms must be the 'holy trinity' of (i) contractual freedom of states; (ii) *pacta sunt servanda*; and (iii) *pacta tertiis*. States are, indeed, free to change their legal relationship with other states (contractual freedom), as long as these other states consent. When they do not consent, these other states cannot be bound (*pacta tertiis*) and any earlier treaty must be complied with (*pacta sunt servanda*), otherwise state responsibility will be incurred. Conflict of norms in international law is governed essentially by priority rules and state responsibility, not by rules invalidating either of the two conflicting norms.

When concluding new norms, or assessing the hierarchy as between existing norms, states ought to be aware of the following eight steps:

(1) Norms cannot deviate from *jus cogens* (Arts. 53 and 64 of the Vienna Convention). Any new norm in conflict with *jus cogens* will be void. The same happens to existing norms contradicting supervening *jus cogens*. The one other instance of 'invalidity' occurs when acts of an international organisation are taken *ultra vires*, i.e., outside the limited competence of the organisation in question.

(2) One norm may constitute in and of itself breach of another, earlier norm. In that event, the later norm is 'illegal'. Also, an *inter se* agreement deviating from a pre-existing multilateral treaty may be 'illegal'. This will be the case not only if the multilateral treaty explicitly prohibits the later treaty, but also in the event that the multilateral obligation derogated from *inter se* is of an 'integral nature'. *Inter se* deviations from 'integral obligations' are not permitted (Arts. 41/58 of the Vienna Convention), essentially because they necessarily affect also third states (against the *pacta tertiis* principle). The very idea of concluding 'integral obligations' is that they continue to apply to all parties to the multilateral treaty (until amended by, in

most cases, consensus). Many environmental and human rights obligations are of an 'integral nature'. Hence, when concluding, for example, new trade agreements states ought to be aware of the limits imposed by Arts. 41/58. Nonetheless, when all parties to the 'integral obligation' agree to change it, Art. 30(3) (*lex posterior*) applies. Then, the only limit is *jus cogens*. Similar limits of 'illegality' must apply in respect of acts of international organisations that constitute a breach of the law that applies to them (to be distinguished from acts that are 'invalid' on the ground that they were taken *ultra vires*).

(3) Treaty norms cannot affect the rights and obligations of third parties and this even if these third party rights and obligations do not derive from 'integral treaties'. An *inter se* agreement deviating from a 'reciprocal obligation' set out in a multilateral treaty will also be illegal to the extent it breaches the rights of third parties (Arts. 41/58 of the Vienna Convention). Moreover, a later agreement as between A and C cannot alter the rights and obligations of B under an earlier AB agreement (*pacta tertiis*).

(4) Account must be had to explicit conflict clauses in existing treaties (especially Art. 103 of the UN Charter). Also, when creating new treaties conflict clauses may be inserted so as to safeguard pre-existing treaties, to make sure that the new treaty prevails over earlier ones, or to regulate the relationship between the new treaty and future treaties, in particular *inter se* deviations from the new treaty. Apart from Art. 103, conflict clauses claiming priority over future treaties are, however, subject to the contractual freedom of states, both as expressed in a new treaty as between all parties to the earlier one and in *inter se* agreements. Such conflict clauses are, in other words, without much practical effect.

Moreover, conflict clauses cannot alter the operation of the first three steps set out above: (i) a slave trade agreement, even if it includes a conflict clause stating that it prevails over the prohibition on the slave trade, remains void; (ii) a conflict clause in an 'illegal' *inter se* agreement stating that it prevails over the earlier multilateral treaty does not deactivate Art. 41 nor the *pacta tertiis* principle; (iii) the same applies in respect of an AC treaty explicitly stating that it prevails over an earlier AB treaty (*pacta tertiis*) or in respect of an act of an international organisation in which it is explicitly set out that the act prevails over any limitations as to the competence of the organ taking the act (such competence could be extended only by changing the constituent instrument of the organ).

(5) In case the previous four steps do not solve the conflict, one must fall back on the contractual freedom of states and look for the 'current expression of state intent'. In many cases, this search will be determined under Art. 30's *lex posterior* rule, applicable to 'successive treaties'. The *latest* expression of state intent is presumed to coincide

with the *current* expression of state intent. Even if an earlier treaty is *lex specialis* vis-à-vis this latest expression, this latest expression should still prevail. Article 30 does not provide for an exception in this regard. Nonetheless, there may be cases where different treaties cannot be seen as 'successive treaties', either because they were concluded at the same time or because they were concluded at different times for different parties or are of a 'continuing' or 'living' nature so that they must be seen as 'parallel' treaties rather than 'successive' treaties. In those cases where it is difficult to apply Art. 30, resort must be had to step 6.

(6) In case the search for the 'current expression of state intent' cannot be resolved by the *lex posterior* principle, other indications as to state consent must be looked to. Here, the *lex specialis* principle plays a pivotal role. The more precise and specific expression of state consent is then considered as coinciding with the strongest and current expression of state intent (overruling a more general norm, even if this norm is, from certain points of view, later in time). *Lex specialis* cannot, however, overrule a *lex posterior* in case Art. 30 finds application. It can only prevail in cases where treaties cannot be said to be 'successive' (e.g., conflicts involving 'continuing treaties'). Other indications as to state intent may also play a role, in particular implicit statements in, for example, the preamble or *travaux préparatoires* as to what the drafters had in mind in terms of the interplay between the treaties in question.

(7) Once the earlier six steps have been exhausted, there may be exceptional cases where an adjudicator would no longer be applying the law but creating it: that is, situations where none of the first five steps above offer a solution and where under the sixth step (*lex specialis*) the search for 'current expression of state consent' cannot be conclusively determined either. In that event, the adjudicator is faced with a lacuna in the field of conflict rules. He or she must then declare a *non liquet*.

(8) Under all seven steps above questions of state responsibility may arise. One norm may, in and of itself, constitute breach of the other and thereby become 'illegal' under the law of state responsibility (see step 2). But the 'illegality' may also be limited to the application or implementation of either norm. State responsibility is of great importance, especially in conflicts of the type AB/AC. It is, in that event, the only solution to conflict given that the *pacta tertiis* principle precludes an adjudicator from letting one rule prevail over the other.

In sum, when concluding new treaties states ought to keep in mind the limits under steps 1 (*jus cogens*), 2 (illegalities) and 3 (*pacta tertiis*). If at all possible, they should include explicit conflict clauses in their new treaties (step 4). Doing so cannot neutralise the limits in steps 1–3, but it will avoid the inherent uncertainties present in steps 5–7. If, for whatever reason, an explicit conflict clause is not set out, states must remember that the rule of first resort is and remains the *lex posterior* principle. Their latest expression of consent will prevail (step 5). Nonetheless, states must be aware of the fact that the *lex posterior* rule has its limits in that it applies only to 'successive treaties'. If, *but only if*, the treaties are, for whatever reason, not 'successive' (but, for example, 'parallel'), the search for 'current expression of state consent' must be widened so as to include also the *lex specialis* principle and any other implicit statements of preference for either norm (step 6). If these additional elements leave the question of 'current state consent' indecisive, the conflict of norms cannot be resolved. States must be cognisant of this risk of *non liquet*. This risk ought to be an incentive for states to provide for explicit conflict clauses under step 4.

8 Conflict of norms in WTO dispute settlement

> If the WTO is to become a vehicle for global governance one thing has to be clear: this vehicle ought not travel without a road map, and should be mindful of other traffic.[1]

The case study used throughout this book has been the law of the WTO. When examining the hierarchy of sources of international law (chapter 3), the concepts of accumulation and conflict of norms (chapter 4) and the available conflict-avoidance techniques (chapter 5), we have made reference to the particular situation in the WTO as well as to the case law developed under WTO dispute settlement. When it comes then to resolving conflicts of norms, be they inherent normative conflicts (chapter 6) or conflicts in the applicable law (chapter 7), we also used conflicts involving WTO norms, including internal WTO conflicts, as the standard example. A major missing link that remains, however, is to see how the ideas developed in previous chapters play out in the concrete setting of WTO dispute settlement. The main tenet of this book has been to portray WTO law as part of the wider corpus of public international law, with which it may either accumulate or conflict, and which it may either prevail over or have to give way to. But what remains of this 'unitary view' of international law when looking at the specifics of WTO dispute settlement? Does, for example, the DSU allow non-WTO norms to be part of the applicable law before a WTO panel? This is what we examine in this final, but crucially important, chapter.

This chapter is based largely on Joost Pauwelyn, 'The Role of Public International Law in the WTO: How Far Can We Go?' (2001) 95 AJIL 535.

[1] Marco Bronckers, 'More Power to the WTO?' (2001) 4 JIEL 41 at 56.

The judicial settlement of disputes

In public international law

As noted in chapters 1 and 3 above, international law lacks a central 'legislator' and an inherent hierarchy of its rules (other than *jus cogens*). In addition, it also lacks a unified international 'judiciary' to which all pertinent disputes could be referred.[2] The jurisdiction of an international court or tribunal cannot be presumed. It must be granted by the consent of states in *explicit* terms.[3] *Peaceful* settlement is the only available means to settle disputes.[4] However, general international law does not actually *obligate* states to settle disputes or, *a fortiori*, to submit all disputes to one given court. States are free to choose the court or tribunal they want.[5] The jurisdiction of an international adjudicator depends on the consent of the parties. States may decide to authorise an *ad hoc* arbitrator to settle their dispute. In that case they will often specify, by consent, both the subject matter in dispute and the applicable law. States may also decide to create a standing judicial body (such as the ICJ, the ITLOS or the WTO Appellate Body) and grant their consent *ex ante* for this body to hear not so much *a given* dispute but a certain *type* of dispute (for example, disputes on certain subjects or claims under a given convention). When doing so, states are required to specify, in advance, certain general procedural rules to be followed by the parties and the court in question. These general procedural rules or statutes may include a provision on the 'applicable law'.[6] Whereas the consent to jurisdiction and the definition of the applicable law in *ad hoc* arbitrations are mostly clear and precise, the reference *ex ante* to a standing judicial body often results in jurisdictional objections by the defending state and makes discussions on applicable law more frequent.

Consequently, despite the lack of a general hierarchy of rules of international law the need for explicit consent for legal claims to be brought before an international court or tribunal means that, in a sense, a 'two-class society' does exist, namely, between rules of international

---

[2] See chapter 1 above, pp. 16–17. There is, of course, the ICJ, the 'principal judicial organ of the United Nations' (UN Charter, Art. 92). But this court only has compulsory jurisdiction as between some states and in respect of certain subject matters (as, for example, defined under the optional clause system of Art. 36(3) of the Statute of the ICJ).
[3] For exceptions, see below, pp. 447–9.
[4] UN Charter, Art. 2(3).   [5] UN Charter, Art. 33(1).
[6] See Art. 38 of the Statute of the ICJ and Art. 291 of UNCLOS.

law under which claims can be judicially enforced before a court with compulsory jurisdiction and those where this is not the case.[7]

In the WTO

At first glance, one may doubt whether the DSU actually provides for the *judicial* settlement of disputes. First, contrary to the Appellate Body, WTO panels are not standing bodies but *ad hoc* tribunals created pursuant to predetermined procedures in the DSU. Panels must be established *ad hoc* for each case by the WTO dispute settlement body (DSB). They cannot be established by the mere will of the disputing parties. However, their establishment by the DSB is virtually automatic pursuant to the negative consensus rule in DSU Art. 6.1. In terms of their *mode of establishment*, panels could thus be qualified as a mixture between arbitration and judicial dispute settlement. Yet, when it comes to their actual function and way of handling disputes, the DSU leaves no doubt that panels are judicial in nature. The Appellate Body has confirmed the judicial nature of WTO panels by making statements such as: 'as a matter of due process, and *the proper exercise of the judicial function* panels are required to..." (emphasis added).[8] Second, the legal findings and conclusions of both panels and the Appellate Body culminate only in 'recommendations' to the defending party. These recommendations must still be adopted by the DSB to obtain their legally binding force as between the parties to the dispute. Once again this adoption occurs by negative consensus, i.e., virtually automatically (DSU Arts. 16.4 and 17.14). This procedure could, at most, mean that the WTO judiciary includes the DSB. In practice, however, both panels and the Appellate Body are established, operate and make their legal conclusions in an entirely independent and law-based fashion. They are judicial tribunals in the international law sense.

WTO members granted *compulsory* jurisdiction to this WTO 'judiciary' *ex ante* and on a claim-specific basis (claims under WTO covered agreements only). It was *not* granted general jurisdiction to adjudicate *all trade disputes* between WTO members (i.e., on a subject-matter basis). Importantly, it is generally accepted that no counter-claims (not even counter-claims under WTO covered agreements) can be made. If a defendant

---

[7] Obviously, the fact that claims under a certain rule cannot be judicially enforced does not mean that the rule will not be complied with. Compliance mechanisms other than judicial settlement of disputes may, in certain cases, be as effective as, or even more effective than, third party adjudication.

[8] Appellate Body report on *Mexico – Corn Syrup (Article 21.5 – US)*, para. 36.

wishes, in turn, to lodge a complaint about the acts of the plaintiff it must start a new procedure.[9] As pointed out in chapter 1 above (pp. 22–3), the importance of the WTO judiciary's holding compulsory jurisdiction for all WTO claims cannot be overestimated. It is a crucial element in the increasing risk of conflicts arising between WTO law and other international law.

The jurisdiction of WTO panels

The substantive jurisdiction of WTO panels

Standard WTO panels

The jurisdiction of WTO panels is limited to certain claims only, namely *claims under WTO covered agreements*. DSU Art. 1.1 provides that the DSU applies to 'disputes brought pursuant to the consultation and dispute settlement provisions of the *agreements listed in Appendix 1 to the [DSU]*' (emphasis added).

These consultation and dispute settlement provisions allow for so-called violation complaints (claims of violation of WTO rules), non-violation and situation complaints[10] (hereinafter referred to jointly as claims under WTO covered agreements or WTO claims). *Ratione temporis*, the jurisdiction of WTO panels is limited to requests for consultations made on or after 1 January 1995 (the date of entry into force of the WTO agreement). What counts is the date of the request, not the date of enactment of the allegedly WTO inconsistent measure (this measure may be pre- or post-1995). The fact that the jurisdiction of WTO panels is limited to claims under WTO covered agreements is confirmed in DSU Art. 3.2, which states that the DSU mechanism 'serves to preserve the rights and obligations of Members under the *covered agreements*'. The standard terms of reference of WTO panels are '[t]o examine, in the light of the relevant provisions in (name of the *covered agreement(s)* cited by the parties to the dispute), the matter referred to the DSB...and to make such findings as will assist the DSB in making the recommendations or in giving the rulings provided for in *that/those agreement(s)*' (DSU Art. 7.1, emphasis added).

Finally, DSU Art. 11 instructs panels to 'make an objective assessment of...the applicability of and conformity with the *relevant covered agreements*, and make such other findings as will assist the DSB in making

---

[9] DSU Art. 3.10. [10] See GATT Art. XXIII.1(a), (b) and (c).

the recommendations or in giving the rulings provided for in the *covered agreements*' (emphasis added).

Consequently, no claims of violation of rules of international law *other than* those set out in WTO covered agreements can be brought to a WTO panel. Similarly, a WTO panel does not have jurisdiction to consider claims under *WTO rules other than those included in WTO covered agreements* (such as the ministerial decisions and declarations that are part of the Final Act, but not of the WTO Agreement; or rules set out in a mutually acceptable solution agreed upon in the context of a WTO dispute). Nor does it have jurisdiction to rule on claims of violation of *non-WTO* rules, such as environmental or human rights conventions or rules of general international law (including rules of customary law and/or *jus cogens*). A WTO panel could only decide these other claims if the parties to the dispute in question were to grant it this jurisdiction *ad hoc* and by mutual consent, for example, by means of explicitly agreeing on special terms of reference pursuant to DSU Art. 7.3 or by referring the dispute, including these other claims, to arbitration under DSU Art. 25.[11] On the basis of, *inter alia*, such mutual consent, one GATT arbitrator examined, for example, claims that were made not under the GATT but under a bilateral agreement between Canada and the European Communities.[12] In the context of the DSU, however, it could be submitted that, based on DSU Arts. 1.1 and 3.2, quoted earlier, any form of dispute settlement – including that under special terms of reference pursuant to DSU Art. 7.3 and special arbitration pursuant to DSU Art. 25 – must be limited to 'disputes brought pursuant to the consultation and dispute settlement provisions of the [WTO covered agreements]' and must, therefore, have a close connection with at least some WTO claims. (A dispute completely unrelated to WTO covered agreements, for example, could not be covered by the DSU, not even under DSU Arts. 7.3 and 25.) The special nature of dispute settlement under DSU Arts. 7.3 and 25 could, indeed, relate also to timing (expedited procedures), the absence of third parties (not

---

[11] DSU Art. 25.1 only requires that the disputes 'concern issues that are clearly defined by the parties'.

[12] See the Arbitration Award on *Canada/European Communities Article XXVIII Rights* (DS12/R), BISD 37s/80. The arbitrator gave the following reasons in support (at p. 84): 'In principle a claim based on a bilateral agreement cannot be brought under the multilateral dispute settlement procedures of the GATT. An exception is warranted in this case given the close connection of this particular bilateral agreement with the GATT, the fact that the Agreement is consistent with the objectives of the GATT, and that both parties joined in requesting recourse to the GATT Arbitration procedures.'

provided for in DSU Art. 25 without mutual agreement of both parties) or the absence of an appeal.

Although a WTO panel has jurisdiction only over WTO claims, it should be recalled that some WTO rules explicitly confirm and incorporate pre-existing *non-WTO* treaty rules. These non-WTO rules have thereby become WTO rules under which claims can be judicially enforced before a panel. Other WTO rules do not *incorporate* non-WTO rules but make an explicit reference to them. These non-WTO rules can thereby become part of a WTO claim (although they have not as such been incorporated and can therefore not be judicially enforced independently of other WTO rules). An example of 'incorporation' is the TRIPS agreement which incorporates, *inter alia*, provisions of the Berne, Paris and Rome Conventions part of WIPO.[13] Examples of 'explicit reference' are the SPS, TBT and Subsidies agreements where reference is made, for example, to international standards adopted in the WHO/FAO Codex Alimentarius Commission (SPS agreement), the IARC[14] (TBT agreement) or the OECD Arrangement on Guidelines for Officially Supported Export Credits (Subsidies agreement).[15] In the TRIPS agreement, the incorporated rules are legally binding as such in the WTO and claims under those rules can be judicially enforced before a WTO panel.[16] In the other WTO agreements, the non-WTO rules serve only as a benchmark or basis for the assessment of a distinct WTO-specific obligation. For example, the international standards referred to in the SPS agreement are not incorporated as binding in the WTO (hence no independent claim of breach of, for example, Codex standards can be brought to a WTO panel). However, when WTO members conform their sanitary measures to such standards, they will be presumed to be in conformity also with the SPS agreement.[17]

Implementation panels under DSU Art. 21.5 and arbitrators on retaliation under DSU Art. 22.6

In the DSU, WTO members agreed also to confer compulsory jurisdiction on WTO panels/arbitrators in respect of two particular types of disputes:

---

[13] See chapter 7 above, pp. 346–7.
[14] International Agency for Research on Cancer, referred to, for example, in the panel report on *EC – Asbestos*, at para. 8.186. See chapter 7 above, pp. 349–50.
[15] Annex I, item (k) of the Subsidies agreement. See chapter 7 above, pp. 348–9.
[16] See, for example, in respect of the Berne Convention, the panel report on *US – Copyright*.
[17] SPS Art. 3.1 and 3.2.

(i) disputes constituting 'disagreement as to the existence or consistency with a covered agreement of measures taken to comply with the recommendations and rulings' adopted by the DSB as a result of standard panel and Appellate Body procedures (so-called 'implementation panels' set up under Art. 21.5 of the DSU); and
(ii) disputes over retaliation as a result of objections to the level of suspension proposed by the winning WTO member faced with non-compliance or claims of violation of the principles and procedures set forth in DSU Art. 22.3 on the sectors and agreements under which retaliation and cross-retaliation may take place (referred to here as 'arbitration on retaliation', pursuant to DSU Art. 22.6).

The jurisdiction of implementation panels has been broadly defined. Such panels may examine (i) whether there *exist* 'measures taken to comply'; and (ii) whether such measures are *consistent* with any provision in WTO covered agreements. The Appellate Body stressed that these panels are 'not confined to examining the "measures taken to comply" from the perspective of the claims, arguments and factual circumstances that related to the measure that was the subject of the original proceedings'.[18]

The jurisdiction of arbitrators on retaliation is much more limited. It covers only (i) the *level* of retaliation, i.e., is it equivalent to the level of nullification or impairment? (as called for in DSU Art. 22.4); and (ii) whether the principles and procedures in DSU Art. 22.3 have been met. DSU Art. 22.7 adds to this (iii) the question of whether the proposed suspension is allowed under the covered agreement (in line with DSU Art. 22.5). Article 22.7 makes it explicit that these arbitrators 'shall not examine the *nature* of the concessions or other obligations to be suspended'. Nonetheless, the arbitrators in *EC – Bananas*, albeit in exceptional circumstances, also considered the *consistency* under WTO covered agreements of EC measures taken to comply (something that should normally be done under Art. 21.5).[19]

Importantly, arbitrators under DSU Art. 22.6 do not have jurisdiction to decide, for example, whether the proposed suspension is in line also with other rules of international law, say, the 2001 Draft Articles on

---

[18] Appellate Body report on *Canada – Aircraft*, Recourse by Brazil to Art. 21.5 of the DSU, para. 40. See also the implementation panel report on *Australia – Salmon*, paras. 7.10–7.22.

[19] Arbitrators report on *EC – Bananas* (US request for retaliation), para. 4.2. This approach was approved by the panel on *US – Certain Products*, paras. 6.121–6.126. However, on appeal the Appellate Body found that the panel had no mandate to make these findings in respect of DSU Art. 22.6 and declared that these findings 'have no legal effect' (para. 90).

State Responsibility which prohibit the taking of countermeasures in the form of suspending obligations for the protection of fundamental human rights or WIPO conventions in case the proposed suspension is one under the TRIPS agreement.[20] The arbitrators in *EC – Bananas* (suspension request by Ecuador) confirmed that they did not have jurisdiction 'to pass judgment on whether Ecuador, by suspending, once authorized by the DSB, certain TRIPS obligations, would act inconsistently with its international obligations arising from treaties other than the agreements covered by the WTO (e.g. the Paris, Berne and Rome Conventions which Ecuador has ratified)'.[21]

Nonetheless, the fact that a WTO panel does not have *jurisdiction* to rule on the conformity with these other norms does not mean that these other norms do not apply to the suspension finally imposed. A WTO arbitrator may well decide that, under the DSU, the proposed suspension is authorised, but this does not mean that it is consistent also under other rules of international law. Hence, although authorised by the WTO, a suspension may still be inconsistent with international law (in case the suspension would, for example, derogate from fundamental human rights). Yet, this inconsistency cannot be challenged before a WTO arbitrator, unless the parties involved were to grant it the additional jurisdiction required.

To legitimise the enforcement mechanism of the WTO further, thought should be given to expanding the jurisdiction of arbitrators under DSU Art. 22.6 so as to include also claims of violation of general international law restrictions that apply to countermeasures, that is, those set out in the 2001 ILC Draft Articles.

The implied or incidental jurisdiction of WTO panels

The substantive jurisdiction of any international court or tribunal must be granted *explicitly* by consent of the parties involved. Nevertheless, once an international court or tribunal has been seized of a specific matter, it also has certain implied jurisdictional powers which derive directly from its very nature as a judicial body. This, what has been called, incidental or implied jurisdiction is an inherent part also of the mandate of WTO panels (WTO panels being international bodies of a judicial nature). Elements of this incidental jurisdiction are: (i) the jurisdiction 'to

---

[20] We discussed how to resolve conflict between a DSB decision and, for example, WIPO conventions in chapter 6 above, pp. 324–6.
[21] Arbitrators report on *EC – Bananas* (request by Ecuador for retaliation), para. 152.

interpret the submissions of the parties' in order to 'isolate the real issue in the case and to identify the object of the claim';[22] (ii) the jurisdiction to determine whether one has substantive jurisdiction to decide a matter (the principle of *la compétence de la compétence*); (iii) the jurisdiction to decide whether one should *refrain* from exercising substantive jurisdiction that has been validly established;[23] and (iv) the jurisdiction to decide all matters linked to the *exercise* of substantive jurisdiction and inherent in the judicial function[24] such as claims under rules on burden of proof, due process or any other general international law rules on the judicial settlement of disputes or state responsibility including the implied jurisdiction to order remedies, i.e. to order cessation of the breach,[25] assurances of non-repetition[26] and reparation for breach.[27] As the ICJ held recently in the *LaGrand* case: 'Where jurisdiction exists over a dispute on a particular matter, no separate basis for jurisdiction is required by the Court to consider the remedies a party has requested for the breach of the obligation.'[28] The jurisdiction to indicate provisional measures, explicitly provided for in respect of some courts and tribunals,[29] is not generally recognized as part of their implied jurisdiction.[30]

That WTO panels have *la compétence de la compétence* was explicitly confirmed by the Appellate Body in *US – Anti-Dumping Act of 1916*. There, the Appellate Body referred to the 'widely accepted rule that an international tribunal is entitled to consider the issue of its own jurisdiction on its own initiative, and to satisfy itself that it has jurisdiction in any case that comes before it'.[31] As noted by the Appeals Chamber of the International Criminal Tribunal for the Former Yugoslavia in the *Tadić* case (which decided, contrary to the Trial Chamber, that it did have

---

[22] *Nuclear Tests* cases, ICJ Reports 1974, 262, para. 29 and 466, para. 30.
[23] In support, see the WTO jurisprudence outlined in chapter 4 above, p. 208.
[24] See the very broad statements on the ICJ's implied jurisdiction in the *Northern Cameroons* case (Judgment), ICJ Reports 1963, 29 and the *Nuclear Tests* cases, ICJ Reports 1974, 259–60, para. 23 and 463, para. 23.
[25] As confirmed in the *Rainbow Warrior* Arbitration Award (30 April 1990), UNRIAA, vol. XX, 217 at 270, para. 114.
[26] See the *LaGrand* case recently decided by the ICJ, at para. 48.
[27] See the *Chorzów Factory* case, PCIJ, Series A, No. 9, 22.
[28] ICJ *LaGrand* case, at para. 48.
[29] See Art. 41 of the ICJ Statute and Art. 290 of UNCLOS.
[30] In this sense, see Hugh Thirlway, 'The Law and Procedure of the International Court of Justice 1960–1989 (Part One)' (1989) 60 BYIL 1 at 19.
[31] Appellate Body report on *US – Anti-Dumping Act of 1916*, note 30. See also the Appellate Body report on *Mexico – Corn Syrup (Article 21.5 – US)*, paras. 36–7.

jurisdiction to review the validity of its establishment by the Security Council), this implied jurisdiction

> is a necessary component in the exercise of the judicial function and does not need to be expressly provided for in the constitutive document of...tribunals ...To assume that the jurisdiction of the International Tribunal is absolutely limited to what the Security Council 'intended' to entrust it with, is to envisage the International Tribunal exclusively as a 'subsidiary organ' of the Security Council.[32]

In addition, the implied jurisdiction to decide whether one should refrain from exercising substantive jurisdiction finds reflection in WTO jurisprudence where the so-called principle of judicial economy plays a prominent role. The principle was referred to in US – Shirts and Blouses as one providing that 'a panel need only address those claims which must be addressed in order to resolve the matter at issue'.[33]

It should be stressed that the question of jurisdiction is one to be examined by the court or tribunal *proprio motu*.[34] In US – Anti-Dumping Act of 1916 the Appellate Body rightly rejected an EC argument that the United States had raised a jurisdictional objection before the panel in an untimely manner, noting that an international tribunal 'is *entitled* to consider the issue of its own jurisdiction on its own initiative'.[35] In Mexico – Corn Syrup (Article 21.5 – US), the Appellate Body went a step further, rightly pointing out that 'panels cannot simply ignore issues which go to the root of their jurisdiction...Rather, panels *must* deal with such issues – if necessary, on their own motion – in order to satisfy themselves that they have authority to proceed.'[36]

What about WTO claims in the context of a wider dispute mainly about non-WTO matters?

The issue may arise as to whether a WTO panel has jurisdiction to hear WTO claims even though the underlying or predominant element of

---

[32] Decision of 2 October 1995, IT-94-1-AR72, paras. 18 and 15. Note that Prof. Abi-Saab, a member of the WTO Appellate Body at the time of writing, was a judge on this Appeals Chamber.
[33] Appellate Body report on *US – Shirts and Blouses*, 19.
[34] Case concerning *Border and Transborder Armed Actions (Nicaragua v. Honduras)*, ICJ Reports 1988, 76, para. 16. In that dispute, the ICJ opened a phase of the proceedings devoted to jurisdiction and admissibility on its own initiative.
[35] Appellate Body report on *US – Anti-Dumping Act of 1916*, note 30 (emphasis added).
[36] Appellate Body report on *Mexico – Corn Syrup (Article 21.5 – US)*, para. 37 (emphasis added).

disagreement derives rather from other rules of international law, under which claims cannot be judicially enforced in the WTO (such as the law of the sea, territorial delimitation or human rights law). Potential examples can be found in the WTO dispute on *Chile – Swordfish*, a dispute that was brought also before the International Tribunal for the Law of the Sea; and the WTO dispute on *Nicaragua – Measures Affecting Imports from Honduras and Colombia*, involving trade sanctions as a result of a maritime delimitation dispute, pending also before the ICJ.[37]

This issue of jurisdiction must, however, be distinguished from the issue of what the role of non-WTO rules is before a WTO panel once such a panel has decided that it will hear a case (discussed below, pp. 456–72).[38] In chapter 3 above, we discussed the problem of conflict between judicial decisions (pp. 114–24).

One should, first, recall that a WTO panel has the implied jurisdiction to decide whether, and to what extent, it has substantive jurisdiction in respect of a given dispute. What is more, it must exercise this jurisdiction on its own initiative. Second, no burden of proof is involved in establishing jurisdiction. As noted by the ICJ in the case concerning *Border and Transborder Armed Actions (Nicaragua v. Honduras)*, '[t]he existence of jurisdiction of the Court in a given case is... not a question of fact, but a question of law'.[39] In respect of questions of law the principle *jura novit curia* applies. The judge knows the law. It is not for either party to establish it. What remains important though is the question of whether, in case of doubt, the Court should decide that it has jurisdiction or rather decline jurisdiction. On this issue, the ICJ noted that it will 'only affirm its jurisdiction provided that the force of the arguments militating in favour of it is preponderant. The fact that weighty arguments can be advanced to support the contention that it has no jurisdiction cannot itself create a doubt calculated to upset its jurisdiction.'[40] Under WTO jurisprudence, this level or degree of proof required may be slightly lower,

---

[37] *Maritime Delimitation between Nicaragua and Honduras in the Caribbean Sea (Nicaragua v. Honduras)*, http://www.icj-cij.org.

[38] The matter here must also be distinguished from that of two agreements dealing with dispute settlement in respect of one given dispute but where only one of the two agreements provides for compulsory jurisdiction. In this respect, see the *Southern Bluefin Tuna* case, and Bernard Oxman, 'Complementary Agreements and Compulsory Jurisdiction' (2001) 95 AJIL 276.

[39] ICJ Reports 1988, 76, para. 16.

[40] Case concerning *Border and Transborder Armed Actions (Nicaragua v. Honduras)*, ICJ Reports 1988, 76, para. 16, quoting and confirming *Chorzów Factory* (Jurisdiction), PCIJ, Series A, No. 9, 32.

namely creating a *presumption* (in favour of the panel having jurisdiction) not sufficiently rebutted by the defendant.[41]

Two possible solutions

With these considerations in mind, one can imagine two possible solutions to the problem of panel jurisdiction over predominantly non-WTO disputes. First, it could be submitted that as soon as a WTO member brings a claim pursuant to the consultation and dispute settlement provisions of WTO covered agreements (i.e., a WTO claim), a WTO panel has jurisdiction to hear and decide the claim notwithstanding the fact that the wider dispute underlying the claim also, or even predominantly, involves other rules of international law. In most (if not all) cases, this will be the preferred solution (unless, of course, the disputing parties 'contracted out' of WTO panel jurisdiction under NAFTA Art. 2005, see pp. 114–15).

The WTO does not provide for compulsory dispute settlement only in the event that a WTO member *wants* to bring a WTO claim to the WTO. DSU Art. 23.1 prescribes that '[w]hen Members seek the redress of a violation of obligations or other nullification or impairment of benefits under the covered agreements or an impediment to the attainment of any objectives of the covered agreements, *they shall have recourse to*, and abide by, the [DSU]' (emphasis added). A WTO panel has interpreted this provision as being an 'exclusive dispute resolution clause'.[42] DSU Art. 11 further supports the competence of panels to examine WTO claims, even if non-WTO rules are of crucial and even higher importance in the context of the wider dispute. This provision directs panels to 'make such *other findings* as will assist the DSB in making the recommendations or in giving the rulings provided for in the covered agreements'.[43] The standard terms of reference of WTO panels are of similar effect.[44] Support

---

[41] See Joost Pauwelyn, 'Evidence, Proof and Persuasion in WTO Dispute Settlement, Who Bears the Burden?' (1998) 1 JIEL 227.
[42] Panel report on *US – Section 301*, para. 7.43. But see, however, the limited exception provided for in SPS Art. 11.3, discussed in chapter 7 above, p. 352.
[43] Thomas Schoenbaum, 'WTO Dispute Settlement: Praise and Suggestions for Reform' (1998) 47 ICLQ 647 at 653 refers to DSU Art. 11 as an 'implied powers' clause which 'should be interpreted broadly so that the panels and Appellate Body can decide all aspects of a dispute'.
[44] DSU Art. 7.1 directs panels 'to make *such findings* as will assist the DSB in making the recommendations or in giving the rulings provided for in [the relevant covered agreement(s)]'.

for such 'salami-slicing' of disputes[45] can be found also in the *Nicaragua* case where the ICJ declared that it did have jurisdiction over certain claims under *customary international law* brought by Nicaragua against the United States. The Court did so even though the United States had not accepted ICJ jurisdiction in respect of 'disputes arising under a multilateral treaty, unless... all parties to the treaty affected by the decision are also parties to the case before the Court' and even though the multilateral treaty rules largely overlapped with the customary law invoked by Nicaragua.[46] Moreover, in the *Hostages* case the ICJ found that 'no provision of the Statute or Rules contemplates that the Court should decline to take cognizance of one aspect of a dispute merely because that dispute has other aspects, however important'.[47]

In chapter 3 above, pp. 118–21, we discussed the possibility for WTO panels and the Appellate Body to seek assistance from other tribunals or organisations through the operation of, for example, DSU Art. 13.1 allowing panels to 'seek information and technical advice from any individual or body which it deems appropriate'. Exercising this power in cases involving non-WTO matters may be particularly helpful.

As a second way of dealing with predominantly non-WTO disputes, one could argue that in certain extreme cases the dispute no longer genuinely concerns WTO claims (even though such claims could technically be made) but rather claims under other rules of international law to which the WTO claims are inextricably linked and independently of which these WTO claims could not be decided.[48] In such extreme cases

---

[45] A term used by Alan Boyle, 'Dispute Settlement and the Law of the Sea Convention: Problems of Fragmentation and Jurisdiction' (1997) 46 ICLQ 37 at 41.

[46] Jurisdiction and Admissibility, ICJ Reports 1984, para. 73 and Merits, ICJ Reports 1986, para. 175. For forceful critique, see the Dissenting Opinions by Schwebel (ICJ Reports 1984, 613 and 616, noting, for example, that 'Nicaragua's claims are so integrally and essentially bound up with the treaty provisions on which they rely that, if those provisions cannot be pleaded, there is no case which the Court can consider' and calling the 'salami-slicing' approach in this instance 'an unreal, artificial, highly constricted – and yet unduly unconstrained – process'), Oda (ICJ Reports 1986, 217) and Jennings (ICJ Reports 1986, 530). Oda had, indeed, a strong point when saying that 'the Court should have proved, not that it can apply customary and general international law independently, but that the dispute referred to it in the Applicant's claims had *not* arisen under these multilateral treaties'. The Court in that case did, indeed, confuse to some extent the issue of applicable law (custom versus treaty) with that of jurisdiction (over certain *disputes*).

[47] *United States Diplomatic and Consular Staff in Teheran*, ICJ Reports 1980, 19, para. 36.

[48] See the Dissenting Opinion of Schwebel, note 46 above. Recall also that a WTO panel cannot hear counter-claims, a restriction that may limit a panel's ability actually to resolve a dispute (see the *Chile – Swordfish* dispute, where in the WTO only the EC complained, but where in ITLOS both parties submitted claims).

it could then be submitted that the history, prior procedures and substantive content of the dispute indicate that the real issue of the case (i.e., the genuine object of the claim) is related to non-WTO claims as to which a WTO panel does *not* have jurisdiction. On these grounds, the WTO panel could either decide that it does *not* have substantive jurisdiction over the dispute or find that it *does* have jurisdiction but that it does not consider it appropriate to exercise this jurisdiction.[49] In this respect, one should recall that WTO panels, like any international court or tribunal, have the implied jurisdiction 'to interpret the submissions of the parties' in order to 'isolate the real issue in the case and to identify the object of the claim'.[50] As was confirmed in WTO jurisprudence on the principle of judicial economy, WTO panels also have the implied jurisdiction to decide whether or not to exercise substantive jurisdiction even if, in theory, this jurisdiction was conferred upon them.

In the *Fisheries Jurisdiction* case (*Spain v. Canada*), for example, the ICJ 'redefined' Spain's complaint relating to Canada's 'lack of entitlement to exercise jurisdiction on the high seas' so as to mean a dispute 'arising out of or concerning conservation and management measures' for which Canada had made a reservation. On that basis, the Court found that it did *not* have jurisdiction to hear the case.[51]

Support for this second solution or 'incorporation' (*auxiliarum principali sequitur*) approach[52] can be found in the recent Arbitration Award on *Southern Bluefin Tuna*. There, the tribunal found that the dispute 'while *centered in* the 1993 [trilateral Convention for the Conservation of Southern Bluefin Tuna], *also arises under* [UNCLOS]'. It continued, nonetheless, by saying that '[t]o find that, in this case, there is a dispute actually arising under UNCLOS which is distinct from the dispute that arose under the [1993 Convention] would be artificial'.[53] Since the tribunal

---

[49] See William Davey, 'Has the WTO Dispute Settlement System Exceeded its Authority?' (2001) 4 JIEL 95 on what he termed 'issue avoidance techniques', such as standing, mootness, ripeness, political appropriateness and judicial economy. Note that, although the WTO dispute settlement body must first 'establish' a panel, it will be difficult for this body not to establish a panel, even if there are potential problems related to jurisdiction or exercising jurisdiction, given that it makes its decision by negative consensus, i.e., the panel will be established unless all WTO members, including the complainant, agree not to establish it. Nonetheless, this virtually automatic DSB decision establishing a panel should not bar panels from properly examining their jurisdiction.

[50] *Nuclear Tests* cases, ICJ Reports 1974, 262, para. 29 and 466, para. 30.

[51] ICJ Reports 1998, 437.

[52] The Appellate Body used this approach, not to decide on jurisdiction but on which WTO rules to apply, in *EC – Asbestos*, para. 62.

[53] *Southern Bluefin Tuna* case, paras. 52 and 54. But see the forceful Separate Opinion by Sir Kenneth Keith.

later declared that it did not have jurisdiction over the 1993 Convention part of the dispute, it automatically declined jurisdiction also over the UNCLOS part (notwithstanding the compulsory jurisdiction in Part XV of UNCLOS) on the ground of its 'single dispute' theory.

Although, for present purposes, the sticking point is a related *subject matter* or *claim* for which WTO panels have no jurisdiction, it is instructive to recall that the ICJ has found that it cannot decide a case in the event that doing so would necessarily imply making a ruling in respect of *states* for which it has no jurisdiction.[54]

In any event, for a WTO panel to dismiss a case because it has no substantive jurisdiction, or because it does not consider it appropriate to exercise this jurisdiction, is not the same as proclaiming a *non liquet*. In a *non liquet* a panel would find that it *has* substantive jurisdiction and that it *is* appropriate to exercise this jurisdiction, but nevertheless conclude that it cannot come to a substantive legal conclusion *on the ground that there is no law to be applied or that the applicable law is unclear*.[55] In the context of WTO dispute settlement, being a claim-specific mechanism, *non liquet* (often portrayed as prohibited under general international law) is generally precluded. Either a WTO claim is valid (and the complainant wins) or a WTO claim is unfounded (and the complainant loses). A panel should *not* normally be allowed to conclude that the WTO rules invoked are unclear (*jura novit curia*) and on that basis proclaim a *non liquet* (except in the extreme circumstances referred to in chapter 7 above, pp. 419–22).

Crucially, the question discussed here – do WTO panels still have jurisdiction and, if so, should they exercise this jurisdiction, in the event the dispute largely concerns other rules of international law? – must be distinguished from the question discussed earlier of overlapping jurisdictions vested in different international tribunals. Under the first question, the one discussed here, there is not necessarily another tribunal to turn to and the lack of jurisdiction on behalf of a WTO panel results, if at all, from the inseparability of WTO claims from other non-WTO rules and claims, not from the fact that the jurisdiction of another international tribunal prevails over that of a WTO panel. In contrast, the

---

[54] *Monetary Gold* case, ICJ Reports 1954, 32 ('Albania's legal interests would not only be affected by a decision, but would form the very subject-matter of the decision. In such a case, the Statute cannot be regarded, by implication, as authorizing proceedings to be continued in the absence of Albania'); confirmed more recently in the *East Timor* case, ICJ Reports 1995, 102, para. 28. See also the panel report on *Turkey – Textile*, paras. 9.4–13.

[55] See chapter 7 above, pp. 419–22, and chapter 3 above, pp. 150–4.

second question of overlapping jurisdictions must, as noted in chapter 3 above (pp. 114–15), be construed as just another conflict of norms issue to which normal conflict rules should apply. As a result, the jurisdiction granted to a non-WTO tribunal may well prevail over that vested in a WTO panel on the ground of, for example, an explicit conflict clause or the *lex specialis* principle (and this notwithstanding the *obligation* in DSU Art. 23 to bring WTO claims to a WTO panel since this obligation may conflict with another treaty clause granting jurisdiction to another tribunal and conflict rules may indicate that this non-WTO rule prevails over DSU Art. 23). Moreover, even if, under the first solution suggested earlier, a WTO panel still decides to have jurisdiction notwithstanding the fact that the wider dispute is predominantly one under non-WTO rules, this WTO panel may still, with reference to other international tribunals, apply the principles of *res judicata* or *lis alibi pendens* or the doctrine of abuse of process (discussed in chapter 3 above) and refuse to answer the claims submitted to it or delay their examination.

The problem of non-violation complaints with reference to a violation of non-WTO rules

The necessity for a WTO panel actually to decide on whether *non-WTO* rules have been *violated* could arise particularly in a so-called non-violation case. It may arise also when the defendant relies on an act of another international organisation (say, the UN Security Council, WIPO or the ILO) in defence of an alleged breach under WTO covered agreements. In reply, the complainant may then challenge the legality of this non-WTO act under the constituent instrument of the decision-maker in question, that is, the complainant may then make claims of violation under norms other than those set out in WTO covered agreements.

In non-violation cases a WTO panel could, indeed, be called upon to refer to non-WTO rules (such as international competition law or international labour or environmental law) in its assessment of whether certain governmental measures, though not in violation of WTO rules, have affected the 'legitimate expectations' that could have been derived from a trade concession. A complainant could invoke these non-WTO rules along the following lines: 'when we obtained your trade concession (duty free access for our computers), we did so with the expectation that you would continue to respect international labour standards (in particular, not to employ children under the age of ten); now you have violated these non-WTO rules (children under the age of ten assemble computers in your country); this violation of labour standards does not violate WTO rules as such, but it nullifies the trade value of your concession, a nullification that we could not have foreseen (you are now able to produce much cheaper computers than before and out-compete our computers which are produced with full respect for international labour standards); so in the WTO we should be compensated for this nullification under the heading of non-violation'.

Such non-violation claims may require that WTO panels decide on whether non-WTO rules have been violated (in our example, a decision as to whether employing children under the age of ten violates international labour standards binding as between the disputing parties), although the focus under non-violation complaints is not a violation of rules, but an upsetting of 'legitimate expectations' (you acted in a certain way when we got the concession, that is, you did not employ children under the age of ten; we had a legitimate expectation that you would continue to do so, but now you do not and employ children under the age of ten; so you upset our expectations and in doing so nullified our concession). The Appellate Body has, however, recently confirmed that the non-violation remedy 'should be approached with caution and should remain an exceptional remedy'.[56] This trend goes against endorsing the wide interpretation paraphrased above.

The applicable law before a GATT/WTO panel

The applicable law before GATT 1947 panels

The law referred to by GATT 1947 panels was very much limited to the 'four corners of GATT'. No distinction was made between (i) the *jurisdiction* of GATT panels; (ii) the law that GATT panels could refer to when *interpreting* GATT treaty terms; and (iii) the law they could *apply* when deciding on the validity of GATT claims. GATT Art. XXIII conferred jurisdiction on panels only in respect of claims under the GATT, not in respect of claims under any other norm of international law. Moreover, as we noted earlier, the (unadopted) GATT panel on *US – Restrictions on Imports of Tuna* correctly pointed out that, in principle, treaty interpretation allows for reference *only* to non-GATT rules of international law that reflect the common intentions of *all* GATT contracting parties.[57] Since CITES was not accepted by all GATT contracting parties, the panel refused to take it into account. However, these restrictions imposed in respect of treaty *interpretation* and, in particular, the limited *jurisdiction*

---

[56] Appellate Body report on *EC – Asbestos*, para. 186.   [57] See chapter 5 above, p. 258.

of GATT panels, were erroneously extended so as to portray GATT dispute settlement as an activity exclusively limited to the 'four corners of GATT', outside the realm of international law.

In the 1984 panel report on *Canada – Administration of the Foreign Investment Review Act*, the United States challenged the GATT consistency of Canadian investment legislation. At the Council meeting, a number of contracting parties had expressed 'doubts whether the dispute...was one for which the GATT had competence since it involved investment legislation, a subject not covered by the GATT'.[58] In response, the United States stressed that it was only challenging 'the two specific trade-related issues mentioned in the terms of reference' of the panel. Canada too was of the view that 'the terms of reference ensured that the examination would touch only on trade matters within the purview of GATT'. On the basis of this discussion, the Council decided that 'it be presumed that the Panel would be limited in its activities and findings to within the four corners of GATT'.[59]

To the extent this decision relates only to panel jurisdiction, it is obviously correct: the parties conferred jurisdiction on the panel only in respect of GATT claims, not claims under, for example, bilateral investment agreements.[60] Nonetheless, the broad scope of the statement surely gave the wrong impression that GATT panels, when interpreting GATT treaty terms and examining the validity of GATT claims, are not allowed to refer to, or apply, any other rules of international law.

The same impression was created by the 1984 panel on *United States – Imports of Sugar from Nicaragua*. There, the United States stated that 'it was neither invoking any exceptions under the provisions of the General Agreement nor intending to defend its actions in GATT terms'.[61] The United States stressed that its reduction in Nicaragua's sugar imports 'was not taken for trade policy reasons' and 'was fully justified in the context in which it was taken'. It concluded that 'attempting to discuss this issue in purely trade terms within the GATT, divorced from the broader context of the dispute, would be disingenuous' and that it 'did not believe that the review and resolution of that broader dispute was within the ambit of the GATT'. In response, the panel stated that the

---

[58] Panel report adopted on 7 February 1984, L/5504, BISD 30S/140, at p. 141, para. 1.4.
[59] Ibid., confirmed by the panel at p. 157, para. 5.1.
[60] For an exceptional GATT case where claims were nonetheless made and examined under a bilateral agreement (not GATT provisions), see the Arbitration Award on Canada/European Communities Article XXVIII Rights (DS12/R), BISD 37S/80.
[61] Panel report adopted on 13 March 1984, BISD 31S/67, L/5607, at p. 72.

US measures 'were but one aspect of a more general problem' and that, pursuant to its terms of reference, it would examine those measures 'solely in the light of the relevant GATT provisions, concerning itself only with the trade issue under dispute'.[62]

Here again, the panel's statement was correct in so far as it related to panel jurisdiction. The panel took the right decision also to examine GATT claims, even if they were set in a broader dispute, the way the ICJ did in the *Teheran Hostages* and *Nicaragua* cases.[63] But, here again, it erroneously limited its examination in terms of treaty interpretation and validity of GATT claims to GATT provisions only. Non-GATT rules could have been referred to in the interpretation of GATT treaty terms. More importantly, the United States should have been allowed also to invoke non-GATT norms, such as those on self-defence or countermeasures, in defence of its action and of any violation of GATT rules. (Whether such defence would have been valid and would have prevailed over GATT under the applicable conflict rules is another question.)

A similarly restrictive approach was taken by the 1988 panel on *Canada – Measures Affecting Exports of Unprocessed Herring and Salmon*, where the panel noted the following at the very end of its report: 'Canada referred in its submission to international agreements on fisheries and the Convention on the Law of the Sea. The Panel considered that its mandate was limited to the examination of Canada's measures in the light of the relevant provisions of the General Agreement. This report therefore has no bearing on questions of fisheries jurisdiction.'[64]

Javier Pons would continue to apply GATT/WTO rules within the 'four corners' of the WTO treaty.[65] He notes that

beyond a panel's particular findings, other rules of international law such as the general international rules on countermeasures could justify certain behaviour in contrast to the special GATT/WTO rules. In such a case, the value of

---

[62] *Ibid.*, p. 73, para. 4.1.   [63] See above, pp. 451–2.
[64] Panel report adopted on 22 March 1988, BISD 35S/98, L/6268, at p. 115, para. 5.3. See also the panel report on *United States – Taxes on Petroleum and Certain Imported Substances*, adopted on 17 June 1987, BISD 34S/136, at p. 162, para. 5.2.6 where the panel noted that its terms of reference did not allow it to examine the consistency of the US Superfund Act with the polluter-pays principle. That this is so should not have prevented the panel from taking account of this principle, for example, in the interpretation of GATT treaty terms to the extent this principle was part of customary international law.
[65] Javier Fernandez Pons 'Self-Help and the World Trade Organization', in Paolo Mengozzi (ed.), *International Trade Law on the 50th Anniversary of the Multilateral Trade System* (Milan, A. Giuffrè, 1999).

a panel/Appellate Body report would be characterized by its relativity, since the 'losing' party could continue to invoke other international law rules, in relation to which it had not operated a third party adjudication, so as to legitimate its conduct.[66]

But this is exactly the 'ostrich' approach that must be avoided. If not, not only would WTO judicial decisions become 'relative', but also the unity of international law as such would be at risk. This is why a treaty must always be applied, and treaty claims be examined, in the context of *other* applicable law. In WTO dispute settlement as well, such other law must be capable of justifying a breach of WTO rules. There is no need for the WTO treaty explicitly to incorporate such non-WTO justifications, nor for the defendant to go to another tribunal to see this non-WTO law applied. This will be explained in the following subsections.

The applicable law before WTO panels: the framework delimited

Once it has been determined that a WTO panel has jurisdiction to hear a case, the question of what law to be applied in order to resolve the WTO claims put before it may arise. The applicable law before a WTO panel is delimited by four factors:

(1) *The claims that can be brought to a WTO panel.* Based on the limited *substantive jurisdiction* of WTO panels, only legal claims under WTO covered agreements can be examined. Only claims set out with sufficient clarity by the complaining party in the panel request upon which the dispute settlement body has established the panel fall within a panel's mandate[67] (no counter-claims within the same procedure are allowed).[68] As pointed out earlier, in order to complete such examination of WTO claims, a panel may also be required, and is allowed, to make other findings either pursuant to its *implied jurisdiction*[69] or in order to come to a legal conclusion under the WTO claims themselves.[70]

(2) *The defences invoked by the defending party.* Except for matters or defences that a WTO panel must examine *ex officio* (such as its own jurisdiction), a WTO panel must limit its examination to defences invoked by the defending party (*non ultra petita*).

(3) *The scope of the relevant rules* ratione materiae, ratione personae *and* ratione temporis. Within the framework of the claims and defences

---

[66] Ibid., p. 102. [67] DSU Arts. 6.2 and 7.1.
[68] DSU Art. 3.10. [69] See above, pp. 447–9.
[70] Of course, in so far as this necessity to decide on non-WTO matters has not led the panel to find that it has no substantive jurisdiction in the first place or that it does not consider it appropriate to exercise such jurisdiction, as discussed above, pp. 452–4.

thus before the panel, a WTO panel can only apply those rules (be they WTO rules or other rules of international law) which apply to the facts and circumstances of the case before it.

(4) *Conflict rules in the WTO treaty, general international law and other non-WTO treaties.*[71] In the event two or more rules apply to the facts and circumstances of the case and these rules are contradictory (pursuant to the definition of conflict described in chapter 4 above), a WTO panel must apply the relevant conflict rules to decide which of the two norms prevails.

'Jurisdiction' distinguished from 'applicable law'

Crucially – and this is one of the main points of this book – the fact that the substantive jurisdiction of WTO panels is limited to claims under WTO covered agreements does not mean that the applicable law available to a WTO panel is necessarily limited to WTO covered agreements. Much has been said above about the creation and continuing existence of the WTO treaty in the wider context of general international law and other non-WTO treaties, be they pre- or post-1994. This context and background (essentially, that WTO rules belong to international law) does not suddenly evaporate when WTO claims are transferred to a WTO panel.

As submitted earlier, it could be argued that there is a 'two-class society' between those rules of international law under which claims can be judicially enforced and those where this is not the case. In that sense, rules of international law may, indeed, operate at two levels: the first and more general level being that of the entire corpus of public international law where all rules of international law freely interact; the second and more specific level being that of a court of international law with jurisdiction to enforce only a limited number of claims under specified rules. Rules in WTO covered agreements operate at both the first and the second level. However, these two levels do not exist in 'splendid isolation'. There is an obvious link between them. In particular, if in the first, more general level of the entire corpus of international law, WTO rules are somehow changed, albeit as between certain WTO members only, such change must necessarily be felt also and penetrate the second, more concrete level of WTO dispute settlement. The exact consequences of such change are discussed below.

In so far as the WTO treaty was not created nor exists in a legal vacuum, neither does its dispute settlement system. That system, providing for the judicial settlement of disputes under certain rules of

---

[71] See chapters 6 and 7 above.

international law, is merely a tool or an instrument to enforce WTO covered agreements *as they were created and necessarily continue to exist in the wider corpus of international law*. It is not a system frozen into April 1994 law, nor is it one that is limited to the four corners of WTO covered agreements (even if it is limited to enforcing claims under these agreements). No treaty can be created outside the system of international law, neither can a court or tribunal enforcing claims under a treaty.

As noted in chapter 3 above (pp. 116–18), the approach suggested here – of allowing all relevant international law to be part of the applicable law before a WTO panel – is not only crucial for WTO dispute settlement. It is, more generally, one of the main instruments that *all* tribunals should use so as to avoid contradictions between judicial decisions. Although different tribunals may be dealing with different claims, the applicable law to examine those claims should be the same no matter where the case is brought. Not to accept this proposition, as many authors seem to do[72] – arguing, for example, that in ITLOS only UNCLOS rules can be applied or in the WTO only WTO rules can be applied – necessarily results in the creation of small isolated pockets of international law, delinked from other branches of the wider corpus of international law. It goes against the unity of international law as well as the principle of *pacta sunt servanda*.

The *Lockerbie* cases perfectly illustrate the crucial distinction to be made between 'jurisdiction' and 'applicable law'. In that dispute, the ICJ had jurisdiction only to consider Libyan claims under the Montreal Convention. However, this did not stop it from also examining other international law, in particular UN Security Council resolution 748 invoked in defence by the United Kingdom and the United States, as part of the applicable law.[73]

The same approach was taken by the ICJ in its Advisory Opinion on *Interpretation of the Agreement of 25 March 1951 between the WHO and Egypt*:

---

[72] See Gabrielle Marceau, 'Conflicts of Norms and Conflicts of Jurisdictions, The Relationship between the WTO Agreement and MEAs and other Treaties' (2001) 35 JWT 1081 at 1116 ('the applicable law before WTO adjudicating bodies is only WTO law'); Gerhard Hafner, 'Risk Ensuing from Fragmentation of International Law', ILC, Report on the work of its fifty-second session, General Assembly, Official Records, Fifty-fifth session, Supplement No. 10 (A/55/10), 321 at 332 ('most mechanisms, in particular the treaty bodies, are restricted only to their own substantive law as a legal basis for the legal evaluation of the dispute').

[73] *Questions of Interpretation and Application of the 1971 Montreal Convention Arising from the Aerial Incident at Lockerbie (Libyan Arab Jamahiriya v. US and UK)*, Provisional Measures, ICJ Reports 1992, at para. 42.

a rule of international law, whether customary or conventional, does not operate in a vacuum; it operates in relation to facts and in the context of a wider framework of legal rules of which it forms only a part. Accordingly, if a question put in the hypothetical way in which it is posed in the request is to receive a pertinent and effectual reply, the Court must first ascertain the meaning and full implications of the question in the light of the actual framework of fact and law in which it falls for consideration. Otherwise its reply to the question may be incomplete and, in consequence, ineffectual and even misleading as to the pertinent legal rules actually governing the matter under consideration.[74]

Or, as it was noted in the *Kronprins Gustaf Adolf* arbitration award, in response to a US argument that the arbitrator's jurisdiction is limited to a consideration of whether two specific treaties have been violated so that the arbitrator cannot base his decisions on other rules of international law:

The decision to be given is undoubtedly to be governed by the treaties, and the Arbitrator is not asked to look for other rules in the field of international law. On the other hand, it is clear that the treaties themselves are part of the international law as accepted by both contracting powers and it may be safely assumed that, when the said treaties were concluded, both parties considered them as being agreed upon as special provisions to be enforced between them in what may be called the atmosphere and spirit of international law as recognized by both of them.[75]

Finally, as to the fact that a treaty (such as the WTO treaty) must not only be considered in the wider context of international law as it existed at the time of its conclusion, but also as this international law continues to develop, note the Separate Opinion of Judge Weeramantry in the *Case Concerning the Gabčíkovo–Nagymaros Project*.[76] In that case, the Court was faced, in 1996, with a 1977 bilateral treaty, on the one hand, and international environmental norms that had developed since, on the other:

This inter-temporal aspect of the present case is of importance to all treaties dealing with projects impacting on the environment. Unfortunately, the Vienna Convention offers very little guidance regarding this matter which is of such importance in the environmental field. The provision in Article 31, paragraph 3 (c)... scarcely covers this aspect with the degree of clarity requisite to so important a

---

[74] ICJ Reports 1980, 73 at 76.
[75] *Arbitration of a Difference Concerning the Swedish Motor Ships Kronprins Gustaf Adolf and Pacific*, 18 July 1932 (1935) 29 AJIL 835 at 839–40.
[76] *(Hungary v. Slovakia)*, ICJ Reports 1997, para. 140.

matter. Environmental concerns are live and continuing concerns whenever the project under which they arise may have been inaugurated. It matters little that an undertaking has been commenced under a treaty of 1950, if in fact that undertaking continues in operation in the year 2000. The relevant environmental standards that will be applicable will be those of the year 2000.

As much as these new environmental norms must be taken into account by the ICJ in a dispute on a 1977 bilateral investment treaty, also in WTO disputes, concerning the WTO treaty, any relevant subsequent norms, binding as between the disputing parties, must be considered as part of the law that may be applied to decide on the validity of the WTO claims before a WTO panel.

Reliance on non-WTO rules as 'facts' versus non-WTO rules part of the applicable law

One other distinction must be made, namely between applying non-WTO rules as legal norms that may decide a dispute and relying on non-WTO rules as facts or evidence in support of, or against, a claim of violation of WTO law. In establishing the relevant facts of a dispute and applying WTO rules to these facts, non-WTO rules may, indeed, constitute proof of certain factual circumstances that must be present, for example, if WTO rules are not to be violated. The standard example is a multilateral environmental convention that calls for the imposition of certain trade restrictions to protect the environment from product X which is considered harmful to human health under the convention. Even if this convention is not binding on all WTO members, or on the disputing parties in the particular case (in particular, the complainant), the fact that, say, ninety countries including half of the WTO membership have ratified the convention may constitute significant factual evidence under GATT Art. XX(b) that the defendant's measure is, indeed, 'necessary for the protection of human health'. The role that non-WTO rules may play as 'facts' can be especially important in defending trade restrictions prescribed in an environmental convention against non-parties. Even if those non-parties (members of the WTO) are not legally bound by the convention and a WTO panel could therefore not apply this non-WTO rule (with a view to its prevailing over the relevant WTO rule, depending on the conflict rule to be applied), the convention could nonetheless constitute strong support for the defendant's contention that the trade restriction is 'necessary' pursuant to GATT Art. XX(b). Nonetheless, in these circumstances, the non-WTO rule then exerts influence not as a legal right or obligation, but as evidence of an alleged fact ('necessary to protect health'), meaning that it may not be conclusive. The complainant may be able to disprove the veracity of, or rebut the factual evidence reflected in, the non-WTO rule. Without such an option, a group of WTO members might conclude a convention stating, for example, that hormone-treated beef is dangerous. In doing so, they might hope to bind non-signatories which could challenge their ban on hormone-treated beef in the WTO. In these circumstances, a WTO panel would not be compelled to accept the premise that hormones are dangerous as an established fact. It would need to weigh that premise in the convention against other evidence on the record and might conclude, as it did in *EC – Hormones*, that science does not support a ban on hormone-treated beef.

A more recent example where the Appellate Body relied on a non-WTO convention as a 'factual reference' is *US – Shrimp (Article 21.5 – Malaysia)*. In that dispute, to avoid 'arbitrary or unjustifiable discrimination' in the sense of the *chapeau* of GATT Art. XX, the United States had to provide all exporting countries 'similar opportunities to negotiate' an international agreement.[77] The panel under DSU Art. 21.5 found that 'the Inter-American Convention [for the Protection and Conservation of Sea Turtles, in force as of 2 May 2001] can reasonably be considered as a benchmark of what can be achieved through multilateral negotiations in the field of protection and conservation'.[78] On appeal, the Appellate Body approved the panel's reliance on the Inter-American Convention as follows: 'The Panel rightly used the Inter-American Convention as a factual reference in this exercise of comparison [as between US efforts to negotiate the Inter-American Convention with one group of exporting countries and US efforts to negotiate a similar agreement with another group of exporting countries, including the complainant Malaysia].'[79] In this case, the non-WTO convention thus played a role, not as a set of norms part of the law applicable to the dispute, but as a factual benchmark to gauge whether the United States had engaged in 'comparable negotiations' as required under GATT Art. XX. Nonetheless, the two issues are related: if the United States can be absolved under GATT Art. XX by concluding an MEA with Malaysia (in which both states agree, for example, on the imposition of certain trade restrictions), would this

---

[77] Appellate Body report on *US – Shrimp (Article 21.5 – Malaysia)*, para. 122.
[78] Panel report on *US – Shrimp (Article 21.5 – Malaysia)*, para. 5.71.
[79] Appellate Body report on *US – Shrimp (Article 21.5 – Malaysia)*, para. 130.

not imply that once such an MEA was concluded, the United States can also rely on it as a legal defence against any future WTO claim that Malaysia may bring? Indeed, if Malaysia were to bring a WTO complaint subsequent to the entry into force of the MEA, targeted at the very trade restrictions agreed on in this MEA, should the United States not be permitted to invoke this MEA as a defence also before a WTO panel? It is suggested here that the United States should be permitted to do this. In this sense, the Appellate Body report on *US – Shrimp (Article 21.5 – Malaysia)* seems to imply that non-WTO rules can play a role not only as factual reference, but also as valid legal defence. This is the issue we examine next with reference to the DSU and relevant WTO case law.

Relevant DSU provisions and WTO jurisprudence

The DSU limits the *jurisdiction* of WTO panels and the Appellate Body. It does not limit the potentially *applicable law* before them. The DSU, unlike UNCLOS or the Statute of the ICJ,[80] does not include an explicit provision on 'applicable law'. The repeated references to 'providing security and predictability to the multilateral trading system', preserving 'the rights and obligations of Members under the covered agreements' (DSU Art. 3.2), 'benefits accruing to it directly or indirectly under the covered agreements', 'proper balance between the rights and obligations of Members' (DSU Art. 3.3) and the panel function of assessing the 'applicability of and conformity with the relevant covered agreements' (DSU Art. 11) relate to the *jurisdiction* or *substantive mandate* of WTO panels to enforce judicially only claims under WTO covered agreements, not to the *law* that may be applied in doing so.

Moreover, as noted earlier, it must be recalled that confirming some rules of public international law – such as DSU Art. 3.2 does in respect of rules on treaty interpretation – does not amount to excluding all others.[81] There is no need to *confirm* that general international law applies to the WTO treaty. Rather, international law continues to apply to the WTO treaty *unless* the WTO treaty has contracted out of it. Equally, as pointed out in chapter 7 above, pp. 352–5, the direction in DSU Arts. 3.2 and 19.2 that panels cannot 'add to or diminish the rights and obligations provided in the covered agreements' relates to a panel's *interpretative* function, not to the law that it can *apply*. Nor do these provisions set out a general *conflict clause* in favour of WTO rules.

---

[80] Respectively, Art. 291 and Art. 38.   [81] See chapter 4 above, pp. 214–15.

More directed at applicable law are DSU Arts. 7.1 and 7.2. Article 7.1, setting out the standard terms of reference of panels, directs panels to examine the matter referred to them 'in the light of the relevant provisions in (name of the covered agreement(s) cited by the parties to the dispute)'. Article 7.2 obliges panels to 'address the relevant provisions in any covered agreement or agreements cited by the parties to the dispute'. Panels have hence *an obligation* to address and, as the case may be, apply those rules referred to by the parties that are part of WTO covered agreements. However, and this again is crucial, *nothing in the DSU or any other WTO rule precludes panels from addressing and, as the case may be, applying* other *rules of international law in order to decide the WTO claims before them*.[82] As was outlined earlier in respect of the WTO treaty, there is no need for the DSU, a judicial system aimed at enforcing certain rules of international law, explicitly to refer to or confirm all *other* potentially relevant rules of international law, be they pre- or post-1994. Such reference or confirmation occurs automatically by virtue of the simple fact that the DSU was created and continues to exist in the wider context of international law. These other rules of international law apply, indeed, automatically *unless* the DSU or any other WTO rule has contracted out of them. As noted by the panel on *Korea – Government Procurement* in respect of rules of customary international law which it referred to in its examination of the non-violation complaint before it (in a footnote!):

---

[82] In support: David Palmeter and Petros Mavroidis, 'The WTO Legal System: Sources of Law' (1998) 92 AJIL 398 at 399 and Lorand Bartels, 'Applicable Law in WTO Dispute Settlement Proceedings' (2001) 35 JWT 499. *Contra*: Joel Trachtman, 'The Domain of WTO Dispute Resolution' (1999) 40 *Harvard International Law Journal* 333 at 342 (stating that the explicit language in the DSU 'would be absurd if rights and obligations arising from other international law could be applied by the DSB' and that '[w]ith so much specific reference to the covered agreements as the law applicable in WTO dispute resolution, it would be odd if the members intended non-WTO law to be applicable'; less categorically: Gabrielle Marceau, 'A Call for Coherence in International Law – Praises for the Prohibition Against "Clinical Isolation" in WTO Dispute Settlement' (1999) 33 JWT 87 at 110 (concluding that '[i]t seems, therefore, that under the DSU not all sources of law may be applied or enforced by WTO adjudicating bodies') and Gabrielle Marceau, untitled, World Bank Seminar on International Trade Law, 24–25 October 2000, 3 ('Under the DSU only provisions of the "covered agreements" can be the "applicable law" applied and enforced by panels and the Appellate Body'); Jonathan Charney, 'Is International Law Threatened by Multiple International Tribunals?' (1998) 271 *Recueil des Cours* 101 at 219 ('sources of general international law outside of the agreements appear to arise only in the context of treaty interpretation rules'); Pons, 'Self-Help', 102; and Eric Canal-Forgues, 'Sur l'Interprétation dans le Droit de l'OMC' (2001) 105 RGDIP 1 at 11–12.

'We do not see any basis for arguing that the terms of reference [in DSU Art. 7.1] are meant to exclude reference to the broader rules of customary international law in interpreting a claim properly before the Panel.'[83]

Unlike UNCLOS Art. 291 or Art. 38 of the ICJ Statute, the DSU does not *explicitly confirm* its creation and existence in international law. However, there was no need for the DSU to do so: it cannot but be created and exist in international law.[84] As noted in chapter 2 above (p. 37), as soon as states contract with one another, they do so automatically and necessarily *within* the system of international law. This is why WTO law is international law. It is not, and cannot be, a 'self-contained regime' in the sense of a regime existing outside of international law. In their treaty relations states can 'contract out' of one, more or, in theory, all *rules* of international law (other than those of *jus cogens*), but they cannot contract out of the *system* of international law. This limitation, directly linked to the *pacta sunt servanda* principle, could be construed as one of *jus cogens*. This limitation is another reason why none of the WTO provisions referred to earlier – in particular DSU Arts. 3.2 and 19.2 – can be seen as an expression of state intent to set up WTO dispute settlement as a mechanism operating outside international law, that is, where non-WTO rules cannot be part of the applicable law that a WTO panel may consider. All of these WTO provisions must be presumed to be consistent with general international law, especially rules of *jus cogens*.[85] If there is a way to give a meaning to those WTO provisions that does not detract from these other rules – a meaning we set out above, that is, relating

---

[83] Panel on *Korea – Government Procurement*, para. 7.101, note 755. One could compare this to a situation where the ICJ, say, pursuant to the optional clause system, has jurisdiction only over a limited set of claims (as occurred in the *Nicaragua* case where it had jurisdiction only over certain claims under customary law and a bilateral treaty: see note 46 above). The fact of not having jurisdiction over claims under *other* rules of law (*in casu*, multilateral treaties) does not prevent the ICJ from referring to and, as the case may be, applying these *other* rules in deciding on the claims which *are* within its jurisdiction (as Judge Singh noted in respect of the claims under the bilateral treaty: 'under the Treaty basis the Court would be free to apply for purposes of interpretation and application of the Treaty the whole sphere of international law, as defined in Article 38' (ICJ Reports 1984, Separate Opinion, 448).

[84] As noted by the First Committee in the *travaux préparatoires* of Art. 38 of the ICJ Statute in respect of the addition in Art. 38 of the obligation for the Court to decide 'in accordance with international law': '[t]he lacuna in the old Statute with reference to this point did not prevent the [PCIJ] from regarding itself as an organ of international law; but the addition will accentuate that character of the new Court' (13 UNCIO 164, 284, 392 (Committee IV/1)).

[85] See chapter 5 above, pp. 240–1.

not to applicable law, but to jurisdiction, panels' mandate and treaty interpretation – such meaning must be preferred.

Moreover, it is one thing to insert a conflict clause to the effect that a treaty prevails over other treaties (with the limited effect this has vis-à-vis future treaties, discussed in chapter 7 above, pp. 335–6), quite another *a priori* to exclude other treaties from the applicable law before an international tribunal. The former can be done (see, for example, UNCLOS Arts. 311.1 and 311.6) and results from the contractual freedom of states; the latter cannot be easily presumed and must in any event give way to the principle of *pacta sunt servanda* as a result of which prior treaties may well have to give way to the new treaty, but future treaties will, in principle, prevail. In the *Continental Shelf* case *(Tunisia v. Libya)*, the ICJ confirmed that disputing parties could, by agreement, add to the applicable law as prescribed in Art. 38 (*in casu*, 'new accepted trends' in the law of the sea) but that they cannot detract from it: 'the Court is, of course, bound to have regard to all the legal sources specified in Article 38'.[86]

For those reasons, the direction in Art. 293 of UNCLOS that ITLOS and UNCLOS tribunals shall apply UNCLOS 'and other rules of international law not incompatible with [UNCLOS]' must not so much be seen as *a priori* excluding all law inconsistent with UNCLOS from the applicable law before an UNCLOS court or tribunal, but rather as a cross-reference to, and confirmation of, the conflict clauses set out in, for example, UNCLOS Art. 311. These conflict clauses do allow for a number of prior treaties to persist, while others have to give way to UNCLOS. They also permit the conclusion of subsequent *inter se* agreements derogating from UNCLOS as long as the conditions in Art. 311(3) are met (conditions that are copied from Art. 41 of the Vienna Convention). Such *inter se* agreement – though derogating from UNCLOS – must also be part of the applicable law before an UNCLOS court or tribunal.

Implicit confirmation that WTO panels, when examining WTO claims, may be required to refer to and apply other rules of international law can be found in DSU Arts. 3.2, 7.1 and 11. As noted earlier, the reference in Art. 3.2 to 'customary rules of interpretation of public international law' implies an obligation for panels to *interpret* WTO rules, taking account of 'any relevant rules of international law applicable in the relations between the parties'.[87] Article 7.1 instructs panels to make '*such findings as*

---

[86] ICJ Reports 1982, 37, 38.
[87] Pursuant to Art. 31(3)(c) of the Vienna Convention. See chapter 5 above.

will assist the DSB in making the recommendations or in giving the rulings provided for in [the relevant WTO covered agreements]'. Article 11 directs panels to 'make an *objective assessment of...the applicability of...the relevant covered agreements'* and to 'make such *other findings* as will assist the DSB in making the recommendations or in giving the rulings provided for in the covered agreements'. The obligation in Art. 11 to assess the applicability of WTO rules objectively may – depending on the claims, defences and facts of the matter before it – require a panel to refer to and apply *other rules* of international law.[88] These other rules may show that the relevant WTO rules *do not apply* (for example, because they must give way to these other rules pursuant to the conflict rules set out above) and have, therefore, *not* been violated. Not to look at these other rules would preclude an 'objective assessment of...the applicability of...the relevant covered agreements'.

The reference in Art. 11 to making all 'other findings' (or, in the words of DSU Art. 7.1, all 'such findings') as will assist the DSB in resolving the WTO claims before it, further acknowledges that WTO panels may need to resort to and apply rules of international law *beyond* the four corners of WTO covered agreements.

Hence, to deduce from the *explicit* reference in DSU Arts. 7.1 and 7.2 (quoted above) to *some law* (i.e., WTO covered agreements) that *all other law* is thereby *implicitly excluded* is erroneous. Indeed, in practice, the terms of reference of WTO panels do not read as requiring an examination 'in the light of the relevant provisions in (name of the covered agreement(s) cited *by the parties to the dispute*)' (DSU Art. 7.1), but rather, an examination 'in the light of the relevant provisions of the covered agreements cited by [the complainant] in [document DS/...]', i.e., the panel request submitted *by the complainant*.

Does this exclusive reference to the provisions invoked *by the complainant* imply that no other law (*not even the defences invoked by the defending party*) can be looked at? Surely not. The same reasoning applies in respect of the explicit references in the DSU to WTO covered agreements. These references cannot be read as excluding all other law. Or does the

---

[88] The Appellate Body in *US – Steel Hot-Rolled* (at para. 54) made it explicit that 'Article 11 of the DSU imposes upon panels a comprehensive obligation which embraces all aspects of a panel's examination of the "matter", both factual and legal. Thus, panels make an "objective assessment of the facts", of the "applicability" of the covered agreements, and of the "conformity" of the measure at stake with those covered agreements.'

law explicitly referred to in Art. 38 of the ICJ Statute preclude the ICJ from looking at and applying other rules of international law? It does not. The ICJ (as WTO panels), being a court under international law, can refer, and regularly does refer, to law not explicitly mentioned in Art. 38, in particular unilateral acts of states and acts of international organisations.[89]

WTO jurisprudence also confirms that the DSU, or any other WTO rule, should *not* be interpreted as limiting the applicable law before a WTO panel to WTO covered agreements. In practice, panels and the Appellate Body alike have frequently referred to and applied other rules of international law in their examination of WTO claims. They did so not only in the process of *interpreting* WTO covered agreements (discussed in chapter 5 above, pp. 268–72). In addition, and more importantly, WTO panels and the Appellate Body have applied other rules of international law *independently* of giving meaning to specific words in a given WTO provision. This case law was summarised in chapter 4 above, pp. 207–12. In their examination of WTO claims, they have applied (1) rules of *general international law*, in particular rules on (i) judicial dispute settlement (such as standing,[90] representation by private counsel,[91] la compétence de la compétence,[92] burden of proof,[93] the treatment of municipal law,[94] the authority to accept *amicus curiae* briefs[95] and to draw adverse inferences[96] and judicial economy);[97] (ii) the law of treaties (such as the principle of non-retroactivity of treaties[98] and error in treaty formation);[99] and (iii) state responsibility (such as rules on countermeasures[100] and attribution),[101] referring each time to the work of the ILC on the subject. Moreover, WTO panels and the Appellate Body alike have applied

---

[89] See Nguyen Quoc Dinh, P. Daillier and A. Pellet, *Droit International Public* (Montreal: Wilson & Lafleur, 1999), 356–81.
[90] Appellate Body report on *EC – Bananas*, para. 133.   [91] *Ibid.*, para. 10.
[92] Appellate Body report on *US – Anti-Dumping Act of 1916*, note 30.
[93] Appellate Body report on *US – Shirts and Blouses*, 14.
[94] Appellate Body report on *India – Patent*, para. 65.
[95] Appellate Body report on *US – Shrimp*, para. 107.
[96] Appellate Body report on *Canada – Aircraft*, para. 202.
[97] Appellate Body report on *US – Shirts and Blouses*, 19.
[98] Appellate Body report on *Brazil – Coconut*, 15. Confirmed in: Appellate Body report on *EC – Bananas*, para. 235 and *Canada – Patent Protection Term*, paras. 71–4.
[99] Panel report on *Korea – Government Procurement*, paras. 7.123–7.126.
[100] Arbitration report (US request for suspension) on *EC – Bananas*, para. 6.16 and arbitration report on *Brazil – Aircraft*, para. 3.44 and notes 45 and 48.
[101] Panel report on *Canada – Dairy Products*, para. 7.77 and note 427 (in support of provincial milk marketing boards being an 'agency' of Canada). See also panel report on *Turkey – Textile*, para. 9.33.

(2) WTO rules not part of WTO covered agreements (such as the Declaration on the Relationship of the WTO and the IMF[102] and acts of WTO organs such as waivers)[103] as well as (3) non-WTO rules which are not part of general international law (such as the Lomé Convention[104] or unilateral acts of WTO members).[105] In the absence of an inherent hierarchy of rules of international law (other than *jus cogens*), there is no reason to apply *general* international law, but not to apply, for example, non-WTO *treaties* (always to the extent, of course, that both disputing parties are legally bound by them and in so far as this is done in the examination of *WTO claims*).[106] Finally, confirmation that the WTO judiciary does not apply only WTO covered agreements can also be found in its repeated reference to GATT/WTO jurisprudence and publicists. These sources do not, in and of themselves, constitute rules of international law. However, as noted in Art. 38(1)(d) of the ICJ Statute (where they are mentioned as two of the five legal sources that the Court must 'apply'), they are 'subsidiary means for the determination of rules of law'.

This case law offers compelling examples of why the applicable law before a WTO panel cannot be, and has not been, limited to WTO covered agreements. If it were so limited, a WTO panel would not be able to perform its judicial function appropriately (to do so it must 'fall back' on certain norms of general international law for matters on which the WTO treaty itself remained silent), nor would it be able take account of, for example, conflict rules provided for by WTO organs *outside WTO covered agreements*, such as those set out by the WTO Ministerial Conference in a waiver or other *sui generis* decisions. Such an approach would be unacceptable. The Appellate Body itself realised this when reverting to the Declaration on the Relationship of the WTO with the IMF, a Ministerial Declaration not part of WTO covered agreements, in *Argentina – Footwear*. The same was done in *EC – Bananas* where a waiver was taken into account as a defence, even though such waiver is not strictly speaking part of WTO covered agreements. *Clearly, if WTO panels and the Appellate Body were not allowed to refer to or apply any source of law other than WTO covered agreements, all of the WTO cases referred to above would be legally incorrect.*

---

[102] Appellate Body report on *Argentina – Footwear*. See chapter 7, above, pp. 347–8.
[103] See Appellate Body report on *EC – Bananas*, para. 164.
[104] *Ibid.*, para. 167. [105] See panel report on *US – Section 301*, para. 7.114.
[106] For a possible exception in respect of treaty interpretation, see chapter 5 above, pp. 260–3.

That the interplay between WTO rules and non-WTO rules, in particular MEAs, as they can be raised before WTO panels, is also very much at the forefront of the political debate, witness the Doha Declaration, adopted in November 2001, which includes the following agenda point for negotiation during the pending Doha Development Round: 'the relationship between existing WTO rules and specific trade obligations set out in multilateral agreements (MEAs). The negotiations shall be limited in scope to the applicability of such existing WTO rules as among parties to the MEA in question.'[107]

An EC submission on this point argued that

> MEAs and WTO are equal bodies of international law...WTO rules should not be interpreted in 'clinical isolation' from other bodies of international law and without considering other complementary bodies of international law, including MEAs...In those rare cases in which interpretation is not sufficient to avoid a potential conflict, there is a need to determine – under rules of public international law – which is the applicable body of law.[108]

The least one can say is that this EC statement implies that the applicable law before WTO panels is *not* necessarily limited to WTO covered agreements. If it were so limited, a conflict could never arise in the first place (since the non-WTO rule would not even be 'applicable') and there would be no need to 'determine...which is the applicable body of law'.

Practical consequences of the approach suggested

'At worst': the WTO rule is not enforced; a WTO panel has no jurisdiction to enforce the non-WTO rule

The jurisdiction of WTO panels is limited. The applicable law before them is not. What is the practical result of WTO defending parties being allowed to invoke other rules of international law, be they part of general international law or non-WTO treaties?

First, it should be stressed that a defending party can only invoke those rules to which both itself and the complaining party are bound.[109] The

---

[107] Doha Ministerial Declaration, paragraph 31(i), adopted on 14 November 2001, WT/MIN(01)/DEC/1, dated 20 November 2001.

[108] *Multilateral Environmental Agreements (MEAS): Implementation of the Doha Development Agenda*, Submission by the European Communities, paragraph 31(i), 21 March 2002 (TN/TE/W/1).

[109] For a possible exception in respect of treaty interpretation, see chapter 5 above, pp. 260–3.

complaining party cannot see its WTO rights diminished on the basis of a rule of international law by which it is not bound. Second, as we have repeated more than once, other rules of international law, including post-1994 treaties, cannot form the legal basis of a WTO complaint. Only claims under WTO covered agreements can be brought.

Within these limits, however, the practical consequences of a defending party being able to invoke, for example, a rule of customary law or an environmental or human rights convention or bilateral treaty to which both disputing parties are bound *in defence against a WTO claim*, must be determined by the relevant conflict rules referred to earlier.[110] These rules may be spelled out in the WTO treaty itself, the treaty from which the contradictory rule derives or general international law. Hence, and this is of paramount importance, even if, as we suggest here, all relevant international law applicable between the disputing parties can be looked at by a WTO panel to decide on WTO claims, this does not necessarily mean that these non-WTO rules *part of the applicable law* must always *prevail* over WTO law. Whether this is the case must be determined by conflict rules.

If the relevant conflict rule indicates that the WTO rule in question *prevails* over the conflicting norm of international law, the WTO rule must be applied (and the complainant wins). If, in contrast, the relevant conflict rule demonstrates that the other rule of international law overrides or even invalidates the WTO rule, the WTO rule then *cannot be applied* (and the defendant wins). Crucially, this will be the case irrespective of whether the WTO treaty itself includes an exception or justification for the measure at hand.[111] The latter case does not result in requiring the WTO panel *to enforce judicially claims under the other rule of international law* (say, breach of the contradictory environmental norm). A WTO panel can only enforce claims under WTO covered agreements. To be able to enforce claims under these other rules, a WTO panel would need expanded jurisdiction.

Recalling the two levels at which WTO covered agreements operate (the general level of the entire corpus of international law and the more

---

[110] See chapters 6 and 7 above.
[111] A defence under a NAFTA provision could, for example, be submitted by Canada against a US complaint before the WTO. If, under the applicable conflict rules, the NAFTA provision prevails over the WTO provision allegedly breached, as between NAFTA members, the NAFTA provision should then constitute a valid defence. This may be the case, for example, based on Art. 103(2) of NAFTA which gives preference to NAFTA over the WTO treaty in the event, and to the extent, of inconsistency, except as otherwise provided in NAFTA. See chapter 7 above, p. 331.

concrete level of WTO dispute settlement), *what has been taken away or overruled at the first level can no longer be enforced either in the second level* (i.e., if a WTO rule no longer exists or has been overruled under international law, it can no longer be enforced either in WTO dispute settlement). What WTO members *themselves* have taken out of WTO covered agreements at the first level (albeit *inter se* only) cannot be put back *by a WTO panel* in the second level. For a panel to do so anyway would amount to (using the wording of DSU Arts. 3.2 and 19.2) 'adding' to obligations of the defendant that, pursuant to other rules of international law and the way these interact with WTO rules, no longer exist. If a panel follows the approach suggested here and disapplies the WTO rule in these circumstances, the panel would not be 'diminishing' the rights of the complainant. Rather, the complaining WTO member itself would have done so by agreeing to the conflicting non-WTO rule in the first place. Thus the WTO panel would not create law but merely give effect to law created elsewhere *by the WTO member itself*. On the other hand, for *claims* under these non-WTO rules to filter through to the second level of WTO dispute resolution, an express intention to expand the jurisdiction of WTO panels would be required.

Is the uniformity of WTO law at risk?

Critics may submit that the WTO treaty explicitly provides as to how it can be amended[112] so that the legal relationships that the treaty establishes can only be changed by the consent of all WTO members. Following this line of thinking, one could argue that for a WTO panel to take cognisance of non-WTO rules as part of a defence, especially rules binding only on the disputing parties, contravenes WTO amendment procedures and threatens the uniformity of WTO law. This reasoning implies, however, that the WTO treaty is an island created and existing outside the sphere of international law. One of the main objectives of this study was to show that it is not. Thus, the WTO treaty can be affected by explicit amendment, but also by the conclusion of other treaties or the existence or emergence of other rules of international law pursuant to, for example, the rules in the Vienna Convention on, *inter alia*, the

---

[112] The general rule is that amendments should be taken by consensus (Art. X:1). However, if consensus is not reached, most amendments can be taken by a two-thirds majority of WTO members (others only upon acceptance by all WTO members) (Art. X:3–5).

application of successive treaties (Art. 30), *inter se* modifications (Art. 41) and treaty interpretation (Art. 31(3)(c)).[113] We discussed the crucial distinction between treaty 'amendment' and treaty 'modification' at length in chapter 6 above, pp. 315–24. The WTO treaty did not contract out of these general international law rules on the interplay of norms, let alone out of the system of international law. Hence, these rules must apply also to the WTO treaty. The WTO treaty changed the 1994 landscape of international law, but post-1994 treaties can also change this landscape, including the legal relationships between WTO members in the WTO.

International law does not comprehend inherent hierarchies of norms, nor does it require an *acte contraire* for a norm to be affected by another one. Moreover, if WTO members could affect the WTO treaty only through a formal amendment (i.e., if the WTO were in essence a separate legal system as domestic or, to some extent, EC law is), it would basically mean that whatever WTO members do in their relationship with other WTO members in the area of trade is regulated exclusively and eternally by the 1994 provisions of the WTO treaty *unless a consensus of WTO members decides otherwise*. Ironically, this immobility in the WTO would then only increase together with the membership of the WTO. Indeed, the more WTO members there are, the more difficult it becomes to muster a consensus for formally amending WTO rules.[114] The WTO would become more than a collection of rules 'written in stone', it would also be transformed into a 'safe haven' for WTO members wanting to backtrack on obligations entered into elsewhere. This is why contracting out of the *system* of international law, or setting up a dispute settlement regime that can look only at 'in-house' rules of law, not at other rules of the same system of international law, goes against the principle of *pacta sunt servanda*. Moreover, as pointed out in chapter 2 above, this 'unitary' view

---

[113] In addition, besides other treaties, subsequent practice and custom can also affect the WTO treaty (irrespective of amendment provisions). See, in this respect, Wolfram Karl, *Vertrag und Spätere Praxis im Völkerrecht* (Berlin: Springer, 1983), 387–9 and Nancy Kontou, *The Termination and Revision of Treaties in the Light of New Customary International Law* (Oxford: Clarendon, 1994). Indeed, if such *implicit* forms of consent as subsequent practice and custom can alter or revise a treaty notwithstanding amendment provisions in the treaty itself or the Vienna Convention, then *a fortiori* formal *inter se* agreements to which certain WTO members *explicitly* agreed (such as a post-1994 environmental convention) must be able to affect WTO rules as between the parties to these agreements.

[114] This point was made by Marceau, 'Coherence', 124.

of international law is not only crucial to uphold the *pacta sunt servanda* principle as between states. It is also essential to avoid international law becoming what Benvenisti calls 'a convenient exit option for those finding domestic controls too stringent', that is to avoid certain domestic actors circumventing domestic controls by fencing off their private (trade) interests in an isolated branch of international law, such as WTO law, detached from other branches of international law (such as MEAs) that could otherwise restrict their conduct.[115] In other words, it goes to the heart of the legitimacy and democratic content of international law.

The effect of the approach suggested here, that WTO rules would apply differently to different WTO members depending on whether or not they have accepted other non-WTO rules, may complicate the matrix of rights and obligations between WTO members. But this is an unavoidable consequence of not having a centralised legislator in international law.[116] In addition, from a practical point of view, should we expect – in our complex world with 144 WTO members of widely diverging interests – each and every WTO member to bear the same obligations vis-à-vis each and every other WTO member? Surely not. Still, this consequence would ensue if formal amendments were required as a prerequisite to affecting the WTO treaty.[117] The WTO seeks to promote non-discrimination and *trade* liberalisation *in the context of regulatory diversity*. Unlike the EC, for example, it does not generally extend its reach to harmonisation in *non-trade* matters in pursuit of some sort of 'federation of nation states'.

Finally, giving effect to non-WTO rules as suggested here must be distinguished from *interpreting* the WTO treaty differently depending on the disputing WTO members involved (discussed in chapter 5 above, pp. 257–63). In my view, the latter is not allowed and would definitely threaten the uniformity of WTO law.

To summarise, the triple distinction between jurisdiction, applicable law and interpretation as it relates to WTO panels – a distinction that runs through this work – can be depicted in the following table:

---

[115] Eyal Benvenisti, 'Exit and Voice in the Age of Globalization' (1999) 98 *Michigan Law Review* 167 at 169.

[116] Even today, each WTO member has quite unique obligations depending, *inter alia*, on the provisions in its schedules of concessions.

[117] See Petros Mavroidis, 'Trade and Environment after the Shrimps–Turtles Litigation' (2000) 34 JWT 73 at 77.

WTO law and other international law before the WTO judiciary

	WTO covered agreements (including amendments)	Other WTO law (e.g., agreements or declarations not part of covered agreements and acts of WTO organs)	General international law and norms binding on all WTO members or reflecting their 'common intentions'	Norms binding on both disputing parties (not all WTO members, nor reflecting their 'common intentions')	Norms binding on only one of the disputing parties
Jurisdiction (to examine claims under these rules)	Yes	No	No	No	No
Applicable law (to be applied in the examination of WTO claims)	Yes	Yes	Yes	Yes	No
Reference material for the interpretation of WTO covered agreements	Yes	Yes	Yes	No	No
Valid defence against a WTO claim	Yes	Yes	Yes	Yes	No
Claims enforced under these rules if they prevail as the applicable law	Yes	No	No	No	No

Not making these distinctions has led to confusion. The limited *jurisdiction* of panels has led to unjustified restrictions on the distinct matter of *applicable law* before a panel.[118] In turn, the realisation by some that a panel should be allowed to consider more than WTO covered agreements (a matter of *applicable law*) has led certain commentators wrongly to accept even those non-WTO rules that do not reflect the 'common intentions' of all WTO members as reference material in *interpreting* WTO treaty terms.[119] Moreover, those authors rightly accepting that potentially all international law may be *applicable law* before a panel have erroneously restricted the impact of these non-WTO rules (in the sense that, in their view, WTO rules always prevail) with reference to restrictions on treaty *interpretation* (e.g., DSU Arts. 3.2 and 19.2).[120] Equally important is the distinction between amending the WTO treaty and accepting *inter se* modifications to it. The strict requirements imposed to *amend* the WTO treaty have been wrongly invoked as a reason to preclude that *inter se* agreements may *modify* WTO rules as between some WTO members only.

A closer look at certain past disputes in the light of the theory presented here

EC – Poultry

WTO panels have sometimes been asked to examine claims under pre-1994 GATT instruments that were *not* included in WTO covered agreements. The answer to such requests is obvious: only those GATT rules that were incorporated into WTO covered agreements (including member-specific schedules of concessions) can be the subject of claims before a panel.[121] The substantive jurisdiction of WTO panels is limited to claims under WTO covered agreements. In *EC – Poultry*, the Appellate Body found that the so-called Oilseeds agreement concluded bilaterally between the EC and Brazil in the framework of GATT Art. XXVIII renegotiations (as part of the resolution of a previous 1990 oilseeds dispute) was *not* a 'covered agreement' subject to the DSU, nor part of the multilateral obligations accepted by Brazil and the EC pursuant to the WTO

---

[118] See, in particular, the case law on applicable law before GATT panels, below, pp. 456–9.
[119] Marceau, 'Coherence'.   [120] Bartels, 'Applicable Law'.
[121] But see the exceptional GATT arbitration award where claims under a bilateral agreement (not part of GATT) were examined: note 12 above.

agreement. As a result, the Appellate Body concluded that 'it is Schedule LXXX [the relevant 1995 EC schedule of concessions attached to the WTO agreement into which only parts of the Oilseeds agreement had been incorporated], rather than the Oilseeds Agreement, which forms the legal basis for this dispute'.[122] The Appellate Body added that, in its view,

it is not necessary to have recourse to either Article 59.1 [termination of a treaty by conclusion of a later treaty] or Article 30.3 [application of successive treaties] of the *Vienna Convention*, because the text of the *WTO Agreement* and the legal arrangements governing the transition from the GATT 1947 to the WTO resolve the issue of the relationship between Schedule LXXX and the Oilseeds Agreement in this case.[123]

The arbitrators in *EC – Hormones* were faced with a similar problem. The United States claimed autonomous beef quota rights on the basis of bilateral US–EC agreements, not incorporated in WTO covered agreements. The arbitrators repeated what was said in *EC – Poultry*, namely that the bilateral agreements do not set out 'rights under any of the WTO agreements covered by the DSU' and that '[t]he rights thus alleged are derived from bilateral agreements that cannot be properly enforced on their own in WTO dispute settlement'.[124]

But had, in these two disputes, the relationship between the bilateral agreement and the relevant GATT rules *not* been addressed in the WTO treaty and if, pursuant to conflict rules of international law, the bilateral agreement would *prevail* over the GATT rule, under the theory presented here such bilateral agreement could operate as a valid *defence* (disapplying the relevant WTO rule); in any event it could not operate as a valid *claim*.

Argentina – Footwear

In *Argentina – Footwear*, the Appellate Body examined whether a 3 per cent statistical tax found by the panel to be in violation of GATT Art. VIII could be excused by means of an allegedly conflicting obligation imposed on Argentina in a Memorandum of Understanding between Argentina and the IMF. In this IMF Memorandum it was set out that the fiscal measures to be adopted by Argentina included 'increases in import

---

[122] Appellate Body report on *EC – Poultry*, para. 81.   [123] *Ibid.*, para. 81.
[124] Arbitration report (US request for suspension) on *EC – Hormones*, para. 50. In support, the arbitrators explicitly referred to the *lex posterior* rule in Art. 30 of the Vienna Convention (*ibid.*, para. 51).

duties, including a temporary 3 per cent surcharge on imports'. The Appellate Body found that, on the basis of the record before the panel, it did 'not appear possible to determine the precise legal nature of this Memorandum'.[125] The Appellate Body found also that 'Argentina did not show an irreconcilable conflict between the provisions of its "Memorandum of Understanding" with the IMF and the provisions of Article VIII of the GATT 1994.'[126] The Appellate Body continued that, even if there were a conflict, 'nothing in the *Agreement Between the IMF and the WTO*, the *Declaration on the Relationship of the WTO with the IMF* or the *Declaration on Coherence*... justifies a conclusion that a Member's commitments to the IMF shall prevail over its obligations under Article VIII of the GATT 1994'.[127] The Appellate Body found that only the Declaration on the Relationship of the WTO with the IMF – a Ministerial Decision which is part of the WTO Final Act, but *not* part of WTO covered agreements – says something about the legal relationship between the WTO and the IMF. This declaration states, in essence, that the relationship between WTO and IMF rules in the area of trade in goods shall continue to be governed by GATT 1947 provisions, i.e., that only the exceptions provided for in these GATT provisions for IMF-related measures can be used as an excuse for GATT violations.[128] On the basis of this conflict rule, the Appellate Body found that since no IMF-related exceptions under GATT Art. VIII are to be found in GATT itself, independent IMF rules, such as the IMF Memorandum, could not justify Argentina's violation of GATT Art. VIII.[129]

If the Appellate Body had thought that the IMF Memorandum could not possibly cure the violation of GATT Art. VIII simply because this Memorandum is *not* part of WTO covered agreements, it could have said so. But it did not. Rather, it made an assessment of whether the IMF Memorandum is *in conflict* with GATT rules and examined which of the two rules should prevail in case such conflict were to arise. The conclusion reached is fully justified and supports the thesis presented in this book. The Appellate Body did not, indeed, limit its examination to WTO covered agreements. It went beyond those agreements and took account also of (i) IMF rules; and (ii) the Declaration on the Relationship of the WTO with the IMF, a legal instrument *not* part of WTO covered agreements. This declaration provides for an explicit conflict clause in

---

[125] Appellate Body report on *Argentina – Footwear*, para. 69.
[126] *Ibid.*   [127] *Ibid.*, para. 70.   [128] See chapter 7 above, pp. 347–8.
[129] Appellate Body report on *Argentina – Footwear*, paras. 69–74.

favour of GATT rules. But had the allegedly conflicting rule not been an IMF rule, but one drawn from, for example, an environmental convention binding on both parties, how would the Appellate Body have reacted? Under the theory suggested here, it should then, as it did in *Argentina – Footwear*, not limit itself to the 'four corners' of WTO covered agreements. It would need to apply the environmental rule as a possible defence and, in the event of conflict between it and WTO rules (say, GATT Arts. III and XX), apply the relevant conflict rules of general international law (in the absence of any treaty-based conflict rules). In the event that the applicable conflict rule determines that the environmental rule prevails, the Appellate Body would then be obliged *not* to apply the contradictory WTO rule and the complainant would lose. It would not, however, have jurisdiction to hear claims of violation of the environmental rule.

EC – Hormones

In *EC – Hormones*, the Appellate Body was faced with an EC claim that the so-called 'precautionary principle' constitutes customary international law, or at least a general principle of law. The Appellate Body found that it was 'unnecessary, and probably imprudent, for [it] in this appeal to take a position on this important, but abstract, question'.[130] It noted though that 'the precautionary principle, at least outside the field of international environmental law, still awaits authoritative formulation'.[131] It further remarked that 'the principle has not been written into the *SPS Agreement* as a ground for justifying SPS measures that are otherwise inconsistent with the obligations of Members set out in particular provisions of that Agreement'. The Appellate Body recognised, however, that the principle 'finds reflection' in several SPS provisions. Noting that 'the precautionary principle does not, by itself, and without a clear textual directive to that effect, relieve a panel from the duty of applying the normal...principles of treaty interpretation', the Appellate Body finally agreed with the panel that 'the precautionary principle does not override the provisions of Articles 5.1 and 5.2 of the *SPS Agreement*'.[132]

[130] Appellate Body report on *EC – Hormones*, para. 123.   [131] *Ibid.*
[132] *Ibid.*, para. 125. It is unclear whether the EC referred to the 'precautionary principle' either (i) as an element to be looked at in the *interpretation* of Art. 5 of the SPS agreement; or (ii) as a non-WTO rule of international law in defence of a violation of Art. 5. Although the former seems more accurate (the EC was claiming that *because* its measures were precautionary in nature they satisfied the requirements of Art. 5), the latter hypothesis is more interesting and it is the one we examine further in this chapter.

This outcome is, in my view, fully justified. But not so the legal reasoning. As noted earlier, there was *no need* for the SPS agreement to refer explicitly to the precautionary principle for this principle to be a possible defence in WTO dispute settlement. In my view, the Appellate Body was obliged to make a ruling on whether this principle is, indeed, part of customary law binding on the disputing parties.[133] If this had been the case, the Appellate Body should have acknowledged that a rule of customary law, if later in time and in conflict with an earlier (SPS) treaty rule, must prevail over that treaty rule (no inherent hierarchy exists between treaty and custom),[134] *unless* there was an intention to continue applying the (SPS) treaty rule as *lex specialis*. In the circumstances, it was, however, difficult to establish (i) that the 'precautionary principle' *is* a rule of customary international law; (ii) that it emerged *subsequent to* the WTO treaty; (iii) that it was, indeed, in conflict with SPS rules (the EC had, for example, *not* invoked SPS Art. 5.7 which explicitly provides for a form of precautionary approach); and (iv) that WTO members did *not* want the SPS agreement to continue applying as *lex specialis* (in particular, given the 'continuing' nature of the WTO treaty).[135] Hence, the Appellate Body was correct in concluding that 'the precautionary principle does not override the provisions of Articles 5.1 and 5.2 of the *SPS Agreement*'. But it did so too categorically and without deciding certain crucial questions it should have answered before coming to that conclusion.

Korea – Government Procurement

As noted earlier, this panel rightly found that '[c]ustomary rules of international law apply to the WTO treaties and to the process of treaty formation under the WTO' and this to the extent that 'the WTO treaty agreements do not "contract out" from it'.[136] The panel applied, more particularly, rules on error in treaty formation under a US claim of non-violation (GATT Art. XXIII:1(b) as referred to in the Government Procurement Agreement (GPA)). The panel saw similarities between the non-violation provision in the WTO and the rules on error in treaty formation in international law: both are based on the principle of good faith. The panel noted that the traditional interpretation of the non-violation

---

[133] Or at least to *assume* that it was customary law and on that basis to examine further, whether it could possibly overrule SPS treaty rules.
[134] See chapter 3 above, pp. 94–6 and 137–43.   [135] See chapter 7 above, pp. 378–80.
[136] Panel report on *Korea – Government Procurement*, para. 7.96, discussed above, pp. 210–11.

provision is aimed at 'protecting the reasonable expectations of competitive opportunities through negotiated concessions'.[137] Hence, it is about good faith *implementation* of what is set out in the WTO treaty. Error in treaty formation, the panel continued, does not address what is set out in the treaty. Rather, it attacks the very validity of the treaty on the ground of error in its negotiation. Thus, the panel found, error in treaty formation is about good faith *negotiation* of the WTO treaty. On the basis of these two legal principles (non-violation and error in treaty formation) the panel found, in my view correctly, that '[p]arties have an obligation to negotiate in good faith just as they must implement the treaty in good faith'.[138] So far so good.

But then the panel, instead of applying these two principles independently to the case at hand, *injected the error in treaty formation principle into the non-violation rule*. It did so on the ground that '[t]o do otherwise potentially would leave a gap in the applicability of the law generally to WTO disputes'. More precisely, the panel stated: 'If the non-violation remedy were deemed not to provide a relief for such problems as have arisen in the present case regarding good faith and error in the negotiation of GPA commitments...then nothing could be done about them within the framework of the WTO dispute settlement mechanism.'[139]

The panel was right to rephrase the US claims somehow. As noted earlier, WTO panels hold an implied jurisdiction 'to interpret the submissions of the parties' in order to 'isolate the real issue in the case and to identify the object of the claim'.[140] Although, in that case, the panel went perhaps *beyond* this mandate by actually deciding a claim that was never put to it by the United States (the United States itself never claimed error, definitely not in its request for a panel, and only vaguely so in its submissions). As far as the specifics of non-violation are concerned, non-violation is about upsetting the competitive opportunities that can be expected *from a concession* against the legitimate expectations that a member can reasonably hold *on the basis of this concession* (even if the upsetting is not as such illegal). However, *in the absence of a concession* (as was the case here, as acknowledged by the panel), there can be no question of upsetting anything. The fact that non-violation, as it is generally understood, does *not* provide relief for error in treaty formation (and in the absence thereof 'nothing could be done about [it]'

---

[137] Ibid., para. 7.98.   [138] Ibid., para. 7.100.   [139] Ibid., para. 7.101.
[140] *Nuclear Tests* cases, ICJ Reports 1974, 262, para. 29 and 466, para. 30: see above, pp. 447–9.

in WTO dispute settlement) is *not* a good enough reason suddenly to expand non-violation so as to include error (especially so if this is done without regard to the actual words of GATT Art. XXIII:1(b)).[141]

Since error in treaty formation does not, therefore, seem to be a claim for which WTO panels have been granted jurisdiction, the panel should not have decided upon it (even if the United States had actually made the claim).[142] That being said, error in treaty formation as a ground of invalidity could well be invoked *as a defence* before a WTO panel (this rule being one of customary international law from which the WTO treaty did not contract out). Moreover, a complaint based on error could be brought also under Art. 66 of the Vienna Convention, at least to the extent both parties were bound by that Convention.

US – Shrimp

Finally, although not a case where the scope of the jurisdiction or applicable law before a WTO panel was examined, nor a case where genuine conflict was at issue, reference could also be made to the US – Shrimp saga. As a follow-up to the infamous 1994 case on *United States – Restrictions on Imports of Tuna*[143] (a GATT panel taking a rather isolationist, trade-only perspective on the trade and environment debate, finding against the United States), the US – Shrimp dispute originally produced a decision against the United States, but then – after minor changes in US policy – went in favour of the US restrictions on imports of shrimp imposed to save turtles.

The US – Shrimp decisions were warmly welcomed by green NGOs. Many academic commentators consider the dispute as the most important systemic case decided in the WTO so far.[144] From the perspective of this book, the case stands witness to the increased openness of the WTO regime to other branches of international law, in particular international environmental law. We referred to the case earlier as a prime

---

[141] This provision requires, for example, that Korea impairs benefits or impedes the attainment of objectives by means of the 'application' of a 'measure', something error in treaty formation does not involve.

[142] The only way it could be said to be within a WTO panel's jurisdiction is to argue that it amounts to Korea impeding the attainment of an objective under the GPA (i.e., the objective of having a valid agreement in the first place) 'as the result of the existence of any other situation' (namely, the situation of error on behalf of the United States) in the sense of GATT Art. XXIII.1(c) pursuant to a so-called situation complaint.

[143] *United States – Restrictions on Imports of Tuna*, DS 29/R, circulated on 10 June 1994, not adopted.

[144] See, for example, John Jackson, 'Comments on Shrimp/Turtle and the Product/Process Distinction', (2000) 11 EJIL 303–7.

example where the Appellate Body *interpreted* WTO law in an evolutionary manner, taking account of non-WTO rules of international law (see chapter 5 above).

In what is so far the only case where the Appellate Body explicitly used Article 31(3)(c) of the Vienna Convention, the Appellate Body, first of all, interpreted the *chapeau* of GATT Art. XX, 'seeking additional interpretative guidance, as appropriate, from the general principles of international law', more particularly the principle of good faith and the related doctrine of *abus de droit*.[145] Secondly, the Appellate Body found that the term 'exhaustible natural resources' in GATT Art. XX(g) 'must be read by a treaty interpreter in the light of contemporary concerns of the community of nations about the protection and conservation of the environment [not as it was understood in 1947]'.[146] In doing so, the Appellate Body referred to a number of multilateral environmental treaties.[147] None of these were binding on all WTO members and some of them were not binding even on all disputing parties in the particular case. Nonetheless, in an attempt to justify this move under the Vienna Convention rules on treaty interpretation, we submitted earlier that the non-WTO treaties referred to, though not legally binding on all WTO members, could be said to reflect the 'common intentions' of all WTO members and/or the 'ordinary meaning' of the term 'exhaustible natural resources' as it is used in Art. XX(g) of the GATT 1994. Thirdly, as noted earlier, in the implementation dispute, the Appellate Body relied heavily on a non-WTO treaty, the Inter-American Convention, as a 'factual reference' or point of comparison in its decision that the new US policy was no longer discriminatory in the sense of the *chapeau* of GATT Art. XX.[148] In doing so, it implied that the conclusion of an MEA can absolve a WTO inconsistency. As a result, once such an MEA is concluded, it would be difficult for the Appellate Body to exclude it from the applicable law in case a WTO complaint were brought, for example, against the very trade restrictions imposed or explicitly permitted in the MEA.

Nonetheless, the *US – Shrimp* decisions have also been heavily criticised by WTO developing country members. They fear that the decisions sanction US unilateralism in that they permit the granting of trade advantages conditional on the adoption of US-style domestic policies in exporting developing countries.

---

[145] Appellate Body report on *US – Shrimp*, para. 158.
[146] *Ibid.*, para. 130.   [147] *Ibid.*, paras. 128–32.
[148] Appellate Body report on *US – Shrimp (Article 21.5 – Malaysia)*, para. 130.

The approach set out in this book would embrace the environmental victory in this decision as well as take account of the fears expressed by certain WTO members. First, the approach suggested here would go further than just referring to MEAs in the *interpretation* of WTO provisions. It would actually *apply* such MEAs as between the disputing parties who are bound by them. Hence, if, for example, the United States and other WTO members conclude an MEA or a human rights convention in which certain trade restrictions are imposed or explicitly permitted (say, trade sanctions in the event of non-compliance) and subsequently those trade restrictions are challenged before a WTO panel, the WTO panel should apply those non-WTO treaties as a possible defence against a claim of WTO violation, irrespective of whether this defence is explicitly set out in the WTO treaty itself (such as in GATT Art. XX). Second, in what should alleviate developing country fears of US unilateralism, the approach suggested in this book would only permit reference to non-WTO rules in case the disputing parties have all accepted those rules in the first place (that is, the requirement for the direct *application* of non-WTO rules by a WTO panel) or in case those rules can be said to express the 'common intentions' of *all* WTO members (the requirement for non-WTO rules to be referred to in the *interpretation* of WTO provisions). WTO members, particularly developing countries who may have different priorities from developed states, should not see their WTO rights affected by non-WTO rules that they did not agree to or accept in the first place. However, once such rules have been accepted, there is no reason why this consent should all of a sudden evaporate when a WTO complaint is examined before a WTO panel (*pacta sunt servanda*).

Conclusions

In the end, it is perhaps a question of whether common ground may be discovered for human attitudes and judgment. In juridical terms, the question is whether common legal principles can gain sufficient acceptance to unite the different systems within one meaningful structure.[1]

Two themes have been developed in this work: first, a centralising or uniting theme, in defence of construing and applying all international law, including the WTO treaty, in the context of other norms of international law, be they customary law or other treaties; second, a theme calling for the recognition of the diversity between states and the contractual freedom of states to change their minds and to decide for themselves to which treaty or norm they want to give preference. This second theme is not a centralising or uniting one, but a centrifugal one allowing for regional and state-to-state differences in legal relationships. The tension between these two themes explains why this thesis, though focusing on conflict and conflict resolution, devoted large parts also to the process of accumulation of norms.

The interplay of norms in international law is no longer of academic interest only. In today's interdependent world, where states must cooperate in pursuit of common objectives and do so under the auspices of an ever increasing number of distinct international organisations, the potential for conflict between norms is very real, indeed. In the absence of a centralised international law-maker, the multitude of law-makers and other actors, be they domestic or international, at work on the international scene fuel the risk of conflict of norms arising (chapter 1).

---

[1] Max Sørenson, 'Autonomous Legal Orders: Some Considerations Relating to a Systems Analysis of International Organisations in the World Legal Order' (1983) 32 ICLQ 559 at 576.

Unlike domestic legal systems, in international law hierarchy of norms is not determined by the particular source of the norms in question. All international law, in one way or the other, derives from the same source, that is, state consent. Hence, there is no inherent hierarchy as between the different sources of international law traditionally referred to (treaties, custom, general principles of law and unilateral acts of states or international organisations). In principle, they all have the same binding force. Even the higher standing of *jus cogens* is unrelated to its source. Only judicial decisions and doctrine, not in and of themselves creating new norms, are secondary in nature. In operational terms, however, it can safely be said that general principles of law (other than those of *jus cogens*) will have to give way to treaties and custom. In most cases, treaties will also prevail over custom, although it must be recognised that custom – being of the same legal standing as treaties – is capable of revising or even terminating pre-existing treaties (chapter 3).

Given that the criterion of source cannot constitute a solid foundation for a theory on conflict of norms, one must turn to an examination of the interplay of norms, regardless of their source. Norms can either accumulate or conflict. As part of the centralising or uniting theme of this book, we stressed that all new law must be seen in the context of pre-existing law. This pre-existing law, be it general international law or other treaties, will apply to any new treaty unless the new treaty 'contracts out' of it. There is, in other words, a presumption of continuity and against conflict. The 'fall-back' on other international law norms may, first of all, take the form of *interpreting* the new treaty in the light of other norms. However, this interpretative process is limited to giving meaning to the terms in the treaty. It cannot extend to revising the treaty. It is limited also to a reference to outside norms that can be said to reflect the 'common intentions' of all parties to the treaty. Secondly, and perhaps more importantly, the 'fall-back' on other norms must take the form also of directly *applying* other norms, be they norms of general international law for matters on which the new treaty remains silent or other treaty norms binding on the disputing parties. The new treaty must be considered also in the context of other norms even if the two sets of norms do not accumulate but conflict. Such conflict will, however, emerge only as a genuine one in case the presumption against conflict has been rebutted, in particular, in case an interpretation of the two norms in the light of each other – if such is called for under the rules of treaty interpretation – does not lead to a harmonious reading. Nonetheless, although there is a presumption against conflict, this is no reason to define conflict strictly. Conflict must be equated with breach. Hence, there is conflict of norms in case one norm breaches, has led or may lead to breach of another norm. Crucially, contradiction as between an obligation and an explicit right (be it a permission or an exemption) must also be recognised as a situation of conflict (chapters 4 and 5).

Once a conflict of norms does arise, a distinction must be made between 'inherent normative conflicts' (that is, situations where one norm, in and of itself, breaches the other, discussed in chapter 6) and 'conflict in the applicable law' (that is, where the implementation or reliance on one norm has led or may lead to breach of the other norm, discussed in chapter 7).

Inherent normative conflict may be resolved in one of two ways: either one of the two norms ceases to exist or one of the two norms is illegal. A norm will cease to exist if it is in conflict with *jus cogens*, if it is implicitly terminated by another one or if it takes the form of an act of an international organisation taken *ultra vires*. A norm is illegal in case it constitutes, in and of itself, a breach under another norm or if it takes the form of an *inter se* agreement deviating from an earlier multilateral treaty obligation of the 'integral type' (that is, an obligation breach of which necessarily affects not just the parties to the *inter se* agreement but also all other parties to the original multilateral treaty) (chapter 6).

Conflict in the applicable law can be resolved in one of four main ways. First, it can be resolved by giving effect to an explicit conflict clause, such as Art. 103 of the UN Charter. Second, in the absence of such clause, priority can be given to the *lex posterior*. In some cases, however, especially those involving 'continuing' or 'living' treaties, it will be difficult to determine which treaty is 'later in time'. The conflicting treaties are then 'parallel' rather than 'successive' so that the *lex posterior* principle cannot apply. Third, in the absence of a conflict clause and in case the *lex posterior* principle cannot be applied, resort must be had to the *lex specialis* principle. This principle cannot apply over and above the *lex posterior* rule, but will be crucial in a number of cases where norms have the same date or can be said to be 'parallel' in time rather than 'successive'. Fourth, one particular type of conflict, that where a state has conflicting obligations vis-à-vis two different states (conflict of type AB/AC) has not been resolved in the law of treaties (both norms are 'equals'). For those conflicts a solution must be found rather in the law on state responsibility under the norm that is finally not complied with. In cases where none of the above conflict rules resolve the conflict, an adjudicator must acknowledge a lacuna and may be forced to pronounce a *non liquet* (chapter 7).

The conflict rules thus provided by international law – based essentially on three principles: contractual freedom of states, *pacta sunt servanda* and *pacta tertiis* – surprisingly perhaps, offer a coherent theory on conflict of norms. The fact that lacunae may arise is not so much an anomaly but should provide an incentive for states to incorporate explicit conflict clauses in the treaties they negotiate or at least to prevent conflict by increased co-operation between different law-making agencies. Hence, it was felt that there was no need to elaborate a 'new theory' on conflict of norms in this book. The solutions provided derive from already existing principles. The only remaining uncertainty resides in conflicts of the type AB/AC (state A having conflicting obligations vis-à-vis B and C) where both norms are equal and only state responsibility offers a way out. Still, a further development in the rules on shared responsibility for assistance or aid in breach by another state as well as the acknowledgement that such conflicts will, in the end, only be resolved by a renegotiation of either norm does not make this conflict of norms a pressing topic for new law-making either.

Applying these conclusions to the example of the WTO treaty (chapters 2 and 8), the centralising or uniting theme of this book advocates an examination of WTO law in the wider context of other norms of international law. WTO law is but a branch of public international law. Hence, WTO law must, first of all, be *interpreted* in a way that takes account of other norms of international law, as long as these other norms represent the 'common intentions' of all WTO members. The normal restrictions of treaty interpretation apply, although 'evolutionary interpretation' can safely be said to be the rule rather than the exception given the 'continuing' or 'living' nature of the WTO treaty. Apart from the process of treaty *interpretation*, other rules of international law must also *apply* to the WTO treaty unless that treaty has 'contracted out' of those rules. In addition, before a WTO panel the 'applicable law' must include all relevant norms of international law binding on the disputing parties, even if the jurisdiction of panels is limited to claims under WTO covered agreements only. Such examination of WTO law in the wider context of international law may lead to 'fall-back' on, especially, general international law rules for matters not regulated in the WTO treaty itself. In addition, other non-WTO treaties may be applicable in the relation between the disputing parties and conflict with WTO law. In that event, the conflict rules set out in this book must determine which rule prevails. Crucially, the current definition of conflict in WTO jurisprudence must be broadened so as to include, in addition, obligations contradicting explicit rights. The presumption against conflict applies also to the WTO treaty, and only in case 'contracting out' or conflict can be proven and treaty interpretation cannot harmonise the two norms in question will a genuine conflict arise.

This brings us to the dividing or centrifugal theme of the book, as it applies to the WTO example. In the event of conflict involving WTO provisions, WTO provisions may not always prevail, including before a WTO panel. The trade obligations in the WTO treaty are of the 'reciprocal type'. They are not of an 'integral nature'. Hence, most WTO provisions can be deviated from as between a limited number of WTO members only, as long as this deviation does not breach third party rights. Affecting the economic interests of other WTO members does not amount to breaching their WTO rights. Recognising that most WTO obligations are of a reciprocal nature allows for the taking into account of the diversity of needs and interests of different WTO members. It shows that in most cases of conflict between, for example, human rights and environmental conventions (generally setting out obligations of an 'integral type'), on the one hand, and WTO obligations (of the 'reciprocal' type), on the other hand, WTO provisions will have to give way. This will be so either on the basis of the rules resolving 'inherent normative conflict' (in particular, the fact that *inter se* deviations from integral obligations are 'illegal') or the rules resolving 'conflict in the applicable law'. In respect of the latter, the *lex specialis* principle in particular must be resorted to. Given the 'continuing' nature of the WTO treaty it will often be difficult to frame the conflict in terms of one of 'successive treaties' so that the *lex posterior* rule is difficult to apply. From this perspective as well, the WTO treaty, being a framework agreement in respect of most trade matters, will often have to give way to, for example, MEAs or other conventions imposing obligations or granting explicit rights in terms of trade restrictions applied to *particular products* or for *particular reasons*.

However, the fact that non-WTO norms may, therefore, prevail over the WTO treaty, even as before a WTO panel, does not mean that WTO panels must judicially enforce compliance with these non-WTO rules. Non-WTO rules may be part of the applicable law before a WTO panel and hence offer, in particular, a valid defence against claims of WTO breach. However, they cannot form the basis of legal claims, the jurisdiction of WTO panels being limited to claims under WTO covered agreements only.

Finally, intra-WTO conflict can often be resolved by the explicit conflict clauses provided for in the WTO treaty itself. In the absence of such clauses (as is the case for GATT/GATS/TRIPS conflicts), the normal conflict rules set out earlier must apply. Given that all WTO provisions are part of one and the same treaty, the *lex posterior* principle will not be of help. *Lex specialis*, in contrast, may resolve a great number of conflicts, say, as between GATT and GATS.

The WTO treaty must be construed and applied in the context of all other international law. This other law may fill gaps or provide interpretative material. But it may also overrule WTO norms. WTO law must thus be united with other public international law, through a process of both vertical integration (that is, in its relationship to other sub-systems) and horizontal integration (that is, vis-à-vis general international law). Other law, in particular *more specific* law, must be recognised as capable of overruling WTO law so as to take account of the diversity between WTO members. There is no need to expand the mandate of the WTO as an international organisation for the WTO to take account of other non-trade concerns (including those going beyond the exceptions provided for in, for example, GATT Art. XX). The fact that the WTO is part of international law should suffice. That way, the WTO can continue to produce trade norms; other international organisations and conferences can produce other types of norms. Each should stay within its field of competence, but once it comes to resolving a particular dispute, all relevant and applicable norms must be resorted to – both WTO norms and other norms – in order to settle the dispute 'in accordance with international law'.

Bibliography

Abbott, Kenneth, 'GATT as a Public Institution: The Uruguay Round and Beyond' (1992) 18 *Brooklyn Journal of International Law* 31

Abi-Saab, Georges, 'De la Jurisprudence: Quelques Réflexions sur son Rôle dans le Développement du Droit International', in *Mélanges Manuel Diez De Velazco* (Madrid: Editorial Tecnos, 1993), 1

'Les Sources du Droit International: Essai de Déconstruction', in *Le Droit International dans un Monde en Mutation, Mélanges E. J. De Arechaga* (Montevideo: Fundación de Cultura Universitaria, 1994), 29

Akehurst, Michael, 'The Hierarchy of the Sources of International Law' (1974–5) 47 BYIL 273

Alkema, Evert, 'The Enigmatic No-Pretext Clause: Article 60 of the European Convention on Human Rights', in J. Klabbers and R. Lefeber (eds.), *Essays in the Law of Treaties* (The Hague: Nijhoff, 1998), 41

Alvarez, José, 'The New Treaty Makers' (2002) 25 *Boston College International and Comparative Law Journal* 213

Aly, S., 'L'Interprétation Evolutive en Droit International Public', dissertation on file at the library of the Institut des Hautes Etudes Internationales, Geneva, Ref. HEIDS 576 (1997)

Arnull, Anthony, 'Private Applicants and the Action for Annulment under Article 173 of the EC Treaty' (1995) 32 *Common Market Law Review* 7

ASIL Bulletin, No. 9, 'Implications of the Proliferation of International Adjudicatory Bodies for Dispute Resolution' (1995)

Aufricht, Hans, 'Supersession of Treaties in International Law' (1952) 37 *Cornell Law Quarterly* 655

Bagwell, Kyle, Mavroidis, Petros and Staiger, Robert, 'It's a Question of Market Access' (2002) 96 AJIL 56

The publisher has used its best endeavours to ensure that the URLs for external websites referred to in this book are correct and active at the time of going to press. However, the publisher has no responsibility for the websites and can make no guarantee that a site will remain live or that the content is or will remain appropriate.

Bagwell, Kyle and Staiger, Robert, 'GATT-Think', NBER Discussion Paper No. 8005 (November 2000)

Barnhoorn, L. A. N. M., 'Diplomatic Law and Unilateral Remedies' (1994) 25 NYIL 39

Bartels, Lorand, 'Applicable Law in WTO Dispute Settlement Proceedings' (2001) 35 JWT 499

'*Non Liquet* in the WTO Dispute Settlement System', paper on file with the author

Bello, Judith, 'The WTO Dispute Settlement Understanding: Less is More' (1996) 90 AJIL 416

Benedek, Wolfgang, *Die Rechtsordnung des Gatt aus Völkerrechtlicher Sicht* (Berlin: Springer, 1990)

Benvenisti, Eyal, 'Exit and Voice in the Age of Globalization' (1999) 98 *Michigan Law Review* 167

Bernhardt, Rudolf, 'Thoughts on the Interpretation of Human-Rights Treaties', in F. Matscher and H. Petzold (eds.), *Protecting Human Rights: The European Dimension, Studies in Honour of G. J. Wiarda* (Cologne: Heymanns, 1988), 65

Bodansky, Daniel, '*Non Liquet* and the Incompleteness of International Law', in Laurence Boisson de Chazournes and Philippe Sands (eds.), *International Law, the International Court of Justice and Nuclear Weapons* (Cambridge: Cambridge University Press, 1999), 153

Boisson de Chazournes, Laurence, *Les Contre-Mesures en Droit International Economique* (Paris: Pedone, 1992)

Bos, Maarten, 'The Recognized Manifestations of International Law' (1977) 20 GYIL 9

'The Hierarchy among the Recognized Manifestations ("Sources") of International Law' (1978) 25 NILR 334

A Methodology of International Law (Amsterdam: Elsevier, 1984)

Boyle, Alan, 'Dispute Settlement and the Law of the Sea Convention: Problems of Fragmentation and Jurisdiction' (1997) 46 ICLQ 37

Brewer, Scott, 'Scientific Expert Testimony and Intellectual Due Process' (1998) 107 *Yale Law Journal* 1535

Brierly, J. L., *The Law of Nations* (Oxford: Clarendon, 1963)

Bronckers, Marco, 'More Power to the WTO?' (2001) 4 JIEL 41

Brownlie, Ian, 'General Course on Public International Law' (1995) 255 *Recueil des Cours* 21

Principles of Public International Law (Oxford: Clarendon, 1998)

Brunnée, Jutta and Toope, Stephen, 'International Law and Constructivism: Elements of an Interactional Theory of International Law' (2000) 39 *Columbia Journal of Transnational Law* 19

Bustamante, Rodrigo, 'The Need for a GATT Doctrine of Locus Standi: Why the United States Cannot Stand the European Community's Banana Import Regime' (1997) 6 *Minnesota Journal of Global Trade* 533

Byers, Michael, *Custom, Power and the Power of Rules* (Cambridge: Cambridge University Press, 1999)

Cahier, P., 'Le Problème des Effets des Traités à l'Egard des Etats Tiers' (1974) 143 *Recueil des Cours* 718
Canal-Forgues, Eric, 'Sur l'Interprétation dans le Droit de l'OMC' (2001) 105 RGDIP 1
Capotorti, F., 'Interférences dans l'Ordre Juridique Interne entre la Convention et d'autres Accords Internationaux', in *Les Droits de l'Homme en Droit Interne et en Droit International* (Brussels: 1968), 123
Carmody, Chi, 'Remedies and Conformity under the WTO Agreement' (2002) 5 JIEL 307
Cass, Deborah, 'The Constitutionalization of International Trade Law: Judicial Norm-Generation as the Engine of Constitutional Development in International Trade' (2001) 12 EJIL 39
Cassese, Antonio, *International Law in a Divided World* (Oxford: Clarendon, 1986)
Cassese, Antonio and Weiler, Joseph (eds.), *Change and Stability in International Law-Making* (Berlin: De Gruyter, 1988)
Charney, Jonathan, 'Is International Law Threatened by Multiple International Tribunals?' (1998) 271 *Recueil des Cours* 101
Charnovitz, Steve, 'Rethinking WTO Trade Sanctions' (2001) 95 AJIL 792
Chayes, Abraham and Chayes, Antonia, *The New Sovereignty – Compliance with International Regulatory Agreements* (Cambridge, Mass.: Harvard University Press, 1995)
Cheng, B., *General Principles of Law as Applied by International Courts and Tribunals* (London: Stevens, 1953)
Churchill, Robin and Ulfstein, Geir, 'Autonomous Institutional Arrangements in Multilateral Environmental Agreements: A Little-Noticed Phenomenon in International Law' (2001) 94 AJIL 623
Cleveland, Sarah, 'Human Rights Sanctions and International Trade: A Theory of Compatibility' (2002) 5 JIEL 133
Cox, Robert and Jacobson, Harold, *The Anatomy of Influence – Decision Making in International Organization* (New Haven: Yale University Press, 1973)
Craig, Paul, 'Legality, Standing and Substantive Review in Community Law' (1994) 14 *Oxford Journal of Legal Studies* 507
Crawford, James, Special Rapporteur to the ILC on State Responsibility, First Report (with addenda), submitted to the ILC, 50th session, UN doc. A/CN.4/490, 4 (1998)
 Second Report (with addenda), UN doc. A/CN.4/498 (1999)
 Third Report (with addenda), UN doc. A/CN.4/507 (2000)
Czaplinski, W. and Danilenko, G., 'Conflict of Norms in International Law' (1990) 21 NYIL 3
Dahl, K., 'The Application of Successive Treaties Dealing with the Same Subject-Matter' (1974) 17 *Indian Yearbook for World Affairs* 305
Davey, William, 'Has the WTO Dispute Settlement System Exceeded its Authority?' (2001) 4 JIEL 95
de Vattel, Emerich, *Le Droit des Gens ou Principes de la Loi Naturelle* (Lyons: Gauthier, 1802)

de Visscher, Charles, *Problèmes d'Interprétations Judiciaire en Droit International Public* (Paris: Pedone, 1963)
  'Cours Général de Droit International Public' (1972) 136 *Recueil des Cours* 116
Declaration on the TRIPS Agreement and Public Health, adopted by the Ministerial Conference at Doha on 14 November 2001, WTO doc. WT/MIN(01)/DEC/2 (20 November 2001)
Degan, V., *L'Interprétation des Accords en Droit International* (The Hague: Nijhoff, 1963)
  Sources of International Law (The Hague: Nijhoff, 1997)
Delbrück, Jost, *New Trends in International Lawmaking – International 'Legislation' in the Public Interest* (Berlin: Duncker & Humblot, 1997)
  'Laws in the Public Interest – Some Observations on the Foundations and Identification of Erga Omnes Norms in International Law', in Volkmar Götz et al. (eds.), *Liber Amicorum Gunther Jaenicke* (Berlin: Springer, 1998) 17
Doha Ministerial Declaration, adopted on 14 November 2001, WTO doc. WT/MIN(01)/DEC/1 (20 November 2001)
Downs, George, Rocke, David and Barsoom, Peter, 'Is the Good News About Compliance Good News About Cooperation?' (1996) 50 *International Organization* 379
Draft Articles on Responsibility of States for Internationally Wrongful Acts, adopted by the ILC at its 53rd session, 2001 (Report of the ILC on the Work of its 53rd Session, General Assembly Official Records, 56th Session, Supplement No. 10 (A/56/10), chapter IV.E.1)
Draft Articles on State Responsibility adopted by the ILC on first reading (Report of the ILC on the Work of its 48th Session, 1996, General Assembly Official Records, 51st Session, Supplement No. 10 (A/51/10), pp. 125 ff.)
Draft Articles on State Responsibility provisionally adopted by the Drafting Committee of the ILC on second reading (ILC 52nd Session, 2000, A/CN.4/L.600)
Dupuy, René-Jean (ed.), *A Handbook on International Organizations* (Dordrecht: Nijhoff, 1998)
Falke, Dirk, 'Vertragskonkurrenz und Vertragskonflikt im Recht der WTO' (2000) 3 *Zeitschrift für Europarechtlicher Studien* 307
Fastenrath, Ulrich, *Lücken im Völkerrecht: zu Rechtscharakter, Quellen, Systemzusammenhang, Methodenlehre und Funktionen des Völkerrechts* (Berlin: Duncker & Humblot, 1991)
  'Relative Normativity in International Law' (1993) 4 EJIL 305
Fitzmaurice, Sir Gerald, 'The Law and Procedure of the ICJ, 1951–54: General Principles and Sources of Law' (1953) 30 BYIL 1
  Special Rapporteur to the ILC, Second Report on the Law of Treaties, UN doc. A/CN.4/107, YBILC 1957, vol. 2, 16
  Third Report on the Law of Treaties, UN doc. A/CN.4/115, YBILC 1958, vol. 2, 20
  'Some Problems Regarding the Formal Sources of International Law', in *Symbolae Verzijl* (The Hague: Nijhoff, 1958) 153

The Future of Public International Law and of the International Legal System in the Circumstances of Today (Institut de Droit International, Special Report, 1973)

The Law and Procedure of the ICJ (Cambridge: Grotius, 1986), I

Franckx, Erik, 'Pacta Tertiis and the Agreement for the Implementation of the Straddling and Highly Migratory Fish Stocks Provisions of the United Nations Convention on the Law of the Sea' (2000) 8 *Tulane Journal of International and Comparative Law* 49

Friedmann, Wolfgang, *The Changing Structure of International Law* (New York: Columbia University Press, 1964)

Gaffney, John, 'The GATT and the GATS: Should they be Mutually Exclusive Agreements?' (1999) 12 *Leiden Journal of International Law* 135

Garcia Rubio, Mariano, *Unilateral Measures as a Means of Enforcement of WTO Recommendations and Decisions* (The Hague: Academy of International Law, 2001)

Gehring, Thomas, 'International Environmental Regimes: Dynamic Sectoral Legal Systems' (1990) 1 YIEL 353

Grané, Patricio, 'Remedies Under WTO Law' (2001) 4 JIEL 755

Grossen, Jacques-Michel, *Les Présomptions en Droit International Public* (Neuchâtel, 1954)

Grotius, Hugo, *Le Droit de la Guerre et de la Paix* (D. Alland and S. Goyard-Fabre, eds.) (Paris: Presses Universitaires de France, 1999)

Guggenheim, Paul, *Traité de Droit International Public* (Geneva: Georg, 1967)

Guillaume, Gilbert, 'The Future of International Judicial Institutions' (1995) 44 ICLQ 848

'The Proliferation of International Judicial Bodies: The Outlook for the International Legal Order', Speech to the Sixth Committee of the General Assembly of the United Nations, 27 October 2000, posted on the internet at http://www.icj-cij.org/icjwww/ipress com/SPEECHES/iSpeechPresident_Guillaume_SixthCommittee_20001027.htm

Hafner, Gerhard, 'Should One Fear the Proliferation of Mechanisms for the Peaceful Settlement of Disputes?', in L. Caflisch (ed.), *The Settlement of Disputes between States: Universal and European Perspectives* (The Hague: Kluwer, 1998), 25

'Risk Ensuing from Fragmentation of International Law' (Report of the ILC on the Work of its 52nd Session, General Assembly Official Records, 55th Session, Supplement No. 10 (A/55/10), 321-39)

Hahn, Michael, *Die einseitige Aussetzung von Gatt-Verpflichtungen als Repressalie* (Berlin: Springer, 1995)

Hart, H. L. A., *The Concept of Law* (Oxford: Clarendon, 1961)

Herczegh, Géza, *General Principles of Law and the International Legal Order* (Budapest: Akadémiai Kiadó, 1969)

Higgins, Rosalyn, 'General Course on Public International Law' (1991-V) 230 *Recueil des Cours* 23

'Some Observations on the Inter-Temporal Rule in International Law', in Jerzey Makarcyk (ed.), *Theory of International Law, Essays in Honour of K. Skubiszewski* (The Hague: Kluwer, 1999), 173

Housman, Robert and Goldberg, Don, 'Legal Principles in Resolving Conflicts Between Multilateral Agreements and the GATT/WTO', in Robert Housman et al. (eds.), *The Use of Trade Measures in Select Multilateral Environmental Agreements* (Nairobi: UNEP, 1995), 297

Howse, Robert, 'From Politics to Technocracy – and Back Again: The Fate of the Multilateral Trading Regime' (2002) 96 AJIL 94

Hulsroj, Peter, 'Three Sources – No River, A Hard Look at the Sources of Public International Law with Particular Emphasis on Custom and "General Principles of Law"' (1999), 54 *Zeitschrift für öffentliches Recht* 219

'The Intertemporal Problem in Public International Law', Resolution of the Institute of International Law of 1975 (1975) *Yearbook of the Institute of International Law* 537

Iynedjian, Marc, 'L'Accord de l'Organisation Mondiale du Commerce sur l'Application des Mesures Sanitaires et Phytosanitaires, Une Analyse Juridique', doctoral thesis (University of Lausanne, 2000)

Jackson, John, *The World Trading System* (Cambridge, Mass.: MIT Press, 1997)

'The WTO Dispute Settlement Understanding – Misunderstandings on the Nature of Legal Obligation' (1997) 91 AJIL 60

'Comments on Shrimp/Turtle and the Product/Process Distinction' (2000) 11 EJIL 303

Jacot-Guillarmod, Olivier, 'La Hiérarchie des Règles dans l'Ordre Constitutionnel de l'Union Européenne', in Piermarco Zen-Ruffinen and Andreas Auer (eds.), *De la Constitution, Etudes en L'honneur de J.-F. Aubert* (Basle: Helbing & Lichtenhahn, 1996)

Jenks, Wilfred, 'Conflict of Law-Making Treaties' (1953) 30 BYIL 401

The Proper Law of International Organisations (London: Stevens, 1962)

Jennings, Sir Robert, 'What Is International Law and How Do We Tell It When We See It?' (1981) 37 ASDI 59

'Universal International Law in a Multicultural World', in TMC Institute, *International Law and the Grotian Heritage* (The Hague, 1985), 187

Jennings, R. and Watts, A., *Oppenheim's International Law* (London: Longmans, 1992), I

Jessup, Philip, *A Modern Law of Nations* (New York: Macmillan, 1948)

Karl, Wolfram, *Vertrag und Spätere Praxis im Völkerrecht* (Berlin: Springer, 1983)

'Conflicts Between Treaties', in R. Bernhardt (ed.), *Encyclopedia of Public International Law* (Amsterdam: North-Holland, 1984), VII, 468

Kelly, Claire, 'The Value Vacuum: Self-enforcing Regimes and the Dilution of the Normative Feedback Loop' (2001) 23 *Michigan Journal of International Law* 673

Kelsen, Hans, *Théorie Pure du Droit* (translation H. Thevenaz) (Neuchâtel: Editions de la Baconnière, 1988)

Théorie Générale des Normes (Paris: Presses Universitaires de France, 1996)

Kennedy, David, 'Theses about International Law Discourse' (1980) 23 GYIL 353

Kingsbury, Benedict, 'Foreword: Is the Proliferation of International Courts and Tribunals a Systemic Problem?' (1999) 31 *New York Journal of International Law and Politics* 679

Klein, Friedrich, 'Vertragskonkurrenz', in Karl Strupp and H.-J. Schlochauer (eds.), *Wörterbuch des Völkerrechts* (Berlin: De Gruyter, 1962), 555

Kontou, Nancy, *The Termination and Revision of Treaties in the Light of New Customary International Law* (Oxford: Clarendon, 1994)

Kopelmanas, Lazar, 'Essai d'une Théorie des Sources Formelles de Droit International' (1938) *Revue de Droit International* 101

Koskenniemi, Martti, 'General Principles: Reflections on Constructionist Thinking in International Law' (1985) 18 *Oikevstiede-Jurisprudentia* 133

   From Apology to Utopia: The Structure of International Legal Argument (Helsinki: Finnish Lawyers' Publishing Company, 1989)

   'Breach of Treaty or Non-Compliance? Reflections on the Enforcement of the Montreal Protocol' (1992) 3 *Yearbook of International Environmental Law* 123

   'The Silence of Law/The Voice of Justice', in Laurence Boisson de Chazournes and Philippe Sands (eds.), *International Law, the International Court of Justice and Nuclear Weapons* (Cambridge: Cambridge University Press, 1999), 488

Krugman, Paul, 'What Should Trade Negotiators Negotiate About?' (1997) 35 *Journal of Economic Literature* 113

Kuijper, Pieter Jan, 'The Law of GATT as a Special Field of International Law, Ignorance, Further Refinement or Self-Contained System of International Law?' (1994) 25 NYIL 227

   'The Court and the Tribunal of the EC and the Vienna Convention on the Law of Treaties 1969' (1998) 25 *Legal Issues of European Integration* 1

Lauterpacht, Elihu, 'The Development of the Law of International Organization by the Decisions of International Tribunals' (1976) 152 *Recueil des Cours* 379

Lauterpacht, Hersch, 'The Chinn Case' (1935) 16 BYIL 162

   'The Covenant as the "Higher Law"' (1936) 17 BYIL 54

   'Restrictive Interpretation and the Principle of Effectiveness in the Interpretation of Treaties' (1949) 26 BYIL 48

   'Report to the Institute of International Law', in (1950-I) *Yearbook of the Institute of International Law* 407

   'Some Observations on the Prohibition of "Non Liquet" and the Completeness of the Law', in *Symbolae Verzijl* (The Hague: Nijhoff, 1958) 196

   'Contracts to Break a Contract', in E. Lauterpacht (ed.), *International Law, Being the Collected Papers of Hersch Lauterpacht* (Cambridge: Cambridge University Press, 1978), 341

Leebron, David, 'Linkages' (2002) 96 AJIL 5

Lennard, Michael, 'Navigating by the Stars: Interpreting the WTO Agreements' (2002) 5 JIEL 17

Lowe, Vaughan, '*Res Judicata* and the Rule of Law in International Arbitration' (1996) 8 *African Journal of International Law* 38

   'Overlapping Jurisdictions in International Tribunals' (2000) 20 *Australian Yearbook of International Law* 1

McDougal, M., *Studies in World Public Order* (New Haven: Yale University Press, 1960)

McDougal, M., Lasswel, H. and Miller, J., *The Interpretation of International Agreements and World Public Order* (Dordrecht: Nijhoff, 1967)

McNair, Arnold, *The Law of Treaties* (Oxford: Clarendon, 1961)

McRae, Donald, 'The Contribution of International Trade Law to the Development of International Law' (1996) 260 *Recueil des Cours* 111

'The WTO in International Law: Tradition Continued or New Frontier?' (2000) 3 JIEL 27

Maki, Peter, 'Interpreting GATT Using the Vienna Convention on the Law of Treaties: A Method to Increase the Legitimacy of the Dispute Settlement System' (2000) 9 *Minnesota Journal of Global Trade* 343

Marceau, Gabrielle, 'A Call for Coherence in International Law – Praises for the Prohibition Against "Clinical Isolation" in WTO Dispute Settlement' (1999) 33 JWT 87

untitled, World Bank Seminar on International Trade Law, 24–25 October 2000, 3, on file with the author

'Conflicts of Norms and Conflicts of Jurisdictions, The Relationship between the WTO Agreement and MEAs and other Treaties' (2001) 35 JWT 1081

'WTO Dispute Settlement and Human Rights' (2002) 13 EJIL 753

Matrix on Trade Measures Pursuant to Selected MEAs, WTO doc. WT/CTE/W/160/Rev.1 (14 June 2001)

Mavroidis, Petros, 'Remedies in the WTO Legal System: Between a Rock and a Hard Place' (2000) 11 EJIL 763

'Trade and Environment after the Shrimps–Turtles Litigation' (2000) 34 JWT 73

Maxwell, Peter, *The Interpretation of Statutes* (Helsinki: Finnish Lawyers' Publishing Company, 1946)

Monaco, R., 'Sources of International Law', in R. Bernhardt (ed.), *Encyclopedia of Public International Law* (Amsterdam: North-Holland, 1984), VII, 424

Montaguti, Elisabetta and Lugard, Maurits, 'The GATT 1994 and Other Annex 1A Agreements: Four Different Relationships?' (2000) 3 JIEL 473

Moravcsik, Andrew, 'Taking Preferences Seriously: A Liberal Theory of International Politics' (1997) 51 *International Organization* 513

Mosler, H., 'General Principles of Law', in R. Bernhardt (ed.), *Encyclopedia of Public International Law* (Amsterdam: North-Holland, 1984), VII, 89

Mosoti, Victor, 'In Our Own Image, Not Theirs: Damages as an Antidote to the Remedial Deficiencies in the WTO Dispute Settlement Process; A View from Sub-Saharan Africa' (2001) 19 *Boston University International Law Journal* 231

Multilateral Environmental Agreements (MEAS): Implementation of the Doha Development Agenda, Submission by the European Communities, 21 March 2002 (TN/TE/W/1)

Neumann, Jan, 'Die Koordination des WTO-Rechts mit anderen völkerrechtlichen Ordnungen – Konflikte des materiellen Rechts und Konkurrenzen der Streitbeilegung', unpublished doctoral thesis (Münster, 2001)

'Die materielle und prozessuale Koordination völkerrechtlicher Ordnungen, Die Problematik paralleler Streitbeilegungsverfahren am Beispiel des *Schwertfisch*-Falls' (2001) 61 *Zeitschrift für ausländisches öffentliches Recht und Völkerrecht* 529

O'Connell, D. P., *International Law* (London: Stevens, 1970), I

Oda, S., 'The International Court of Justice from the Bench' (1993) 244 *Recueil des Cours* 9

Oxman, Bernard, 'Complementary Agreements and Compulsory Jurisdiction' (2001) 95 AJIL 276

Palmeter, David and Mavroidis, Petros, 'The WTO Legal System: Sources of Law' (1998) 92 AJIL 398

Dispute Settlement in the WTO, Practice and Procedure (The Hague: Kluwer, 1999)

Panitchpakdi, Supacha, 'Keynote Address: The Evolving Multilateral Trade System in the New Millennium' (2001) 33 *George Washington International Law Review* 419

Parry, Clive, *The Sources and Evidences of International Law* (Manchester: Manchester University Press, 1965)

Pauwelyn, Joost, 'The Concept of a "Continuing Violation" of an International Obligation: Selected Problems' (1995) 66 BYIL 415

'Evidence, Proof and Persuasion in WTO Dispute Settlement, Who Bears the Burden?' (1998) 1 JIEL 227

'Enforcement and Countermeasures in the WTO: Rules are Rules – Toward a More Collective Approach' (2000) 94 AJIL 335

'The Role of Public International Law in the WTO: How Far Can We Go?' (2001) 95 AJIL 535

'Cross-agreement Complaints before the Appellate Body: A Case Study of the EC – *Asbestos* Dispute' (2002) 1 *World Trade Review* 63

'The Nature of WTO Obligations', Jean Monnet Working Paper No. 1/2002, posted on the internet at http://www.jeanmonnetprogram.org

'The Use of Experts in WTO Dispute Settlement' (2002) 51 ICLQ 325

'A World Environment Court?', Working Paper for the United Nations University, in *International Environmental Governance – Gaps and Weaknessses, Proposals for Reform* (Tokyo, 2002)

PCIJ, Advisory Committee of Jurists, *Procès-Verbaux* of the Proceedings of the Committee, 16 June–24 July 1920, with Annexes (1920), 306

Pellet, Alain, 'The Normative Dilemma: Will and Consent in International Law-Making' (1991) 12 *Australian Yearbook of International Law* 22

'Can a State Commit a Crime? Definitely, Yes!' (1999) 10 EJIL 425

Penalver, E., 'The Persistent Problem of Obligation in International Law' (2000) 36 *Stanford Journal of International Law* 271

Perelman, Chaim, 'Les Antinomies en Droit, Essai de Synthèse', in Chaim Perelman (ed.), *Les Antinomies en Droit* (Brussels: Bruylant, 1965), 392

Petersmann, E.-U., *The GATT/WTO Dispute Settlement System* (London: Kluwer, 1997)

'Constitutionalism and International Adjudication: How to Constitutionalize the UN Dispute Settlement System?' (1999) 31 *New York Journal of Law and Policy* 753

'Dispute Settlement in International Economic Law – Lessons for
   Strengthening International Dispute Settlement in Non-Economic Areas'
   (1999) 2 JIEL 189
'Human Rights and International Economic Law in the 21st Century – The
   Need to Clarify their Interrelationships' (2001) 4 JIEL 3
Pierros, Philip and Maciejewski, Mariusz, 'Specific Performance or
   Compensation and Countermeasures – Are These Alternative Means of
   Compliance Under the WTO Dispute Settlement System?' (2001) 6
   International Trade Law Review 167
Pinto, M., 'From Dispute Resolution to Dispute Avoidance: Some Thoughts on
   Collective Management of Treaty Performance', in Volkmar Götz et al.
   (eds.), *Liber Amicorum Gunther Jaenicke* (Berlin: Springer, 1998), 353
Pons, Javier Fernandez, 'Self-Help and the World Trade Organization', in Paolo
   Mengozzi (ed.), *International Trade Law on the 50th Anniversary of the
   Multilateral Trade System* (Milan: A. Giuffrè, 1999), 67
Posner, Richard, *Overcoming Law* (Cambridge, Mass.: Harvard University Press,
   1995)
'Problems Arising from a Succession of Codification Conventions on a
   Particular Subject', Resolution of the Institute of International Law of 1
   September 1995, (1995–I) 66 *Yearbook of the Institute of International Law* 245
Quoc Dinh, Nguyen, 'Evolution de la Jurisprudence de la Cour Internationale
   de La Haye Relative au Problème de la Hiérarchie des Normes
   Conventionnelles', in *Mélanges Offerts à Marcel Waline, Le Juge et Le Droit Public*
   (Paris: Librairie générale de droit et de Jurisprudence, 1974, 2 vols.) I, 215
Quoc Dinh, Nguyen, Daillier, P. and Pellet, A., *Droit International Public*
   (Montreal: Wilson & Lafleur, 1999)
Ragazzi, Maurizio, *The Concept of International Obligations* Erga Omnes (Oxford:
   Clarendon, 2000)
Rauschning, Dietrich, *The Vienna Convention on the Law of Treaties, Travaux
   Préparatoires* (Frankfurt: Metzner, 1978)
Reisman, Michael, 'International Law after the Cold War' (1990) 84 AJIL 859
Reuter, Paul, *Institutions Internationales* (Paris: Presses Universitaires de France,
   1972)
Riphagen, W., Special Rapporteur to the ILC on State Responsibility, Third
   Report on the Content, Forms and Degrees of International Responsibility,
   YBILC 1982, vol. 2, part 1
   Special Rapporteur to the ILC on State Responsibility, Fourth Report, YBILC
   1982, vol. 2, 202
Roessler, Frieder, 'The Institutional Balance between the Judicial and the
   Political Organs of the WTO', paper presented at the Center for Business
   and Government, Harvard University, June 2000, on file with the author
Rosenne, Shabtai, 'Bilateralism and Community Interest in the Codified Law of
   Treaties', in W. Friedmann, L. Henkin and O. Lissitzyn (eds.), *Transnational
   Law in a Changing Society, Essays in Honor of Philip C. Jessup* (New York:
   Columbia University Press, 1972), 203
   Breach of Treaty (Cambridge: Grotius, 1985)

Roucounas, Emmanuel, 'Engagements Parallèles et Contradictoires' (1987-VI) 206 *Recueil des Cours* 9

Rousseau, Charles, 'De la Compatibilité des Normes Juridiques Contradictoires dans l'Ordre International' (1932) 39 RGDIP 133

Ruggie, John, 'Embedded Liberalism and the Postwar Economic Regimes', in *Constructing the World Polity: Essays on International Institutionalization* (London: Routledge, 1998), 62

Rutsel, Martha, 'The Duty to Exercise Judgment on the Fruitfulness of Actions in World Trade Law' (2001) 35 JWT 1035

Salmon, J.-A., 'Les Antinomies en Droit International Public', in Chaim Perelman (ed.), *Les Antinomies en Droit* (Brussels: Bruylant, 1965), 285

Sands, Philippe, 'Treaty, Custom and the Cross-fertilization of International Law' (1998) 10 *Yale Human Rights and Development Law Journal* 3

Sato, Tetsuo, *Evolving Constitutions of International Organizations* (Dordrecht: Kluwer, 1996)

Schachter, Oscar, 'The Relation of Law, Politics and Action in the United Nations' (1963) 109 *Recueil des Cours* 165

'Entangled Treaty and Custom', in Yoram Dinstein and Mala Tabory (eds.), *International Law at a Time of Perplexity – Essays in Honour of Shabtai Rosenne* (Dordrecht: Nijhoff, 1998), 717

Schermers, Henry and Blokker, Niels, *International Institutional Law, Unity Within Diversity* (The Hague: Nijhoff, 1995)

Schilling, Theodor, *Rang und Geltung von Normen in gestuften Rechtsordnungen* (Berlin: Nomos, 1994)

Schloemann, Hannes and Ohlhoff, Stefan, 'Constitutionalization and Dispute Settlement in the WTO: National Security as an Issue of Competence' (1999) 93 AJIL 242

Schoenbaum, Thomas, 'WTO Dispute Settlement: Praise and Suggestions for Reform' (1998) 47 ICLQ 647

Schwarzenberger, Georg, *International Law as Applied by International Courts and Tribunals* (London: Stevens, 1957), I

'The Principles and Standards of International Economic Law' (1966-I) 87 *Recueil des Cours* 1

Seidl-Hohenveldern, Ignaz, *International Economic Law* (Dordrecht: Nijhoff, 1989)

Sicilianos, Linos-Alexander, 'The Relationship between Reprisals and Denunciation or Suspension of a Treaty' (1993) 4 EJIL 341

Siederman, Ian, *Hierarchy in International Law – The Human Rights Dimension* (Antwerp: Intersentia, 2001)

Simma, Bruno, 'Reflections on Article 60 of the Vienna Convention on the Law of Treaties and its Background in General International Law' (1970) 20 *Österreichische Zeitschrift für öffentliches Recht* 5

'Self-Contained Regimes' (1985) 16 NYIL 115

Simon, Denys, *L'Interprétation Judiciaire des Traités d'Organisations Internationales* (Paris: Pedone, 1981)

Sinclair, Sir Ian, *The Vienna Convention on the Law of Treaties* (Manchester: Manchester University Press, 2nd edn, 1984)

Skubiszewski, Krzysztof, 'The International Court of Justice and the Security Council', in Vaughan Lowe and Malgosia Fitzmaurice (eds.), *Fifty Years of the International Court of Justice: Essays in Honour of Sir Robert Jennings* (Cambridge: Cambridge University Press, 1996), 606

Slaughter, Anne-Marie, 'International Law in a World of Liberal States' (1995) 6 EJIL 503

Société Française pour le Droit International, Colloque d'Orléans, *Aspects du droit international économique* (1972)

Sohn, L. B., 'Enabling the United States to Contest "Illegal United Nations Acts"' (1975) 69 AJIL 852

Sørenson, Max, *Les Sources du Droit International* (Copenhagen: E. Munksgaard, 1946)
 'Autonomous Legal Orders: Some Considerations Relating to a Systems Analysis of International Organisations in the World Legal Order' (1983) 32 ICLQ 559
 'Le Problème dit du Droit Intertemporel dans l'Ordre International' (1984) 55 *Yearbook of the Institute of International Law* 1

Spelliscy, Shane, 'The Proliferation of International Tribunals: A Chink in the Armor' (2001) 40 *Columbia Journal of Transnational Law* 143

Stone, Julius, '*Non Liquet* and the Function of Law in the International Community' (1959) 35 BYIL 135

Teraya, Koji, 'Emerging Hierarchy in International Human Rights and Beyond: From the Perspective of Non-derogable Rights' (2001) 12 EJIL 917

Thirlway, Hugh, *International Customary Law and Codification* (Leiden: Sijthoff, 1972)
 'The Law and Procedure of the International Court of Justice 1960–1989 (Part One)' (1989) 60 BYIL 1
 'The Law and Procedure of the International Court of Justice 1960–1989 (Part Two)' (1990) 61 BYIL 1

Trachtman, Joel, 'The Domain of WTO Dispute Resolution' (1999) 40 *Harvard International Law Journal* 333

Tunkin, G., 'General Principles of Law in International Law', in R. Marcic et al. (eds.), *Internationale Festschrift für Alfred Verdross* (Munich: Fink, 1971) 523
 International Law (Moscow: Progress Publishers, 1990)

Van Hoof, D., *Rethinking the Sources of International Law* (Deventer: Kluwer, 1983)

Verzijl, J., *International Law in Historical Perspective* (Leiden: Sijthoff, 1968), I

Vierdag, E. W., 'The Time of the "Conclusion" of a Multilateral Treaty' (1989) 60 BYIL 75

Villiger, Mark, *Customary International Law and Treaties, A Manual on the Theory and Practice of the Interrelation of Sources* (The Hague: Kluwer, 1997)

Virally, M., 'Panorama du Droit International Contemporain' (1983) 83 *Recueil des Cours* 171

Weil, Prosper, 'Towards Relative Normativity in International Law?' (1983) 77 AJIL 413

'The Court Cannot Conclude Definitively... *Non Liquet* Revisited' (1997) 36 *Columbia Journal of Transnational Law* 109

Weiler, Joseph, 'The Rule of Lawyers and the Ethos of Diplomats: Reflections on the Internal and External Legitimacy of Dispute Settlement', in Roger Porter, Pierre Sauvé, Arvind Subramanian and Americo Zampetti (eds.), *Efficiency, Equity, and Legitimacy: The Multilateral Trading System at the Millennium* (Washington: Brookings Institution Press, 2001), 334

Weiler, Joseph and Paulus, A. L., 'The Structure of Change in International Law or Is There a Hierarchy of Norms in International Law?' (1997) 8 EJIL 545

Weinberger, Sheila, 'The Wimbledon Paradox and the World Court: Confronting Inevitable Conflicts between Conventional and Customary International Law' (1996) 10 *Emory International Law Review* 397

Wilting, Wilhelm, *Vertragskonkurrenz im Völkerrecht* (Cologne: Heymanns, 1996)

Wolfke, Karol, *Custom in Present International Law* (Wroclaw, 1964)

Wolfrum, Rüdiger and Matz, Nele, 'The Interplay of the United Nations Convention on the Law of the Sea and the Convention on Biological Diversity' (2000) 4 *Max Planck Yearbook on United Nations Law* 445

WTO Secretariat, *The Results of the Uruguay Round of Multilateral Trade Negotiations, The Legal Texts* (Geneva, 1995)

Zamora, S., 'Is there Customary International Economic Law?' (1989) 22 GYIL 9

Zdouc, Werner, 'The Triangle of GATT/GATS and TRIPS', in Thomas Cottier, Petros Constantinos Mavroidis and Marion Panizzon (eds.), *Intellectual Property: Trade, Competition, and Sustainable Developments The World Trade Forum*, vol. III (University of Michigan Press, forthcoming)

Zuleeg, M., 'Vertragskonkurrenz im Völkerrecht, Teil I: Verträge zwischen souveränen Staaten' (1977) 20 GYIL 246

Index

AB/AC type conflict 281, 300
  bilateral 18, 147, 166
  examples of 300–1, 422
  inherent normative 423, 489
  multilateral treaties, growth due to 423
  norms, renegotiation of 490
  resolution 426–7, 428, 429, 434, 435–6, 489
  state responsibility and 427, 429, 432–3, 438, 489
  WTO examples of 433–4
Abi-Saab, Georges 92
academics, custom, creation by 16
acte contraire 133
  customary law and 137
actio popularis 55, 80, 85
Agreement on Trade-Related Intellectual Property Rights (TRIPS) 42
  dispute settlement provisions 346
  suspension of 347
  WIPO conventions incorporated into 346
Akehurst, Michael 17
Alvarez, José 20
Appellate Body *see* WTO Appellate Body
applicable law 178, 278, 327, 489
  pacta sunt servanda and 328
  pacta tertiis and 328
  priority rules for resolving 327–8
  state responsibility and 327
  states, contractual freedom of 328, 335
arbitration, WTO bilateral settlements and 44
Aréchaga, Jiménez de
  AB/AC conflicts, state responsibility and 429
armed conflict, law on 408–9
authoritative interpretations, WTO agreements and 112, 216

avoidance of conflict
  international adjudicator, techniques of 240
  international law and 247
  international organisations, role in 238
  states, negotiation, role in 239

Bello, Judith 27
  WTO, purpose of 33
  WTO rules, views on 26
Benvenisti, Eyal 15, 476
bilateral, AB/AC conflicts 18, 147, 166
Bodansky, Daniel
  non liquet, justification for 152
border disputes, WTO and 23
Bos, Maarten 7
  international law, normative concept of 90
  treaty and custom, mutual exclusivity of 156
Brownlie, Ian, international law, sources, ICJ Statute in 94

Capotorti, Francesco 165
  conflict, interpretation of 168
case law, WTO Appellate Body 52
cessation
  secondary obligation of 299
  WTO obligations, sanction for breach of 27
Charney, Jonathan
  international tribunals, number of 123
  states bound by norms, independent of explicit consent 105
Cheng, Bin
  customary law, general practice of states 132
  general principles of international law: derogation from 129; superior value of 127

INDEX 507

choice of law, applicable law, conflict in 327
Codex Alimentarius Commission 349
collective rights and obligations 10
command and prohibition, conflict between 184
communitarianism 10
competence
  attributed, doctrine of 286
  international organisations: implied powers of 287; lacking 286
compulsory dispute settlement systems, conflict and 22
conflict clauses
  applicable law, conflict in 489
  illegal *inter se* agreements and 437
  lacunae, avoidance of 490
  a priori exclusion, treaty provisions 468
conflict rules 328–9
  DSU, limited scope of 354, 355
  European Convention on Human Rights 334
  future treaties, priority over 342–3, 437
  GATT, Agriculture Agreement, priority of 359
  GATT and GATS provisions 351
  hierarchy of 329
  internal treaty conflicts 355, 356
  lex posterior and 335
  lex specialis and 385, 387, 391
  new treaties, pre-existing treaty subject to 332
  non liquet in absence of 419
  pacta sunt servanda limiting 335
  UN Charter Art. 103 337, 437; *lex posterior* and 339; non-UN members and 338; obligations under 338–9
  WTO, summary of 361
  WTO treaty 344, 345; lack of 354
conflicts of interest 15
constructivism, international law and 14–15
continuing treaties 379
'contracting out' 236
contractual freedom of states 183
countermeasures 53
  contracting out 218; WTO treaty and 228, 232, 233, 236
  DSU in 219, 220
  general international law, objective of 271
  lex specialis and 389–90
  proportionality of 271
  state responsibility 106, 229
  third parties, effect on 233
  WTO members, available to 231
Crawford, James 39, 61

AB/AC conflicts, resolution of 428
bilateral and multilateral obligations, distinguishing 61
contracting out 218, 220
DSU, status of 39
environmental obligations 62
erga omnes obligations 61, 62
human rights obligations 62
integral obligations, view on 65
jus cogens, norms of 98–9
legal interest, standing and 81
state responsibility, acts of other states and 430, 431, 432
customary international law
  acte contraire and 137
  creation of 92
  'fall-back', general international law, onto 210–11
  general principles of law, subordinate nature of 128
  jus cogens 394; creation of 98
  lex specialis as 407; nature of 129, 394
  norms: codification of 48; general principle of law, derogation from 127; identification 92; later prevailing over earlier treaty norm 134; later treaty, conflict with 137; public interest and 105; states bound without consent 105; treaty norm subsequently modified by 138
  opinio juris 136
  precautionary principle as part of 481–2
  primary status of 129
  state practice, dependence on 136
  state responsibility, rules on 271
  subsequent practice, modification of treaties by 50
  treaties: basis in 48; dilemma between 156, 157; distinction from 131–2; evolution to 156; termination or revision by 138
  treaty interpretation rules, contracting out and 214–15
  UN Charter Art. 103 340
  Vienna Convention, preserved application of 407
  WTO 47, 48
  WTO law, source of 48
customary practice, Marrakesh Agreement, provision in 49

Daillier, P.
  public international law, definition of 28
de Vattel, Emerich
  international law, domestic principles transposed into 174–5
  lex specialis and 387

508   INDEX

definition of conflict 5–6, 329–30
  norms 167, 168, 169–70, 176, 183, 188,
    199–200; definition advocated by this
    work 169–70, 176, 199–200
Delbrück, Jost
  environmental protection, *erga omnes*
    and 101–2
Descamps, Baron
  customary law, primary status of 129
diplomatic law
  respect for 36
  self-contained regime of 36
  status of 107
dispute settlement
  DSU and 359–60
  SPS agreement 352
  TRIPS agreement 346
  WTO and 5
Dispute Settlement Understanding *see* DSU
domestic factors in conflict 15
Draft Articles on State Responsibility 2001
  countermeasures prohibited by 107
  diplomatic law and 107
  erga omnes obligations 61, 62–3, 101
  general international law, contracting out
    of 213
  integral obligations: breach of 54;
    prohibited suspension of 53
  lex specialis 232, 392
  reciprocal and integral obligations,
    distinction between 64
droit supplétif 149
DSB
  Appellate Body recommendations, legally
    binding force of 442
  authority of 287
  decisions: forms of 46; WTO organ status
    46
  dispute settlement 45
  WTO panel recommendations, binding
    force of 442
DSB authorisation, WIPO convention,
  priority over 346
DSU 42
  Appellate Body and panels competency,
    basis for 289
  arbitrators: compulsory jurisdiction of
    445–6; jurisdiction, expansion under 447
  authoritative interpretation 112
  bilateral settlements, unenforceable
    under 44
  breach, presumption of 86
  conflict clause, limited effect of 354, 355
  conflicting obligations, interpretation
    under 196
  contracting out, remedies and 220
  countermeasures, remedy 76

covered agreements: definition of 345,
  443; impairment, redress for 451;
  jurisdiction and 465; operation, levels of
  460, 473
dispute resolution 51, 359–60
DSB, authority established by 287
international law, status in 467–8
jurisdiction, WTO panels and Appellate
  Body 465
legal interest, standing and 81, 82
lex specialis 220
provisions covering conflict of norms
  196
remedies 218–19, 220, 222
repeat claims procedure 121
retaliation, arbitrators' jurisdiction in
  relation to 446–7
state responsibility, countermeasures,
  contracting out of 216
suspension: arbitrators' jurisdiction in
  relation to 447; WTO members,
  unilateral acts of 235
treaty norms, customary
  countermeasures, contracting out of 137
working procedures, WTO panels and
  Appellate Body, consistency with 361
WTO panels: compulsory jurisdiction
  conferred by 445–6; creation of 442;
  international law, application of 468–70;
  status of 442

EC law, positive integration, example of 75
EC treaties
  domestic law, form of 75
  objective nature of 74–5
economic development 19
economic interdependence, breach of WTO
  obligations, effect of 80
economic state, emergence of 30
economics, science of 34
effet utile, WTO treaty and 402
embedded liberalism 34
GATT seclusion from public international
  law 34
environment 19, 20
environmental protection: free-riders and
  101; global common as 102
'exhaustible natural resources', WTO
  Appellate Body interpretation of 485
standard enforcing, trade barriers by 20
trade liberalisation and 20
treaties, object and implementation 72
treaty-based obligations 62
erga omnes partes obligations 53, 54, 55,
  81–2, 100–1
environmental protection and 101–2
jus cogens and 100–1

INDEX 509

European Convention on Human Rights, earlier treaties, priority accorded to 334
European Union
 conflicts within 285
 decisions, annulment of 291, 296
 treaties: domestic law, form of 75; objective nature of 74-5
expressio unius est exclusio alterius 126

Fastenrath, Ulrich 93
Final Act 41
Fish Stocks Agreement
 flag states, high seas competency of 104
 third parties bound by 103, 104
fishing, WTO dispute resolution 23
Fitzmaurice, Sir Gerald
 interdependent nature, treatise of 58-9
 reciprocal and integral obligations, distinction between 58
 treaties, invalidity of 280
 treaty obligations, distinction between 61
 Vienna Convention and 59
forum shopping, international disputes 115

GATS *see* General Agreement on Trade in Services (GATS)
GATT
 Agreement on Agriculture, priority of 359
 breach: state responsibility and 276-7; suspension in response to 228-9
 effet utile 402
 embedded liberalism, effect on 34
 GATS: accumulation with 403; conflict, *lex specialis*, resolution by 405, 492; not mutually exclusive 399-401; overlapping provisions of 401-2, 403; pre-existing conflict rule 351
 individuals, relevance to 68
 institutional ethos of 34-5
 inter se agreements, prohibited by 303
 international law, branch of 37
 interpretation 267-8, 269; *abus de droit*, doctrine of 269
 necessity requirement under 108
 norms, permissive and prescriptive elements of 160
 panel reports 51; judicial decisions, status as 51; legitimate expectations 51; status of 46
 remedies under 231
 schedules and provisions, priority 358
 state responsibility, contracting out and 229
 WTO members, UN Charter obligations 351
 GATT 1947 34
 panels: applicable law before 456; GATT claims, jurisdiction of 458
 GATT 1994 41
 WTO treaty, effect on 345
General Agreement on Trade in Services (GATS) 41
 effet utile of 402
 GATT: accumulation with 403; conflict, *lex specialis*, resolution by 405, 492; not mutually exclusive 399-401; overlapping provisions of 401-2, 403; pre-existing conflict rule 351
 schedules and provisions, conflict between 357-8
general international law
 conflict: broader definition in 197; WTO treaty, resolution by 404
 contracting out 158, 236; *expressio unius est exclusio alterius* and 218; *lex specialis* and 214; *pacta sunt servanda*, compatibility with 475-6; presumption against 236; WTO treaty 218, 228
 corpus of 148
 countermeasures, objective of 271
 fall-back 201, 273; countermeasures, third parties, effect on 233; customary international law and 210-11; forms of 201-2, 208; treaties, 'gaps' in 273-4; WTO Treaty and 205, 207
 graduation, custom from treaty 156, 157
 jus cogens 149
 norms of 147-8
 particular international law: complemented by 155; prevalence of 150, 391
 secondary rules of 149
 state responsibility 271
 treaties 'contracting out' of 212, 213
 weakest and strongest forms of 150
 WTO treaty, interpretation of 268, 269
general principles of law 127, 130, 131
 customary law and 128, 132, 394
 definition of 128-9
 derogation from 127, 129
 jus cogens and 127
 lex generalis, nature of 129
 secondary nature of 128, 129, 394, 488
 WTO, role in 130
generalia specialibus non derogat 405, 406, 407
 lex specialis, basis for 407-8
genocide, prohibition on 21
Genocide Convention, objects of 56, 74
global common
 environmental protection 102
 fundamental human rights 154
 high seas 154

globalisation 19–20, 21
graduated normativity 99
Grossen, Jacques-Michel, conflict, presumption against 243
Grotius, Hugo, *lex specialis*, reference to 387
Grundnorm 172
Guggenheim, Paul, public international law, definition of 28
Guillaume, Gilbert, treaty interpretation, divergent case law on 123–4

Hafner, Gerhard 19
Hahn, Michael 70
Hardie, Sir Andrew 339
Higgins, Rosalyn
  international law, view of 7
  later custom modifying earlier treaty 138
high seas
  flag states, competency on 104
  global common 154
horizontal nature of conflict 11
Howse, Robert 34
Hulsroj, Peter 8
  customary law, state practice 132
  treaties prevailing over custom 135
human rights 19, 20, 21, 62
  derogations permitted under International Covenant on Civil and Political Rights 21
  enforcing, trade barriers by 20
  fundamental 126, 154
  fundamental obligations, non-suspension of 77
  global common 154
  inter se agreements: detracting from 309; modifying 322
  non-derogable: norms of 21; obligations of 108
  obligations: breach, standing to invoke 65; collective promise to uphold 65; trade liberalisation and 20
  treaties: object and implementation of 72; purpose of 74
  WTO dispute resolution 23
  WTO treaty, *inter se* treaty modifications to 322–3

IMF rules, WTO treaty, relationship between 347–8
implicit expressions of intent 330–1
implied jurisdiction
  of international courts and tribunals 447–8
  WTO panels and 450
in dubio mitius 186
in foro domestico, international law, source of 125

inconsistent adjudication of norms 17
inherent nature of conflict 12
inherent normative conflict 178, 275, 489
  AB/AC conflict types and 423
  illegality and 277
  inter se agreements and 321
  international organisations, inconsistent acts by 285
  invalidity and 277
  later norm prohibited by earlier 299–300
  norms breaching other norms 276
  one norm illegal under another 298–9
  solutions for 278
  state responsibility and 276
  termination, norms of 278
  intellectual property, WTO protection standards 71
inter se agreements
  conflict clauses in 437
  human rights and 309, 322
  modifying multilateral treaties: contextual differences 321, 322; prohibition on 280–1, 302, 304, 305–7
  pre-existing treaties, deviation from 436
  third party rights, affecting 309, 312, 320, 332
  treaties, supplementing 342
  Vienna Convention, prohibition on 280–1, 302, 304, 305–7, 310, 314
  WTO: trade liberalisation and 316, 317–18, 320; trade restricting 316
  WTO members: conflict of norms and 321; contractual freedom to change 318, 320
  WTO treaty 316, 332; deviating from 315
  WTO treaty, modifications to 478
interest groups 15, 16
international agreements, *inter se* agreements affecting 309
International Convention on Civil Aviation, non-parties, public interest bound by 105
International Court of Justice
  advisory opinion by 118–19
  judgments, authority of 121
  judicial review, United Nations decisions 292–3
  jurisdiction of 16–17
  leading role of 123
  non liquet, ruling on 151
  Statute of, international law, source of 89, 94
  UN Charter Art. 103 and 339–40
international courts, resort to 22
international courts and tribunals
  advisory opinion of ICJ sought by 118–19
  binding preliminary rulings by 121, 124
  contradictory statements by 122–3

INDEX 511

declining jurisdiction 115
ICJ, leading role of 123
implied jurisdictional powers of 447–8
inconsistent decisions: abuse of
  process 115, 116; *lis alibi pendens* and 115;
  same facts 115
  increase in number of 123
jurisdiction, determination of 114, 115
International Covenant on Civil and
  Political Rights 21
international law
  applicable law, conflicts in 178, *see also*
    customary international law, general
    international law, norms 178
  central legislator, lack of 13, 92, 441
  centralised adjudication, lack of 17, 93, 441
  co-existence of states in 17, 19, 31
  co-operation of states, development of 17, 18, 19, 31, 32, 66, 154
  co-ordination, different branches between 120
  completeness of 151
  conflict, resolution of 275
  conflicting commands in 180
  constructivism and 14–15
  'contract out' by states 37
  customary, variety of actors involved in 16
  decentralised nature of 95
  definitions of 28
  divergent law-making process 97
  diversity and conflict 13
  division of powers, lack of 92
  dual function of 13
  enforcement mechanisms 36–7
  equitable principles of 126
  erga omnes partes obligations in 66
  evolution from custom to treaty 156
  expressio unius est exclusio alterius 126
  fundamental human rights 126
  general and particular, distinguishing norms of 147–8
  general principles 92, 124; customary law and 128, 132; definition of 128–9; derogation from 127, 129; induction, process of 126; legal logic 126; meta principles 125; 'necessary' 127; role of 130; secondary nature of 128, 129; source of 125; WTO, role in 130
  inconsistencies in 13
  international organisations, bound by 324–5
  international trade law 29–31
  interpretation, conflict avoidance and 247
  intertemporal, problem of 165, 242
  judicial decisions: abuse of process 115, 116; contradictory 114, 115, 117; *lis alibi pendens* and 115; status of 110, 112

lacunary character of 19, 152
legitimacy and democratic content of 38
lex generalis 129
lex posterior 126, 173
lex specialis 126
liberal theories 14
neutrality of 13
non liquet 13, 151; justification for 152
normative concept of 90
obligations, suspension of 106
pacta sunt servanda 125
particular 155; binding nature of 155; corpus of 155; prevailing over general 150
pre-normative elements 6
presumption, new law and pre-existent, consistency in 241
principle and rule, difference between 132
realist theories 14
residual negative principle 150, 154
rights and obligations under 10
rules of: equal binding force 96; WTO treaty, interpretation 274
self-contained regime of 35, 36, 37
sources 89, 93, 125; conflict between 92–3; formal 91; inherent hierarchy lacking 94; international organisations, acts of 256; material 91; municipal law 125, 174–5; normativity threshold 91; state consent and 13, 133; traditional 94; uncertainty as to 90, 91
state aiding breach by another 430
state consent, derived from 441, 488
state sovereignty: consequence of 33; hierarchies created by 38; limit on 154
states: consumers as 7–8, 91; equality in 13; free-riders 101; legal relationships of 487; subjects of 95
sub-systems 38, 40; WTO law as 38
temporal nature of 14
treaties, role of 9
UN Charter, status of 99
unitary view of 38
WTO: covered agreements, status of 460; contracting out 40; law, as part of 25, 26, 27, 29, 37, 38; norms, overruled by 492
International Law Commission 12
1996 Draft Art. 27 430, 431, 432
jus cogens 98
state aiding another to commit breach 430
treaties, later custom modifying, view on 140–1
International Monetary Fund, WTO, relationship between 480
International Office of Epizootics 349

512 INDEX

international organisations
  acts incompatible with constituent
    instrument 285
  acts of 256, 290, 291
  annulment of organs' decisions,
    availability of 291
  attributed competence, doctrine of 286
  co-operation between 238
  competence: implied powers of 287; lack
    of 286; 'limited' or 'special' 415
  decisions: conflict between 141; norms,
    conflict with 146–7
  implied powers, theory of 415
  international law, extent bound by 324–5
  judicial review and 290
  jus cogens, respect for 324
  legally binding acts: internal operations
    144–5; *jus cogens*, consistency with 146;
    members' rights and obligations
    affecting 145; status of 145, 146
  multilateral treaties, *inter se* deviation
    from 325
  non-consenting members, ability to bind
    105
  norms: acts inconsistent with 324;
    created by 416; created within 96
  presumption of legality 241
  ultra vires acts of 436
  UN Economic and Social Council,
    co-ordination and consultation role
    238
  UN Security Council 100
  WTO 44
  WTO, co-operation agreements 238–9
interpretation, WTO treaty, members'
  common intentions of 260, 263
Islamic law, state responsibility, view of
  432

Jackson, John 27
Jenks, Wilfred 8, 15, 19
  conflict, strict interpretation of 167, 170,
    171; criticism of 173–4, 183
  Conflict of Law-Making Treaties 8
  conflict of norms, presumption against
    242–3
  general principles of law 131
  legislative intent 370
  treaties, negotiators' responsibilities
    237–8
Jennings, Sir Robert 91
  international law, sources of 93
judicial decisions
  amicus curiae, use of 119
  application of law in particular case 112
  conflicting 122; interpreting same law 117;
    res judicata and 110, 115
  contradiction between 114

inconsistent, WTO 121
status of 51, 110
temporal nature of 124
judicial review
  European Union, decisions of 291, 296
  International Court of Justice, United
    Nations decisions 292–3
  international organisations, decisions by
    290
  United Nations, decisions of 287, 292–3
  WTO organs, decisions of 293, 298
  WTO panels, waiver decisions of 296
jus cogens 13, 14, 21
  binding effect, state consent
    notwithstanding 105
  conflict: source of 22; treaty norm with
    134
  customary international law, creation by
    98
  erga omnes obligations and 100–1
  general international law and 149
  general principles of law, status of 127
  hierarchical supremacy of 98
  integral treaties, type of 60
  International Law Commission view on 98
  international organisations: consistency
    with 146; respect for 324
  invalid treaty, conflict with 279, 280, 281,
    282
  lex specialis and 394
  no deviation from 22
  non-derogable nature of 37
  norms 67; in conflict with 278, 279;
    non-deviation by 436
  pacta sunt servanda, principle of 37, 467
  preference in conflict with treaty 173
  special customary law and 394
  standing 81–2
  UN Charter and 99
  Vienna Convention 60, 98, 134, 149

Karl, Wolfram
  AB/AC conflicts, resolution of 427
  criticism of 183
  future treaties, priority claims over 336
  treaty obligations, conflicting 167
Kelsen, Hans
  conflict of norms, rejection of 172
  Grundnorm 172
Kingsbury, Benedict
  ICJ, leading role of 123
Kontou
  criticism of 141
  later custom modifying earlier treaty
    139–40
Kopelmanas, Lazar 92
  customary international law, creation
    of 92

INDEX 513

Kuijper, Pieter Jan
GATT, branch of international law, theory of 37
WTO, self-contained legal system, emergence of 39, 40

lacuna
conflict rules in 438, 490
non liquet, declaration of 419, 421, 490
Lauterpacht, Hersch
conflict, broad interpretation of 168
inter se agreements, contracting parties' consent for 315
treaties, void where breach earlier 280, 425
law-making
international law, norms of 12
'over-inclusion' and 12
'under-inclusion' and 12
law-takers, states as 7–8
Leebron, David 21
legal standing
bilateral obligations, breach of 63
human rights obligations 65
multilateral obligations, breach of 63
'specially affected' states 63, 64
legislative intent
date of 374
later prevailing 368–9, 370
lex posterior rule and 369–70
legitimate expectation, GATT panel reports, creation by 51
lex generalis
lex specialis, accumulation with 410; earlier giving way to later 412; supplemented by 410
WTO obligations 87
lex mercatoria 48
lex posterior 14, 96, 97, 374
conflict: applicable law in 489; primary function in 439
conflict clause, priority over future treaties and 335
continuing treaties and 380, 406
detecting 388–9
general principle of law as 126
legislative intent and 369–70
lex specialis, coinciding with 395, 396; interaction with 392; priority of 407
municipal law, origins in 97
norms, application to 380
regional and multilateral treaties, conflict between 377
treaties, priority to earlier treaty and 333
UN Charter Art. 103 and 339
Vienna Convention and 362, 375–6, 408
WTO treaty and 375–6
lex specialis 126, 232

conflict: applicable law in 489; GATT and GATS 405
conflict rules, application of 385, 396
continuing treaties 406, 408
contracting out, general international law and 213, 214
contractual freedom of states and 388
countermeasures 389–90, 393; WTO obligations, breach of 389
customary international law as 407
detecting 388–9
general norms, interpretation of 410
general principles of law, secondary nature of 394
generalia specialibus non derogat, basis in 407–8
indeterminate, *non liquet* declaration 421
international tribunals, jurisdiction determined by 455
lex generalis, accumulation with 410; precedence of 412; supplementing 410
lex posterior, interaction with 392, 395, 396; prevailing over 405, 407
norms: general norms prevailing over 387–8; subject matter 389
self-defence and armed conflict 408
special customary law and 394
SPS treaty, application under 482
state consent, determination of 438
treaty interpretation, role in 414
treaty norm, general international law, conflict between 391–2
UN Charter Art. 103 and 387
Vienna Convention 392
wider credence, dangers of 408
WTO 389–90; agreements and 142, 411
lex specialis derogat legi generali, WTO treaty and 233, 397–9
liberal theories
change to domestic legal system, international law, effect on 14
international law and 14
lis alibi pendens 115
living treaties *see* treaties, continuing
Lowe, Vaughan
inconsistent tribunal decisions 115
international tribunals, jurisdiction of 114, 115

McRae, Donald
criticism of 31, 32, 33
economic state, emergence of 30
GATT/WTO, international law, place in 29–31, 34
international trade and economic law 29, 31
state sovereignty, views on relevance of 33

514   INDEX

Marceau, Gabrielle
 criticism of 316
 WTO law, self-contained view of 316
margin of discretion 176
Marrakesh Agreement 41, 42, 146
 amendment procedures under 43, 45
 conflict, prevailing nature of 356
 contracting out, general international law 216
 customary practice, guidance by 49
 WTO, scope and function of 287
 WTO organs, competence of 287
Marrakesh Protocol 357–8
Mavroidis, Petros, contracting out, DSU and 220
MEAs, WTO treaty, relationship between 350
Mosler, Hermann, general principles of law, customary law and 132
Most Favoured Nation (MFN) 69
 obligations 69, 79, 160
multilateral treaties
 conflict between 375
 conflicting with bilateral 375
municipal law, international law, source of 125

NAFTA, dispute settlement 115
national interests, international law, effect on 14
negative integration
 bilateral obligations 66
 WTO rules 73, 184
neutrality, international law in 13
non-governmental organisations 16
non liquet
 avoidance of 129, 151
 conflict of norms and 151
 conflict rules, lacunae in 419, 438, 490
 ICJ ruling on 151
 indeterminate *lex specialis*, declaration due to 421
 justification for 152
 lacuna, declaration due to 419, 421
 non-resolvable conflict and 421
 views on 151
 WTO legal system in 152–3
 WTO panels, declaration by 454
normative feedback loop 239–40
norms *see also* treaty norms
 accumulation 161, 162, 182, 201, 487; complementary 162
 avoidance of conflict, limitations of 272
 breach, state responsibility for 278, 299
 broad interpretation of conflict 168
 command and prohibition, conflict between 184

conditional obligations imposing 160
conflict: between norms 5, 6, 7, 10, 13, 94, 115, 163; identification of 166; *jus cogens* with 278, 280; lacuna, law in 173, 278, 331, 419; *ratione personae*, limitations and 254; *ratione temporis*, limitations and 254; resolution of 173, 436
conflict clauses, priority to earlier norms 22
constituent elements, identification of 93
continuing treaties, treatment of 378–9
contracting out 236
contractual freedom of states and 183
creation, determinate point in time lacking 97
creation and identification of 91
decision of international organisations 146–7
definition of conflict 167, 168, 169–70, 172, 176, 183, 188, 199–200
derogation from another 237
doctrinal writing contradicting 110
earlier customary, conflict with later treaty 137
earlier norm terminated by new norm 282–3
empowering 159
enforcement, vital interests and 108, 109
environmental, bilateral treaty, conflict with 462
evolutionary nature of 136
exempting 159, 160
explicit right, prohibition on 187
explicit termination or suspension by another norm 283
fall-back position 488
forum shopping and conflict 115
functions of 158
general 160
general international law 147–8
general principles of law, status of 124
hierarchy of 5, 7, 278
identification of 91
illegal 436
implementation leading to breach of another 272
imposing negative obligations 160
incorporation of 237
individual 159
inherent conflict, breach causing 176
inherent normative conflict 178, 489
inter se 106; agreements and 321
interaction of 158, 161
international communications treaties 108
international organisations: acts inconsistent with 324; created by 96, 416

interpretation: application as distinct from 204; multilateral treaties, derived from 263
interpretation by *lex specialis* 410
interpretation in light of other norms 262
invalidity 278; *jus cogens*, conflict with 278, 279
jus cogens, non-deviation from 436
later derogating from earlier 185
lex posterior and 380
lex specialis: general norm prevailing over 387–8; subject matter 389
margin of discretion 176
mutual exclusivity 163, 175, 183
necessary conflict 184
negative permission 161
negotiation stage and conflict 237, 239
new, change in law, purpose of 242
non liquet in conflict 151
'objective' question of conflict 176
one breaching another 276
one illegal under another 298–9
outcomes, classification by 278
particular international law 147–8, 156
permissive 159, 160
positive obligations, 184, 186
positive permission 161
prescriptive 158
presumption against conflict 240–1, 242–3, 251
prohibitive 158
public interest of 101, 102, 104–5
ratione materiae 161, 165
ratione personae 162, 165
ratione temporis 165
reference to another 237
regulatory 159
renegotiation of 490
rights and obligations under 171
secondary 159
sources of 89
speciality, principle of 416, 418
state consent 133; created by 95
state or body bound by both rules 165
states creating 418
subject and parties, overlapping 165
subject matter of 96
suspension/termination under Vienna Convention Art. 60 106–7
teleological interpretation 420
terminated 278
terminating other norms 162
treaties: drafting 237; interpretation in light of other norms 251; interpretation of 247
unconditional obligations imposing 160
unilateral acts and 144

vague nature of 94
validity, earlier detracting from later norm 424
WTO Appellate Body interpretations 190–1, 193–4
WTO panel interpretations 190–1, 193–4
WTO treaty and 463, 491

OECD Arrangements on export credits 348
opinio juris 48, 136
Oxford English Dictionary, treaty interpretation, use in 262, 268

pacta sunt servanda 27, 37, 117
AB/AC conflicts, resolution of 426
conflict in applicable law and 328
conflict clauses, limitation on 335
conflict of norms, resolution of 436
contracting out, compatibility of 475–6
general principle of law 125
international tribunals, applicable law of 461
jus cogens, standing of 37, 467
treaty provisions, *a priori* exclusion of 468
WTO members, contractual freedom 38
pacta tertiis 14, 95
AB/AC conflicts, resolution of 426
conflict in applicable law and 328
conflict of norms, resolution of 436
conflict rules, restriction on 332
inter se agreements, illegality of 307, 312
pre-existing treaty, non-derogation from 332–3
treaty interpretation and 257
treaty norms and 103
Vienna Convention and 363
particular international law 155
binding nature of 155
complementary nature of 155
corpus of 155
general international law, prevailing over 150, 391
norms of 156
Pellet, Alain
public international law, definition of 28
Perelman, Chaim
conflict, interpretation of 168
permissions/exemptions, conflict between 163
politics, WTO rules and 79
positive integration
EC law 75
international law, growth of *erga omnes partes* obligations in 66
WTO rules embodying 71

pre-normative elements, international law of 6
presumption against conflict 212–13, 215, 488
  WTO treaty and 491
prevention of conflict 490
private interest groups, transnational paradigm 16
public international law disciplines involved in resolution of conflict 275
  regional and multilateral treaties, between 377
  time, factor in 14
  treaty clauses, priority over earlier norms 333
  treaty interpretation, presumption against 207
  treaty norms: between 18, 19; supervening custom and 384
principle of contemporaneity, treaty interpretation and 264
principle of effectiveness
  conflict, presumption against, limiting 251
  treaty interpretation, use in 248–50
public interest norms 67
  criticism of 101, 102
  custom, transformed into 105
  pacta tertiis and 106
  third parties bound by 104–5, 106
public international law, WTO law, relationship with 5
Pufendorf, Samuel von 387
  lex specialis and 387

Quoc Dinh, Nguyen
  public international law, definition of 28

ratione materiae 161
  WTO panels, applicable law before 459–60
ratione personae 162, 254
  WTO panels, applicable law before 459–60
ratione temporis 254
  WTO panels: applicable law before 459–60; jurisdiction subject to 443
realist theories, state interests, international law and 14
relative normativity 21
res judicata 110
  conflicting judicial decisions and 115
  homogenous legal relations and 115
  judicial decisions in international law 110
  new facts, discovery of 111
  WTO, non-application to 111
  Resolution of the Institute of International Law 1995
  jus cogens, norm of, preference for 134

later custom, treaty modified by 138
particular international law and 155
Riphagen, Willem 217
  treaty norms, implicit derogation by 217
Ruggie, John 34

Salmon, Jean 144
  lacunae and 419
Sands, Philippe
  Vienna Convention Art. 31(3)(c), treaty interpretation, role in 253, 254, 269
Schachter, Oscar 48, 54, 70
  treaties, prominence over custom 134–5
Schermers, Henry
  international organisations, international law, bound by 324–5
Schoenbaum, Thomas 118
Secretariat of the International Plant Protection Convention 349
self-defence, law on 408–9
Simma, Bruno 12
Sinclair, Sir Ian
  lex specialis principle, view on 366
  treaties, timing of 372
  Vienna Convention Art. 30, view on 364
  Vienna Convention Art. 31(3)(c), view on 255
Spelliscy, Shane
  divergent international case law 124
SPS agreement 352
standing judicial body, state consent to 441
state consent
  current expression, defining 388
  legal claims for 441
  norms created by 95
  source of international law 13, 133, 441, 488
state practice 90
state responsibility 39
  AB/AC conflict and 427, 429, 432–3, 438, 489
  acts of other states and 430
  applicable law, conflict in 327
  conflict and 275, 276
  countermeasures 106, 229
  diplomatic law and 36
  GATT: breach of 276–7; contracting out of 229
  general international law, rules of 271
  Islamic law and 432
  norms, breach of 278, 299
  remedies, countermeasures 53
  self-contained law of 39
state sovereignty 33
  contractual freedom, international law hierarchy and 38

INDEX 517

international law, consequence of 33
limit in international law 154
trade law, underlying assumption 33
states
co-existence, international law in 17, 19
co-operation, evolution in international law 17, 18, 19, 31, 32
conflict avoidance, negotiation and 239
contractual freedom of 183, 328, 331, 487; AB/AC conflict resolution 426; conflict clause conflicting with 335; conflict of norms, resolution of 436; current expressions of intent 437; factual/subjective elements of 388; *lex posterior* and 362, 381; *lex specialis* and 388; treaty conflict clauses and 437
diversity of 487
domestic law, origin of *lex posterior* rule in 97
equality of 13, 95, 126
erga omnes partes obligations, owed to 100
free-riders 101; environmental protection and 101; political considerations 105
freedom of 185
intent of 437
international law, subjects as 95
jus cogens, bound by consent notwithstanding 105
law-takers 7-8
legal relationships between 487
legislative intent 374
norms created by 418
self-defence, right of 126
self-help, right of 126
unilateral acts: binding obligations 92, 143, 144; existing obligations, detracting from 144; later norm, prevailing over 144
subsequent practice
international organisations and 49, 50
treaty norms, change by 50
treaty rules, further clarification by 50
Vienna Convention 49
WTO 49
synallagmatic obligations 65

third parties
public interest norms binding 104-5
treaties binding 103, 332
treaty norms not affecting 437
time, international law, effect on 14
trade
concessions, legitimate expectation and 455
instrumental form of 73
international and bilateral nature of 72
liberalisation, beneficial effects of 78
obligations, reciprocal nature of 65
restrictions 20
Trade Policy Review Mechanism 42
travaux préparatoires 6
treaties
bilateral 18, 22; AB/AC conflicts 18; international environmental norm, conflict with 462
bilateral obligations 66, 67; legal standing to invoke 63
breach allowing suspension of 53-4
conclusion, date of 370, 371, 373
conflict: AB/AC type 423; amendments, caused by 376; multilateral conflicting with bilateral 375; same subject matter 367
conflict rules 328-9, 331-2; *pacta tertiis* and 332
consensus and 13
continuing 378-9, 380, 406, 408, 438
contracting out: explicit 216, 488; *expressio unius est exclusio alterius* and 214; general international law 212; presumption against 212-23, 488
custom: prominence over 134-5; source of 48
customary international law: dilemma between 156, 157; distinction between 131-2; evolution from 156
definition of 41
desuetude 143
distinction 61
drafting, norms, conflict avoidance and 237
erga omnes obligations 61
error in, defence based on 484
'fall-back', to general international law 201-2
human rights and environmental, object and implementation of 72
increased use of 17
inter se agreements: legality of 436; prohibition on 280-1, 302, 304, 305-7; supplemented by 342; third party rights affected by 309, 312, 320
interdependent nature type 58-9
international communications, norms of 108
international organisations, *inter se* deviation from 325
international tribunals, jurisdiction of 114, 115
interpretation *see* treaty interpretation
invalidity 280, 282; *jus cogens*, conflict with 279, 280, 281, 282
later custom modifying 138, 139-40; ILC view on 140-1

treaties (cont.)
  later terminating earlier, same subject matter 284
  legislative intent, fiction of 368–9, 372
  lex specialis 129
  modern international law, role in 9
  modification: implied consent by 143; subsequent practice by 50, 143
  multilateral 22; conflict between 375; 'contracting out' of 37; *inter se* modifications to 53, 280–1; *inter se* suspension of 60
  multilateral obligations: distinguishing 67; legal standing to invoke 63, 64
  negative integration 161
  negotiation 237–8
  norms *see* treaty norms
  objects, determination of 56
  obligations *see* treaty obligations
  pre-existing, non-derogation 332–3
  prevailing over custom 134–6
  a priori exclusion of 468
  private interest groups, effect on 15, 16
  reciprocal and integral, breach, remedies for 69
  reciprocal obligations 53, 58, 64, 65, 66, 67; breach of 65
  regional and multilateral, conflict between 377
  sub-regimes 9
  subsequent, effect on existing customary law 136–7
  third parties bound by 103, 104, 105
  timing of 370, 371, 372
  voidable, breach of earlier treaty obligation 425
treaty interpretation
  application and, distinction 204
  bilateral treaties, use of 258–9
  canons of 126
  conflict, presumption against 207
  contemporaneity, principle of 264, 266
  divergent case law on 123–4
  effectiveness, principle of 248–50
  evolutionary basis for 267–8
  general international law, fall-back 273–4
  historical background and 252
  international law, relevant rules and 253, 254–5, 263–4
  international norms and 490
  lex specialis, role in 414
  limitation on 254
  limits of 245
  Oxford English Dictionary, use in 262, 268
  pacta tertiis, principle of 257
  parties, common intentions of 257, 258
  pre-normative elements and 6
  subsequent practice 223, 252, 258
  travaux préparatoires and 252, 330
treaty norms
  change by subsequent practice 50
  conflict 18, 19, 134, 364–5
  contracting out 217
  fall-back position 488
  general principle, derogation from 127
  general rule, prevailing over custom 134
  hierarchical role of 133
  increase in 18
  integral nature of 64
  interpretation, Vienna Convention and 251–2
  interpretation of 247, 251
  lex specialis 134, 391–2
  negotiation of 328–9
  pacta tertiis and 103
  precedence given to later customary norm 134
  public interest 67
  state consent and 133
  subsequent custom modifying 138
  supervening custom, conflict with 384
  third party rights and obligations and 437
treaty obligations
  global commons 66
  integral 53, 58, 65, 67
  reciprocal 53, 58, 64, 65
  reciprocal and integral, distinction 54, 55, 58, 64, 65–6, 67
  suspension of 106
  WTO MFN obligation 69
TRIPS agreement *see* Agreement on Trade-Related Intellectual Property Rights

UNCLOS
  existing norms, prevailing over 331, 468
  inter se agreements, acceptability of 342
  undertakings, WTO members by 52
United Nations
  conflict, attribution of power between organs 285–6
  decisions, judicial review of 292
  Economic and Social Council, co-ordination and consultation function 238
  organisation, limits of 287
  UN Security Council, mandate of 100
  WTO, source of conflict 20, 21, 24, 403
  WTO judiciary, risk created by conflict 443
United Nations Charter
  Art. 103: conflict clause 337, 437, 489; customary international law and 340; ICJ judgments and 339–40; interpretation of

339, 340–2; *lex posterior* and 339; *lex specialis* and 387; non-UN members and 338; obligations under 338–9 international law, status in 99
United States, unilateralism 485
Uruguay Round 24, 41
use of force, obligation to refrain from 107

Vienna Convention on the Law of Treaties 29, 41
AB/AC conflict, resolution under 426–7
Art. 30: *lex specialis* and 412; priority rules, successive treaties 363–4; treaties, different parties to 381; treaties, same subject matter 364, 367
Art. 31(3)(c) 251–2, 253, 254–5; temporal scope of 264, 267–8
customary international law rules and 407
integral obligations, no *inter se* deviation from 436
inter se modification, multilateral treaties 280–1, 302, 304, 305–7, 310, 314, 321
jus cogens: conflict, preference for 173; peremptory norm 60, 98, 134, 149; treaty in conflict with 279
lex posterior rule in 96, 173, 362, 366, 367, 375–6, 380, 408, 437
lex specialis 392
material breach: termination/suspension as remedy for 59; treaty suspended for 53–4
norms, suspension/termination under 106–7
pacta tertiis rule in 363
reciprocal and integral obligations, distinction 64
reservations, prohibition on 56–7
state intent, *lex posterior*, determination by 437, 438
states, contractual freedom of 183, 381
subsequent practice and 49
suspension permitted by 60
treaties: distinction 59; interpretation under 245; termination 284, 285
treaty formation, error in 484
treaty norms, interpretation of 251–2
WTO treaty, amendments and modifications to 474–5
Vierdag, E. W.
conflict, amended treaties and 376
lex posterior, effect of 374
treaty norms, two conflicting 365
Vienna Convention, termination of treaties by 284
Vienna Convention Art. 30, criticism of 377

Vienna Convention Art. 59, termination of treaties by 284, 285
Villiger, Mark E.
criticism of 140
subsequent treaties, pre-existing customary law and 136–7
treaties, revision and termination by later custom 140

Waldock, Sir Humphrey
conflict, interpretation of 168
inter se agreements, Vienna Convention prohibition on 305
invalid treaty, *jus cogens*, conflict with 279, 280
treaty interpretation, subsequent practice and 258
Weil, Prosper 21
graduated normativity, view of 99
non liquet, views on 151
public interest norms, criticism of 102
relative normativity 21
Weiler, Joseph
GATT, institutional ethos 34–5
WIPO conventions
subsequent DSB authorisation, conflict with 384
TRIPS agreement, incorporation into 346
Wolfke, Karol, treaty rules, prevailing over custom 135–6
World Trade Organization (WTO)
accessions, covered agreements, status of 43
actio popularis, no basis for 85
advisory opinions, lack of 293
amicus curiae procedures 119
Appellate Body *see* WTO Appellate Body
arbitrators 445–7
bilateral settlements: arbitration clauses and 44; unenforceable under DSU 44
co-operation agreements, with international organisations 238–9
compulsory dispute resolution 8
compulsory jurisdiction of 442, 443
conflict: potential for 24; source of 20; within 286
countermeasures: *lex specialis* 389; remedy as 76
covered agreements: applicable international law and 460, 470; operation, levels of 460, 473; panel and Appellate Body jurisdiction 465; WTO panels, substantive jurisdiction of 478
customary international law 47, 48, 49
dispute settlement 5; decisions, binding effect 27, 28; remedial measures 27
dispute settlement rules, intention of 297

520 INDEX

World Trade Organization (WTO) (cont.)
 Doha Declaration, WTO rules and MEAs, application of 472
 enforcement mechanism 447
 fishing disputes and 23
 human rights disputes and 23
 IMF, legal relationship between 480
 implementation panels, jurisdiction of 446
 inconsistent judicial decisions in 121
 integral rules 70, 71
 intellectual property 71
 international agreements, concluded by 45
 jurisprudence: judicial economy, principle of 449; jurisdiction, presumption in favour of 450–1
 jurisprudence and publicists, judicial references to 471
 law see WTO law
 legal structure 44
 legal system: nature of 35; non liquet in 152–3
 lex specialis, examples of 389–90, 393
 members see WTO members
 most favoured nation obligations: breach, consequences of 69; collective bilateral concessions and 79; norm of 160
 obligations see WTO obligations
 Oilseed agreement, status of 345
 organs see WTO organs
 panels see WTO panels
 permissions and exemptions, health reasons 160
 pillars of 24
 practice, treaty interpretation, role in 50
 purpose of 33
 regional integration agreement, examination by WTO panels 295
 res judicata, non-application of 111
 scope and functions of 287
 specialised international tribunals, binding preliminary rulings 121, 124
 SPS and TBT agreements: dispute settlement provisions 352; mutual exclusivity 360; national measures, consistency with 349
 standing: burden of proof 83; 'legal interest' and 81, 82; proof of breach and 86
 Subsidies agreement, export credits, treatment of 348
 suspension, remedy of 77
 territorial border disputes 23
 Tokyo Round Codes 23
 waiver 45

WTO agreements
 authoritative interpretation of 112, 113
 breach, bilateral nature of 87
 concluded post-1994 43
 conflict: definition of 188; regulation of 188–9
 country-specific schedules of concessions 42, 43
 covered agreements enforceable under DSU 42, 43, 44, 451, 460
 Final Act 41
 legal norms, status as 29, 42
 lex specialis and 142
 Marrakesh Agreement 41, 42; amendment procedures in 43, 45
 member-specific schedules 42
 multilateral nature of 52
 non-static nature of 43
 plurilateral agreements 42, 43
 supervening custom, revision by 142
 Uruguay Round 24, 41
WTO Appellate Body
 case law of 52
 competence derived from DSU 289
 conflict, definition of 194, 195
 'exhaustible natural resources', interpretation of 485
 expert opinion, use by 119
 general international law, 'fall-back' to 208
 IMF rules, application of 480–1
 judicial decisions by 51
 jurisdiction of 465
 non-WTO convention, reliance upon 464–5
 precautionary principle, application of 481–2
 recommendations by 442
 working procedures 361
WTO law 5, see also DSB, DSU, GATT, General Agreement on Trade in Services (GATS), WTO treaty 5
 breach of 68
 compliance, worldwide welfare increase 80
 conflict, broader definition in 197, 198, 199
 conflicting commands in 180
 customary international law, engine of growth for 48
 Doha Declaration and 472
 GATT 1947 panels, applicable law before 456
 general principles of international law and 130, 461
 indirect effect of 68

individual economic operators, effect on 68
individuals, relevance to 68
inter se agreement modifying human rights or MEA obligations 322
interpretation: members' common intentions 490; practice, role in 50
lex prior, later *inter se* modification 323
negative integration 184
non-WTO rules: facts, as 463–5; impact of 478; incorporation of 445
norms: international law overruling 492; negative obligations 160
political considerations 79
public international law, part of 25, 26, 27, 29, 37, 38
reciprocal obligations under 69
rules of law, subsidiary means for determining 471
sources of 40–1, 91
specific market access 73
state responsibility, exclusion of 39
state sovereignty and self-interest 33
status of 467–8
sub-system, international law of 38
subsequent practice, development of 49
suspension, breach, as response to 228–9
WTO members
acts inconsistent with rules, burden of proof 241
agreement, act of organ, distinction between 47
claims on others' behalf 84, 85
collective non-compliance mechanism established by 78
common intention of, WTO treaty interpretation and 260, 263
compulsory jurisdiction granted by 442
consensus of 47
countermeasures, availability of 231
developing countries, priorities of 486
economic interests of 491
free-riders 101
inter se relations, contractual freedom to change 318, 320
international standards: Codex Alimentarius Commission 349, 445; International Office of Epizootics 349; Secretariat of the International Plant Protection Convention 349
legally binding act of organisation, effect on 145
national measures, conformity with SPS or TBT agreements 349
organs, acting as 45, 286
pacta sunt servanda and 38
schedules, standing in WTO legal order 357
self-interest of 33
standing: no objection to lack of 84; trade flows and 83; wide standard of 84
state responsibility incurred by 914
trade obligations, bilateral nature of 65–6
trade restrictions imposed by 276–7
treaty amendment, agreement to 45
UN Charter, obligations under 351
undertakings by 52
unilateral action by 52, 235
unilateral statements by 143–4
WTO panels, compulsory jurisdiction conferred on 445–6
WTO obligations 52
AB/AC type conflicts: examples of 433–4; resolution of 435–6
bilateral: enforcement 76; negotiation 75–6
binding nature of 26
breach, economic effects of 72
cessation, sanction for breach of 27
definition of 52, 53
erga omnes partes, inter se modifications to 54
lex generalis 87
MFN 69
multilateral, *inter se* modifications to 54
reciprocal nature of 13, 54, 55, 75, 76, 83, 491
WTO organs 44
acts of 44–5; Marrakesh Agreement, consistent with 146
agreement by, distinction between agreement of members 47
competence of 287
customary practice 49
decisions, validity of 296
DSB, decisions of 46
judicial acts, *ultra vires* 289
judicial review, decisions of 293, 298
norms enacted by 45
other international organisations, relations with 344
WTO panels
ad hoc jurisdiction granted by parties 444
ad hoc tribunals 442
applicable law 459–60, 476; interpretation of 476
competency 286, 289
compulsory jurisdiction conferred by members 445–6
conflict, definitions adopted by 190–1, 193–4
covered agreements, applicable law and 470

522 INDEX

WTO panels (cont.)
　defences, treaty formation, error in 484
　implied jurisdiction of 450
　international law rules, application of 468-70, 473
　judicial review, waiver decisions of 296
　jurisdiction 353, 443, 465, 472, 476; covered agreements and 443, 473; non-WTO law claims 449-50, 451, 453, 455, 456, 459-60; presumption in favour of 450-1
　legal standing, breach of reciprocal obligation 54
　non liquet, declaration by 454
　non-violation cases, applicable law of 455, 456
　non-WTO treaties, application of 486
　non-WTO tribunal having greater jurisdiction 455
　norms emerging subsequent to WTO treaty 463
　other international tribunals and 120
　recommendations by, legally binding force of 442
　repeat claim under DSU Art. 9 121
　reports: inconsistencies between 122; judicial decisions, status as 51
　status of 442
　substantive jurisdiction 45, 460, 478; lack of 454
　unilateral statements, member bound by 143-4
　working procedures 361
WTO jurisprudence and publicists, application of 471
WTO treaty *see also* DSB, DSU, GATT, General Agreement on Trade in Services (GATS), WTO law
　amendment procedure 45
　amendments and modifications to 474-5
　application, public international law context of 413
　binding nature of 28
　cessation 218
　composition of 23
　concessions, suspension of 222
　conflict: definition of 189, 190
　conflict clauses: internal 6, 354, 355, 356, 399; summary of 361
　conflict rules in 459-60
　'continuing' nature of 379
　contracting out: countermeasures 228, 232, 233, 236; general international law of 215; remedies 218, 226

countermeasures, *lex specialis* and 231
'fall-back', to general international law 205, 207
GATT 1994 effect on 345
general conflict clause, absence of 344, 345
general international law, resolution by 404
General Interpretative Note: conflict between SCM and GATT 1994 197; conflict definition in 189, 190-1, 192, 199; *lex specialis* and 397-9
IMF rules, relationship between 347-8
inter se agreements: deviating from 315; modifying 53, 316, 322-3; trade, effect on 316, 317-18, 320
inter se modifications to 478
international law, contracting out of 40
interpretation 245, 258-9, 269, 270, 271; *abus de droit*, doctrine of 269; customary international trade usage 272; international law and 253-4, 255, 256, 263-4, 274; members, common intention of 260, 263; non-WTO rules and 252, 256, 268; principles of 249, 268, 269; state responsibility and 271; subsequent agreement and practice and 223, 252; *travaux préparatoires* and 252
lex posterior rule in relation to 375-6
lex specialis 233, 397-9, 411
Marrakesh Agreement and conflict 356
multilateral environmental agreements, relationship between 350
negative integration and 161
negotiation 26
non-WTO norms, prevalence of 491
non-WTO rules, defence relying on 473
norms: distinguished from acts of organs 45; effectiveness, principle of 249-50; GATT panel reports as 46; interpretation 247; MFN obligations 160
organs acting contrary to 45
overlapping provisions, GATT and GATS 401-2, 403
presumption against conflict 491
remedies 218-19
reparation, for past damage 221
subsequent norms and 463
travaux préparatoires 189
WTO organ decisions, validity under 296

CAMBRIDGE STUDIES IN INTERNATIONAL AND COMPARATIVE LAW

Books in the series

Conflict of Norms in Public International Law
How WTO Law Relates to other Rules of International Law
Joost Pauwelyn

The Search for Good Governance in Africa
Making Constitutions in the States of the Commonwealth
Peter Slinn and John Hatchard

Transboundary Damage in International Law
Hanqin Xue

European Criminal Procedures
Edited by Mireille Delmas-Marty and John Spencer

The Accountability of Armed Opposition Groups in International Law
Liesbeth Zegveld

Sharing Transboundary Resources
International Law and Optimal Resource Use
Eyal Benvenisti

International Human Rights and Humanitarian Law
René Provost

Remedies against International Organisations
Basic Issues
Karel Wellens

Diversity and Self-Determination in International Law
Karen Knop

The Law of Internal Armed Conflict
Lindsay Moir

International Commercial Arbitration and African States
Amazu A. Asouzu

The Enforceability of Promises in European Contract Law
James Gordley

International Law in Antiquity
David J. Bederman

Money Laundering
Guy Stessens

Good Faith in European Contract Law
Reinhard Zimmermann and Simon Whittaker

On Civil Procedure
J. A. Jolowicz

Trusts
A Comparative Study
Maurizio Lupoi

The Right to Property in Commonwealth Constitutions
Tom Allen

International Organizations before National Courts
August Reinisch

The Changing International Law of High Seas Fisheries
Francisco Orrego Vicuña

Trade and the Environment
Damien Geradin

Unjust Enrichment
Hanoch Dagan

Religious Liberty and International Law in Europe
Malcolm D. Evans

Ethics and Authority in International Law
Alfred P. Rubin

Sovereignty over Natural Resources
Nico Schrijver

The Polar Regions and the Development of International Law
Donald R. Rothwell

Fragmentation and the International Relations of Micro-States
Jorri Duursma

Principles of the Institutional Law of International Organisations
C. F. Amerasinghe

Lightning Source UK Ltd.
Milton Keynes UK
UKOW05f2216230813

215884UK00001B/107/P